The Asyut Project

Edited by
Jochem Kahl, Ursula Verhoeven,
Mahmoud El-Khadragy and Andrea Kilian

Volume 18

2022
Harrassowitz Verlag · Wiesbaden

Jochem Kahl and Andrea Kilian (Eds.)

Asyut - The Capital That Never Was

2022

Harrassowitz Verlag · Wiesbaden

Bibliografische Information der Deutschen Nationalbibliothek
Die Deutsche Nationalbibliothek verzeichnet diese Publikation in der Deutschen
Nationalbibliografie; detaillierte bibliografische Daten sind im Internet
über https://dnb.de/ abrufbar.

Bibliographic information published by the Deutsche Nationalbibliothek
The Deutsche Nationalbibliothek lists this publication in the Deutsche
Nationalbibliografie; detailed bibliographic data are available on the internet
at https://dnb.de/.

For further information about our publishing program consult our
website https://www.harrassowitz-verlag.de/

Printed on permanent/durable paper.
Printing and binding: Hubert & Co., Göttingen
Printed in Germany

ISSN 1865-6250   eISSN 2701-5610
ISBN 978-3-447-11909-2   eISBN 978-3-447-39323-2

Contents

Preface

The present volume of *The Asyut Project* series contains a collection of articles on ancient Asyut, which offer insight into latest research on topical issues. Although, or perhaps precisely because, four major officially sanctioned excavations took place at Asyut between 1903 and 1914, this book would never have been written twenty years ago – simply due to the fact that there would not have been enough available data about Asyut. It is only thanks to the enthusiasm, the high level of commitment and the constant support of the international team of *The Asyut Project* that so much new knowledge on ancient Asyut could be accumulated and that this volume can be published. Covering a time span of several millennia, dealing with evidence from Pharaonic and Coptic culture, with texts, objects, history and material culture from the third millennium BCE to the first millennium CE, the present volume is a current snapshot of the variety of ongoing research on Asyut.

Several research activities have been carried out since 2003 under the name *The Asyut Project*. After a first survey on the Gebel Asyut al-gharbi in 2003, conducted by Jochem Kahl and Mahmoud El-Khadragy, it became clear that by resuming archaeological fieldwork on this mountain, many new insights into the regional history of Asyut as well as the history of Egypt in general would be gained. Supported by the Johannes Gutenberg University of Mainz in 2004, the fieldwork project *The ancient Egyptian necropolis of Asyut: documentation and interpretation* was funded by the DFG (German Research Foundation) from mid-2005 until the end of 2019. Directed by Ursula Verhoeven (Johannes Gutenberg University of Mainz; project director since 2004) and Jochem Kahl (Johannes Gutenberg University of Mainz and Freie Universität Berlin; field director since 2004 and project director since 2010), this project focused on mapping the Gebel Asyut al-gharbi, recording inscriptions, paintings and reliefs associated with the nomarchs' tombs of the First Intermediate Period and the Middle Kingdom, retrieving an animal tomb, studying pottery, tracing the reuse and recontextualization of tombs during Pharaonic, Byzantine and Islamic history and identifying the various functions of the Gebel Asyut al-gharbi. Based on this previous research, beginning in 2020, the German-Polish project *Asyut – centre of ancient trade* (directed by Jochem Kahl, Freie Universität Berlin, and Teodozja Rzeuska, Polish Academy of Sciences) followed suite in order to define the role of Asyut as a centre of merchandise during the Pharaonic Period and Late Antiquity. Both projects have been supported by colleagues from Sohag University, in particular Mahmoud El-Khadragy, Mohamed Abdelrahiem, Ahmed Alansary and Mahmoud El-Hamrawi, as well as the State Ministry of Antiquities in Egypt, represented by Zahi Hawass, Mamdouh Eldamaty and Khaled El-Anani over the years. Another project which has been running since 2016 is the study of objects from both early and illicit excavations in Asyut city and on Gebel Asyut al-gharbi, which are now stored at the Antiquities magazine at Shutb. This project is financed by the Egyptological Seminar of the Freie Universität Berlin and directed by Jochem Kahl and Mohamed Abdelrahiem. We are grateful to Paul-Michael Spielhagen for additional funding. For their constant support with publishing, we thank Harrassowitz Verlag and its former and current directors Michael Langfeld, Barbara Krauss, and Stephan Specht. Thanks are also due to the staff of the Museo Egizio, Turin, and the British Museum, London, for their support and the access to the objects provided by them. Special thanks further go to the General Directors of Asyut Antiquities, Hany Sadek Metri, Abdel-Satar Ahmed Mohamed and Mahmoud El-Sayed Mahdy. We are also grateful to the former and current General Directors of Foreign Missions Affairs & P. Committees Nashwa Gaber, Hany Abo El-Azam and Mohamed Ismail.

Fifteen seasons of fieldwork reduced the statements of early travellers (e.g. Anton, Graf Prokesch-Osten, Sohn, in 1874) and archaeologists (e.g. Nestor L'Hôte in 1839; David George Hogarth after his own excavations in 1907) to absurdity, who wrote that the site was nearly exhausted. Today, after twenty years of constant research in the field, in libraries and museums, we can say: the work will go on. Nineteen published books and nearly sixty articles bear witness that we have set our knowledge about Asyut on a new foundation. A foundation, which enables us to add substantial information to the history of one of the regional centres of ancient Egypt. We extend special gratitude to all the scholars and students who participated in fieldwork or contributed with research on libraries and museums to *The Asyut Project*. It is a pleasure to mention them here below:

List of participants in fieldwork in chronological order:
Jochem Kahl, Egyptologist (2003–2012, 2014, 2016–2019)
Mahmoud El-Khadragy, Egyptologist (2003–2012, 2014)
Mahmoud El-Hamrawi, Egyptologist (2003, 2016–2019)
Eva-Maria Engel, Egyptologist (2003–2005)
Sameh Shafik, Epigrapher (2003–2009, 2011, 2014, 2016–2018)
Ahmed Atitou, Archaeologist, "Qufti" (2003–2019, 2021)
Ursula Verhoeven, Egyptologist (2004–2012, 2014, 2016)
Ulrike Fauerbach, Surveyor (2004–2006, 2012)
Monika Zöller-Engelhardt, Egyptologist (2004–2008, 2010–2012, 2014, 2017–2018)
Yasser Mahmoud Hussein, Egyptologist (2004–2008, 2010)
Omar Nour el-Din, Egyptologist (2004, 2014)
Meike Becker, Egyptologist (2005–2008, 2014, 2017)
Dietrich Klemm, Geologist (2005)
Rosemarie Klemm, Egyptologist (2005)
Christiane Dorstewitz, Egyptologist (2005)
Diana Kleiber, Egyptologist (2005)
John Moussa Iskander, Egyptologist (2005, 2007)
Ilona Regulski, Epigrapher (2006–2007, 2014, 2016, 2018)
Ammar Abu Bakr, Draughtsman (2006–2011)
Fritz Barthel, Photographer (2006–2007, 2010, 2012, 2014, 2016–2018, 2021)
Hazim Saleh Abdallah, Egyptologist (2006–2007)
Eva Gervers, Egyptologist (2006–2012, 2014, 2016–2018)
Andrea Kilian, Egyptologist (2006–2012, 2014, 2016–2018)
Mohamed Naguib Reda, Egyptologist (2006–2007)
Laura Sanhueza-Pino, Egyptologist (2006–2008, 2010–2011)
Abd el-Naser Yasin, Scholar of Islamic Studies (2007–2009, 2012, 2014, 2016–2018)
Jan Moje, Egyptologist (2007)
Manja Maschke, Architect (2007–2008)
Magdalena Patolla, Anthropologist (2007–2009)
Ibrahim Kedees, Egyptologist (2007–2008)
Hytham Aly Madkour, Egyptologist (2007–2008)
Ahmed Ali El-Khatib, Botanist (2008–2009)
Hesham Faheed Ahmed, Egyptologist (2008–2012, 2014, 2016–2018)
Nadine Deppe, Archaeologist (2008, 2011)
Chiori Kitagawa, Zoo-Archaeologist (2008, 2010–2011, 2014, 2016–2017)
Mohamed Al-Shafey, Egyptologist (2008–2012, 2014, 2016–2019, 2021)
Mohamed Helmi, Egyptologist (2008–2012, 2014)

Veronika Wagner, Egyptologist (2008)
Mohamed Abdelrahiem, Egyptologist (2009–2012, 2014, 2016–2019, 2021)
Ina Eichner, Byzantine Archaeologist (2009)
Thomas Beckh, Egyptologist (2009)
Silvia Prell, Egyptologist (2009–2010)
Corinna Garbert, Egyptologist (2009)
Josephine Malur, Egyptologist (2009–2012)
Josuah Pinke, Egyptologist (2009)
Cornelia Lehrle (née Goerlich), Architect (2009–2012, 2014)
Barbara Reichenbächer, Egyptologist (2009–2010, 2012)
Teodozja Rzeuska, Egyptologist (2010–2012, 2014, 2016–2018)
Edyta Klimaszewska-Drabot, Byzantine Archaeologist (2010)
Michael van Elsbergen, Egyptologist (2010–2012, 2014)
Svenja A. Gülden, Egyptologist (2010, 2012, 2014)
Mohamed Farag, Egyptologist (2010–2012, 2014)
Agatha Wiek, Illustrator (2010)
Aid Abu Hamid, Archaeologist, "Qufti" (2011–2018)
Aneta Cedro, Archaeologist (2011–2012, 2014, 2016–2018)
Tina Beck, Egyptologist and Social and Cultural Anthropologist (2011–2012, 2014, 2016, 2018–2019)
Anne Herzberg, Egyptologist (2012)
Ann-Cathrin Gabel, Egyptologist (2012)
Rudaina Bayoumi Hasan, Egyptologist (2012)
Dana Jacoby, Egyptologist (2012)
Alexandra Winkels, Conservator (2012)
Ewa Czyżewska-Zalewska, Byzantine Archaeologist (2012, 2014, 2016–2018)
Günter Vittmann, Egyptologist (2014)
Stephan Hartlepp, Egyptologist (2014, 2016)
Rebekka Pabst, Egyptologist (2014)
Marcus Stecher, Anthropologist (2014)
Metoda Peršin, Archaeologist (2014)
Philipp Jansen, Architect (2014, 2016–2018)
Adel Refat, Egyptologist (2014, 2016–2018, 2021)
Ahmed Alansary, Egyptologist (2016–2018)
Ana Sofia de Carvalho Gomes, Egyptologist (2016–2018)
Katarzyna Molga, Archaeologist (2016–2018)
Alice Sbriglio, Egyptologist (2016)
Ulrike Dubiel, Egyptologist (2017–2018)
Judit Garzón Rodríguez, Egyptologist (2017–2018)
Walid Azab, Veterinarian (2017)
Anja Buhlke, Architect (2018)
Esmeralda Lundius, Egyptologist (2018)

List of accompanying inspectors and conservators in fieldwork and in the Magazine of Antiquities at Shutb:

Ahmed Abdeldayem
Islam Mohamed Al-Amir Abdelhamid
Ahmed Abdelrahiem Abdelmageed
Rafat Fakher Karas Abdelmeseeh

Mohamed Farghali Abdelrahiem
Mohamed Abdollah Mohamed Ahmed
Hussein Hashim Sayed Ali
Mohamed Mustafa Alshafey
Mohamed Abou Daif Amer
Emad Bostan Ata
Helal Qeli Attalan
Abdrabuh Sayed Atyah
Kamil Ezzat Awadallah
Heba Ramadan Mohamed Badawy
Abou Bakr
Mustafa Bekhit Mohamed Bekhit
Lisa Khalil Bishay
Michel Nabil Gendi
Osama Samir Ghaly
Mohamed Ismail Mahmoud Ghanim
Samy Kamal Hamdy
Enas Mohamed Hassan
Tarek Hassan
Sameh Khalaf Hemdan
Hussein Mustafa Hussein
Rageh Darwish Khalaf
Taher Ahmed Madkur
Howaida Mahar
Niazy Mustafa Mohamed Mahmoud
Ghada Ali Maray
Suzy Hosny Youssef Masaoud
Adly Garas Matta
Dalia Mohamed
Esraa Saber Mohamed
Mohamed Khalifa Mohamed
Mohamed Refaat Mohamed
Rehab Mohamed Abuserir Mohamed
Tarik Mahmoud Mohamed
Manar Mohamed Naguib
Nadja Naguib
Khaled Omar
Ahmed Mohamed Ahmed Omran
Hassan Saad Hassan Osman
Hamada Rifat
Ayman Ahmed Salam
Khaled Gomaa Sayed
Magdy Shaker
Medhat Fayez Tadros
Kabil Kamil Girgis Tanious
Khaled Abdelmalek Abu Zed

List of contributors to *The Asyut Project* by translation work, graphic work or studies in libraries or museums:

Anna Arpaia
Youssef Ahmed-Mohamed
Sabrina Mercedes Benz
Martin Bleisteiner
Dieter Blohm
Hannah Jade Cope
Rebecca Diewitz
Anke Ebel
Douglas Fear
Dora Goldsmith
Nadine Gräßler
Oliver Hasselbach
Janine Höhne
Jessica Jancziak
Elisabeth Kruck
Claire Malleson
Antonio Morales
Mohamed Abdollah Osman
Iris Rodenbüsch
Philipp Scharfenberger
Nora Abdelhamid Shalaby
Jeff Simpson
Rebecca Van Es
Madita Voß
Petra Weschenfelder
Benjamin Wortmann
Anissa Zoubir

Last but not least, our thanks go to our driver Sobhi and the numerous local workmen without whom the project would never have been possible.

Berlin, May 2022   Jochem Kahl and Andrea Kilian

Asyut – The Capital That Never Was[1]

Jochem Kahl

1. Asyut: The "Capital of Dreamland"?

In 1873, the English writer and Egyptologist Amelia Blandford Edwards described how she approached the city of Asyut by boat from the north; how, time and again, the seemingly endless bends of the Nile delayed her arrival (Fig. 1); how beautiful the city appeared to her, as its minarets kept re-emerging like a mirage, sometimes to the left and sometimes to the right of the river; how the mountains looked as transparent as the sunshine, and how every last detail of the panorama seemed to belong in a painting.

What she also described, however, is how this romantic idea of Asyut was shattered and replaced by disenchantment the minute she stepped off the boat:

> So our mirage turns to sordid reality, and Siût, which from afar off looked like the capital of Dreamland, resolves itself into a big mud town as ugly and ordinary as its fellows.

(Edwards 1877: 101)

Asyut, the object of Amelia Edwards' unrealised vision, has a chequered history that reaches back more than 5,000 years – a history so rich that it is rarely matched in Egypt, and indeed anywhere in the world; a history, moreover, that continues to be written even today. In fact, this episode of the "capital of dreamland" that failed to materialise is but one of many stories the city can tell – there is Asyut, the capital of the 13th Upper Egyptian nome throughout the Pharaonic Period, where the city's chief deity Wepwawet and the god Anubis were worshipped; there is the Asyut to which pilgrims flocked in the 4th century CE; there is the Asyut which is right in the geographical centre of Egypt, but nevertheless a border city – a *wounded* city, ravaged by wars and crises, but also a *creative* city, whose writings, images, statues and architecture – whose whole cultural life, in fact – were often ground-breaking and highly influential. The following is intended to present a number of small snippets from the densely written pages of the incredibly diverse histories of this fascinating city.

2. Asyut: The Lost City

Today, Asyut is home to about 400,000 people. The airy vista from the mountain Gebel Asyut al-gharbi that presented itself to the traveller still in the 19th century[2] has given way to quite a different sight: what the modern visitor observes from the same spot is basically a sea of houses (Fig. 2). The modern city (Fig. 3) stretches from the western banks of the Nile all the way to the mountain range on the fringes of the Libyan Desert, which begins with Gebel Asyut al-gharbi right on the city's outskirts. This sprawling concrete jungle has swallowed Early Modern gardens and palaces along with the last traces of the ancient city. Closely packed buildings cover Old Asyut completely; the alluvial deposits left by the annual

1 Lecture given on the 20th July 2017 at The British Museum, London (The Raymond and Beverly Sackler Distinguished Lecture in Egyptology). I would like to thank Martin Bleisteiner for correcting my English.
2 Cf. for example Kahl 2013: 360, Fig. 20; 411–412, pls. 1–2.

flooding of the Nile over millennia have done their part as well. As a result, what remains of the ancient settlement is, quite literally, buried metres deep – the ruins from Late Antiquity can be found at a depth of about 5 metres, those from the New Kingdom at about 8 metres below ground level.[3]

The growth of modern Asyut is nothing short of rampant – slowly but surely, its grey-on-grey urban landscape is about to devour even the last remains of open farmland. Whereas the city kept a respectful distance to Gebel Asyut al-gharbi and its burial sites as late as 2012 (Fig. 2), both legal and *il*legal construction work has since covered the remaining open areas (Fig. 4). The modern cemetery, too, is intruding ever more deeply into the mountain, and thus into the ancient necropoleis (Fig. 5). A large number of modern tombs have been erected on top of the ancient burial sites, in many cases making use of existing shafts and openings.

If we are to attempt the writing of Asyut's history – or rather, one of Asyut's many histories – we will have to rely mostly on evidence from outside the city's perimeter. This evidence could, for example, consist of textual sources. In addition to that, we could also focus our attention on the numerous objects and monuments – excavated legally and *il*legally on Gebel Asyut al-gharbi during the 19th and 20th centuries – that lend an air of splendour and mystique to the collections of modern western museums in Paris, Turin, Berlin, New York and London; these items are universally regarded as priceless masterpieces, but sadly they were not adequately documented on site. Here are a number of particularly striking examples:

1. Two wooden statues depicting a Dynasty 12 nomarch called Djefai-Hapi; today, the statues are located at the Louvre in Paris[4] and at the Egyptian Museum in Turin.[5] These statues are unique for the Middle Kingdom because of their considerable size. They are both over 2 metres tall and bear eloquent witness to the impressive standard of workmanship at that time.
2. Asyuti statues from the New Kingdom also display a high craftsmanship, as do a statue group of Isis-Hathor and Wepwawet (Fig. 6)[6] and the double statue of Iuny and his wife Renenut (Figs. 7–8),[7] both from the Ramesside Period.
3. Museums in Japan house also statues from Asyut as, for example, the well-preserved wooden statue of Nakht in the Miho Museum.[8]
4. A final example is a remarkable statue of a dog from the Ptolemaic or Roman Period, today at the Louvre.[9]

3. Asyut – Retracing the City

Since 2003, a joint German-Egyptian mission has been carrying out research on Gebel Asyut al-gharbi – the objectives being to remedy the shortage of source material, to shed light on Asyut's identity and individual character, and ultimately to allow the city to assume – at long last – its rightful place in Egyptian history.[10]

The tasks we set ourselves include the following:

---

3 Kahl 2007: 3, 44.

4 Paris, Louvre E 26915, h: 205 cm (Delange 1987: 76–77; Kahl 2007: 130, Fig. 104).

5 Turin S.08650, h: 207 cm (Del Vesco 2015: 78, no. 73).

6 New York, Metropolitan Museum of Art 17.2.5, limestone, h: 129 cm (Hayes 1959: 348–350).

7 New York, Metropolitan Museum of Art 15.2.1, limestone, h: 84,5 cm (Winlock 1919).

8 Miho Museum, h: 168 cm. Style and workmanship point to Asyut as origin of this statue (Inagaki 2007: 50–51).

9 Paris, Louvre E 11657, h: 101,5 cm (Bénédite 1923: 129–136; Kahl 2007: 153, Fig. 111; David 2015: 33–35).

10 Together with Ursula Verhoeven from the University of Mainz and our Egyptian colleagues from Sohag University – especially Mahmoud El-Khadragy, Mohamed Abdelrahiem, Ahmed Alansary and Mahmoud El-Hamrawi – I am responsible for coordinating and directing the fieldwork on the mountain.

— to describe the various functions the mountain fulfilled over the millennia – this goal is accomplished via talks and presentations as well as via essays, exhibitions and monographs, for the purpose of which a dedicated publication series has been established.[11]
— to investigate change and continuity from the Pharaonic Period to the Byzantine and in some cases even the Islamic Period
— to document endangered monuments and other architectonic structures
— to question western perspectives on Asyut, and to come to a better understanding of our own archaeological activities by making sure that the voice of the local population is heard
— and finally, to reconstruct the history of the ancient city of Asyut.

In order to achieve these objectives, an international research team with about 25 members is deployed on Gebel Asyut al-gharbi from mid-August to mid-October every year. This team is supported by inspectors and guards provided by the Egyptian Antiquities Organisation, by highly-skilled restorers, and around 80 local workers.

Given that parts of the excavation area belong to a restricted military zone, and given that Asyut saw a spate of terrorist incidents in the 1990s, we are constantly accompanied by the police, and sometimes by the military.

About one kilometre long and rising to a height of up to 200 metres on Asyut's western outskirts, Gebel Asyut al-gharbi (Figs. 9–10) quite literally constitutes a field of research that raises a multitude of fascinating questions – fortunately, it also supplies clues that allow us to answer at least some of them.

The mountain's peculiar shape is quite remarkable: with a little imagination, it resembles a nose pointing towards the city (Figs. 11–12). The population of Asyut has used the Gebel continuously since the Archaic Period, that is, since 3000 BCE. As the finds of our recent excavation campaigns suggest, human activity on the mountain began even earlier, around 4000 BCE.[12] The mountain served as:

— cemetery for humans,[13] but also for animals[14]
— quarry[15]
— site of the temple of Hathor[16]
— destination for literate visitors[17]
— place of prayer[18]
— dwelling of Christian anchorites[19]
— site of Christian monasteries[20]
— place of school[21]
— military base[22]

---

11 *The Asyut Project*, Harrassowitz Verlag, https://www.harrassowitz-verlag.de/reihe_412.ahtml
12 Rzeuska 2014: 84–100; Rzeuska 2017: 27–61.
13 Cf. Kahl 2007: 59–106; Zitman 2010; Kahl, Sbriglio, Del Vesco & Trapani 2019.
14 Cf. Kitagawa 2016.
15 Cf. Kahl 2007: 61–63; Kahl 2013: 79–85, 126.
16 Cf. Verhoeven 2013a.
17 Verhoeven 2013b; Verhoeven 2020.
18 Tomb N13.1, for example, was used as place of prayer during the Islamic Period, cf. Ahmed-Mohamed 2020: 411, 422–426.
19 Cf. Kahl 2007: 103–106; Kahl 2014a; Kahl 2015; Eichner 2020: 4.
20 Kahl 2007: 99–103; Kahl 2014a; Eichner 2020: 11–54..
21 Coptic school exercises written on a wall were found near the mausoleum of Sheikh Abu Tug.
22 Today as well as during the third Persian occupation of Egypt (618/619–629 CE; Richter 2003). Cf. also the large numbers of military personnel attested on the stelae from the Salakhana Trove (DuQuesne 2009: 62).

Based on the work of Dietrich and Rosemarie Klemm, the limestone mountain's geological structure can be divided into 11 steps.[23] In the area of the burial sites, this division corresponds quite closely to the archaeological stratification of the Gebel: for static reasons, ancient Egyptian tombs were cut from a solid limestone layer wherever possible.

Enormous mountains of debris caused by extensive quarrying and earlier excavations determine the appearance of the mountain today (Figs. 9–10, 13); steep escarpments are the result of the use of explosives – not only by quarry workers, but also by archaeologists.[24] Metaphorically speaking, the mountain was stripped of its skin and flesh down to its bare bones – when Jean François Champollion visited the mountain in 1828, he aptly compared the tombs to abandoned skeletons. On the slope pointing towards Asyut, around 10 to 15 metres of the mountain's surface has been quarried away – this means that whenever we examine the tombs and their architecture, we must keep in mind that their frontmost areas may be damaged, or even lost altogether as this is the case with Tomb II (Figs. 14–15).[25]

What remains today, apart from the quarries and ruined monasteries, are tombs filled with debris, abandoned objects and all kinds of osteoarchaeological material. Parts of their architecture may have been blown to pieces, their images and inscriptions exposed to the elements and to vandalism, but they still contain invaluable information concerning the regional history of Asyut. What is more, a steady stream of fresh finds (Figs. 16–18) – sometimes of a type or nature as yet unknown in Egyptology – has increased and consolidated our knowledge of Ancient Asyut considerably.[26]

From the rich inventory of research results established by *The Asyut Project*, the follwoing chapters will focus on three particularly interesting aspects of the city's history:

– Asyut as a wounded city
– as a border city
– and as a city of culture.

4. Asyut – A City of War and Terror, a Wounded City

Badly damaged by quarrying, the tombs of Asyut's nomarchs from the First Intermediate Period (Fig. 19) contain inscriptions that testify to Asyut's crucial role in the civil war between Herakleopolis and Thebes during the 21st century BCE.

The royal house of Herakleopolis in the north of the country represented the traditions of the Old Kingdom; Thebes, on the other hand, located in the country's south, was a nome that pursued a highly aggressive policy of expansion, seeking – and ultimately gaining – control over all of Egypt. The decisive battle in this power struggle took place at Asyut: supported by the royal family of Herakleopolis, the nomarchs of Asyut were the last bulwark against the approaching Thebans.

The autobiographical inscriptions in Tombs III and IV (Figs. 20–21) – commissioned by the nomarchs Iti-Ibi and Khety II, respectively – give us a graphic description of the civil war, a description that is more or less unparalleled elsewhere in Egypt in its stunning intensity. Here are some of the terms that were used:

---

23 KAHL 2007: 59–61; KLEMM & KLEMM 2008: 112–115.
24 KAHL 2013: 79–95; RYAN 1988: 79.
25 Cf. BECKER 2012; KAHL 2013: 79–85.
26 Cf. magical bone: KAHL 2016a; Dosoo 2021; ceiling decoration: KAHL 2016b; hippopotamus figurine: KAHL 2018a; statue: KAHL 2019.

"act of violence", (*3wḥ* IV, 34),
"aggressor" (*3dw* III, 6),
"battleground" (*pg3* III,5),
"civil war" (*ḏ3iś* III, 7),
"to die" (*mwt* IV, 4),
"enemy" (*ḫrw.i* III, 51),
"to fall" (*ḫr* III, 23),
"fight" (*ʿḥ3* III, 21),
"to fight" (*ʿḥ3* III, 16, 34; IV, 33, 48),
"flame" (*nśr.t* IV, 14),
"fleet" (*ḥʿw*; III, 23),
"insurgent" (*bšṯ* III, 25),
"painful" (*ḳśn* IV, 14, 52),
"to protect" (*mk(i)* III, 63),
"to repel" (*ḫśf* III, 6),
"robber" (*ḥʿḏ* IV, 12),
"to shoot" (*śṯi* IV, 33),
"to suppress" (*ś:ḫr* III, 17),
"to tremble" (*śd3* IV, 12),
"to unleash" (*ś:tw3* IV, 50)

"to be afraid" (*ś:ʿb3* IV, 12),
"arrow" (*śśr* IV, 33),
"to burn" (*hwt* IV, 14),
"crime" (*bt3* III, 39),
"to drive away" (*ḫśf* IV, 12),
"to expel" (*dr* III, 5, 7, 25),
"fear" (*ḫry.t* III, 20, 36; *śnḏ* III, 10, 36; IV, 10, 13, 54; *śnḏ.t* IV, 13),
"fighter" (*ʿḥ3.w* III, 7),
"fire" (*ḫt* III, 24),
"to flash" (*ś:šd* IV, 12),
"fortress" (*ḫtm* III, 35),
"to land" (*mini* IV, 16),
"protection" (*mkw.t* III, 10),
"refugee" (*tšw.ti* IV, 18),
"to rob" (*ḥʿḏ* IV, 33),
"shield" (*ikm* IV, 54),
"to strike (dead)" (*sḫ* IV, 33),
"terror" (*nḫ3.t* III, 32; *šfy.t* IV, 13),
"troops" (*ʿḥ3* III, 10; *mšʿ* III, 16, 20, 23, 26, 34, 36),

Alarming as it sounds, this list captures only a fraction of the terror, the atrocities and the suffering that must have befallen the city.

The horrors of civil war found their way into the tombs' imagery as well: a wall painting that we discovered in 2004 depicts an Egyptian in the act of striking and killing another (Fig. 22).

The depictions of tomb owners with their troops that we encounter in several places at Asyut are another reflection of the civil war.[27] The images from Tomb IV (Fig. 23) are certainly from the same period when the hostilities took place.

The images in Tomb N13.1, on the other hand, were probably created after Asyut's final defeat by the Theban ruler, Mentuhotep II.[28] The painting on the eastern wall (Fig. 24) shows the nomarch Iti-ibi(-iqer) leading his troops, the number of which – there are 40 soldiers all told – corresponds exactly to the number of wooden model soldiers found in the tomb of Mesehti[29] (Fig. 25). The inscriptions we discovered in Tomb N13.1 tell us that Mesehti succeeded Iti-ibi(-iqer) as Asyuti nomarch. This crucial piece of information allows us to date Mesehti's tomb to Dynasty 11 with a high degree of certainty, most likely to the reign of Mentuhotep II.[30]

The fragmentary images (Fig. 26) in the Northern Soldiers-Tomb[31] (H11.1) – a tomb heavily damaged by quarrying – can also be dated to the final stages of Dynasty 11, or possibly to the period of transition between Dynasties 11 and 12.

Warfare and the exercise of command over their own troops were of the highest importance for the Asyuti nomarchs, not only during the civil war in the First Intermediate Period, but also for some time – even for generations – after the reunification of Egypt.

Our knowledge of the civil war during the First Intermediate Period has enabled us for the first time to grasp Asyut's special status as a "wounded city", a status that the following 4,000 years held in

---

27 Cf. El-Khadragy 2012.
28 Cf. El-Khadragy in print.
29 El-Khadragy 2012: 38.
30 Kahl 2019a: 26–32.
31 Abdelrahiem 2020.

store for the city on more than one occasion.[32] The fight for Asyut lasted for almost two decades,[33] but the city did not perish – it survived conquest by the Thebans under the reign of Iti-ibi, liberation from Theban rule under Khety II, and a further – and this time final – defeat at the hands of the Thebans under Khety II or Iti-ibi(-iqer). It seems that the city recovered quickly from the devastations of war – at least that is what the monumental nomarchs' tombs that were constructed from the end of Dynasty 11 onward suggest.

Asyut met a similar fate several times over the course of its history:[34] in the Second Intermediate Period, Asyut was pillaged once again – we know this because statues looted from Asyut were found at places as far away as Kerma (statues of Djefai-Hapi I and his wife Sennwy)[35] and Gebel Barkal (statue of Djefai-Hapi I)[36] in modern-day Sudan; there is evidence that an armed uprising took place at Asyut during the Assyrian occupation in the first half of the 7th century BCE;[37] in the civil war between the Theban anti-king Ankhwennefer and the Ptolemies in the 2nd century BCE, Asyut yet again signified a major turning point: Ankhwennefer's campaign apparently failed to penetrate northwards past the city[38]. Incursions by marauding Blemmyes from Nubia in the middle of the 5th century CE, as well as raids by other Nubian invaders on Asyut's monasteries, are further instances where Asyut's character as a "wounded city" becomes manifest.[39]

5. Asyut – A Border City in the Middle of Egypt

The reason for Asyut's special fate is to be found in its specific geographic circumstances: although it is located in the middle of Egypt, it was always a border city.

S3ww.ti – "guardian city" – is Asyut's ancient Egyptian name (Fig. 27),[40] a name that lives on in the modern Arabic toponym. The epithet "guardian city" evidently derives from the city's location and its strategic significance. 375 kilometres south of modern Cairo and Memphis, the erstwhile capital of ancient Egypt, Asyut marks the halfway point for travellers to Thebes about 300 kilometres further to the south – the logistic and strategic implications of this are obvious.

Asyut is located to the south of Gebel Abu el-Feda, the most dangerous section of the Nile north of the First Cataract. According to Early Modern travelogues, the current was particularly strong there, and Asyut offered shelter from adverse winds and inclement weather until conditions had improved enough to negotiate the narrow passage.[41]

Even more important was the fact that Asyut was the gateway to a caravan route that Early Modern sources refer to as Darb al-Arba'in, which translates into English as "Forty Days Road". This important trade route leads to the oasis of Kharga and all the way on to Darfur in modern-day Sudan, 1,767 kilometres to the south. Asyut offered much-needed shelter and supplies at the beginning or at the end of a long and dangerous voyage through the desert. In the 19th century CE, there were occasions on which more than 10,000 people embarked on the route at the same time, although not all of them did so voluntarily: many of them were slaves.[42]

---

32 Cf. Kahl 2007: 3–20.
33 For a chronology of the fight, see Kahl 2019b: 25, Table 4.
34 See Kahl 2007: 9–12.
35 Boston, MFA 14.724 and 14.720; Kahl 2007: 116–119.
36 Dunham 1937–38: 14–15.
37 Onasch 1994: 36, 55, 118–121; Kahl 2007: 11–12.
38 Kahl 2007: 12 (cf. Trinity College Dublin Pap. Gr. 274).
39 Kahl 2007: 12.
40 Osing 1976: 320, 866 note 1377.
41 Ebers 1880: 198; Kahl 2007: 14.
42 Kahl 2013: 48–54.

There is evidence that a network of fortresses guarded the caravan route during the Graeco-Roman Period.[43] The hypothesis[44] that the third expedition to Nubia under the leadership of the Old Kingdom official Harkhuf travelled on the Darb al-Arba'in remains highly plausible: research conducted by Mohamed Osman has demonstrated that the terrain in the vicinity of Asyut is passable, that is to say, suitable for a caravan route. In all likelihood, the entrance to the desert route was located between Asyut and Beni Ghaleb and donkeys were used as pack animals (see Mohamed Osman & Jochem Kahl, The Desert Route of Darb el Arba'in at Asyut, in this volume).

While Asyut gave access to the oases and to Nubia, by the same token it was also a natural gateway for invaders. It is very likely that the the above-mentioned marauding Blemmyes made use of the Darb al-Arba'in,[45] and it is just as likely that the looted statues of the Asyuti nomarch Djefai-Hapi I and his wife Sennwy travelled in the opposite direction on the same route.

Based on numerous finds of Roman and Late Roman pottery from the oases Dakhla and Kharga, Teodozja Rzeuska's research[46] for The Asyut Project has demonstrated that the caravan route was in use during the Late Period and the Roman Period.[47] It is safe to assume that Asyut served as an important commercial hub for goods that were transported from the oases to the Nile delta during that time.[48]

Situated right at the junction of the Nile and the caravan route, Asyut was, of course, also an important way station for merchandise and imported goods coming from the north:

A Canaanite amphora (Fig. 28) found in the reused tomb of the nomarch Khety I can be dated to the late Middle Kingdom or the Second Intermediate Period. It originates from the region between Akko in Israel and Akkar in Lebanon.[49] Phoenician amphoras from the Persian Period, that is from around 500 BCE, have been found as well.[50] Another spectacular find dating from the Persian Period is a hoard of more than 870 coins from all over the Mediterranean: from Italy and the Cyrenaica in the west to Caria and Asia Minor in the east.[51] Pottery from the Ptolemaic Period found on Gebel Asyut al-gharbi by The Asyut Project includes items from the Greek islands (Fig. 29).[52] Finds of pottery from the Roman and Byzantine Periods illustrate Asyut's role as a major distribution centre for merchandise from Italy, Northern Africa, the Eastern Mediterranean and the southern oases.[53]

Allegedly found in a monastery close to Asyut, a hoard of high-carat gold jewellery consisting of almost 40 gemmed pieces can also be dated to Late Antiquity or the Byzantine Period, to between the end of the 4th century and the beginning of the 7th century CE. One theory is that the jewellery originated from the Imperial Treasury of Constantinople – exactly how, why and by whom they were brought to Asyut is still unclear.[54] What we do know is that links between Asyut and Constantinople existed as

---

43 Vivian 2000: 359: "massive fortresses".

44 Cf. Obsomer 2007: 45.

45 The Blemmyes advanced as far as Cynopolis (Leipoldt 1902/03, 129; Emmel 1998: 86–88). More than 20,000 people sought refuge at the White Monastery close to Sohag.

46 Rzeuska 2017: 648, Fig. 350: mainly water kegs (known as siga, in production since the Late Period up to the present day) and flasks made with a hard limestone temper; content: wine; larger quantities found than at other archaeological sites.

47 It is hard to determine whether pottery originates from Dakhla or Kharga without detailed petrographic analysis.

48 Rzeuska 2017: 651.

49 Rzeuska 2017: 425, pl. 8.

50 Rzeuska 2017: 503.

51 The coins were found in 1969 by Egyptian workers, who subsequently sold their finds piece by piece to various antique dealers. Today, the coins are spread over almost 100 different collections. As far as can be reconstructed, they were brought to Egypt over a period of less than 15 years (c. 490–475 BCE). The owner of the hoard and his or her origins (Greek or Egyptian?) are unknown: Price & Waggoner 1975: 121.

52 Rzeuska 2017: 563–565 (amphorae, 3rd to 2nd century BCE).

53 Rzeuska 2017: 627–731.

54 See Platz-Horster 2004: 286, who assumes that the artefacts were brought to Egypt because Constantinople was under imminent threat of being conquered. The reasons why they ended up in, of all places, Asyut remains shrouded in mystery. See also Williams 2014.

early as the 4th century: The prophet and seer St John of Lycopolis not only attracted pilgrims from all over Egypt – even the Byzantine Emperor Theodosius sought his advice.[55]

In light of Asyut's geopolitical significance, it is no surprise that the city was characterised by a strong military presence throughout its history. The modern military camp on Gebel Asyut al-gharbi has many precursors: in the 4th and 5th centuries CE, Mauretanian cavalrymen were stationed at Asyut;[56] during the third Persian occupation of Egypt from 618/19 to 627 CE, the city served as a Persian military base.[57]

As early as in the New Kingdom, in the second half of the 2nd millennium BCE, soldiers must have been a common sight in Asyut: members of the military are frequently mentioned on the stelae from what is known as the Salakhana Trove,[58] a hoard of votive offerings found in the tomb of the Middle Kingdom nomarch Djefai-Hapi III.

6. Asyut – A City of Culture

It has become clear at this point that the city was not only a commercial hub, but also a melting pot of local and royal artisans, soldiers and foreign merchants – or in other words, of people and ideas from vastly different cultural backgrounds. Therefore, Asyut's specific geopolitical situation has not resulted in suffering alone: its location lent the city lasting importance. It not only allowed it to recover from armed conflicts time and again, but also to achieve remarkable progress and innovation in the arts, in literature and architecture – in short, to develop its very own intellectual culture.

There is no better example for this than Tomb I, the final resting place of the Asyuti nomarch Djefai-Hapi I (Fig. 30). The tomb was constructed during the reign of Senwosret I – that is, in the 20th century BCE. Djefai-Hapi I served as the mayor of Asyut, as overseer of the priests of the temple of the Asyuti main god Wepwawet, and as the overseer of the priests of the temple of Anubis. Given that he held the office of high priest, he had probably received thorough philological training and was well educated in medicine and astronomy.[59] Djefai-Hapi I was married twice, to women named Sennwy and Wepay. He had a brother who was also called Djefai-Hapi, and a mother named Idy, the elder. Djefai-Hapi's daughter was called Idy like his mother, and his two sons again carried his own name.

Unlike his predecessors, Djefai-Hapi did not have his tomb installed at mid-height of the mountain in solid limestone of good quality, but rather in the lower part (Fig. 13), which already had a natural scattering of karst caves. According to the geologist Dietrich Klemm, Djefai-Hapi made use of these existing cavities to build the largest non-royal rock tomb of his time.[60]

With an original depth of 70 metres, a ceiling height of up to 11 metres and a massive causeway connecting it to the edge of the cultivated land, the rock tomb was a monument to Djefai-Hapi's power and ability that was visible from afar. A reconstruction was prepared in 2004 (Fig. 31) based on archaeological and textual evidence – for example, we can be reasonably sure that the chapel with pond and trees existed because it is described in the tomb's inscriptions.[61] A three-dimensional model from 2018 shows the result of cleaning operations that took place in the years before (Fig. 32).

---

55 Kahl 2007: 138–140; Kahl 2015.
56 Timm 1984: 240.
57 Richter 2003: 228–229.
58 DuQuesne 2009: 62.
59 Cf. *Book of the Temple*. On the curriculum for the children of high priests, see Quack 2002: 170. Quack argues that the origins of the *Book of the Temple* date back as far as the 2nd millennium BCE.
60 Cf. Kahl 2007: 60–61.
61 Engel & Kahl 2009.

Today, the tomb still extends 55 metres deep into the mountain; the missing 15 metres fell victim to quarrying prior to 1799, when the French Expedition arrived in Asyut. Research concerning the causeway and the tomb's substructure is still ongoing.

Tomb I was – and is – a fascinating sight: Its architectural concept, including a chapel and a causeway, is reminiscent of the pyramid layouts of the Old Kingdom. Its architecture is truly monumental – the first hall was about 11 metres high, as the remaining parts of the ceiling show (Fig. 33). The first corridor (Fig. 34) with a height of more than 10 metres is particularly noteworthy: A wooden door, about 6 metres high, gave access to the Great Transverse Hall, which retains a stunningly rich decor even today. The imagery on its northern wall include a scene where cattle is presented to the tomb owner, and an illustration of boys and various animals in trees.[62] The eastern wall contains a catalogue of more than 100 epithets that form an idealised biography. There is also a depiction of Djefai-Hapi I in front of the name of his king, Senwosret I.[63] Another outstanding feature is the ceiling decoration in the Great Transverse Hall with its fascinating geometric patterns. Thanks to an Egyptian restoration team led by Niazy Mostafa Mohamed and Khaled Abd el Malek Abu Zed, the original colours were uncovered (Pls. 1–2a). The second corridor, too, is adorned with exceptionally fine decorations – for example a beautifully detailed rendition of vessels in a scene that depicts the bearers of gifts and offerings (Pl. 2b).[64] The innermost area of the tomb housed a shrine, which has been damaged rather badly by quarrying. It could once be sealed with a double-wing door, a symbol for the gates of heaven. The walls of the shrine were decorated with offering scenes and a false door. There was also a statue of the deceased in the shrine.[65]

A system of corridors descends into the depths of the mountain from the southern rear section of the tomb and leads to the decorated, but heavily destroyed burial chamber at a depth of c. 28 m below ground level.[66] Presumably, this sprawling underground structure was inspired by the cult of Osiris, a religious practice for which we have ample evidence from Asyut for the time of Djefai-Hapi I. According to the autobiographical epithets in his tomb, Asyut, too, maintained a tomb of Osiris like the one that is known to have existed at Abydos during the Middle Kingdom.[67]

The texts and images Djefai-Hapi I used in his burial site are unique in their radiance. Refined, augmented and reworked time and again, the pictorial and textual agenda of his tomb contributed to his being venerated as a god in the late Middle Kingdom, during Dynasty 18 and probably as late as the 1st millennium BCE.[68] One example for the long afterlife of texts from Djefai-Hapi's tomb are ten contracts that ensured that the cult of the deceased would be properly carried out by Asyut's priesthood and necropolis staff. The monumental inscription covers an area of 40 square metres (4 m x 10 m) on one of the walls, and was probably intended as a kind of biographical testimony, but also as a reminder to posterity to respect the stipulations of the contracts. These contracts (Fig. 35) were recopied as late as the Roman Period – that is, more than 2,000 years later – as manuscripts found at Tebtynis on the edge of the Fayum basin suggest.[69]

Other texts and images developed or used in the political, social and cultural environment of Djefai-Hapi I and his predecessors from the end of the First Intermediate Period were greatly admired and frequently copied all over Egypt hundreds and even thousands of years later.[70] High-ranking civil servants such as Senen-mut, Rekh-mi-Ra and Pui-em-Ra (all from Dynasty 18 in the 15th century BCE), Pa-di-Amenope, Mont-em-hat and Ibi (from Dynasties 25 and 26 in the 7th century BCE), reused ex-

---

62 El-Khadragy 2007a: 131–133, 139, 144.
63 Cf. Kahl 2014b.
64 El-Khadragy 2007a: 126–131, 140–143.
65 El-Khadragy 2007b.
66 Beck 2017; Kilian 2017; Kahl 2018b.
67 Kahl 2019a: 47–48; Végh 2019.
68 Kahl 2012.
69 Osing 1998. Kahl 2014b.
70 Kahl 1999; Kahl 2014b: 168–169.

cerpts from biographic formulas, liturgical texts, and decan lists found in Asyut in their own tombs or on statues.[71]

One example of the high regard in which the products of Asyuti artists and craftsmen were held are the beautiful ceiling paintings in Djefai-Hapi's tomb (Pls. 1–2a). A spiral pattern on the ceiling (Pl. 2a) shows an Aegean influence, probably from Crete.[72] This demonstrates yet again just how international a place Asyut must have been as early as during Dynasty 12. 1,200 years later and 300 kilometres further to the south in Upper Egyptian Thebes, the ceiling patterns were reused in a scaled-down format in the tomb of the lector priest Pa-di-Amenope (TT 33).[73] Indeed, the influence of these ornaments reached as far as 19th-century Britain, as could be demonstrated in 2016 based on previous research undertaken by Stephanie Moser on the designer and architect Owen Jones. His book *The Grammar of Ornament* from 1856 contains patterns that are remarkably similar to the ceiling painting in Djefai-Hapi's tomb.[74]

Another case of pictorial transfer is the above-mentioned painting on the eastern wall of the Great Transverse Hall, which shows Djefai-Hapi I standing in a respectful pose in front of the names of his king, Senwosret I (c. 1956–1910 BCE). Some 450 years later, this motif was adapted by the Theban official Senen-mut and reused in his tomb.[75]

Houses of Scroll stored Asyut's collection of knowledge. Texts, images and architectural designs from the city circulated all over Egypt: in Thebes, Naga'el-Hasaya (near Edfu), Memphis/Saqqara, Sais, Rhoda, Athribis (in the Delta), Kom Abu-Yasin and Tuna el-Gebel. According to current research, the above-mentioned Roman Period library in Tebtynis is the last traceable station of the lore from Asyut. Asyut's epistemic heritage formed an integral part of the cultural memory of the ancient Egyptians – or rather, of the collective memory of a powerful group of civil servants and priests. It belonged to a body of knowledge that allowed the Egyptian elites to stabilise and project their self-image and their sense of unity and uniqueness.[76] It is thus fully justified to refer to Asyut as an archive of knowledge. Yet the Houses of Life, the libraries and temples where this knowledge was once preserved have long since disappeared.

The main temple of the city was dedicated to the canid-shaped god Wepwawet. There were also temples for Anubis, Hathor, Osiris and Thot, as well as cults for other gods and kings.[77] As we know from chance finds, the temple of Wepwawet is buried underneath the modern city. For example, a block that surfaced a couple of years ago on the art market, and that has since been returned to Egypt thanks to the efforts of Marcel Marée of the British Museum, certainly originates from Asyut, and very likely from the city's temple of Wepwawet.[78]

What little we know about the main temple of the city is mostly due to an illicit excavation during the 1930s, when a house owner found the temple walls below his cellar while looking for gold, and neighbours called the police after the walls of the house threatened to collapse.[79] We know from Sami Gabra's report on this illicit excavation where the temple of Wepwawet is located, and that it lies at a depth of 8 metres below the modern buildings. Unfortunately, the whereabouts of the blocks that were confiscated at the time were unknown for decades. In 2008, a number of crates were shipped from Cairo to the magazine of the Egyptian Antiquities Organisation at Shutb (see Mohamed Abdelrahiem, *The*

---

71 KAHL 1999.
72 KAHL 2016b.
73 KAHL 2016b.
74 KAHL 2016b: 38–40.
75 KAHL 2014b: 161–163. Senen-mut also reused astronomical imagery known from a 12th Dynasty coffin at Asyut in his burial site at Thebes (Tomb TT 353, constructed in the reign of Queen Hatshepsut, Dynasty 18): see DORMAN 1991: 138–146, Tab. 84–85. On the coffin of Heny (Dynasty 12) from Asyut, see: GUNN 1926.
76 KAHL 1999. See ASSMANN 1988: 15.
77 KAHL 2007: 35–58.
78 http://english.ahram.org.eg/NewsContent/9/40/152042/Heritage/Ancient-Egypt/Egypt-recovers-Stolen-relief-of-King-Seti-I-from-L.aspx
79 GABRA 1931.

Coffin of Nakhti (S1Shu) at the Shutb Storage Museum in Asyut in this volume). They had not been opened for 50 years, and contained, among other things, the blocks examined by Gabra. As the numbering of the blocks suggests, there were probably over 90 of them, significantly more than the 20 described in Gabra's article. At present, I am in the process of cataloguing and examining these finds together with my colleague Mohamed Abdelrahiem from Sohag University in a project funded by the Freie Universität Berlin (see Jochem Kahl & Mohamed Abdelrahiem, *Der verschollene Tempel des Upuaut, des Herrn von Assiut* in this volume).

Concluding this overview, the question remains: why is it that Asyut never became the official capital of Egypt despite its cultural and military significance? The answer is clear: the city's geographical location is what made it important in the first place, but it also made it unsuitable as the nation's seat of government – throughout the millennia, Asyut was simply too vulnerable to attacks from the desert, and too remote from the arena of international politics.

As a result, Asyut ultimately remained a "capital of dreamland"...

...a "capital of dreamland" for the ancient scribe, who – consciously or not – included a highly place-specific detail in one of his texts: on a Middle Kingdom coffin currently located at the Ruhr Museum in Essen,[80] the determinative for the word "necropolis" is not, as could be expected, the usual hieroglyph for mountainous terrain, but nothing other than the outline of Gebel Asyut al-gharbi (Fig. 36).

Asyut also remains, as it has always been, the "capital of dreamland" for treasure hunters of all stripes – medieval or modern, in the city or on the Gebel. This dream, however, is not without dangers – the last fatal incident took place in 2016 right next to the Tomb of the Dogs.

Last but not least, Asyut is the "capital of dreamland" for all team members of *The Asyut Project* and *The Shutb Magazine Project*, whose great hope it is to answer as many questions concerning the city as possible, and to return to it at least some of its many histories.

Bibliography

AHMED-MOHAMED 2020: Y. Ahmed-Mohamed, Texte und Zeichnungen aus islamischer Zeit, in: U. Verhoeven (ed.), Dipinti von Besuchern des Grabes N13.1 in Assiut (The Asyut Project 15; Wiesbaden 2020), 409–444.

ABDELRAHIEM 2020: M. Abdelrahiem, The Northern Soldiers-Tomb (H11.1) at Asyut (The Asyut Project 14; Wiesbaden 2020).

ASSMANN 1988: J. Assmann, Kollektives Gedächtnis und kulturelle Identität, in: J. Assmann & T. Hölscher (eds.), Kultur und Gedächtnis (Frankfurt 1988), 9–19.

BECK 2017: T. Beck, Tomb I, Shaft 1, in: J. Kahl, A. Alansary, U. Verhoeven, T. Beck, E. Czyzewska-Zalewska, E. Gervers, A. Kilian, The Asyut Project: Twelfth Season of Fieldwork (2016), Studien zur Altägyptischen Kultur 46, 2017, 131–141.

BECKER 2012: M. Becker, The Reconstruction of Tomb Siut II from the Middle Kingdom, in: J. Kahl, M. El-Khadragy, U. Verhoeven & A. Kilian (eds.), Seven Seasons at Asyut. First Results of the Egyptian-German Cooperation in Archaeological Fieldwork. Proceedings of an International Conference at the University of Sohag, 10th-11th of October, 2009 (The Asyut Project 2; Wiesbaden 2012), 69–90.

BÉNÉDITE 1923: G. Bénédite, Un „chien" égyptien du Nouvel Empire au Musée du Louvre, in: Gazette des Beaux-Arts 65, Paris 1923, 129–136.

DAVID 2015: É. David, La statue Louvre E 8059, un chien typiquement non-égyptien, in: L. Gabolde (ed.), Un savant au pays du fleuve-dieu. Hommages égyptologiques à Paul Barguet. Kyphi 7, Paris 2015, 32–43.

DELANGE 1987: E. Delange, Catalogue des statues égyptiennes du Moyen Empire (Paris 1987).

DORMAN 1991: P. F. Dorman, The Tombs of Senenmut. The Architecture and Decoration of Tombs 71 and 353 (Publications of the Metropolitan Museum of Art (Egyptian Expedition) 24; New York 1991).

---

80 Ruhr Museum Essen, Inv.-Nr. 2002:2 (formerly known as S2Tü).

Dosoo 2021: K. Dosoo, The Powers of Death: Memory, Place and Eschatology in a Coptic Curse, in: Religion in the Roman Empire 7, 2021, 167–194.

Dunham 1937–38: D. Dunham, An Egyptian Statuette of the Middle Kingdom, in: Worcester Art Museum Annual 3, 1937–38, 9–16.

DuQuesne 2009: T. DuQuesne, The Salakhana Trove: votive stelae and other objects from Asyut (Oxfordshire Communications in Egyptology 7; London 2009).

Del Vesco 2015: P. Del Vesco, The provincial burials of Gebelein and Asyut, in: Museo Egizio (Modena 2015), 70–83.

Ebers 1880: G. Ebers, Aegypten in Bild und Wort dargestellt von unseren ersten Künstlern beschrieben von Georg Ebers (Stuttgart – Leipzig 1880).

Edwards 1877: A. B. Edwards, A Thousand Mile up the Nile (London 1877).

Eichner 2020: I. Eichner, Der Survey der spätantiken und mittelalterlichen christlichen Denkmäler in der Nekropole von Assiut/Lykopolis (Mittelägypten) (The Asyut Project 14; Wiesbaden 2020).

El-Khadragy 2007a: M. El-Khadragy, Fishing, Fowling and Animal-handling in the Tomb of Djefaihapi I at Asyut, in: The Bulletin of the Australian Centre for Egyptology 18, 2007, 125–144.

El-Khadragy 2007b: M. El-Khadragy, The Shrine of the Rock-cut Chapel of Djefaihapi I at Asyut, in: Göttinger Miszellen. Beiträge zur ägyptologischen Diskussion 212, 2007, 41–62.

El-Khadragy 2012: M. El-Khadragy, The Nomarchs of Asyut During the First Intermediate Period and the Middle Kingdom, in: J. Kahl, M. El-Khadragy, U. Verhoeven & A. Kilian (eds.), Seven Seasons at Asyut. First Results of the Egyptian-German Cooperation in Archaeological Fieldwork. Proceedings of an International Conference at the University of Sohag, 10th–11th of October, 2009 (The Asyut Project 2; Wiesbaden 2012), 31–46.

El-Khadragy in print: M. El-Khadragy, Tomb N13.1 of the Nomarch Iti-ibi(-iqer) at Asyut, with collaboration of U. Dubiel and E. Gervers (The Asyut Project; Wiesbaden in print).

Emmel 1998: S. Emmel, The Historical Circumstances of Shenute's Sermon God Is Blessed, in: M. Krause & S. Schaten (eds.), ΘΕΜΕΛΙΑ. Spätantike und koptologische Studien. Peter Grossmann zum 65. Geburtstag (Sprachen und Kulturen des Christlichen Orients 3; Wiesbaden 1998), 81–96.

Engel & Kahl 2009: E. - M. Engel & J. Kahl, Die Grabanlage Djefaihapis I. – Ein Rekonstruktionsversuch, in: J. Popielska-Grzybowska, O. Białostocka & J. Iwaszczuk (eds.), Proceedings of the Third Central European Conference of Young Egyptologists. Egypt 2004: Perspectives of Research. Warsaw 12–14 May 2004 (Acta Archaeologica Pultuskiensia 1, Pułtusk 2009), 55–60.

Gabra 1931: S. Gabra, Un temple d'Aménophis IV à Assiout, in: Chronique d'Égypte 6, 1931, 237–243.

Grébaut 1890–1900: E. Grébaut, Le Musée Égyptien. Recueil de monuments et de notices sur les fouilles d'Égypte. Tome premier (Le Caire 1890–1900).

Gunn 1926 : B. Gunn, The Coffins of Heny, in: Annales du Service des Antiquités de l'Égypte 26, 1926, 166–171.

Hayes 1959: W. C. Hayes, The Scepter of Egypt. A Background for the Study of the Egyptian Antiquities in The Metropolitan Museum of Art. Part II: The Hyksos Period and the New Kingdom (1675–1080 B.C.) (New York 1959).

Inagaki 2007: H. Inagaki, The South Wing. Art of the Ancient World, in: Miho Museum (exhibition catalogue) (Shigaraki 2007), 47–97.

Jomard 1820–1830: E. – F. Jomard et al., Description de l'Égypte ou recueil des observations et des recherches qui ont été faites en Égypte pendant l'Expédition de l'armée française, Seconde edition (Paris 1820–1830).

Kahl 1999: J. Kahl, Siut – Theben. Zur Wertschätzung von Traditionen im alten Ägypten (Probleme der Ägyptologie 13; Leiden – Boston – Köln 1999).

Kahl 2007: J. Kahl, Ancient Asyut. The First Synthesis after 300 Years of Research (The Asyut Project 1; Wiesbaden 2007).

Kahl 2012: J. Kahl, Regionale Milieus und die Macht des Staates im Alten Ägypten: Die Vergöttlichung der Gaufürsten von Assiut, in: Studien zur Altägyptischen Kultur 41, 2012, 163–188.

Kahl 2013: J. Kahl, Die Zeit selbst lag nun tot darnieder. Die Stadt Assiut und ihre Nekropolen nach westlichen Reiseberichten des 17. bis 19. Jahrhunderts: Konstruktion, Destruktion und Rekonstruktion (The Asyut Project 5; Wiesbaden 2013).

Kahl 2014a: J. Kahl, Gebel Asyut al-gharbi in the First Millennium AD, in: E. R. O'Connell (ed.), Egypt in the First Millennium AD: Perspectives from New Fieldwork (British Museum Publications on Egypt and Sudan 2; Leuven – Paris – Walpole, MA 2014), 127–138.

KAHL 2014b: J. Kahl, Assiut – Theben – Tebtynis. Wissensbewegungen von der Ersten Zwischenzeit und dem Mittleren Reich bis in römische Zeit, in: Studien zur Altägyptischen Kultur 43, 2014, 159–172.

KAHL 2015: J. Kahl, The Cave of John of Lykopolis, in: G. Gabra & H. N. Takla (eds.), Christianity and Monasticism in Middle Egypt: Al-Minya and Asyut (Cairo – New York 2015), 255–264.

KAHL 2016a: J. Kahl, Magical Bone, in: J. Kahl, N. Deppe, D. Goldsmith, A. Kilian, C. Kitagawa, J. Moje & M. Zöller-Engelhardt, Asyut, Tomb III: Objects (The Asyut Project 3; Wiesbaden 2016), 333–337.

KAHL 2016b: J. Kahl, Ornamente in Bewegung. Die Deckendekoration der Großen Querhalle im Grab von Djefai-Hapi I. in Assiut (The Asyut Project 6; Wiesbaden 2016).

KAHL 2018a: J. Kahl, Ewiges Leben: Nilpferdfigurinen aus Assiut, in: A. I. Blöbaum, M. Eaton-Krauss & A. Wüthrich (eds.), Pérégrinations avec Erhart Graefe. Festschrift zu seinem 75. Geburtstag (Ägypten und Altes Testament 87; Münster 2018), 239–247.

KAHL 2018b: J. Kahl, Tomb I (P10.1): Causeway, first hall, and main shaft, in: J. Kahl, M. El-Hamrawi & U. Verhoeven, The Asyut Project: Thirteenth Season of Fieldwork (2017), in: Studien zur Altägyptischen Kultur 47, 2018, 137–142.

KAHL 2019a: J. Kahl, Die Statue S10/16. Ein Regionalstil und seine Bewertung (The Asyut Project 11; Wiesbaden 2019).

KAHL 2019b: J. Kahl, Asyut, in: J. Kahl, A. M. Sbriglio, P. Del Vesco & M. Trapani, Asyut. The Excavations of the Italian Archaeological Mission (1906–1913) (Studi del Museo Egizio 1; Modena 2019), 7–38.

KAHL, SBRIGLIO, DEL VESCO & TRAPANI 2019: J. Kahl, A. M. Sbriglio, P. Del Vesco & M. Trapani, Asyut. The Excavations of the Italian Archaeological Mission (1906–1913) (Studi del Museo Egizio 1; Modena 2019).

KILIAN 2017: A. Kilian, Pottery from P10.1, main shaft (inner hall), in: J. Kahl, A. Alansary, U. Verhoeven, T. Beck, E. Czyżewska-Zalewska, E. Gervers, A. Kilian, The Asyut Project: Twelfth Season of Fieldwork (2016), Studien zur Altägyptischen Kultur 46, 2017, 141–145.

KITAGAWA 2016: C. Kitagawa, The Tomb of the Dogs at Asyut: Faunal Remains and Other Selected Objects (The Asyut Project 9; Wiesbaden 2016).

KLEMM & KLEMM 2008: R. Klemm & D. D. Klemm, Stones & Quarries in Ancient Egypt (London 2008).

LEIPOLDT 1902/03: J. Leipoldt, Berichte Schenutes über Einfälle der Nubier in Ägypten, in: Zeitschrift für Ägyptische Sprache und Altertumskunde 40, 1902/3, 126–140.

OBSOMER 2007: C. Obsomer, Les expéditions d'Herkhouf (VIe dynastie) et la localisation de Iam, in: M.-C. Bruwier & R. Betz (eds.), Pharaons Noirs, sur la piste des quarante jours (Musee Royal de Mariemont 2007), 39–52.

ONASCH 1994: H.-U. Onasch, Die assyrischen Eroberungen Ägyptens. Teil 1: Kommentare und Anmerkungen (Ägypten und Altes Testament. Studien zu Geschichte, Kultur und Religion Ägyptens und des Alten Testaments 27/1; Wiesbaden 1994).

OSING 1976: J. Osing, Die Nominalbildung des Ägyptischen (Mainz 1976).

OSING 1998: J. Osing, PSI inv. I 3 + pCarlsberg 305 + pTebt. Tait Add. 2 e PSI inv. I 4 + pCarlsberg 306 + pTebt. Tait Add. 3. Copie delle iscrizioni nelle tombe di Assiut, in: J. Osing & G. Rosati (eds.), Papiri geroglifici e ieratici da Tebtynis (Firenze 1998), 55–100.

PLATZ-HORSTER 2004: G. Platz-Horster, Schmuck und Private Frömmigkeit: Der Goldschmuck von Assiût, Ägypten, in: L. Wamser (ed.), Die Welt von Byzanz – Europas östliches Erbe. Glanz, Krisen und Fortleben einer tausendjährigen Kultur (München 2004), 286–304.

PRICE & WAGGONER 1975: M. Price & N. Waggoner, Archaic Greek Coinage. The Asyut Hoard (London 1975).

QUACK, 2002: J. F. Quack, Die Dienstanweisung des Oberlehrers im Buch vom Tempel, in: H. Beinlich, J. Hallof, H. Hussy & C. von Pfeil (eds.), 5. Ägyptologische Tempeltagung Würzburg, 23. – 26. September 1999 (Ägypten und Altes Testament 33,3; Wiesbaden 2002), 159–171.

RICHTER 2003: S. G. Richter, Beobachtungen zur dritten persischen Eroberung und Besetzung Ägyptens in den Jahren 618/19 bis 629 n. Chr., in: A. I. Blöbaum, J. Kahl & S. D. Schweitzer (eds.), Ägypten – Münster: Kulturwissenschaftliche Studien zu Ägypten, dem Vorderen Orient und verwandten Gebieten – donum natalicium viro doctissimo Erharto Graefe sexagenario ab amicis collegis discipulis ex aedibus Schlaunstraße 2/ Rosenstraße 9 oblatum (Wiesbaden 2003), 221–232.

RYAN 1988: D. P. Ryan, The Archaeological Excavations of David George Hogarth at Asyut, Egypt (Cincinnati 1988).

RZEUSKA 2014: T. Rzeuska, In the Shadow of Wepwawet: An Early Necropolis on Gebel Asyut al-gharbi?, in: Studies in Ancient Art and Civilization 18, 2014, 84–100.

RzEUSKA 2017: T. Rzeuska, Chronological Overview of Pottery from Asyut. A contribution to the history of Gebel Asyut al-gharbi (The Asyut Project 7; Wiesbaden 2017).

TIMM 1984: S. Timm, Das christlich-koptische Ägypten in arabischer Zeit. Teil 1 (A-C) (Beihefte zum Tübinger Atlas des Vorderen Orients, Reihe B (Geisteswissenschaften) 41/1; Wiesbaden 1984).

VÉGH 2019: Z. Végh, The $m^cḥ^c.t$ of Osiris in Asyut, in: I. Regulski (ed.), Abydos: The Sacred Land at the Western Horizon (British Museum Publications on Egypt and Sudan 8; Leuven – Paris – Bristol, CT 2019), 301–313.

VERHOEVEN 2013a: U. Verhoeven, New Kingdom Temple Remains and Other Religious Objects from the Mountain Plateau, in: J. Kahl, M. El-Khadragy, U. Verhoeven, M. Abdelrahiem & E. Czyzewska, The Asyut Project: Tenth Season of Fieldwork (2012), Studien zur Altägyptischen Kultur 42, 2013, 126–138.

VERHOEVEN 2013b: U. Verhoeven, Literatur im Grab: Der Sonderfall Assiut, in: G. Moers, K. Widmaier, A. Giewekemeyer, A. Lümers & R. Ernst (eds.), Dating Egyptian Literary Texts (Lingua Aegyptia – Studia Monographica 11; Hamburg 2013), 139–158.

VERHOEVEN 2020: U. Verhoeven (ed.), Dipinti von Besuchern des Grabes N13.1 in Assiut (The Asyut Project 15; Wiesbaden 2020).

VIVIAN 2000: C. Vivian, The Western Desert of Egypt. An Explorer's Handbook (Cairo 2000).

WILLIAMS 2014: E. D. Williams, "Into the hands of a well-known antiquary of Cairo": The Assiut Treasure and the Making of an Archaeological Hoard, West 86th: A Journal of Decorative Arts, Design History, and Material Culture , 21, No. 2, 2014, 251–272.

WINLOCK 1919: H. E. Winlock, The Statue of Iny and Rennut, The Metropolitan Museum of Art Bulletin, 14 (2), 1919, 32–35.

ZITMAN 2010: M. Zitman, The Necropolis of Assiut: A Case Study of Local Egyptian Funerary Culture from the Old Kingdom to the End of the Middle Kingdom, 2 vols. (Orientalia Lovaniensia Analecta 180; Leuven–Paris–Walpole, MA 2010).

Internet References

http://english.ahram.org.eg/NewsContent/9/40/152042/Heritage/Ancient-Egypt/Egypt-recovers-Stolen-relief-of-King-Seti-I-from-L.aspx

https://www.metmuseum.org/art/collection/search/544740

https://www.metmuseum.org/art/collection/search/544742

The Asyut Project, Harrassowitz Verlag, https://www.harrassowitz-verlag.de/reihe_412.ahtml

Fig. 1: The Asyut region (Map: Oliver Hasselbach; © The Asyut Project).

Fig. 2: The city of Asyut in 2012 (photo: Fritz Barthel; © The Asyut Project).

Fig. 3: Google view on Asyut and Gebel Asyut al-gharbi in 2006.

Fig. 4: The city of Asyut in 2016 (photo: Fritz Barthel; © The Asyut Project).

Fig. 5: Asyut, modern cemetery in 2010 (photo: Fritz Barthel; © The Asyut Project).

Fig. 6: Statue of Isis-Hathor and Wepwawet (New York, Metropolitan Museum of Art 17.2.5,
Rogers Fund, 1917; https://www.metmuseum.org/art/collection/search/544742).

Fig. 8: Statue of Iuny and Renenut, back (New York, Metropolitan Museum of Art 15.2.1, Rogers Fund, 1915; https://www.metmuseum.org/art/collection/search/544740).

Fig. 7: Statue of Iuny and Renenut, front (New York, Metropolitan Museum of Art 15.2.1, Rogers Fund, 1915; https://www.metmuseum.org/art/collection/search/544740).

Fig. 9: Gebel Asyut al-gharbi in 2012 (photo: Fritz Barthel; © The Asyut Project).

Fig. 10: Gebel Asyut al-gharbi in 2018 (photo: Fritz Barthel; © The Asyut Project).

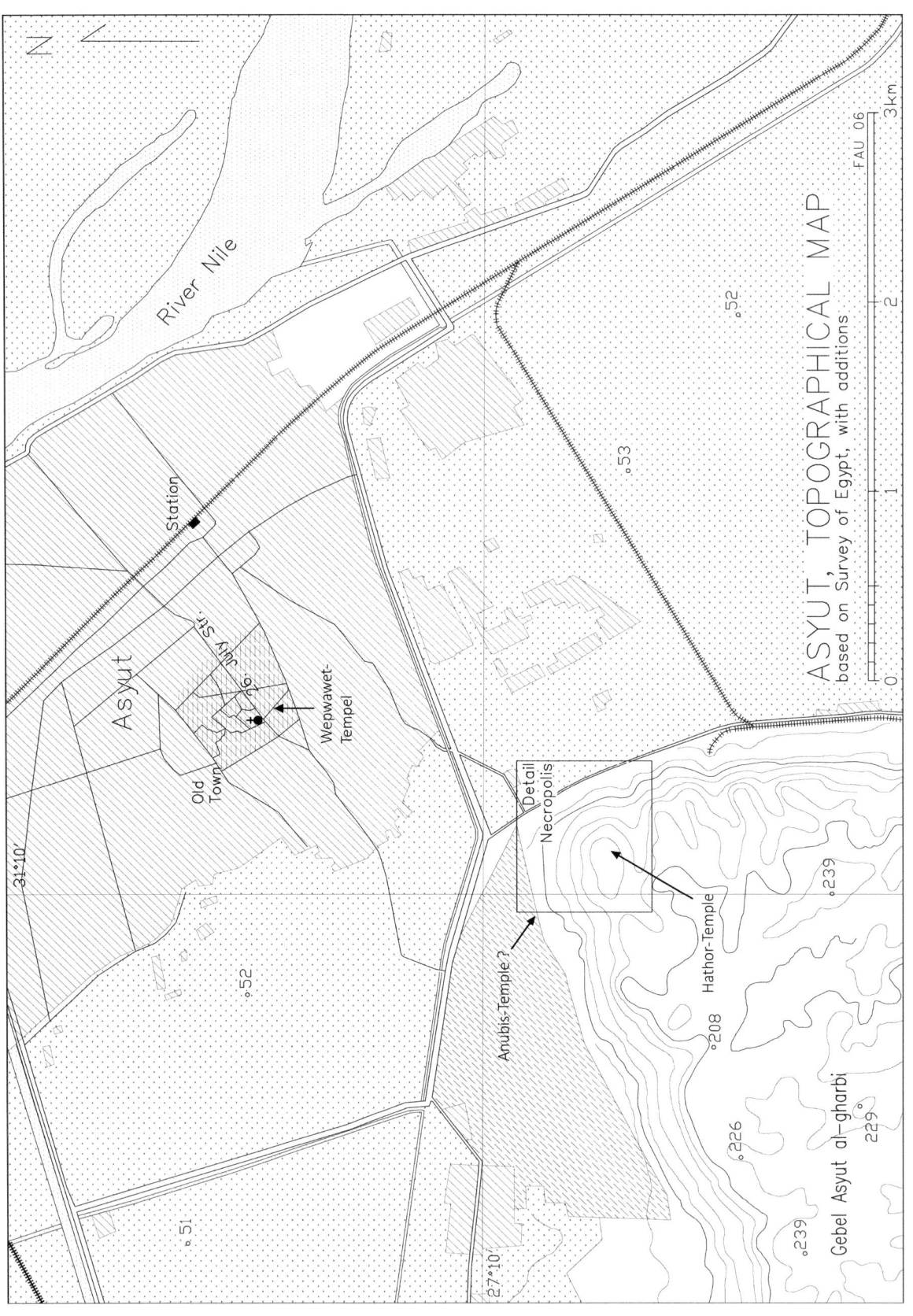

Fig. 11: Map of Asyut (© The Asyut Project).

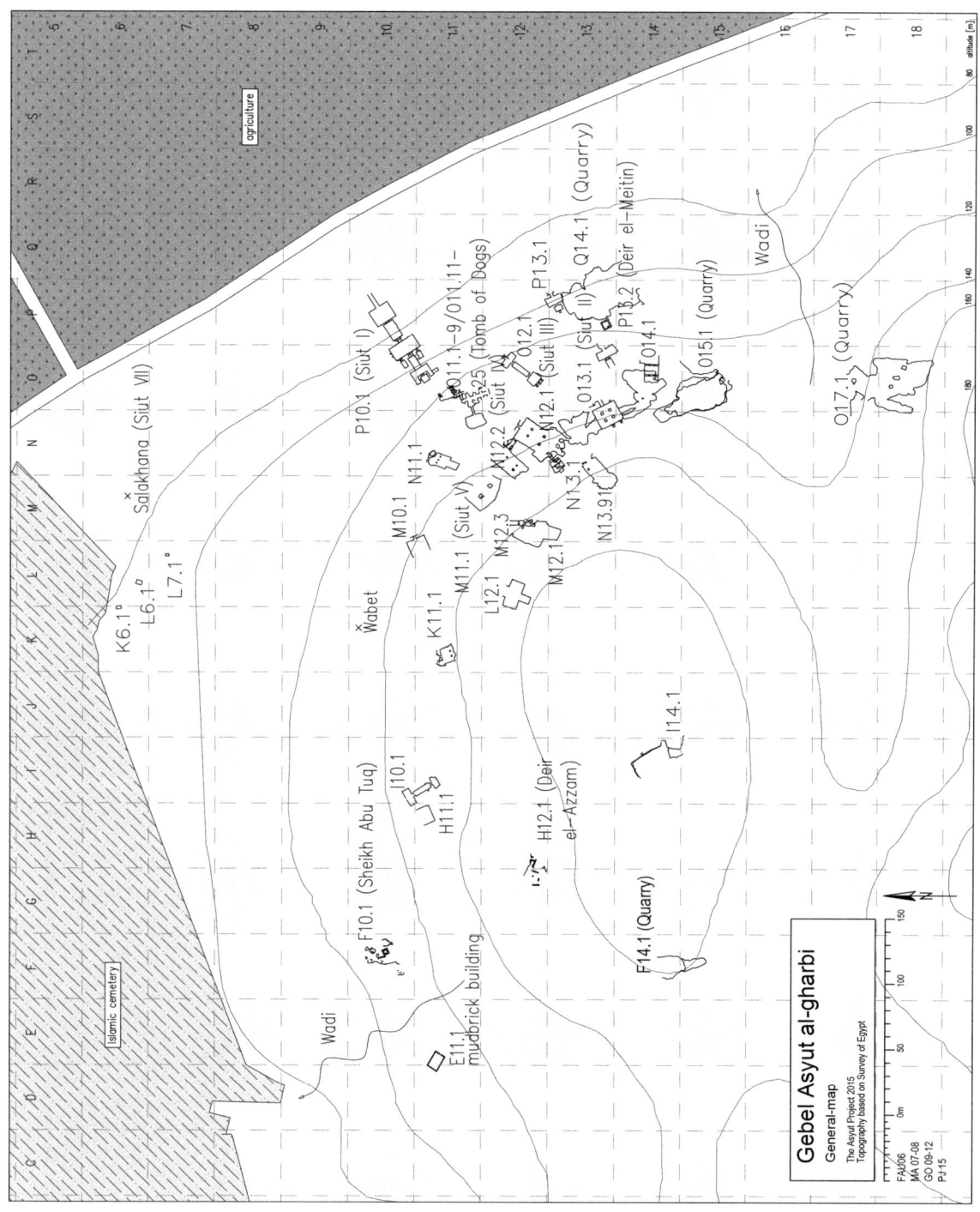

Fig. 12: Gebel Asyut al-gharbi (© The Asyut Project).

Fig. 13: Gebel Asyut al-gharbi in 2010 (photo: Fritz Barthel; © The Asyut Project).

Fig. 14: Tomb II in 1799 (Jomard 1820–1830: pl. 46.10).

Fig. 15: Tomb II in 2005 (photo: Jochem Kahl; © The Asyut Project).

Fig. 16: Statue S10/16 (photo: Fritz Barthel;
© The Asyut Project).

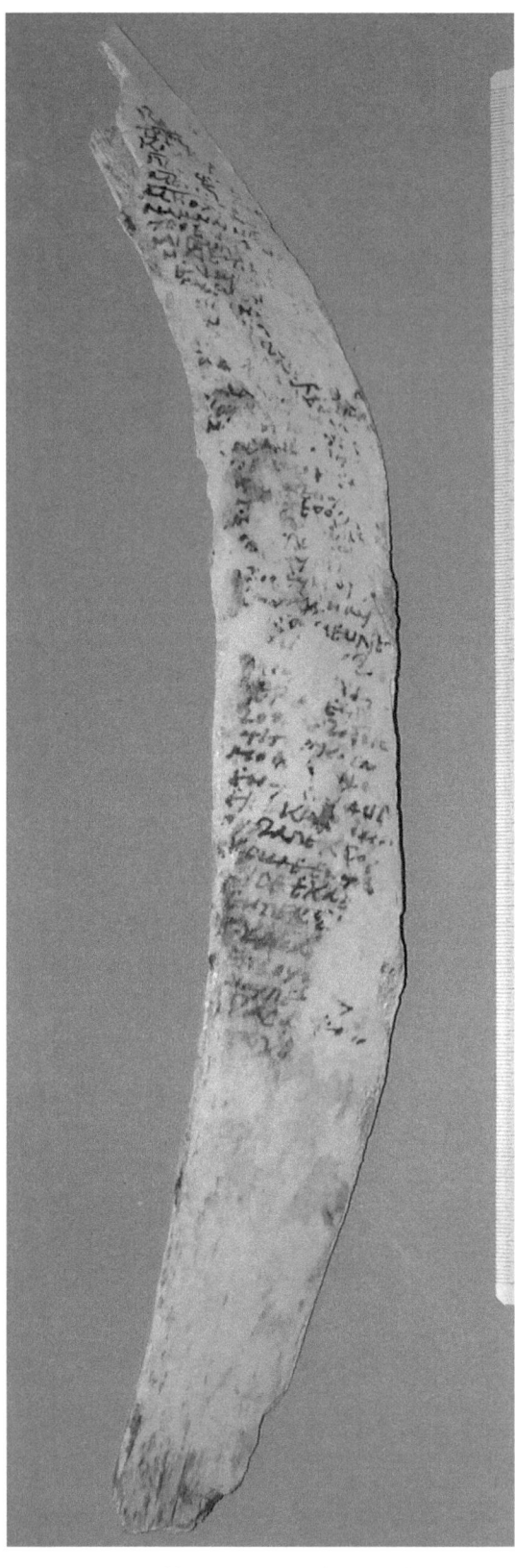

Fig. 17: Figurine of a hippopotamus (S10/4, photo:
Fritz Barthel; © The Asyut Project).

Fig. 18: Magical bone (S05/46, photo: Jochem Kahl;
© The Asyut Project).

Fig. 19: Asyut, Tomb III, IV, and V (from left to right) from the late First Intermediate Period, 2007
(photo: Fritz Barthel; © The Asyut Project).

Fig. 20: Tomb III, northern wall, autobiographical inscription of Iti-ibi, 2006 (photo: Fritz Barthel; © The Asyut Project).

Fig. 21: Tomb IV, northern wall, autobiographical inscription of Khety II, 2006 (photo: Fritz Barthel; © The Asyut Project).

Fig. 22: Tomb III, northern wall, fighting soldiers (drawing: Ilona Regulski; © The Asyut Project).

Fig. 23: Tomb IV, southern wall, marching soldiers, 2006 (photo: Jochem Kahl; © The Asyut Project).

Fig. 24: Tomb N13.1, eastern wall, southern part, nomarch and marching soldiers, 2007
(photo: Fritz Barthel; © The Asyut Project).

Fig. 25: Tomb of Mesehti, models of soldiers (Grébaut 1890–1900: pl. 33).

Fig. 26: Northern Soldiers-Tomb, H11.1, 2010 (photo: Fritz Barthel; © The Asyut Project).

Fig. 27: Tomb I, Great Transverse Hall, ceiling inscription with the name of Asyut in hieroglyphs, 2014
(photo: Fritz Barthel; © The Asyut Project).

Fig. 28: Canaanite amphora found in Tomb V
(photo: Aneta Cedro; © The Asyut Project).

Fig. 29: Rhodian amphora stamp (S04/st307; photo:
Jochem Kahl; © The Asyut Project).

Fig. 30: Tomb I, 2014 (photo: Fritz Barthel; © The Asyut Project).

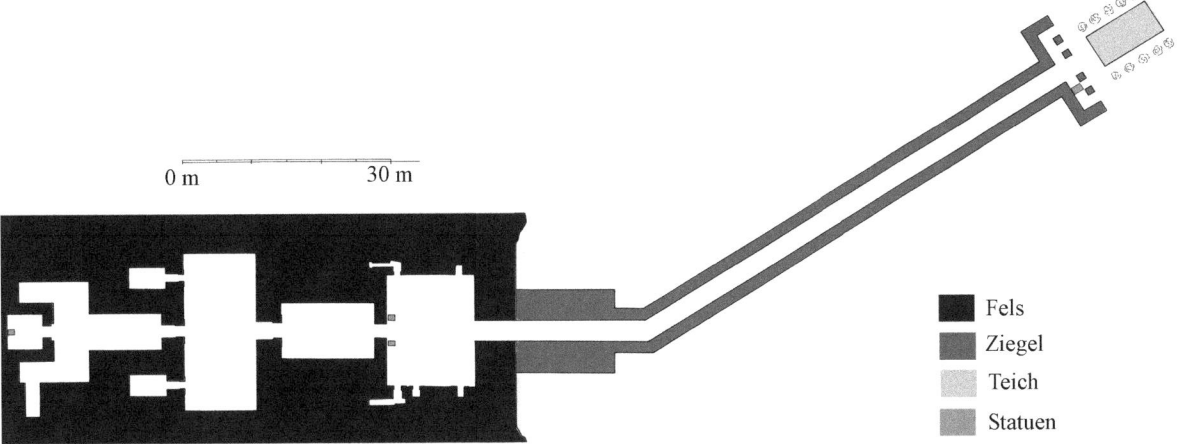

Fig. 31: Tomb I, reconstruction of the architecture according to archaeological and textual evidence, 2004
(Eva-Maria Engel & Jochem Kahl; © The Asyut Project).

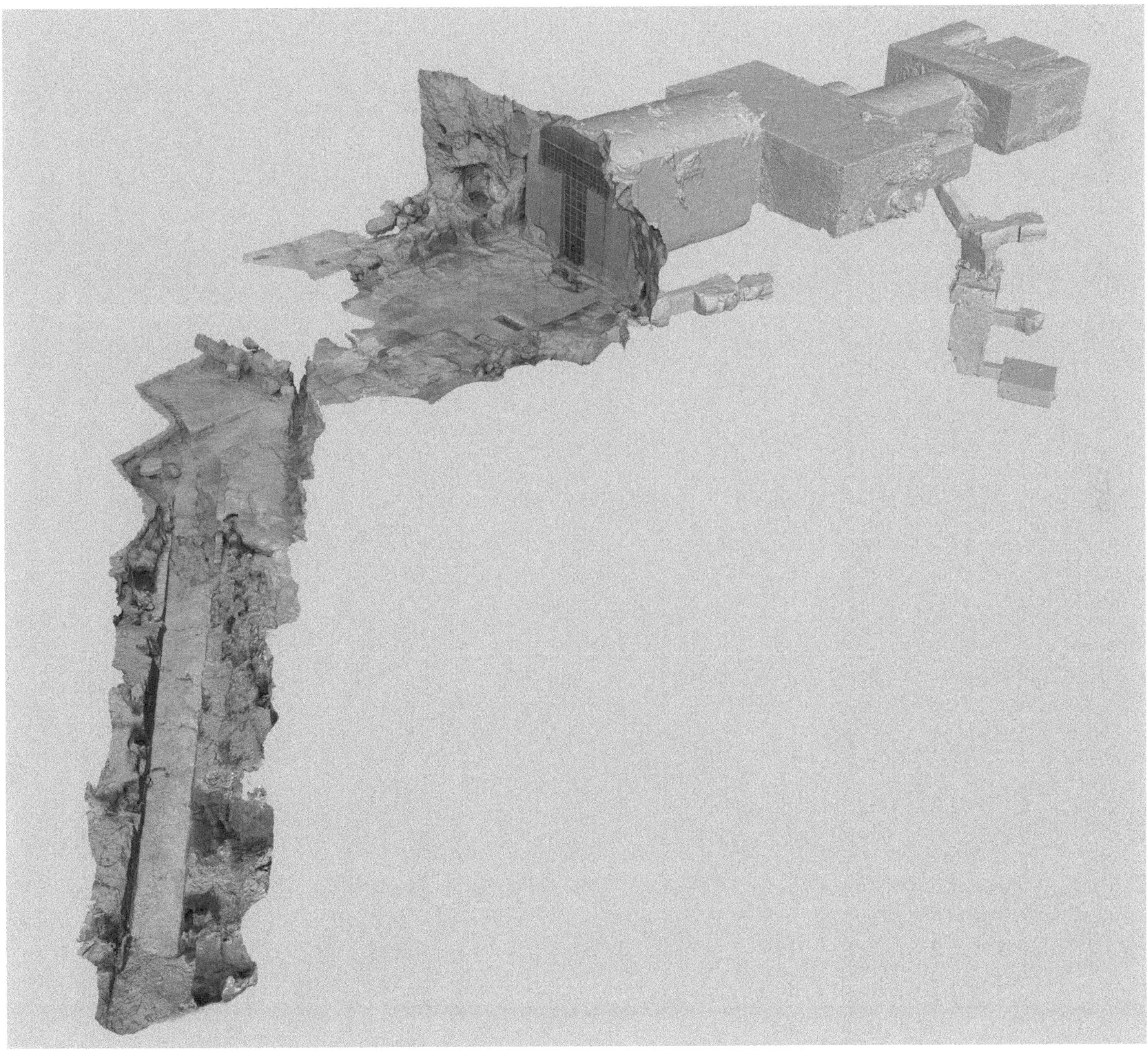

Fig. 32: Tomb I, 3D-model (Philipp Jansen; © The Asyut Project).

Fig. 33: Tomb I, First Hall, 2007 (photo: Fritz Barthel; © The Asyut Project).

Fig. 34: Tomb I, First Corridor and entrance to Great Transverse Hall, 2018 (photo: Fritz Barthel; © The Asyut Project).

Fig. 35: Tomb I, Great Transverse Hall, eastern wall, the ten contracts (photo: Fritz Barthel 2007; © The Asyut Project).

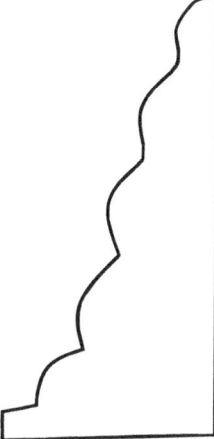

Fig. 36: Hieroglyph depicting Gebel Asyut al-gharbi on coffin of the Middle Kingdom
in the Ruhr Museum, Essen, Inv.-Nr. 2002:2 (drawing: Chiori Kitagawa).

The Desert Route of Darb el-Arba'in at Asyut*

Mohamed Osman & Jochem Kahl

1. Introduction

Darb el-Arba'in is one of the well-known trade routes that was once active in the north-eastern African Sahara.[1] It is known, thanks to several travel reports, that this route was used at least during the Early Modern and Modern Period. This established camel route was described and illustrated on old maps of Egypt and Sudan as starting in Asyut (Siut) and ending in El-Fasher in Darfur (or *vice versa*). So far, the significance of the route during antiquity has not been solidly confirmed, however, it has always been appealing to the Egyptologists to correlate Darb el-Arba'in with the ancient Egyptian route that once connected Egypt to the land of Yam.

This paper intends to investigate the possibilities of considering Asyut as one of the starting points of the desert route, which once took caravans towards southern destinations such as Yam and later towards Darfur, from the landscape-archaeology point of view. It will also try to correlate the spatial analysis results with the related material culture. This attempt will be possible through the usage of both preliminary and advanced spatial analysis, using old and modern maps, satellite images, travel reports and GIS spatial analysis.

2. Asyut as a center of trade

Asyut, situated c. 375km to the south of modern Cairo and half way between the ancient Egyptian capitals of Memphis and Thebes, was a political and cultural center in Middle Egypt from the First Intermediate Period (c. 2100 BCE) at the latest until the end of the Pharaonic Period.[2] The city formed part of the cultural memory of Ancient Egypt[3] and also had a highly strategic importance. Moreover, during the Byzantine and Islamic Periods, Asyut played an important supraregional role in Christianity.[4]

In early modern times, Asyut was also well known as a fertile area, where especially grain was cultivated. In 1844, for example, the city was located in Egypt's most extensively cultivated province and therefore of economic importance.[5] We may assume that already during the Pharaonic Period, Asyut produced a rich amount of grain, as it was, for example, mentioned in the First Intermediate Period inscription of the nomarch Khety I.[6]

For the Pharaonic Period and Late Antiquity, the role of the city as a hub of trade became clear during the most recent research on Gebel Asyut al-gharbi. Despite the lack of any material from the Pharaonic

---

* This article was written within the research project „Asyut – centre of ancient trade" funded by the Deutsche Forschungsgemeinschaft (DFG) - Project-number 426702318 and Narodowe Centrum Nauki.
1 Cf. MORKOT 1996; ROE 2005/6; DUCÈNE 2007; MORENO GARCÍA 2017: 118.
2 Cf. KAHL 2007.
3 KAHL 1999; KAHL 2014.
4 Cf. TIMM 1984: 235–251; VAN DER VLIET 2015.
5 WALZ 1978: 117.
6 SCHENKEL 1978: 29–32. LICHTHEIM 1988: 26–29.

city of Asyut, which is completely overbuilt by modern houses, the objects found at Gebel Asyut al-gharbi (Fig. 2 in the contribution of J. Kahl) constitute Asyut as a center of trade during the Pharaonic and Byzantine Periods.

The archaeological investigation of Gebel Asyut al-gharbi brought many vessels to light, which prove the supraregional relations of Asyut. Only some individual imports from Syro-Palestine have been attested for the third and second millennium BCE so far.[7] The situation, however, changes for the first millennium BCE, as trade between Asyut and Phoenicia during the Late Period is attested by so-called "torpedo amphorae" of the Cypro-Phoenician tradition[8]. Amphorae from Rhodes, which was part of the Ptolemaic Empire,[9] and from Kos,[10] as well as fine ware from Asia Minor (Knidos or Pergamon?)[11] point to relations with the Aegean and the Eastern Mediterranean regions. The goods which were transported in these vessels cannot be determined exactly. The Asyut hoard of about 900 silver coins "is a classic illustration of international trade relations"[12] and attests direct or indirect connections with the Mediterranean region. Coins from Italy, Sicily, Macedonia, Thrace, Central Greece, Athens, Aegina, Corinth, the Greek Islands, Asia Minor, Caria, Sardes, Lycia, Cyprus and Cyrenaica seem to have been accumulated over a period of not more than fifteen years (c. 490–475 BCE).[13] The owner of this hoard and his/her ethnic background—Greek or Egyptian—remain unknown[14]. During the Roman Period (first century BCE–mid third century CE), imports from Asia Minor (probably Knidos) and Campania came to Asyut.[15]

Late Roman Period (mid-third–seventh century CE) brought intensive trade activity with the Mediterranean. Amphorae of the type Carthage Late Roman 1 amphorae (LR 1) are more numerously attested at Asyut than at any other site in Egypt.[16] These amphorae indicate trade relations with the eastern part of the Mediterranean Basin: Cilicia, Cyprus, Rhodes and the Greek mainland are possible areas of origin.[17] Goods could have been grain, wine and resin. Carthage Late Roman 4 amphorae (LR 4) are also well represented at Asyut, which leaves no doubt that both types were mass imported.[18] These amphorae (early fourth–early eighth century CE; from Gaza and Palestine) were probably containers for fish, olive oil, sesame oil, cereals and wine.[19] Less numerous are LR 3 amphorae (fourth–seventh century CE) at Gebel Asyut al-gharbi. Their exact provenance still has to be determined; presumably they were produced in Asia Minor.[20] The contents of LR 3 amphorae may have been unguents and/or wine.[21]

The hoard of Byzantine gold jewelry from the fifth to early seventh century CE indicates a connection to the imperial family in Constantinople.[22] The enormous value of the high-carat gold and the precious stones—sometimes imported from afar, even from Ceylon—as well as the restricted use of the so-called Berlin collar by female members of the imperial family[23] suggest that the commissioner, bearer and gold-

---

7 A fragment of a Levantine jar from the Old Kingdom (Rzeuska 2017: 86–87, 148–149) and a Second Intermediate Period Amphora from the region between Akko in present day Israel and Akkar in Lebanon (Rzeuska 2017: 425).
8 Rzeuska 2017: 503, 546–549.
9 Rzeuska 2017: 563–565, 618–623.
10 Rzeuska 2017: 565, 624–625.
11 Rzeuska 2017: 566, 624–625.
12 Alram 2016: 70.
13 Kahl 2007: 117.
14 Price & Waggoner 1975: 121; cf. Duyrat 2005: 10–51; Kahl 2007: 117–118.
15 Rzeuska 2017: 652–653, 708–711.
16 Rzeuska 2017: 653.
17 Rzeuska 2017: 654.
18 Rzeuska 2017: 653.
19 Rzeuska 2017: 655–656.
20 Rzeuska 2017: 654.
21 Rzeuska 2017: 654.
22 Dennison 1918.
23 Stolz 2006: 554–555.

smith were most likely located in the capital of Byzantium. When and how the jewelry was transferred to Asyut remains unclear.[24] The situation of the presumed find spot of the nearly forty pieces of jewelry in a monastery close to Asyut—exact information is missing—points to intentional hoarding. A connection with the Arabic conquest of Egypt (639–642 CE) is conceivable.[25]

3. Description of the landscape

The desert hinterland of Asyut is basically a part of the Eocene limestone plateau, which dominates the northern part of the Egyptian Western Desert[26]. One of the main attributes of the plateau is the steep and relatively high eastern escarpments, which define the western edges of the Nile Valley. In other locations, the Nile Valley often includes a low desert area that expands behind the alluvial fertile fields, before the steep escarpment of the plateau defines the western ends of the Nile Valley and the beginning of the high desert. However, in the Asyut region, the low desert area does not exist, as the alluvial land extends to end almost at the foot of the plateau. In Asyut, the plateau curvature takes a projecting shape towards the east, before it retreats towards the west/north-west. This projection forms what is called Gebel Asyut, where all the rock-cut tombs were found (Fig. 9–10 in the contribution of J. Kahl). Geologically, Gebel Asyut is part of what is known as the Drunka Formation (Gebel Drunka/Jabal Durunkah).[27] The slope angle/grade of the Gebel Asyut escarpment is between 13° and 27° (Pl. 3) and it is dissected with several watersheds[28] that vary in size and steepness between small steep watersheds and watersheds big enough to form ascending wadis to the summit of the plateau.

At the summit of the plateau, the terrain is undulating in general. On the top of the plateau, as Kassas and Said described, the surface consists of a thin eroded layer of alluvial and limestone gravel or what is called the Hamada terrain.[29] Bubenzer and Bolton during their survey in Darb el Tawil (another trial leads from Asyut to Dakhla), detected long tracks of caravans, which are preserved within the areas where Hamada surface exists.[30] These tracks remained preserved through ages, as the terrain developed over time with the constant usage of the route by caravans. The dynamics of this landscape change was caused by pack animals, during their repeating march, clearing the fragments of stones and gravel of the Hamada surface in their way, creating relatively deep tracks with accumulated cleared gravel on both sides and with aeolian sand accumulating in these worn paths. At this stage the landscape became rigid and preserved the tracks on the surface.[31] These tracks can be seen on satellite images in the areas where there are Hamada surfaces, because these areas are not interrupted by modern activity or sand dunes. Usually, it is visible as many wide parallel lines going in the same direction.

The summit of the Eocene plateau at the Asyut desert hinterlands and up to Kharga Oasis can be described as an undulating surface, which includes several medium/wide to narrow watersheds. Most of the watersheds are shallow and do not represent a wadi formation and almost all of them are oriented

---

24 For a critical view on the hoard see Williams 2014: 251–272.

25 Platz-Horster 2004: 286; cf. Kahl 2007: 119–120.

26 Said 1990: 11–14.

27 Kahl 2007: 59; cf. Klemm & Klemm 2008: 112–115.

28 Watershed can be described as: "the upslope area that contributes flow—generally water—to a common outlet as concentrated drainage. It can be part of a larger watershed and can also contain smaller watersheds, called sub-basins. The boundaries between watersheds are termed drainage divides. The outlet or pour point, is the point on the surface at which water flows out of an area. It is the lowest point along the boundary of a watershed". See: http://pro.arcgis.com/en/pro-app/tool-reference/spatial-analyst/how-watershed-works.htm (accessed 19-9-2021).

29 Said 1990: 14; Kassas 1953: 195–196.

30 Bubenzer & Bolton 2013.

31 Bubenzer & Bolton 2013: 70.

from north to south (Pl. 4). This last attribute was noticed partially by L. Giddy in her description of one of the passes that leads outside of Kharga Depression:

> "… a terrain desolate and rugged to the extreme. The stark, limestone surface is cut into deep gullies, all orientated north-south, owing to the prevailing wind. To head eastwards across these gullies is indeed difficult, but the least arduous route is clearly marked out by a line of cairns, leading off to the north-east as far as the eye can see".[32]

As for water sources in this part of the Sahara, as part of the Eocene plateau, the only aquifer located in this area is what is known as the Carbonate aquifer system. Very little is known about this aquifer and the depth of it. However, it is known that its recharging process depends on upward leaking coming from the lower Nubian Sandstone aquifer; the only known access to this aquifer is via the natural springs in the Siwa oasis.[33] This means practically an almost completely arid situation at the limestone plateau, where the first segment of Darb el-Arba'in was supposed to have passed through and the closest reliable water source would be the Kharga Oasis in the west or the Nile Valley itself in the east.

3.1 The traveler's records

Several travelers recorded their journeys through Egypt and Sudan between the eighteenth and the twentieth centuries. One of the well-known journeys was the one that was taken by the British traveler William George Browne in 1793.[34] His journey to the kingdom of Darfur covered several segments of Darb el-Arba'in, where he encountered and recorded several facts and events of desert traveling before the age of cars. Moreover, he was one of several Europeans who wrote about Asyut as a main city in Middle Egypt, describing its landscape and the surrounding towns and villages.[35] In fact, Browne started his journey from Bulaq-Cairo, where he took a boat to Asyut on the 21st of April, 1793. He arrived in Asyut after 8 days, but nevertheless, he had to stay in Asyut 50 days before the caravan to Darfur was ready, as the caravan had to prepare for the journey by buying camels and provisions. He described how it was not easy to find camels and the five camels that he eventually bought.

The first segment of the journey took one week for the caravan to arrive at the access point to Kharga Depression (Rumlie Pass).[36] This descent point from the plateau to Kharga Depression was described by Giddy. It is located on the most northern point of Kharga Depression. Travelers would cross around 210km from Asyut to this point, where there was no chance to access any water sources on the way.[37] Giddy mentions the experiences of both Blundell (1890s) and Moritz (1900) descending Rumlie Pass, which was attributed with *"vast amounts of accumulated sand there, forming a gently inclined plane"*; however, the existence of accumulated aeolian sand at this descent proved not to be an advantage, as *"all camels sunk forlornly up to their knees in the loose sand"*[38]. Browne also mentions a considerably difficult descent from Rumlie, to the extent that the caravan had to unload the camels in order to make them rest. They *"were employed four hours and a half, the following morning, in passing from the foot of the mountain"* to Ain el-Diz and then they marched for another eight hours to reach Kharga.[39] Rossi and Ikram, during their survey of Kharga Depression, found several pieces of evidence of caravan mobility

---

32 GIDDY 1987: 9.
33 EL TAHLAWI, FARRAG & AHMED 2008: 647; GIDDY 1987: 1 mentions the impossibility of digging wells in the Eocene plateau, as it is too thick to reach the groundwater.
34 BROWNE 1799: 180–215. For his 1792 journey to Asyut see KAHL 2013: 185–188.
35 BROWNE 1799: 120.
36 BROWNE 1799: 184.
37 GIDDY 1987: 7.
38 GIDDY 1987: 7.
39 BROWNE 1799: 185.

across Rumlie Pass (Aqabet el-Remilya), such as donkey and camel skeletons, along with the occasional occurrence of second and third century CE pottery fragments.[40]

The segment between Asyut and Kharga was described by Beadnell as *"the last and the worst portion of Darb el Arba'in"*, mentioning that this 200km segment is attributed with difficult surfaces, full of sharp stone fragments (Hamada). He also describes the considerable big number of camel skeletons that were seen on the road, sometimes in groups, taking this as additional evidence of how difficult the route was.[41] Browne also mentions losses of camels in the caravan he was traveling with, as well.[42]

In 1884, E. J. Montague-Stuart-Wortley was appointed as an army officer to travel through Darb el-Arba'in to Sudan, this time for security reasons. He says:

> "Early in May, 1884, it was decided to send a reconnoitering force, composed of Arabs, from Assiut a distance of some hundreds of miles through the oases of the western desert, in order to see whether it was possible for a hostile force from Kordofan or Darfur to advance by the desert on the delta, without touching the Nile. A route was known to exist from Assiut to Darfur by which slave-dealing caravans were accustomed to travel, called the "Arba'in" or the Forty Days Route."[43]

He started his journey from Asyut, specifically from Manqabad army camps. He ascended the plateau through Wadi Mehattar, most likely close to Kulit el-Edissiyah (Pl. 5a). He mentioned a Bedouin tribe called the Jawazi tribe, which used to live around the hinterlands of Asyut.

Roughly 100 years after Browne's journey, A. R. Guest describes the segment between Asyut and Kharga:

> "The roads through the desert to the oases are broad, well-beaten tracks worn into furrows by long usage. The desert is generally hard and rocky, consisting of plain after plain separated by slight rises and hollows. In some places the road winds between rocks or passes through heavy sand, and in these it is difficult to find the way without a guide. There is generally good going for a camel, but broken ground in each road would render it almost impassable for any kind of vehicle".[44]

Besides the descriptions of European travelers, several maps of Egypt and Sudan mark the route of Darb el-Arba'in. A historical map of Egypt from 1584, which was illustrated by Abraham Ortelius, *"Aegyptus Antiqua"*[45] shows the Nile Valley and a clear separator between the oases and the Nile Valley and the surrounding desert. The map, referring to Plinius, shows the Asyut region (*"Lycopolites Lybycon"*) and a route that connects the Asyuti area with the oasis. Although the geospatial relations in this map are obviously not correct, it still provides an early hint about a caravan route, which connected Asyut with the oases, Kharga and Dakhla, probably denoting the first segment in Darb el-Arba'in (Pl. 5b).

Another early map dates back to 1707[46] and illustrates the marginal borders of Egypt, the Kingdom of Sennar and the Kingdom of Abyssinia (Pl. 6a). The map records a route that starts from Cairo, going southwards along the Nile to reach Asyut (*"Siout"*). From there, the route starts crossing the Western Desert between hills, reaching Kharga Oasis (*"El-Ouah"*) through a northern approach called *"M de Ramlie"*[47]. The map also depicts Kharga (*"Hargue"*) as a town, as well as other locations such as Baris. The route continues to the south to reach Selima Oasis and then turns to the south-east to meet the Nile Valley again at Mocho, which is located not far from Amara-west in Sudan. The route reaches Dongola and transcends it crossing Bayuoda Desert (*"Desert de Bahiouda les Chanedi"*) to meet the Nile Valley

---

40 Rossi & Ikram 2013: 275.
41 Beadnell 1909: 33–34.
42 Browne 1799: 187.
43 Montague-Stuart-Wortley 1953: 22.
44 Guest 1900: 657.
45 Schilder 1987: 8–9. Meurer 1998: 133–159.
46 Carte de l'Egypte, de la Nubie, de l'Abissinie &c. Par Guillaume de L'Isle de l'Academie Royale des Sciences; Desrosiers sculp. (to accompany) Atlas Geographique contenant la Mappemonde et les quatre partie, 1707.
47 Toponym as it is written on the map.

again in the Chanedi region. Crossing the Nile, the route reaches Sennar. From Sennar, the route takes a dramatic turn towards the east, as it crosses the border to Abyssinia and reaches the Red Sea at Arkiko ("*Arquico*"), in the regions east of Asmara. This route is obviously not the traditional Darb el-Arba'in, although it overlaps with it in the first three segments. Although the geospatial relations and proportions are not correct in such an old attempt at cartography, the geographers recorded some important aspects of topography and several toponyms, which are still known to us today and we can orient our modern maps on them. A clear example is the descend point to Kharga Depression at Rumlie Pass, which was mentioned in Browne's journey memoire.

Another more accurate map of the Turkish Empire, which was published in 1715, mentions in detail toponyms along the Nile Valley and the southern extension in Ethiopia. The map includes a route that starts in Asyut ("*Siot*") towards the oasis ("*Elouah*"). From there, with a general southern direction and in parallel to the Nile Valley, it reaches Dongola, then Corti and continues southwards through Bayuoda Desert to reach Sennar and eventually reaches the shores of the Red Sea at Arkiko ("*Arquico*") in "*Abissinie*" or modern Eretria (Pl. 6b).[48] This map shows a better sense of spatial relations between the geographical units, nevertheless, it is not accurate in illustrating the geographical attributes of the Nile curvature.

During the nineteenth century, more accurate maps of Egypt and the rest of the Nile Valley were published. The earliest to be printed was the "*Charte vom Nil Strome, Aegypten, Nubien und Habesch*" (*Map of the Nile River, Egypt, Nubia and Abyssinia*) in 1817 (Pl. 6c).[49] On this map, the caravan route between Asyut ("*Siut*") and Kharga ("*Charje Grosse Oasis od. El Wah*") specifies different locations within the oasis, such as Bulaq and Baris. The route heads towards Selima Oasis and from there it forks to reach the Nile Valley at "*Moschu*" right north of Saï Island. The left branch continues towards the south to reach Darfur, via Laqiyah and Bir Malha. The route was named as "*Karawanen Strasse von Sudan über Darfur nach Kahira*"[50].

In the "*Description de l'Egypte*", another interesting map (Fig. 1)[51] was published showing the area of Asyut and the surrounding villages. One of the details of this map is two trails, which start in Asyut and proceed to the west. One of them turns to the south-southwest to ascend the plateau at one of the illustrated wadis. Worth mentioning is that the cartographers did not illustrate all the wadis dissecting the plateau, in general they only illustrated the bigger wadis. The location of this wadi is, more or less, to the south-west of Manqabad village. This corresponds with the location of the wadi starting at Bani Ghalib. The text written to this route is: "*Route des Caravanes du Darfur et du Dongola dans la haute Egypte*". The other trail continues following the Nile Valley to reach al-Qusiya further to the north. The text written to this route is: "*Marche du Général Desaix pour se rendre à Bani Adin le 1 Compl. An 6 (17 Septembre 1798)*". Among the maps published with the *Description de l'Egypte* (Fig. 2)[52] is a map that illustrates all of Upper Egypt, providing a bigger scene of the caravan route between Asyut and Kharga. The significance of this map is that it records the topographical aspects of the steep escarpments of the Eocene plateau in the east and the west, defining the western edge of the Nile Valley. Accordingly, the cartographers also illustrated the access point of the caravan route to ascend the plateau, which was located at some place west of Manqabad (according to the map). The topographical curvature of the plateau also clearly shows Gebel Asyut in this part of the map. The other significant aspect is the mention of

48 Nicolas de Fer, L'Empire des Turcs en Europe, en Asie, et en Afrique (Paris 1715).
49 Adam Christian Gaspari, Allgemeiner Hand-Atlas der Ganzen Erde: nach den besten astronomischen Bestimmungen, neuesten Entdeckungen und kritischen Untersuchungen entworfen und zu A.C. Gaspari vollstaendigem Handbuche der neuesten Erdbeschreibung bestimmt. Weimar, Verlag des Geographischen Instituts, 1817.
50 Toponym as it is written on the map.
51 Jacotin, Pierre, Description de l'Égypte ou recueil des observations et des recherches qui ont été faites en Égypte pendant l'Expédition de l'armée française. Seconde édition. Dediée au Roi. Publiée par C.L.F. Panckoucke, Chevalier de la Legion d'Honneur. Atlas geographique. Paris, Imprimerie de C.L.F. Panckoucke, 1827, Flle. 12.
52 Ibid, Flle. 3.

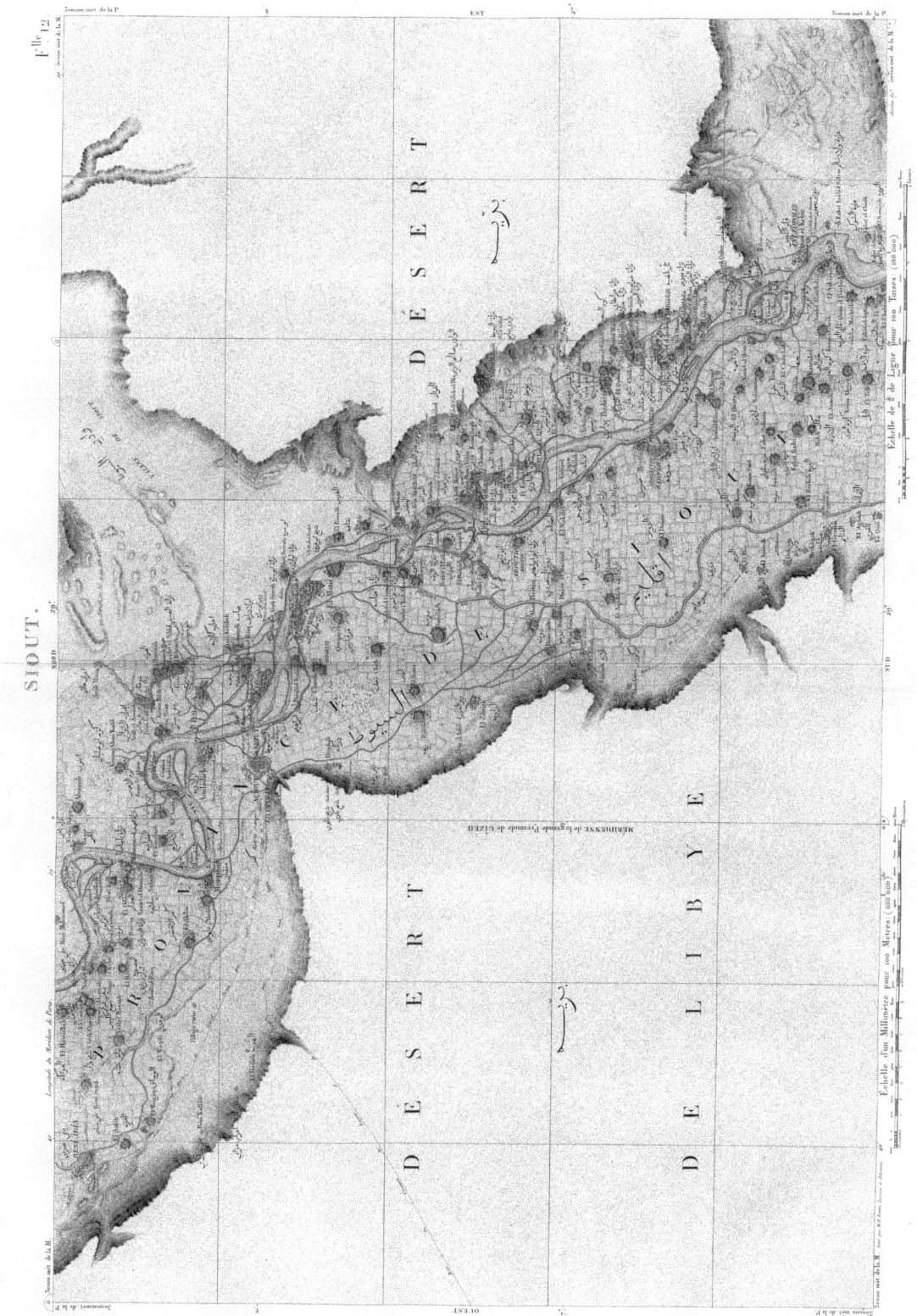

Fig. 1: Jacotin, Pierre, Description de l'Égypte ou recueil des observations et des recherches qui ont été faites en Égypte pendant l'Expédition de l'armée française. Seconde édition. Dediée au Roi. Publiée par C.L.F. Panckoucke, Chevalier de la Legion d'Honneur. Atlas géographique. Paris, Imprimerie de C.L.F. Panckoucke, 1765–1827, Flle. 12.

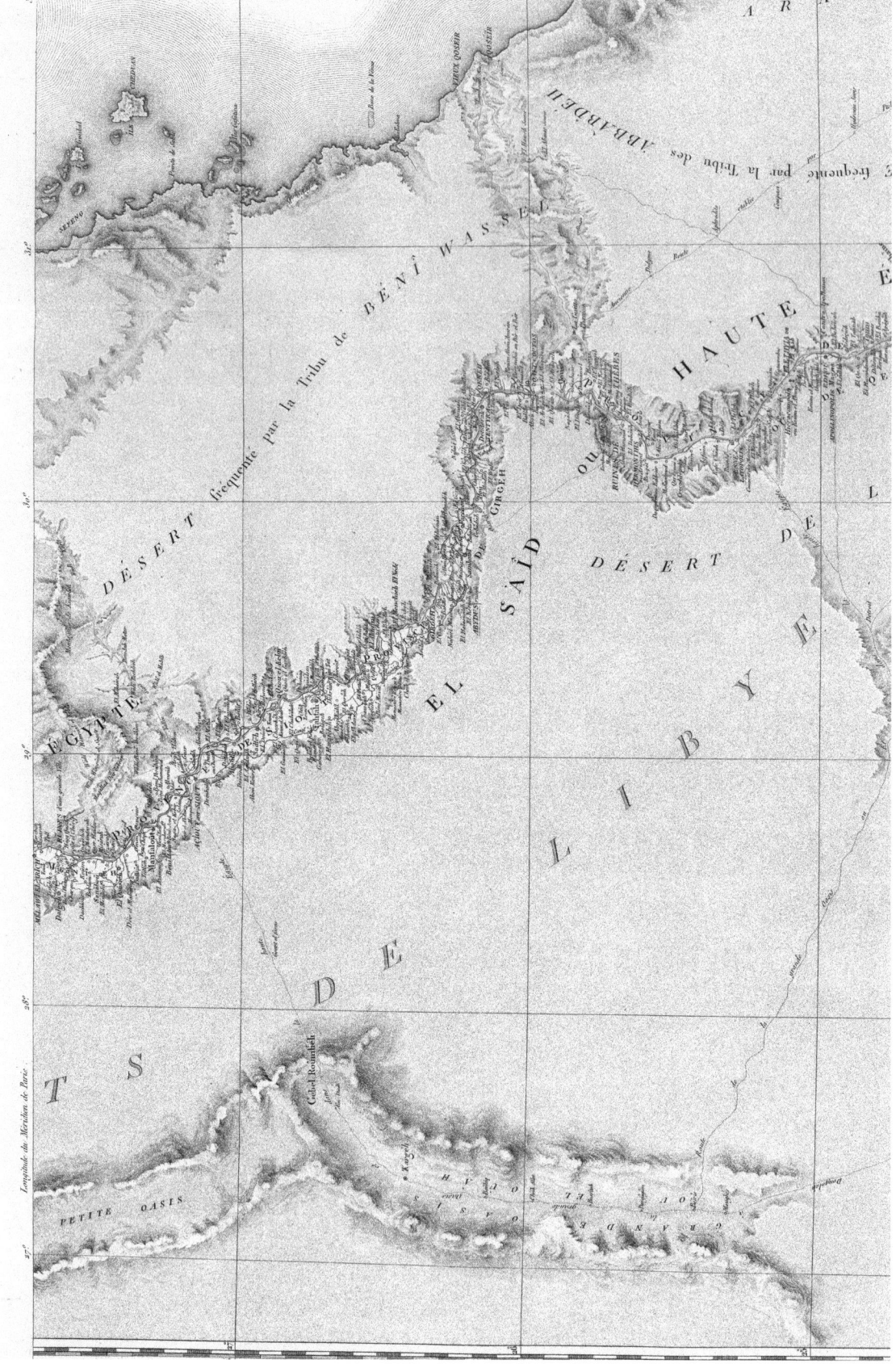

Fig. 2: Jacotin, Pierre, Description de l'Égypte ou recueil des observations et des recherches qui ont été faites en Égypte pendant l'Expédition de l'armée française. Seconde édition. Dediée au Roi. Publiée par C.L.F. Panckoucke, Chevalier de la Legion d'Honneur. Atlas géographique. Paris, Imprimerie de C.L.F. Panckoucke, 1765–1827, Flle. 3, detail.

the name of the descent point at *"Gebel Rumlieh"* north of Kharga, which is compatible with traveler's descriptions as mentioned above. Yet, the geospatial relations of locations and topography are still not representing the actual situation, as Kharga was illustrated as shifting to the north, away from its real location. Accordingly, the route between Asyut and Kharga was mistakenly diverged to be oriented towards the west, while the actual route would be attributed with a southern direction.

Other maps published during the first half of the nineteenth century show a development in recording the geospatial relations between the topographical units. This accordingly meant locating these units more properly, which can be seen in the adjusted location of Kharga Depression and the existence of Dakhla Depression, as well as the more specific perimeters of the Eocene plateau. Moreover, another caravan route was added to these maps, which is the Darb el-Tawil route. This route starts in Asyut and ends up at Dakhla Oasis (Pl. 7).[53]

3.2 The archaeological and textual evidence

According to the above-mentioned maps and travelers' memoirs, the Darb el-Arba'in route was an important caravan route, which provided a stable and probably continuous connection between Egypt and the other cultural identities in (early) modern day Sudan and Ethiopia. This old caravan route was steadily recorded on more than 15 maps that span more than 300 years, before the radical change in travel methods by using cars. Yet, the possibility that ancient Egyptians actually traveled on the same route is still to be discussed.

The archaeological record, so far, does not provide us with a lot of evidence that can prove the usage of Darb el-Arba'in by the ancient Egyptians. But, here, one must consider the lack of systematic archaeological work in these areas. One of the hints about the connections between Asyut and the western oases, which consequently means the usage of the first segment of Darb el-Arba'in, can be found in the pottery fragments that date back to the Late Roman Period. This assemblage of pottery was collected from different locations on Gebel Asyut al-gharbi and studied by Teodozja Rzeuska.[54]

Evidence of ceramics, which was mentioned in some detail above, shows that Asyut was also an important center for the distribution of foreign goods, which found their way through the southern and western oases. Continuous and intense trade relations between Dakhla and Kharga oases and Asyut are attested from the end of the Late Period to Roman times.[55] Ceramics from the oases, especially water kegs (large, barrel-shaped storage vessels), but also other vessels, were found on Gebel Asyut al-gharbi.[56] Also, local imitations of ceramics from the oases are attested at Gebel Asyut al-gharbi.[57] Asyut, connected with the southern oases by the ancient caravan routes, Darb el-Arba'in and Darb el-Tawil, may have been a redistribution center for merchandise imported from the oases to the Nile Valley.[58]

Asyut continued to function as a trade hub for the western and southern oases during the Late Roman Period (mid third–seventh century CE). Imports arrived from as far as North Africa, especially fine wares and amphorae. As Teodozja Rzeuska could show, the African Red Slip Ware (especially Hayes's forms 82 and 84) proves trade relations with the area of present-day Tunisia. African amphorae made in Graeco-Roman tradition point to relations with Zeugitana, Southern Byzacena, Sahel, Nabeul and

---

53 Carte de l'Egypte, de la Nubie, de l'Abissinie, du Kourdofan et d'une partie de l'Arabie. Dressee par M. Lapie, 1er. Geographe du Roi et M. Lapie Fils, Geographe de S.A.R.M. le Dauphin. Paris, 1829. Chez Eymery Fruger et Cie., Rue Mazarine No. 30. La gravure dirigee et executee par Lallemand.

54 Cf. Rzeuska 2015: 144, 148–151.

55 Rzeuska 2017: 651.

56 Rzeuska 2017: 649–651, 700–703.

57 Rzeuska 2017: 651.

58 Kahl 2007: 15; Rzeuska 2017: 651.

the Gulf of Hammamat. Traded products may have been olive oil, wine or garum.[59] Presumably, North African merchandise reached the Nile Valley (i.e. Asyut) through the oases.[60]

One may assume the use of the desert route to Nubia for raids and plundering several times in the history of Asyut. Writings by the monk Shenute inform us about the marauding Blemmyes, a people from Nubia, who penetrated Egypt as far north as Kynopolis during the middle of the fifth century CE.[61] More than 20,000 people from different cities found refuge at Shenute's monastery, the White Monastery, near Sohag, where they remained for three months: People from Kynopolis and Panopolis, from Hermopolis and Antinoopolis, and also from Hypsele and Lykopolis/Asyut.[62] The Nubian invasion caused Shenute to *"entertain the possibility that the end of days had come"*[63]. The invaders probably arrived via the desert route. The Copto-Arabic Synaxarion, which is a formal compilation of the lives of the martyrs, saints and religious heroes of the Coptic church, reports that Nubian invaders murdered forty nuns at a monastery in the mountains close to Asyut.[64]

This narrative is supported by Alan Roe's conclusion in his article about Darb el-Arba'in, which mentioned that, on the one hand, there is a lack of material culture or textual evidence that can support the assumption of direct contact between Egypt and Darfur through Darb el-Arba'in in early antiquity. On the other hand, however, there is indirect evidence that trade may have arisen during the later Roman Period and this is consistent with the beginnings of regular trans-Saharan trade elsewhere in Africa. However, the more solid conclusion would be the high probability that considerable caravan traffic passed through the first segment of Darb el-Arba'in between Asyut and Kharga Oasis, at least from the first century CE onwards[65].

As a matter of fact, there are more traces of an earlier use of the desert road, which is later known as Darb el-Arba'in. During the Second Intermediate Period, the Hyksos maintained trade and diplomatic relations with the kingdom of Kush in Nubia to the south of Egypt. The statues of the Asyuti Twelfth Dynasty nomarch Djefai-Hapi I and his wife Sennwy were found in Kerma, in Upper Nubia on the third cataract. The function of the building in which they stood is disputed. Another statue of Djefai-Hapi was discovered in the temple of Gebel Barkal, in Upper Nubia. Since these statues bear titles and epithets that clearly refer to Asyut and which do not show any relation to Nubia, they must have been brought from Asyut to Nubia.[66] The most plausible explanation therefore is that the Hyksos donated or sold these statues to their Nubian allies.[67] This would mean that the Hyksos plundered the Asyuti necropolis and eventually even the city itself. But, a Kushite invasion and looting of Asyut should also be taken into account: Kushites used the desert roads for penetrating deep into Upper Egypt according to Davies.[68] In whichever way the historical events happened in detail, the plundered statues might have been transported from Asyut to Nubia via the desert road, because the way up the Nile was partially controlled by Egyptian forces and crossing the cataracts was not an easy task.

Even if Nubian pottery is still missing in the corpus of finds at Asyut, other finds suggest connections with the south and would also suggest the use of the desert roads during several periods of Pharaonic history. During the New Kingdom (c. 1550–1070 BC), literate people visited a tomb from the time of King Mentuhotep II (c. 2000 BC) and left inscriptions and paintings on the walls. This tomb (Asyut Tomb N13.1) was situated higher up in the Gebel Asyut al-gharbi and belonged to the nomarch Iti-ibi(-iqer).

---

59 Cf. Rzeuska 2017: 657–658.
60 Rzeuska 2017: 658.
61 Leipoldt 1902/03: 129.
62 Emmel 1998: 87.
63 Emmel 1998: 91.
64 Timm 1984: 238.
65 Roe 2005/6: 129.
66 Kahl 2007: 10.
67 Säve-Söderbergh 1941: 103–116; Helck 1976; Kendall 1997: 24–27; Valbelle 2004.
68 Davies 2003: 53.

Fig. 3: King Darius I dedicates an offering to Wepwawet in a shrine with Hathor of Medjeden; temple of Hibis; Hypostyle M, North Wall, Register I (after Davies 1953: pl. 30, detail).

About 500 years after his death, the tomb became a meeting point for people of a scribal class, who, for example, wrote literary texts and visitors' formulae on the walls, but who also made some exercises in writing and drawing.[69] One depiction represents a giraffe.[70] These animals were not native in Egypt anymore during the New Kingdom. Also, they did not have a religious significance, which might have explained their choice as a motif for a *dipinto*. There are some New Kingdom tomb paintings showing giraffes (e.g. in the tombs of Rekhmire and Huy), which in these cases belonged to gifts brought from Nubia and Punt. One may assume that only a painter, who was familiar with the shape and proportions of giraffes, could draw this animal. The attestation of the *dipinto* showing a giraffe in Tomb N13.1 means that the draftsman had good knowledge of this animal, which was widespread in Sub-Saharan Africa.

Another *dipinto* from Tomb N13.1 proves a direct connection between Asyut and the Western Desert. What may be the earliest *dipinto* in the tomb (and thus dating to the end of the Seventeenth Dynasty or the beginning of the Eighteenth Dynasty) was written in a tight, narrow script by a visitor from the oases of the Egyptian Western Desert. He reports that he came to see this tomb, that he read the tomb in-scriptions and that he recited an offering formula for the Ka of the tomb owner. The visitor calls himself *"scribe of the chief of the oases Ipu"*.[71] This *dipinto* gives a hint about the use of the desert route from the Western oases to Asyut and vice versa at the very beginning of the New Kingdom.

The Hibis-temple from Kharga Oasis provides further evidence for a relation between Asyut and the Western Desert. On the north wall of Hypostyle M, King Darius I is depicted dedicating an offering to Hathor of Medjeden, the Asyuti form of the Egyptian goddess Hathor. Hathor of Medjeden is standing in a shrine behind the sitting Asyuti main god Wepwawet (Fig. 3).[72] Hathor of Medjeden was the local

---

69 Verhoeven 2020; Verhoeven 2013a; Verhoeven 2013b; Verhoeven 2012a; Verhoeven 2012b; Verhoeven 2009; Kahl 2006.
70 Gervers 2020: 350–351, pl. 162d, 361d.
71 Verhoeven 2020: 45–46.
72 Kahl 2007: 38; Davies 1953: pl. 30.

consort of Wepwawet. She is rarely attested outside of Asyut:[73] in the New Kingdom tomb of Tutu at Rifeh in the neighboring nome, in New Kingdom monuments from Thebes, which show a direct relation to Asyut, so that one can expect some links,[74] and on a colossal statue from Ramesses II found at Tanis. Hathor of Medjeden's veneration at the Hibis-temple may result from a close connection between Asyut and Kharga Oasis.

Finally, there is other evidence, already intensively discussed several times, which might support an ancient usage of the route or at least some segments of it. This evidence comes from the autobiography of Herkhuf, who made several journeys to the south during the Sixth Dynasty. After the first two journeys of Herkhuf to Yam starting from Elephantine and taking the *ꜣbw* road, he conducted his third journey traveling via *wḥꜣ.t* road.[75] The starting point of this third journey is known only through the hieroglyphic sign within the text, which is not in a good state of preservation. The transcription of this sign by Sethe showed it as a sail resting on a stand (Gardiner sign number P5), however, it seemed to be a rather uncertain transcription. Later, the door was open for several interpretations of this sign.

A discussion was presented by Elmar Edel in the 1950's trying to define the toponym that was mentioned as the starting point of this journey.[76] The discussion was an attempt to decide whether the sign represents Thinis (*tꜣ-wr*) or maybe another location in another Upper Egyptian nome. Yet, he suggested that Herkhuf, coming from Memphis, took the shorter route from Abydos or Thinis to Kharga (c. 160km), rather than taking the longer route from Asyut to Kharga (c. 200km). In both cases, Edel was convinced that *wḥꜣ.t* route was more or less following Darb el-Arba'in segments from Kharga Depression to reach Yam.[77] Later, in 2008, the translation of the full text of Herkhuf by Edel was published interpreting the sign in the text as referring to Thinis.[78] Edel's suggestion that *wḥꜣ.t* road overlaps with Darb el-Arba'in was also in agreement with other scholars, such as Cooper and Obsomer.[79] Nevertheless, the latter considers Asyut as a possible starting point of the route.

3.3 Ancient destinations (Yam)

According to the biographical text of the caravan leaders during the Old Kingdom, such as Herkhuf[80], one of the main trade destinations during the second half of the Old Kingdom was Yam[81]. Like Punt, the location of Yam is an issue of ongoing discussion among Egyptologists. The location was identified differently by several scholars. Although there is no consensus on the interpretations, several of them tend to locate Yam in the Upper Nubian territory. According to the interpretations of the biographical text of Herkhuf, as well as other textual sources, it is more or less where the later major center of Kerma was located. The proponents of this interpretation vary between different suggestions, conceiving Yam as an ambiguous wide entity, which used to cover Upper Nubia from the third cataract upstream to the fourth cataract[82], which is approximately where the medieval kingdom of Sennar was. Others describe Yam specifically as centralized at Kerma, the destination Herkhuf aimed for in his journeys[83]. Egyptian pottery and stone vessel fragments found in Kerma and the Deffufa support Kerma as the location of Yam[84].

---

73 DuQuesne 2008.
74 Cf. Kahl 1999.
75 Sethe ²1933: 125.10–11.
76 Edel 1955: 62–63, 72–73.
77 Edel 1955: 63.
78 Edel 2008: 624.
79 Goedicke 1981: 9; Cooper 2012: 9; Obsomer 2007: 45.
80 Sethe ²1933: 120–131.
81 For a more recent translation of Herkhuf's biography, see: Edel 2008: 620–628.
82 Balanda 2005–6: 42.
83 Edel 1955: 51–57; Obsomer 2007: 49–50.
84 Pottery found in Kerma cemetery. See: Bourriau 2004: 3–13; stone vessels found in Kerma and the Deffufa, see: Reisner 1923: 56–69, 506–510.

On the other hand, another suggestion was hinted at, locating Yam further to the south-west around Darfur. In his description of the Darb el-Arba'in route, which ends up with Darfur, Beadnell suggests that Darb el-Arba'in was one of the communication routes between the oases and the Nile Valley in ancient times.[85] Kendall also mentioned that travelers, who escorted one caravan from Darfur in the late eighteenth and nineteenth century and even further from Kordofan, noted all the products which came from these lands.[86] Both scholars discussed late antiquity and modern desert trade routes, considering a much earlier usage of these routes. The main argument of such discussion was the existence of the imported commodities in Darfur region, which made it a good candidate as the source from where ancient Egyptians imported these goods. No evidence, however, can support this possibility. Nevertheless, these hints encouraged scholars to consider Darb el-Arba'in with all its segments as the ancient route to Yam or Kerma.

3.4 Why was Darb el-Arba'in the route to Yam/ Kerma?

Now, if the starting point and the destination are located within the Nile Valley, another related question needs to be raised here, which is: Why did the ancient Egyptians choose to travel across the desert instead of traveling through the Nile Valley or close to it?

It is understood that when the destination is located away from the Nile Valley in the Sub-Saharan desert, such as Darfur, that part of the route should cross this desert. Moreover, it is mentioned in Browne's memoir that crossing Lower Nubia was practically impossible because of the local violent turmoil, which prevented him from his original plan to travel to Ethiopia. Relatively speaking, according to the 1707 map (Pl. 6a), other destinations such as Sennar, which is also located within the Nile Valley, were connected to Egypt by the first three segments of Darb el-Arba'in. This fact might turn the attention to another factor that made traders and caravan leaders choose desert routes: the speed of traveling through the desert and being away from the complications of having a valley full of settlements and fields. Nevertheless, another geospatial reason should also be considered. The Nile Valley as a space for movement offered a high speed route to the south by transportation on the Nile River. However, this route is not clear, as the cataracts along the Nile represent a serious obstacle for big trade vessels to travel through. On the other hand, the valley itself is mainly occupied with settlements and agricultural fields, which in several cases would prevent caravans from mobilizing without problems and the low desert areas along the Nile Valley are not continuous on one bank in the same width, which also make it unreliable. The ancient Egyptians most likely suffered from the same problems and desert routes were a suitable solution.

3.5 Donkeys vs camels

A trade caravan that potentially started from Asyut or Abydos, taking the desert route southwards, should have seriously considered where to find water and how long it would spend in the desert. According to traveler's notes, during modern times, caravans to Darfur exclusively used camels, so there was no use of horses or donkeys. The reputation of camels as "ships of the desert" actually comes from them being able to survive traveling in arid landscapes for a week or two without the need to drink water. Also, the fact that they can carry a considerably big load of goods, as well as people, is important. However, it seemed that the caravan leaders of the eighteenth century were pushing the very limits of the abilities of these animals. Browne mentions the extreme exhaustion of the camels in some phases of the trip via Darb el-Arba'in, to the extent of losing camels. This was only due to the caravan leaders not wanting to spend a longer time in the desert, which is understood as a strategy, if we consider the amount of supplies needed

---

85 BEADNELL 1909: 34; also mentioned by: OSING 1994: 159–173, fig. 1.
86 KENDALL 1989: 702–703.

for everyday survival in the desert. Today, one can still see a camel caravan crossing a similar distance between Kufra Oasis and Abeche in Chad.[87]

However, although camels were known in Egypt, at least since the New Kingdom,[88] ancient Egyptians did not use them as pack animals. Instead, they used donkeys on their journeys. Several attestations mention donkeys as pack animal in caravans that traveled in both Eastern and Western Deserts. Herkhuf mentions 300 donkeys in his report as the pack animal that was used on his third trade journey to Yam[89]. The usage of donkeys to carry supplies was mentioned in the inscription of Henw in Wadi Hammamat[90]. Another rock inscription in Wadi Hammamat dates back to the Eighth Dynasty and belongs to Idy son of Shemai (No. 152).[91] The text mentions dispatching an expedition to bring a stone for a high official called Tjauti. The expedition consisted of 200 men, 50 donkeys and 2 oxen. Donkeys can carry around 60kg on their backs and they need to drink every three or four days, while the average daily travel rate of a donkey caravan is ca. 25–40km[92]. However, since the caravan itself probably included men on foot, then human speed and the influence of marching in big numbers should be considered here as well. Consequently, the speed of a caravan is suggested to be reduced to around 30 to 35km per day.

4. Spatial analysis

4.1 Geospatial sources

Beside the historical maps that were exhibited above, other geospatial sources were used in the spatial analysis. These sources mainly provided topographic data: The first source is topography geo-referenced paper maps, which were created by the National Egyptian Survey Authorities for the Eastern Desert and the Nile Valley, scale 1:50,000. Also, US and Russian military maps of the Western Desert, scale 1:250,000 were useful. The second source of data is the U.S. Geological Survey Digital Elevation Models (DEM) (called ASTER Global DEM ver.3) along with NASA Shuttle Radar Topography Mission Global 3 arc second (SRTMGL3). However, there is also the archaeological sites location data, which was taken from several sources, such as publications and online maps from archaeological excavation missions, also some data was digitized from older published maps, which were geo-referenced and used for that purpose, also historical maps are included. Most of the data was initially verified against medium resolution satellite images. And all of the data was plotted and analyzed using three software programs – ArcGIS, QGIS, Grass GIS – and Google Earth.

4.2 The approach

Although geospatial analysis seems to be a pure GIS process, the fact is that different GIS based spatial analyses are mainly structured and designed according to a number of theoretical approaches. This is especially true for the analyses which involve the detection and reconstruction of human behavior, such as pathway finding analysis. The main set of spatial analysis used in order to reconstruct routes is the

---

87 Meerpohl 2013: 167–191.
88 Köpp-Junk 2013: 111; 2015: 112–115.
89 Sethe ²1933: 126.17.
90 Couyat & Montet 1912: 83, No. 114; translation: Lichtheim 1988: 52–54.
91 Couyat & Montet 1912: 92, No. 152; translation: Mostafa 2014: 109.
92 Förster, Riemer & Maher 2013: 212; Förster 2015: 385–434.

Least Cost Path analysis and Corridor analysis, which mainly follows Zipf's concept "the Least Effort principle"[93] and the discussion around it[94].

However, the Least Cost Path (LCP) analysis consists of two main steps. The first one is to calculate the accumulated cost surface in order to find the shortest and least steep zones with the lowest grades. The second step is to identify the LCP by tracking back the path from the destination point to the starting point(s). Obviously, these two steps are executed considering a specific critical slope to avoid, which in general is around 12° and a maximum of 20°.

The shortest distance between two points is always a straight line. However, being surrounded by a landscape imposes another factor, which is the topography of the terrain or the elevation and the slope angle/grade, as higher elevations require effort and even more effort is necessary if the slope angle/grade is steeper. Consequently, human behavior, according to Zipf's concept, tends to avoid unnecessary steep elevations and follow the less steep paths considering the shortest path at the same time, which might be an issue of compromise.

Higher elevations usually do not entirely limit movements as long as the slope angle/grade is smooth enough. The grade of a slope is the acting feature of elevation, which defines the limitations of movements in the landscape. As humans, animals and even cars cannot ascend very steep slopes; obviously the human maximum limits are different than those for some animals and cars. The limitation of walking up a slope for humans and pack animals is relative and calculations vary according to the purposes of ascent. Here, we should take into consideration that in this study, we talk about trade caravans of travelers, which most likely were a mixture of humans, pack animals (donkeys), goods and supplies. Considering that land cover, the second landscape attribute, would influence the critical grade degree for the traveling caravan according to the Least Cost concept, it would be preferable that all the phases of the route between any starting point and destination are attributed with an undulating surface. In very rare occasions, when another factor is involved, walking on steeper surfaces is the last choice to be made. One can imagine the difficulties that could face a caravan of hundreds of pack animals loaded with commodities and supplies ascending the Eocene plateau through a steep or medium-grade watershed, while another wider and undulating surface is available in another wadi.

Least Cost Path analysis usually gives one or more resulted route(s). However, illustrating these routes as single tracks on the landscape can be misleading. In some cases, for example the Eastern Desert, the Red Sea Hills limit the choices of the traveling caravans within narrow wadis that have high sides. On the other hand, an undulating surface, such as the summit of the Eocene plateau, offers a wider terrain to move through. This attribute can be responsible for wider movement choices within the same direction between the starting point and the destination. Therefore, it is important to consider another approach, which can be called "directional intentionality".

Lock and Pouncett present this concept as:

> "The combination of directional intentionality based on a known destination and the visibility of intermediate waypoints creates a "corridor of intentionality" through which movement proceeds, rather than a well-defined pathway. Progress is based on mid-distance targets which aggregate to achieve the final aim even if each waypoint is not actually reached but is bypassed once it gets close enough for the next one to be in view and become the next aim."[95]

---

93 In the late 1940s, G. K. Zipf defined his concept as a social principle and called it "the Least Effort principle", as he believed that "human behavior tends to minimize the average rate of probable work-expenditure over time". This concept has been adapted by many geographers and geo-archaeologists as a main concept of the least cost path finding analysis, although S. Surface-Evans & D. White would argue that there are many reasons humans do not follow the least effort principle. See Zipf 1949: 6.

94 Surface-Evans & White 2012.

95 Lock & Pouncett 2010: 193.

This concept widens the understanding of traveling routes from specific narrow paths to include buffer zones around these suggested paths, which cover the other possible route options and choices that share the same attributes and direction. As it will be shown later, GIS Least Cost Path analysis always results in more than one path between two points, however, all of them go in the same direction and with similar spatial attributes, with slight differences between the several turning points. An example of the use of Corridor analysis in GIS was done by Kondo *et.al.* in Japan, combined with a ground check verification process.[96] The experimental study put more support to the validity of Corridor intentionality as a concept to understand the movement between two points in a landscape, which offers multiple possible least cost paths.

4.3 Analysis

There is a certain amount of archaeological and textual evidence available, despite the different opinions about whether Darb el-Arba'in was used by the ancient Egyptians to reach southern destinations in Nubia or partially used to reach Kharga Oasis during the Roman Period. Based on this, it is promising to conduct geospatial analysis on the first segment of the road between Asyut and Kharga. The goal of this analysis is to detect specific possibilities for the starting point(s) in the Asyut area or the ascending points from the alluvial land to the summit of the plateau and to illustrate the possible route southwards towards Kharga Depression.

Unfortunately, the route between Asyut and Kharga and Dakhla is not yet properly surveyed and, in several locations, what could be surviving from it is disturbed with modern activity of roads construction and soil mining. However, some remote sensing studies were conducted by the team of the ACACIA project from the University of Cologne, trying to detect caravan tracks, which are preserved on the Hamada surface of the Eocene plateau, using satellite images and several sets of geological and topographical maps and in some cases ground checking methodology.[97] This method was able to identify a network of caravan trails across the Eocene plateau, running between Kharga and Dakhla Depressions and the Nile Valley. The network that was detected represents camel and donkey tracks, as well as caravan tracks, that were recorded on maps. The southern part of the first segment of Darb el-Arba'in was one of the tracks that was detected, however, the northern part, including the starting point was not published.

Using the same methodology and Google Earth satellite images, it was possible to detect some tracks at the very beginning of the route, including some tracks which can signify the ascending location from the low desert to the summit of the plateau (Pl. 9a–b). The tracks detected are located at the mouth of a wadi south of Manqabad, which is significantly consistent with the description of Montague-Stuart-Wortley that he started his journey from Manqabad, ascending a wadi to the summit of the plateau[98]. Other tracks were also detected coming most likely from Bani Ghalib.

On the other hand, sets of spatial analysis were done to examine the first segment of Darb el-Arba'in. Both Least Cost Path and Corridor analysis were able to identify more than one ascending point in the area to the north-west of Gebel Asyut. The corridor analysis produced a wide variety of routes/corridors. These corridors can be categorized as: 1) "most likely path", which follows the most undulating surface and the shortest distance; 2) "credible path", which chooses the next steeper or longer routes; and finally 3) "likely" category, which chooses the least desirable path, but still could be used for caravan or human mobility. The corridor identified as running between Asyut city and Kharga resulted in a descent down the plateau from more than one wadi and watershed. The main and most likely ascending points went through two wadis that are facing the town of Manqabad (Pl. 8). The same result can be confirmed through the satellite image analysis (Pl. 9a) and more importantly through the notes of the British

---

96 Kondo et al. 2008.
97 Striwanek 2007: 136–137.
98 Montague-Stuart-Wortley 1953: 22, 24.

officer Montague-Stuart-Wortley. The second possible ascending point was through Kulit el-Edissiyah Watershed. The last possible route goes through a wadi located further to the west, in front of Bani Ghalib (Pl. 9b). This route is also confirmed with satellite image analysis.

At the south, the corridor analysis produced a descent point from the Eocene plateau towards Kharga Depression through Naqab el-Rufuf Watershed (Pl. 10). This descent is also known for the routes coming from Abydos and Nawahid. However, the modern traveler's notes about the descent point to Kharga refer to a different point, which is Naqab el-Ramlie at the northernmost extent of Kharga Depression. In this case, the LCP and Corridor analyses did not consider this descent as part of the least exerting route and preferred Naqab el-Rufuf. One should consider here that spatial analysis generated by GIS software does not consider the human behavior variations as a factor in its algorithms. In order to complete the picture, it is crucial to import the variations in human behavior into the process of analysis. LCP and Corridor analyses suggested the routes that are least steep and the shortest in distance. This means slope steepness/grade varies between 0° and 6° in the Naqab el-Rufuf case.

At el-Ramlie (north of Kharga Depression), the steep escarpment of the Eocene plateau does not have such an undulating descent itself, only aeolian sand dunes provide such a descent. Looking at the slope model of this area, it shows no trace of the effect of these dunes on the steepness of the escarpment in this area, which explains why the Corridor analysis did not illustrate any route through this part. On the other hand, one can recall what Browne mentioned in his memoir about the difficulties of descending this part of the route at el-Ramlie and the loss of camels and time in this phase. This note is confirmed with the citations of camel bones found in this sandy descent by C. Rossi & S. Ikram. In fact, the aeolian sand surface in this area is one of the least favorable land covers for donkeys and camels. The first ones to cross such a surface always have problems walking with loads on their backs on such sand, sinking their feet deep in it. Also, although camels can walk in sandy terrain easier than donkeys, they do not deal well with steep slope angles/grade.

The last point to be mentioned in this argument, that away from the spatial analysis results and the capabilities of pack animals, one should consider that the aeolian sand accumulated at el-Ramlie is part of the big barchan train of Abu el-Mahariq. Barchan dunes (Ghorud), which are an aeolian formation, occur in the form of north-south trending belts in several parts of the depression. Barchan dunes are also the most dynamic landform in the area, as they shift with the wind direction and in time change their locations covering other areas in the depression with a rate that varies between 20.8 to 100 meters per year. The Barchan dunes are usually convex-concave shaped from the windward side, as the slope angle/grade of these dunes varies between 12°, 13–15° and 32–34°. It is worth mentioning the difficulty of ascending and descending from these dunes, as their aeolian nature makes human and pack animal feet sink in the fine sand. Due to this, it requires a lot of effort and good balance to climb and descend the dune. Usually, the low slope side is easier to climb.[99] A noteworthy story about Barchans was mentioned by Beadnell, as he reported in the beginning of the twentieth century about the impact of the sand dunes movement in Kharga Oasis and the almost disappearance of palm trees and houses in northern Kharga under the shifting sand coming from the Abu el-Mahariq dune belt.[100]

5. Conclusions

Finally, it is possible to conclude the geospatial credibility of the use of the segment between Asyut and Kharga for trade caravans. According to the GIS spatial analysis and the verification process through satellite imagery analysis, both of them illustrate several features of the route between Asyut and Kharga.

---

99 EMBABI 1982: 146.
100 See BEADNELL 1909: 70.

This segment might have had close destinations, such as the Kharga or Dakhla oases, or much further destinations such as Upper Nubia. The historical evidence of old maps and traveler's records support the existence of a stable and repetitively used caravan route between Egypt and Darfur and Sennar in Sudan through the Darb el-Arba'in route during the late medieval period and through the modern period. This route started with the Asyut-Kharga segment. This evidence can be combined with the textual sources that suggest Asyut as one of the starting points of the route that led to Yam in the autobiography of Herkhuf. The archaeological evidence also shows possible direct connections between Asyut and the oases. Accordingly, one may assume that ancient Egyptians used Asyut as the main center of Middle Egypt to start some of their journeys towards the south. However, one should consider Asyut as one of several starting points within the Darb el Arba'in route and it is the northernmost starting point.

Bibliography

ALRAM 2016: M. Alram, The Coinage of the Persian Empire, in: William E. Metcalf (ed.), The Oxford Handbook of Greek and Roman Coinage (Oxford 2012), 61–87.

BALANDA 2005–6: St. Balanda, The so-called "Mine of Punt" and its location, in: Journal of the American Research Center in Egypt 42, 2005–6, 33–44.

BEADNELL 1909: H. J. Llewellyn Beadnell, An Egyptian Oasis, an account of the oasis of Kharga in the Libyan Desert, with special reference to its history, physical geography, and water-supply (London 1909).

BOURRIAU 2004: J. Bourriau, Egyptian pottery in Kerma Ancien, Kerma Moyen and Kerma Classique graves at Kerma, in: T. Kendall (ed.), Nubian studies 1998: Proceedings of the 9th Conference of the International Society of Nubian Studies, August 21–26, 1998 (Boston, Massachusetts 2004), 3–13.

BROWNE 1799: W. G. Browne, Travels in Africa, Egypt, and Syria, from the year 1792 to 1798 (London 1799).

BUBENZER & BOLTON 2013: O. Bubenzer & A. Bolton, Top down: New satellite data and ground-truth data as base for a reconstruction of ancient caravan routes. Examples from the Western Desert of Egypt, in: F. Förster & H. Riemer (eds.), Desert Road Archaeology in Ancient Egypt and Beyond (Africa Praehistorica 27; Köln 2013), 61–75.

COOPER 2012: J. Cooper, Reconsidering the Location of Yam, in: Journal of the American Research Center in Egypt 48, 2012, 1–21.

COUYAT & MONTET 1912: J. Couyat & P. Montet, Les inscriptions Hiéroglyphiques et Hiératiques du Ouâdi Hammâmât (Cairo 1912).

DAVIES 1953: N. De Garis Davies, The Temple of Hibis in El Khārgeh Oasis. Part III. The Decoration, edited by Ludlow Bull and Lindsley F. Hall (Publications of The Metropolitan Museum of Art Egyptian Expedition 17; New York 1953).

DAVIES 2003: V. Davies, Kush in Egypt: a new historical inscription, in: Sudan and Nubia. The Sudan Archaeological Research Society Bulletin 7, 2003, 52–54.

DENNISON 1918: W. Dennison, A Gold Treasure of the Late Roman Period (Studies in East Christian and Roman Art 2; New York 1918).

DUCÈNE 2007: J.-Ch. Ducène, Le Darb al-arba'în à l'époque musulmane, in: M.-C. Bruwier (ed.), Pharaons noirs, sur la Piste des Quarante Jours (Mariemont 2007), 245–252.

DUQUESNE 2008: T. DuQuesne, The Great Goddess and her Companions in Middle Egypt: new findings on Hathor of Medjed and the local deities of Asyut, in: B. Rothohler & A. Manisali (eds.), Mythos & Ritual. Festschrift für Jan Assmann zum 70. Geburtstag (Religionswissenschaft: Forschung und Wissenschaft 5; Berlin 2008), 1–26.

DUYRAT 2005: F. Duyrat, Le trésor de Damanhour (IGCH 1664) et l'évolution de la circulation monétaire en Égypte hellénistique, in: F. Duyrat & O. Picard (eds.), L'exception égyptienne? Production et échanges monétaires en Égypte hellénistique et romaine. Actes du colloque d'Alexandrie, 13–15 avril 2002 (Études alexandrines 10; Cairo 2005), 10–51.

EDEL 1955: E. Edel, Inschriften des Alten Reiches, V. Die Reiseberichte des ḥrw-ḫwif (Herchuf), in: O. Firchow (ed.), Ägyptologische Studien (Berlin 1955), 51–75.

EDEL 2008: E. Edel, Die Felsgräbernekropole der Qubbet el-Hawa bei Assuan, Band I (Paderborn 2008).

EL TAHLAWI, FARRAG & AHMED 2008: M. R. El Tahlawi, A. A. Farrag & S. S. Ahmed, Groundwater of Egypt: "an environmental overview", in: Environmental Geology 55, 2008, 639–652.

EMBABI 1982: N. Embabi, Barchans of the Kharga Depression, in: F. El-Baz & T. A. Maxwell (eds.), Desert landforms of southwest Egypt: A basis for comparison with Mars – NASA-CR-3611 (Washington 1982), 765–774.

EMMEL 1998: St. Emmel, The Historical Circumstances of Shenute's Sermon God Is Blessed, in: M. Krause & S. Schaten (eds.), ΘΕΜΕΛΙΑ. Spätantike und koptologische Studien. Peter Grossmann zum 65. Geburtstag (Sprachen und Kulturen des Christlichen Orients 3; Wiesbaden 1998), 81–96.

FÖRSTER 2015: F. Förster, Der Abu Ballas-Weg. Eine pharaonische Karawanenroute durch die Libysche Wüste (Africa Praehistorica 28; Köln 2015).

FÖRSTER, RIEMER & MAHER 2013: F. Förster, H. Riemer & M. Maher, Donkeys of El-Fasher, in: F. Förster & H. Riemer (ed.), Desert Road Archaeology (Africa Praehistorica 27; Köln 2013), 193–220.

GERVERS 2020: E. Gervers, Zeichnungen von Besuchern des Neuen Reiches, in: U. Verhoeven (Hg.), Dipinti von Besuchern des Grabes N13.1 in Assiut (The Asyut Project 15; Wiesbaden 2020), 325–405.

GIDDY 1987: L. L. Giddy, Egyptian oases: Bahariya, Dakhla, Farafra and Kharga during Pharaonic times (Warminster 1987).

GOEDICKE 1981: H. Goedicke, Harkhuf's Travels, in: Journal of Near Eastern Studies 40, 1981, 1–20.

GUEST 1900: A. R. Guest, The Oases of the Mudirieh of Assyut, in: The Geographical Journal 16, 1900, 655–662.

HELCK 1976: W. Helck, Ägyptische Statuen im Ausland – ein chronologisches Problem, in: Ugarit Forschungen 8, 1976, 101–115.

KAHL 1999: J. Kahl, Siut–Theben: zur Wertschätzung von Traditionen im alten Ägypten (Probleme der Ägyptologie 13; Leiden – Boston – Köln 1999).

KAHL 2006: J. Kahl, Ein Zeugnis altägyptischer Schulausflüge, in: Göttinger Miszellen 211, 2006, 25–29.

KAHL 2007: J. Kahl, Ancient Asyut. The First Synthesis after 300 Years of Research (The Asyut Project 1; Wiesbaden 2007).

KAHL 2013: J. Kahl, Die Zeit selbst lag nun tot darnieder, Die Stadt Assiut und ihre Nekropolen nach westlichen Reiseberichten des 17. bis 19. Jahrhunderts: Konstruktion, Destruktion und Rekonstruktion (The Asyut Project 5; Wiesbaden 2013).

KAHL 2014: J. Kahl, Assiut – Theben – Tebtynis. Wissensbewegungen von der Ersten Zwischenzeit und dem Mittleren Reich bis in Römische Zeit, in: Studien zur Altägyptischen Kultur 43, 2014, 159–172.

KASSAS 1953: M. Kassas, Landforms and Plant Cover in the Egyptian Desert, in: Bulletin de la Société de Géographie d'Égypte 26, 1953, 193–205.

KENDALL 1989: T. Kendall, Ethnoarchaeology in Meroitic studies, in: S. Donadoni & St. Wenig (eds.), Studia Meroitica 1984. Proceedings of the fifth international conference for Meroitic studies, Rome 1984 (Berlin 1989), 702–703.

KENDALL 1997: T. Kendall, Kerma and the Kingdom of Kush, 2500–1500 B.C.: The archaeological discovery of an ancient Nubian empire (Washington 1997).

KLEMM & KLEMM 2008: R. Klemm & D. D. Klemm, Stones and Quarries in Ancient Egypt (London 2008).

KÖPP-JUNK 2013: H. Köpp-Junk, Desert travel and transport in ancient Egypt. An overview based on epigraphic, pictorial and archaeological evidence, in: F. Förster & H. Riemer (eds.), Desert Road Archaeology in Ancient Egypt and Beyond (Africa Praehistorica 27; Köln 2013), 107–132.

KÖPP-JUNK 2015: H. Köpp-Junk, Reisen im Alten Ägypten: Reisekultur, Fortbewegungs- und Transportmittel in pharaonischer Zeit (Göttinger Orientforschungen. IV. Reihe: Ägypten 55; Wiesbaden 2015).

KONDO ET AL. 2008: Y. Kondo et. al., "FIELDWALK@KOZU: A Preliminary Report of the GPS/GIS-aided Walking Experiments for Re-modelling Prehistoric Pathways at Kozushima Island (east Japan)," paper presented at the 36th Annual Conference on Computer Applications and Quantitative Methods in Archaeology, Budapest, Hungary, April 2–6, 2008.

LEIPOLDT 1902/03: J. Leipoldt, Berichte Schenutes über Einfälle der Nubier in Ägypten, in: Zeitschrift für Ägyptische Sprache und Altertumskunde 40, 1902/03, 126–140.

LICHTHEIM 1988: M. Lichtheim, Ancient Egyptian autobiographies chiefly of the Middle Kingdom, a study and anthology (Orbis Biblicus et Orientalis 84; Fribourg/Göttingen 1988).

Lock & Pouncett 2010: G. Lock & J. Pouncett, The Methodological and Theoretical Implications of Scale Dependency for the Derivation of Slope and the Calculation of Least-Cost Pathways, in: B. Frischer, J. Webb Crawford & D. Koller (eds.), Making History Interactive. Computer Applications and Quantitative Methods in Archaeology (CAA). Proceedings of the 37th International Conference, Williamsburg, Virginia, United States of America, March 22–26 (BAR International Series S2079; Oxford 2010), 192–203.

Meerpohl 2013: M. Meerpohl, Footprints in the sand: recent long-distance camel trade in the Libyan Desert (Northern Chad/Southern Libya), in: F. Förster, H. Riemer (eds.), Desert Road Archaeology (Africa Praehistorica 27; Köln 2013), 61–75.

Meurer 1998: P. H. Meurer, Ortelius as the Father of Historical Cartography, in: M. van den Broecke, P. van der Krogt & P. H. Meurer (eds.), Abraham Ortelius and the First Atlas. Essays commemorating the quadricentennial of his death, 1598–1998 (Utrecht 1998), 133–159.

Montague-Stuart-Wortley 1953: E. J. Montague-Stuart-Wortley, My Reminiscences of Egypt and the Sudan (from 1882 to 1899), Sudan Notes and Records 34, 1953, 17–46, 172–188.

Moreno García 2017: J. C. Moreno García, Trade and Power in Ancient Egypt: Middle Egypt in the Late Third/Early Second Millennium BC, in: Journal of Archaeological Research 25, 2017, 87–132 (DOI 10.1007/s10814-016-9097-4).

Morkot 1996: R. Morkot, The Darb el- Arbain, the Kharga Oasis and its forts, and other desert routes, in: D. M. Bailey (ed.), Archaeological Research in Roman Egypt: The Proceedings of The Seventeenth Classical Colloquium of The Department of Greek and Roman Antiquities, British Museum, held on 1–4 December, 1993 (Journal of Roman Archaeology, Ann Arbor, 1996), 82–94.

Mostafa 2014: M. F. Mostafa, The Mastaba of Shemai at Nag' Kom el-Koffar, Vol 1 (Cairo 2014).

Obsomer 2007: C. Obsomer, Les expéditions d'Herkhouf (VIe dynastie) et la localisation de Iam, in: M.-C. Bruwier & R. Betz (eds.), Pharaons Noirs, sur la piste des quarante jours (Musee Royal de Mariemont 2007), 39–52.

Osing 1994: J. Osing, Les voies de communication entre les oasis égyptiennes et la vallée du Nil, in: Voyages et voyageurs au proche-orient ancien, Les Cahiers de CEPOA 6, Paris 1994, 159–173.

Platz-Horster 2004: G. Platz-Horster, Schmuck und Private Frömmigkeit: Der Goldschmuck von Assiût, Ägypten, in: Ludwig Wamser (ed.), Die Welt von Byzanz – Europas östliches Erbe. Glanz, Krisen und Fortleben einer tausendjährigen Kultur (München 2004), 286–304.

Price & Waggoner 1975: M. Price & N. Waggoner, Archaic Greek Coinage. The Asyut Hoard (London 1975).

Reisner 1923: G. Reisner, Excavations at Kerma, Parts IV–V (Cambridge 1923).

Roe 2005/6: A. Roe, The Old "Darb al Arb'in" Caravan Route and Kharga Oasis in Antiquity, in: Journal of the American Research Center in Egypt 42, 2005/6, 119–129.

Rossi & Ikram 2013: C. Rossi & S. Ikram, Evidence of Desert Routes across Northern Kharga (Egypt's Western Desert), in: Frank Förster & Heiko Riemer (eds.), Desert Road Archaeology in Ancient Egypt and Beyond (Africa Praehistorica 27; Köln 2013), 265–282.

Rzeuska 2015: T. Rzeuska, Pottery from Tomb III/N12.1, V/M11.1 and shaft P10.4, in: J. Kahl, M. El-Khadragy, H. Faheed Ahmed, U. Verhoeven, M. Abdelrahiem, I. Regulski, M. Becker, E. Czyżewska-Zalewska, A. Kilian, M. Stecher & T. Rzeuska, The Asyut Project: Eleventh Season of Fieldwork (2014), in: Studien zur Altägyptischen Kultur 44, 2015, 144–151.

Rzeuska 2017: T. I. Rzeuska, Chronological Overview of Pottery from Asyut. A contribution to the history of Gebel Asyut al-gharbi (The Asyut Project 7; Wiesbaden 2017).

Säve-Söderbergh 1941: T. Säve-Söderbergh, Ägypten und Nubien. Ein Beitrag zur Geschichte altägyptischer Aussenpolitik (Lund 1941).

Said 1990: R. Said, Geomorphology, in: R. Said (ed.), The Geology of Egypt (Rotterdam 1990), 11–25.

Schenkel 1978: W. Schenkel, Die Bewässerungsrevolution im alten Ägypten (Mainz 1978).

Schilder 1987: G. Schilder, Monumenta Cartographica Neerlandica II (Alphen aan den Rijn 1987).

Sethe ²1933: K. Sethe, Urkunden des Alten Reiches (Urkunden des aegyptischen Altertums, Abt. I; Leipzig ²1933).

Stolz 2006: Y. Stolz, Eine kaiserliche Insignie? Der Juwelenkragen aus dem so genannten Schatzfund von Assiût, in: Jahrbuch des Römisch-Germanischen Zentralmuseums 53, 2006, 521–577.

Striwanek 2007: J. Striwanek, Caravan routes – discovered with satellite eyes, in: O. Bubenzer, A. Bolten & F. Darius (eds.), Atlas of Cultural and Environmental Change in Arid Africa (Africa Praehistorica 21; Köln 2007), 136–137.

Surface-Evans & White 2012: S. L. Surface-Evans & D. A. White, An Introduction to the Least Cost Analysis of Social Landscapes, in: D. A. White & S. L. Surface-Evans (eds.), Least Cost Analysis of Social Landscapes (Salt Lake City 2012).

Timm 1984: St. Timm, Das christlich-koptische Ägypten in arabischer Zeit. Teil 1 (A–C) (Beihefte zum Tübinger Atlas des Vorderen Orients, Reihe B (Geisteswissenschaften) 41/1; Wiesbaden 1984).

Valbelle 2004: D. Valbelle, The Cultural Significance of Iconographic and Epigraphic Data Found in the Kingdom of Kerma, in: T. Kendall (ed.), Nubian Studies 1998. Proceedings of the Ninth Conference of the International Society of Nubian Studies, August 21–26, 1998, Boston, Massachusetts (Boston 2004), 176–183.

Verhoeven 2009: U. Verhoeven, Von der 'Loyalistischen Lehre' zur 'Lehre des Kairsu' – Eine neue Textquelle in Assiut und deren Auswirkungen, in: Zeitschrift für Ägyptische Sprache und Altertumskunde 136, 2009, 87–98.

Verhoeven 2012a: U. Verhoeven, The New Kingdom Graffiti in Tomb N13.1: An Overview, in: J. Kahl, M. El-Khadragy, U. Verhoeven & A. Kilian (eds.), Seven Seasons at Asyut. First Results of the Egyptian-German Cooperation in Archaeological Fieldwork. Proceedings of an International Conference at the University of Sohag,10th–11th of October, 2009 (The Asyut Project 2; Wiesbaden 2012), 47–58.

Verhoeven 2012b: U. Verhoeven, Tomb N13.1: New Kingdom Graffiti, in: J. Kahl, M. El-Khadragy, U. Verhoeven, M. Abdelrahiem, M. van Elsbergen, H. Fahid, A. Kilian, Ch. Kitagawa, T. Rzeuska & M. Zöller-Engelhardt, The Asyut Project: Ninth Season of Fieldwork (2011), in: Studien zur Altägyptischen Kultur 41, 2012, 206–209.

Verhoeven 2013a: U. Verhoeven, Literatur im Grab – Der Sonderfall Assiut, in: G. Moers, K. Widmaier, A. Giewekemeyer, A. Lümers & R. Ernst (eds.), Dating Egyptian Literary Texts (Lingua Aegyptia – Studia Monographica 11; Hamburg 2013), 139–158.

Verhoeven 2013b: U. Verhoeven, New Kingdom temple remains and other religious objects from the mountain plateau, in: J. Kahl, M. El-Khadragy, U. Verhoeven, M. Abdelrahiem & E. Czyżewska, The Asyut Project: Tenth Season of Fieldwork (2012), in: Studien zur Altägyptischen Kultur 42, 2013, 126–138.

Verhoeven 2020: U. Verhoeven (Hg.), Dipinti von Besuchern des Grabes N13.1 in Assiut (The Asyut Project 15; Wiesbaden 2020).

van der Vliet 2015: J. van der Vliet, Snippets from the Past. Two Ancient Sites in the Asyut region: Dayr al-Gabrawi and Dayr al-'Izam, in: G. Gabra & H. N. Takla (eds.), Christianity and Monasticism in Middle Egypt. Al-Minya and Asyut (Cairo – New York 2015), 161–168.

Walz 1978: T. Walz, Asyūṭ in the 1260's (1844–53), in: Journal of the American Research Center in Egypt 15, 1978, 113–126.

Williams 2014: E. Dospěl Williams, "Into the hands of a well-known antiquary of Cairo": The Assiut Treasure and the Making of an Archaeological Hoard, in: West 86th: A Journal of Decorative Arts, Design History, and Material Culture 21 (No. 2), 2014, 251–272.

Zipf 1949: G. K. Zipf, Human Behaviour and the Principle of Least Effort: An Introduction to Human Ecology (New York 1949).

Der verschollene Tempel des Upuaut, des Herrn von Assiut

Jochem Kahl & Mohamed Abdelrahiem

Die Geschichte der Stadt Assiut kann bislang nur mittels außerhalb von ihr gefundener Textquellen sowie anhand der archäologischen Erforschung des im Westen der Stadt gelegenen Gebel Assiut al-gharbi geschrieben werden. Aus Schriftquellen bekannte Tempel, Wohnbauten, Straßen und Aufzuchtplätze für heilige Tiere liegen ebenso wie Deiche und Ländereien für die moderne Forschung derzeit unerreichbar unter dem modernen Assiut.[1] Aus den vorhandenen Quellen ergibt sich, dass dem zumeist canidengestaltig dargestellten Gott Upuaut der Haupttempel der Stadt geweiht war und dass für den Nekropolengott Anubis, die Götter Thot und Osiris sowie andere Gottheiten weitere Tempel in bzw. am Rande der Stadt angelegt waren.[2] Zudem gab es einen Hathor-Tempel, der vermutlich auf dem Berg am Westrand der Stadt zu lokalisieren ist,[3] und einen Tempel (ḥw.t-nṯr) für Djefai-Hapi I.[4]

Lediglich bekannt durch seine schriftlichen Erwähnungen und durch Raubgrabungen erfuhr der Upuaut-Tempel von Assiut dementsprechend bislang wenig Beachtung.[5] Seine architektonischen Überreste liegen mehrere Meter tief unter der modernen Stadt begraben (Pl. 11). Moderne Häuser und Straßenzüge dehnen sich dicht gedrängt über dem antiken Tempelareal aus. Der einzige veröffentlichte archäologische Fund stammt aus einer illegalen Grabung, die 1930 der ägyptischen Altertümerverwaltung gemeldet wurde (Fig. 1): eine Anzahl beschlagnahmter Blöcke, welche Sami Gabra in einem Bericht kursorisch vorstellte.[6] Demnach grub ein Einwohner Assiuts im Keller seines Hauses nach Gold, stieß aber in ca. 8 m Tiefe auf Kalksteinblöcke des Neuen Reiches, die aufgrund der Inschrift eines der Blöcke dem Upuaut-Tempel zugeordnet werden können und einen bislang einmaligen Einblick in den Haupttempel der Stadt bieten.[7] Aus Gabras Publikation geht hervor, dass neben ramessidenzeitlichen Blöcken auch solche aus der Amarnazeit im Tempel verbaut waren.[8] Sie ergänzen damit schriftliche Hinweise aus der Zeit des Neuen Reiches, wonach während der Regierungszeiten von Thutmosis III., Amenhotep II., Haremhab und Ramses III. Restaurierungsarbeiten am Upuaut-Tempel durchgeführt wurden.[9] Insbesondere Papyrus Harris I bietet ein eindrucksvolles Bild des Haupttempels von Assiut: Hier wird u. a. geschildert, dass eine über 15 Meter hohe Umfassungsmauer mit Rampen, Türmen, steinernen Türpfosten und Türen aus Zedernholz errichtet wurde.[10] Die Anfänge des Tempels lassen sich derzeit anhand schriftlicher Quellen bis in die Zeit Königs Merikare am Ende des 3. Jahrtausends v. Chr. zurückverfolgen: In der autobiographischen Inschrift des Gaufürsten Cheti II. wird der Upuaut-Tempel als "der Himmel dessen, der den Himmel schuf" bezeichnet.[11] Hierbei dürfte es sich um den Namen des Tempels handeln.

---

1 Kahl 2007: 107–128.
2 See Kahl 2007: 35–58; Verhoeven 2020: 281–291.
3 Vgl. Ursula Verhoeven, New Kingdom temple remains and other religious objects from the mountain plateau, in: Kahl et al. 2013, 126–138; Verhoeven 2020: 284–286.
4 Vgl. Kahl 2012; id., Tomb I, First Hall, Shaft 3, in: Kahl et al. 2015: 124–127; Verhoeven 2020: 286–287.
5 Der Tempel ist beispielsweise nicht erwähnt in Arnold 1996.
6 Gabra 1931: 237–243.
7 Cf. Kahl 2007: 39–48.
8 Gabra 1931: 237–243.
9 Cf. J. Kahl 2007: 43.
10 pHarris I, 58,12–59,3; Grandet 1994: 306.
11 Siut IV, 21.

Fig. 1: Illegale Grabung im Keller eines Hauses in der Rue Amir Farouk, 1930 (GABRA 1931: 237, fig. 1).

Fig. 2: Tempelblöcke aus illegaler Grabung in der Rue Amir Farouk, 1930 (GABRA 1931: 239, fig. 3).

Sami Gabra veröffentlichte die konfiszierten Blöcke bald nach ihrer Entdeckung, doch blieben ihr damaliger Aufbewahrungsort bzw. späterer Verbleib unbekannt. Im Jahre 2008 allerdings gelangten 60 große Holzkisten vom Ägyptischen Museum Kairo in das Magazin der Ägyptischen Altertümerverwaltung in Shutb (6 km südlich von Assiut). Eine erste Durchsicht dieser Kisten ergab, dass sowohl Objekte aus der Nekropole im Westgebirge von Assiut (Gebel Assiut al-gharbi) als auch ein Teil der von Gabra veröffentlichten Tempelblöcke aus der Stadt in diesen Kisten aufbewahrt waren.

Die Geschichte der Tempelblöcke von ihrer illegalen Ausgrabung bis zu ihrem Eintreffen im Magazin der Ägyptischen Altertümerverwaltung in Shutb ist noch nicht vollends geklärt. Sie lässt sich derzeit wie folgt rekonstruieren: Die Blöcke wurden zunächst für Jahrzehnte in einem Magazin in oder bei Assiut (sogenanntes Magazin no. 3) gelagert. Im Jahre 1961 wurden sie vom Inspektorat von Minia, dem auch die Gegend von Assiut unterstand, in Kisten verpackt und irgendwann ab diesem Zeitpunkt zusammen mit Objekten aus der Nekropole von Assiut in das Ägyptische Museum Kairo geschickt, dort allerdings nie geöffnet. Im Jahre 2008 wurden sie – immer noch original verpackt – wieder von Kairo zurück nach Shutb bei Assiut gesandt, wo sie nun offiziell registriert im Magazin der Ägyptischen Altertümerverwaltung aufbewahrt sind[12] und im Rahmen einer Unternehmung des Ägyptologischen Seminars der Freien Universität Berlin bearbeitet werden. Mindestens 14 der 60 aus Kairo nach Shutb verfrachteten Kisten beinhalteten Kalksteinblöcke, die aus dem Tempel des Upuaut in der Altstadt von Assiut stammen. Die Durchsicht der Kisten ergab, dass wesentlich mehr Blöcke aus dieser illegalen Grabung existieren, als es Gabras Publikation vermuten ließ. Sind in der Publikation aus dem Jahre 1931 auf dem Übersichtsfoto nur 20 Blöcke abgebildet (Fig. 2) und ist auch in Gabras beschreibendem Text nicht die Anzahl der Tempelblöcke vermerkt, so konnten bislang 56 Blöcke mit Sicherheit als solche aus dem Upuaut-Tempel identifiziert werden. Denn neben der rezenten Inventarnummer des Ägyptischen Antikenmagazins von Shutb ist auf diesen Blöcken eine weitere, ältere Nummer angebracht; dieser ist jeweils noch die Abkürzung „TA" vorangestellt, was als „Temple Assiout" gedeutet werden darf. Diese TA-Nummern dürften aus der Registrierung der Blöcke durch Sami Gabra resultieren. Allerdings sind nicht mehr alle TA-Nummern auf den Blöcken erkennbar, manchmal ist nur noch ein Teil der Buchstaben oder der folgenden Ziffern lesbar. Die TA-Nummern reichen von TA 2 bis TA 93. Dies lässt darauf schließen, dass ursprünglich 93 + x Tempelblöcke von Sami Gabra erfasst worden waren. Nicht alle TA-Nummern sind in den Kisten erkennbar vertreten. Bislang sind mindestens 52 Blöcke aufgrund der TA-Nummern eindeutig dem Tempel zuzuweisen; zusätzlich waren mindestens vier Blöcke mit ursprünglicher, aber heute nicht genau lesbarer TA-Nummer in den Kisten aufbewahrt. Eventuell gehören weitere Blöcke aus den Kisten zum Tempel, deren TA-Nummern heute komplett verblasst sein mögen.

Eine Dokumentation der Blöcke erfolgt seit dem Jahr 2015 im Antikenmagazin in Shutb.[13] Neben bereits bei Gabra abgebildeten Blöcken aus der Amarnazeit bzw. Ramessidenzeit sind auch bislang unbekannte Blöcke faksimiliert und fotografiert worden. Im folgenden seien einige wenige Beispiele vorgestellt.

---

12 Die Blöcke sind mit anderen beschrifteten Objekten in einem Registerbuch (Arabisch: دفتر حرف ز) erfasst, welches zur besseren Unterscheidung von anderen Registerbüchern intern als Z-Registerbuch geführt wird. Die darin enthaltenen Objekte werden entsprechend mit einem Z und einer nachfolgenden Nummer zitiert.

13 An den ersten Sichtungen beteiligt waren: Mohamed Abdelrahiem (2015–2018), Adel Refaat (2015–2018), Sameh Shafik (2015), Fritz Barthel (2016–2018), Anja Hilbig (2016), Andrea Kilian (2016–2018), Reis Ahmed Atitou und Aid Abu Hamid (2016–2018), sowie Jochem Kahl (2016–2018). Wir danken in diesem Zusammenhang dem Direktor des Antikenmagazins von Shutb, Herrn Medhat Fayez Hana, und seinen Mitarbeiterinnen und Mitarbeitern für ihre Unterstützung. Für seine Mithilfe in landschaftsarchäologischen Fragestellungen danke ich zudem Dr. Mohamed Osman (Freie Universität Berlin/College of Archaeology and Cultural Heritage, The Arab Academy for Science, Technology and Maritime Transport, Aswan).

Shutb, Antikenmagazin, SCA Z36/4, alte Nummer: TA 4

Block aus der Zeit Echnatons mit Inschrift in vertieftem Relief (Pl. 12a–b), Kalkstein

Maße: H: 24 cm; B: 33 cm; T: 20 cm

GABRA 1931: 239, fig. 3 (2. Stapel von links, 2. Block von oben)

Eine senkrechte Inschriftenkolumne mit Kartusche der Nofretete:

[nfr-]nfr.w[-ꞽtn] Nfr.tꞽ-ꞽy.tꞽ	„[Schön ist] die Vollkommenheit [des Aton], Nofretete.
ꜥnḫ.tꞽ ḏ.t	Sie lebe ewig".

Shutb, Antikenmagazin, SCA Z49, alte Nummer: TA 64

Block aus der Zeit Echnatons mit vertieft gearbeiteter, nachträglich ausradierter Inschrift (Figs. 3–4), Kalkstein

Maße: H: 21 cm; B: 54 cm; T: 22 cm

GABRA 1931: 240, fig. 4

Vier Kolumnen mit Inschriften, daneben Strahlenaton

1 [ꜥnḫ Rꜥw ḥḳꜣ] ꜣḫ.tꞽ [ḥ]ꜥ.y m ꜣḫ.t	„[Es lebe Re,] der zum Lichtland gehörige [Herrscher], der im Lichtland [ju]belt,
2 ⌈m rn=f m⌉ […] ⌈m ꞽtn⌉	⌈in seinem Namen als⌉ […] ⌈als Aton⌉.
3 […]	[…]
4 […] nb tꜣ m ꜣḫ.t-ꞽtn	[…] Herr der Erde in Achet-Aton."

Shutb, Antikenmagazin, SCA Z41/1, alte Nummer: TA 16

Block aus der Zeit Ramses II. mit Inschrift in vertieftem Relief (Pl. 13a–b), Kalkstein

Maße: H: 21 cm; B: 39 cm; T: 24 cm

GABRA 1931: 240, fig. 4

Reste von vier Inschriftenkolumnen, die in folgender Reihenfolge zu lesen sein dürften:

1 ḏ(d) mdw.w in Wpꞽ-wꜣꞽ.wt	„Worte zu sprechen seitens Upuaut,
2 šmꜥ.wꞽ sḫm tꜣ.wꞽ	des Oberägyptischen, der Macht der Beiden Länder:
3 čꞽ.n=i n=k nsw.y[t…]	„Hiermit gebe ich das Königt[um…] Dir,
4 nb tꜣ.wꞽ Wsr[-Mꜣꜥ.t-]Rꜥw [stp.n-Rꜥw]	Herr der Beiden Länder, User[-Maat-]Re [Setep-en-Re]"

Shutb, Antikenmagazin, SCA Z37/5, alte Nummer: TA 15

Block aus der Zeit Echnatons mit vertieft gearbeiteter Inschrift (Fig. 5), Kalkstein

Maße: H: 19 cm; B: 38 cm; T: 20 cm

GABRA 1931: 239, fig. 3 (li., 2. Block von oben)

Sechs Inschriftenkolumnen mit Nennung der ursprünglich beim Kom el-Nana in Amarna gelegenen Kultanlage der Nofretete Rudj-Anchu-Iten[14]:

1 ꞽm(.ꞽ) [ḫꜣb.w nb]	„der im [Fest] ist, [Herr]
2 šnn nb ꞽtn	all dessen, was Aton umkreist,
3 nb p.t nb tꜣ	Herr des Himmels, Herr der Erde,
4 ḥr(.ꞽ)-ꞽb	der residiert in
5 rwḏ-	„Rudj-
6 ꜥnḫ.w-ꞽtn	Anchu-Iten""

---

14 Vgl. WILLIAMSON 2013: 145–152; WILLIAMSON 2016: 150–175.

Fig. 3: Tempelblock, Antikenmagazin Shutb SCA Z49 (TA 64)
(Foto: Fritz Barthel 2016; © Ägyptologisches Seminar, Freie Universität Berlin).

Fig. 4: Tempelblock, Antikenmagazin Shutb SCA Z49 (TA 64)
(Foto: Fritz Barthel 2016; © Ägyptologisches Seminar, Freie Universität Berlin).

Zusätzlich zu den derzeit 56 identifizierten Blöcken aus pharaonischer Zeit sind im Magazin der Altertümerverwaltung in Shutb noch Säulenfragmente aus der Spätantike gelagert, die ebenfalls aus dem Areal des früheren Tempels stammen (u.a. gefunden in den Kellern moderner Wohnhäuser).[15] Sie belegen die kontinuierliche Nutzung des Areals als Tempel wie auch als Kirche und zeugen damit von einer über die Kulturen und Religionen hinausgehenden Bedeutung dieses Platzes als geistigem Zentrum Assiuts (Pl. 11).

---

15 KAHL 2007: 44, Fig. 24.

Fig. 5: Tempelblock, Antikenmagazin Shutb SCA Z37/5 (TA 15)
(Foto: Fritz Barthel 2016; © Ägyptologisches Seminar, Freie Universität Berlin).

Weiterhin ergab die Durchsicht von Berichten des lokalen Inspektorats, dass gelegentlich illegale Grabungen in der Altstadt Assiuts von der Polizei unterbunden bzw. aufgedeckt wurden. Zwar sind keine konfiszierten Blöcke zugänglich (diese wurden in aller Regel an ihrem ursprünglichen Fundplatz gelassen), aber eine Kartierung der Ortsangaben in diesen Berichten gibt nochmals Hinweise auf die Lage des Upuaut-Tempels in der Altstadt von Assiut. Häufig wurde in den Kellern von Wohnhäusern illegal nach Tempelblöcken gegraben. Solche Häuser wurden dann zwar von den ägyptischen Behörden geschlossen, wie z. B. das Haus in der Sh. Harat el-Canisa in der Altstadt von Assiut (Fig. 6), jedoch scheinen diese Maßnahmen allein nicht den Raubgrabungen völlig Einhalt gebieten zu können. Ein im Jahre 2015 in London aufgetauchter und von Marcel Marée bekannt gemachter Block eines Tempels kann aufgrund der dargestellten Gottheiten ebenfalls Assiut zugewiesen werden.[16] Der Block, auf dem König Sethos I. vor Hathor von Medjeden und Upuaut dargestellt ist, wurde inzwischen wieder nach Ägypten zurückgebracht und ist im Museum von Sohag ausgestellt (Pl. 14a). Zusätzlich zu pharaonenzeitlichen Blöcken kommen gelegentlich auch spätantike Bauteile in der Altstadt Assiuts zu Tage, so z. B. eine ca. 2,70 m hohe Granitsäule, die 2018 auf der Straße beim Gemüsemarkt von Assiut lag (Sh. Soukh; Fig. 7).

Das Areal, auf dem nach derzeit vorliegenden Informationen Blöcke des Upuaut-Tempels lokalisiert werden können, hat eine Ausdehnung von mindestens 200 m Länge. Es stellt den antiken Kern der Stadt dar und ist ca. 1,5 km Luftlinie vom Gebel Assiut al-gharbi entfernt. Eine Konturanalyse, basierend auf Satellitenaufnahmen (Beilagen 1–2), zeigt, dass die heutige Altstadt von Assiut mit den Resten

---

16 http://english.ahram.org.eg/NewsContent/9/40/152042/Heritage/Ancient-Egypt/Egypt-recovers-Stolen-relief-of-King-Seti-I-from-L.aspx

Fig. 6: Haus in der Sh. Harat el-Canisa
(Foto: Jochem Kahl 2017; © Ägyptologisches Seminar,
Freie Universität Berlin).

Fig. 7: Spätantike Granitsäule, Assiut, Sh. Soukh
(Foto: Jochem Kahl 2017; © Ägyptologisches Seminar,
Freie Universität Berlin).

des Upuaut-Tempels einen bis zu 72 m über NN liegenden Siedlungshügel bildet, der sich deutlich von seiner Umgebung abhebt (Beilage 3a–b). Nach derzeitigem Forschungsstand sind Bautätigkeiten aus folgenden Zeiten im Tempelareal belegt:

- Cheti II. (z. Zt. König Merikare) (schriftlich)[17]
- Sesostris I. (schriftlich)[18]
- Thutmosis III. (schriftlich)[19]
- Amenhotep II. (schriftlich)[20]
- Echnaton? (Blöcke: verschleppt aus Amarna oder ursprünglich aus Assiut[21])
- Haremhab (schriftlich und Blöcke)[22]
- Sethos I. (Block)
- Ramses II. (Blöcke)
- Ramses III. (schriftlich)[23]

17 Siut IV, 19–20.
18 Siut I, 235–236.
19 Helck 1956: 1443.3.
20 Eissa 1996: 85. Ullmann 2002: 98–101.
21 Es bleibt zu klären, ob die amarnazeitlichen Blöcke ursprünglich zu einem Gebäude in Assiut gehörten, wie dies S. Gabra, in: Gabra 1931: 237–241 annahm, oder ob sie erst nachträglich aus Amarna abtransportiert und in Assiut verbaut wurden. Der Block Z37/5 deutet auf eine Herkunft aus Amarna.
22 Eissa 1996: 84–85.
23 pHarris I, 58,12–59,3, 61a, 15 (Grandet 1994: 306, 311).

Der Upuaut-Tempel selber bzw. sein Personal sind von der Ersten Zwischenzeit (Grabinschrift des Gaufürsten Cheti I., Siut V, 14) bis in römische Zeit in Texten und Inschriften greifbar.[24] Von seiner Rolle als Haupttempel von Assiut, seiner langen Nutzungsdauer und seiner sich uns erst nach und nach erschließenden Ausdehung vermögen die nun wiedergefundenen Tempelblöcke ein erstes greifbares Zeugnis zu geben.

Bibliographie

Arnold 1996: D. Arnold, Die Tempel Ägyptens. Götterwohnungen, Baudenkmäler, Kultstätten (Augsburg 1996).

Eissa 1996: A. Eissa, Zwei königliche Stelen der 18. Dynastie aus Siût, in: Mitteilungen des Deutschen Archäologischen Instituts Abteilung Kairo 52, 1996, 83–85.

Gabra 1931: S. Gabra, Un temple d' Amenophis IV à Assiout, in: Chronique d'Égypte 6, 1931, 237–243.

Grandet 1994: P. Grandet, Le Papyrus Harris I (BM 9999), Bibliothèque d'Étude 109, Le Caire 1994.

Helck 1956: W. Helck, Urkunden der 18. Dynastie. Heft 18. Biographische Inschriften von Zeitgenossen Thutmosis' III. und Amenophis' II. (Berlin 1956).

Kahl 2007: J. Kahl, Ancient Asyut. The First Synthesis after 300 Years of Research (The Asyut Project 1; Wiesbaden 2007).

Kahl 2012: J. Kahl, Regionale Milieus und die Macht des Staates im Alten Ägypten: Die Vergöttlichung der Gaufürsten von Assiut, in: Studien zur Altägyptischen Kultur 41, 2012, 163–188.

Kahl et al. 2013: J. Kahl, M. El-Khadragy, U. Verhoeven, M. Abdelrahiem & Ewa Czyżewska, The Asyut Project: Tenth Season of Fieldwork (2012), in: Studien zur Altägyptischen Kultur 42, 2013, 123–153.

Kahl et al. 2015: J. Kahl, M. El-Khadragy, H. Faheed Ahmed, U. Verhoeven, M. Abdelrahiem, I. Regulski, M. Becker, E. Czyżewska-Zalewska, A. Kilian, M. Stecher & T. Rzeuska, The Asyut Project: Eleventh Season of Fieldwork (2014), in: Studien zur Altägyptischen Kultur 44, 2015, 103–161.

Ullmann 2002: M. Ullmann, König für die Ewigkeit. Die Häuser der Millionen von Jahren. Eine Untersuchung zu Königskult und Tempeltypologie in Ägypten (Ägypten und Altes Testament 51; Wiesbaden 2002).

Verhoeven 2020: U. Verhoeven (Hg.), Dipinti von Besuchern des Grabes N13.1 in Assiut (The Asyut Project 15; Wiesbaden 2020).

Williamson 2013: J. Williamson, Two Names, One Compound: The rwd anxw itn and the Sunshade of Re at Kom el-Nana, in: Journal of the American Research Center in Egypt 49, 2013, 143–152.

Williamson 2016: J. Williamson, Nefertiti's Sun Temple. A New Cult Complex at Tell el-Amarna (Harvard Egyptological Studies 2; Leiden – Boston 2016).

---

24 Kahl 2007: 39–48.

The Fragmentary Wall Paintings in Tomb I10.1 at Asyut

Ursula Verhoeven

1. Outline

This paper presents views of the architecture and the painted decoration and inscriptions of eight remaining fragmentary areas in Tomb I10.1 in the northwestern part of the necropolis of Asyut which in 1799 was described as the most beautifully painted tomb therein. The owner was a *ḥꜣtj-ꜥ* whose name is only partly preserved as *Mr*[...] or [...]*mr*[...]. The west wall of the large hall must have borne several registers of scenes showing craftsmen at work and other activities, together with a biographical text. Its north wall is decorated with several registers showing officials (heralds, stewards, a scribe) with their personal names possibly accompanied by a sunshade bearer. In the vaulted corridor, fragments of the ceiling decoration with stars and some single hieroglyphs on the walls still remain. Evidence for dating the tomb in Dynasty 11 or early Dynasty 12 is discussed at the end of the article.

2. Location and architecture

Tomb I10.1 is situated in the northern part of the necropolis at Gebel Asyut al-gharbi, on the geological step 6. A visitor passing Tomb V (M11.1, First Intermediate Period) and Tomb M10.1 (Dynasty 11 or early 12)[1] on their left will reach it after another 150m, just before the so-called Northern Soldiers-Tomb H11.1 (late Dynasty 11)[2]; cf. the map in the contribution of J. Kahl, Fig. 12. Jochem Kahl has proposed that Tomb I10.1 is most seemingly to be identified with one described and planned by two engineers of the French Expedition who visited Asyut in 1799 and summed up: « Cet hypogée est, de tous ceux que nous avons vus dans la montagne de Syout, le plus richement décoré et le plus soigné ».[3] Recently Kahl and Sbriglio also found architectural sketches by Piero Molli ('Assiut 1913') which belong to this tomb.[4] Griffith did not reach the tombs in this northern part of the necropolis.[5] Marcel Zitman has mentioned the tomb and called it 'Tomb XVIII', according to his own numbering system.[6]

As there are no plans to excavate the tomb in the near future, the currently available material is published here. Restorers of the Ministry of State for Antiquities worked on the tomb during our seasons in 2004 (outside) and 2016 (inside), but the walls continue to suffer from weather conditions, modern graffiti and vandalism.

Ulrike Fauerbach has drawn a new ground plan, section and elevation of the tomb, for which see Kahl 2007, 98, fig. 81; a simplified version was used for our Figs. 1 and 8. Due to its distant location

---

1 Cf. Kahl 2007: 95–96; for the inscriptions, see Verhoeven 2013: 221–228.
2 El-Khadragy 2006: 147–164; Kahl et al. 2011; 2012; Abdelrahiem 2020.
3 See Kahl 2013: 120–121 with Figs. 74–76.
4 National archive/Archivio di stato, Turin: 'secondo versamento, mazzo 3, fascicolo 12'; cf. Kahl, Sbriglio, Del Vesco & Trapani 2019: 244, Pl. 76a–e.
5 Cf. Kahl 2013: 121.
6 Zitman 2010a: 42; 2010b: 4, map 2.

around the curvature of the mountain, this tomb faces north-northwest. I regard this tomb as facing local east, like the other tombs on step 6, and hereafter I shall label its walls accordingly.

The full length of the tomb, with its three consecutive rooms which are preserved nowadays, is some 27.5 m. The large hall (A) has an approximate width of 12.5 m and its maximum height was 6.5 m. Access to the tomb is currently hampered by large heaps of debris, and our view of hall A (Fig. 2) shows only the higher parts of its walls exposed. The ground floor seems to be about 1,50 m deeper. Fig. 3 shows a view of the local south wall with its two corners. According to the ground plan of Piero Molli,[7] there seems to be a rectangular shaft with a burial chamber towards west in front of the south-west corner. The west and north walls in hall A still bear remains of painted decoration on gypsum plaster, marked as areas 1–6 in Fig. 1 and presented in detail below. The engineers of the French Expedition described the ceiling of hall A as follows: « Le plafond du vestibule est décoré d'ornements peints. Un cadre d'étoiles forme la première bordure: le reste est rempli de dessins en échiquier, dans le goût des Grecs, des Étrusques et des Arabes. »[8] With such patterns, the ceiling must have been very similar to that of the great transverse hall in Tomb I of Djefai-Hapi I from the time of Senwosret I.[9]

Hall A provides access to a corridor B, which has a vaulted ceiling that is 4.2 m high (for a recent view of this room see Fig. 4). Corridor B was also decorated with paintings on plaster, but small parts remain only in one area where the south wall meets the ceiling which was decorated with stars as well (area 7 in Fig. 1; cf. Pl. 26, Fig. 14) and in tiny fragments on the north wall (area 8 in Fig. 1), see below. Two side doors at the back of corridor B give access to shafts, which slope down to burial chambers, for the entrance on the south wall see Fig. 5, for the one on the north wall see Fig. 6. In former times, yellow coffins of the Third Intermediate Period were found here which are kept in the magazine at El-Ashmunein. The third room, hall C, probably once contained a rock-cut shrine like the one in Tomb I of Djefai-Hapi I.[10] Nowadays it shows several niches (Fig. 7).

After this raw sketch of the architecture and the state of preservation, the remaining decoration will be presented and discussed according to the numbers in our groundplan (Fig. 1) as well as in the elevation plan (Fig. 8).

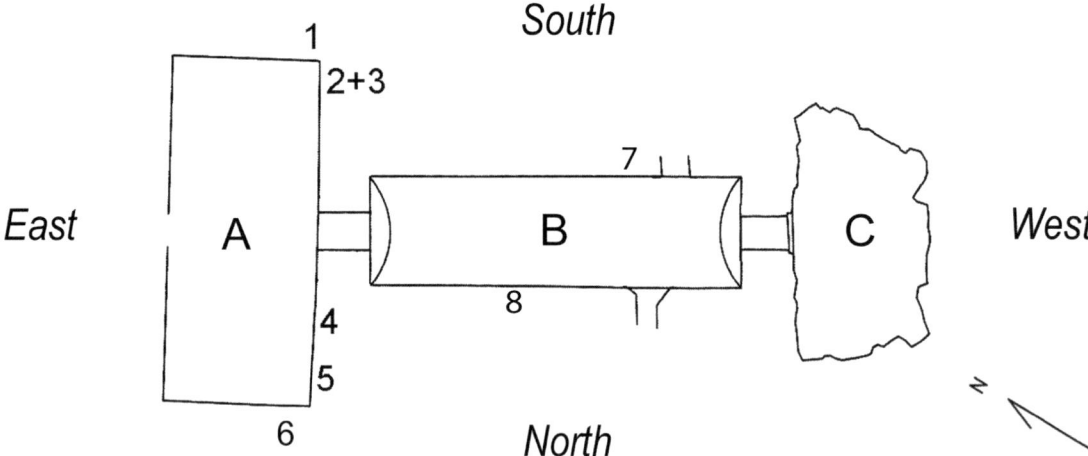

Fig. 1: Ground plan of Tomb I10.1, showing the locations of preserved decoration (areas 1–8).
The arrow indicates true north, the text labels mark local directions (© The Asyut Project).

---

7 Cf. note 4.
8 Cf. Jollois & Devilliers 1818: 13. Cf. also Kahl 2013: 121.
9 Kahl 2016.
10 El-Khadragy 2007: 57, fig. 2; Kahl 2007: 89, fig. 71.

Fig. 2: View of Tomb I10.1 from local east (photo: Svenja A. Gülden 2010; © The Asyut Project).

Fig. 3: View of the south wall of hall A (photo: Fritz Barthel 2016; © The Asyut Project).

Fig. 4: View into corridor B facing local west (photo: Fritz Barthel 2016; © The Asyut Project).

Fig. 5: Entrance to the shaft on the south wall of corridor B (photo: Ursula Verhoeven 2016; © The Asyut Project).

Fig. 6: Entrance to the shaft on the north wall of corridor B (photo: Ursula Verhoeven 2016; © The Asyut Project).

Fig. 7: View into hall C facing north (photo: Ursula Verhoeven 2016; © The Asyut Project).

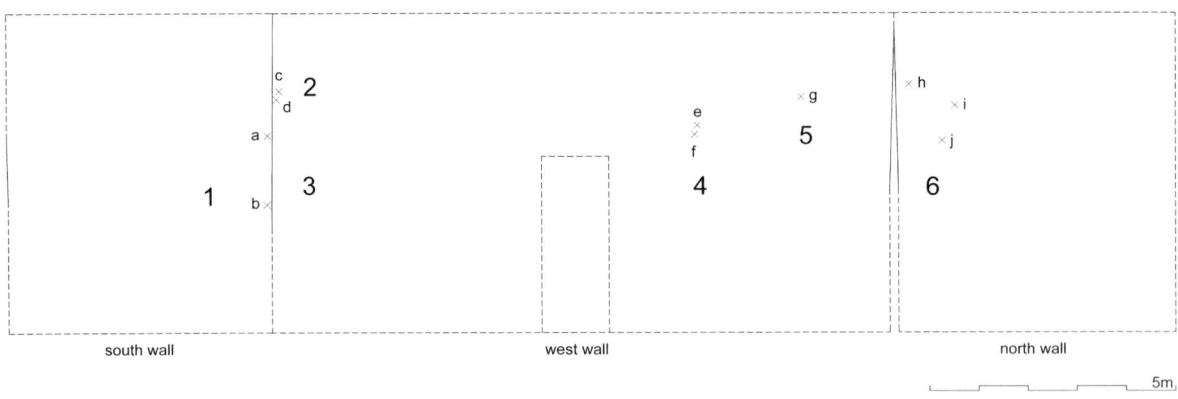

Fig. 8: Sketch of the remaining walls of hall A, showing the locations of preserved decoration (areas 1–6).
Points a–j are those in the drawings on Figs. Fig. 9–13 (© The Asyut Project).

2.1 Hall A

Area 1: Fragmentary decoration on the south wall, west end (Fig. 8: no. 1 a–b)

Where the south and west walls meet (cf. Fig. 2–3, Pl. 14b) there remains a narrow strip of plaster with painted decoration. The extant decoration on the south wall, at its west end, comprises a vertical column of text with a green border line near the corner of the wall (Fig. 9). The polychrome hieroglyphs were drawn in red outlines and painted on a yellow background. The ꜣ-vultures have a white neck, blue wings and yellow claws, the kꜣ-arms are red (Pl. 15a), as are the legs of the sitting man and the ꜥ-arm. The t-loaf and the n-water ripple are coloured blue-green. Yellow was used for the w-quail chick, the ḥꜣt-forepart of a lion (Pl. 15b), the mr-hoe (which has red dots; see Pl. 15b) and the ḥ-wick. The j-reed has yellow awns and a green stem (Pls. 15b and 16). The red outlines, the overall colour scheme and the style of the signs are very similar to those painted in Tomb III (N12.1) of Iti-ibi after its incised biographical inscription about the battles at Asyut was covered with stucco and replaced by a more traditional biography (EL-KHADRAGY 2012, 32–33 with fig. 1; cf. the colour plates in KAHL 2007, pl. 3, and KAHL 2013, 427, pl. 17). However, the painted hieroglyphs in the tomb of Djefai-Hapi I (P10.1/Tomb I) from the reign of Senwosret I are also quite similar in style. The palaeography of hieroglyphs in the tombs of Asyut's nomarchs is being documented by Jochem Kahl, and the resultant overview will enable more detailed comparison.[11]

The surviving column 1, perhaps once followed by others, reads (cf. the drawing in Fig. 9):

---

11 Cf. KAHL ET AL. 2011: 183–185. Some Siutian coffins also show partly similar hieroglyphs, cf. HANNIG 2006: 186 (S6C), 210 (S13C), 221 (S16C), 226 (S17C), 240 (S1Hil), 312 (S37L).

Area 1, column 1:

Area 1, col. 1: *[mꜣꜣ kꜣt nt ḥmw[w]* (a) *j[n] ḥꜣ[tj]-ꜥ [...]mr[...]*(b) *ḥ[s]y*(c) *[.?.]*

Area 1, col. 1: [Wat]ching the work of the craftsm[en] by the *ḥꜣtj-*ꜥ(d) [...]mer[...](e) (?), pra[ise]d [.?.]

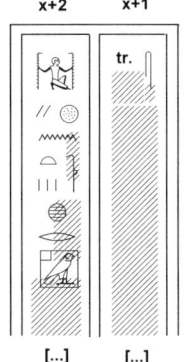

(a) For the form of the drill hieroglyph (Gardiner Sign-list U24), cf. the example in the contemporary Siutian tomb P13.1 (Verhoeven 2011: 187, fig. 3).

(b) The reading of the name is uncertain. The sign of the hoe is clear, but the surrounding space is covered with mud (cf. Pl. 15b). The leftward position of the *mr*-hoe might indicate that it was preceded on the right by a tall vertical sign, as for instance in the name *Sn-mrj* (Ranke 1935: 308, 23), although that name is not otherwise attested at Asyut.

(c) The position of the sitting man (A1 or more likely A2) between the *ḥ* and the reeds (cf. Pl. 16) is puzzling.

(d) Harco Willems has discussed the title *ḥꜣtj-*ꜥ and its interpretations as either a signifier of rank or as a function title denoting a mayor. He notes, "[W]here the title *ḥꜣtj-*ꜥ is followed by a name, this could imply an abbreviation of any title string containing the element *ḥꜣtj-*ꜥ. This implies that the title could in principle refer to a mayor, but does not necessarily always do so." (Willems 2014: 56–57).

(e) We have various attestations of the name Merer/Mereru at Asyut: Four wooden statues, now in New York, belonged to a man called *Mrr*, who had the title *sẖꜣ ḥtp-nṯr*, 'scribe of god's offerings', and lived during the early Middle Kingdom. Another *Mrr*, known from an offering table, was *jmj-rꜣ pr*, 'steward'. The form *Mrrw* is known for two men without documented titles, whose coffins (S6Tor, S1Tor) were found by Ernesto Schiaparelli in 1908.[12] Unfortunately, no *ḥꜣtj-*ꜥ with a similar name is known from Asyut.

The text in area 1 identified the subject of images divided between the south wall on the left, which would have included a large figure of the tomb owner, and the west wall on the right. A similar phrase 'watching all work in the workshop of the craftsmen' occurs, e. g., in Davies 1902a: 18, pl. 13 (cf. also pl. 24). For the construction *mꜣꜣ ... jn ḥꜣtj-*ꜥ *...* NN, see, e. g., Davies 1902a: 14, pl. 5.

To the left of the final pair of reeds there are traces of a large representation that seemingly included part of a human body coloured light red. Other elements are painted in darker red and light blue.

Area 2: Fragmentary decoration on the west wall, south end, upper part (Fig. 8: no. 2 c–d)

Points c and d locate the position of this area on the wall. There are traces of two columns of hieroglyphs, again drawn in red outlines but this time entirely filled with blue colour (photo in Pl. 17; drawing in Fig. 10):

Area 2, columns x+1–2:

Area 2, col. x+1: *s[...]*

Area 2, col. x+1: ... [...]

Area 2, col. x+2: *ḥḥ*(a) *sp 2 n [rn]pwt*(b) *[ḥ]r Ḥwt-ḥr [...]*

Area 2, col. x+2: millions and millions of [yea]rs [ne]ar Hathor [...]

(a) The *ḥḥ*-hieroglyph has an unusual ground line and the ends of the two plants are bent together upon the head.

(b) The *rnp*-sign is mostly destroyed, but the context makes this the most plausible reading.

---

12 All these men and relevant sources are listed by Zitman 2010b: 180.

Area 3: Fragmentary decoration on the west wall, south end, lower part (Fig. 8: no. 3)
Area 3 lies some distance below area 2, beneath a plaster gap of about 70 cm. It preserves the left ends of six registers (drawing in Fig. 9 and photo in Pl. 18). Of the highest detectable register x+1, only a trace of the baseline remains. The second to fourth registers show the figures of standing men. The man in register x+2 has short-cropped hair (painted blue) and wears a short kilt, part of which curves up around his backward leg. The heel of his rear foot is raised and he holds a long stick or rope in a near-horizontal direction. In register x+3 stands another man in a short kilt, and he also had the heel of his rear foot off the ground, but the rest of his figure is lost. Register x+4 features a man in a short, straight kilt with his feet planted firmly on the ground. He bows forward and had both his arms in front of him.

Register x+5 shows a rectangular yellow object or structure within two bands or frames, the inner one in red colour, the outer one in light grey-blue. The bands are of the same width, while the bottom lines are narrower than the three others (see Pl. 19). Inside it stands the figure of a man, facing right, who wears a blue pointed kilt and he holds a long staff and sceptre ( ). In front of him, still inside the frames, there may be traces of hieroglyphs, as yet illegible.[13] Should the full composition be read as *ḥwt-sr*, 'estate of the nobleman'?

At the bottom of area 3 there is a remnant of a sixth register (see Pl. 18). It shows the head of a man with short-cropped hair. He stood straight with his arms reaching forward.

The lively postures of all these men in area 3 fit well with scenes of craftsmen, as may be expected based on the text in area 1.

Area 4: Fragmentary decoration on the west wall, north of the doorway (Fig. 8: no. 4 e–f)
All that remains is traces of blue hieroglyphs arranged in three columns (Pl. 20a). This seems to have been a biographical inscription (see drawing in Fig. 11):

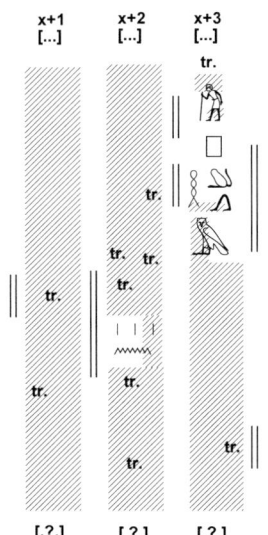

Area 4, columns x+1–3:

Area 4, col. x+1: *[...]*
Area 4, col. x+1: [...]

Area 4, col. x+2: *[...]w* (plur.) *n [...]*
Area 4, col. x+2: [...] (plur.) of/for [...]

Area 4, col. x+3: *[... jꜣw(?)]* (det. old man) *pḥ m [...]*
Area 4, col. x+3: [... old age (?)] reached in [...]

Area 5: Fragmentary decoration on the west wall, north end (Fig. 8: no. 5 g)
In this area three patches of painted plaster remain (photo in Pl. 20b, drawing in Fig. 12). The upper two (fragm. 1–2) feature a blue baseline of a pictorial register, which on the right-hand fragment (fragm. 2) is accompanied by a parallel stroke in light red below – perhaps this was part of the draughtsman's initial outline sketch. The same fragment shows also a man's rear foot with its heel raised off the ground. The

---

13 I thank Andrea Kilian for this observation.

figure seems to have been of a similar size to those in area 6 and larger than the men in area 3. The last fragment (fragm. 3), at the bottom, preserves part of a man's chest, belly and forward arm. Both men, like all the surviving figures on these walls, faced to the right.

Area 6: Fragmentary decoration on the north wall, west end (Fig. 8: no. 6 h–j)

The main area with fragments of painted plaster on the west part of the north wall (cf. overview Pl. 21, drawing Fig. 13) preserves parts of four registers. In register x+1 only two fragments indicate the position of standing men (see below). The upper two registers are completed on the left side with a single text column (col. x+1) followed by the figure of a man holding an object on a long staff (Pl. 22a–b, see below). The hieroglyphs of col. x+1 being placed between blue vertical lines are larger than the others on this wall and polychrome like the hieroglyphs on the south wall. The first recognisable sign in his hieroglyphic caption is a yellow quail chick *w*, followed by a red seated man in a white kilt (A1), then by the left part of a red mouth *r*. A lacuna ends with unclear traces, followed by a partly preserved brazier (Q7), which was typically used as a determinative in words concerning 'fire' and 'heat'. The bird below this is without a head now and open to different interpretations. Its white body and blue wing match those of the *ꜣ*-vulture in area 1 (south wall), but the same colour scheme is to be expected for a polychrome depiction of an owl (*m*). In fact, the bird's feet are fully preserved and lack a backward toe or hallux, which suggests that this is indeed an owl. In Egyptian representations, including hieroglyphs, the owl is consistently depicted without a hallux (cf. Pl. 24a), unlike the other birds of prey (cf. the *ꜣ*-vulture in Pl. 15a). The last preserved sign is clearly a dark red door-bolt *s*.

x+1   Area 6, column x+1:

Area 6, col. x+1: *[j]w=j r [...]n(=j) m s[...](?)*
Area 6, col. x+1: I shall [... (something involving heat)]... with(?) ...[...]

This text must relate to the man shown behind this column at the far left, in the corner. The man has slightly darker skin than the others. His arms hang down and apparently held a long yellow stick. Maybe the blue lines in the uppermost part of the area (Pl. 22a, Fig. 13) belong to the object he is holding, which could therefore be a sunshade.[14] It is odd that this man with the possible sunshade in the left part should be shown following other subordinates of the tomb owner who are represented in front of him, rather than the tomb owner himself. However, there are other examples of sunshade bearers accompanied by texts expressing speech or chant. In the tomb of Ibi in Deir el-Gebrawi (Dynasty 6), two such men have a caption that is now incomplete and hard to understand but ending with *ḏd=sn*, 'they say'.[15] In the tomb of Djau, a text inscribed below the owner's palanquin is evidently sung by his carriers and/or the carriers of his sunshades: 'Those who carry the palanquin are pleased. It (i. e. the palanquin) is more beautiful when full than when it is empty!'[16]

The main area preserves parts of four registers containing figures of men (Fig. 13, Pls. 22b–23b), all dressed in calf-length kilts and walking to the right. Each places the hand of his rear arm on the forward shoulder, while the other hand supports the elbow of that arm. This is a pose of respect, undoubtedly towards the tomb owner, who must once have been depicted further to the right.[17] The men's hair is always painted blue, their bodies are red, their kilts white. Three heads are

---

14 For depictions of sunshades, see Fischer 1972: 151–156; 1984, 1104–1105; Moussa and Altenmüller 1977: pl. 55; Schenkel and Gomaà 2004: Beilage 15; Kanawati 2005: pl. 47; Kormysheva et al. 2010: 143, fig. 32; Kanawati & Evans 2014: pl. 91.

15 Davies 1902a: pl. 8; Kanawati 2007: pls. 14 and 49.

16 Davies 1902b: 11, pl. 8; Kanawati 2013: 46, pls. 24 and 63 (the text is now incomplete); Grunert 2015 interprets this as the song of the palanquin carriers, but those carrying the sunshades may well be singing along – the six of them form a tight group.

17 See Dominicus 1993: 7, table 1, and 8, fig. 1, notably pose 4/5.

almost fully preserved and display a fine drawing style (Pls. 24a–25). The figures were drawn in dark red outlines while the skin is a lighter red. This combination of two shades of red is, again, closely paralleled in the painted decoration of Tomb III (N12.1; Iti-ibi).[18] The baselines of the registers are blue as usual, and so are the men's hieroglyphic captions.[19]

The highest confirmed register x+1 exhibits only traces of a foot and a small part of another man, but the second register x+2 has fared better (Pl. 22b). It showed at least five identical looking men, the first of whom is now lost, apart from a trace of the back of his head. The next three men assume the pose of respect but they are the only ones who also hold, against their chest, a long wooden sceptre-like baton of authority (painted dark red) with a tapering terminal (same colour as the background).[20] These staves are attested by a variety of sources from late Dynasty 11 and early Dynasty 12 (Fischer 1979, 17, nn. 74–78; cf. Fischer 1986, 53, fig. 1G; 55 (C 2), nn. 49–50). The five men each had their own captions, only the first being completely lost (cf. the drawing in Fig. 13):

Area 6, register x+2, columns x+1–5:

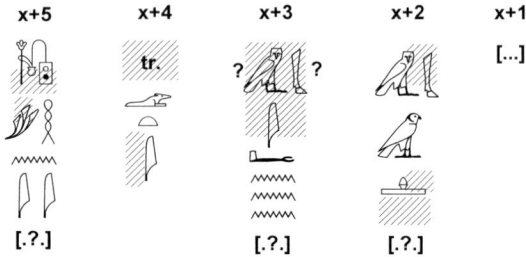

Area 6, reg. x+2, col. x+1: *[...]*   [...]

Area 6, reg. x+2, col. x+2: *[wḥ]m Ḥr-[ḥ]tp*   [the messen]ger[(a)] Hor[h]otep[(b)]

Area 6, reg. x+2, col. x+3: *[wḥm(?) Jꜥ[.?.]*   [the messenger(?) I]a[.?.][(c)]

Area 6, reg. x+2, col. x+4: *[...] Msḥtj*   [the ...] Mesehti[(d)]

Area 6, reg. x+2, col. x+5: *s[ḥꜣ] Ḥny*   the scr[ibe][(e)] Heny[(f)]

(a) The reading of the title *wḥm* seems plausible, as a tiny part of a hoofed leg is apparently visible at the bottom right of a hole (Pl. 22b). The title was in use since the Old Kingdom. In tomb B2 in Meir, from the reign of Senwosret I, the title is associated with men in the same long kilts and holding the same authority baton as they lead, or accompany, other people to the tomb owner.[21]

(b) Cf. Pl. 24a. The name Horhotep is already attested in Asyut: see coffin S2Mal (Mallawi no. 567) of a man with the title *jmj-rꜣ ḥtmt*, 'sealer' (Zitman 2010b: 189).

(c) I reconstruct the title *wḥm*, because this man carries the same baton as Horhotep; see comment (a) above. The name *Jꜥy* occurs on an offering table from Asyut in the filiation (*jr.n Jꜥy*) of a man whose father is called *Ḥty*; Zitman must therefore be right in taking *Jꜥy* as the mother's name (Zitman 2010b: 164), *contra* Ranke 1935: 12, 2.

(d) The name *Msḥtj* was common in Asyut, written mostly with phonetic signs but sometimes, as here, with the crocodile (Zitman 2010b: 180–181).

---

18 Cf. the colour illustration of the forearm in Kahl 2013: 428, pl. 18.

19 The blue colour of the hieroglyphs in areas 1, 4 and 6 recall again the description by the French Expedition, see Kahl 2013: 121.

20 The terminal is only preserved with the second man.

21 Blackman 1915: 22, pl. 11 (a *wḥmw* behind a herdsman presenting cattle); 24, pl. 15 (a *wḥmw* leading a temple overseer and three musicians); cf. Ward 1982: 89, no. 741. For another man in the same kilt and holding the same baton, but with no stated title, see Blackman 1914: 25, pl. 3.

(e) The sign for 'scribe' is incomplete and a bit small, but the top of the reed-holder and a trace of the palette seem clear.

(f) The name *Ḥny* is attested in Asyut for a steward, who owned coffins S1X, S2X and S8X, and statue Cairo JE 47240. He was buried in the First Hall of Tomb I of the nomarch Djefai-Hapi I (temp. Senwosret I)[22] and was probably a retainer of the latter (KAHL 2007: 91; cf. also ZITMAN 2010a: 344).

The third register showed at least four men in the usual pose and kilt (Pl. 23a). Only three of their captions are partly preserved (cf. again the drawing in Fig. 13):

Area 6, register x+3, columns x+1–5:

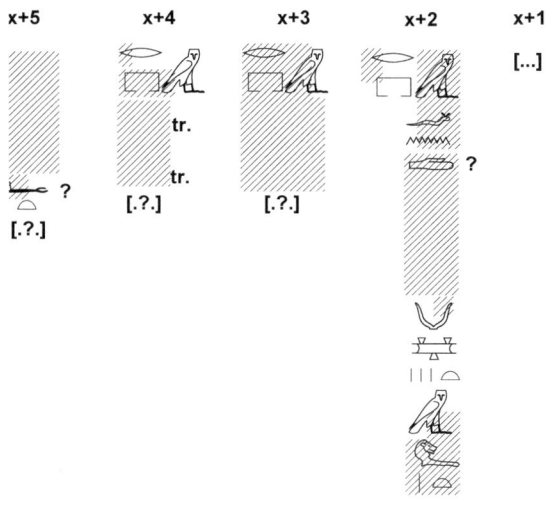

Area 6, reg. x+3, col. x+1: *[...]*
Area 6, reg. x+3, col. x+1: [...]

Area 6, reg. x+3, col. x+2: *[jmj]-rꜣ pr Fn[d(?) sꜣ] Wp-wꜣwt-m[-ḥꜣt]*
Area 6, reg. x+3, col. x+2: [the stew]ard Fene[d(?)'s[(a)] son] Wepwawetem[hat][(b)]

Area 6, reg. x+3, col. x+3: *[j]m[j-rꜣ pr...]*
Area 6, reg. x+3, col. x+3: [the ste]w[ard ...][(c)]

Area 6, reg. x+3, col. x+4: *jmj-rꜣ [pr ...]r[...]*
Area 6, reg. x+3, col. x+4: the stew[ard ...][(d)]

Area 6, reg. x+3, col. x+5: *[...]ꜥ(?)t[...]*
Area 6, reg. x+3, col. x+5: [...] ... [...][(e)]

(a) For the name *Fnd*, see RANKE 1935: 142, 20.

(b) The placement of the name *Wp-wꜣwt-m-[ḥꜣt]* after *Fn[d]* suggests a filiation. In Dynasty 11 and early Dynasty 12, paternal filiation would be expressed in the form NN father + *sꜣ* ('son') + NN son, so Fened would have been the father of Wepwawetemhat. The name Wepwawetemhat was common at Asyut. Zitman lists 15 people of this name as owners of Siutian coffins and two statues (ZITMAN 2010b: 173).

(c) All that remains of this man's caption is a hieroglyphic trace that fits the *m*-owl perfectly, and it sits exactly where it does in the two neighbouring captions. Like the men who flank him, this person too was probably a steward.

22 WAINWRIGHT 1926: 160–166; GUNN 1926: 166–171; cf. also ZITMAN 2010a: 339–344; 2010b: 187 [1].

(d) The signs *m* and *r* and their relative positions suggest the reconstruction *jmj-r₃ [pr]*. Only the tiniest blue traces show where the name would have been (Pl. 24b). Was the first sign a bird, with extant traces of its beak and feet?

(e) Column x+5 is behind the last man. All that remains is what seems to be the hand of an ⸢ and an almost complete *t*. Was this a separate inscription, or were these signs a continuation of column x+4, i. e. a part of the caption that identifies the last man?

The lowest detectable register (cf. Fig. 13) still shows traces of three men, with ample space between the second and the last man for restoring a fourth. Each man would again have been identified by hieroglyphic captions, but only the smallest traces of two such captions now remain. Those in front of the second man may include a *t*, and a yellow trace behind his head[23] is likely a bird's claw (cf. Pl. 25). As with the other walls, decoration fragments may still be hidden further down, beneath the accumulated debris (Pl. 21).

2.2 Corridor B

The vault (cf. Fig. 4) had been decorated with painted plaster, but nowadays only fragments adorned with stars against a yellow background are still preserved. The stars having five points are arranged in horizontal bands (Fig. 14). Thin red guidelines were used for the shape of the stars as well as for the vertical and horizontal position. After the partial cleaning by conservators of the Ministry of State for Antiquities in 2016, the points of these stars proved to be of black colour and the circles in the middle of red (Pl. 26). In Tomb I (P10.1) of Djefai-Hapi I from the time of Senwosret I, the vaulted first passage was also entirely decorated with stars whose colour could not yet be recognized.[24]

Area 7: Fragmentary decoration on top of the south wall of corridor B (cf. Pl. 27b, Fig. 14)

Area 7, line 1:   [...]   [...]

Area 7, line 1: *[...] f [...] s₃ (?) [...]*
Area 7, line 1: [...] ef [...] son (?) [...]

Maybe a name with filiation was written, but two signs are not enough to present an interpretation. Further to the right, fragments of a third hieroglyph are to be seen, but cannot be identified (Pl. 27b).

Area 8: Fragmentary decoration on the north wall of corridor B (cf. Pl. 28a, Fig. 15)

On the other side of the corridor, several small fragments are still preserved on the middle part of the wall. The largest area shows coloured decoration with the end of two columns of hieroglyphs. The reconstruction and translation is almost tentative:

Area 8, col. x+1: *[...] j₃[w]* Det. (?)
Area 8, col. x+1: [...] old (?)

Area 8, col. x+2: *[...] ḫftjw / ḫ[s]fwt / ḫf[₃]wt ⸢₃.w* (?)
Area 8, col. x+2: [...] great adversaries/penalties/repasts (?)

Traces of red lines right of the standing man can maybe identified as the sign or .

---

23 It is noteworthy that this trace should be yellow at all, because the hieroglyphs in the captions on this wall are usually monochrome blue, apart from the larger inscription with the sunshade-bearer.
24 Kᴀʜʟ 2016: 25.

South wall   West wall

col. 1

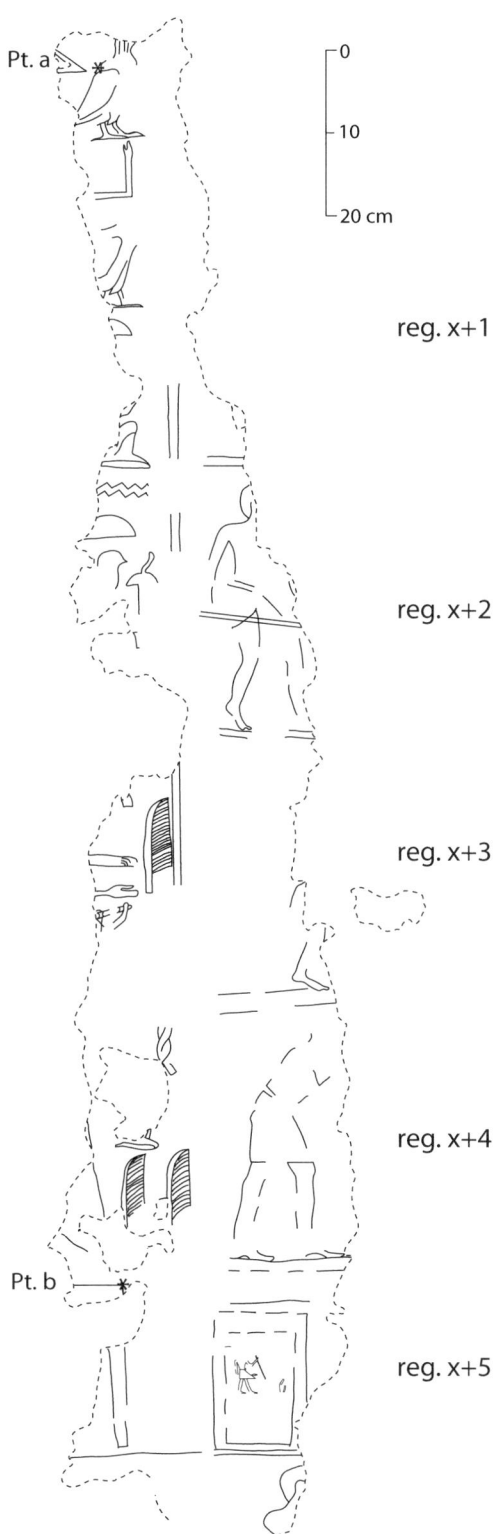

Pt. a

0

10

20 cm

reg. x+1

reg. x+2

reg. x+3

reg. x+4

Pt. b

reg. x+5

reg. x+6

Fig. 9: Area 1 on the south wall (left) and area 3 on the west wall
(right). The two walls meet at right angles but are here shown in the
same plane (drawing: Ursula Verhoeven, Andrea Kilian).

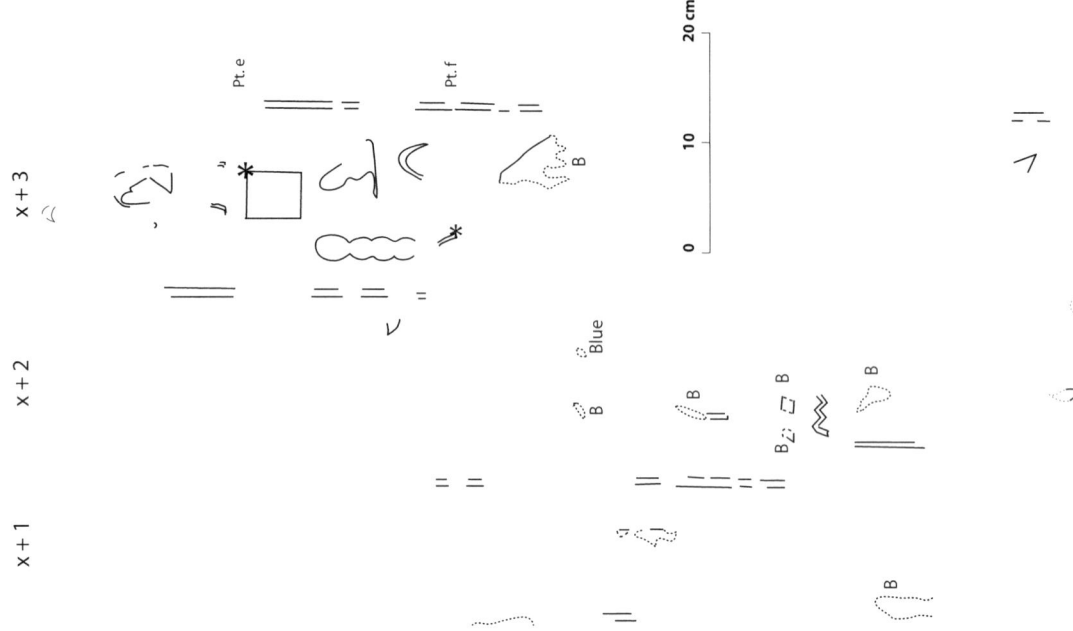

Fig. 11: Area 4 on the west wall, north of the doorway
(drawing: Ursula Verhoeven, Andrea Kilian).

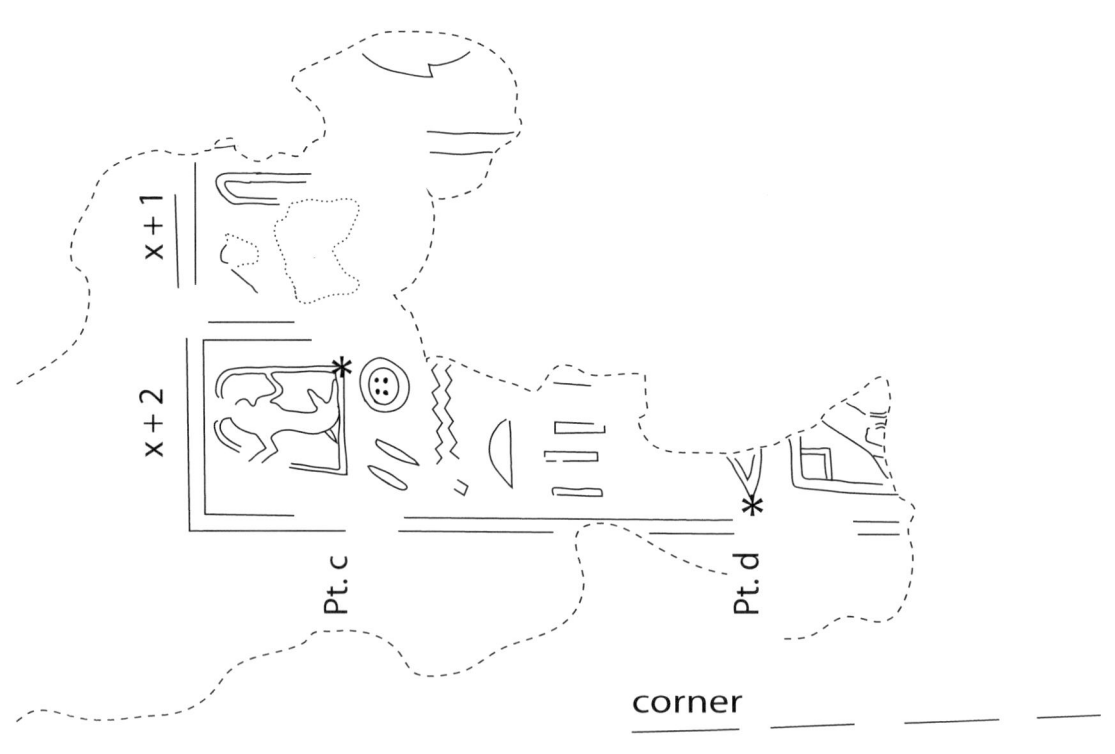

Fig. 10: Area 2 on the west wall, at the south end
(drawing: Ursula Verhoeven, Andrea Kilian).

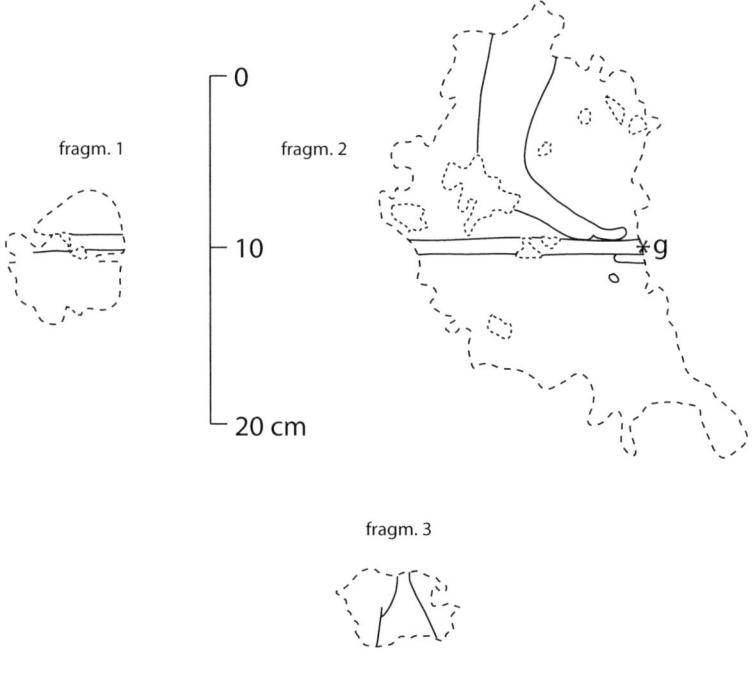

Fig. 12: Area 5 on the west wall, at the north end
(drawing: Ursula Verhoeven, Andrea Kilian).

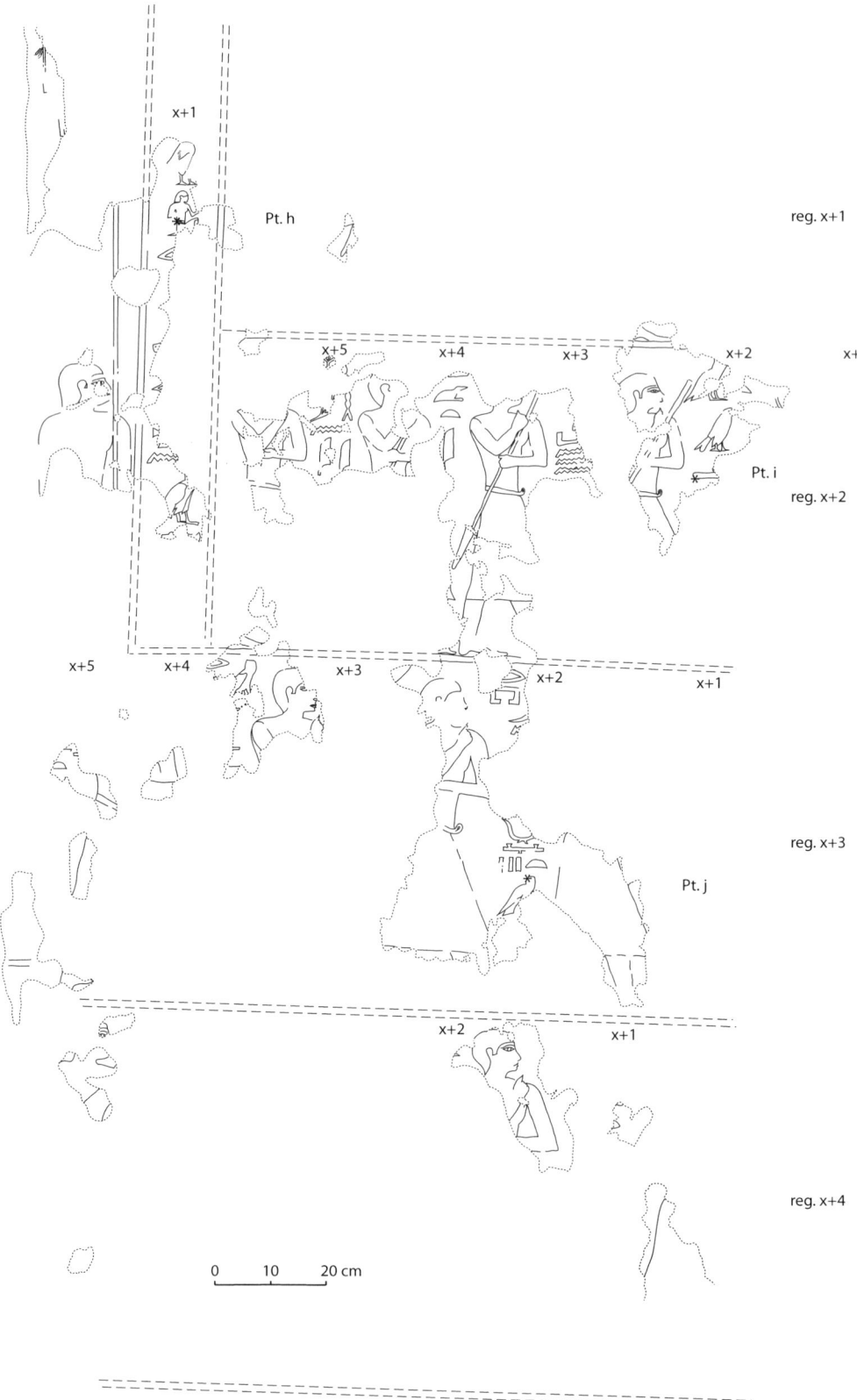

Fig. 13: Area 6 on the north wall, at the west end (drawing: Ursula Verhoeven, Andrea Kilian).

line 1

Fig. 14: Area 7 in corridor B, south wall, ceiling and upper part of the wall (drawing: Ursula Verhoeven, Andrea Kilian).

col. x+2   col. x+1

Fig. 15: Area 8 in corridor B, north wall (drawing: Ursula Verhoeven, Andrea Kilian).

3. Dating

It is unfortunate that so little information can help us date Tomb I10.1 with any precision before the rooms and shafts are fully excavated, which could yield diagnostic pottery and other finds. A survey on the surface by Andrea Kilian in 2016 only showed pottery from the Graeco-Roman periods. Other large tombs at step 6 of Gebel Asyut al-gharbi are from the First Intermediate Period (in chronological order M11.1/Tomb V, N12.1/Tomb III, N12.2/Tomb IV), Dynasty 11 (H11.1) and early Dynasty 12 (O13.1/ Tomb II and M10.1).[25] The architecture of the present tomb, with its three rooms and the middle one is vaulted, is only to be found again in P10.1/Tomb I within the necropolis of Asyut, while all the earlier tombs have one or two broad rooms and flat ceilings. As said, the type of baton held by three of the tomb owner's staff in area 6 points to late Dynasty 11 or early Dynasty 12.[26] As Marcel Maree proposed in a personal communication, the elongated proportions of the figures' bodies and faces better match the artistic style of Dynasty 11, as stockier figures prevail from Amenemhat I and Senwosret I onwards. But the style in Asyut is not so easily comparable with the style in other regions of the country. If the tomb I10.1 had been built during the late Dynasty 11, it would have been the first example for the new

25 See Fig. 12 in the contribution of J. Kahl and the publications cited above in nn. 1 and 2.
26 KAHL ET AL. 2006: 245, wrote that the tomb's decoration 'emphasises once more the military character of Asyut, even after the reunification of Egypt by the Theban ruler Mentu-hotep Neb-hepet-re', because in the 'today roofless large hall people are depicted holding spears'. This view, repeated by ZITMAN 2010a: 21, is incorrect, because the supposed spears are just the afore-mentioned batons of authority, held by three non-military officials in area 6.

type of tomb architecture in Asyut, which maybe Djefai-Hapi II[27] and surely Djefai-Hapi I took over and monumentalized during the time of Amenemhet I and Senwosret I. If the Tomb I10.1 had been built only during the beginning of Dynasty 12, the tomb owner was maybe a contemporary of the two Djefai-Hapis and could profit from their new ideas for tomb architecture. The exact date must remain an open question until new data become available.[28]

Acknowledgements

Thanks are due to the team of 'The Asyut Project', namely Ulrike Fauerbach, Svenja A. Gülden, Jochem Kahl, Andrea Kilian and Monika Zöller-Engelhardt, our photographer Fritz Barthel, and to the late chief ghafir Mohammed Saad Moursi ('Quraim') for their input. Jeff Simpson kindly revised the first version of my English text. Marcel Maree very carefully read the article and added several useful commentaries, for which I am very thankful.

Bibliography

ABDELRAHIEM 2020: M. Abdelrahiem, The Northern Soldiers-Tomb (H11.1) at Asyut (The Asyut Project 13; Wiesbaden 2020).

BECKER 2012: M. Becker, The reconstruction of Tomb Siut II from the Middle Kingdom, in: J. Kahl, M. El-Khadragy, U. Verhoeven & A. Kilian (eds), Seven Seasons at Asyut. First Results of the Egyptian-German Cooperation in Archaeological Fieldwork. Proceedings of an International Conference at the University of Sohag, 10th–11th of October, 2009 (The Asyut Project 2; Wiesbaden 2012), 68–90.

BLACKMAN 1914: A. M. Blackman, The rock tombs of Meir I: The tomb-chapel of Ukh-Hotp's son Senbi (Archaeological Survey of Egypt 22; London 1914).

BLACKMAN 1915: A. M. Blackman, The rock tombs of Meir II: The tomb-chapel of Ukh-Hotp's son Senbi (B, No.2) with two appendixes on hieroglyphs and other details in B, Nos. 1, 2, 4 (Archaeological Survey of Egypt 23; London 1915).

DAVIES 1902a: N. de G. Davies, The rock tombs of Deir el Gebrâwi I: Tomb of Aba and smaller tombs of the southern group (Archaeological Survey of Egypt 11; London 1902).

DAVIES 1902b: N. de G. Davies, The rock tombs of Deir el Gebrâwi II. Tombs of Zau and tombs of the Northern Group (Archaeological Survey of Egypt 12; London 1902).

DOMINICUS 1993: B. Dominicus, Gesten und Gebärden in Darstellungen des Alten und Mittleren Reiches (Studien zur Archäologie und Geschichte Altägyptens 10; Heidelberg 1993).

FISCHER 1972: H. G. Fischer, Sunshades of the marketplace, in: Metropolitan Museum Journal 6, 1972, 151–156.

FISCHER 1979: H. G. Fischer, Notes on sticks and staves in ancient Egypt, in: Metropolitan Museum Journal 13, 1979, 5–32.

FISCHER 1984, H. G. Fischer, in: W. Helck et al. (eds), Lexikon der Ägyptologie V, Wiesbaden 1984, s. v. Sonnenschirm, 1104–1105.

FISCHER 1986: H. G. Fischer, in: W. Helck et al. (eds), Lexikon der Ägyptologie VI, Wiesbaden 1986, s. v. Stöcke und Stäbe, 49–57.

GRUNERT 2015: S. Grunert, Lied der Sänftenträger. Grabinschriften des Alten Reiches, Ostwand, Grab des Djau, Deir el-Gebrawi, Strukturen und Transformationen des Wortschatzes der ägyptischen Sprache, Berlin-Brandenburgische Akademie der Wissenschaften, in: Thesaurus Linguae Aegyptiae. http://aaew.bbaw.de/tla/servlet/GetTextDetails?u=esdsfd&f=0&l=0&tc=11068&db=0 [31.05.2015].

GUNN 1926: B. Gunn, The coffins of Heny, in: Annales du Service des Antiquités de l'Égypte 26, 1926, 166–171.

---

27 BECKER 2012: 86, presumes that also O13.1/Tomb II could have been reconstructed with three rooms and a vaulted ceiling.

28 Cf. also KAHL 2019: 34: „Ende 11. Dynastie/Anfang 12. Dynastie."

HANNIG 2006: R. Hannig, Zur Paläographie der Särge aus Assiut (Hildesheimer Ägyptologische Beiträge 47; Hildesheim 2006).

JOLLOIS AND DEVILLIERS 1818: M. Jollois and E. Devilliers, Description de Syout, et des antiquités qui paroissent avoir appartenu à l'ancienne ville de Lycopolis. In Description de l'Égypte: Ou recueil des observations et des recherches qui ont été faites en Égypte pendant l'expédition de l'armée française, publié par les ordres de Sa Majesté l'Empereur Napoléon le Grand II, 1.2: Texte 2. Antiquités, E. F. Jomard (ed.), 1–16. Paris. (http://digi.ub.uni-heidelberg.de/diglit/jomard1818bd2_1_2/0145?sid=a680e6ce496ddb56441a9ef9c28bd2e0 [31.05.2015])

KAHL 2007: J. Kahl, Ancient Asyut. The first synthesis after 300 years of research (The Asyut Project 1; Wiesbaden 2007).

KAHL 2013: J. Kahl, Die Zeit selbst lag nun tot darnieder. Die Stadt Assiut und ihre Nekropolen nach westlichen Reiseberichten des 17. bis 19. Jahrhunderts: Konstruktion, Destruktion und Rekonstruktion (The Asyut Project 5; Wiesbaden 2013).

KAHL 2016: J. Kahl, Ornamente in Bewegung. Die Deckendekoration der Großen Querhalle im Grab von Djefai-Hapi I. in Assiut (The Asyut Project 6; Wiesbaden 2016).

KAHL 2019: Die Statue Assiut S10/16. Ein Regionalstil und seine Bewertung (The Asyut Project 11; Wiesbaden 2019).

KAHL ET AL. 2006: J. Kahl, M. El-Khadragy & U. Verhoeven, The Asyut Project: Third season of fieldwork (2005), in: Studien zur Altägyptischen Kultur 34, 2006, 241–249.

KAHL ET AL. 2010: J. Kahl, M. El-Khadragy, U. Verhoeven, M. Abdelrahiem, H. Faheed Ahmed, C. Kitagawa, J. Malur, S. Prell & T. Rzeuska, The Asyut Project: Eighth season of fieldwork (2010), in: Studien zur Altägyptischen Kultur 40, 2010, 181–209.

KAHL ET AL. 2011: Kahl, J., M. El-Khadragy, U. Verhoeven, M. Abdelrahiem, M. van Elsbergen, H. Fahid, A. Kilian, C. Kitagawa, T. Rzeuska and M. Zöller-Engelhardt, The Asyut Project: Ninth season of fieldwork (2011), in: Studien zur Altägyptischen Kultur 41, 2011, 189–234.

KAHL, SBRIGLIO, DEL VESCO & TRAPANI 2019: J. Kahl, A. M. Sbriglio, P. Del Vesco & M. Trapani, Asyut. The Excavations of the Italian Archaeological Mission (1906–1913) (Studi del Museo Egizio 1; Modena 2019).

KANAWATI 2005: N. Kanawati, Deir el-Gebrawi I: The northern cliff (The Australian Centre for Egyptology Reports 23; Oxford 2005).

KANAWATI 2007: N. Kanawati, Deir el-Gebrawi II: The southern cliff: The tombs of Ibi and others (The Australian Centre for Egyptology Reports 25; Oxford 2007).

KANAWATI 2013: N. Kanawati, Deir el-Gebrawi III: The southern cliff: The tomb of Djau/Shemai and Djau (The Australian Centre for Egyptology Reports 32; Oxford 2013).

KANAWATI & EVANS 2014: N. Kanawati & L. Evans, The cemetery of Meir II: The tomb of Pepyankh the black (The Australian Centre for Egyptology Reports 34; Oxford 2014).

EL-KHADRAGY 2006: M. El-Khadragy, The Northern Soldiers-Tomb at Asyut, in: Studien zur Altägyptischen Kultur 35, 2006, 147–164.

EL-KHADRAGY 2007: M. El-Khadragy, The shrine of the rock-cut chapel of Djefaihapi I at Asyut, in: Göttinger Miszellen 212, 2007, 41–62.

EL-KHADRAGY 2012: M. El-Khadragy, The nomarchs of Asyut during the First Intermediate Period and the Middle Kingdom, in: J. Kahl, M. El-Khadragy, U. Verhoeven & A. Kilian (eds), Seven Seasons at Asyut. First Results of the Egyptian-German Cooperation in Archaeological Fieldwork. Proceedings of an International Conference at the University of Sohag, 10th–11th of October, 2009 (The Asyut Project 2; Wiesbaden 2012), 31–46.

KORMYSHEVA ET AL. 2010: E. Kormysheva, S. Malykh & S. Vetokhov, The tomb of Khafraankh (Giza Eastern Necropolis I; Moscow 2010).

MOUSSA AND ALTENMÜLLER 1977: A. Moussa, and H. Altenmüller, Das Grab des Nianchchnum und Chnumhotep (Archäologische Veröffentlichungen 21; Mainz 1977).

RANKE 1935: H. Ranke, Die ägyptischen Personennamen I (Glückstadt 1935).

SCHENKEL AND GOMAA 2004: W. Schenkel and F. Gomaà, Scharuna I (Mainz 2004).

VERHOEVEN 2011: U. Verhoeven, Tomb P13.1 of a certain Djefai-Hapi, in: KAHL ET AL. 2011: 186–191.

VERHOEVEN 2013: U. Verhoeven, "Der lebt nach dem Tod". Orthographisches und Biographisches in den Inschriftenfragmenten der Grabanlage M10.1 in Assiut, in: H.-W. Fischer-Elfert & R. B. Parkinson (eds), Studies on the Middle Kingdom in memory of Detlef Franke (Philippika 41; Wiesbaden 2013), 221–228.

WAINWRIGHT 1926: G. A. Wainwright, A subsidiary burial in Hapi-Zefi's tomb at Assiut, in: Annales du Service des Antiquités de l'Égypte 26, 1926, 160–166.

WARD 1982: W. A. Ward, Index of Egyptian administrative and religious titles of the Middle Kingdom (Beirut 1982).

WILLEMS 2014: H. Willems, Historical and archaeological aspects of Egyptian culture (Culture and History of the Ancient Near East 73; Leiden, Boston 2014).

ZITMAN 2010a: M. Zitman, The necropolis of Assiut I (Orientalia Lovaniensia Analecta 180; Leuven 2010).

ZITMAN 2010b: M. Zitman, The necropolis of Assiut II (Orientalia Lovaniensia Analecta 180; Leuven 2010).

The Head of a Female Statuette from Asyut

Mohamed Abdelrahiem

The head of the limestone statuette, which I am herewith privileged to publish, has been found on 29 August 2012 by *The Asyut Project*. The head was found at the northern part of Gebel Asyut al-gharbi, in the vicinity of two neighboring tombs, the Northern Soldiers-Tomb (H11.1) and Tomb I10.1. The head is stored in the magazine of Shutb at Asyut under the No. SCA 245. This paper gives a thorough presentation and examination of the head and also aims to shed a new light on the Ancient Egyptian sculpture in the timespan between the Old Kingdom and the early 12th Dynasty.

1. Introduction

In the campaign of 2012 at Gebel Asyut al-gharbi, *The Asyut Project*, a joint Egyptian-German Mission of Sohag University (Egypt), Mainz University (Germany) and Free University Berlin (Germany) discovered a large number of objects of great artistic and scientific significance[1] in the debris of the Northern Soldiers-Tomb and its neighboring area. The objects dating to different periods are ranging from artifacts which might belong to the original inventory to remnants of later burials and reuse of the tomb. The majority of these finds were isolated, without proper context. However, much of this material is not as well known as it deserves, and its variety and its range provide of themselves important evidence for the history of the site.

This paper is a publication of one of these finds, a limestone head of a statuette found on 29 August 2012 at the northern part of the necropolis in the Gebel Asyut al-gharbi, about 8 meters in front of two neighboring tombs, the Northern Soldiers-Tomb (H11.1)[2] and Tomb I10.1[3]. The head was registered in the official register book of the Mission at the magazine of Shutb at Asyut under the number SCA 245.[4] The paper also aims to shed a new light on the Ancient Egyptian sculpture in the timespan between the Old Kingdom and the early 12th Dynasty.

---

1 Since September 2003, *The Asyut Project* has conducted fifteen successive seasons of fieldwork and surveying in the cemetery at Asyut, aiming at documenting the architectural features and decorations of the First Intermediate Period and Middle Kingdom tombs, see KAHL ET AL. 2015.

2 This newly rediscovered Middle Kingdom tomb (Northern Soldiers-Tomb, H11.1) at Asyut is located on the northern part of Gebel Asyut al-gharbi on geological step 6, in the same terrace containing the three First Intermediate Period tombs (Tomb III/N12.1, Tomb IV/N12.2 and Tomb V/M11.1), about 330 m to the north of Tomb IV. M. EL-KHADRAGY 2006 published a preliminary report on the tomb, M. ABDELRAHIEM 2020 presented the final publication.

3 Tomb I10.1 is situated also on the northern part of the necropolis, just next to the Northern Soldiers-Tomb, see the contribution of U. Verhoeven in this volume.

4 Acknowledging the generous fund of the Deutsche Forschungsgemeinschaft without which the project would not have been possible. I need to offer our thanks to our colleagues in the Supreme Council for Antiquities whose assistance and support during the fieldwork since 2003 has been outstanding. Directed by Prof. Dr. U. Verhoeven, Prof. Dr. J. Kahl, Prof. Dr. M. El-Khadragy and the author, the mission was assisted by a number of individuals who deserve all my thanks.

2. Description

The head represents a youthful lady, whose face still preserves the yellow colour of the lady's skin, which conforms with the Egyptian custom of covering most sculptures with paint to make them as life-like as possible. The lady wears a shoulder-length, striated wig, which is not slightly flared, revealing the portion of the small ears. The hair is rendered by means of parallel lines with median line. The lines of the eyes are carved, but lines for eyebrows are missing. The nose is broad and round, but the mouth is small.

The head has been roughly executed, although evident care is given to the face, which is amazingly naturalistic by the energetically and smiling mouth. The feature of the face does not reveal the ideal type of beauty of the period, but seems to portray the individual features of the original. The head is characterized by specific features of the owner, there is obviously a will to individualize the owner, to give her "personal" features, even if we cannot be sure that these features are the true portrait of the individual.

Whatever, the head shows a poor skill in technique and the depiction of proportions. The right eye and the helix of the right ear are projecting. The exact measurements of the two eyes indicate that they are not identical, the width of the left eye is 1.2 cm, while the right is 1.3 cm. The measurements indicate that the head and accordingly the statuette were a small-size. The height of the head is 7.5 cm, while the width from tip to tip of the wig is 6.3 cm.

The preservation of the head is good, nose and mouth are undamaged, although in many Egyptian statues the nose has been knocked off or is partially missing. Only some scratches, however, could be seen around the nose (Pl. 28b–e).

At this point an important question arises, when was the head made? Unfortunately there is no inscription to give us an unequivocal answer to this question. The head was found out of its context, the absence of any definite information about its original place has left us without firm grounds for discerning its exact date. If we knew in what tomb the sculpture once stood, our question could easily be answered, even without inscription. When so unusual a sculpture as the Asyut head is torn from its ancient context without record, a convincing identification can be made only by detailed examination of its features, comparing and contrasting them with documented sculptures. Unfortunately for this method, the head is unique and individual in style, so that typical parallels are not to be found. On this point we are reminded of the following limestone statues and statuettes which have been assigned to the timespan between the Old Kingdom and the early 12th Dynasty.

3. Comparative Material

The comparison of the already known portraits from the Old Kingdom and the early 12th Dynasty with the Asyutian head reveals that the facial features of the head, e. g. the formation of the eyes and ears, do not offer a basis for an exact dating of our head, and are therefore of no use for a specific dating. If we had a representative selection of the sculpture for comparison, the wig might be an important clue in dating the head. Our parted shoulder-length wig could be compared with the following types of wigs.

Type 1: Flared shoulder-length wigs covering the ears, striated, with a parting in the center are shown on the following sculptures:

1. The famous princess Nofret (Cairo Museum CG 4) from the reign of Sneferu is sitting beside her husband Rahotep and wearing the shoulder-length wig covering her ears. The wig is striated, flared,

parted and is encircled by a diadem ornamented with rosettes. One catches a glimpse of her natural hair under the wig.[5]

2. The two standing rock-cut statues of queen Meresankh III, wife of Khufu, and her mother Hetepheres show the two ladies wearing a striated, flared and parted wig, covering their ears.[6]

3. The seated female statue (Louvre A.109) dating back to the 4th Dynasty represents the woman wearing the striated and flared shoulder-length wig, which covers the ears.[7]

4. The standing statuette of the queen Meritites I, wife of Khufu[8] (Leiden, inv. no. D.125),[9] shows her twice repeated wearing the flared wig, with median line, striated and covering her ears. The hair is evidently kept completely beneath the wig and is laid out smoothly over the forehead.[10]

5. The couple statue of Mersuankh and his wife (Cairo JE 66619) dating to the end of the 5th Dynasty represents the wife standing beside Mersuankh and wearing the normal shoulder-length striated, flared wig, which covers her ears.[11]

6. A standing female statue (Cairo JE 72214, CG 50) from the 5th Dynasty represents the lady wearing the short striated and flared wig of the 5th Dynasty, along with a sheath dress.[12]

7. The Leiden statue (inv. no. AST9) dates to the late 5th or early 6th Dynasty representing two identical standing female figures accompanied by small-scaled nudes (circumcised). The women are wearing the striated, flared and parted wig, covering the ears.[13]

Type 2: Non-flared shoulder-length wigs covering the ears, striated, with a parting in the center, are shown on the following sculptures:

8. The statue of Ankhoudjes and his wife Tepemnefert (JE 25368) dates to the end of the 4th Dynasty or the first half of the 5th Dynasty (Mycerinus/Niuserre) and is representing the lady, who sits beside her husband wearing the striated, parted, non-flared wig, which reaches just above the shoulders, covering her ears.[14]

9. The famous statue of the dwarf Seneb and his family (Cairo JE 51280) dates to the 4th or beginning of the 5th Dynasty, representing his wife Senetites sitting beside him and wearing a black wig over the natural hair, which remains partly visible. The wig is shoulder-length, striated, and covers the ears, but is not flared.[15]

---

5 This couple statue was found by Mariette in 1871 in the Mastaba of Rahotep and Nofret at Meidum, cf. Borchardt 1911–1936: 3–5, pl. 1; Aldred 1968: 28; Vandier 1958: 28; Smith 1949: 85; Saleh & Sourouzian 1987: no. 27.

6 The Mastaba of Queen Meresankh III at Giza (G7530–7540) includes two standing rock-cut female figures of Meresankh and her mother Hetepheres executed in the center of the west wall of the offering room, in the shallow false door, cf. Dunham & Simpson 1974: 18, pl. 11; Vandier 1958: pl. 14.1; Reisner 1955: 68, fig. 19; Reisner 1942: 68, fig. 19; Shoukry 1951: fig. 77.

7 The statue was found by Mariette at Saqqara about 500 m from the great pyramid at Abusir, cf. Porter & Moss 1974: 370; Boreux 1932a: 450; Vandier 1958: 55–56, 573, pl. 15.5; Ziegler 1997: 173; Bolshakov 2005: 28.

8 For dating, cf. Smith 1949: 79.

9 The Statue was found at Giza, cf. Boeser & Holwerda 1905–1908: pl. 24.

10 Speidel 1990: 199; Riefstahl 1952: 14.

11 The statue was found by Selim Hassan in the Mastaba of Mersuankh at Giza, cf. Porter & Moss 1974: 270; Hassan 1932: 115–116, pl. 73; Vandier 1958: pl. 74; Saleh & Sourouzian 1987: no. 50.

12 The statue was found by Mariette at Saqqara, probably in Mastaba D5, cf. Borchardt 1911–1936: 45, pl. 13; Vandier 1958: 104–105, pl. 19.2–3.

13 The provenance of this statue is unknown, cf. Porter & Moss 1927: 727; Capart 1902–1905: pl. 4.5; Fechheimer 1920: fig. 1; Schäfer & Andrae 1925: 258; Eaton-Krauss 1995: 74 (Cat. 32), pl. 15b.

14 The statue was found at Giza, cf. Vandier 1958: 78, pl. 27.5; Cherpion 1989: 112; Vandier 1957: 145, pls. 9–10; Ziegler 1997: 82–86 (Cat. 23); Rzepka 2000: 469.

15 The statue was found by Junker in 1926–1927 in the Mastaba of Seneb at Giza, cf. Junker 1941: 107–114, pl. 9; Porter & Moss 1978: 102; Smith 1981: fig. 133; Cherpion 1984; Saleh & Sourouzian 1987: no. 39.

10. The family group statue (Giza 48) dates to the late 6th Dynasty and represents a wife sitting beside her husband encircling him with her right arm. Unfortunately, the left hand portion of the wife's face including her nose is broken. Yet it is clear that she is wearing the striated, parted wig which reaches just above the shoulders, but it is not flared.[16]

Type 3: A Non-flared shoulder-length wig revealing the ears, striated, with a parting in the center is shown on the following sculpture:

11. The head of the queen or daughter of King Amenemhat II (Brooklyn Museum, Charles Edwin Wilbour Fund, 56.85) is representing the queen wearing the non-flared shoulder-length wig, striated, with a parting in the center and revealing the ears.[17]

4. Dating

The first two types of the shoulder-length wigs, either flared (nos. 1–7) or non-flared (nos. 8–10) (Figs. 1–2), were predominant among women during the Old Kingdom from the 4th Dynasty to the late 6th Dynasty and are not known after this period.[18] They appeared together in the tomb of Metri at Saqqara (near Unas causeway) from the reign of Unas. The two female statues there wear the two coiffures. The first lady (MMA 26.2.3) wears the normal flared and striated wig, reaching just above the shoulder, while the other (MMA 26.2.5) wears the similar, but non-flared wig.[19]

The wig of our statuette is really a shoulder-length wig, striated and non-flared like type 2, but it reveals the ears (Fig. 3). Thus it belongs to type 3 (Parallel 11), which is known during the Middle Kingdom. Revealing the ears does not appear in the three-dimensional sculptures of wigs during the Old Kingdom, rather a smooth variant of Type 1, revealing the ears (Fig. 4), does appear in the representations of statues from this period.[20]

---

16 The statue was found in the Mastaba of Itf at Giza, cf. Junker 1951: 91ff; Vandier 1958: 80, pl. 28. 4.

17 This sculpture was found probably in Heliopolis and the Roman emperor Hadrian (117–138 C.E.) brought it from Egypt to Italy in 130 C.E. to be displayed alongside other Egyptian antiquities at his villa in Tivoli, near Rome, cf. Aldred 1962: 221(29), Taf. 29.

18 Cf. Harvey 1989: 115.

19 The two types are widely used on women wooden statutes of the Old Kingdom, for example: the bust of Ka-aper's wife (CG33) dates to the beginning of the 5th Dynasty, probably reign of Userkaf (Porter & Moss 1974: 459–460; Ranke 1935: 338.24; Borchardt 1911–1936: 31–32, pl. 9; Mariette 1889: 127–129; Aldred 1968: 34; Vandersleyen 1983; Cherpion 1989: 99; Saleh & Sourouzian 1987: no. 41); female standing statuette CG 269 (JE 22073) dates to the 5th Dynasty, end of reign of Niuserre or slightly later (Harvey 1989: 150 (Cat. A7), pl. 6; Staehelin 1966: 124; Shoukry 1951: 92, n. 4, 104, n. 2, 105 n. 2; Wilkinson 1971: 47); highly decorated striding female's statuette (Cairo CG 139) dates to the end of the reign of the king Niuserre or slightly later (Harvey 1989: 272 (Cat. B1), pl. 71; Borchardt 1911–1936: 103, pl. 31; Staehelin 1966: 124, fig. 57; Shoukry 1951: 86 (n. 2), 90 (n. 1), 92 (n. 3), 100 (n. 6), 104 (n. 3, 8–10); standing female statue of Akhtihotep's wife (Cairo JE 93174) dates to the reign of Unas (Harvey 1989: 165 (Cat. A22), pl. 13a; Zayed 1958: pl. 7 (left); Badawi 1940: 495, pl. 47); standing female statue (New York, Metropolitan Museum of Art, MMA 26.2.3) dates to the reign of Unas (Harvey 1989: 137 (Cat. A30), pl. 22; Firth 1926: 101; Zayed 1956: 14–22, pl. 10; Peterson 1984; Davenport 1948: 21, pl. 48; Brooklyn Museum 1960: 90; Smith 1981: 77, pl. 52b); striding female statuette (Boston, Museum of Fine Arts, MFA 13.3462) dates to the reign of Unas (Harvey 1989: 274 (Cat. B3), pl. 73a, cf. p. 115; Smith 1959: 59–60); standing nude female's statuette Cairo Museum JE 10892 (CG 121) dates to the reign of Unas (Harvey 1989: 280 (Cat. B9), pl. 74c; Smith 1959: 59–60; Shoukry 1951: 90 (n.1), 92 (n.4), 104; couple statue of husband and wife (Louvre N2293) dates to the reign of Unas (Vandier 1958: 111, pl. 18.3, cf. p. 74 (n. 2); Smith 1959: 60; Boreux 1932b: 453, pl. 63; Aldred 1968: 34, pl. 41; Harvey 1989: 116); standing female statue (Metropolitan Museum of Art, MMA 26.2.5) dates to the reign of Unas (Harvey 1989: 174 (Cat. A31), pl. 23; Firth 1926: 101; Porter & Moss 1978: 632; Smith 1959: 60; Zayed 1956: 14–22).

20 Eaton-Krauss 1984: Cat. no. 1, 109–110, no. 3, 111, 30, 40, 58–59.

Fig. 1: Flared shoulder-length wig covering the ears, striated, with a parting in the center (after HARVEY 1989: 432, fig. 2a, Wf.1).

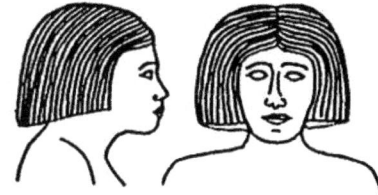

Fig. 2: Non-flared shoulder-length wig covering the ears, striated, parting in the center (after HARVEY 1989: 432, fig. 2a, Wf.1a).

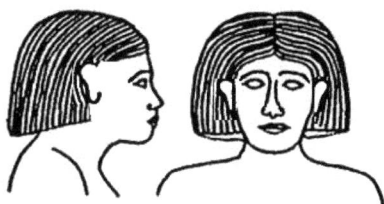

Fig. 3: Non-flared shoulder-length wig revealing the ears, striated, parting in the center (adapted from HARVEY 1989: 432, fig. 2a, with modifications by the author).

Fig. 4: Flared shoulder-length wig revealing the ears, smooth, parting in the center (adapted from HARVEY 1989: 432, fig. 2a, with modifications by the author).

Apparently, this highly stylized treatment of our wig is not known in the Old Kingdom, and while our present state of knowledge does not permit a certain statement of its earliest use, its date most probably falls within the Middle Kingdom, which produced a parallel (Fig. 5a–c)[21]. The relationship of the wig of our statuette to the first two types of wigs and its variations from them would seem to identify the statuette as a reflection of the style established by the 4th Dynasty sculpture, and it is therefore later. If my argument that our head belongs to the Middle Kingdom is accepted, then its date must be within the second half of 11th Dynasty and the early 12th Dynasty, because the head was found in the vicinity of two Middle Kingdom tombs, the Northern Soldiers-Tomb (H11.1), which dates within the second half of the 11th Dynasty and the early 12th Dynasty[22] and Tomb I10.1, which dates in the timespan between the end of 11th Dynasty and the early 12th Dynasty[23].

21 For permission to reproduce photographs, I am grateful to Brooklyn Museum, New York.
22 Cf. EL-KHADRAGY 2006: 155; ABDELRAHIEM 2020: 39–47.
23 Cf. VERHOEVEN, this volume.

Fig. 5a–c: Head of the queen or daughter of King Amenemhat II
(Brooklyn Museum, Charles Edwin Wilbour Fund, 56.85).

Bibliography

ABDELRAHIEM 2020: M. Abdelrahiem, The Northern Soldiers-Tomb (H11.1) at Asyut (The Asyut Project 13; Wiesbaden 2020).

ALDRED 1962: C. Aldred, Ägypten (Köln 1962).

ALDRED 1968: C. Aldred, Old Kingdom Art in Ancient Egypt (London 1968).

BADAWI 1940: A. Badawi, Denkmäler aus Sakkarah, in: Annales du Service des antiquités de l'Égypte 40, 1940, 495–401.

BOESER & HOLWERDA 1905–1908: A. Boeser & A. Holwerda, Die Denkmäler des Alten Reiches I (Beschreibung der Ägyptischen Sammlung des Niederländischen Reichsmuseums der Altertümer in Leiden; Leiden 1905–1908).

BOLSHAKOV 2005: A. Bolshakov, Studies on Old Kingdom Reliefs and Sculpture in the Hermitage (Wiesbaden 2005).

BORCHARDT 1911–1936: L. Borchardt, Statuen und Statuetten von Königen und Privatleuten im Museum zu Kairo I, Nr. 1–1294, Berlin 1911–1936.

BOREUX 1932a: C. Boreux, Musée National du Louvre, Département des Antiquités Égyptiennes, Guide-catalogue sommaire I: Salles du Rez-de-Chaussée; escalier et palier du premier étage; Salle du Mastaba et Salle de Baouît (Paris 1932).

BOREUX 1932b: C. Boreux, Musée National du Louvre, Département des Antiquités Égyptiennes, Guide-catalogue sommaire II: Salles du premier étage (Salles Charles X) (Paris 1932).

BROOKLYN MUSEUM 1960: Egyptian Sculpture of the Late Period. 700 B.C. to A.D. 100 (New York 1960).

CAPART 1902–1905: J. Capart, Recueil de monuments égyptiens: cinquante planches phototypiques avec texte explicative (Bruxelles 1902–1905).

CHERPION 1984: N. Cherpion, De quand date la tombe du nain Seneb?, in: Bulletin de l'Institut français d'archéologie orientale 84, 1984, 35–54.

CHERPION 1989: N. Cherpion, Mastabas et hypogées d'Ancien Empire. Le problème de la datation (Bruxelles 1989).

DAVENPORT 1948: M. Davenport, The Book of Costume1 (New York 1948).

DUNHAM & SIMPSON 1974: D. Dunham & W. Simpson, Giza Mastabas. The Mastaba of Queen Mersyankh III (G7530-7540) I (Boston 1974).

EATON-KRAUSS 1984: M. Eaton-Krauss, The Representations of Statuary in Private Tombs of the Old Kingdom (Ägyptologische Abhandlungen 39; Wiesbaden 1984).

EATON-KRAUSS 1995: M. Eaton-Krauss, Pseudo-Groups, in: Deutsches Archäologisches Institut Abteilung Kairo (ed.), Kunst des Alten Reiches. Symposium im Deutschen Archäologischen Institut Kairo am 29. und 30. Oktober 1991 (Sonderschriften des Deutschen Archäologischen Instituts Kairo 28; Mainz 1995) 57–74.

EL-KHADRAGY 2006: M. El-Khadragy, The Northern Soldiers-Tomb at Asyut, in: Studien zur Altägyptischen Kultur 35, 2006, 148–164.

FECHHEIMER 1920: H. Fechheimer, Die Plastik der Ägypter (Berlin 1920).

FIRTH 1926: C. Firth, Preliminary Report on the Excavations at Saqqara 1925–1926, in: Annales du Service des antiquités de l'Égypte 26, 1926, 97–101.

HARVEY 1989: J. C. Harvey, A Typological Study of Egyptian Wooden Statues of the Old Kingdom, (unpubl. Ph.D., University College London 1989).

HASSAN 1932: S. Hassan, Excavations at Giza I. 1929–1930 (Oxford 1932).

JUNKER 1941: H. Junker, Gîza V. Bericht über die von der Akademie der Wissenschaften in Wien auf gemeinsame Kosten mit Dr. Wilhelm Pelizaeus unternommenen Grabungen auf dem Friedhof des Alten Reiches bei den Pyramiden von Gîza (Vienna/Leipzig 1941).

JUNKER 1951: H. Junker, Gîza X. Bericht über die von der Akademie der Wissenschaften in Wien auf gemeinsame Kosten mit Dr. Wilhelm Pelizaeus unternommenen Grabungen auf dem Friedhof des Alten Reiches bei den Pyramiden von Gîza (Vienna/Leipzig 1951).

KAHL ET AL. 2015: J. Kahl et al., The Asyut Project: Eleventh Season of Fieldwork (2014), in: Studien zur Altägyptischen Kultur 44, 2015, 103–161.

MARIETTE 1889: A. Mariette, Les mastabas de l'Ancien Empire (Paris 1889).

PETERSON 1984: B. Peterson, Eine wiederentdeckte Statue aus Sakkara, in: Medelhavsmuseet Bulletin 19, 1984, 10–18.

PORTER & MOSS 1927: R. Porter, R. L. B. Moss, Topographical bibliography of ancient Egyptian hieroglyphic texts, reliefs, and paintings. 1: The Theban Necropolis (Oxford 1927).

PORTER & MOSS 1974: R. Porter, R. L. B. Moss, Topographical bibliography of ancient Egyptian hieroglyphic texts, reliefs, and paintings. 3.1: Abû Rawâsh to Abûsîr (Oxford ²1974).

PORTER & MOSS 1978: R. Porter, R. L. B. Moss, Topographical bibliography of ancient Egyptian hieroglyphic texts, reliefs, and paintings. 3.2: Saqqâra to Dashûhr (reprint, Oxford 1978).

RANKE 1935: H. Ranke, die ägyptischen Personennamen. 1: Verzeichnis der Namen (Glückstadt 1935).

REISNER 1942: G. A. Reisner, A History of the Giza Necropolis I (Cambridge MA 1942).

REISNER 1955: G. A. Reisner, A History of the Giza Necropolis II. The Tomb of Hetep-heres the Mother of Cheops (Cambridge MA 1955).

RIEFSTAHL 1952: E. Riefstahl, An Ancient Egyptian Hairdresser, in: Brooklyn Museum Bulletin 13.4, 1952, 7–16.

RZEPKA 2000: S. Rzepka, Methods of Optimizing Sculptor's Work during the Old Kingdom, in: Z. Hawass (ed.), Egyptology at the Dawn of the Twenty-first Century. Proceedings of the eighth International Congress of Egyptologists in Cairo, 1,2 (Cairo/New York 2000) 467–473.

SALEH & SOUROUZIAN 1987: M. Saleh & H. Sourouzian, The Egyptian Museum Cairo: official catalogue (Mainz 1987).

SCHÄFER & ANDRAE 1925: H. Schäfer & W. Andrae, Die Kunst des alten Orients (Berlin 1925).

SHOUKRY 1951: M. Shoukry, Die Privatgrabstatue im Alten Reich (Annales du Service des antiquités de l'Égypte, Supplement 15; Cairo 1951).

SMITH 1949: W. S. Smith, A History of Egyptian Sculpture and Painting in the Old Kingdom (Oxford 1949).

SMITH 1981: W. S. Smith, The Art and Architecture of Ancient Egypt (Hardmonthsworth 1981).

SPEIDEL 1990: M. Speidel, Die Friseure des ägyptischen Alten Reiches. Eine historisch-prosopographische Untersuchung zu Amt und Titel (*jr-šn*) (Konstanz 1990).

STAEHELIN 1966: E. Staehelin, Untersuchungen zur ägyptischen Tracht im Alten Reich (Münchner Ägyptologische Studien 8; Berlin 1966).

VANDERSLEYEN 1983: C. Vandersleyen, La Date du Cheikh el-Beled, in: Journal of Egyptian Archaeology 69, 1983, 61–65.

VANDIER 1957: J. Vandier, Le groupe et la table d'offrandes d'Ankhoudjès, in: Revue d'Égyptologie 11, 1957, 145–155.

VANDIER 1958: J. Vandier, Manuel d'archéologie égyptienne III. Les grandes époques. La statuaire (Paris 1958).

WILKINSON 1971: A. Wilkinson, Ancient Egyptian Jewellery (London 1971).

ZAYED 1956: A. Zayed, Trois études d'égyptologie (Cairo 1956).

ZAYED 1958: A. Zayed, Le tombeau d'Akhti-hotep à Saqqara, in: Annales du Service des antiquités de l'Égypte 55, 1958, 127–137, pls. I–XVII.

ZIEGLER 1997: Ch. Ziegler, Les statues égyptiennes de l'Ancien Empire (Paris 1997).

Augen aus Assiut – Zu einem Stilmerkmal der Darstellungsweise von Augen auf funerären Objekten aus Assiut

Nadine Gräßler

Einleitung

Das Auge kommt in der ägyptischen Kunst häufig vor, sei es als Bestandteil des Gesichts bei Menschen und Tieren, als Schriftzeichen oder in der Form des Udjatauges, das auf verschiedenen Objekten oder in der Wandmalerei abgebildet sein kann. Neben der stilisierten Darstellungsweise des Auges mit schwarzer Umrahmung, weißer Sklera und einem schwarzen Kreis für Iris und Pupille wurde das Auge in der ägyptischen Kunst auch sehr detailliert gestaltet mit geröteten Augenwinkeln und/oder einem differenzierten Iris-Pupillen-Bereich. Diese detaillierten Gestaltungsmerkmale sind teilweise Stilmerkmale einer bestimmten Epoche oder Region.[1]

Insbesondere die Udjataugen auf Särgen aus Assiut aus der Ersten Zwischenzeit und dem Mittleren Reich können nach Rainer Hannig in drei Typen eingeteilt werden, wodurch ihre Wichtigkeit als Stil- und Datierungsmerkmal hervortritt.[2] Typ A benennt die „klassische Form", die nach Hannig im Alten Reich und ab der 12. Dynastie auf Särgen vorkommt. Typ B, die „assiutische Form", ist auf Särgen vom Übergang der Ersten Zwischenzeit zur 12. Dynastie belegt. Dieser Typ zeichnet sich dadurch aus, dass der Spiralbogen und der senkrechte Fortsatz am unteren Augenlid zusammengefügt sind und erst etwas unterhalb des unteren Lidrands ansetzen. Typ C bezeichnet die „groteske Form", die in Assiut nur einmal belegt ist (S22Tor), allerdings auch nicht außerhalb von Assiut vorkommt.[3] Darüber hinaus können die verschiedenen Typen in Kombination mit anderen Merkmalen wie bspw. der Ausführung des Götterdeterminativs nach Hannig auf eine bestimmte Werkstatt hindeuten (siehe dazu auch unten).[4]

Für die Augendarstellungen dieser Epoche auf Objekten aus Assiut kommt noch ein weiteres Merkmal hinzu, das in anderen Nekropolen der gleichen Zeit nicht belegt ist. Es handelt sich um die Einzeichnung von zwei bis fünf dünnen, roten Strichen auf der Sklera, d.h. dem Weißen zwischen Iris-Pupillen-Bereich[5] und innerem und äußerem Augenwinkel (siehe Abb. 1–5, Pl. 29a–32a). Bislang ist

---

1 Siehe mit einigen grundsätzlichen Beobachtungen Grässler 2017: 215–226; die Darstellungsweise der Augen in den einzelnen Epochen wartet noch einer eingehenderen Untersuchung, die sehr lohnenswert wäre, da die jeweiligen Augenformen als Datierungskriterium herangezogen werden könnten, teilweise sogar für einzelne Regierungsperioden spezieller Herrscher, siehe z. B. Bothmer 2004 mit seiner Analyse zu den Augenformen bei Statuen Amenophis' III. Die Angabe absoluter Jahreszahlen richtet sich nach Shaw 2000: 480.

2 Die Typologie der Särge aus Assiut von Hannig 2006 muss dennoch durchaus kritisch betrachtet werden, vor allem da sie vornehmlich auf subjektiven Kriterien des Autors beruht und nur wenige Erläuterungen und Definitionen bietet; siehe insbesondere Kahl 2008: 320–328, sowie Grajetzki 2010: 287–289, und Willems 2010: 359–366. Die bei Hannig erfolgte Gruppenzugehörigkeit von Särgen, die u.a. auf der Typeneinteilung der Udjataugen basiert, ist zudem nicht ausreichend; siehe dazu Willems 2010: 364, der darauf aufmerksam macht, dass ein stilistisches Element zum typologischen Indikator von Särgen wird, die darüber hinaus nur wenig gemeinsam haben. Allerdings ist die Paläographie von Hannig neben Zitman 2010 bislang die einzige Arbeit, die sich mit typologischen Fragen zu dem Konvolut der Särge aus Assiut beschäftigt.

3 Zu den Udjataugentypen im Einzelnen siehe Hannig 2006: 41–45.

4 Hannig 2006: 41; vgl. auch Anm. 2. Wie sich dies in anderen Nekropolen der Ersten Zwischenzeit bzw. des Mittleren Reiches verhält, ist bislang noch nicht weiter untersucht worden, was allerdings an der dortigen Fundlage liegt. Assiut bildet daher mit seinem umfangreichen Sargkorpus eine solide Basis für etwaige Analysen.

5 Im Folgenden abgekürzt als „Irisbereich".

dieses Detail bei einigen Udjataugenpaaren auf Särgen und bei Augen auf Mumienmasken zu fassen.[6] Bei den roten Strichen könnte es sich, wie schon häufiger in der Literatur vermutet, um Blutgefäße handeln, die von Natur aus im Weißen des Auges mehr oder weniger ausgeprägt zu sehen sind.[7] Die Einzeichnung der Striche lässt die Augendarstellung noch natürlicher wirken und zeugt von einer sehr detaillierten Beobachtung des natürlichen Vorbilds durch den jeweiligen Künstler.

In diesem Beitrag soll versucht werden, die Objekte – soweit bekannt und publiziert – mit der Darstellung von Blutgefäßen im Auge zusammenzustellen und ihre Herkunft innerhalb der Nekropole näher zu spezifizieren. Aus dieser Zusammenstellung lassen sich dann Überlegungen zur Herstellung der Objekte und Werkstattgedanken in Assiut ableiten.[8]

Objekte mit Blutgefäßen im Auge

Bislang ist die Einzeichnung roter Blutgefäße bei Darstellungen von Udjataugen auf Särgen und bei menschlichen Augen auf Mumienmasken belegt. Auf Bootsmodellen, auf denen ebenfalls Udjataugen am Bug aufgemalt sein konnten, ist diese Darstellungsweise der Autorin nicht bekannt.[9]

Eine Übersicht der der Autorin bislang bekannten Objekte mit Einzeichnung der Blutgefäße im (Udjat-)Auge bieten Tab. 1 (Särge)[10], 2 (Masken) und 3 (unsicher). Aus Tab. 4 wird ersichtlich, dass bei den Udjataugen der Typ B, der assiutische Typ nach Hannig, vorherrscht. Ausnahme bildet der Sarg S5Tor (vgl. Pl. 29b), der den klassischen Udjataugentyp (Typ A) aufweist.[11] Da Typ B bei den Udjataugenpaaren auf Särgen aus Assiut generell am häufigsten vorkommt, ist dieser Befund nicht überraschend.[12]

Alle Augendarstellungen bis auf die der Maske Paris, Louvre E 11995 und vermutlich auch die der Maske Baltimore, Walters Art Museum 78.4[13] sowie des Sarges S10Tor (vgl. Pl. 30b) weisen auch rotgefärbte Augenwinkel auf (vgl. Tab. 1–3). Entweder ist der Augenwinkel dabei punktuell eingefärbt oder verläuft als Linie entlang des Augenwinkels. In allen Fällen ist die Rotfärbung scharf abgegrenzt vom Weißen des Auges.

Bei allen Augendarstellungen ist der Irisbereich undifferenziert, d.h. er weist keine erkennbare Trennung von Iris und Pupille auf, wie dies bei einigen Särgen des Mittleren Reiches der Fall sein kann,[14] sondern ist als schwarz ausgemalter Kreis wiedergegeben.

Für die Striche im Weißen des Auges lassen sich zwei Typen fassen (vgl. Tab. 1–3): Zum einen längere schmale Striche (vgl. Abb. 1 und 2), von denen drei bis fünf parallel, horizontal oder leicht schräg

---

6 Siehe Tabelle 1–3. Aus Hannigs Paläographie wird nicht deutlich, ob er diese roten Strichzeichnungen schon bemerkt hat. Zumindest berücksichtigt er dieses Merkmal nicht bei seiner Zuordnung zu verschiedenen Werkstätten. Bei seinen Ausführungen zur Terminologie des Udjatauges erwähnt er „rötliche Striche im Augenweiß: innere Augenröte" bzw. „äußere Augenröte", wobei jedoch nicht ersichtlich ist, ob er die einzelnen Striche oder die Rötung der Augenwinkel (oder beides?) meint, siehe Hannig 2006: 42.

7 Vgl. Grässler 2017: 222; Oppenheim et al. 2015: 235 („veins"); Casini 2017: 60 („veins"); Brovarski 1988: 119.

8 Die Sammlung in den Tabellen stellt die Objekte dar, die anhand der Sekundärliteratur und bei Museumsbesuchen zusammengetragen werden konnten. Eine absolute Zusammenstellung der spezifischen Objekte wird erschwert durch die schlechte Publikationslage. Zudem sind nicht alle Objekte in den Museen ausgestellt. Die Objekte befinden sich zwar zum größten Teil im Ägyptischen Museum Kairo, im British Museum London und im Museo Egizio Turin, allerdings sind die meisten nicht so publiziert, dass Einzelheiten in den Augen erkennbar sind. Erschwerend kommt der Erhaltungszustand hinzu: Durch Absplitterungen des Holzes oder Farbabrieb könnten bei einigen Objekten die Einzeichnungen auch verloren gegangen sein.

9 Es ist jedoch nicht auszuschließen, dass es hier ebenfalls Objekte mit dieser Einzeichnung gegeben haben könnte.

10 Mein großer Dank geht an Dr. Paolo Del Vesco (Museo Egizio, Turin), der mir hoch aufgelöste Detailbilder der Turiner Särge mit Einzeichnung von Blutgefäßen in den Udjataugen zur Recherche überlassen und den Abdruck dieser Bilder genehmigt hat.

11 Bei Hannig 2006: 43, dem Typ Aj zugeordnet, den er als „unklar" bestimmt.

12 Vgl. Hannig 2006: 43f.

13 Im inneren Augenwinkel des rechten Auges der Maske ist eine flächige Rötung zu erkennen, in den anderen Augenwinkeln allerdings nicht; vgl. Tab. 3, Anm. h.

14 Siehe dazu mit Beispielen Grässler 2017: 220, Anm. 1160.

ins Weiße des inneren und äußeren Augenwinkels gesetzt sind (S2Br; S2Hil; S12C; S13C; S4–5Tor; S10Tor; S13Tor; Maske Hildesheim, RPM 6226; Maske Boston, MFA 1987.54). Zum anderen kurze (fast tupfenähnliche) Striche, die im inneren und äußeren Augenwinkel (S7Tor; S11Tor; S12Tor; S9Mi) und einmal sogar über und unterhalb des Irisbereichs (S11Tor; vgl. Abb. 3; Pl. 31a) eingezeichnet sind.

Abb. 1: Auge auf dem Sarg des Anchef,
Kairo, Ägyptisches Museum,
JdE 45065, S12C. Umzeichnung:
N. Gräßler.

Abb. 2: Auge auf dem Sarg des J, Museo
Egizio, Turin, S. 8875, S4Tor (vgl. Pl. 29a).
Umzeichnung: N. Gräßler.

Abb. 3: Auge auf dem Sarg Museo Egizio,
Turin, S. 8807, S11Tor (vgl. Pl. 31a).
Umzeichnung: N. Gräßler.

Herkunft und Datierung der Särge und Masken mit Einzeichnung der Blutgefäße

Die exakte Provenienz der in Tab. 1 und 2 aufgelisteten Särge und Mumienmasken ist heute leider nur schwer zu rekonstruieren, da zu vielen Objekten aus Assiut nur wenig genaue Aufzeichnungen über die Fundumstände existieren: entweder, weil die Fundumstände gänzlich unbekannt sind und somit auch der Ausgräber nicht bekannt ist, oder weil von den Ausgräbern keine bzw. nur wenige Aufzeichnungen mit Zuordnung der Objekte zum jeweiligen Grab angefertigt wurden. Dennoch lassen sich die hier behandelten Särge und Masken zumindest grob den verschiedenen Ausgrabungen in Assiut zuweisen, wodurch es möglich ist, die Datierung der Objekte einzugrenzen. Im Folgenden wird daher anhand der Ausgräber und deren Grabungsgebiet innerhalb der Nekropole vorgegangen.

a) Die Grabung Schiaparelli 1908

Das Konvolut der Turiner Särge (S4–5Tor, S7Tor, S10–13Tor; siehe Tab. 1) bietet die beste Möglichkeit, eine Näherbestimmung des Herkunftsorts anzugeben. Alle Särge stammen aus der Grabung Ernesto Schiaparellis 1908.[15] Diese Grabung fokussierte den nordöstlichen Teil der Nekropole, wie schon Marcel Zitman darlegte. Wie Jochem Kahl kürzlich herausgearbeitet hat, kann der Fundort vermutlich noch genauer auf die geologische Stufe 3 über dem Grab von Djefai-Hapi I. eingegrenzt werden.[16] In diesem Teil der Nekropole befinden sich Gräber der späten 11. und frühen 12. Dynastie, u.a. auch das Grab des Minhotep, aus dem die Särge S7Tor und S11Tor sowie möglicherweise S10Tor (Sarg des Minhotep)[17] stammen.[18]

---

15 Vgl. die Einträge bei D'Amicone et al. 2009: 90 (S4Tor); 94 (S5Tor); 173 (S7Tor); 174 (S11Tor); 176 (S10Tor); 178 (S12Tor). Die Grabung ist unpubliziert. Zur Grabung allgemein siehe Zitman 2010: I, 63f.; 217–231; Zitman 2010: II, 273–278 (Appendix 5); aktuell zudem Kahl et al. 2017: 114–116.

16 Kahl et al. 2017: 116; Kahl 2019: 13, Fig. 3.

17 Möglicherweise auch noch Sarg S8Tor; siehe zur Verknüpfung der Särge Zitman 2010: I, 218–222; vgl. ferner Zitman 2010: II, 117 (Eintrag S8Tor), 139f. (Eintrag S7Tor), bzw. 141 (Eintrag S10Tor bzw. S11Tor); vgl. auch die Fundliste ebd.: 274.

18 Eine Datierung kann aufgrund der aus dieser Grabung bekannten Grabausstattungen des Schemes, der Rehuerausen und eben des Minhotep vorgenommen werden, siehe dazu Zitman 2010: I, 222 (zum Grab des Minhotep); 227f. (zum Grab

b) Die Grabung von Hogarth 1906/07

Der Sarg S2Br[19] (Tab. 1) und die Mumienmaske London, BM EA 46631[20] (Tab. 3), lassen sich dieser Grabung zuordnen. Während Schiaparellis Konzession den nordöstlichen Teil des Berges beinhalte- te, lag Hogarths Schwerpunkt im nordwestlichen Teil der Nekropole.[21] Für den Sarg S2Br lässt sich die Herkunft innerhalb der Nekropole über das grobe Ausgrabungsgebiet hinaus nicht bestimmen.[22] Die Mumienmaske London BM EA 46631 stammt aus Grab 9 der Hogarth-Grabung und wurde im Sarg S6L des Anchef gefunden.[23] Dieser Originalbefund wird heute im British Museum dargestellt.[24] Grab 9 liegt ziemlich weit oben auf dem Berg, unterhalb des Grabes von Mesehti (Hogarth Grab 3).[25] Die Gräber in dieser Zone stammen aus unterschiedlichsten Zeiten (Altes bis spätes Mittleres Reich).[26] Aufgrund der Funde wird Grab 9 von Zitman in das frühe Mittlere Reich (11./12. Dynastie) einsor- tiert.[27] Die Typologie des Sarges S2Br lässt darauf schließen, dass er ebenfalls aus dieser Zeit (frühe 12. Dynastie) stammt.[28]

c) Die Grabung A. Kamal 1913–1914

Der Grabung Ahmed Kamals im Jahr 1913–14 lassen sich vermutlich der Sarg S12C[29] (Tab. 1) und die Mumienmaske Baltimore, Walters Art Museum 78.4[30] (Tab. 3) zuweisen. Die Grabung wurde von Kamal und Sayed Khashaba im nordöstlichen Teil der Nekropole durchgeführt.[31] Auch wenn die ge- naue Herkunft aus diesem Bereich unklar bleibt und nicht rekonstruiert werden kann, kann Sarg S12C aufgrund seiner Gestaltung in das frühe Mittlere Reich (12. Dynastie) datiert werden.[32] Die Maske könnte aufgrund ihrer stilistischen Ähnlichkeit zu den anderen Masken ebenfalls in die späte 11. bzw. frühe 12. Dynastie datiert werden.[33]

---

von Schemes und Rehuerausen); 228–230 (zu den Särgen S4–5Tor, S12–13Tor); vgl. auch Kahl et al. 2017: 116. Der Sarg S5Tor scheint etwas früher anzusetzen mit dem Ende der Ersten Zwischenzeit, vgl. Zitman 2010: I, 229, allerdings weist der Sarg ein klassisches Udjataugenpaar auf, das nach Hannig 2006: 41, im Alten Reich und dann erst wieder ab der 12. Dynastie auf den Särgen zu finden ist; Hannig 2006: 79, lässt die Datierung für S5Tor offen. Die Datierung in die Erste Zwischenzeit für die hier behandelten Turiner Särge bei Hannig 2006: 131 (S11Tor = hier S4Tor); 135 (S7Tor und S4Tor = hier S11Tor) (S12Tor wurde nicht eingeordnet); sowie bei D'Amicone et al. 2009: siehe Anm. 15 oben, scheint insgesamt etwas zu früh anzusetzen.

19 Zur Zuordnung siehe Delvaux & Therasse 2015: 34; Zitman 2010: II, 122; Hannig 2006: 428; The Global Egyptian Museum, http://www.globalegyptianmuseum.org/record.aspx?id=468 [Zugriff 08/2018].

20 Zur Zuordnung siehe die Webseite des British Museums: https://www.britishmuseum.org/collection/object/Y_EA46631 [Zugriff 02/2021]; Zitman 2010: II, 214 (BM 46631-542).

21 Siehe zur Grabung allgemein Zitman 2010: I, 49–56; Zitman 2010: II, 209–243 (Appendix 1); vgl. zum Gebiet Zitman 2010: II, 3, Map 1; 4, Map 2, und 6, Map 3.

22 Vgl. Delvaux & Therasse 2015: 34; PM IV, 268.

23 Zitman 2010: II, 214.

24 Vgl. auch die Webseite: https://www.britishmuseum.org/collection/object/Y_EA46631 [Zugriff 02/2021].

25 Vgl. Zitman 2010: II, 6, Map 3. Zur exakten Lokalisierung des Grabes des Mesehti siehe nun Kahl 2018: 145–148.

26 Zitman 2010: I, 157.

27 Zitman 2010: I, 157; siehe auch die Datierungsangabe auf der Webpage des British Museums: https://www.britishmuse-um.org/collection/object/Y_EA46631 [Zugriff 02/2021]: „12th Dynasty (?); 11th Dynasty (?)".

28 Zitman 2010: I, 180; 313–318 (S. 318: Sesostris I./Amenemhet II.); Lapp 1993: 125–131 (§284–293); Blatt 20; vgl. auch Delvaux & Therasse 2015: 34. Hannig 2006: 112, datiert den Sarg aufgrund seiner Paläographie in die Erste Zwischenzeit.

29 Der Sarg S12C wird in der Fundauflistung des Grabungsberichts von Kamal 1916: 65–114, nicht genannt. Wie Zitman 2010: I, 66; 313, darlegt, ist er allerdings 1914 zusammen mit den Särgen S5C und S15C, die aus der Grabung A. Kamals stammen, im Kairener Museum angekommen und wird daher von Zitman dieser Grabung zugewiesen.

30 Auf der Webpage des Walters Art Museums werden als Herkunft Grabungen von Sayed Khashaba Pacha in Assiut 1913–1914 (?) angegeben. Es könnte sich dabei um die Grabung A. Kamals 1913–14 gehandelt haben; siehe https://art.thewalters.org/de-tail/29816/mummy-mask-of-a-high-official/ (Provenance) [Zugriff 08/2018]. Allerdings ist die genaue Zuweisung unsicher.

31 Kamal 1916: 66; zur Grabung allgemein und den Problemen mit dem unvollständigen Bericht siehe Zitman 2010: I, 64–68; Zitman 2010: II, 4, Map 2 (blaue Markierung); Zitman 2010: II, 281 (Appendix 7).

32 Siehe Zitman 2010: I, 313–318 (Sesostris I./Amenemhet II.); Lapp 1993: 125–131 (§§284–293). Hannig 2006: 113, datiert in die Erste Zwischenzeit.

33 Siehe Schulz 2009: 36; Oppenheim et al. 2015: 234f.; Casini 2017: 60f.

d) Die Grabung M. Kamal 1932

Durch Hinweise des Einheimischen Ahmed Mahmoud El-Mellawech aus Dronka auf Särge im „montagne occidentale d'Assiout" wurde 1932 von M. Kamal unter anderem der Sarg S9Mi der Imi aufgefunden (Tab. 1).[34] Zitman nimmt daraufhin an, dass mit „montagne occidentale" vermutlich die Nordwesthälfte der Nekropole gemeint sein könne.[35] „Montagne occidentale" könnte sich aber genauso gut ganz allgemein auf das westliche Gebirge von Assiut, also den Gräberberg insgesamt, beziehen, vor allem, da der allgemeine Hinweis eines Einheimischen wiedergegeben wird. Eine Datierung aufgrund des Nekropolengebietes lässt sich daher nicht vornehmen. Aufgrund seiner Epigraphie und Typologie wird der Sarg S9Mi von Lapp und Zitman in das frühe Mittlere Reich (12. Dynastie, Sesostris I.) eingeordnet.[36]

e) Die Grabung Chassinat/Palanque 1903

Sarg S13C (Tab. 1) stammt aus der Grabung von Émile Chassinat und Charles Palanque im Jahr 1903. Die Grabung fand im nordöstlichen Teil der Nekropole, genauer unter dem Kloster von Deir el-Metin, statt.[37] Er wurde in Grab 6 (nach der Zählung von Chassinat und Palanque) gefunden und kann einem Mann namens Nachti zugeordnet werden.[38] Bei Grab 6 handelte es sich um ein bis dahin ungeöffnetes Grab, das sieben Bestattungen enthielt.[39] In dem hier besprochenen Sarg wurde zudem die Mumienmaske Louvre E 11995 (Tab. 3) gefunden, wo sie Kopf und Schulterpartie der Mumie bedeckte.[40] Aufgrund der Typologie wird der Sarg von Zitman und Lapp in die frühe 12. Dynastie (Sesostris I.) eingeordnet.[41]

f) Die Särge und Maske aus Hildesheim

Die Herkunft der Särge S1Hil (Tab. 3) und S2Hil (Tab. 1) aus dem Roemer- und Pelizaeus-Museum Hildesheim kann auf Assiut festgelegt werden. Sie stammen aus der Sammlung Sayed Khashaba[42] und wurden 1989 vom Roemer- und Pelizaeus-Museum angekauft. Da Khashaba 1913–14 mit A. Kamal in Assiut gegraben hat, könnten sie aus dieser Grabung stammen. Ihre Herkunft ließe sich daher möglicherweise zumindest auf den nordöstlichen Teil der Nekropole eingrenzen (siehe oben c). Aufgrund der Gestaltung der Särge können sie in die späte 11. bis frühe 12. Dynastie datiert werden.[43]

Für die Mumienmaske RPM 6226 (Tab. 2) wird Assiut als Herkunftsort nur mit Fragezeichen angegeben.[44] Sie wurde 1991 vom Museum erworben;[45] ihre Herkunft oder gar ihr genauer Fundkontext ist jedoch nicht bekannt. Aufgrund ihrer Stilistik wird sie vom Museum selbst in die 11. Dynastie einge-

---

34 Siehe den Bericht von Kamal 1934: 49–53 (Zitat auf S. 49); außerdem Zitman 2010: I, 58.

35 Zitman 2010: I, 58.

36 Lapp 1993: 125–131 (§§284–293); Zitman 2010: I, 291f.; Hannig 2006: 113, setzt den Sarg zeitlich früher an, und zwar in die Erste Zwischenzeit.

37 Siehe die Grabungspublikation von Chassinat & Palanque 1911; allgemein siehe auch Zitman 2010: I, 59–61; Zitman 2010: II, 4, Map 2 (rote Markierung); 8, Map 5; 255–268 (Appendix 3)

38 Siehe zu Grab 6 Chassinat & Palanque 1911: 4–28. Dieser Nachti ist nicht zu verwechseln mit dem Nachti aus Grab 7.

39 Siehe zur Grabausstattung Zitman 2010: II, 255f.; PM IV, 266.

40 Chassinat & Palanque 1911: 12; Tf. 3.1; vgl. Zitman 2010: II, 255. Zur Maske siehe auch unten „Bemerkungen zur Produktion".

41 Zitman 2010: I, 212f.; Lapp 1993: 125–131 (§§284–293). Hannig 2006: 113, datiert in die Erste Zwischenzeit.

42 Nach dem Eintrag zur „Object's History" auf der Webseite des Global Egyptian Museums: http://www.globalegyptianmuseum.org/record.aspx?id=11510 (S1Hil), sowie http://www.globalegyptianmuseum.org/record.aspx?id=11511 (S2Hil) [Zugriff 02/2021]. In den Hildesheimer Katalogeinträgen (siehe Anm. e zu Tab. 1 und Anm. a zu Tab. 3) wird dies nicht erwähnt.

43 Zu S1Hil siehe Zitman 2010: I, 283; Hannig 2006: 100 (11. Dyn.). In den Museumskatalogen findet sich ebenfalls eine Datierung in die 11./12. Dynastie, siehe Hannig 1990: 58; Schulz 1993: 41, sowie The Global Egyptian Museum, http://www.globalegyptianmuseum.org/record.aspx?id=11510 [Zugriff 08/2018]. Zu S2Hil siehe Zitman 2010: I, 254, mit Anm. 1788 und 1789; 274; sowie Hannig 2006: 88. Für den Sarg wird von Seidel 1990: 94, eine Datierung in die 11. Dynastie vorgeschlagen, die aber aufgrund der Problematik der fehlenden Fundkontexte und unzureichenden Publikationslage „nur als Eckwert zu betrachten" ist; dieser Datierung schließt sich The Global Egyptian Museum, http://www.globalegyptianmuseum.org/record.aspx?id=11511 [Zugriff 08/2018], an.

44 Seidel 1990: 44; The Global Egyptian Museum, http://www.globalegyptianmuseum.org/record.aspx?id=11074 [Zugriff 08/2018].

45 Vgl. The Global Egyptian Museum, http://www.globalegyptianmuseum.org/record.aspx?id=11074 [Zugriff 08/2018].

ordnet.[46] Ihre Ähnlichkeit zu den anderen Masken aus Assiut (vgl. die Masken aus London, Boston und Baltimore) bestätigt eine Datierung in das frühe Mittlere Reich (11./12. Dynastie).[47] Die Einzeichnung der Blutgefäße im Auge der Maske ist zudem ein weiterer Hinweis auf ihre Herkunft aus Assiut.

g) Die Mumienmaske Boston, MFA 1987.4 (Tab. 3)

Die Maske wurde 1987 vom Museum of Fine Arts in Boston erworben.[48] Die genauen Fundumstände sind unbekannt. Aufgrund ihrer Stilistik und Ähnlichkeit zu den anderen Masken aus Assiut (vgl. die Masken aus Hildesheim, London und Baltimore) kann sie in das frühe Mittlere Reich (11./12. Dynastie) datiert werden.[49]

Die betreffenden Objekte stammen demnach alle aus einem Zeitraum von der mittleren/späten 11. bis frühen 12. Dynastie. Die Blutgefäße im Auge scheinen daher ein synchrones Stilelement zu sein, das bei einer Zeitspanne von ca. 2055 bis 1870 v. Chr. unter mehreren Generationen von Künstlern/Werkstätten weitertradiert wurde. Augendarstellungen aus späterer Zeit mit diesem Detail sind der Autorin bislang nicht bekannt.

Die Objekte kommen sowohl aus dem nordöstlichen als auch nordwestlichen Teil der Nekropole, sie lassen sich somit nicht auf ein bestimmtes Gebiet festlegen. Abschließend lässt sich jedoch feststellen, dass Objekte mit Blutgefäßen im (Udjat-)Auge aus Assiut mit derzeit unbestimmtem Fundort und unsicherer Datierung einem der zeitlich entsprechenden Gebiete der Nekropole zugewiesen und so ihr Fundkontext und ihre Datierung besser fixiert werden können.

Sarg-Nr.	Museum + Inventarnr.	Ausgräber + Fundjahr	Inhaber und Datierung	Augenwinkelfärbung	Irisbereich	Anzahl und Art der Blutgefäße (Striche)
S2Br	Brüssel, MRAH, E 3035[a]	Hogarth 1906–1907	*Ḥnw*; frühes Mittleres Reich (12. Dyn.)	Winkel ausfüllend, klar abgetrennt vom Weißen	undifferenziert, schwarz	beide Augen: je 4 dünne, längere Striche mittig zw. Irisbereich und innerem und äußerem Augenwinkel
S12C	Kairo, JdE 45065[b]	A. Kamal 1913–14[c]	*ꜥnḫ=f*; frühes Mittleres Reich (12. Dyn.)	Winkel blockartig ausfüllend, klar abgetrennt vom Weißen	undifferenziert, schwarz	beide Augen: 2-mal 3 dünne, längere Striche zw. Irisbereich und äußerem Augenwinkel, die einander entgegengesetzt laufen und einen Winkel bilden; linkes Auge: 3 dünne, längere Striche mittig zw. Irisbereich und innerem Augenwinkel; rechtes Auge: 1-mal 3 sowie 1-mal 2 dünne, längere Striche zw. Irisbereich und innerem Augenwinkel, die einander entgegengesetzt laufen und einen Winkel bilden (vgl. Abb. 1)
S13C	Kairo, CG 28130[d]	Chassinat/ Palanque 1903, Grab 6	*ꜥnḫ=f*; wiederbenutzt von *Nḫt*; frühes Mittleres Reich (12. Dyn.)	Winkel blockartig ausfüllend, leicht nach innen gebogen, klar abgetrennt vom Weißen	undifferenziert, schwarz	beide Augen: je 3 dünne, längere Striche mittig zw. Irisbereich und innerem und äußerem Augenwinkel

46 Seidel 1990: 44; The Global Egyptian Museum, http://www.globalegyptianmuseum.org/record.aspx?id=11074 [Zugriff 08/2018].
47 So auch aktuell Oppenheim et al. 2015: 234, Kat. 172.
48 Vgl. die Informationen auf der Webseite des Museums: https://www.mfa.org/collections/object/mummy-mask-164600 [Zugriff 08/2018].
49 Brovarski 1988: 119; vgl. auch Oppenheim et al. 2015: 234f.; Casini 2017: 60f.

Sarg-Nr.	Museum + Inventarnr.	Ausgräber + Fundjahr	Inhaber und Datierung	Augenwinkel-färbung	Irisbereich	Anzahl und Art der Blutgefäße (Striche)
S2Hil	Hildesheim, RPM 6000[e]	A. Kamal 1913–14 (?)[f]	*Wpj-w3.wt-nḫt*; frühes Mittleres Reich (11./12. Dyn.)	Winkel blockartig ausfüllend, klar abgetrennt vom Weißen	undifferen-ziert, blau mit schwarzer Umrandungs-linie	beide Augen: je 3 dünne, längere Striche mittig zw. Irisbereich und innerem und äußerem Augenwinkel
S9Mi	Minya M3[g]	M. Kamal 1932	*Jmy*; frühes Mittleres Reich (12. Dyn.)	Rötung mit schmaler flächiger Linie parallel zum Augenwinkel, klar abgetrennt vom Weißen	undifferen-ziert, schwarz	rechtes Auge: 2-mal 2 kurze Striche zw. Irisbereich und äußerem Augenwinkel[h]
S4Tor	Turin, Museo Egizio, S. 8875[j]	Schiaparelli 1908	*J*; frühes Mittleres Reich (11./12. Dyn.)	Winkel blockartig ausfüllend, klar abgetrennt vom Weißen	undifferen-ziert, schwarz	beide Augen: 4 längere, dünne Striche mittig zw. Irisbereich und äußerem Augenwinkel; linkes Auge: 5 längere, dünne Striche mittig zw. Irisbereich und innerem Augenwinkel; rechtes Auge: 3 längere, dünne Striche mittig zw. Irisbereich und innerem Augenwinkel (vgl. Abb. 2; Pl. 29a)
S5Tor	Turin, Museo Egizio, S. 8876[j]	Schiaparelli 1908	*B3s3* (?); Ende 1. ZwZt.; frü-hes Mittleres Reich (11. Dyn.)	Rötung mit schmaler flächiger Linie parallel zum Augenwinkel, klar abgetrennt vom Weißen	undifferen-ziert, schwarz	beide Augen: je 2 mittellan-ge, dünne Striche mittig zw. Irisbereich und innerem und äußerem Augenwinkel (vgl. Pl. 29b)
S7Tor	Turin, Museo Egizio, S. 8912+8922[k]	Schiaparelli 1908	*Wpj-w3.wt-m-ḥ3.t*; frühes Mittleres Reich (11./12. Dyn.)	Rötung mit schmaler flächiger Linie parallel zum Augenwinkel, klar abgetrennt vom Weißen	undifferen-ziert, schwarz	beide Augen: je 2-mal 3 kurze Striche zw. Irisbereich und äußerem Augenwinkel; linkes Auge: 3 kurze Striche mittig zw. Irisbereich und innerem Augenwinkel; rechtes Auge: 4 kurze Striche mittig zw. Irisbereich und äußerem Augenwinkel (vgl. Pl. 30a)
S10Tor	Turin, Museo Egizio, S. 8919[l]	Schiaparelli 1908	*Mnw-ḥtp* (II)	Rötung nicht erkennbar – ob überhaupt vorhanden?	undifferen-ziert, schwarz	linkes Auge: innerer Augenwinkel abgesplittert (2 kurze Striche erkennbar), 4 kurze, dünne Striche mittig zw. Irisbereich und äußerem Augenwinkel; rechtes Auge: 3 kurze Striche mittig zw. Irisbereich und innerem Augenwinkel, 3 kurze, dünne Striche mittig zw. Irisbereich und äußerem Augenwinkel (vgl. Abb. 4; Pl. 30b)

Sarg-Nr.	Museum + Inventarnr.	Ausgräber + Fundjahr	Inhaber und Datierung	Augenwinkel-färbung	Irisbereich	Anzahl und Art der Blutgefäße (Striche)
S11Tor	Turin, Museo Egizio, S. 8807[m]	Schiaparelli 1908	?; frühes Mittleres Reich (11./12. Dyn.)	Rötung mit schmaler flächiger Linie parallel zum Augenwinkel, klar abgetrennt vom Weißen	undifferen-ziert, schwarz	beide Augen: 3 kurze Striche mittig zw. Irisbereich und äußerem Augenwinkel; je 2 kurze Striche über und unter dem Irisbereich; linkes Auge: 3 kurze Striche mittig zw. Irisbereich und innerem Augenwinkel; rechtes Auge: keine Striche zw. Irisbereich und innerem Augenwinkel (vgl. Abb. 3; Pl. 31a)
S12Tor	Turin, Museo Egizio, S. 8923+8962+8929[n]	Schiaparelli 1908	*Msḥ.tj*; frühes Mittleres Reich (11./12. Dyn.)	Winkel blockartig ausfüllend, klar abgetrennt vom Weißen	undifferen-ziert, schwarz	beide Augen: 2 kurze Striche mittig zw. Irisbereich und innerem Augenwinkel; linkes Auge: 2-mal 2 kurze Striche zw. Irisbereich und äußerem Augenwinkel; rechtes Auge: 2 kurze Striche mittig zw. Irisbereich und äußerem Augenwinkel (vgl. Pl. 31b)
S13Tor	Turin, Museo Egizio, S. 8924+8927[o]	Schiaparelli 1908	*Wpj-wꜣ.wt-m-ḥꜣ.t* (II)	tw. zerstört, wo erkenn-bar: Rötung mit schmaler flächiger Linie parallel zum Augenwinkel, scharf abge-grenzt vom Weißen	undifferen-ziert, blau mit schwarzer Umrandungs-linie	beide Augen: 2-mal 4 dünne, längere Striche zw. Irisbereich und äußerem Augenwinkel (beim rechten Auge nicht sicher erkennbar); linkes Auge: 3 dünne längere Striche mittig zw. Irisbereich und innerem Augenwinkel, 4 dünne längere Striche unten an der Rundung des Irisbereichs; rechtes Auge: 4 dünne längere Striche mittig zw. Irisbereich und innerem Augenwinkel, unten an der Rundung des Irisbereichs noch 2 Striche erkennbar, Rest zerstört (vgl. Abb. 5; Pl. 32a)

Tab. 1: Udjataugen auf Särgen mit Einzeichnung von Blutgefäßen[50]

Anmerkungen zur Tabelle:

a   Zum Sarg des Henu siehe DELVAUX & THERASSE 2015: 34f.; ZITMAN 2010: II, 122f.; HANNIG 2006: 432–434; LAPP 1993: 125–131 (§§284–293); 296f. (S53); Blatt 20; PM IV, 268; The Global Egyptian Museum, http://www.globalegyptianmuseum.org/record.aspx?id=468 [Zugriff 08/2018]; vgl. auch die Konkordanz bei WILLEMS 2014: 276f.

b   Im Ägyptischen Museum Kairo als JdE 45066 ausgewiesen. Durch Abgleich der Fotos bei Hannig allerdings als JdE 45065 zu identifizieren; ebenso in der Konkordanz von WILLEMS 2014: 276f. Zum Sarg des Anchef siehe ZITMAN 2010: II, 122f.; WILLEMS 1988: 28; HANNIG 2006: 482–484; LAPP 1993: 125–131 (§§284–293); 135–137 (§§306–310); 292f. (S17); Blatt 22; Tf. 26; vgl. auch die Konkordanz bei WILLEMS 2014: 276f.

c   Zur Zuordnung zur Grabung A. Kamals 1913–14 siehe oben, Abschnitt „Herkunft und Datierung", c.

d   Kein Katalog zur CG-Nummer vorhanden. Zum Sarg siehe die Grabungspublikation von CHASSINAT & PALANQUE 1911: 7–13; siehe außerdem ZITMAN 2010: II, 122f.; WILLEMS 1988: 28; HANNIG 2006: 485–490; LAPP 1993: 125–131 (§§284–293); 135–137 (§§306–309); 294f. (S43); Blatt 21; PM IV, 266; vgl. auch die Konkordanz bei WILLEMS 2014: 276f.

50 Die Datierung basiert zum einen auf dem Fundkontext der Objekte, zum anderen auf der typologischen Einordnung; siehe dazu jeweils oben Abschnitt „Herkunft und Datierung".

e   Der Sarg des Upuaut-Nacht ist wie S1Hil im Inneren bemalt und weist eine Diagonalsternuhr im Deckel auf. Zum Sarg siehe Seidel 1990: 94–96; Zitman 2010: II, 112f.; Hannig 2006: 576–585; The Global Egyptian Museum, http://www.globalegyptianmuseum.org/record.aspx?id=11511 [Zugriff 08/2018]; vgl. auch die Konkordanz bei Willems 2014: 278f.

f   Zur Zuordnung zur Grabung A. Kamals 1913–14 siehe oben, Abschnitt „Herkunft und Datierung", f.

g   Alte Inventar-Nr.: Minya 635; zum Sarg der Imi siehe den Grabungsbericht von Kamal 1934: 49–51 (I); außerdem siehe Zitman 2010: II, 136f.; Hannig 2006: 765–769; Lapp 1993: 125–131 (§§284–293); 292f. (S1); Blatt 21; vgl. auch die Konkordanz bei Willems 2014: 286f.

h   Grundlage ist die Abbildung bei Hannig 2006: 768. Das Foto in schwarz/weiß ist leicht unscharf und lässt für den inneren Augenwinkel keine Aussage zu; das linke Auge ist nicht abgebildet. Der Sarg ist ansonsten unpubliziert. Möglicherweise lassen sich auch auf Sarg S10Mi Blutgefäße ausmachen, allerdings ist die Abbildung bei Hannig 2006: 770, ebenfalls zu unscharf, um eine konkrete Aussage treffen zu können. Der Sarg wurde daher hier nicht aufgenommen.

i   Zum Sarg des J siehe D'Amicone et al. 2009: 84f. (Großaufnahme der Udjataugen); 90f. (Beschreibung); 92f. (zugehörige Funde); Zitman 2010: II, 138f.; Hannig 2006: 857f. (hier S11Tor [sic!]); vgl. auch die Konkordanz bei Willems 2014: 290f.

j   Zum Sarg des Basa siehe D'Amicone et al. 2009: 94–97 (mit zugehörigen Funden); 99; Zitman 2010: II, 138f.; Hannig 2006: 847f.; vgl. auch die Konkordanz bei Willems 2014: 290f.

k   Siehe zum Sarg der Upuautemhat D'Amicone et al. 2009: 173f.; Zitman 2010: II, 138f.; Hannig 2006: 850; vgl. auch die Konkordanz bei Willems 2014: 290f.

l   Siehe zum Sarg des Minhotep D'Amicone et al. 2009: 176f.; Zitman 2010: II, 140f.; Hannig 2006: 855f.; vgl auch die Konkordanz bei Willems 2014: 290f.

m   Zu diesem Sarg siehe D'Amicone et al. 2009: 174–176; Zitman 2010: II, 140f.; Hannig 2006: 845f. (hier S4Tor [sic!]); vgl. auch die Konkordanz bei Willems 2014: 290f.

n   Siehe zum Sarg des Mesehti D'Amicone et al. 2009: 178f.; 282f. (Großaufnahme der Augen) [hier nur Inventarnr. S. 8929 angegeben]; Zitman 2010: II, 140f. [Inventarnr. S. 8923, S. 8929 und S. 8936]; Hannig 2006: 859 [hier nur Name und Inventarnr. S. 8923 angegeben]; vgl. auch die Konkordanz bei Willems 2014: 290f. [hier Inventarnr. S. 8923 angegeben].

o   Siehe zu S13Tor Hannig 2006: 859; Zitman 2010: II, 140f.; vgl auch die Konkordanz bei Willems 2014: 290f.

Museum und Inventar-Nr.	Ausgräber und Fundjahr	Inhaber/Datierung	Augenwinkel-färbung	Irisbereich	Anzahl und Art der Blutgefäße (Striche)
Hildesheim, RPM 6226[a]	unbekannt[b]	frühes Mittleres Reich (11./12. Dyn.)	Rötung mit schmaler flächiger Linie parallel zum Augenwinkel, klar abgetrennt vom Weißen	undifferenziert, schwarz	beide Augen: 3 dünne, längere Striche mittig zw. Irisbereich und innerem Augenwinkel; linkes Auge: 5 schräge, längere Striche mittig zw. Irisbereich und äußerem Augenwinkel; rechtes Auge: 4 schräge, längere Striche mittig zw. Irisbereich und äußerem Augenwinkel
Boston, MFA 1987.54[c]	unbekannt[d]	frühes Mittleres Reich (11./12. Dyn.)	Rötung mit schmaler flächiger Linie parallel zum Augenwinkel, klar abgetrennt vom Weißen	undifferenziert, schwarz	beide Augen: 4 schräge, längere Striche mittig zw. Irisbereich und äußerem Augenwinkel; 3 Striche mittig zw. Irisbereich und innerem Augenwinkel

Tab. 2: Mumienmasken mit Einzeichnung von Blutgefäßen im Auge[51]

Anmerkungen zur Tabelle:

a   Siehe zur Maske aus Hildesheim Seidel 1990: 44f.; The Global Egyptian Museum, http://www.globalegyptianmuseum.org/record.aspx?id=11074 [Zugriff 08/2018]; Oppenheim et al. 2015: 234f., Kat. 172; vgl. auch Casini 2017: 60f.; 62, Abb. 4.2.

b   Siehe oben Abschnitt „Herkunft und Datierung", f.

c   Siehe zu dieser Maske Brovarski 1988: 119, Kat. 46; Webseite des Museums of Fine Art: https://www.mfa.org/collections/object/mummy-mask-164600 [Zugriff 08/2018]; Freed et al. 2009: 55, Abb. 22; 204 (Fig. 22); vgl. auch Oppenheim et al. 2015: 234f., Kat. 172, sowie Casini 2017: 60f.

d   Siehe oben Abschnitt „Herkunft und Datierung", g.

---

51   Die Datierung basiert zum einen auf dem Grabungs- und Fundkontext der Objekte, zum anderen auf der typologischen Einordnung; siehe dazu jeweils oben Abschnitt „Herkunft und Datierung".

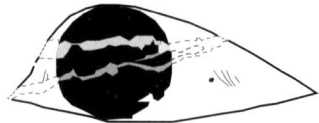

Abb. 4: Augen auf dem Sarg des Minhotep, Museo Egizio, Turin, S. 8919,
S10Tor. Umzeichnung: N. Gräßler (vgl. Pl. 30b).

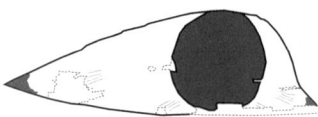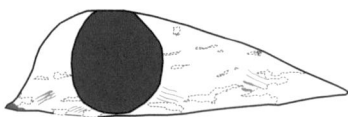

Abb. 5: Augen auf dem Sarg der Upuautemhat, Museo Egizio, Turin,
S. 8924+8927, S13Tor. Umzeichnung: N. Gräßler (vgl. Pl. 32a).

Mögliche weitere Belege

Tab. 3 listet einige Mumienmasken und Särge auf, die in der Literatur oder auf Abbildungen Einzeichnungen von roten Strichen im Auge vermuten lassen. Die Augen der Objekte konnten nicht am Original überprüft werden, daher werden sie hier als „unsicher" gekennzeichnet.

Museum und Inventar-Nr.	Ausgräber und Fundjahr	Inhaber/ Datierung	Augenwinkelfärbung	Irisbereich	Anzahl und Art der Blutgefäße (Striche)
Sarg S1Hil: Hildesheim, RPM 5999[a]	A. Kamal 1913–14 (?)[b]	*Nḫt*; frühes Mittleres Reich (11./12. Dyn.)	Winkel ausfüllend, klar abgegrenzt vom Weißen	undifferenziert, schwarz	auf Abbildung nicht erkennbar[c]
Maske London, British Museum, EA 46631[d]	Hogarth 1906–7 (Grab 9)	*ꜥnḫ=f*; frühes Mittleres Reich (11./12. Dyn.)	Winkel ausfüllend, klar abgegrenzt vom Weißen	undifferenziert, schwarz	rechtes Auge: Reste von Strichen zw. Irisbereich und äußerem Augenwinkel (?)[e]
Maske Baltimore, Walters Art Museum 78.4[f]	A. Kamal 1913–14 (?)[g]	frühes Mittleres Reich (11./12. Dyn.)	leichte Rötung im inneren Winkel des rechten Auges (?), ansonsten keine geröteten Augenwinkel erkennbar	undifferenziert, schwarz	keine Striche erkennbar[h]
Maske Paris, Louvre E 11995[i]	Chassinat/ Palanque 1903, Grab 6	frühes Mittleres Reich (12. Dyn.)	keine roten Augenwinkel	undifferenziert, schwarz	keine Striche erkennbar[j]

Tab. 3: Mumienmasken und Särge mit unsicherer Einzeichnung von Blutgefäßen im Auge[52]

Anmerkungen zur Tabelle:

a   Der Sarg gehört zusammen mit S2Hil zu den auch im Inneren bemalten Särgen. Beide weisen zudem am Sargdeckel eine Diagonalsternuhr auf. Zum Sarg des Nacht siehe HANNIG 1990: 58–61 (nur Innenseiten abgebildet); SCHULZ 1993: 41–43 (nur Innenseiten abgebildet); ZITMAN 2010: II, 112f.; HANNIG 2006: 565–575; The Global Egyptian Museum, http://www.globalegyptianmuseum.org/record.aspx?id=11510 [Zugriff 08/2018]; vgl. auch die Konkordanz bei WILLEMS 2014: 278f.

b   Zur Zuordnung zur Grabung A. Kamals 1913–14 siehe oben, Abschnitt „Herkunft und Datierung", f.

---

52 Die Datierung basiert zum einen auf dem Grabungs- und Fundkontext der Objekte, zum anderen auf der typologischen Einordnung; siehe dazu jeweils oben Abschnitt „Herkunft und Datierung".

c   Der Sarg wird bei Oppenheim et al. 2015: 235, Anm. 4, als Beleg für die Einzeichnung von „veins" im Auge auf Assiuter Särgen benannt. Da der Sarg im Inneren reich dekoriert ist, werden in der Regel nur die Innenseiten abgebildet. Zum Udjataugenpaar auf der Außenseite siehe die Abbildung auf der Webseite des Museums: http://www.rpmuseum. de/presse/dauerausstellungen/aegypten/tod-in-der-wueste/bildmaterial.html [Zugriff 08/2018; ziemlich weit unten auf der Seite]; das Bildmaterial auf der Seite des Global Egyptian Museum, http://www.globalegyptianmuseum.org/record. aspx?id=11510 [Zugriff 08/2018]; sowie bei Hannig 2006: 567. Auf den Abbildungen sind keine Striche zu erkennen.

d   Zur Maske des Anchef siehe die Webseite des British Museums: https://www.britishmuseum.org/collection/object/Y_ EA46631 [Zugriff 02/2021]. Siehe außerdem Zitman 2010: II, 214; PM IV, 268; vgl. auch Oppenheim et al. 2015: 234f., Kat. 172. Bei Casini 2017: 60, nicht mit aufgelistet.

e   Die Blutgefäße im Auge werden bei Oppenheim et al. 2015: 234f., Kat. 172, als gemeinsames Merkmal der Masken aus Boston, Hildesheim, Baltimore und London genannt. Auf dem Foto der Maske auf der Webseite des British Museums scheinen im äußeren Augenwinkel des rechten Auges drei kleine rote Punkte bzw. die Reste von roten Strichen zu sehen zu sein. Es ist jedoch wahrscheinlicher, dass es sich hierbei um Abreibungen oder Ähnliches handelt, da in den anderen (unzerstörten) Augenwinkeln keine Striche zu erkennen sind, vgl. Tab. 3, Anm. h.

f   Zu dieser Maske siehe Schulz 2009: 36f.; die Webseite des Walters Art Museums: https://art.thewalters.org/detail/29816/ mummy-mask-of-a-high-official/ [Zugriff 08/2018]; vgl. auch Oppenheim et al. 2015: 234f., Kat. 172, sowie Casini 2017: 60f.; 62, Abb. 4.2.

g   Siehe Fußnote 30.

h   Die Blutgefäße im Auge werden bei Oppenheim et al. 2015: 234f., Kat. 172, und Casini 2017: 60, als gemeinsames Merkmal der Masken aus Boston, Hildesheim, London und eben Baltimore genannt. Dies sollte revidiert werden: Auf der Abbildung bei Schulz, in: Schulz & Seidel 2009: 37, sind keine Einzeichnungen im Auge erkennbar. Auch auf dem vom Museum bereit gestellten, hoch aufgelösten Foto sind keine roten Striche auszumachen. Die Fotos der Masken London, BM EA46631 und Baltimore, Walters Art Museum 78.4 wurden von der Verfasserin mit verschiedenen Filtern bearbeitet, um rote Farbe herauszufiltern und so möglicherweise Reste von roten Strichen im Auge erkennbar zu machen. Bei beiden Masken ist keine rote Farbe auf dem Weißen des Auges nachweisbar. Auch die drei rötlich erscheinenden Punkte auf der Maske aus London erscheinen mit Filter eher braun, was wiederum für Abreibungen spricht. Es ist zudem unklar, ob die Augenwinkel der Baltimore-Maske gerötet sind, da nur der innere Augenwinkel des rechten Auges leicht rot (eher pink), aber verwaschen, erscheint.

i   Chassinat & Palanque 1911: 12; Tf. 3.1; Vercoutter & Grimal 1981: 134, Kat. 133; Rigault 2009: 149f., Kat. 115; Webseite des Louvre, https://www.louvre.fr/en/oeuvre-notices/mummy-mask [Zugriff 09/2018].

j   Die Maske wird hier mit aufgenommen, da die Blutgefäße im Auge bei Casini 2017: 60, als gemeinsames Merkmal der Masken aus Boston, Hildesheim, Baltimore und eben aus dem Louvre gelten. Allerdings wird die Maske des Nachti aus dem Louvre nur bei Casini in engem Zusammenhang mit den anderen Masken genannt. Oppenheim et al. 2015: 235, Anm. 3, und Schulz 2009: 36, erkennen zwar ebenfalls eine gewisse Vergleichbarkeit mit den Masken aus Baltimore, Hildesheim, Boston und London an, jedoch ordnen sie sie stilistisch einer anderen Werkstatt zu (siehe auch unten „Bemerkungen zur Produktion").

Bemerkungen zur Produktion der Särge in Zusammenhang mit der Einzeichnung in den Augendarstellungen

Es ist in der ägyptologischen Forschung häufig beobachtet worden, dass Särge des Mittleren Reiches aus Nekropolen Ober- und Mittelägyptens eigene lokale Typen verkörpern, die sich in ihrer Dekoration und Typologie von den „Standardsärgen des Mittleren Reiches" unterscheiden[53] und somit nicht zentralisiert hergestellt wurden.[54] Diese lokale Herstellung und Tradierung lokaler Traditionen wird auch durch das Merkmal der Blutgefäße in Augendarstellungen aus Assiut bestätigt.

Wie die Herstellung der Särge und Masken aussah, ist bislang nur in Ansätzen untersucht.[55] Eine solche Untersuchung ist generell schwierig, da nur die fertigen Objekte Aufschluss darüber geben kön-

53 Willems 1988: 50. Dennoch lässt sich nachweisen, dass auch die lokalen Typen einer Nekropole sich untereinander beeinflussten oder Ähnlichkeiten zur Standardform aufweisen können, siehe im Falle Assiuts Willems 1988: 102–104.

54 Generell wird zwischen zentralisierter und lokaler Organisation der Herstellung von Objekten unterschieden; siehe dazu die kurze Zusammenfassung bei Ilin-Tomich 2018: 82, mit weiterer Literatur.

55 Aktuell beschäftigt sich ein Sammelband anhand von Fallbeispielen speziell mit der Funktion und den Handwerkertraditionen von Särgen, siehe Taylor & Vandenbeusch 2018 (insb. Kap. 4 und 5); vgl. ebenfalls aktuell die Beiträge in Strudwick & Dawson 2019. Caroline Joan Arbuckle hat in ihrer Dissertation „A Social History of Coffins and Carpenters in Ancient Egypt" (University of California 2018) Praktiken der Holzherstellung insbesondere in Bezug

nen, archäologische Strukturen jedoch kaum vorhanden sind und bildliche Quellen nur wenig Auskunft darüber geben.[56]

In der Forschung wird bislang vor allem versucht, die Produktion von Objekten wie Stelen, Opfertellern, Särgen oder Mumienmasken verschiedenen lokalen Werkstätten oder einer von der Residenz ausgehenden, zentralisierten Herstellung zuzuordnen. Eine „Werkstatt" wird dabei nicht anhand einer individuellen Künstlergruppe, sondern über mehrere Objekte, die den gleichen „Werkstattstil" aufweisen, identifiziert.[57] D.h., dass vor allem typologische und stilistische Gemeinsamkeiten eine Rolle bei der Zuordnung von Objekten zu gemeinsamen Werkstätten spielen.[58] Allerdings könnte es sich bei Objekten mit gleichen stilistischen Merkmalen auch um einen individuellen Künstler gehandelt haben. Der Begriff „Werkstatt" muss daher nicht unbedingt, wie oben schon angedeutet, auf eine größere Künstlergruppe schließen lassen, sondern könnte auch nur einen einzelnen Künstler beinhalten.[59]

Für das Mittlere Reich ist derzeit die Erforschung von Stelenwerkstätten am weitesten fortgeschritten,[60] andere Objektgattungen, wie z. B. Skulptur oder Modelle, rücken aber ebenfalls immer mehr in den Fokus.[61] Die Untersuchung von Werkstätten wird von vielen Fragen begleitet, die sich vornehmlich auf die Organisation und Zusammensetzung sowie die Mobilität einzelner Künstler derselben bzw. der fertiggestellten Objekte beziehen.[62] Biographische Texte auf Stelen belegen, dass Künstler nicht lokal fest angesiedelt sein mussten, sondern auch zu anderen Orten gereist sind bzw. geschickt wurden.[63] Bei einer zeitlich sehr engen Spanne wie den hier behandelten Särgen und Masken aus Assiut stellt sich zudem die Frage, wie viele Werkstätten generell in einer Region existiert haben könnten bzw. ob es eine Werkstatt gab, die mehrere Handwerker und Dekorateure beschäftigte, mehrere Typen im Angebot hatte und deren Stil sich diachron ebenfalls weiterentwickelte.[64]

Tabelle 4 zeigt eine Übersicht der in Tab. 1 aufgeführten Särge und ihre Zuordnung zu Werkstätten bei Hannig sowie ihre Einordnung in Gruppen bei Zitman.[65]

---

auf Särge untersucht. Die Dissertation ist Open Access über die University of California verfügbar: https://escholarship. org/uc/item/1b81337z [Zugriff 02/2021]. Ein weiteres Projekt von ihr betrifft speziell die Untersuchung des Holzes und der Konstruktion der Särge des Mittleren Reiches aus dem Museo Egizio Turin (persönliche Mitteilung von M. Zöller-Engelhardt; siehe auch https://carriearbuckle.wordpress.com/ [Zugriff 01/2018]).

56 Zu bildlichen Quellen zur Sargproduktion siehe DRENKHAHN 1976: 103–105.

57 FREED 1996: 298; siehe auch ILIN-TOMICH 2017: 71; ein kurzer Gesamtüberblick zum derzeitigen Forschungsstand findet sich ebenfalls bei ILIN-TOMICH 2018: 81–83; speziell zu Sargwerkstätten in Assiut siehe HANNIG 2006: 146–150. Siehe auch die Kritik an der Theorie von Werkstätten und dem Begriff Werkstattstil bei DOHRMANN 2004: 440–446, die daher „Werkstätten" (feste Verbindungen von Künstlern) und „Schulen" (lockere Verbindungen im Meister-Schüler-Verhältnis) unterscheidet. Einer Werkstatt könnten damit mehrere Schulen, d.h. Meister mit einer Gruppe von Schülern, unterstellt sein, die unterschiedliche bzw. Varianten von Stilen aufweisen, wodurch Objekte unterschiedlichen Stils entstehen könnten, die aber alle aus einer Werkstatt stammten. Deshalb seien an verschiedenen Stilen nur die jeweiligen Schulen abzulesen (S. 441). Die Identifizierung einer Werkstatt anhand stilistischer Merkmale sei daher abzulehnen (S. 443).

58 Vgl. auch WILLEMS 1988: 53f., zu den Problemen bei typologischen Vergleichen.

59 FREED 1996: 298; zur Problematik des Begriffs „Werkstatt" vgl. auch ESCHENBRENNER-DIEMER 2017: 135f., sowie DOHRMANN 2004: 442.

60 Siehe zur Produktion von Stelen und Stelenwerkstätten aktuell ILIN-TOMICH 2017; vgl. außerdem FREED 1996: 297–336; FRANKE 1994: 105–117.

61 Siehe z. B. aktuell zu Skulpturwerkstätten CONNOR 2018: 11–30; zu Opfertellern ILIN-TOMICH 2018: 81–100; zu Holzmodellen ESCHENBRENNER-DIEMER 2017: 133–191.

62 Vgl. z. B. die Übersicht zu Künstlern und Werkstätten bei OPPENHEIM 2015: 23–27, siehe auch FRANKE 1994: 108, der drei Möglichkeiten zur Identifizierung von Werkstätten innerhalb eines Korpus benennt: 1. lokale Handwerker, 2. nicht lokale königliche und Residenz-Handwerker, 3. Objekte wurden an einem Ort produziert und nach Fertigstellung zum Aufstellungsort versendet.

63 Siehe Belege z. B. bei FRANKE 1994: 105–108; vgl. auch DOHRMANN 2004: 444f.; vgl. zur Mobilität von Handwerkern auch OPPENHEIM 2015: 24f.; und in Bezug auf Stelenherstellung ILIN-TOMICH 2017: 163.

64 Vgl. zur diachronen Komponente auch LORAND 2012: 47–55, insb. 49–52, zu den von Vandier zugeordneten Schulen/ Stilen der Statuen Sesostris' I.; vgl. auch die Ausführungen zur Erstellung einer Typologie bei WILLEMS 1988: 53f.

65 Die Einordnung der Särge zu Werkstätten bei Hannig ist jedoch durchaus kritisch zu sehen, da die Gemeinsamkeiten der Särge nicht erläutert werden und es fraglich sein muss, ob der Udjataugentyp tatsächlich als Kriterium für eine in Zusammenhang stehende Sarggruppe herhalten kann. Er selbst bemerkt, dass die Einordnung subjektiv ist und nur seine

Sarg	Augentyp Hannig	Sargtyp nach Hannig und ggf. Werkstattzugehörigkeit	Gruppe Zitman[a]	Dekorationstyp Zitman[b]
S2Br	B	Bc1; verwandt mit S9C, S13C, S15C (von einem Dekorateur), mit diesen Werkstatt bildend[c]	16	As. I.b.a.a /-
S12C	B	Bc1; verwandt mit S1Br[d]	16	As. II.b.a.b /-
S13C	B	Bc1; verwandt mit S2Br, S9C, S15C[e]	14	As. II.b.a.a-1 /-
S2Hil	B	Ba4[f]	10	As. II.b.a.a-1 /*As. ?
S9Mi	B	Bc1; verwandt mit S1Tan[g]	14	As. II.b.a.a-1 /-
S4Tor[h]	B	Typ Ca, keine Werkstatt erkennbar, da Einzelstück[i]	?	nicht klassifiziert
S5Tor	Aj	Ab2; verwandt mit S16L, S36L, S48L, S54L, S57L; keine Werkstatt eindeutig feststellbar[j]	3	I/-
S7Tor	B	Dc; verwandt mit S11Tor; möglicherweise Werkstatt bildend mit S11Tor aufgrund der Udjataugenform[k]	6	As. I.b.a.a /-
S10Tor	B	nicht zugewiesen	8	As. I.b.a.a /-
S11Tor[l]	B	Dc; verwandt mit S7Tor; siehe bei S7Tor	6	As. I.a.a.a /-
S12Tor	B	nicht zugewiesen	6	As. I.b.a.a /-
S13Tor	B	nicht zugewiesen	8	As. I.a.a.a /-

Tab. 4: Übersicht über die Werkstättenzuordnung nach Hannig und die Klassifizierung nach Zitman; nur die Särge mit sicherer Augeneinzeichnung werden hier gelistet (nähere Informationen zu den Objekten siehe Tab. 1)

Anmerkungen zur Tabelle:

a   Siehe zur jeweiligen Angabe ZITMAN 2010: II, 112 (List 1, Part I) für S2Hil; 122–140 (List I, Part II) für die anderen Särge; die Auflösung der Kürzel befindet sich auf S. 106f. Eine ausführliche Diskussion der Klassen und Gruppen soll erst im angekündigten Folgeband erscheinen.

b   Siehe zur jeweiligen Angabe ZITMAN 2010: II, List 1; die Dekorationstypen werden auf S. 153–162 erklärt.

c   HANNIG 2006: 112–120, insb. 112f., Tab. 8; 148f.

d   HANNIG 2006: 112–120, insb. 112f., Tab. 8; 148f.

e   HANNIG 2006: 112–120, insb. 112f., Tab. 8; 148f.

f   HANNIG 2006: 88, Tab. 6; 93f.; 146f.

g   HANNIG 2006: 112–120; insb. 112f., Tab. 8; 148f.

h   Turin, Museo Egizio S. 8875; bei Hannig S11Tor (sic!), siehe HANNIG 2006: 857f.

i   HANNIG 2006: 131; 150 (hier S11Tor [sic!]).

j   HANNIG 2006: 79, Tab. 5; 84. Da es sich bei S16L, S36L, S48L, S54L und S57L um sehr kleine Sargfragmente handelt, nimmt Hannig anhand der ähnlichen Zeichen eine Verwandtschaft an, jedoch kann dadurch keine eindeutige Werkstatt festgestellt werden.

k   HANNIG 2006: 135, Tab. 11; 138; 150 mit Anm. 1 (S4Tor bei Hannig ist eigentlich S11Tor).

l   Turin, Museo Egizio S. 8807; bei Hannig S4Tor (sic!), siehe HANNIG 2006: 845f.

Auch wenn sich die von Hannig und Zitman jeweils identifizierten Werkstätten und Gruppen unterscheiden, wird ersichtlich, dass die Särge mit Blutgefäßen im Auge anhand ihrer paläographischen, epigraphischen und typologischen Merkmale häufig nicht in Beziehung zueinander stehen. Die Blutgefäße im Auge können daher nicht als ein Merkmal einzelner Werkstätten, sofern es mehrere gegeben hat (siehe oben), gewertet werden, sondern sind als Stilmerkmal eines individuellen Künstlers oder mehrerer spezifischer Künstler/Dekorateure zu werten. Dass mehrere Künstler dieses Detail übernommen haben, wird auch durch die verschiedenen Typen von Blutgefäßeinzeichnungen deutlich. So zeichnete ein Künstler die Blutgefäße als längere Striche auf jeder Seite im Weißen des Augenwinkels ein, ein anderer Künstler bevorzugte kurze Striche, die auch zu mehreren Gruppen im Weißen des Auges auftreten konnten (siehe oben Abschnitt „Objekte").

Vermutung darstellt, siehe HANNIG 2006: 78, Anm. 1. Da Hannig den Werkstattbegriff nicht definiert, ist bei ihm viel eher von „Gruppen" an Särgen auszugehen, die möglicherweise in Verbindung standen; siehe dazu und darüber hinaus ausführlich KAHL 2008: 323–326; vgl. auch GRAJETZKI 2010: 289; WILLEMS 2010: 364.

Die Einordnung der Särge von Hannig und Zitman in bestimmte Gruppen lässt sich unter der Berücksichtigung der Augeneinzeichnung bestätigen bzw. spezifizieren: So werden die Särge S2Br, S12C und S13C von Hannig dem Sargtyp Bc1 zugewiesen (vgl. Tab. 4), wobei S2Br und S13C eine besonders enge Verbindung aufweisen. Die Zusammengehörigkeit der beiden Särge bestätigen auch die Striche in den Udjataugenpaaren: S2Br und S13C weisen eine fast identische Einzeichnung der Blutgefäße sowie der Rötung des Augenwinkels auf. Dadurch lässt sich für diese beiden Särge vielleicht sogar ein und derselbe Künstler fassen.[66] Die Einzeichnung bei S12C ist zwar mit länglichen, schmalen Strichen ebenfalls ähnlich, allerdings wurden hier im äußeren und inneren Augenwinkel je zwei Gruppen mit drei Strichen angeordnet (vgl. Abb. 1), was auf einen anderen Künstler schließen lassen könnte.[67] Der bislang als Einzeltyp gekennzeichnete Sarg S4Tor (vgl. Abb. 2; Pl. 29a) könnte aufgrund der Augeneinzeichnung (lange schmale, schräge Linienführung) ebenfalls zu dieser Gruppe dazugezählt werden.

Ferner werden S11Tor[68] (vgl. Abb. 3; Pl. 31a) und S7Tor (vgl. Pl. 30a) von Hannig zu einer Werkstatt gezählt; Zitman teilt beide Särge ebenfalls in die gleiche Gruppe ein (vgl. Tab. 4). Die Särge weisen den gleichen Udjataugentyp auf; die Strichführung in den Augen mit kurzen, schmalen Strichen ähnelt sich ebenfalls. Allerdings variiert die Einzeichnung der Blutgefäße (vgl. Tab. 1). Dies kann entweder auf verschiedene Künstler zurückgeführt werden oder ein und derselbe Künstler hat die Einzeichnung in den Augen selbst variiert. Geht man nur von der Strichart aus, könnte auch S12Tor (vgl. Pl. 31b), der von Hannig generell nicht einer Gruppe zugeteilt, von Zitman aber der gleichen Gruppe zugeordnet wurde, zu dieser Gruppe dazugehören.

Von der Einzeichnung komplett von den anderen Särgen zu unterscheiden ist S5Tor (vgl. Pl. 29b), der auch von Hannig und Zitman in gänzlich andere Werkstätten bzw. Gruppen eingeteilt wird: Dieser Sarg weist zwei parallele, dünne, nahezu horizontale Linien sowohl im inneren als auch äußeren Augenwinkel auf. Diese Einzeichnung kommt bei den anderen Särgen nicht vor, so dass dies möglicherweise ein Indiz dafür ist, dass S5Tor tatsächlich zeitlich früher anzusetzen ist.[69]

Die Mumienmasken Hildesheim, Boston, Baltimore und London sind einander stilistisch so ähnlich, dass sie aus einer Werkstatt stammen könnten.[70] Eine Ausnahme bildet die Mumienmaske des Nachti, die stilistisch zwar vergleichbar ist, sich im Detail aber doch von den anderen unterscheidet.[71] Da die Maske zeitlich etwas später angesiedelt zu sein scheint als die anderen (vgl. Tab. 2–3 sowie Abschnitt „Herkunft und Datierung", e), könnte hier auch der Fall vorliegen, dass sich der Stil der Werkstatt mit der Zeit etwas gewandelt hat (siehe auch oben zur Frage nach dem diachronen Verlauf einer Werkstatt), es sich aber dennoch um die gleiche Werkstatt handelt, in der auch die anderen Masken aus Tab. 2–3 gefertigt wurden.

Die Augen der Mumienmasken weisen nicht alle die charakteristischen roten Striche im Auge auf (vgl. Tab. 2–3). Da die Masken (bis auf die des Nachti) relativ zeitnah zueinander entstanden sind, kann hier möglicherweise von unterschiedlichen Künstlern, die mit der Dekoration der Masken betraut waren, ausgegangen werden. Die Masken aus Hildesheim und Boston, die als einzige der Masken auch

---

66 Siehe auch HANNIG 2006: 148, der für die Särge S9C, S2Br, S15C und S13C mindestens einen gemeinsamen Dekorateur annimmt. Die Särge S9C und S15C sind leider zu schlecht publiziert, als dass hier eine Aussage zu einer möglichen Einzeichnung von Blutgefäßen getroffen werden kann. Sollten sie keine Augeneinzeichnung haben, könnte dies entweder doch für einen anderen Künstler sprechen oder die jeweiligen Künstler selbst haben nach Lust und Laune oder nach Vorgabe des Auftraggebers variiert.

67 Vgl. auch HANNIG 2006: 146–148. Auch bei Holzmodellen dieser Zeit lassen sich verschiedene „Hände" fassen, siehe ESCHENBRENNER-DIEMER 2017: 163. Zur Arbeitsteilung in Werkstätten bzw. Schulen siehe DOHRMANN 2004: 436–463, am Beispiel der Sitzstatuen Sesostris' I. aus Lischt.

68 Achtung: bei Hannig S4Tor (sic!), siehe HANNIG 2006: 845f.

69 Vgl. Anm. 18.

70 OPPENHEIM ET AL. 2015: 234f.; vgl. auch CASINI 2017: 60, der allerdings die Maske des Anchef aus London (BM EA46631, vgl. Tab. 3) nicht berücksichtigt.

71 Die Maske unterscheidet sich zum einen im Halsschmuck, da hier das Halsband mit Karneol fehlt. Zum anderen ist der Haarschmuck nicht als Haarband an der Stirn angebracht, sondern legt sich über den Kopf; vgl. OPPENHEIM ET AL. 2015: 235, Anm. 3; CASINI 2017: 60, weist die Maske ebenfalls dieser Werkstatt zu.

die Einzeichnung der Blutgefäße aufweisen, sind sich im Vergleich aller hier behandelten Masken am ähnlichsten. Sogar die Strichführung und Anordnung der Blutgefäße im Auge ist nahezu identisch. Vielleicht ist auch hier ein individueller Künstler am Werk gewesen.

Bei der Herstellung der Särge und Masken stellt sich zudem die Frage, ob eine Werkstatt oder Künstlergruppe für die Produktion beider Objekttypen zuständig war oder verschiedene, auf die jeweiligen Objekte spezialisierte Werkstätten anzunehmen sind. Die Frage lässt sich hier nicht eindeutig beantworten. Allerdings weisen sowohl Mumienmasken als auch Särge die charakteristische Einzeichnung der Blutgefäße in den Augen auf, was zumindest für eine Verbindung zwischen der Herstellung beider Objekte spricht. Die Künstler der Objekte waren daher entweder für beide Produkte zuständig oder haben sich untereinander beeinflusst.

Interessant hierbei ist, dass sich bei den Masken und Särgen, die sich einer Person zuweisen lassen und als Ensemble aufgefunden wurden, keine einheitliche Gestaltung der Augen in Hinblick auf die Einzeichnung der Blutgefäße feststellen lässt. So weist der Sarg des Nachti (S13C) aus Grab 6 in Assiut (siehe oben „Herkunft und Datierung", e) die Einzeichnung von Blutgefäßen im Auge auf (vgl. Tab. 1), die im Sarg gefundene und ebenfalls Nachti gehörende Maske (Louvre E11995, vgl. Tab. 3) jedoch nicht. Da der Sarg S13C ursprünglich einer anderen Person gehörte (Anchef) und von Nachti wiederverwendet wurde, könnte diese Abweichung auch daran liegen, dass der Sarg in einer Zeit hergestellt wurde, als die Einzeichnung der Blutgefäße noch in Mode war; zur Zeit der Fertigung der Maske des Nachti, die ja zeitlich etwas später als die anderen Masken angesiedelt werden kann, jedoch nicht mehr.

Schluss

Die Einzeichnung der Blutgefäße in Augen aus Assiut lässt sich für einen eng umrissenen Zeitraum belegen (Mitte/Ende 11. Dynastie bis ca. Ende der Regierungszeit Sesostris' I. in der 12. Dynastie). Daher stellen die Blutgefäße im Auge im Gegensatz zu z. B. der Einfärbung der Augenwinkel, die in vielen Regionen des Mittleren Reiches zu finden ist, eine lokale Tradition dar, die über mehrere Generationen unter spezifischen Künstlern weitertradiert wurde (ca. 2055–1870 v. Chr.). Dieses Charakteristikum ist nicht in anderen Regionen derselben Zeit zu finden,[72] so dass davon ausgegangen werden kann, dass zumindest die Künstler, die Blutgefäße im Auge einzeichneten, nicht zwischen den Nekropolen umherreisten, sondern lokal fest angesiedelt waren.[73] Dies belegt noch einmal die Hypothese einer lokalen und eben nicht zentralisierten Produktion von Särgen. Die Einzeichnung der Blutgefäße ist ferner nicht als spezifisches Merkmal einer einzelnen Werkstatt zu identifizieren, sondern mit individuellen Künstlern, die dieses Detail bei der Dekoration der Särge hinzufügten.

Einige Merkmale der Dekoration der Udjataugen auf Särgen im Mittleren Reich scheinen innerhalb der verschiedenen künstlerischen Zentren Ober- und Unterägyptens allgemein verbreitet gewesen zu sein. Dazu gehört die rote Färbung der Augenwinkel sowie die Ausarbeitung des Irisbereichs, der oftmals differenziert gestaltet wurde, also mit Abtrennung von Iris und Pupille. Beides wurde häufig

---

72 Vgl. ähnlich in Bezug auf die Stelenherstellung Ilin-Tomich 2017: 163, der aufzeigt, dass Elemente lokaler Tradition nicht über den Einflussbereich des jeweiligen Zentrums hinaus zu finden sind. Dennoch wurden die lokalen Handwerker und Künstler durch die künstlerischen Zentren dieser Zeit (Memphis und Theben) beeinflusst, wie Objekte aus verschiedenen Nekropolen, die stilistische Ähnlichkeiten und gleiche Produktionsweisen/Herstellungsprozesse aufweisen, zeigen; siehe dazu in Bezug auf Holzmodelle Eschenbrenner-Diemer 2017: 165f.

73 Einen ähnlichen Befund konnte Ilin-Tomich 2018: 88–93, für die Opferteller aus Assiut feststellen. Die Mobilität von Künstlern aus regionalen Zentren stellt Ilin-Tomich 2017: 163, auch in Bezug auf Stelen in Frage: „The available evidence rather speaks against the models implying the high degree of artists' mobility. The long-term persistence of local artistic traditions suggests that most artists producing private memorial stelae were neither trained at the royal residence, nor moved around Egypt within teams of artisans. One would rather assume that artists were trained locally, learning their trade directly from the predecessors."

umgesetzt, war jedoch anscheinend nicht verpflichtend, da auf Särgen auch Udjataugen ohne gefärbte Augenwinkel und/oder differenziertem Irisbereich belegt sind.[74]

Die Ausarbeitung der Augenwinkel und/oder des Irisbereichs konnte innerhalb der einzelnen Regionen unterschiedlich umgesetzt werden, wodurch sich regionalspezifische Details fassen lassen.[75] Nur in Assiut wurde den Augen mit der Einzeichnung der Blutgefäße aber ein individuelles Detail hinzugefügt, das sich nicht in anderen Regionen findet und somit heute ein Alleinstellungsmerkmal Assiuts bildet.

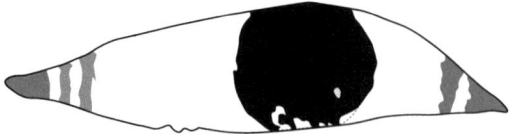

Abb. 6: Auge auf dem Sarg des Senebni, Kairo, Ägyptisches Museum, JdE 29339 (Sheikh Abd'el-Gournah). Umzeichnung: N. Gräßler.

Abb. 7: Auge auf dem Sarg der Nub-her-redi, Kairo, Ägyptisches Museum, JdE 31632 (Deir el-Bahari). Umzeichnung: N. Gräßler.

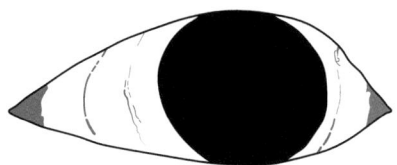

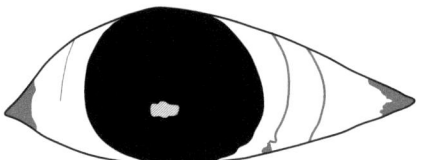

Abb. 8: Rechtes Auge auf dem Sarg Kairo, Ägyptisches Museum, CG 28001 (Achmim). Umzeichnung: N. Gräßler.

Abb. 9: Linkes Auge auf dem Sarg Kairo, Ägyptisches Museum, CG 28001 (Achmim). Umzeichnung: N. Gräßler.

74 Siehe z. B. ohne gerötete Augenwinkel und mit schwarzem stilisiertem Irisbereich: Sarg der Imi, Assiut, Turin, Museo Egizio S. 14457; innerer Sarg des Djehutinacht, Deir el-Bersha, Boston, Museum of Fine Arts 21.962a; mit geröteten Augenwinkeln, aber schwarzem, stilisiertem Irisbereich siehe z. B.: Sarg der Neby, Beni Hassan, Boston, Museum of Fine Arts 04.2058; Sarg des Ameny, Meir, New York, Metropolitan Museum 11.150.39a, b; Sarg des Wah, Theben, New York, Metropolitan Museum 20.3.202a, b; mit geröteten Augenwinkeln und differenziertem Irisbereich siehe z. B.: Sarg des Chnumnacht, Meir (?), New York, Metropolitan Museum 15.2.2a, b; Sarg der Nephthys, Meir, New York, Metropolitan Museum 11.150.15a–c; auch bei Einlegeaugen: Augeneinlage aus Deir el-Bersha, Boston, Museum of Fine Arts 21.10548.

75 Aus der Region Theben sind der Autorin drei Särge der 13./14. Dynastie bekannt, bei denen die Rotfärbung der Augenwinkel sehr charakteristisch ist: Sarg T6C der Chonsu aus Sheikh Abd'el-Gournah, Kairo, Ägyptisches Museum, CG 28028 (JdE 29340; Lacau 1906: 75f.); Sarg T10C des Senebni aus Sheikh Abd'el-Gournah, Kairo, Ägyptisches Museum, CG 28029 (JdE 29339; Lacau 1906: 77f.; Tf. 15) (beide Särge im Museum mit Fundort „Bersha" ausgewiesen!), und der Sarg T7C der Nub-her-redi aus Deir el-Bahari (angekauft), Kairo, Ägyptisches Museum, CG 28030 (JdE 31632; Lacau 1906: 79–81; Tf. 16). Die Augenwinkel sind bei allen Särgen rot eingefärbt. Direkt daneben wurden dann aber noch ein bis zwei senkrechte rote, entweder durchgehende oder gepunktete Linien angefügt, die vielleicht eine Schattierung oder Auslaufen der Rötung darstellen sollen (vgl. Abb. 6 und 7). Eine weitere Besonderheit ist charakteristisch für die Särge der 10. Dynastie aus Achmim: Hier wurden um den Irisbereich noch zwei bis drei parallele, halbkreisförmige, dünne rote Linien gezogen. Ob hier ebenfalls Blutgefäße imitiert werden sollten? Siehe die Särge Kairo, Ägyptisches Museum, CG 28001 (vgl. Abb. 8 und 9); CG 28013; CG 28015.

Bibliographie

Brovarski 1988: E. Brovarski, Mummy Mask, in: S. D'Auria et al. (Hgg.), Mummies & Magic. The Funerary Art of Ancient Egypt (Boston 1988), 119.

Bothmer 2004: B. Bothmer, Eyes and Iconography in the Splendid Century: King Amenhotep III and his Aftermath, in: M. Cody (Hg.), Egyptian Art: Selected Writings of Bernard V. Bothmer (Oxford 2004), 443–464.

Casini 2017: E. Casini, Remarks on Ancient Egyptian Cartonnage Mummy Masks from the Late Old Kingdom to the End of the New Kingdom, in: J. Chyla et al. (Hgg.), Current Research in Egyptology 2016 (Oxford 2017), 56–73.

Chassinat & Palanque 1911: É. Chassinat & Ch. Palanque, Une campagne de fouilles dans la nécropole d'Assiout (Mémoires publiés par les membres de l'Institut Français d'Archéologie Orientale du Caire 24; Kairo 1911).

Connor 2018: S. Connor, Sculpture Workshops: Who, Where and for Whom?, in: G. Miniaci et al. (Hgg.), The Arts of Making in Ancient Egypt. Voices, Images, and Objects of Material Producers 2000–1550 BC (Leiden 2018), 11–30.

D'Amicone et al. 2009: E. D'Amicone et al. (Hgg.), Egitto mai visto. La montagna dei morti: Assiut quattromila anni fa (Trento 2009).

Delvaux & Therasse 2015: L. Delvaux & I. Therasse, Sarcophages – Sous les étoiles de Nout (Brüssel 2015).

Dohrmann 2004: K. Dohrmann, Arbeitsorganisation, Produktionsverfahren und Werktechnik – eine Analyse der Sitzstatuen Sesostris' I. aus Lischt (Diss. Göttingen 2004).

Drenkhahn 1976: R. Drenkhahn, Die Handwerker und ihre Tätigkeiten (Ägyptologische Abhandlungen 31; Wiesbaden 1976).

Eschenbrenner-Diemer 2017: G. Eschenbrenner-Diemer, From the Workshop to the Grave: the Case of Wooden Funerary Models, in: G. Miniaci et al. (Hgg.), Company of Images: Modelling the Imaginary World of Middle Kingdom Egypt (2000–1500 BC) (Orientalia Lovaniensia Analecta 262; Leuven u.a. 2017), 133–191.

Franke 1994: D. Franke, Das Heiligtum des Heqaib auf Elephantine (Studien zur Archäologie und Geschichte Altägyptens 9; Heidelberg 1994).

Freed et al. 2009: R. Freed et al. (Hgg.), The Secrets of Tomb 10A (Boston 2009).

Freed 1996: R. Freed, Stela Workshops of Early Dynasty 12, in: P. Der Manuelian (Hg.), Studies in Honor of William Kelly Simpson, Bd. 1 (Boston 1996), 297–336.

Grässler 2017: N. Gräßler, Konzepte des Auges im alten Ägypten (Studien zur altägyptischen Kultur, Beihefte 20; Hamburg 2017).

Grajetzki 2010: W. Grajetzki, Rezension zu Rainer Hannig, Zur Paläographie der Särge aus Assiut, in: The Journal of Egyptian Archaeology 96, 2010, 287–289.

Hannig 1990: R. Hannig, Sarg des Nacht, in: A. Eggebrecht (Hgg.), Suche nach Unsterblichkeit. Totenkult und Jenseitsglaube im Alten Ägypten (Mainz 1990), 58–61.

Hannig 2006: R. Hannig, Zur Paläographie der Särge aus Assiut (Hildesheimer ägyptologische Beiträge 47; Hildesheim 2006).

Ilin-Tomich 2018: A. Ilin-Tomich, Centralized and Local Production, Adaption, and Imitation. Twelfth Dynasty Offering Tables, in: G. Miniaci et al. (Hgg.), The Arts of Making in Ancient Egypt. Voices, Images, and Objects of Material Producers 2000–1550 BC (Leiden 2018), 81–100.

Ilin-Tomich 2017: A. Ilin-Tomich, From Workshop to Sanctuary. The Production of Late Middle Kingdom Memorial Stelae (Middle Kingdom Studies 6; London 2017).

Kahl 2008: J. Kahl, Rezension zu Rainer Hannig, Zur Paläographie der Särge aus Assiut, in: Orientalistische Literaturzeitung 103, 2008, Sp. 320–328.

Kahl et al. 2017: J. Kahl, A. Alansary, U. Verhoeven, T. Beck, E. Czyżewska-Zalewska, E. Gervers & A. Kilian, The Asyut Project: Twelfth Season of Fieldwork (2016), in: Studien zur Altägyptischen Kultur 46, 2017, 113–151.

Kahl 2018: J. Kahl, The Tomb of Mesehti, in: J. Kahl, M. El-Hamrawi & U. Verhoeven, The Asyut Project: Thirteenth Season of Fieldwork (2017), in: Studien zur Altägyptischen Kultur 47, 2018, 137–148.

Kahl 2019: J. Kahl, Asyut, in: J. Kahl, A. M. Sbriglio, P. Del Vesco & M. Trapani, Asyut. The Excavations of the Italian Archaeological Mission (1906–1913) (Studi del Museo Egizio 1; Modena 2019), 7–38.

Kamal 1916: A. Bey Kamal, Fouilles à Deir Dronka et à Assiout, in: Annales du Service des antiquités de l'Égypte 16, 1916, 65–114.

KAMAL 1934: M. Moharram Kamal, Trois sarcophages du Moyen Empire provenant de la nécropole d'Assiout, in: Annales du Service des antiquités de l'Égypte 34, 1934, 49–53.

LACAU 1906: P. Lacau, Catalogue général des antiquités égyptiennes du Musée du Caire, 28087/28126: Sarcophages antérieurs au Nouvel Empire, 2 Bde. (Kairo 1906).

LAPP 1993: G. Lapp, Typologie der Särge und Sargkammern von der 6. bis 13. Dynastie (Studien zur Archäologie und Geschichte Altägyptens 7; Heidelberg 1993).

LORAND 2012: D. Lorand, The 'Four Schools of Art' of Senwosret I. Is it Time for a Revision?, in: K. A. Kóthay (Hg.), Art and Society. Ancient and Modern Contexts of Egyptian Art (Budapest 2012), 47–55.

OPPENHEIM 2015: A. Oppenheim, Artists and Workshops. The Complexity of Creation, in: OPPENHEIM ET AL. 2015: 23–27.

OPPENHEIM ET AL. 2015: A. Oppenheim et al. (Hgg.), Ancient Egypt Transformed. The Middle Kingdom (New York 2015).

RIGAULT 2009: P. Rigault, Masque de momie avec plastron, in: M. Étienne (Hg.), Les portes du ciel. Visions du monde dans l'Égypte ancienne (Paris 2009), 149–150.

SCHULZ 1993: R. Schulz, Sarg des Nacht, in: A. Eggebrecht (Hg.), Antike Welt im Pelizaeus-Museum. Die ägyptische Sammlung (Mainz 1993), 41–43.

SCHULZ 2009: R. Schulz, Mummy Mask, in: SCHULZ & SEIDEL 2009: 36f.

SCHULZ & SEIDEL 2009: R. Schulz & M. Seidel (Hgg.), Egyptian Art: The Walters Art Museum (Baltimore 2009).

SEIDEL 1993: M. Seidel, Mumienmaske eines Beamten, in: A. Eggebrecht (Hg.), Antike Welt im Pelizaeus-Museum. Die ägyptische Sammlung (Mainz 1993), 44f.

SEIDEL 1990: M. Seidel, Kastensarg des Upuaut-nacht, in: A. Eggebrecht (Hg.), Suche nach Unsterblichkeit. Totenkult und Jenseitsglaube im Alten Ägypten (Mainz 1990), 94–96.

SHAW 2000: I. Shaw (Hg.), The Oxford History of Ancient Egypt (Oxford 2000).

STRUDWICK & DAWSON 2019: N. Strudwick & J. Dawson (Hgg.), Ancient Egyptian Coffins. Past – Present – Future (Oxford – Philadelphia 2019).

TAYLOR & VANDENBEUSCH 2018: J. Taylor & M. Vandenbeusch (Hgg.), Ancient Egyptian Coffins. Craft Tradition and Functionality (British Museum Publications on Egypt and Sudan 4; Leuven u.a. 2018).

VERCOUTTER & GRIMAL 1981: J. Vercoutter & J. Grimal (Hgg.), Un siècle de fouilles francaises en Égypte. 1880–1890. A l'occasion du Centenaire de l'École du Caire (IFAO) (Kairo 1981).

WILLEMS 1988: H, Willems, Chests of Life. A Study of the Typology and Conceptual Development of Middle Kingdom Standard Class Coffins (Mededelingen en Verhandelingen van het Vooraziatisch-Egyptisch Genootschap "Ex Oriente Lux" 25; Leiden 1988).

WILLEMS 2010: H. Willems, Rezension zu Rainer Hannig, Zur Paläographie der Särge aus Assiut, in: Lingua Aegyptia 18, 2010, 359–366.

WILLEMS 2014: H. Willems, Historical and Archaeological Aspects of Egyptian Funerary Culture. Religious Ideas and Ritual Practice in Middle Kingdom Elite Cemeteries (Culture and History of the Ancient Near East 73; Leiden – Boston 2014).

ZITMAN 2010: M. Zitman, The Necropolis of Assiut. A Case Study of Local Egyptian Funerary Culture from the Old Kingdom to the End of the Middle Kingdom, I: Text, II: Maps, Plans of Tombs, Illustrations, Tables, Lists (Orientalia Lovaniensia Analecta 180; Leuven – Paris – Walpole, MA 2010).

The Coffin of Nakhti (S1Shu) at the Shutb Storage Museum in Asyut

Mohamed Abdelrahiem

The coffin of Nakhti, published fully in the present article for the first time, is stored in the Storage Museum of the village of Shutb at Asyut under No. 1, and measures 1.99 m in length, 49.50 cm in width, and the overall height is c. 60.0 cm. The coffin is said to come from an undocumented excavation at "Gebel Asyut al-gharbi", therefore, the exact find-spot of this piece is not mentioned. The present study gives a detailed description of the coffin's construction, decoration, and the translation of the inscriptions on the bands. Based on the parallels, textual reasons, epigraphical and paleographical features, the coffin is most probably dated to the early 12th Dynasty, reaching into the early years of Senwosret I. Furthermore, the study pinpoints the significance of the Middle Kingdom coffins in their general aspect of being a funerary object.[1]

1. Introduction

According to the plan of the Egyptian Supreme Council of Antiquities for developing the Storage Museums, thousands of objects stored in the Egyptian Museum at Cairo for long time, were sent back to the sites in which they were discovered. Among these objects are 60 sealed wooden boxes which were sent back to Asyut on 30th November 2008, and stored in the Storage Museum of the village of Shutb.[2] The boxes have serial numbers from 1 to 80, however, the boxes Nos. 2 to 22 are not among the collection. I do not know whether they do not belong to the Asyutian sites and, therefore, they were sent to somewhere else in the nearby, or they are still in the Egyptian Museum in Cairo.[3] Whatever, the box No. 1, which contains the coffin under discussion, is labeled "Magazine of Asyut Coffins, Al-Minya" (Fig. 1a), while all the other boxes have the uniform label "Magazine No. 3, Monuments of Gebel Asyut" (Fig. 2).

On 16th June 2014, the boxes were opened and their contents were registered in a special book entitled "Register Book of the Boxes at the Basement of the Egyptian Museum in Cairo". This hard work was accomplished in October 2015 by the following SCA members, to whom I would like to express my deep appreciation: Mr. Abdelsatar Ahmed, Director General of Asyut, Mrs. Nadia Naguib, Director of Shutb Storage Museum, Mrs. Magda Shawki, Chief Inspector of Abhnoub, Mr. Medhat Fayez, Inspector of Asyut inspectorate and Mr. Osama Sadak, SCA Photographer.

Worn inventories, recording the number of the pieces, were found inside the boxes. The inventories entitled "Magazines of Al-Minya, Magazine No. 3, Monuments of Gebel Asyut", were signed by the three SCA members who have packed the objects on 18th July 1961. As the signatures show, this committee included Mr. Gamal Abdelhamid, Mr. Motawa Elbalbwshey and was headed by Mr. Ali Elkhouly, who sealed the boxes with his private seal (Fig. 3). Noteworthy, the year 1961 in which the objects were packed is confirmed by many humbled papers (pieces of newspaper, envelopes and packets of cigarettes)

---

1   I am very grateful to Professor Jochem Kahl (Freie Universität Berlin) for a critical review, all remaining mistakes are entirely my responsibility.

2   The village of Shutb locates ca. 5.5 km to the south of Asyut on the western bank of the Nile. The modern town is identified with the Ancient Egyptian city *Šзs-ḥtp*, which is very often mentioned together with its ram-headed god Khnum, as capital of the 11th Nome of Upper Egypt, see GARDINER 1947: 67 [367]; GOMAÀ 1986: 250–251.

3   Unfortunately, there is a box, which bears also No. 1, including four wooden faces and four hands of anthropoid coffins, probably, it was erroneously sent to Shutb Magazine, although it definitely belongs to Meir as its label indicates: "Magazine 3, Monuments of Meir".

Fig. 1a: Box No. 1 packed the coffin of Nakhti (S1Shu) (Photo: Osama Sadak 2014; © Shutb Magazine Project).

Fig. 1b: The coffin of Nakhti (S1Shu) enveloped by the fragments of other coffins
(Photo: Osama Sadak 2014; © Shutb Magazine Project).

Fig. 2: Sample of the boxes transferred from Cairo to Shutb Storage Museum at Asyut
(Photo: Osama Sadak 2014; © Shutb Magazine Project).

found in some boxes (Fig. 4). As I have been informed, around that time there was only one inspectorate for Middle Egypt located in Al-Minya. The areas under this inspectorate's supervision used to use a
closed tomb as a magazine. Three of these magazines were known at that time: Magazine (1) in Malawi,
Magazine (2) in Meir and Magazine (3) in Gebel Asyut.[4] This could clarify why the inventories were
labeled "Magazines of Al-Minya", whereas the objects came from Asyut.

---

4   Personal communication by the Director of Shutb Storage Magazine, Mr. Medhat Fayez Hana in 2017. It is worth noting
    that after discovering the Tomb of Nakhti in 1903, Émile Chassinat used Tomb IV/N12.2 of Khety II as a magazine because
    it was secured with iron bars. It is interesting that traces of this relocation were unearthed by *The Asyut Project*, see KAHL
    2007: 31; J. Kahl, in: KAHL ET AL. 2016: xi–xii, 339–343.

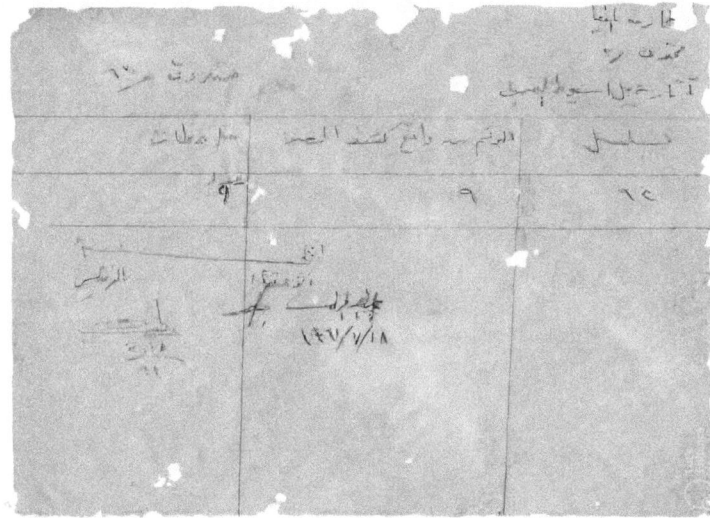

Fig. 3: Sample of the worn inventories found in box No. 63
(Photo: Mohamed Abdelrahiem 2017; © Shutb Magazine Project).

The material of the boxes is relatively disparate, as it includes temple blocks, stelae, figurines, offering tables, pottery, ushabtis, coffins and coffin fragments. The diversity of the objects shows that they came from different areas of Asyut and not exclusively from Gebel Asyut. The inscribed blocks of the Wepwawet-temple, for instance, are derived from an illicit excavation in the city.[5] Except some other objects which could be identified,[6] all other materials, unfortunately, came from undocumented excavations. The approval to study the material of the boxes was given in 2015 to the *Shutb Magazine Project*,[7] funded by Freie Universität Berlin[8] and directed by Prof. Jochem Kahl and the author. As already mentioned, the coffin of Nakhti which I deal with, was found in box No. 1, enveloped by a lid, front, back and bottom panels of other coffins (Fig. 1b).[9] The coffin is registered in the Storage Museum of Shutb under No. 1, and henceforth referred to as S1Shu.[10]

---

5 During illicit excavation, some decorated blocks from the reigns of Ramesses II and Akhenaton occurred eight meters under a modern house at Alwet el-Nasara "the mound of the Christians", see Gabra 1931; Kahl 2007: 44, 58.

6 On closer inspection, however, the material might reveal more information. For instance, the bulk of Wepwawet stelae and canid figurines packed together in box No. 57, might belong to the "Salakhana Trove" discovered by Gerald Wainwright in 1922 in the so called "Salakhana Tomb" of Djefai-Hapi III. About 500 to 600 stelae and more than 50 figurines of this cache have been collected and published by Terence DuQuesne in DuQuesne 2009. There was also an earlier exhibition of some of these stelae in Cairo, published in DuQuesne 2007.

7 The project is the offspring of *The Asyut Project*, a joint Egyptian-German mission, which has conducted fourteen successive seasons of fieldwork at Gebel Asyut al-gharbi since September 2003. For the publications of *The Asyut Project*, see the website: https://www.aegyptologie.uni-mainz.de/publikationenpublications/

8 On behalf of the *Shutb Magazine Project*, I would like to express my indebtedness for the generosity of our sponsor Ägyptologisches Seminar, Freie Universität Berlin, without which the realization of this project would have been practically impossible. I would like also to express my deep appreciation and sincere thanks to the staff of the Ministry of State for Archaeology who helped us in various ways. Special thanks to the State Minister of Archaeology Prof. Dr. Khaled El-Anany, to the former Chairman, Dr. Mostafa Amin and the present Dr. Mostafa Waziry, to the former Head of the Foreign and Egyptian Mission Affairs and Permanent Committee, Dr. Mohamed Ismail and to the present Dr. Nashwa Gaber, to the former Director General of Asyut, Mr. Abdelsatar Ahmed and to the present Mr. Mahmoued Mahdy, to the Director of Shutb Storage Magazine, Mr. Asam Maghazy, to the staff of the Magazine, Mr. Medhat Fayez and Mr. Adly Garas, to our accompanying inspector Mr. Tarek Hassan. The staff of *Shutb Magazine Project* was most co-operative in the work. In this connection my thanks are due to Prof. Jochem Kahl, Director of the project, to Dr. Teodozja Rzeuska, Dr. Andrea Kilian, Mrs. Aneta Cedro, Mr. Adel Refat, Mr. Fritz Barthel, the photographer, Reis Ahmed Atitou, Reis Aid, and our driver, Sobhey.

9 Supposing that all these fragments belong to a single coffin, they are registered together under No. 2.

10 This sigla (S1Shu) means, (S) Asyut (Siut), coffin number (1) in (Shu) Shutb Magazine.

Fig. 4: Sample of humbled paper found inside different boxes (Photo: Mohamed
Abdelrahiem 2017; © Shutb Magazine Project).

2. Description

S1Shu measures 1.99 m in length, 49.5 cm in width, and the height is 49.0 cm. It is set on four legs,
therefore the length of ca. 4.0 cm must be added to the preserved height of 49.0 cm of the coffin. On
adding the height of the lid, which in all known cases is more substantial and thicker than side panels,
the overall height of the coffin comes up to ca. 60.0 cm. The rectangular coffin with its flat lid is made of
several wooden panels held together by wooden pegs.[11] The dowels on the upper and lower parts of the
side panels are used to construct the panels together. The coffin was supported by four wooden curved
blocks used as legs (Pl. 32b), the inner side of the lid was also supported by three wooden props, but one
of them has fallen (Pl. 33a).

---

11 Middle Kingdom coffins are usually made from several pieces of wood constructed together. For this technique, cf. ARNOLD
   1988: 34–39, 147–149, pls. 13–14.

The coffin is substantially well preserved, notwithstanding that the wood is cracked at some points, especially on the lid and the floor panel. The plaster flaked off and the blue colour of the inscription vanished on some parts leaving the original brown colour of the wood visible. The interior of the coffin is undecorated;[12] the wood is left untreated and covered with stucco (Pl. 33b). The outside is plastered and then painted yellow; the decoration and the hieroglyphic signs are painted in blue after they were accurately drawn in black ink. The lid is inscribed with three horizontal lines of hieroglyphs down the centre (Pl. 33c). On the top of the four outer sides there are two horizontal lines of hieroglyphs with four sets of double vertical columns placed underneath on the front and back sides (Pl. 34a–b); one set of double columns is placed in the middle of the two short sides (Pl. 35a–b). The hieroglyphic signs on the lid, the front side and the foot end are oriented from the right to the left, while the signs on the back side and the head end are starting from left to right.[13] As suggested by some scholars, the textual layout of the coffin must be read in relation to the Egyptian mortuary conceptions.[14] Hence, Leonard Lesko[15] suggested that the horizontal band of texts intersected by vertical bands on the exterior of the coffin gives the impression of a wrapped package. Harco Willems, however, has understood the orientation of the text in the way that they are legible from the corpse's "viewpoint", running from head to foot on the long sides and the lid.[16] The horizontal and vertical edges of the coffin are lined by bands composed of white coloured rectangles.[17] The front panel is decorated with a pair of wedjat-eyes over a white coloured square. The eyebrow and the eyelash are painted blue, while the sclera and the pupil are painted white and black respectively.[18] Depicting the pair of the eyes near the head end on the front side, just in front of the deceased's face, confirms that the body was to be laid on his left side.[19] This side was oriented to the East, hence, the deceased could watch sunrise by these magical eyes which enable him to participate in the solar cycle and to see the offerings in the tomb chapel.[20]

The two short ends of the coffin include a representation of the four sons of Horus squatting to the right and left of the text columns.[21] Above their heads, just beneath the second line, are small squares containing their names;[22] *Ḥˁpy* "Hapi" and *Jmst* "Amset" are placed at the head end, while *Qbḥ-snw=f* "Qebehsenuef" and *Dwꜣ-mwt=f* "Duamutef" are on the foot end.[23]

---

12 Some scholars suggested that the choice between a coffin with or without inner decoration is a deliberate choice depending on the wealth of the coffin's owner and maybe also his connection to the local governors and the royal court, see GRAJETZKI 2016: 25–26, 29–30. In fact, the Asyutian coffins with a highly elaborated decoration on the outside indicate that their owners have had some resources, but the coffins with the inner decoration are generally less common at Asyut. From the 292 coffins studied by M. Zitman (ZITMAN 2010: II, 110–151, List 1), only 58 coffins have had interior decoration. For the main study of the interior decoration of Asyutian coffins, see NEUGEBAUER & PARKER 1960, 1964, 1969.

13 According to L. Lesko (LESKO 1982: 41), the coffins were ordinarily laid out by the artists before having the texts filled, and the scribes, in this case, did write either from left to right or right to left, cf. FISCHER 1977: 5, 36, n. 98.

14 In his publication of the sarcophagus of pharaoh Merenptah, J. Assmann (ASSMANN 1972a: 127–130; ASSMANN 1972b: 47–73) arrived at this conclusion, cf. also R. Nyord (NYORD 2014: 29–44), who has adopted these conceptions in his analysis of the Middle Kingdom Coffins.

15 LESKO 1982: 39.

16 WILLEMS 1988: 119.

17 These frames can take various forms, e.g. gilded or monochrome, see WILLEMS 1988: 120, n. 15.

18 The magical eyes became a regular feature on the outside of the Middle Kingdom coffins, see HOFFMEIER 1991: 70.

19 LESKO 1982: 39.

20 Cf. WILLEMS 1988: 120 and see below.

21 As the coffin of *Mrj-jb* shows, the head and foot panels during the Old Kingdom were discerned by the hieroglyph (*tp*) of the head in the north and the hieroglyph (*rdwj*) of feet in the south, see DONADONI ROVERI 1969: fig. 19.

22 These components seem to be optional, as some similar coffins have only added the squatting gods, or the squares with the name of the four sons of Horus, or omitted both, see ZITMAN 2010: I, 265.

23 Representing the four sons of Horus is highly remarkable, being one of the earliest examples for figures of major deities in private contexts in Egypt, see GRAJETZKI 2016: 33.

As already mentioned, S1Shu has come from an undocumented excavation and, accordingly, its find-spot is unknown.[24] However, the coffin is definitely derived from Gebel Asyut al-gharbi, as it has the typical style of Asyutian coffins. The above-mentioned outer decoration or the so-called "Siutian style of the coffin's exterior decoration" and the textual programme or "Siutian coffin textual programme" indicate Asyut as the place of the coffin's origin.[25] S1Shu, as will be further discussed below, is also dis-tinguished by its own paleography or its "Siutian traits".[26] For example, (1) the wedjat-eye on the front panel with a combined thorn and spiral is a typical rendition of the wedjat-eye in Asyut,[27] (2) the title *nb R₃-qrr.t* (Texts 3, 6) is a typical Asyutian epithet designating Anubis as the lord of the necropolis,[28] (3) the *jm₃ḫj ḥr* formula and the self-laudatory phrases (Text 4) are the typical combination on coffins from the Asyutian region, (4) the placement of *Bitte* 33a, (5) the Asyutian reversal of the epithets of Anubis *ḫntj zḥ-nṯr nb zp₃* on the lid (Text 1), and (6) the proper position of *nb R₃-qrr.t* in the *ḥtp-dj-nzw* for-mula with Anubis on the back (Text 6),[29] all these features combine some of the aspects unique to the Asyutian traditions.[30]

Another prominent feature of S1Shu is the extensive use of expletive or "filler" strokes in the middle of the words.[31] It appears in many words such as [hieroglyphs] , [hieroglyphs] (Text 6) and in [hieroglyphs] (Texts 10, 12). This feature may look trivial at first sight because the absence of this random stroke is not consistent in such words. Nevertheless, this phenomenon was chronologically in excess during the Old Kingdom[32] and became more limited in the course of the First Intermediate Period at various Upper Egyptian sites.[33] In Asyut, however, it was also extensively employed in the tombs of the late Heracleopolitan Period.[34] The phenomenon seems to have culminated in the 11th Dynasty, beginning with the reign of Intef II.[35] Wolfgang Schenkel observed that the texts of the early 12th Dynasty also exhibit this phenomenon.[36] Examining the citations provided by Schenkel, Edward Brovarski added a modification that the exple-tive strokes continue to appear into the period of the co-regency of Senwosret I with Amenemhat I.[37] Nevertheless, the appearance of this feature sporadically in the texts of Dynasties 10–12, may weaken its ability as a dating criterion.[38]

The last feature to be observed on S1Shu, is the writing of the same word in two different forms. For example, *nṯr-ꜥ₃* in the Osiris formula (Text 4), is written with horizontal [hieroglyph] and vertical [hieroglyph] *ꜥ₃*. The word *prt-ḫrw* has the determinative of the bread-sign [hieroglyphs] in the festival context (Text 2), on the con-trary, it is written with the *ḥb*-sign [hieroglyphs] on Osiris formula (Text 2).

---

24 Asyut is the site with the highest number of Middle Kingdom coffins. They mostly came from undocumented excavations. In fact, the Asyutian coffins form the largest collection of all examples known today. H. Willems counts 277 Asyutian coffins, mentioning that new coffins from Asyut "appear on the art market or in private collections almost every year" (WILLEMS 2014: 156, 160), while Zitman, who studied the largest database of the Asyutian coffins, raises the number to 292 (ZITMAN 2010: II, 110–151, List 1), see BOMMAS 2017: 149, n. 1.

25 ZITMAN 2010: I, 367–368; II, 155–158 (appendix 2).

26 R. Hannig dealt with a database of 90 Middle Kingdom coffins from Asyut, which helped to identify the main features of the paleography of the region (HANNIG 2006: 34–40A), cf. the critical review from J. Kahl (KAHL 2008).

27 This is the specific feature of wedjat-eye of Asyut following category (B) of HANNIG 2006: 43–44.

28 HANNIG 2006: 93.

29 ZITMAN 2010: I, 368.

30 It is often easy to assign a single coffin to a certain place as specific details are typical for specific places. It can be assumed that most coffins were produced locally, perhaps in workshops attached in some way to the local governors or the local temples, see GRAJETZKI 2016: 26.

31 For the random stroke, see COUYAT & MONTET 1912: 13–14; SCHENKEL 1962: § 5 a–d; BROVARSKI 1989: 740–741.

32 For the function of the stroke in the Old Kingdom, see EDEL 1964: §§ 65–68; GARDINER 1957: 34, § 25, 534.

33 Cf. SCHENKEL 1962: 35–36; MAGEE 1983: 248.

34 GRIFFITH 1889: Siût III (pl. 11, line 30); IV (pl. 13, lines 8, 34); V (pl. 15, lines 7, 9, 33, 35, 37).

35 BROVARSKI 1998: 47, n. 50.

36 SCHENKEL 1962: § 5.

37 See BROVARSKI 1998: 47, cf. PETRIE 1907: pl. 9.

38 For using the stroke as a dating criterion, see BROVARSKI 1998: 47–51.

3. Text

The main textual programme of S1Shu is composed of a series of *ḥtp-dj-nzw, ḥtp-dj-(n)* and *ḏd-mdw-jn-Rˁ* formulas, followed by *jmꜣḥy-ḥr* and self-laudatory phrases, it runs as follows.

3.1 The Lid (Pl. 33c, Fig. 5)

Oriented from right to left, the lid includes three lines of inscriptions. Taking up the first line and a part of the second line, the *ḥtp-dj-nzw* formula asks Anubis for a happy passage to the Netherworld (Text 1). The *ḏd-mdw-jn-Rˁ* formula occupies the second line and a part of the third line; it requests an invocation offering on certain religious festivals (Text 2). The *ḥtp-dj-(n)* formula on the third line asks Anubis for a good burial in the West (Text 3).

Text 1: *ḥtp-dj-nzw* formula asking Anubis for a happy passage to the Netherworld, followed by *jmꜣḥy-ḥr* formula.

[1]*ḥtp-dj-nzw ꞽnpw*[(a)] *ḫntj zḥ-nṯr nb zpꜣ*[(b)]	An offering which the king and Anubis, Foremost of the God's Booth, Lord of Sepa, give:
šms sw kꜣ=f r swt wˁbwt jmjwt pt	May he be accompanied well by his ka to the pure places which are in the heaven,
zmꜣ=f tꜣ ḏꜣj=f bjꜣ dj zmjt ˁwj=sj r=f[(c)]	may he be committed to the earth, when he sails across the sky, that the western desert may extend its arms toward him,
[2]*jmꜣḥ(w)*[(d)] <N>*ḫtj jmꜣḥy ḥr*[(e)] *zmjt špswt ꜣḫw jmj=s*[(f)]	the revered one, <Na>khti, the revered one in the necropolis in which the glorious *ꜣḫw* exist.

(a)   The writing of the *ḥtp-dj-nzw* formula is the most common one on the Middle Kingdom monuments, see Barta 1968: 43, 53; A. Ilin-Tomich 2011; Franke 2003; Satzinger 1997; Bennett 1941.

(b)   *nb zpꜣ m swt=f nbwt* "Lord of Sepa in all his places" is expected here according to the most frequently attested use, the last three words of which are missing, see Barta 1968: 56. The order of Anubis' epithet *nb zpꜣ ḫntj zḥ-nṯr* is quite common on coffins from other sites. At Asyut, this series is only rarely found on the lid of some coffins datable to the late 11th and the beginning of the 12th Dynasties, see Lapp 1993: 266 (§ 475–476), n. 1, Blatt 19. The reversed order *ḫntj zḥ-nṯr*[39] *nb zpꜣ*[40] starts to gain the upper hand on the coffins of the 12th Dynasty, producing the typical Asyutian series with *ḫntj zḥ-nṯr* in the front which would be the only mode henceforth, see Zitman 2010: I, 241.

(c)   These formulas are encoded as Barta's *Bitten* 33a (*zmꜣ=f tꜣ*), 30a (*ḏꜣj=f bjꜣ*) and 32b (*dj zmjt ˁwj. sj r=f*), see Barta 1968: 40. As remarked by some scholars (Lapp 1986: 71 (§ 117), Folge 7W; Barta 1968: 38), these *Bitten* normally appear on the lids of the Asyutian coffins followed by the Asyutian formula *šms sw kꜣ=f r swt wˁbwt jmjwt pt* encoded as Barta's *Bitte* 33a, cf. Zitman 2010: I, 250.

(d)   According to W. Helck, the original meaning of *jmꜣḥy* is not "to be revered", but "to be well-provided" with offerings, rituals, etc. (Helck 1956: 68–70).

---

[39] For Anubis "Foremost of the *zḥ-nṯr*", see Willems 1988; 146. For *zḥ-nṯr* as the place where mummification was ceremonially re-enacted prior to the journey to Sais, see Altenmüller 1971–1972; Altenmüller 1972: 46–47; H. Altenmüller 1975: 755–756. For *zḥ-nṯr* as "purification tent", see Willems 1988: 146 and cf. Hoffmeier 1981: 176. For the writing of *zḥ-nṯr* on Middle Kingdom coffins, see Brovarski 1998: 69–61 (O21).

[40] For *zpꜣ* of which Anubis was frequently said to be the lord from the Old Kingdom onwards, see Gardiner 1947: 127–128 [395] and cf. Kees 1923: 90–92, who believes that *zpꜣ* might be an actual town, but he did not refer to its location. The word *zpꜣ* lacks here the phonetic complement ⌗, which usually recurs on coffins from the Old Kingdom onwards, see Lapp 1993: 210 (§ 488); Zitman 2010: I, 282. For the development of the writing of *zpꜣ*, see Brovarski 1998: 65–66.

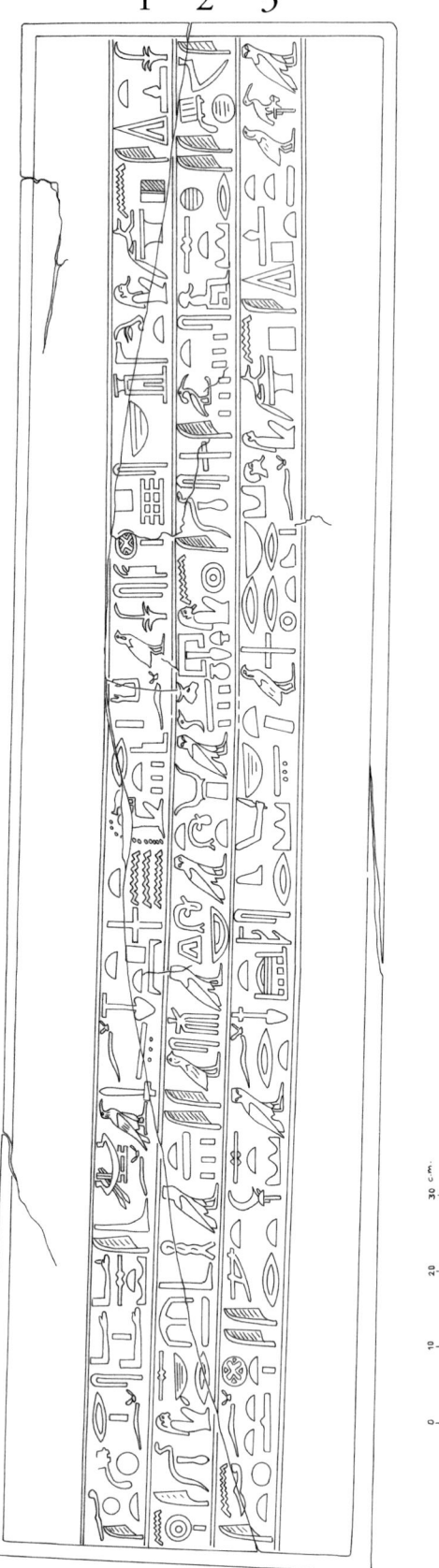

Fig. 5: Lid of S1Shu, Texts 1–3; © Shutb Magazine Project (Drawing: S. Shafik).

(e)   Writing *jmзḫ(w)* side by side with *jmзḫy* was common on Asyutian coffins,[41] this combination might reduce the value of this epithet for dating purposes.[42] As will be further discussed, it is quite common, however, for *jmзḫy ḫr* to occur several times in the same inscription, each time referring to a different god or goddess by whom the individual is said to be venerated, see DOXEY 1998: 95–96.

(f)   Cf. also the Asyutian coffins with the self-laudatory phrase *jmзḫy zmjt jmntt* "revered one within the western necropolis" in LAPP 1993: 130 (§ 291). For the effectiveness of *зḫw*-beings as well as the *зḫ*-deceased, see JANSEN-WINKELN 1996, cf. SCHULMAN 1986: 317; FRIEDMAN 1981.

Text 2: *ḏd-mdw-jn-Rᶜ* formula requesting an invocation offering on certain festivals.

[hieroglyphic text] 2
[hieroglyphic text] 3

²*ḏd-mdw-jn-Rᶜ*⁽ᵃ⁾ *prt-ḥrw t ḥnqt kзw зpdw m Wpt-wзt*⁽ᵇ⁾ *m Wзg*⁽ᶜ⁾ *m Msjt*⁽ᵈ⁾ *m Ḥb-Skr*⁽ᵉ⁾

ḏd-mdw-jn-Rᶜ ³*m Ḏḥwtt*⁽ᶠ⁾

Recitation by Ra: An invocation offering of bread, beer, oxen and fowl, in *Wpt-wзt*-feast, Wag-feast, *Msjt*-feast and Sokar-feast.

Recitation by Ra in Thoth-feast.

(a)   For the composition of *ḏd-mdw-jn-Rᶜ* formula on the Asyutian coffins of the 12th Dynasty, see LAPP 1993: 129 (§ 290).

(b)   For *Wpt-wзt* as a festival of the dead in the first month of the inundation, see GRAEFE 1986: 863; BONNET 1952: 843, cf. DUQUESNE 2003.

(c)   Wag-feast is the principal festival of the dead known as early as the 4th Dynasty and was celebrated during the Middle Kingdom on the 18th of the first month of the year, see ALTENMÜLLER 1977: 174; POSENER-KRIÉGER 1986.[43]

(d)   For the translation of *Msjt*-feast as "Supper of the beginning of the year", see PARKER 1952 and cf. R. El-Sayed (EL-SAYED 1975: 162 n. d, Appendix C [no. 17]), who reads *msjt* as *mswt* and translates it "feast of birth".[44] *Msjt*-feast was celebrated on the 30th of the fourth month of *šmw*. Judging from the data of the later New Kingdom which talk about *Msjt-tpj*, it might be expected that at least two such celebrations existed, see SPALINGER 1996: 32, n. 2., 59, n. 10.[45]

(e)   From the Middle Kingdom at least, two Sokar-festivals are known, one on 14th of the fourth month of the first season *зḫt*, and the other on 16th of the second month of the second season *prt*. In many ways, the festival of Sokar served the duty of completing the first season of the Egyptian year *зḫt*, see ALTENMÜLLER 1977: 175–176; BLEEKER 1967: 69–90; WOHLGEMUTH 1957; GABALLA & KITCHEN 1969: 1–76.

(f)   Significant is the location of the Thoth-feast after the Wag-feast. By the 12th Dynasty, if not earlier, the Thoth-feast was eventually associated with the Wag-feast on the 19th day, and this became the regular order after the Old Kingdom, see PARKER 1950: 36 (§§ 179–180); SPALINGER 1996: 37.[46]

---

41 See ZITMAN 2010: I, 100, n. 658–659; LAPP 1993: 129–130 (§ 291) and cf. DOXEY 1998: 95–96, who mentions that *jmзḫ* and *jmзḫy ḫr* have never appeared side by side in the same text in all known examples of coffins, tombs and statue bases.

42 For using *jmзḫw* and *jmзḫj* as dating criterion, see BROVARSKI 1998: 47–50. According to Zitman (ZITMAN 2010: I, 99–100), the tomb of Khety II (Tomb IV/N12.2) might be one of the first Asyutian examples showing the transition from *jmзḫw* to *jmзḫj*, cf. EDEL 1984: 98–99; SCHENKEL 1962: 49.

43 For the Wag-feast, see also BORCHARDT 1935: 34; WINTER 1951; KRAUSS 1998: 53–57; VYMAZALOVÁ 2008: 137–143; SPALINGER 2013: 616–624, cf. also U. Luft, who revised the date to day 18th of the second lunar month (LUFT 1994: 39–44). For the difference between civil calendar and lunar calendar, see DEPUYDT 1997.

44 Cf. ASSMANN 1984, 286; SETHE 1919: 303; HARI 1985: pl. 40, line 228.

45 Cf. the reference to a *msjt* in the "Annals" of Amenemhet II published by ALTENMÜLLER & MOUSSA 1991: 19 (M27).

46 For Thoth-feast and its conjunction with Wag-feast, see POSENER-KRIÉGER 1985: 35–43; SCHOTT 1950: 82.

Text 3: *ḥtp-dj-(n)* formula asking Anubis for a good burial in the West, followed by self-laudatory phrase.

[hieroglyphic inscription]

³*ḥtp-dj-Jnpw*[a] *tpj ḏw=f nb R3-qrr.t*[b]
jmj-wt[c] *nb t3 ḏsr*

qrst nfrt m zmjt jmntt

mry njwt=f twt[d] *Nḫtj*[e]

An offering which Anubis, who is on his mountain, lord of Ra-qereret, who is in *wt*, Lord of the Holy land, gives:

A good burial in the western desert,

the beloved of his entire township, Nakhti.

(a)   For reading *ḥtp-dj-Jnpw* as relative form like *ḥtp-dj-nzw* formula, implies that the mentioned god "gives" the offering "an offering which Anubis has given", instead of being the recipients "an offering given to Anubis", see WILLEMS 1996: 333 and cf. Zitman (ZITMAN 2010: I, 265, n. 1870), who supported this translation by referring to the Anubis formula on the back side (Text 6) which is a duplicate of that one, having the same meaning, although the later starts with *ḥtp-dj-nsw*.[47]

(b)   Ra-qereret is a name used for the Asyut necropolis (MONTET 1961: 136, 139; GOMAÀ 1956: 170–172; MAGEE 1988: 176–179), which is usually translated "Entrance of the Cavern" (B. ALTENMÜLLER 1975: 328), but Bommas (BOMMAS 2017: 168) translates it "tomb shafts" in a more general sense which are safeguarded by Anubis, suggesting that the name does not denote one particular locality, even though it is only attested with reference to Asyut.

(c)   Determining *wt* with the Land-sign ▱ (GARDINER 1957: Sign-list N21) suggests that it is a place. However, because the title *jmj-wt* has its special function in embalming (B. ALTENMÜLLER 1975: 328), it is usually translated "who is in the mummy wrappings/bindings" or "who is in the embalming place", see BOMMAS 2017: 168, 165.

(d)   The epithet "beloved of his township" is the most common epithet concerned with the township; it appears in tombs from Asyut, Deir Rifeh, El-Bersheh and Beni Hasan. Its use might have been restricted to the highest ranking local nobility to the period just prior the reunification to the early 12ᵗʰ Dynasty, see DOXEY 1998: 186–187, 307.

(e)   RANKE 1935: 212.2. For the owner of Asyutian coffins bearing the same name cf. List 1 in ZITMAN 2010: II, 184 [3], 185 [11].

3.2 The Front Side (Pl. 34a, Fig. 6)

The front panel shows two sections of hieroglyphic inscriptions oriented from right to left. The upper section displays two rows of inscription, while the lower one shows four sets of double vertical columns. The inscription on the first row comprises the *ḥtp-dj-nzw* formula requesting Osiris an invocation offering (Text 4). Taking up the second line and most of the columns, the series of brief *ḥtp-dj-(n)* phrases list the deities of the Great Ennead of Heliopolis (Text 5).

Text 4: *ḥtp-dj-nzw* formula requesting Osiris an invocation offering, followed by self-laudatory phrase.

¹*ḥtp-dj-nzw Wsjr*[a] *nb Ḏdw*[b] *nṯr ˁ3*[c] *nb 3bḏw*[d]
m swt=f nb(wt)[e]

prt-ḫrw[f] *t ḥnqt k3w 3bdw*

n k3 n jm3ḫy ḫr[g] *nṯr ˁ3 nb pt m swt=f nb(wt)*
w3ḥ tpj t3[h] *Nḫtj*

An offering which the king and Osiris, Lord of Busiris, the Great God, Lord of Abydos in all his places, give:

An invocation offering of bread, beer, oxen and fowl,

for the ka of the revered one by the Great God, Lord of the Heaven in all his places, enduring on earth, Nakhti.

---

47 Cf. also LAPP 1986: 32–33.

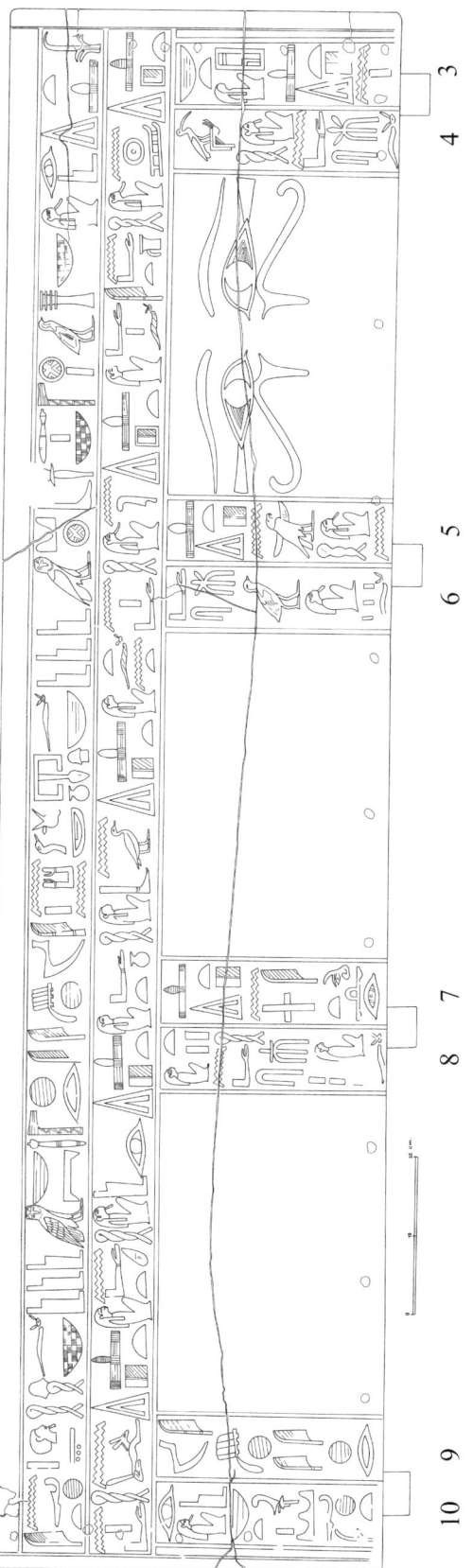

Fig. 6: Front side of S1Shu, Texts 4–5; © Shutb Magazine Project (Drawing: S. Shafik).

(a) According to Lapp (LAPP 1993: 144–146 (§ 322–324), 125–131 (§ 284–293), 197 (§ 453), Blatt 19), the series of epithets *nb Ḏdw nṯr ꜥ3 nb 3bḏw* is typical of the 12ᵗʰ Dynasty coffins, but he also remarked that *nṯr ꜥ3* in the *ḥtp-dj-nzw* formula of Osiris is already known since the end of the First Intermediate Period, as it appears on the façade of Tomb (IV/N12.2) of Khety II, cf. EDEL 1984: 98–99, figs. 14–15; ZITMAN 2010: I, 279–280. For the Osiris formula without *dj=f*, cf. *Bitte* 2 of BARTA 1968: 57, and for Osiris epithets, see BARTA 1968: 56, 74.

(b) For *Ḏdw* "Busiris" as part of the Osiris epithet *nb Ḏdw*, see BENNETT 1941: 77–82. For the filler stroke under the *njwt*-sign and its use as dating criterion, cf. BROVARSKI 1998: 50 and see below.

(c) The title *nṯr ꜥ3* is written in the same formula with horizontal ⊤ and vertical ⊤ *ꜥ3*. This combination is very rare on Asyutian coffins, cf. ZITMAN 2010: I, 280, and see below.

(d) For the different writing of *3bḏw* on the bases of Upper Egyptian sources, see BROVARSKI 1998: 50.

(e) Asyutian coffins frequently add some words after the phrase *m swt=f nb(wt)*, such as *m swt=f nb(wt) wꜥbwt, m swt=f nb(wt) wꜥbwt jmjt jmnt* or *jmjt ḥrt-nṯr*. Comparable phrases with *m swt=f nb(wt)* are quite common on documents from Upper Egypt, mainly during the First Intermediate Period and early Middle Kingdom, cf. ZITMAN 2010: I, 254. For *m swt=f nb(wt)* "in all his places" after the name of Osiris, as characteristic feature of the 11ᵗʰ Dynasty onwards, see BENNETT 1941: 80.

(f) *prt-ḥrw* is determined here with the *ḥb*-sign and with bread-sign on the lid (Text 2). Both writings are attested on Asyutian coffins from the Old Kingdom henceforth, see ZITMAN 2010: I, 279–280.

(g) For using *n k3 n jm3ḫy* from the reign of Amenemhat II onwards, eclipsing the old form *jm3ḫj* of the early Middle Kingdom, see BENNETT 1941: 79; DOXEY 1998: 94.

(h) For the self-laudatory phrase *w3ḥ tpj t3*, see DOXEY 1998: 282.

Text 5: Series of *ḥtp-dj-(n)* phrases list the deities of the Heliopolitan Great Ennead, followed by *jm3ḫy-ḥr* formula.

²*ḥtp-dj-n Rꜥ-Jtm ḥnꜥ Ḏrtj=f*⁽ᵃ⁾		An offering which Ra-Atum and his hand give.
ḥtp-dj-n Šw ḥnꜥ Tfnt⁽ᵇ⁾		An offering which Shu and Tefnut give.
ḥtp-dj-n Gb ḥnꜥ Nwt		An offering which Geb and Nut give.
ḥtp-dj-(n) Wsjr ḥnꜥ 3st		An offering (which) Osiris and Isis give.
ḥtp-dj-n Stḫ ḥnꜥ ³Nbt-ḥwt		An offering which Seth and Nephthys give.
ḥtp-dj-n ⁴Ḏḥwtt ḥnꜥ msjw=f		An offering which Thoth and his children give.
⁵*ḥtp-dj-n Dwn-ꜥnwj*⁽ᶜ⁾ *ḥn⁶ꜥ msjw=f*		An offering which Dunanui and his children give.
⁷*ḥtp-dj-n Jmj-Ḫntj-(n)-jr⁸tj*⁽ᵈ⁾ *ḥnꜥ msjw=f*		An offering which Imy-Chentienirty and his children give,
⁹*jm3ḫy ḥr ¹⁰Wsjr nb jmnt <N>ḫtj*		the revered one by Osiris, Lord of the West, <Na>khti.

(a) The female element or partner of the creator deity, often identified as the goddesses Iusaas or Hathor Nebet-hetepet, was referred to as the Hand of Atum, see PINCH 2002: 136.

(b)   The text names the gods of the Great Ennead of Heliopolis in their basic form. For the list of the Great Ennead members, see Barta 1973: 61–72. For naming the Great Ennead on the Asyutian coffins of the 12th Dynasty, see Lapp 1993: 126–128 (§ 289), Abb. 138–139 and cf. Lepsius 1865: 1866, pls. 1–2.

(c)   For *Dwn-ꜥnwj* "He who spreads out his arms", see Leitz 2002: VII, 525–526 with further references.

(d)   For *Jmj-Ḫntj-(n)-jrtj* "He who is in Chentienirty", see Leitz 2002: III, 394–396, n. 30 with further references.

3.3 The Back Side (Pl. 34b, Fig. 7)

The textual programme of the back side is nearly identical to the one of the front side, but deviations do occur. In this case, the inscription oriented from left to right, the *ḥtp-dj-nzw* formula in the first line asks Anubis for a good burial in the tomb in the West (Text 6), the brief series of *ḥtp-dj-(n)* phrases occupies the second row and the first columns, and enumerates the gods of the Little Ennead of Heliopolis (Text 7). The rest of the columns record a *ḏd-mdw-jn-Rꜥ* formula addressing Ha, the god of the West (Text 8) and a *ḥtp-dj-nzw* formula addressing the coffin's owner himself (Text 9).

Text 6: *ḥtp-dj-nzw* formula asking Anubis for a good burial in the tomb in the West, followed by *jmꜣḫ(y)* formula.

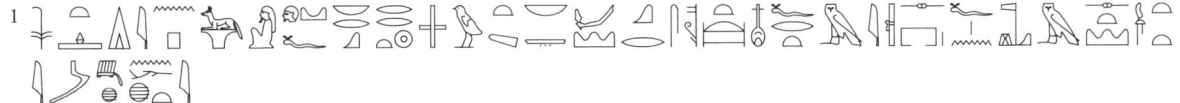

[1]*ḥtp-dj-nzw Jnpw*[(a)] *tpj ḏw=f nb Rꜣ-qrr.t jmj-wt nb tꜣ ḏsr*[(b)]	An offering which the king and Anubis, who is upon his hill, lord of Ra-qereret, who is in *wt*, lord of the sacred land, give:
qrst nfrt m jz=f n ḥrt-nṯr m zmjt jmntt	A good burial in his tomb of the necropolis in the western desert,
jmꜣḫ(w) Nḫtj	the revered one, Nakhti.

(a)   The offering formula invoking Anubis a good burial in the west is attested also on the lid (Text 3), but on the back side, it introduces a novelty by adding the phrase *m jz=f n ḥrt-nṯr*. According to Zitman (Zitman 2010: I, 93, n. 607), the epithet *nb Rꜣ-qrr.t* designating Anubis as the lord of the city necropolis only receives its proper place in the Anubis formula on the back of Asyutian coffins during the latter half of the 11th Dynasty.[48] It occurs on the lid of the coffin S8L dating back to the end of the Old Kingdom.[49] For repeating the texts of the front and the back sides on the lid of the Asyutian coffins since the First Intermediate Period, see Zitman 2010: I, 96. For the meaning of the offering formula *ḥtp-dj-nzw Jnpw* and its stylistic and orthographic features, see DuQuesne 2005: 175 (§§ 209–222).

(b)   For the epithets of Anubis *tpj ḏw=f, jmj-wt, nb tꜣ ḏsr*, see DuQuesne 2005: 135 (§§ 159–175).

Text 7: Series of *ḥtp-dj-(n)* phrases enumerating the deities of the Heliopolitan Little Ennead, supplemented by a number of deities of local importance.

---

[48] This contrasted with the First Intermediate Period Tombs III–IV (N12.1/N12.2) of Iti-ibi and Khety II, where the title *nb Rꜣ-qrr.t* is regularly attested (Edel 1984: 27, fig. 5, line 61, 79, fig. 12, col. 53, 99, fig, 15, col. 69, 159, fig. 19, line 42, cf. Franke 1987: 54), according to Zitman (Zitman 2010: I, 93, n. 607) the Asyutian tomb inscriptions and coffins did not develop along similar lines in this particular field.

[49] The coffin S8L of *Ḥtp-nb=j* (BM 46629) was found by D. Hogarth in 1906/1907, see Budge 1924: 38–39; Taylor 1989: 15, fig. 5; Davies 1995: 146 (n. 1), pl. 31.1; Lapp 1993: 294–295 9S*41, Blatt 18, 121 (§ 272), cf. Zitman 2010: II, 112–113.

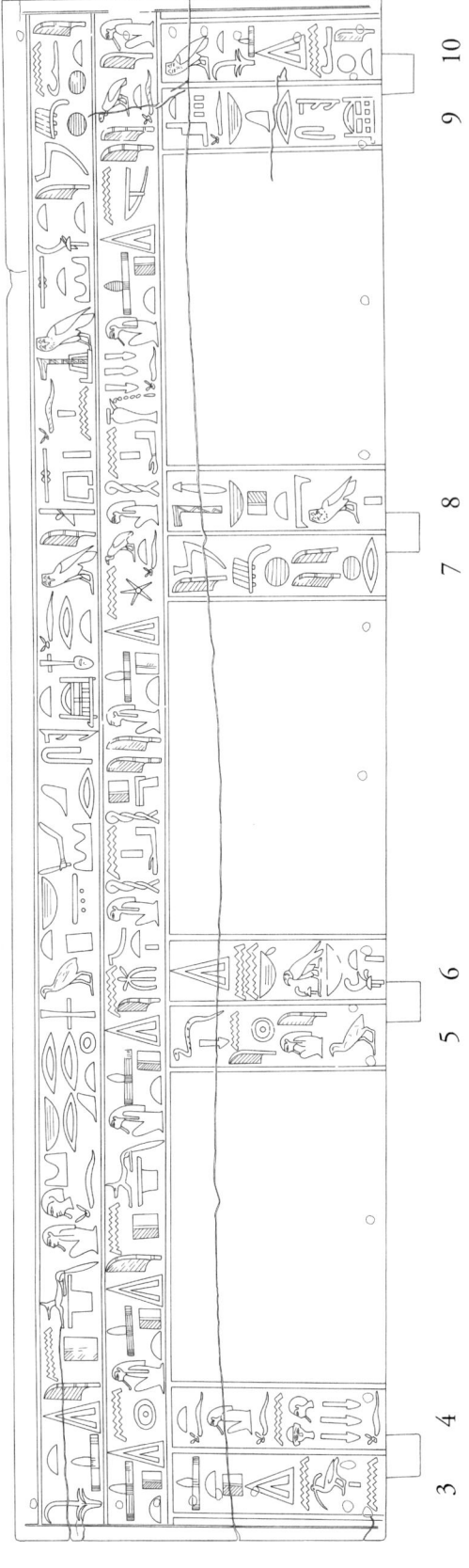

Fig. 7: Back side of S1Shu, Texts 6–9; © Shutb Magazine Project (Drawing: S. Shafik).

[2]*ḥtp-dj-n Rꜥ*	An offering which Ra gives.
ḥtp-dj-(n) Jnpw	An offering which Anubis gives.
ḥtp-dj-n Jmst ḥnꜥ Ḥꜥpy	An offering which Amset and Hapi give.
ḥtp-dj-n Dwꜣ-mwt=f ḥnꜥ Qbḥ-snw=f[(a)]	An offering which Duamutef and Qebehsenuef give.
ḥtp-dj-n Mrj-mwt=f[(b)]	An offering which Merymutef gives.
[3]*ḥtp-dj-n ꜣḫ-n-*[4]*jt=f*[(c)]	An offering which Akhenitief gives.
<ḥtp dj>n Ḥrj-tp-snw=f[(d)]	<An offering> which Heritepsenuef gives.

(a)   Text 7 represents the Little Ennead of Heliopolis, supplemented by deities of *Ḥꜥjt* or Manqabad.[50] For the composition of the little Ennead, cf. Barta 1973: 53seq and see below. For the local deities of Manqabad, see Zecchi 1996: 7–14.

(b)   For *Mrj-mwt=f* "Beloved of his mother", the lord of *Ḥꜥjt*, cf. Leitz 2002: III, 338 with further references; Zecchi 1996: 7–4.

(c)   For *ꜣḫ-n-jt=f* "Glorious one of his father", cf. Leitz 2002: II, 24 with further references; Zecchi 1996: 10–11.

(e)   For *Ḥrj-tp-snw=f* "Chief over his brothers", see Leitz 2002: V, 399 with further references; Zecchi 1996: 10–11.

Text 8: *ḏd-mdw-jn-Rꜥ* formula addressing Ha, God of the West, followed by *jmꜣḥy-ḥr*.

[5]*ḏd-mdw-jn-Rꜥ*[(a)] *jw* [6]*dj.n(=j) n=k Ḥꜣ nb jmnt*[(b)] [7]*jmꜣḥy ḥr* [8]*nṯr ꜥꜣ nb pt m* [9]*swt=f nb(wt)*

qrst [10]*m*[(c)] *<...>*

Recitation by Ra: I have given you Ha, Lord of the West, the revered one by the Great God, Lord of the Heaven in all his places:

A good burial in <...>.

(a)   For *ḏd-mdw-jn-Rꜥ* formula on Asyutian coffins, see Lapp 1993: 129 (§ 290).

(b)   For the god Ha, Lord of the West, see Leitz 2002: V, 10–11 with further references; Roeder 1929: 191.

(c)   A good burial "*m jz=f n ḥrt-nṯr m zmjt jmntt*" is to be expected here. The last words which are attested on Texts 3 and 6, are missing due to the limited available space.

---

50 On *Ḥꜥjt* or Manqabad; see Gardiner 1947: 75–76 [372 A]; Gauthier 1928: 166; Kessler 1980; Helck 1974: 104.

Fig. 8: Head end of S1Shu, Texts 10–11; © Shutb Magazine Project (Drawing: S. Shafik).

Text 9: ḥtp-dj-nzw formula addressing the coffin owner himself.

¹⁰ḥtp-dj-nzw <n> Nḫtj(a)   An offering which the king gives <to> Nakhti.

(a)   For ḥtp-dj-nsw NN or ḥtp-dj-nsw n k3 n NN, see Lapp 1986: 33 (§ 52).

3.4 The head end (Pl. 35a, Fig. 8)

The inscription on the head end starts from left to right. It comprises a ḏd-mdw-jn-Rˤ formula on the uppermost rows and the left hand column, aiming to place Isis at the head (Text 10). The last column includes the ḥtp-dj-n phrase of goddess Seshat (Text 11).

Text 10: ḏd-mdw-jn-Rˤ formula aiming to place Isis at the head.

Fig. 9: Foot end of S1Shu, Texts 12–13; © Shutb Magazine Project (Drawing: S. Shafik).

¹ḏd-mdw-jn-Rꜥ jw dj.n=(j) n=k ꜣst⁽ᵃ⁾ ²ḥr tp=k
rmj⁽ᵇ⁾=s ṯw jꜣ³kb=s ṯw

Recitation by Ra: I have given you Isis under your head, she will shed tears over you, she will mourn you.

(a)   The name of Isis is written with flesh-sign 🔲 (Gardiner 1957: sign-list, F51), which differs from the egg-sign 🔲 (sign-list, H8) on most Asyutian coffins of the Middle Kingdom, cf. Zitman 2010: I, 268, n. 1893. For the different writing of Isis' name, see Leitz 2002: I, 61.

(b)   The verb *rmj* is written without the phonetic complement 🔲, and with a determinative that only has two tears (sign-list D22). For this feature which is common on Asyutian coffins, cf. Zitman 2010: I, 268 and see below.

Text 11: *ḥtp-rdj-(jn)* phrase of the goddess Seshat.

3   4

⁴ḥtp-dj-n Sšꜣt⁽ᵃ⁾   An offering which Seshat gives.

(a)   Writing the name of Seshat without her accompanying title is not common on Asyutian coffins, which often record "*ḫntt pr-mḏꜣt-nṯr* Mistress of the House of the God's Book", see Zitman 2010: I, 267; Leitz 2002: VI, 608–609 with further references.

3.5 The foot end (Pl. 35b, Fig. 9)

Unlike the head end, the inscriptions on the foot end starts from right to left. The texts are nearly almost identical to the last, except that the *ḏd-mdw-jn-Rꜥ* formula here aims to place Nephthys at the feet (Text 12) and the *ḥtp-dj-n* phrase addresses the gods Tatenen and Tatem (Text 13).

Text 12: *ḏd-mdw-jn-Rꜥ* formula aiming to place Nephthys at the feet.

¹*ḏd-mdw-jn-Rꜥ jw dj.n=(j) n=k Nbt-ḥwt* ²*ḥr rdwj=k rmj=s ṯw jꜣ*³*kb=s ṯw*

Recitation by Ra: I have given you Nephthys under your feet, she will shed tears over you, she will mourn you.

Text 13: *ḥtp-dj-n* phrase of the gods Tatenen and Tatem

⁴*ḥtp-dj-n Tꜣ-tnn*⁽ᵃ⁾ *(dj-)n Tꜣ-tm*⁽ᵇ⁾

An offering which Tatenen and Tatem give.

(a)   Writing *Tꜣ-tnn* with *nw*-jar and *pt*-sign is unusual, but reading the name depends on the contextual comparison with other coffins (ZITMAN 2010: I, 268, n. 1868) on which the name is attested recognizable by ⊥⊥, see SCHLÖGL 1980: 13seq; LEITZ 2002: VII, 346.

(b)   For the god *Tꜣ-tm* "The entire land", see LEITZ 2002: VII, 346. On Asyutian coffins, the complex of the Earth Deities usually includes *Tꜣwj-tmwy* "The entirely two lands" (ZITMAN 2010: I, 267), but in all cases *Tꜣ-tnn* as the primeval earth, always introduces the board, see SCHLÖGL 1980: 15.

4. Layout and Textual Programme

The main characteristic feature of S1Shu is its layout and its textual programme on the exterior. As already mentioned, the lid includes three horizontal lines of text, the sides are composed of a double line around the upper edge to which four sets of double columns on the front and back sides, and one set of double columns on the head and foot ends were added.[51] The main textual programme is composed of series of *ḥtp-dj-nzw*, *ḥtp-dj-n* and *ḏd-mdw-jn-Rꜥ* formulas. They focus on the deceased's happy passage to the Netherworld, his good burial, and the offerings presented to him during the offering ritual that serve as a future reference during the festivals of the dead. Except for some novelty recurring on S1Shu (Text 9), there is a relatively high number of Asyutian coffins that share the same features and provide the same sequence of texts. These coffins show nothing more than the following layout illustrated by S1Shu (Fig. 10).[52] The textual programme of S1Shu introduces the coffin as it would be a "model" of the universe.[53] The first Anubis formula on the lid (Text 1) asks the "Foremost of the God's Booth" some favors that show a measure of variation, they are perhaps an experimental or garbled combination of Barta's *Bitten* 33a, 29a, 30a and 32a.[54] These *Bitten* are usually concerned with the deceased's happy passage to the

---

51 The development of the exterior decoration on Asyuti coffins starts with coffins showing a single line of inscription, known at Asyut towards the end of the Old Kingdom and still in use until the early Middle Kingdom, when Asyut has developed its own coffin style, see WILLEMS 1988: 122. Now, the text lines on the coffin exteriors are doubled or even tripled and columns of text are added on the outside, the feature which is known from other parts of Egypt later, at the beginning of the 12ᵗʰ Dynasty, see GRAJETZKI 2016: 33. Against the views of Willems and Lapp, Zitman (ZITMAN 2010: I, 368–369) has pointed out that the development of the exterior decoration is not linked to a specific time, e.g., all three types of exterior decoration are coexistend during the reigns of Senwosret I and Amenemhat II. For the 11ᵗʰ Dynasty, Zitman suggests the existence of type Assiut I and Assiut II (ZITMAN 2010: I, 367).

52 Cf. ZITMAN 2010: II, 155–158, fig. 31.

53 For this expression, see WILLEMS 1988: 141.

54 For the typical Asyutian *Bitten*, cf. LAPP 1993: 126 (§ 287).

Lid

(Text 1) *ḥtp-dj-nzw Jnpw* formula asking Anubis for a happy passage to the Netherworld ⟵ 1

(Text 2) *ḏd-mdw-jn-Rꜥ* formula requesting an offering in certain religious festivals 2

(Text 3) *ḥtp-dj-(n)* formula asking Anubis a good burial in the West 3

Front side

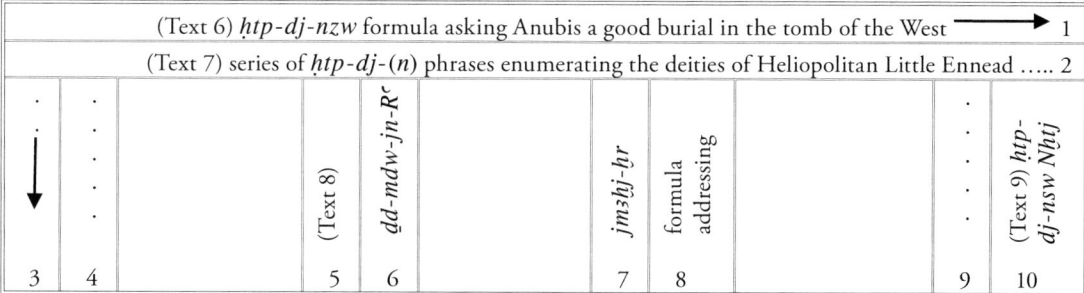

⟵ (Text 4) *ḥtp-dj-nzw* formula requesting Osiris an invocation offering 1

(Text 5) series of *ḥtp-dj-(n)* phrases list the deities of Heliopolitan Great Ennead 2

| 10 | 9 | | 8 | 7 | | 6 | 5 | wedjat-eyes | 4 | 3 |

Back side

(Text 6) *ḥtp-dj-nzw* formula asking Anubis a good burial in the tomb of the West ⟶ 1

(Text 7) series of *ḥtp-dj-(n)* phrases enumerating the deities of Heliopolitan Little Ennead 2

| 3 | 4 | | (Text 8) | *ḏd-mdw-jn-Rꜥ* 5 | 6 | | *jmꜣḫj-ḫr* 7 | formula addressing 8 | | 9 | (Text 9) *ḥtp-dj-nsw Nḥtj* 10 |

Head end

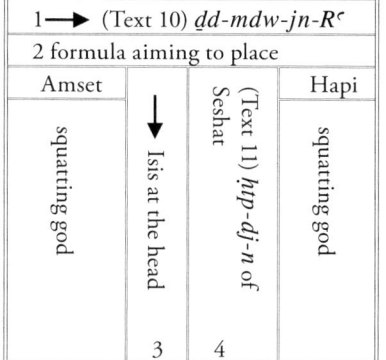

1 ⟶ (Text 10) *ḏd-mdw-jn-Rꜥ*

2 formula aiming to place

Amset		(Text 11) *ḥtp-dj-n* of Seshat	Hapi
squatting god	Isis at the head		squatting god
	3	4	

Foot end

1 (Text 12) *ḏd-mdw-jn-Rꜥ* ⟵

2 formula aiming to place

Dua-mutef		(Text 13) *ḥtp-dj-n* of Tatenen and Tatem	Kebeh-senuef
squatting god	Nephthys at the feet		squatting god
	3	4	

Fig. 10: The layout and textual programme of S1Shu.

Netherworld[55] "may he be accompanied well by his ka to the pure places which are in the heaven, etc".[56] The second Anubis formula on the lid (Text 3) asks the god for "A good burial in the western desert". This formula occupies its proper position on the back side (Text 6) with some novelty: "A good burial in his tomb of the necropolis in the western desert". The back side seems to be the main place of this formula, for this side is the Western side of the coffin. It is not coincidental that Anubis figures here in a text aiming at ensuring a good burial in the West.[57]

The offering formula of Osiris on the front side (Text 4) follows the combination of Osiris and *prt-ḥrw* (*Bitte* 2) attested during the 12th Dynasty.[58] The *prt-ḥrw* ritual was a part of the offering ritual carried out near the tomb during the burial. It aims to offer the food during the offering ritual, and also to serve as a future reference during the festivals of the deceased mentioned on the lid (Text 2).[59]

It is worth noting that the representation of Osiris "Lord of the West" (Text 5) in the offering formula inscribed on the coffin's front side, which was supposed to be the East, is understandable in relation to the tradition of the Old Kingdom,[60] where the traditional position of the offering table was on the East side of the tomb.[61] Since the East is also the place of sunrise, Osiris' syncretistic ties with the rising sun are also worth mentioning here.[62] However, the purpose of the two correlative formulas of Anubis on the back and of Osiris on the front[63] runs in parallel, as they were part of the funerary cult. While the former aims at ensuring a good burial and the correct execution of the necessary rituals, the latter guarantees the deceased's food supplies.[64]

The rest of the texts on the front side are composed of series of *ḥtp-dj-(n)* phrases naming the gods of the Great Ennead of Heliopolis (Text 5). The deities are introduced in their genealogical order, consisting of Ra-Atum, Shu, Tefnut, Geb, Nut, Osiris, Isis, Seth and Nephthys, supplemented by Thoth and his children, Dunanui and his children and Imy-Chentienirty and his children.[65] The Great Ennead is represented here as a part of the *Götterformel*.[66] According to an achievement that occurs during the judgment of the dead,[67] the deceased might be enabled to join the sun god Ra and also eat from offerings presented on his altar as M. Bommas suggests. In his opinion, the Ennead as a whole is equally responsible for funerary offerings since the Middle Kingdom.[68] Moreover, the important role of the Heliopolitan Great Ennead in the celestial rebirth of the deceased, his celestial journey and his invention to ascend to the sky must be taken into consideration.[69]

The exact composition of the Little Ennead of Heliopolis on the back side is unknown (Text 7). They are apparently a random selection of deities, but it has been suggested that the four Sons of Horus form

55 Formulas of that kind are widely attested on the coffins of Middle Egypt around the time of Amenemhat II, but they are known at Asyut as early as the 11th Dynasty, cf. WILLEMS 1988: 172–173.

56 The precursors of such texts during the Old Kingdom dealt with the transport of the coffin to the tomb *sḏꜣ=f nfr ḥr wꜣt nfrt nt ḥrt-nṯr* "may he proceed well on the good roads of the necropolis", cf. LAPP 1993: 89–90; WILLEMS 1988: 172–174.

57 Cf. WILLEMS 1988: 124; LAPP 1993: 39–192, n. 18.

58 BARTA 1968: 57.

59 Cf. LAPP 1986: 39seq.

60 WILLEMS 1988: 124, 233.

61 See HELCK 1982.

62 KEES 1956: 144, 156seq.

63 The two formulas are standard in occupying the first line on the front and back sides. The changes, whatever, involve the second line, the text columns and the expanded layout on the short sides and the lid, see ZITMAN 2010: I, 165.

64 WILLEMS 1988: 124. The Asyutian coffin S19Tor of *Ḥpšt* or *Ṯ(ꜣ)nm* (Turin, Museo Egizio S. 14381, unpl., see GRILLETTO 1991: 36), is unique in changing the role of the two deities. Hence, the Osiris formula on the front asks for a good burial, while the one with Anubis on the back features the invocation offering instead (ZITMAN 2010: I, 143, n. 927). Deviation occurs also on the lid, where the Osiris formula is inscribed on the last line instead that of Anubis (ZITMAN 2010: I, 269, n. 1900).

65 For the basic form of the Great Ennead, see BARTA 1973: 61–72.

66 BARTA 1973: 73seq.

67 ASSMANN 2002: 127.

68 BOMMAS 2017: 158–159,

69 For the celestial journey of the deceased, see WILLEMS 1988: 133–134.

part of it.[70] The most characteristic function of the Sons of Horus is their role as the protectors of the mummy, and especially of its inner organs. In this role, they are usually combined with the goddesses Isis and Nephthys at the head and foot of the deceased, guarding his corpse and acting as the female mourners on behalf of him (Texts 10, 12).[71] Hapi and Amset are equaled with the head, while Qebehsenuef and Duamutef are identified with the opposite end.[72]

The Little Ennead is supplemented by three gods of local significance (Merymutef, Akhenitief and Heritepsenuef), whose connection to the Great Ennead is still unclear. As Marcel Zitman suggested, they seem to represent a Little Ennead composing of the offspring of the Great one.[73] In fact, these minor deities have most likely played the part of a pre-eminent deity of Manqabad.[74] Their relation to Heliopolitan deities has been already pointed out by Marco Zecchi, who argued that the deities are probably intended to be local children of Geb and Nut, as the meaning of their names eloquently suggests. They are similar to Osiris, Isis, Seth and Nephthys, who are also the children of Geb and Nut.[75] At least, the names of Merymutef and Heritepsenuef, in particular, are quoted in the list of Memphite gods inscribed in the chapel of Ptah-Sokar in the temple of Sety I at Abydos.[76] Generally, the religious traditions of the 13th Upper Egyptian Nome were partly influenced by the Heliopolitan theology as Hermann Kees pointed out.[77]

On the other hand, the content of the standard formulation of the Ennead seems trivial at first sight, however, a closer look reveals that both the selection of the gods and the way in which they are arranged are highly significant.[78] While Ra-Atum is added, Horus is overlooked.[79] The absence of the god Horus on Asyutian coffins is highly peculiar, because Horus as the son of Osiris and Isis forms the genealogical link between the Great Ennead and his four Sons of the Little ennead.[80]

The *ḏd-mdw-jn-Rꜥ* formula on the back side (Text 8) is frequently depicted on the back sides or the western sides of the Asyutian coffins, where the creator god Ra places Ha, Lord of the West, at the western side,[81] probably for his role in protecting the deceased and looking after his needs.[82] To fill the space after the above mentioned *ḏd-mdw-jn-Rꜥ* formulas of Isis and Nephthys on the short sides, two *ḥtp-dj-n* formulas were added. The goddess Seshat is placed on the head (Text 11) opposite to the gods Tatenen and Tatem on the foot end (Text 13). The occurrence of these deities is common on the Asyutian coffins, where Seshat is frequently recorded as *ḫntt pr-mḏꜣt-nṯr* "Mistress of the House of the God's Book".[83] In this capacity, Seshat was said to descend into the underworld to record everything in the realm of the dead. She was, even, depicted sometimes helping Nephthys to revive the deceased in the afterlife in preparation for their judgment by Osiris in the Hall of Truth.[84]

Being buried under ground, the gods *Tꜣ-tnn* "The primeval/risen land" and *Tꜣ-tm* "The entire land", and sometimes *Tꜣwj-tmwy* "The entire two lands",[85] were intimately involved with the future of the deceased. Earth Deities, at least Tatenen, made the deceased welcome and helped him on his way in the Netherworld.[86]

---

70 Barta 1973: 53seq.

71 See Münster 1968: 47–53, n. 637–639, 61, cf. Lapp 1993: 131, Abb. 140, 129, § 290.

72 Willems 1988: 139–141.

73 Zitman 2010: I, 265.

74 Kahl 2007: 38.

75 Zecchi 1996: 9–11.

76 Kees 1915: 70, 75; Kitchen 1969: 173 (12)–176 (9); Baines 1988: 124–133.

77 Kees 1941: 326–328.

78 Willems 1988: 139.

79 For the list of the Great Ennead, see Barta 1973: 53–57, 127seq.

80 Zitman 2010: I, 265, n. 1872.

81 On a number of Asyutian coffins, another *ḏd-mdw-jn-Rꜥ* formula is frequently depicted on the front side (ideally the East), aiming to place *Spdw*, Lord of the East at the eastern side, cf. Zitman 2010: I, 266.

82 See Kees 1956: 29. 267. 270; Bonnet 1952: 268–269; Wildung 1977.

83 Zitman 2010: I, 267.

84 Pinch 2002: 190; Helck 1984; Bonnet 1952: 699–701; Wainwright 1940.

85 Zitman 2010: I, 267.

86 During the New Kingdom, Tatenen became particularly important, taking on a protective role towards the royal dead, guarding the kings and their family on their path through the Underworld. In the Book of Gates, Tatenen personifies the entire

Lastly, *jmꜣḫy-ḫr* formulas and self-laudatory phrases, typical combination of texts that prevailed on Asyutian coffins, are added after each formula on the lid (Texts 1, 3) and in the space left in the columns on the front (Texts 4–5) and back (Texts 6, 8) sides.

5. Dating

The Asyutian rectangular coffins generally range in date from the end of the Old Kingdom to the middle of the 12th Dynasty, roughly up to the reign of Senwosret III. The high percentages of the coffins seem to belong to the time around the end of the 11th and early 12th Dynasties.[87] Coffins datable after the reign of Senwosret I are much fewer.[88] In order to define the date of S1Shu, three main features have to be taken into consideration. First, is the general outline of the decoration. Second, are the textual programme and the phraseology. Third, are the epigraphical and paleographical traits.

Based on this evidence, it can be assumed that S1Shu belongs typologically to Lapp's *Typ der 12. Dynastie*,[89] and to Willems' Standard Class Type IV with a combination of Type VI, dating to the late 12th Dynasty.[90] According to the layout and the number of lines and text columns on the coffin sides, Zitman has classified the Asyutian coffins into three Types from I to III.[91] Because of its doubling lines and columns, S1Shu fits neatly into Zitman's group Assiut II.b.[92] Type Assiut II includes a substantial number of coffins that stand close in time within a few generations from the reign of Mentuhotep II Nebhepetre (late 11th Dynasty) to the early years of Senwosret I (early 12th Dynasty), and might be as Zitman suggested, the output of the same workshop.[93]

For dating purposes, Zitman has divided the coffins of this type into two groups; "Siutian Coffins of the early M.K. (3) and (4)".[94] According to him, the first group (3), which includes the coffins coined by him as: S3C, S6C, S7C, S8C, S16C, S17C, S22C, S1Chass, S2Chass, S2Chic, S1Hil, S1L, S13L, S14L, S26L, S28L, S50L, S4Ly, S1P, S2P, S3P, S15Tor, S60Tor, S62Tor, S1Tü,[95] is datable to the end of

　　area of the Netherworld, protecting the deceased in the Beyond, cf. Schlögl 1980: 32seq; Schlögl 1986; Bonnet 1952: 769–770; Assmann 1969: 60seq.

87 Cf. Schenkel 1962: 117–118; Willems 1988: 102–102.
88 Zitman 2010: I, 370.
89 Lapp has already studied the paleography and composition of offering formulas in the tombs and compared them with the offering formulas on the coffins for dating purposes, for his *Typ Dyn. 12.*, see Lapp 1993: 144 (§ 322).
90 For these two types, cf. Willems 1988: 136–161, 163.
91 Zitman 2010: II, 153–162, figs. 30–32.
92 Zitman 2010: II, 155–158, fig. 31.
93 Zitman 2010: I, 279, 283, 367. The majority of these coffins came from one excavation of Charles Palanque conducted in 1903 in the northeast half of Gebel Asyut al-gharbi (Palanque 1903: 119–128; Chassinat & Palanque 1911), while the other came from the excavations of Schiaparelli in 1908 and Hogarth in 1906–1907, conducted also in the northern part of the necropolis, see Zitman 2010: II, 263, 284.
94 Zitman 2010: II, 263–292.
95 The mentioned sigla follow Zitman 2010: II, 105–151 (List 1).
　　S3C *Jt-jb* (JE 36444; Chassinat & Palanque 1911: 191–214; Willems 1988: 28; Lapp 1993: 292–293 (S4).
　　S6C *Ḥwj n=j Skr/Ḥtj* (JE 36320; Chassinat & Palanque 1911: 125–134; pls. 24–25; Lapp 1993: 125–132 (S63).
　　S7C *Dꜣg* (Cairo 21/11/16/24; Chassinat & Palanque 1911: 185–188; pl. 30.2; Lapp 1993: 125–132 (S74).
　　S8C *Mshtj* (JE 36446; Chassinat & Palanque 1911: 138–143; pl. 30.2; Willems 1988: 20; Lapp 1993: 294 (S37).
　　S16C *Nḫtj* (CG 28128; Chassinat & Palanque 1911: 218–219; Willems 1988: 28; Lapp 1993: 294–295 (S47b).
　　S17C *Nḫtj* (CG 28129; Chassinat & Palanque 1911: 135–137; Willems 1988: 28; Lapp 1993: 294–295 (S47a).
　　S22C *Jnj* (Cairo 1/10/14/11; Lefebvre 1912: 90–92, § 5; Willems 1988: 28; Lapp 1993: 292–293 (S2).
　　S1Chass *Nḫtj* (Unknown location; Chassinat & Palanque 1911: 35–46; Willems 1988: 28; Lapp 1993: 294 (S45).
　　S2Chass *Mꜣꜥt* (Unknown location; Chassinat & Palanque 1911: 114–122; Willems 1988: 28; Lapp 1993: 294 (S34).
　　S2Chic *Nḫtj* (Chicago, Field Mus. of Nat. Hist. 881917; Chassinat & Palanque 1911: 23–25; Lapp 1993: 294 (S44).
　　S1Hil *Nḫtj* (Hildesheim, Pelizaeus Mus. 5999; Eggebrecht 1993: 41–44).
　　S1L *Ḥnj* (BM 29576.5; Budge 1924: 79, pls. 10–11; Lapp 1993: 296–297 (S52).
　　S13L *Mgj* (BM 46645.564 (H) and 46645.563 (F); unpl., cf. Zitman 2010: II, 112–113).

the 11th Dynasty and the early beginnings of the 12th Dynasty, possible reaching into the early years of Senwosret I. Meanwhile the second group (4) with the siglum: S4C, S13C, S1Chic, S51L, S9Min, S5P, S1Tan, SiWar, S21X, S24X and S30X,[96] is of a later date, from the reign of Senwosret I to the early years of his successor Amenemhat II.

In fact, a closer inspection of the coffins in both groups reveals that they stand close not only in time, but also in many distinctive epigraphical and paleographical features. To distinguish the two groups, Zitman depends on two main textual grounds. First, is the inclusion of the name of the god *T3-tnn* or *T3-tnnt* on the short sides which is limited to group (3).[97] Second, and more important, is the slight difference in the phrasing of the *dd-mdw-jn-R^c* formula on the lid. While group (3) omitted the *W3g*-feast and inserted a redundant *dd-mdw-jn-R^c* between the festival of *Skr* and *Dhwtt* (e.g. *dd-mdw-jn-R^c prt-hrw m Wpt-w3t m Msjt m Hb-Skr dd-mdw-jn-R^c m Dhwtt*), group (4) recorded the normal or canonical formula that reads: *dd-mdw-jn-R^c prt-hrw m Wpt-w3t m W3g m Msjt m Hb-Skr m Dhwtt*.[98]

From this perspective, S1Shu might stand as a distinctive example between the two groups as it includes a combination of both formulas. It inserted the *W3g*-feast and still kept the redundant *dd-mdw-jn-R^c* (Text 2). This rare feature appears in Asyut once on the coffin S3P found in Tomb 7 of the treasurer Nakhti.[99] As it was a unique example, Zitman considered S3P as an exception which belongs to his group (3).[100] These two examples/exceptions, S1Shu and S3P, might represent an intermediate period between Zitman's two groups, in which the coexistence of the new and the old formulas results in a fusion between their traditions. Also, both coffins share some rare epigraphical traits attested on a few Asyutian coffins in both groups. The first is the writing of *ntr ^c3* on Osiris formula (Text 4), with the horizontal ⊓ and vertical *^c3* 𓉴.[101] The former writing is common on Siutian coffin of group (3), while the latter is very rare as it only occurs twice on the lid of the coffin S1Hil which also belongs to group (3), and on the interior

---

S14L *Mshtj* (BM 47590.598; unpl., cf. Zɪᴛᴍᴀɴ 2010: II, 112–113).

S26L Name lost (BM 46650.571; unpl., cf. Zɪᴛᴍᴀɴ 2010: II, 128–129).

S28L Name lost (BM 46655.576; Pᴀʀᴋɪɴꜱᴏɴ 1999: 75).

S50L *Mshtj* (BM 4661.582 (F) and 47607 (H); unpl., cf. Zɪᴛᴍᴀɴ 2010: II, 114–115).

S4Ly *Htj* (Lyon, Mus. des Beaux-Arts 1972.114; Cʜᴀꜱꜱɪɴᴀᴛ & Pᴀʟᴀɴǫᴜᴇ 1911: 15–18; Lᴀᴘᴘ 1993: 296–297 (S62).

S1P *Nhtj* (Louvre E 11981; Cʜᴀꜱꜱɪɴᴀᴛ & Pᴀʟᴀɴǫᴜᴇ 1911: 53–79, pls. 17–20; Lᴀᴘᴘ 1993: 294 (S46a).

S2P *Nhtj* (Louvre E 11936; Cʜᴀꜱꜱɪɴᴀᴛ & Pᴀʟᴀɴǫᴜᴇ 1911: 79–114, pls. 16, 21; Lᴀᴘᴘ 1993: 294 (S46b).

S3P *Hnn/Hwj n=j Skr/Nhtj* (Louvre E 12036; Cʜᴀꜱꜱɪɴᴀᴛ & Pᴀʟᴀɴǫᴜᴇ 1911: 143–154, pl. 28; Lᴀᴘᴘ 1993: 294 (S54).

S15Tor *Pjpj?* (Turin, Museo Egizio S. 8931; unpl., cf. Zɪᴛᴍᴀɴ 2010: II, 140–141).

S60Tor Name lost (Turin, Museo Egizio (no number); unpl., cf. Zɪᴛᴍᴀɴ 2010: II, 144–145).

S62Tor Name lost (Turin, Museo Egizio (no number); unpl., cf. Zɪᴛᴍᴀɴ 2010: II, 144–145).

S1Tü *Jdj* (Tübingen, Inv. Nr. 6; Bʀᴜɴɴᴇʀ-Tʀᴀᴜᴛ & Bʀᴜɴɴᴇʀ 1981: 209–227; II, pls. 8–9, 40–47).

96 The mentioned sigla follow Zɪᴛᴍᴀɴ 2010: II, 105–151 (List 1).

S4C *Hwj* (JE 36445; Cʜᴀꜱꜱɪɴᴀᴛ & Pᴀʟᴀɴǫᴜᴇ 1911: 156–157, pl. 29.2; Wɪʟʟᴇᴍꜱ 1988: 28; Lᴀᴘᴘ 1993: 296–297 (S37).

S13C *^cnh=f/Nhtj?* (CG 28130; Cʜᴀꜱꜱɪɴᴀᴛ & Pᴀʟᴀɴǫᴜᴇ 1911: 7–13; Wɪʟʟᴇᴍꜱ 1988: 28; Lᴀᴘᴘ 1993: 294–295 (S43).

S1Chic *Jtj-jb* (Chicago, Field Mus. of Nat. Hist. 91068; Cʜᴀꜱꜱɪɴᴀᴛ & Pᴀʟᴀɴǫᴜᴇ 1911: 123–124; Lᴀᴘᴘ 1993: 294 (S44).

S51L Name lost (BM 47606.615 (H) and 47606.614 (F); unpl., cf. Zɪᴛᴍᴀɴ 2010: II, 114–115).

S9Min *Jmj* (Minia Mus. M3; Kᴀᴍᴀʟ 1934: 49–50 (I); Lᴀᴘᴘ 1993: 292–293 (S1).

S5P *Df3=j H^cpj* (Louvre E 12031 and E 12039; Cʜᴀꜱꜱɪɴᴀᴛ & Pᴀʟᴀɴǫᴜᴇ 1911: 233–236, pl. 40; Lᴀᴘᴘ 1993: 296 (S77).

S1Tan *Hq3* (Tanta Mus. No. 549; Kᴀᴍᴀʟ 1916: 77–79 (no. 54); Lᴀᴘᴘ 1993: 296–297 (S58).

S1War Name lost (Warsaw, Nat. Mus. inv. No. 142140; Dᴀʙʀᴏᴡꜱᴋᴀ-Sᴍᴇᴋᴛᴀʟᴀ 1984: no. 8.

S21X *Wp-w3wt-nhtj* (Unknown location; Cʜᴀꜱꜱɪɴᴀᴛ & Pᴀʟᴀɴǫᴜᴇ 1911: 158–159; Lᴀᴘᴘ 1993: 294–295 (S30).

S24X *T3* (Unknown location; Cʜᴀꜱꜱɪɴᴀᴛ & Pᴀʟᴀɴǫᴜᴇ 1911: 169–171; Lᴀᴘᴘ 1993: 296–297 (S69).

S30X *Hnj* (Unknown location; Cʜᴀꜱꜱɪɴᴀᴛ & Pᴀʟᴀɴǫᴜᴇ 1911: 220–212; Lᴀᴘᴘ 1993: 294–295 (S49).

97 Zɪᴛᴍᴀɴ 2010: I, 266–267, 286.

98 As Zitman (Zɪᴛᴍᴀɴ 2010: I, 269, n. 1899) mentioned, this slight difference has been overlooked by Lapp (Lᴀᴘᴘ 1993: 129, § 290, Deckel) and Barta (Bᴀʀᴛᴀ 1968: 41).

99 The coffin S3P of *Hnn/Hwj n=j Skr / Nhtj* (Louvre E12036), was found in 1903 by Charles Palanque in Tomb 7 located in the northeastern half of Gebel Asyut al-gharbi, see Cʜᴀꜱꜱɪɴᴀᴛ & Pᴀʟᴀɴǫᴜᴇ 1911: 143, pl. 28. For the location of this tomb, cf. Zɪᴛᴍᴀɴ 2010: II, Map 5 on page 8.

100 Zɪᴛᴍᴀɴ 2010: I, 269, n. 1898.

101 Other Asyutian coffins usually prefer one of both writings, cf. Lᴀᴘᴘ 1993: Blatt 22–23, 25–26.

front of the coffin S1Chic in group (4).[102] The second trait is the peculiar writing of the name *Tȝ-tnn* on the foot end (Text 13), where the name is written with the *nw*-jar and *pt*-sign ⎯°⏐⎯. This feature recurs on some coffins from the reign of Senwosret I.[103]

The above mentioned evidence might exclude a date of S1Shu before the early 12th Dynasty, possibly into the early years of Senwosret I. This date matches with the date of S3P suggested by Zitman to the end of the 11th and early of the 12th Dynasties, with some margin into the reign of Senwosret I. Zitman's suggested date is close to the work of Schenkel and Lapp, although they have used different lines and different criteria.[104] Noteworthy, the reign of Mentuhotep II to the co-regency of Amenemhat I and Senwosret I forms a unity, and it is often difficult to assign a monument to one dynasty or the other on strictly epigraphical, paleographical evidence and textual grounds.[105] However, the following discriminated phraseology, epigraphical and paleographical traits might support our suggested date.

5.1 Phraseology

1. The coffins without titles follow a pattern typical of the early Middle Kingdom whereby lower officials did not place titles on monuments.[106] Most of the Asyutian coffins attested no titles datable to the early Middle Kingdom.[107]

2. The majority of the coffins combining the writing of *jmȝḫ(w)* side by side with *jmȝḫy* (Text 1) are datable to the end of the 11th and the early 12th Dynasties. According to Zitman,[108] the last presence of this combination dates to the end of the reign of Senwosret I (S13L, S1P, S2P) and the subsequent reign of Amenemhat II (S14X, S15X).[109]

3. Changing the series of Anubis' epithets on the lid from *nb zpȝ ḫntj zḥ-nṯr* into *ḫntj zḥ-nṯr nb zpȝ* (Text 1), occurs on Asyutian coffins dating back to the end of the 11th Dynasty onwards. According to Zitman, the phrase *ḫntj zḥ-nṯr nb zpȝ* was virtually the only option on Asyutian coffins of the 12th Dynasty with a few exceptions.[110]

4. The title *nb Rȝ-qrr.t* already occurs on the lid (Texts 3), it apparently receives its proper place in the Anubis formula on the back (Texts 6) only during the 11th Dynasty.[111]

5. In his study of the phraseology of the offering formula in the Middle Kingdom, John Bennett observed that the phrase *m swt⸗f nb(wt)* "in all his places" (Text 4) placed after the name of Osiris, is characteristic of the 11th Dynasty.[112] According to Brovarski, the phrase falls out in use during the 12th Dynasty, appearing only once in a dated formula, in the reign of Senwosret I.[113]

---

102 ZITMAN 2010: I, 280.

103 ZITMAN 2010: I, 268.

104 Zitman (ZITMAN 2010: I, 210) suggested that all coffins from the tomb of Nakhti probably date to that period, the date which is already proposed by Schenkel (SCHENKEL 1962: 118, § 44a) and Lapp (LAPP 1993: 142, § 320). There is, however, some strong paleographical evidence for dating Nakhti earlier. See KAHL 2016.

105 BROVARSKI 1998: 44. At Asyut and Ch. Lilyquist observed that the archaeological material seems fairly unified between the time of the reunification and the early 12th Dynasty (LILYQUIST 1979: 19). Also, at Thebes, it is often impossible to distinguish the relief style of the late 11th and early 12th Dynasties as R. E. Freed has remarked (FREED 1996: 302).

106 Cf. the Dossier in FRANKE 1984.

107 See GRAJETZKI 2016: 27–28 and cf. ZITMAN 2010: I, 367, n. 2657.

108 ZITMAN 2010 I, 100, n. 658–659.

109 The location of the coffins S14X and S15X is unknown, both coffins have been found by Ahmed Bey Kamal at Asyut, see KAMAL 1916: 102–103, 109–110, nos. 130, 138, cf. WILLEMS 1988: 29; LAPP 1993: 296–297 (S67), 296–297 (S79). Some Egyptologists erroneously assign Kamal's discoveries to Deir Drunka, even though Kamal himself (KAMAL 1916: 66), and later on Henri Wild (WILD 1971, 307–309), explicitly pointed out that they are originated in Asyut, see KAHL 2007: 29.

110 ZITMAN 2010: I, 100, n. 138, n. 899.

111 See ZITMAN 2010: I, 93, n. 607.

112 BENNETT 1941: 80.

113 BROVARSKI 1998: 51.

6. Bonnet[114] pointed out that by the reign of Amenemhat II, the expression *n kꜣ n jmꜣḫy* in the invocation offering (Text 4) had become the more common designated. Through the reign of Senwosret I, the expression replaced the form *jmꜣḫy* of the early Middle Kingdom.[115]

7. Replacing Osiris' title from *ḫntj jmntjw*, preferred since the Old Kingdom into *nb ꜥꜣ* resulted in the new series of Osiris' epithets *nb Ḏdw nṯr ꜥꜣ nb ꜣbḏw* (Text 4). At Asyut, this series would be typical of the 12th Dynasty coffins as Zitman suggested.[116]

5.2 Epigraphical and Paleographical features

1. The word *ḫntj* in the title *ḫntj zḥ nṯr* was written as ⟨glyph⟩ (Text 1) instead of the old form ⟨glyph⟩ which had been used on the coffins since the Old Kingdom. The new form according to Lapp and Schenkel gains its upper hand on coffins of the 12th Dynasty.[117] It is attested on some Asyutian coffins of Zitman's group (4), datable to the 12th Dynasty, reign of Senwosret I and the early years of Amenemhat II.[118]

2. Writing *nb zpꜣ* ⟨glyph⟩ without the phonetic complement ⟨glyph⟩ (Text 1) is according to Lapp a characteristic feature of the coffins datable to 12th Dynasty.[119]

3. (3) Writing the shape of *šms*-sign as ⟨glyph⟩ (Text 1) instead of the fairly common shape ⟨glyph⟩, is much rare at Asyut and mainly appears on Asyutian coffins in the first half of the 12th Dynasty, reign of Senwosret I.[120]

4. (4) Writing *wꜥbt* ⟨glyph⟩ with the seated priest receiving purification (Text 1) is attested on the Asyutian coffin (S7) and (S1Tü), assigned by Lapp to the 12th Dynasty.[121]

5. (5) The form *bjꜣ* ⟨glyph⟩ (Text 1) is first attested on the coffins (S29X) and (S24Tor)[122] datable to the late 11th or the early 12th Dynasties. From then on ⟨glyph⟩, and its variants ⟨glyph⟩ and ⟨glyph⟩ can be followed through the reign of Senwosret I into the mid 12th Dynasty, when their frequency apparently diminished. The preference for this writing, apparently, excludes any date much before the end of the 11th Dynasty.[123]

6. The shape of the pustule ⟨glyph⟩ in *jmj-wt* (Texts 3, 6) has its consistent usage on Asyutian coffins during the reign of Senwosret I and shortly thereafter as Schenkel suggested.[124] It is also attested on the Asyutian coffins of Zitman's group (4).[125]

7. Adding the hill-sign as a determinative of location in *nb tꜣ ḏsr* ⟨glyph⟩ (Texts 3, 6)[126] is apparent on the Asyutian coffin (X2Y) datable to the early years of Senwosret I,[127] and on other Asyutian coffins of

---

114 Zitman 2010: I, 79, cf. Doxey 1998: 94 and see López 1974: figs. 7, 10–11, 13; Abdalla 1992, fig. 2b; Lapp 1986: (§ 355).

115 On basis of the inscriptions of Khety II (Tomb IV/N12.2), it is generally assumed that the use of *n kꜣ n* with the invocation offering *prt-ḫrw* was already current at Asyut in the First Intermediate Period, see Zitman 2010: I, 136, n. 888 with further references, and cf. Edel 1984: 98–99, figs. 14–15, col. 69.

116 Zitman 2010: I, 241, cf. Schenkel 1962: 118 (ad 3); Fischer 1976a: 47; Fischer 1976b: 57, n. 9; Gardiner 1908: 125a, pl. VI, line 1; Habachi 1985: 42, fig. 4, pl. 30–37.

117 Lapp 1993: 210 (§ 487); Schenkel 1962: 118 (§ 44a).

118 Zitman 2010: I, 282, 289.

119 Lapp 1993: 210 (§ 488).

120 Zitman 2010: I, 282, n. 2031.

121 Lapp 1993: 292, (S7). For the different writings of *wꜥbwt* on Asyutian coffins of the Middle Kingdom, see Zitman 2010: I, 282 and cf. Brovarski 1998: 56–57 (D60).

122 The location of the coffin S29X of *ꜥnḫ=f* is unknown, cf. Chassinat & Palanque 1911: 189–190; Lapp 1993: 292–293, (S20), Blatt 19, 122–125 (§ 275seq), 142 (§ 320). The coffin S24Tor of *Jm* is exhibited in Turin, Museo Egizio S. 14457 (unpl.), cf. Grilletto 1991: 36; M. Zitman 2010: II, 140–141.

123 Zitman 2010: I, 283.

124 Schenkel 1962: 118 (§ 44a).

125 Zitman 2010: I, 282, 289.

126 For this writing, cf. Lapp 1993: 144 (§ 322).

127 Cf. Zitman 2010: I, 281–282. The coffin X2Y of *Rḥw-r-ꜣw-sn/Nḫt/Wp---n---/ Wp-wꜣwt-nḫtj?/Ḥnw-kꜣ* is presently in Bonn. On the basis of its exterior, Lapp attributed the coffin to Meir or to Asyut (Lapp 1993: 288–289 (M*22), Blatt 14, 97–99 (§ 220seq), 132–135 (§ 295seq); Lapp 1985: 7–10, pls. 12–19, 38–39), while Willems attributed it on the basis of the typology of its exterior to Meir, suggesting that its interior was decorated by a visiting artist from Asyut (Willems 1988:

Zitman's group (4).[128] Similar writing is attested in (Tomb I/P10.1) of Djefai-Hapi I during the reign of Senwosret I.[129]

8. According to Schenkel, the writing of the toponym *Ḏdw* 𓊽𓅱𓊖 with a stroke after the final radical (Text 4), appeared in the toponyms at the end of the 11th Dynasty, during the reign of Montuhotep IV.[130] On the basis of Upper Egyptian sources, Brovarski, conversely, suggested an earlier date from the reign of Montuhotep II onwards.[131] Henry Fischer thinks that this trait appeared no later than the end of the 11th Dynasty, even though he admits the possibility that it might be as late as the very beginning of the 12th Dynasty.[132] Whatever, as Zitman observed, the matter in Asyut appears to be slightly different. Here, with few exceptions, the coffins of the late 11th Dynasty hardly ever include a expletive stroke with *Ḏdw*, instead, it apparently only became popular in the 12th Dynasty.[133]

9. Determining *prt-ḫrw* 𓉼𓏤𓆄 (Text 4) with a sign resembling the *ḥb*-bowl 𓎱 instead of the oblong *psn* loaf 𓏐, is according to Lapp, a trait exclusive to Asyutian coffins of the 12th Dynasty.[134]

10. As has been observed by Lapp and Schenkel, the combination of 𓏙 and 𓉼𓆄 or 𓉼𓆄 (Text 4), prevails on Asyutian coffins of the 12th Dynasty.[135]

11. Writing the verb *rmj* 𓂋 without the phonetic complement 𓅓, with a determinative that only has two tears (Texts 10, 12), and with distinctive place at the corners of the eyes, is most common on Asyutian coffins datable to the first half of the 12th Dynasty.[136]

Bibliography

ABDALLA 1992: A. Abdalla, The Cenotaph of the Sekwaskhet Family from Saqqara, in: JEA 78, 1992, 93–111.

ALTENMÜLLER 1971–1972: H. Altenmüller, Die Bedeutung der "Gotteshalle des Anubis" im Begräbnisritual, in: JEOL 7.22, 1971–1972, 307–317.

ALTENMÜLLER 1972: H. Altenmüller, Die Texte zum Begräbnisritual in den Pyramiden des Alten Reiches (Wiesbaden 1972).

H. ALTENMÜLLER 1975: H. Altenmüller, Bestattungsritual, in: LÄ I, Wiesbaden, 1975, 745–765.

B. ALTENMÜLLER 1975: B. Altenmüller, Anubis, in: LÄ I, Wiesbaden, 1975, 327–333.

ALTENMÜLLER 1977: H. Altenmüller, "Feste", in: LÄ II, Wiesbaden, 1977, 171–191.

ALTENMÜLLER & MOUSSA 1991: H. Altenmüller, A. Moussa, Die Inschrift Amenemhets II. aus dem Ptah-Tempel von Memphis. Ein Vorbericht, in: SAK 18, 1991, 1–48.

ARNOLD 1988: D. Arnold, The Pyramid of Senwosret I. The South Cemeteries of Lisht, 1 (Publications of the Metropolitan Museum of Art Egyptian Expedition 22, New York 1988).

ASSMANN 1969: J. Assmann, Liturgische Lieder an den Sonnengott. Untersuchungen zur altägyptischen Hymnik, I (MÄS 19, Berlin 1969).

ASSMANN 1972a: J. Assmann, Neith spricht als Mutter und Sarg. Interpretation und metrische Analyse der Sargdeckelinschrift des Merenptah, in: MDAIK 28.2, 1972, 127–130.

34, (X2Bas), 103, 131, n. 38, 133, n. 39, 173, n. 180, 182 (H2), 237, n. 239). However, Zitman remarked that at least two of the coffin's owners (*Rḥw-r-ꜣw-zn/Wp-wꜣwt-nḫtj?*) have names attested at Asyut (ZITMAN 2010: II, 120–121). For this coffin, see also LOCHER 1992.

128 ZITMAN 2010 I, 282, 289.

129 GRIFFITH 1889: pl. 1, line 3; MONTET 1928: 55, line 3.

130 SCHENKEL 1962: 40 (§ 10d).

131 BROVARSKI 1998: 50.

132 FISCHER 1996: 32, fig. 3.

133 ZITMAN 2010: I, 281.

134 Lapp (LAPP 1993: 144 (§ 322), 213 (§ 496), admits, however, at Asyut the *ḥb*-bowl determinative already occurs with the invocation offering in the Heracleopolitan tomb inscriptions of Iti-ibi (Tomb III/N12.1) and of Khety II (Tomb IV/N12.2), cf. ZITMAN 2010: I, 130–131.

135 LAPP 1993: 201–202 (§§ 460–461), Blatt 20–23; SCHENKEL 1962: 30–31 (§ 4a), 118 (§ 44a).

136 ZITMAN 2010: I, 268.

ASSMANN 1972b: J. Assmann, Die Inschrift auf dem äusseren Sarkophagdeckel des Merenptah, in: MDAIK 28.2, 1972, 47–73.

ASSMANN 1984: J. Assmann, Das Grab mit gewundenem Abstieg. Zum Typenwandel des Privat-Felsgrabes im Neuen Reich, in: MDAIK 40, 1984, 277–290.

ASSMANN 2002: J. Assmann, Altägyptische Totenliturgien 1. Totenliturgien in den Sargtexten des Mittleren Reiches (Supplemente zu den Schriften der Heidelberger Akademie der Wissenschaften, Philosophisch-historische Klasse 14, Heidelberg 2002).

BAINES 1988: J. Baines, An Abydos List of Gods and an Old Kingdom Use of Texts, in: J. Baines et al. (eds), Pyramid Studies and Other Essays Presented to I.E.S. Edwards (London 1988).

BARTA 1968: W. Barta, Aufbau und Bedeutung der altägyptischen Opferformel (ÄgForsch 24, Glückstadt 1968)

BARTA 1973: W. Barta, Untersuchungen zum Götterkreis der Neunheit (MÄS 28, München–Berlin 1973).

BENNETT 1941: C. Bennett, Growth of the *htp-di-nsw* formula in the Middle Kingdom, in: JEA 27, 1941, 77–82.

BLEEKER 1967: J. Bleeker, Egyptian Festivals. Enactment of Religious Renewal (Studies in the History of Religions. Supplement to no. 13, Leiden 1967).

BONNET 1952: H. Bonnet, Reallexikon der Religionsgeschichte (Berlin 1952).

BOMMAS 2017: M. Bommas, Middle Kingdom Box Coffin Fragments from Assiut. The Unpublished Coffin Boards Birmingham S1Bir and S1NY, in: S. Bickel, L. Díaz-Iglesias (eds.), Studies in Ancient Egyptian Funerary Literature (OLA 257, Leuven – Paris 2017) 149–180.

BORCHARDT 1935: L. Borchardt, Die Mittel zur zeitlichen Festlegung von Punkten der ägyptischen Geschichte und ihre Anwendung (Kairo 1935).

BROVARSKI 1989: E. Brovarski, The Inscribed Material of the First Intermediate Period from Naga-ed-Dêr (Ph.D. Thesis, University of Chicago 1989).

BROVARSKI 1998: E. Brovarski, A Coffin from Farshût in the Museum of Fine Arts, Boston, in: H. Lesko (ed.), Ancient Egyptian and Mediterranean Studies in Memory of William A. Ward (Rhode Island 1998) 37–69.

BRUNNER-TRAUT & BRUNNER 1981: E. Brunner-Traut, H. Brunner, Die ägyptische Sammlung der Universität Tübingen. I: Textband (Mainz 1981).

BUDGE 1924: E. Budge, A Guide to the 1st, 2nd, and 3rd Egyptian Rooms (British Museum, London 1924).

CHASSINAT & PALANQUE 1911: É. Chassinat, Ch. Palanque, Une campagne des fouilles dans la nécropole d'Assiout (MIFAO 24, Le Caire 1911).

COUYAT & MONTET 1912: J. Couyat, P. Montet, Les inscriptions hiéroglyphiques et hiératiques du Ouadi Hammâmât (MIFAO 34, Cairo 1912).

DABROWSKA-SMEKTALA 1984: E. Dabrowska-Smektala, Middle Kingdom Coffins and their Fragments from the National Museum on Antiquities in Warsaw (unpublished Dissertation, Warsaw 1984).

DAVIES 1995: W. Davies, Ancient Egyptian Timber Imports. An Analysis of Wooden Coffins in the British Museum, in: W. V. Davies and L. Schofield (eds.), Egypt, the Aegean and the Levant – Interconnections in the Second Millennium BC (London 1995) 146–156.

DEPUYDT 1997: L. Depuydt, Civil Calendar and Lunar Calendar in Ancient Egypt (OLA 77, Leuven 1997).

DONADONI ROVERI 1969: A. Donadoni Roveri, I sarcofagi egizi dalle origine alla fine dell'Antico Regno (Università di Roma – Istituto di Studi del Vicino Oriente. Serie archeologica 16, Roma 1969).

DOXEY 1998: M. Doxey, Egyptian Non-royal Epithets in the Middle Kingdom (Probleme der Ägyptologie 12, Leiden 1998).

DUQUESNE 2003: T. DuQuesne, Exalting the god. Processions of Upwawet at Asyut in the New Kingdom, in: DE 57, 2003, 21–45.

DUQUESNE 2005: T. DuQuesne, The Jackal Divinities of Egypt I. From the Archaic Period to dynasty X (Oxfordshire Communications in Egyptology VI, London 2005).

DUQUESNE 2007: T. DuQuesne, Anubis, Upwawet, and Other Deities. Personal Worship and Official Religion in Ancient Egypt (Cairo 2007).

DUQUESNE 2009: T. DuQuesne, Votive Stelae and other Objects from Asyut (London 2009).

EDEL 1964: E. Edel, Altägyptische Grammatik I (AO 34, Rome 1964).

EDEL 1984: E. Edel, Die Inschriften der Grabfronten der Siut-Gräber in Mittelägypten aus der Herakleopolitenzeit. Eine Wiederherstellung nach den Zeichnungen der Description de l'Égypte (ARWAW 71, Opladen 1984).

EGGEBRECHT 1993: A. Eggebrecht, Pelizaeus-Museum Hildesheim. Die ägyptische Sammlung (Mainz 1993).

EL-SAYED 1975: R. El-Sayed, Documents relatifs à Sais et ses divinités (Cairo 1975).

FISCHER 1976a: H. Fischer, Archaeological Aspects of Epigraphy and Palaeography, in: H. Fischer, R. Caminos (eds.), Ancient Egyptian Epigraphy and Palaeography (New York 1976) 29–50.

FISCHER 1976b: H. Fischer, Varia, Egyptian Studies I (New York 1976).

FISCHER 1977: H. Fischer, The Orientation of Hieroglyphs I. Reversals (The Metropolitan Museum of Art, New York 1977).

FISCHER 1996: H. Fischer, The Tomb of Ip at El Saff (New York 1996).

FRANKE 1984: D. Franke, Personendaten aus dem Mittleren Reich (20.–16. Jahrhundert v. Chr.). Dossiers 1–976 (ÄA 41, Wiesbaden 1984).

FRANKE 1987: D. Franke, Zwischen Herakleopolis und Theben: Neues zu den Gräbern von Assiut. Besprechung von: Elmar Edel, Die Inschriften der Grabfronten der Siut-Gräber in Mittelägypten aus der Herakleopolitenzeit. Eine Wiederherstellung nach den Zeichnungen der Description de l'Egypte, in: SAK 14, 1987, 49–60.

FRANKE 2003: D. Franke, The Middle Kingdom Offering Formulas. A challenge, in: JEA 89, 2003, 45–50.

FREED 1996: R. E. Freed, Stela Workshops of Early Dynasty 12, in: P. Der Manuelian (ed.), Studies in Honor of William Kelly Simpson (Boston 1996) 297–336.

FRIEDMAN 1981: F. Friedman, On the Meaning of Akh (ꜣḫ) in Egyptian Mortuary Texts (Ph.D. diss., Brandeis University, 1981).

GABALLA & KITCHEN: G. Gaballa, A. Kitchen, The festival of Sokar, in: Orientalia 38, 1969, 1–76.

GABRA 1931: S. Gabra, Un temple d'Aménophis IV à Assiout, in: CdE 6, 1931, 237–243.

GARDINER 1908: A. Gardiner, Inscriptions from the Tomb of Sirenpowet I. Prince of Elephantine, in: ZÄS 45, 1908, 127–128.

GARDINER 1947: A. Gardiner, Ancient Egyptian Onomastica II (Oxford 1947).

GARDINER 1957: A. Gardiner, Egyptian Grammar (Oxford 1957).

GAUTHIER 1928: H. Gauthier, Dictionnaire des noms géographiques contenus dans les textes hiéroglyphiques IV (Le Caire 1928).

GOMAÀ 1986: F. Gomaà, Die Besiedlung Ägyptens während des Mittleren Reiches I. Oberägypten und das Fayyum (Beihefte zum Tübinger Atlas des Vorderen Orients. Reihe B (Geisteswissenschaften) 66/1, Wiesbaden 1986).

GRAEFE 1986: E. Graefe, Upuaut, in: LÄ VI, Wiesbaden, 1986, 862–864.

GRAJETZKI 2016: W. Grajetzki, Places of Coffin Production in the Early and Late Middle Kingdom, in: EVO 39, 2016, 25–44.

GRIFFITH 1889: F. L. Griffith, The Inscriptions of Siût and Dêr Rîfeh (London 1889).

GRILLETTO 1991: R. Grilletto, Materiali antropologici e zoologici provenienti dall'Egitto e conservati nel Museo Egizio di Torino e nel Museo di Antropologia dell' Università di Torino – Catalogo Generale del Museo Egizio di Torino. Serie Seconda, Supplemento al Volume VI (Turin 1991).

HABACHI 1985: L. Habachi, The Sanctuary of Heqaib (AV 33, Mainz am Rhein 1985).

HANNIG 2006: R. Hannig, Zur Paläographie der Särge aus Assiut (HÄB 47, Hildesheim 2006).

HARI 1985: R. Hari, La tombe thébaine du père divin Neferhotep (TT 50) (Geneva 1985).

HELCK 1956: W. Helck, Wirtschaftliche Bemerkungen zum privaten Grabbesitz im Alten Reich, in: MDAIK 14, 1956, 63–75.

HELCK 1974: W. Helck, Die altägyptischen Gaue (Wiesbaden 1974).

HELCK 1982: W. Helck, Opferstelle, in: LÄ IV, Wiesbaden 1982, 589–590.

HELCK 1984: W. Helck, Seschat, in: LÄ V, Wiesbaden 1984, 884–888.

HOFFMEIER 1981: J. Hoffmeier, The Possible Origins of the Tent of Purification in the Egyptian Funerary Cult, in: SAK 9, 1981, 167–177.

HOFFMEIER 1991: J. Hoffmeier, The Coffins of the Middle Kingdom. The Residence and Regions, in: S. Quirke (ed.), Middle Kingdom Studies (New Malden 1991) 69–86.

ILIN-TOMICH 2011: A. Ilin-Tomich, Changes in the ḥtp-dj-nsw Formula in the Late Middle Kingdom and the Second Intermediate Period, in: ZÄS 138, 2011, 20–34.

JANSEN-WINKELN 1996: K. Jansen-Winkeln, "Horizont" und "Verklärtheit". Zur Bedeutung der Wurzel ꜣḫ, in: SAK 23, 1996, 201–215.

KAHL 2007: J. Kahl, Ancient Asyut. The First Synthesis after 300 Years of Research (The Asyut Project 1, Wiesbaden 2007).

KAHL 2008: J. Kahl, Rezension von Rainer Hannig, Zur Paläographie der Särge aus Assiut, in: OLZ 103, 2008, 320–328.

Kahl 2016: J. Kahl, Zum Alter der Sargtext-Artefakte aus Assiut, in: Peter Dils, Lutz Popko (eds.), Zwischen Philologie und Lexikographie des Ägyptisch-Koptischen. Akten der Leipziger Abschlusstagung des Akademienprojekts „Altägyptisches Wörterbuch" (Abhandlungen der Sächsischen Akademie der Wissenschaften zu Leipzig, Philologisch-historische Klasse 84, Heft 3, Stuttgart–Leipzig) 29–55.

Kahl et al. 2016: J. Kahl et al., Asyut, Tomb III: Objects. Part 1 (The Asyut Project 3, Wiesbaden 2016).

Kamal 1916: A. Kamal, Fouilles à Deir Dronka et à Assiout (1913–1914), in: ASAE 16, 1916, 65–114.

Kamal 1934: M. Kamal, Trois sarcophages du Moyen Empire provenant de la nécropole d'Assiout, in: ASAE 34, 1934, 49–53.

Kees 1915: H. Kees, Eine Liste memphitischer Götter im Tempel von Abydos, in: RT 37, 1915, 57–76.

Kees 1923: H. Kees, Anubis "Herr von Sepa" und der 18. oberägyptische Gau, in: ZÄS 58, 1923, 79–101.

Kees 1941: H. Kess, Der Götterglaube im alten Ägypten (Leipzig 1941).

Kees 1956: H. Kees, Totenglauben und Jenseitsvorstellungen der alten Ägypter. Grundlagen und Entwicklung bis zum Ende des Mittleren Reiches (Berlin 1956).

Kessler 1980: D. Kessler, Manqabad, in: LÄ III, Wiesbaden 1980, 1182.

Kitchen 1969: K. A. Kitchen, Ramesside Inscriptions. Historical and Biographical I (Oxford 1969).

Krauss 1998: R. Krauss, Wenn und aber: das Wag-Fest und die Chronologie des Alten Reiches, in: GM 162, 1998, 53–63.

Lapp 1985: G. Lapp, Särge des Mittleren Reiches aus der ehemaligen Sammlung Khashaba. In Zusammenarbeit mit C. Müller-Winkler, M. Schneider, B. Lüscher (Wiesbaden 1985).

Lapp 1986: G. Lapp, Die Opferformel des Alten Reiches. Unter Berücksichtigung einiger späterer Formen (SDAIK 21, Mainz 1986).

Lapp 1993: G. Lapp, Typologie der Särge und Sargkammern von der 6. bis 13. Dynastie (SAGA 7, Heidelberg 1993).

Lefebvre 1912: G. Lefebvre, A travers la moyenne-égypte. Documents et notes, in: ASAE 12, 1912, 81–94.

Leitz 2002: Ch. Leitz, Lexikon der ägyptischen Götter und Götterbezeichnungen I–VIII (OLA 112, Leuven 2002).

Lepsius 1865: R. Lepsius, Die altägyptische Elle und ihre Einteilung (APAW: philol.-hist. Kl. 1865).

Lesko 1982: L. Lesko, The Texts on Egyptian Middle Kingdom Coffins, in: L'Égyptologie en 1979. Axes prioritaires de recherche. Tome 1 (Editions du Centre National de la Recherche Sientifique, Paris 1982) 39–43.

Lilyquist 1979: Ch. Lilyquist, Ancient Egyptian Mirrors from the Earliest Times through the Middle Kingdom (MÄS 27, München–Berlin 1979).

Locher 1992: K. Locher, Two Further Coffin Lids with Diagonal Star Clocks from the Egyptian Middle Kingdom, in: JHA 23.3, 1992, 201–207.

López 1974: J. López, Rapport préliminaire sur les fouilles d'Héakléopolis (1966), in: Oriens Antiquus 13; 1974, 299–316.

Luft 1994: U. Luft, The Date of the wꜣgy feast. Considerations on the Chronology of the Old Kingdom, in: A. Spalinger (ed.), Revolutions in Time (San Antonio 1994) 39–44.

Magee 1983: D. Magee, An Early Middle Kingdom Coffin from Akhmim in the Ashmolean Museum (No. 1911.477), in: JSSEA 13.4, 1983, 241–248.

Magee 1988: D. Magee, Asyût to the End of the Middle Kingdom I (unpl. Ph.D. Thesis, Oxford 1988).

Montet 1928: P. Montet, Les tombeaux de Siout et de Deir Rifeh, in: Kêmi 1, 1928, 53–68.

Montet 1961: P. Montet, Géographie de l'Égypte ancienne II (Paris 1961).

Münster 1968: M. Münster, Untersuchungen zur Göttin Isis vom Alten Reich bis zum Ende des Neuen Reiches (MÄS 11, Berlin 1968).

Neugebauer & Parker 1960, 1964, 1969: O. Neugebauer, R. Parker, Egyptian Astronomical Texts I–III (Providence 1960, 1964, 1969).

Nyord 2014: R. Nyord, Permeable Containers. Body and Cosmos in Middle Kingdom Coffins, in: R. Sousa (ed.), Body, Cosmos and Eternity. New Research Trends in the Iconography and Symbolism of Ancient Egyptian Coffins (Archaeopress Egyptology 3, Oxford 2014) 29–44.

Palanque 1903: Ch. Palanque, Notes de fouilles dans la nécropole d'Assiout, in: BIFAO 3, Le Caire 1903, 119–128.

Parker 1950: R. Parker, The Calendars of Ancient Egypt (Studies in Ancient Oriental Civilization 26, Chicago 1950).

Parker 1952: R. Parker, Review of Schott, Altägyptische Festdaten, in: BiOr 9, 1952, 100–101.

Parkinson 1999: R. Parkinson, Cracking Codes: the Rosetta Stone and Decipherment (London 1999).

PETRIE 1907: W. M. F. Petrie, Gizeh and Rifeh (British School of Archaeology in Egypt VII, London 1907).

PINCH 2002: G. Pinch, Handbook of Egyptian Mythology (Oxford 2002).

POSENER-KRIÉGER 1985: P. Posener-Kriéger, Remarques préliminaires sur les nouveaux papyrus d'Abousir, in: Ägypten. Dauer und Wandel (Mainz 1985) 35–43.

POSENER-KRIÉGER 1986: P. Posener-Kriéger, Wag-Feast, in: LÄ VI, Wiesbaden 1986, 1135–1139.

RANKE 1935: H. Ranke, Die ägyptischen Personennamen. 1. Verzeichnis der Namen (Glückstadt 1935).

ROEDER 1929: G. Roeder, Ein namenloser Frauensarg des Mittleren Reichs um 2000 v. Chr. aus Siut (Oberägypten) im Städtischen Museum zu Bremen, in: Schriften der Bremer Wissenschaftlichen Gesellschaft, Reihe D, Abhandlungen und Vorträge 3, Bremen 1929, 191–243.

SATZINGER 1997: H. Satzinger, Beobachtungen zur Opferformel. Theorie und Praxis, in: LingAeg 5, 1997, 1–13.

SCHENKEL 1962: W. Schenkel, Frühmittelägyptische Studien (Bonn 1962).

SCHLÖGL 1980: H. Schlögl, Der Gott Tatenen. Nach Texten und Bildern des Neuen Reiches (OBO 29, Freiburg, Schweiz 1980).

SCHLÖGL 1986: Tatenen, in: LÄ VI, 1986, 238–240.

SCHOTT 1950: S. Schott, Altägyptische Festdaten (Abhandlungen der Geistes- und Sozialwissenschaftlichen Klasse, Jahrgang 1950, Nr. 10, Wiesbaden 1950).

SCHULMAN 1986: A. Schulman, Some Observations on the ꜣḫ iḳr n Rꜥ-Stelae, in: BiOr 43, 1986, 302–348.

SETHE 1919: K. Sethe, Die Zeitrechnung der alten Aegypter im Verhältnis zu der der andern Völker. Eine entwicklungsgeschichtliche Studie, in: NGWG: philol.-hist. Kl. 1919, 287–320.

SPALINGER 1996: A. Spalinger, The Private Feast Lists of Ancient Egypt (ÄA 57, Wiesbaden 1996).

SPALINGER 2013: A. Spalinger, Further thoughts on the feast of Wꜣgj, in: ÉT 26, 2013, 616–624.

TAYLOR 1989: J. Taylor, Egyptian Coffins (Aylesbury 1989).

VYMAZALOVÁ 2008: H. Vymazalová, Some remarks on the wꜣg-festival in the papyrus archive of Raneferef, in: M. Bárta, H. Vymazalová (eds.), Chronology and Archaeology in Ancient Egypt. The Third Millennium B.C. (Prague 2008) 137–143.

WAINWRIGHT 1940: G. A. Wainwright, Seshat and the Pharaoh, in: JEA 26, 1940, 30–40.

WILDUNG 1977: D. Wildung, Ha, in: LÄ II, Wiesbaden 1977, 923.

WILLEMS 1988: H. Willems, Chests of Life. A Study of the Typology and Conceptual Development of Middle Kingdom Standard Class Coffins (MVEOL 25, Leiden 1988).

WILLEMS 1996: H. Willems, The Coffin of Heqata (Cairo JdE 36418). A Case Study of Egyptian Funerary Culture of the Early Middle Kingdom (OLA 70, Leuven 1996).

WILLEMS 2014: H. Willems, Historical and Archeological Aspects of Egyptian Funerary Culture: Religious Ideas and Ritual Practice in Middle Kingdom Elite Cemeteries (Culture and History of the Ancient Near East 73, Leiden – Boston 2014).

WINTER 1951: E. Winter, Das ägyptische Wag-Fest (unpl. Ph.D. Thesis, Wien 1951).

WILD 1971: H. Wild, Note concernant des antiquités trouvées, non à Deir Dronka, mais dans la nécropole d'Assiout, in: BIFAO 69, 1971, 307–309.

WOHLGEMUTH 1957: H. Wohlgemuth, Das Sokarfest (unpl. Ph.D. Thesis, Göttingen 1957).

ZECCHI 1996: M. Zecchi, In Search of Merymutef, "Lord of Khayet", in: Aegyptus. Rivista italiana di egittologia e di papirologia 76, 1996, 7–14.

ZITMAN 2010: M. Zitman, The Necropolis of Assiut. A case Study of Local Egyptian Funerary Culture from the Old Kingdom to the end of the Middle Kingdom. I. Text. II. Maps, Plans, Tables, Lists (OLA 180, Leuven–Paris 2010).

Die Torpassagen des Zweiwegebuchs in Assiut*

Jochem Kahl & John Moussa Iskander

Der ägyptische Archäologe Ahmed Bey Kamal unternahm kurz vor dem Ersten Weltkrieg im Auftrag des Sammlers Sayed Bey Khashaba Ausgrabungen auf dem am Wüstenrand gelegenen Gräberberg von Assiut, dem Gebel Assiut al-gharbi. Im Gegensatz zu anderen frühen Ausgräbern, die vor dem Ersten Weltkrieg in Assiut ohne jegliche Publikationstätigkeit unterwegs waren, veröffentlichte Kamal zumindest eine Liste ausgewählter Funde.[1] Unter der Nummer 158 erwähnte Kamal einen mit gemalten Palastfassaden dekorierten, „très joli cercueil en bois" eines Iti-ibi.[2] Hinweise auf die weitere Dekoration des Sarges gab er jedoch nicht. Heute wird der Sarg im Museum von Mallawi unter der Inventarnummer 566 aufbewahrt (Pl. 36a).[3] Er hat dort glücklicherweise auch die Plünderung des Museums am 14. August 2013 überstanden.[4] Nach der von Harco Willems erstellten Typologie der Außenwände von „Middle Kingdom Standard Class Coffins" kann der Sarg dem Typ VI/2 zugewiesen werden und somit der 12. Dynastie.[5]

Der 2,145 m lange und 53 cm breite Holzsarg S1Mal – so die ägyptologische Sigle für den Sarg – war einst für den *im.i-r' ś.t* und *im.i-r' šn^c.w 'Iti-ib=i* hergestellt worden. Bis heute wurde der Sarg nicht ausführlich beschrieben oder bearbeitet, Informationen über seine Innendekoration lagen nicht vor. Eine von den Autoren dieses Artikels veranlasste photographische Dokumentation aller Sargwände im Jahre 2019 erbrachte erstmals einen Überblick über das Text- und Bildprogramm des Sarges. In diesem Zusammenhang von besonderem Interesse scheint die Unterseite des Deckels zu sein, die im Folgenden genauer vorgestellt werden soll. Eine endgültige Bearbeitung des Sarges wird durch John Moussa Iskander erfolgen.[6]

Die Unterseite des Deckels ist mit zwei waagerechten, sich über die gesamte Länge des Deckels erstreckenden Textblöcken beschriftet, welche oben und unten von einer Farbleiter eingerahmt und durch eine mittig verlaufende horizontale Schriftzeile getrennt sind. Die Farbleiter besteht aus alternierenden blauen, roten, grünen und gelben Rechtecken, welche ihrerseits durch schmale weiße Rechtecke unterteilt sind; alle Rechtecke sind schwarz umrandet. Die Hieroglyphen der Horizontalzeile sind in der für Assiut typischen blauen Farbe auf gelbem Grund ausgeführt. Die darüber und darunter angeordneten Textblöcke bestehen aus schwarz bzw. rot geschriebenen Kursivhieroglyphen auf weißem Untergrund und vermitteln – bestärkt durch die gerundeten hölzernen Querleisten des Sargdeckels – den Anschein eines ausgerollten Papyrus (Pl. 36b).

* Dieser Artikel entstand im Rahmen des Forschungsprojektes „Asyut – centre of ancient trade", gefördert durch die Deutsche Forschungsgemeinschaft (DFG) - Projektnummer 426702318 und Narodowe Centrum Nauki.

1 KAMAL 1916.
2 KAMAL 1916: 113.
3 MESSIHA & ELHITTA 1979: 23, pl. XXVII. Der Sarg ist mit wenigen Detailphotos der Außenseite auch erwähnt bei HANNIG 2006: 742–743. Eine kurze Besprechung gibt auch ZITMAN 2010: Text, 339–344, Maps, 114–115. Vgl. weiterhin LAPP 1993: 131–132 (§ 294), 137 (§ 310), 141 (§ 318), Blatt 23, dort als S6 bezeichnet.
4 Ein Bild des Sarges in einer zerstörten Vitrine: https://www.nationalgeographic.com/news/2013/8/130823-museum-mallawi-egypt-looting-artifacts-archaeology-science-antiquities (Zugriff 2020-05-13).
5 WILLEMS 1988: 28, 161–164. Vgl. ALLEN 1996: 3, wonach der Sarkophag MH1A des Mentuhotep aus der Zeit Sesostris I. ebenfalls eine Typ VI-Dekoration aufweist.
6 Für die Publikationserlaubnis danken wir Dr. Nashwa Gaber, General Director of Foreign Missions Affairs and Permanent Committees; Unterstützung in Mallawi erhielten wir von Gehan Naseem Samy, General Director of Malawi Museum und Dr. Nassef Abdelwahed, General Director of the Selection Unit, the Grand Egyptian Museum.

Während im oberen Textblock eine Fassung von Sargtextspruch 335 wiedergegeben ist, ist im unteren Textblock eine 64 Kolumnen einnehmende Fassung der Sargtextsprüche 1100–1103 und 1108–1110 angebracht (Pls. 37–38, Abb. 1a–c). Damit ist der Sarg S1Mal nun der erste Textzeuge aus Assiut für die sieben Torpassagen, die aus den Sargtextsprüchen 1100–1110 bekannt sind.[7] Die Torpassagen sind in der Grabkammer von Chesu, dem Älteren in Kom el-Hisn[8] (KH1KH) und auf der von Wael Sherbiny in Bearbeitung befindlichen Lederrolle Kairo JdE 69292 belegt.[9] Sie sind auch auf den Särgen BH3C, BH4C und BH1Br aus Beni Hasan bezeugt, bei De Buck allerdings separat als Sargtextsprüche 901 bzw. 579 aufgeführt.[10] Die Sargtextsprüche 1100–1110 sind insbesondere aber aus Berscheh bekannt, wo sie einen Teil der Komposition des Zweiwegebuches bilden. Sie werden von Leonard Lesko als „Section VIII", von Burkhard Backes als Teil von „Abschnitt 6" und von Wael Sherbiny als „Part 11" und „Part 12" des Zweiwegebuches bezeichnet.[11]

Die auf dem Sarg S1Mal bezeugte Textfassung der Torpassage gibt die Folge von sieben Toren wieder, die in Berscheh in eine „erste Torfolge" mit vier Toren mit Wächtern und eine „zweite Torfolge" mit drei Toren und Wächtern unterteilt ist.[12] Im einzelnen sind folgende Sprüche auf dem Sargdeckel angebracht:

S1Mal, Kol. 1–16: CT 1100; CT 901; KH1KH, Kol. 255–268
S1Mal, Kol. 16–28: CT 1101; KH1KH, Kol. 269–279
S1Mal, Kol. 28–36: CT 1102; KH1KH Kol. 280–288
S1Mal, Kol. 36–48: CT 1103; CT 579; KH1KH, Kol. 288–300
S1Mal, Kol. 49–52: CT 1108; KH1KH, Kol. 301–303
S1Mal, Kol. 53–58: CT 1109; KH1KH, Kol. 304–307
S1Mal, Kol. 59–64: CT 1110; KH1KH, Kol. 308–311

Der Aufbau der Tornennungen und der Torwächter ist unterschiedlich zu der Zweiwegebuch-Fassung aus Berscheh/Hermopolis gegliedert. Auf S1Mal wird ein neues Tor stets mit der Angabe „Wächter des n-ten Tores" (in numerisch aufsteigender Reihenfolge) angegeben. Dann folgt ein Passierspruch bzw. ein Schutzspruch. Zuletzt wird der Name des jeweiligen Torwächters bekannt gemacht. Die Nennung der Wächter der jeweiligen Tore sowie ihre Namen sind dabei rot geschrieben:

S1Mal, Kol. 1–16: <Nennung „Wächter des ersten Tores"> – Passierspruch – Name des Wächters.[13]
S1Mal, Kol. 16–28: Nennung „Wächter des zweiten Tores" – Passierspruch – Name des Wächters.[14]
S1Mal, Kol. 28–36: Nennung „Wächter des dritten Tores" – Passierspruch – Name des Wächters.[15]
S1Mal, Kol. 36–48: Nennung „Wächter des vierten Tores" – Passierspruch – Name des Wächters.[16]
S1Mal, Kol. 49–52: Nennung „Wächter des fünften Tores" – Schutzspruch vor dem Wächter – Name des Wächters.[17]
S1Mal, Kol. 53–58: Nennung „Wächter des sechsten Tores" – Schutzspruch vor dem Wächter – Name des Wächters.[18]

---

7 De Buck 1961: 416 –440.
8 Silverman 1988: 73 –77, Abb. 60 –64.
9 Sherbiny 2017a: 22, 37; Sherbiny 2017b.
10 De Buck 1961: 107–108 (CT VII, 107k–108r, Spruch 901); De Buck 1956: 194 (CT VI, 194j–q, Spruch 579).
11 Lesko 1972: 109–119; Backes 2005: 100–107, 379–409; Sherbiny 2017a: 424–473.
12 Backes 2005: 100–107.
13 Zu der Fassung auf den Särgen aus Berscheh vgl. Backes 2005: 100.
14 Zu der Fassung auf den Särgen aus Berscheh vgl. Backes 2005: 101.
15 Zu der Fassung auf den Särgen aus Berscheh vgl. Backes 2005: 101–102.
16 Zu der Fassung auf den Särgen aus Berscheh vgl. Backes 2005: 102–103.
17 Zu der Fassung auf den Särgen aus Berscheh vgl. Backes 2005: 104–105.
18 Zu der Fassung auf den Särgen aus Berscheh vgl. Backes 2005: 105–106.

S1Mal, Kol. 59–64: Nennung „Wächter des siebten Tores" – Schutzspruch vor dem Wächter – Name des Wächters.[19]

Die Namen der Torwächter auf S1Mal unterscheiden sich von denen, die auf den Särgen aus Berscheh belegt sind. Teilweise sind jedoch Gemeinsamkeiten erkennbar, insbesondere beim Namen des ersten, sechsten und siebten Torwächters:

Wächter des ersten Tores (Kol. 14–16): *Wnn-m-3ḫ.t ḥwn.w-śpd-ḥr wnn-m-ḥ3.t*

„der im Lichtland ist, der Jüngling, der mit scharfem Gesicht,[20] der an der Spitze ist"

Berscheh-Särge (CT VII, 416a; Wächter des ersten Tores der ersten Torfolge): *Dwn-ḫ3.t* (B3C, B1C, B9C, B1L, B3L)

Wächter des zweiten Tores (Kol. 27–28): *K3-ḫri.t / K3-ḫr* (?)

„der niederfallende Stier; der Opferstier"[21] / „der fällende Stier"[22] (?)

Berscheh-Särge (CT VII, 420a; Wächter des zweiten Tores der ersten Torfolge): *Mdś-śn* (B9C, B1L), *Ikn.ti* (B3C)

Wächter des dritten Tores (Kol. 35–36): [...] *wr.t i3b.t* [...]

„[…] die Große, Osten […]"

Berscheh-Särge (CT VII, 423b; Wächter des dritten Tores der ersten Torfolge): *Wnm-ḫ3m.t-pḫ.wi=f* (B3C); *Wnm-ḫ3m.t-n-pḫ.wi=f* (B1L); *Wnm-ḫ3m.t-n-n-pḫ.wi=f* (B9B)

Wächter des vierten Tores (Kol. 48): *Dd-ḥr H3-ḫrw ꜥnḫ*

„der mit beständigem Gesicht, der mit jubelnder Stimme,[23] Lebender"

Berscheh-Särge (CT VII, 426d; Wächter des vierten Tores der ersten Torfolge): *Ḫśf-ḥr ꜥ3-ḫrw* (B3C, B9C, B1L, B3L)

Beni Hasan-Särge (CT VI, 194q): *Ḫśf-nḥm-ḫr.w* (BH3C)

Wächter des fünften Tores (51–52): *ir.w* [...] *Ḫśf-ḥr-ḫm.y*

„Gestalten (?) […], der die Umstürzler abwehrt"[24]

Berscheh-Särge (CT VII, 436h; Wächter des ersten Tores der zweiten Torfolge): *Śḫd-ḥr ꜥ3-ir.w* (B3C, B1L), *Śḫd-ḥr ꜥ3-ir.w* (B2Bo), *Śḫr-ḥr ꜥ3-ir.w* (B3L), *Śdd-ḥr ꜥ3-ir.w* (B9C),

Wächter des sechsten Tores (55–58): *wdn* [...] *ꜥnḫ-m-iw-r-ꜥk* [...] *n.t-ḥr(.w){t}-śmś.w* [...] *m-fnṯ.w*

„gewichtig an […], der lebt von dem, der kommt, um einzutreten […] des Älteren Horus, der von Würmern […]"[25]

Berscheh-Särge (CT VII, 437f; Wächter des zweiten Tores der zweiten Torfolge): *ꜥnḫ-m-fnṯ.w* (B9C, B1L, B3L, B3C[?])

---

19 Zu der Fassung auf den Särgen aus Berscheh vgl. Backes 2005: 106–107.
20 Vgl. CT VII, 296 g und 502 g und Leitz 2002c: 284.
21 Vgl. Wb III, 322.11.
22 Vgl. *ḫr* als transitives Verb „fällen, niederwerfen": Wb III, 321.4.
23 *H3-ḫrw* ist als Torwächter aus dem Totenbuch (Kapitel 144 und 147) bekannt; vgl. Leitz 2002a: 789–790.
24 Vgl. im Zweiwegebuch CT VII, 286d und 499a; auch als Torwächter aus dem Totenbuch Kapitel 144 bekannt; vgl. Leitz 2002b: 957.
25 Der Name kann vermutlich ergänzt werden zu *ꜥnḫ-m-fnṯ.w* „der von Würmern lebt" (in CT VII, 437f ist dies der Wächter des zweiten Tores in der zweiten Torfolge; vgl. Backes 2005: 105).

Wächter des siebten Tores (61–64): *ikw ḥm-ḫrw ꜥnḫ-[m?]-śḏ.t śti[-n?]-nb[=f? ...]*

„Angreifer,[26] mit brennender Stimme,[27] der lebt [vom?] Feuer, der [für seinen?] Herrn schießt ---"

Berscheh-Särge (CT VII, 439a; Wächter des dritten Tores der zweiten Torfolge): *Ikn.ty kḫꜣ-ḫrw m śḏ.t* (B3C, B4C), *Ikn.t kḫ[...]* (B3L), *[...] kꜣ ḫrw m śḏ.t* (B2P), *Ikn.t kḫꜣ śḏ.t ḫrw=f* (B9C), *Ikn.t kḫꜣ ḫrw=f m śḏ.t* (B1L)

Die Sargtextsprüche 1100–1103 und 1108–1110 bilden einen Bestandteil der Komposition des Zweiwegebuches, wie sie aus Bersheh bekannt ist.[28] Das neben Beni Hasan (BH3C und BH4C) und Kôm el-Hisn (KH1KH) nun auch für Assiut belegte Vorkommen dieser Sprüche bzw. von Teilen dieser Sprüche bestätigt abermals die überregionale Verbreitung des Spruchguts in Mittelägypten wie in Unterägypten.[29] Der nach Auskunft des heutigen Besitzers aus der Gegend von Assiut stammende Sarg des *Jmnj*[30] (S8X) weist weitere Sprüche auf, die mit solchen aus dem Zweiwegebuch vergleichbar sind: Die Sargtextsprüche 1040, 1078 und 1079, die auf diesem Sarg allerdings in einer Fassung zwischen Sargtext- und Totenbuchtradition vorzuliegen scheinen.[31] Vermutlich waren also mehrere Sprüche des Zweiwegebuchs in Assiut im Umlauf, allerdings in anderen bzw. isolierten Kontexten. Der Sarg L1NY aus el-Lischt[32] (Sargtextspruch 1040) und die Pyramide des Merenre in Saqqara[33] (Sargtextspruch 1030) bieten zudem Belege für einzelne Sprüche, die schon aus der Zeit des Alten Reiches stammen bzw. auf dieses zurückgehen[34] und in der Komposition des Zweiwegebuchs Verwendung fanden.

Der Textzeuge S1Mal und die durch ihn erstmalig attestierte Bedeutung der auch aus dem Zweiwegebuch bekannten Torfolgen für die Jenseitsvorstellungen im Assiut des Mittleren Reiches wirft abermals die Frage nach dem Ursprung, Transfer und den Variationen der Textkomposition des Zweiwegebuches auf. Die Textfassung auf S1Mal scheint den aus Beni Hasan und Kom el-Hisn bekannten näher zu stehen als den aus Berscheh bezeugten, weist dennoch auch deutliche Unterschiede zu erstgenannten auf.

Die Särge aus Berscheh nennen in der Ersten Torfolge beim vierten Torwächter (Sargtextspruch 1103, CT VII, 429b) den Gott Thot, dessen häufige Erwähnung im gesamten Zweiwegebuch als Begründung galt, den Ursprung des Zweiwegebuches in Hermopolis zu suchen. Auffällig ist, dass die überregionalen Varianten S1Mal, BH3C und KH1KH an dieser Stelle aber nicht Thot, sondern *ntr* „Gott" lesen.[35] Dies deutet darauf hin, dass das Zweiwegebuch in seiner aus Berscheh/Hermopolis bekannten Fassung aus einer Umarbeitung bereits überregional bestehender Sprüche entstanden ist.[36] Dazu passt eine andere Beobachtung: Beim Passierspruch zum vierten Wächter in der ersten Torfolge (CT VII, 427a–d; CT VI, 194j–p) stimmt S1Mal stark mit BH3C und KH1KH überein. Die Fassung von BH3C und KH1KH wurde von Backes als sinnvoller und ursprünglicher gegenüber der Lesart der Textzeugen aus Berscheh erachtet (dort Auslassung von *ḏśr p.t ḏśr tꜣ* vor der Nennung der Gottheiten Schu und Ruti).[37] Auch

---

26 Van der Molen 2000: 56; Wb I, 139.1

27 Zu *ḥm* vgl. Wb II, 489.15; zu dieser Bezeichnung des Torwächters vgl. *Kꜣꜣ-ḫrw-m-śḏ.t* „mit feuerlohender Stimme" in der Version aus Berscheh (Backes 2005: 106).

28 Zu den Versionen aus Berscheh s. unlängst Willems 2018 mit dem Textzeugen B4B der Dame Anch.

29 Silverman 1996: 133–137.

30 Lapp 1986: 135.

31 Lapp 1986: 144–145; Sherbiny 2017a: 22–23 sieht darin allerdings bereits Versionen der Totenbuch-Kapitel 117 und 118.

32 Allen 2006: 25.

33 Pierre-Croisiau 2004: 268, 278 (Fig. 17); Pierre-Croisiau 2019: 318; Mathieu 2019: 260–261 (TP 1129).

34 Sherbiny 2017a: 17.

35 BH3C: Sargtextspruch 579, CT VI, 194o; KH1KH, 297: Silverman 1988: 76, Fig. 63. Vgl. dazu bereits Hoffmeier 1996: 50.

36 Vgl. Backes 2005: 437, der skeptisch ist bezüglich eines Zusammenhangs der häufigen Nennung des Thot und der Überlieferung in Berscheh: „Jede Erwähnung des Thot in den Texten läßt sich ohne Hinweis auf Berscheh erklären." CT VII, 429b deutet nun aber doch auf eine bewusste, auf Thot zugeschnittene Redaktion der Texte in Berscheh hin.

37 Backes 2005: 161–162.

S1Mal scheint an dieser Stelle den Urtext zu überliefern, wenn auch nicht ohne leichte Veränderung: *ḏśr p.t tȝ śdȝ Šw Rw{rw}.tj r p.t tȝ* (CT VII, 427a–b).[38]

Der Ursprung der Texte des Zweiwegebuchs dürfte somit außerhalb von Hermopolis zu suchen sein.[39] Dies wird durch die Bezeugung von Sargtextspruch 1130 in der Pyramide des Merenre in Saqqara bestätigt. Die Fassung(en) von Hermopolis/Berscheh stellen nach derzeitigem Stand eine lokale Neukonfiguration dar, vermutlich eine Adaption und lokale Redaktion eines schon existierenden Textes bzw. schon existierender Textstücke, wie die oben genannten Beobachtungen nahelegen. In Assiut kursierten spätestens seit der zweiten Hälfte der 12. Dynastie mehrere Teile aus dem Zweiwegebuch (S1Mal und Sarg des *Jmnj*) in einer von Berscheh/Hermopolis unterschiedlichen Tradition, wobei sie in verschiedenen Zusammenhängen separat benutzt wurden.

Bibliographie

Allen 1996: J. P. Allen, Coffin Texts from Lisht, in: H. Willems (Hg.), The World of the Coffin Texts. Proceedings of the Symposium Held on the Occasion of the 100th Birthday of Adriaan de Buck, Leiden, December 17–19, 1992 (Egyptologische Uitgaven 9; Leiden 1996), 1–15.

Allen 2006: J. P. Allen, The Egyptian Coffin Texts: Volume 8. Middle Kingdom Copies of Pyramid Texts (Oriental Institute Publications 132; Chicago 2006).

Backes 2005: B. Backes, Das altägyptische »Zweiwegebuch«. Studien zu den Sargtext-Sprüchen 1029–1130 (Ägyptologische Abhandlungen 69; Wiesbaden 2005).

De Buck 1956: A. De Buck, The Egyptian Coffin Texts VI (Oriental Institute Publications 81; Chicago 1956).

De Buck 1961: A. De Buck, The Egyptian Coffin Texts VII (Oriental Institute Publications 87; Chicago 1961).

Hannig 2006: R. Hannig, Zur Paläographie der Särge aus Assiut (Hildesheimer Ägyptologische Beiträge 47; Hildesheim 2006).

Hoffmeier 1996: J. K. Hoffmeier, Are there regionally-based theological differences in the Coffin Texts?, in: H. Willems (Hg.), The World of the Coffin Texts. Proceedings of the Symposium Held on the Occasion of the 100th Birthday of Adriaan de Buck, Leiden, December 17–19, 1992 (Egyptologische Uitgaven 9; Leiden 1996), 45–54.

Kamal 1916: A. Bey Kamal, Fouilles à Deir Dronka et à Assiout (1913–1914), in: Annales du Service des Antiquités de l'Égypte 16, 1916, 65–114.

Lapp 1993: G. Lapp, Typologie der Särge und Sargkammern von der 6. bis 13. Dynastie (Studien zur Geschichte und Archäologie Altägyptens 7; Heidelberg 1993).

Leitz 2002a: C. Leitz (Hg.), Lexikon der ägyptischen Götter und Götterbezeichnungen IV (Orientalia Lovaniensia Analecta 113; Leuven – Paris – Dudley, MA 2002).

Leitz 2002b: C. Leitz (Hg.), Lexikon der ägyptischen Götter und Götterbezeichnungen V (Orientalia Lovaniensia Analecta 114: Leuven – Paris – Dudley, MA 2002).

Leitz 2002c: C. Leitz (Hg.), Lexikon der ägyptischen Götter und Götterbezeichnungen VI (Orientalia Lovaniensia Analecta 115; Leuven – Paris – Dudley, MA 2002).

Lesko 1972: L. H. Lesko, The Ancient Egyptian Book of Two Ways (Berkeley – Los Angeles 1972).

Mathieu 2019: B. Mathieu, Traduction et translittération des formules nouvelles (TP 1101–1151), in: I. Pierre-Croisiau, Les textes de la Pyramide de Mérenrê. Édition, description et analyse (Mémoires publiés par les membres de l'Institut Français d'Archéologie Orientale du Caire 140; Mission archéologique Franco-Suisse de Saqqâra IX; Le Caire 2019), 239–270.

Messiha & Elhitta 1979: Hishmat Messiha and Mohamed Elhitta, Mallawi Antiquities Museum. A Brief Description (Cairo 1979).

---

38 Die Schreibung auf S1Mal resultierte offensichtlich aus falsch aufgelösten gespaltenen Kolumnen: *ḏśr p.t (ḏśr) tȝ śdȝ Šw r p.t (śdȝ) Rw{rw}.tj r tȝ.*

39 Vgl. Hoffmeier 1996; Silverman 1996.

Pierre-Croisiau 2004: I. Pierre-Croisiau, Nouvelles identifications de Textes des Sarcophages parmi les "nouveaux" Textes des Pyramides de Pépy Ier et de Mérenrê, in: S. Bickel & B. Mathieu (Hgg.), D'un monde à l'autre. Textes des Pyramides & Textes des Sarcophages. Actes de la table ronde internationale "Textes des Pyramides versus Textes des Sarcophages". Ifao – 24–26 septembre 2001 (Bibliothèque d'Étude 139; Cairo 2004), 263–278.

Pierre-Croisiau 2019: I. Pierre-Croisiau, Les textes de la Pyramide de Mérenrê. Édition, description et analyse (Mémoires publiés par les membres de l'Institut Français d'Archéologie Orientale du Caire 140; Mission archéologique Franco-Suisse de Saqqâra IX; Le Caire 2019).

Sherbiny 2017a: W. Sherbiny, Through Hermopolitan Lenses. Studies on the So-called Book of Two Ways in Ancient Egypt (Probleme der Ägyptologie 33; Leiden – Boston 2017).

Sherbiny 2017b: W. Sherbiny, The so-called Book of Two Ways on a Middle Kingdom religious leather roll, in: G. Rosati & M. C. Guidotti (Hgg.), Proceedings of the XI International Congress of Egyptologists, Florence, Egyptian Museum Florence, 23–30 August 2015 (Archaeopress Egyptology 19; Oxford 2017), 594–596.

Silverman 1988: D. P. Silverman, The Tomb Chamber of Ḥsw The Elder: The Inscribed Material at Kom el-Hisn. Part 1: Illustrations (American Research Center in Egypt, Reports 10; Winona Lake 1988).

Silverman 1996: D. P. Silverman, Coffin Texts from Bersheh, Kom el Hisn, and Mendes, in: H. Willems (Hg.), The World of the Coffin Texts. Proceedings of the Symposium Held on the Occasion of the 100th Birthday of Adriaan de Buck, Leiden, December 17–19, 1992 (Egyptologische Uitgaven 9; Leiden 1996), 129–141.

Van der Molen 2000: R. van der Molen, A Hieroglyphic Dictionary of Egyptian Coffin Texts (Probleme der Ägyptologie 15; Leiden – Boston – Köln 2000).

Wild 1971: H. Wild, Note concernant des antiquités trouvées, non à Deir Dronka, mais dans la nécropole d'Assiout, in: Bulletin de l'Institut Français d'Archéologie Orientale 69, 1971, 307–309.

Willems 1988: H. Willems, Chests of Life. A Study of the Typology and Conceptual Development of Middle Kingdom Standard Class Coffins (Mededelingen en Verhandelingen van het Vooraziatisch-Egyptisch Genootschap "Ex Oriente Lux" 25; Leiden 1988).

Willems 2018: H. Willems, A Fragment of an Early Book of Two Ways on the Coffin of Ankh from Dayr al-Barsha (B4B), in: The Journal of Egyptian Archaeology 104, 2018, 145–160.

Zitman 2010: M. Zitman, The Necropolis of Assiut. A Case Study of Local Egyptian Funerary Culture from the Old Kingdom to the End of the Middle Kingdom, 2 vols. (Orientalia Lovaniensia Analecta 180; Leuven – Paris – Walpole, MA 2010).

Internetquelle:

https://www.nationalgeographic.com/news/2013/8/130823-museum-mallawi-egypt-looting-artifacts-archaeology-science-antiquities (Zugriff 2020-05-13).

Abb. 1a: Inschriften auf dem unteren Teil der Deckelunterseite von S1Mal (Sargtextsprüche 1100–1102 [Anfang]).

Abb. 1b: Inschriften auf dem unteren Teil der Deckelunterseite von S1Mal (Sargtextsprüche 1102 [Fortsetzung]–1110 [Anfang]).

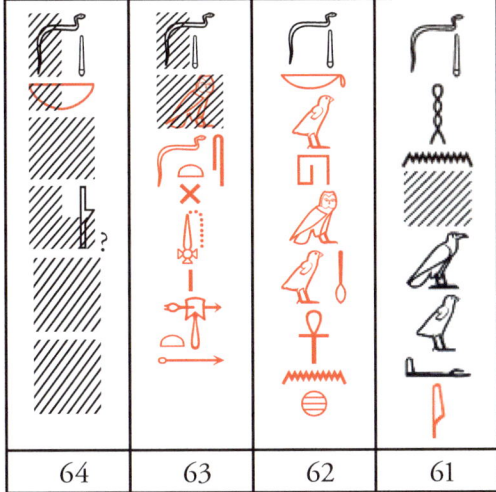

Abb. 1c: Inschriften auf dem unteren Teil der Deckelunterseite von S1Mal (Sargtextspruch 1110 [Fortsetzung]).

Correlations of Wooden Model Equipment and Wall Decorations in Asyut[1]

Monika Zöller-Engelhardt

During the fieldwork of the Asyut Project in the necropolis near the middle Egyptian city of Asyut numerous fragments of wooden model material came to light. They comprise an interesting cross section of the model equipment of burials from the First Intermediate Period and the Early Middle Kingdom, supported by representative finds of early excavators in the Gebel Asyut al-gharbi. In correlation with newly discovered and documented scenes on the walls in the tombs of Asyuti high officials, the material can provide further insight into the question of possible correlations between wall decorations and wooden model material and give new information on the compilation and composition of wooden model equipment of the First Intermediate Period and the Early Middle Kingdom.

1. Introduction

Models are a complex and varied category among the Ancient Egyptian artifact classes.[2] The term 'model' can designate a wide array of object types in the Egyptological literature, ranging from "small-scale representations of objects and people from everyday life"[3] up to a closed class of representations of single (non-wooden) figures, parts of figures as well as architectural elements in three-dimensional manufacturing or raised relief.[4] Thus a designation as funerary models seems more fitting to designate the typical small-scale representations of objects and people made of wood[5] found in funerary contexts.[6] Following the seminal studies of Tooley, these wooden models can be classified into five main categories:[7]

— agriculture and animal husbandry
— food preparation
— industrial processes
— boats
— offering bearers/estate figures[8]

---

1 I am grateful to the directors of the Asyut Project, Prof. Dr. Jochem Kahl, Prof. Dr. Ursula Verhoeven-van Elsbergen, Prof. Dr. Mahmoud el-Khadragy and Prof. Dr. Mohamed Abdelrahiem, for enabling me to analyze the wooden model material and wall decorations from Asyut and additionally wish to thank Prof. Dr. Jochem Kahl for his helpful comments on the manuscript. I am also thankful for additional support and proofreading by Dr. Andrea Kilian and detailed information regarding the decoration of tomb N13.1 by Eva Gervers M. A. Moreover, I thank Tina Beck M. A. for information and fruitful discussions and Tobias Konrad M. A. for a literature reference on the coffins of Mesehti.
2 For a concise definition of artifact class, type and variant cf. Odler 2016: 13–20. In regard to archaeological object classes compare also Feugère 2018.
3 Tooley 2001: 424.
4 Liepsner 1982: 168–180.
5 Even within the definition as wooden funerary models, further materials like cloth, rope or grain must be added (cf. Barker 2016: 69). Regarding model tools and weapons, metal and leather is to be taken into account, as well.
6 Cf. Barker 2016; Eschenbrenner-Diemer 2017: 134–135.
7 Tooley 2001: 425. Tooley extrapolates the main categories for Middle Kingdom models in particular. Cf. also Tooley 1989; 1995.
8 The terms are used parallel here, designating "Figures, predominantly young females, although males do occur, depicted bringing supplies of food and drink […]" (Tooley 1989: 175). In model form, they are often singular (female) figures with tight colorful dresses, striding forward, carrying supplies (in Asyut typically a bird by its wings in one hand, while

All categories have been documented for the region of Asyut with various representations in the sparse early publications,[9] as well as in collections and museums all over the world.[10] The recent fieldwork of the Asyut Project established further evidence for nearly all of these categories apart from clear examples of industrial processes and animal husbandry.[11]

A further category of wooden models is of special interest for Asyut: soldier models, especially in comparison to model tools and weapons,[12] the latter of which the Asyut Project team discovered a great amount of fragmentary material in the main tomb shafts of the nomarchs Khety I (Tomb V/M11.1) and Iti-ibi (Tomb III/N12.1).

The following chapter compiles samples of the model material discovered during the fieldwork of the Asyut Project as well as selected contexts found by early excavators mostly at the beginning of the twentieth century. The next section gives descriptions of a selection of relevant wall decorations from Asyut that comprise objects, figures and scenes comparable with the thematic scopes present in the model material. The focus lies on iconographic and typological features of weaponry, tools and boats, which are the categories best represented and preserved in the model material and wall decorations.[13] In a fourth section the evidence will be compared, while the last chapter presents the findings of the comparison as well as thoughts on further correlations of the material.

The analysis in general is limited by several factors: As far as can be said, only a few tombs in the Gebel Asyut al-gharbi were (fully) decorated.[14] Among these are the large tombs of the nomarchs of the First Intermediate Period and the Early Middle Kingdom, above all Tomb V (M11.1/Khety I), Tomb III (N12.1/Iti-ibi) and Tomb IV (N12.2/Khety II), Tomb I (P10.1/Djefai-Hapi I), Tomb II (O13.1/Djefai-Hapi II), H11.1 ("Northern Soldiers-Tomb") and the recently discovered Tomb N13.1 (Iti-ibi(-iqer)). In most cases the decoration is only partly preserved and in poor condition, exceptions are the well-known Tomb I and the Tomb N13.1.[15] Therefore, the comparison between the model material and the wall decorations is limited

a) by the extent to which the wall decorations are preserved,

b) by the extent to which the model equipment is preserved,

---

the other is raised to support a characteristic yellow basket with black lines and white flour summit on their head [cf. Eschenbrenner-Diemer 2017: 160, fn. 128]). Usually, they are much taller than model figures incorporated in scenes, ranging from 0.6–0.7 m up to over 1 m. Additionally, there exist processions of (smaller) offering bearers (e. g. the well-known "Bersha-Procession", today in the Museum of Fine Arts, Boston, Acc.no. 21.326 [Freed & Doxey 2009: 152–154], or the procession from the tomb of Meketre, today in the Metropolitan Museum, New York, No. 20.3.8 [Roehrig 2015: 225]), which can carry additional supplies like funerary furniture, textiles/cloth, or sometimes weaponry. Estate figurines/ offering bearers are interpreted as representations of funerary estates or members of funerary estates, respectively, as well as symbols for Upper and Lower Egypt. Furthermore, they may allude to the goddesses Isis and Nephthys and generally indicate the fertility and abundance of the Egyptian land. On the discussions and interpretations cf. Jacquet-Gordon 1962; Eggebrecht 1977: 370–371; Vandier 1958: 147–153; Tooley 1989: 175–248; Freed & Doxey 2009: 155–158; Roehrig 2015: 226–227.

9 Cf. e. g. Chassinat & Palanque 1911; Ryan 1988 (on the excavations of David G. Hogarth); Kahl, Sbriglio, Del Vesco & Trapani 2019 (on the excavations of Ernesto Schiaparelli).

10 Cf. Zitman 2010; Eschenbrenner-Diemer 2017.

11 Cf. Zöller-Engelhardt 2007; 2012a; 2012b; 2016.

12 Concerning the 'model' character of the items cf. footnote 25.

13 Another well-represented category in the wall decorations, vessels, have been compared to the archaeological evidence including selected model material by Kilian 2018.

14 The decoration in almost all cases seems limited to the superstructure of the Asyuti tombs; the only evidence for the decoration of a tomb's substructure has recently been discovered in the lowest chamber of the complex substructure of Tomb I/P10.1 of Djefai-Hapi I (Kahl 2018: 139 with fig. 5a; Zöller-Engelhardt forthcoming in *Studien zur Altägyptischen Kultur*).

15 The publications of both tombs are in preparation in The Asyut Project series by Mahmoud el-Khadragy and Jochem Kahl. I thank Eva Gervers M. A. for her information regarding details of the wall decorations of Tomb N13.1 and Dr. Andrea Kilian for her information on specifics of the decorations in Tomb I/P10.1 and N13.1.

c) by the disturbed find contexts, which can lead to uncertain allocations of model material,

d) and poorly documented find contexts by early excavators, which can also lead to uncertain allocations of model material or incomplete compilations of grave goods from individual burials.

Additionally, for Asyut the evaluation is complicated by the fact that the wall decorations in tombs which still yielded a greater variety of model material are very poorly preserved, while the tombs with better preserved wall decorations (Tomb N13.1 and Tomb I) held only some material, which often cannot be assigned to the original tomb equipment with certainty.[16] (Table 1) Therefore, the comparison of the material has to take place across tombs and a time period spanning the First Intermediate Period to the Early Middle Kingdom.

2. Compilation of selected model material from Asyut (Table 2)

The following section comprises model material discovered by the Asyut Project, listed in chronological order according to tomb owner.[17]

Tomb V (M11.1/dating: FIP, nomarch Khety I)

Shaft 2, side chamber (dating: FIP, nomarch Khety I):[18]
In a depth of 10.5 m the central Shaft 2 in Tomb V revealed a side chamber of quite large proportions (5.2 x 5.2 m) with unusual architecture. It is structured by one central pillar supporting a tapered architrave dividing the ceiling of the chamber.[19] At the bottom of the shaft and inside the side chamber several wooden fragments were detected. Their state of preservation was so poor that only some of the larger fragments could be identified, while most of the material was too decayed for a functional reconstruction. Regarding the model material, noteworthy are

— the model of a *ḥs.t*-vase with minimal traces of a golden coating,
— and the heavily decayed hulls of maybe three model boats.

The poor state of preservation of the model boat hulls did not allow an accurate identification of their type. Interesting, however, was the discovery of a larger quantity of wooden handles of (model)[20] tools which led to an overall count of

— at least 20 axes,
— at least 40 adzes,
— and 15 chisels or gravers.

The presence of numerous tool and weapon handles is reflected in the find context of the side chamber of Shaft 3 of Tomb III.

---

16 The selected model material discovered by early excavators presented in this article was found in undecorated tombs.
17 For the latest information on the chronological sequence cf. KAHL 2019: 33–37 with further references.
18 The architecture and the find context are described by KAHL & MALUR 2011: 182–183; the wooden model material by ZÖLLER-ENGELHARDT 2012b: 190–194.
19 KAHL & MALUR 2011: 183; KAHL 2012: 190.
20 Cf. footnote 25.

Tomb III (N12.1/dating: FIP, nomarch Iti-ibi)[21]

Tomb III features four vertical burial shafts arranged inside its large hall, each exhibiting one side chamber branching off to the south. The deepest and largest shaft, Shaft 3, is arranged on the tomb axis in front of the west wall. One of the remaining shafts, Shaft 4, had been unknown to modern science and was undisturbed since the Byzantine Period.

Shaft 1, shaft filling (dating: unknown):

The first shaft cleaned by the Asyut Project contained various fragments of wooden models, among others scattered arms of model figures, some nautical and architectural elements. The material, discovered in a low depth of 0.3–0.9 m inside the shaft filling, proved to be discarded remains of early excavations, most likely Chassinat and Palanque.[22]

Shaft 2, bottom of shaft and side chamber (dating: probably FIP[23]):

As was the case in Shaft 1, Shaft 2 contained a mixture of ancient finds and modern remnants of early excavators. The bottom of the shaft yielded a few model arms, which do not resemble the model material discovered in the side chamber. The side chamber, however, provided a small number of homogeneous fragments, among others model figure parts, a wooden model vessel, the wings of the bird from an offering bearer/estate figure as well as some oar fragments and a part of a rudder. Thus, the fragments point to the original presence of at least

– one food producing/processing scene,
– one model boat,
– and one offering bearer/estate figure.

Shaft 3, side chamber (dating: probably FIP, nomarch Iti-ibi):

Shaft 3 is the largest and deepest of the four shafts in Tomb III. It has the largest side chamber, as well, and held most of the wooden model remnants discovered by the Asyut Project. The filling of the shaft contained only little material, while the side chamber offered a broad variety of fragmentary model equipment. Although fragmentary, the remnants of the model material point to the original presence of the following objects of equipment:

– two or maybe three model boats (including a funerary barque, a travel/transport ship with cabin[24] and a rowing boat),
– one granary,
– one brewery/bakery scene,
– maybe one slaughtering scene,
– and one offering bearer/estate figure.

Most notably is the great amount of (model)[25] tool and weapon handles. The side chamber held numerous fragments, which lead to a minimum number of:

---

21 Kahl 2016b. For the model material see Zöller-Engelhardt 2007; Zöller-Engelhardt 2012a; Zöller-Engelhardt 2016.

22 Among the material discovered by the Asyut Project were several sheets of notes mentioning the division of finds between the French excavators and the Egyptian Museum Cairo (Kahl 2007: 31–32; Kahl 2016a: 339–343; Zöller-Engelhardt 2016: 5).

23 Kahl 2016b: xx; Zöller-Engelhardt 2016: 30.

24 Comparable to examples from Deir el-Bersha, e. g. the 'pilgrimage boat' MFA Acc.no. 21.406 a–b, Freed & Doxey 2009: 177, fig. 136.

25 The model character of these tools and weapons may be worthy of discussion: The Egyptological literature usually presupposes that models are of reduced size compared to the real-world entities, may consist of different material, and/or may lack some of the originals' functionality (cf. Tooley 2001: 424; Odler 2016: 14–19 with further references). Allen (2006: 20–22) distinguishes 'model' vessels and 'miniature' vessels, of which the former have no functional abilities, while the

- 56 adzes (of two different types),
- 28 axes,
- 4 chisels or gravers,
- 41 model shields,
- probably at least one model quiver/spear case,
- and maybe some model arrows.

Thus, the wooden model equipment of Shaft 3 shows a clear distinction to the other shafts: The material is more numerous and seems more diverse than comparable assemblages. Shaft 3 is the only one that also contained a multitude of model tools and weapons. This might reflect the high social status of the tomb owner.[26]

Shaft 4, bottom of shaft and side chamber (dating: probably FIP):

During the cleaning of Tomb III, the Asyut Project discovered a fourth shaft, which was previously unknown to modern science. The most recent finds from Shaft 4 dated to the Byzantine Period and were undisturbed since that time.[27] The bottom of the shaft and especially the side chamber contained various model material, albeit in a smaller quantity than the side chamber of Shaft 3. Although fragmentary and scattered, the material obviously belonged to one group of equipment, which could be established by the workmanship and the distinctive coloring. The fragments point to the original existence of at least the following structures:

- one or probably two model boats,
- one food producing/processing scene,
- one granary,
- and one offering bearer/estate figure.

As stated elsewhere,[28] the few model figures from Shaft 4 show a stylistic resemblance to one model figure found in the second shaft of Tomb IV.

Surface and niches (dating: unknown):

The surface and the niches of Tomb III held some further wooden model fragments. The sporadic material seemed to consist of objects that the early excavators rejected and left behind. Some items resembled objects from the side chamber of Shafts 3 and 4, but could not be assigned to these assemblages with certainty.

Tomb IV (N12.2/dating: FIP, nomarch Khety II)[29]

Tomb IV has two burial shafts, which were also previously unknown to modern science,[30] and a niche that was added at a later date and does not belong to the original layout of the architecture. The first shaft, Shaft 1, is positioned in the front section of the tomb, while the second is placed more centrally in

---

latter are true functional miniatures (further amended by Odler 2016: 15). Traces of corroded metal on some of the tool items from Asyut suggest that most of them were originally equipped with metal blades, thus they were equipped 'functionally'. Questionable might be the reduced size of the items, which will be discussed in the respective sections of weapons and tools below. Clearly of model character are the model shields, since they are of reduced size and consist of a different material (and different construction) in comparison to the wall decorations and life-size examples, see below.

26 Cf. Zöller-Engelhardt 2016. It is noteworthy that criteria like quantity, but especially diversity or 'quality' (in terms of careful and accurate elaboration or choice of material) can be elusive factors and must not necessarily indicate the status of the owner. Cf. Tooley 1984: 373–376.

27 Cf. Kahl 2016b: xxi.

28 Zöller-Engelhardt 2012a: 101–102 with fig. 16.

29 For information on Tomb IV and the progress of the works conducted by the Asyut Project cf. El-Khadragy 2006a; Kahl 2007: 77–79; Kahl 2012: 11–12; for the model material see Zöller-Engelhardt 2012a: 98–100. pl. 7.

30 Kahl, El-Khadragy & Verhoeven 2005: 163; Kahl, El-Khadragy & Verhoeven 2006: 244; Kahl 2019: 33.

front of the rear pillars. The niche is cut in the south wall of the tomb. Both shafts and the niche yielded wooden model material, albeit much less than Tomb III or Tomb V.

Niche (dating: unknown)
The niche turned out to be a depot of rejected finds, which were left behind by early excavators, too.[31] Thus, the finds form a small conglomerate of haphazardly arranged fragments.

The shafts, however, contained only a few, but interesting items:

Shaft 1, shaft filling and southern side chamber (dating: probably FIP)
The filling of Shaft 1 contained several nautical fragments, among others a rudder and the fragment of a mast rest, while the side chamber offered an oval shaped vessel as well as two cylindrical vats.

Shaft 2, shaft filling and upper northern side chamber (dating: probably FIP)
The filling of Shaft 2 yielded several male wooden model figures in poor condition. Interesting is one figure of a larger size, of which only the upper rear part was preserved. Although just a few features like the broken connection at the top of the head and the diagonally painted stripe across the back are still recognizable, they point to a carrier figure or offering bearer/estate figure, which originally held a basket on its head.[32] The upper northern side chamber contained two smaller model figures, a male and an interesting female figure with dark yellow skin and a long white strap dress. Her long black hair is parted and falls on her shoulders. The right arm is missing, the left arm is bent in front of the body. As stated above, its facial features strongly resemble the figures found in Shaft 4, Tomb III, which might establish a connection between the two model groups.[33]

Tomb N13.1 (dating: FIP/11th Dynasty, nomarch Iti-ibi(-iqer))[34]

Tomb N13.1 shows three burial shafts. The first is centered in the middle axis of the tomb near the western niche, while the second is unusually hewn into the south wall and descends in a sloping passage before leading to a side chamber. This second shaft does not belong to the original configuration of the tomb.[35] The third shaft is centered in the front part of the tomb, south of the middle axis. At the time of discovery, Tomb N13.1 was filled with debris,[36] in which some fragmented wooden model material was discovered. A few more fragments came to light in the filling of the central Shaft 1 and its side chamber as well as the filling of Shaft 2.

The model finds include five male model figures or larger fragments of these, respectively.[37] They were found scattered in the surface debris around the mouth of Shaft 1 and the north-east corner as well as in the filling of Shaft 2. Their posture identifies them as regular oarsmen, yet the design of the figures is remarkable (Pl. 39a–d): Their upper bodies are flat with stick-like arms cut directly from the torso by means of a small gap between arm and upper body. The lower part of the body is shaped triangular and includes the lower arms – which are only formed as small protrusions left and right of the leg area – as well as the legs, which are painted as two red stripes on the white background of the apron. The heads are irregularly shaped, displaying short wigs and large painted eyes. This design is unique so far for the

---

31 Cf. EL-KHADRAGY 2006a: 90.
32 The Museo Egizio in Turin has several comparable examples in its open storage displays, e. g. Prov. 1730.
33 Cf. ZÖLLER-ENGELHARDT 2012a: 102, fig. 16.
34 For detailed information on Tomb N13.1 and the progress of the works conducted by the Asyut Project cf. EL-KHADRAGY 2007a: 105–135; KAHL, EL-KHADRAGY & VERHOEVEN 2007: 84–88; KILIAN 2019: 17–19. 83–88.
35 EL-KHADRAGY 2007a: 106, fn. 6; KAHL 2008: 200–201; VAN ELSBERGEN 2019: 29; KILIAN 2019: 85.
36 VAN ELSBERGEN 2019: 17.
37 Find numbers S06/8.1 and S06/8.2, S06/st300, S07/7.

entire necropolis of Asyut. However, a close stylistic parallel is offered in the vast model equipment of king Mentuhotep II: The rowing crews "H" and "G" exhibit a strikingly similar design.[38]

A further fragmentary model figure from Tomb N13.1[39] (Pl. 40a–b) was found in the surface debris around the mouth of Shaft 1. Unfortunately, the head is missing, but the body posture is upright with the left leg striding forward. The body is painted red with a high-waste white apron. The figure exhibits the characteristic stylistic features of Asyuti model figures with a more lifelike execution in contrast to the flat bodies of the oarsmen. This does not necessarily imply that the latter did not belong to the same model equipment as the former, as comparable stylistically mixed crews from the Mentuhotep II compilation show.[40] As surface finds from a disturbed context, however, it cannot be said with certainty that they originated from Tomb N13.1.

Only one seated model figure[41] in poor condition was found in the side chamber of Shaft 2 (Pl. 40c–d). The stylistic features of the body and legs differ from the figures described above, while the manufacturing of the head with the short, flat hair and the facial features resemble the other specimens, which might be an indicator for a broader variety within this model material.

Further model fragments from the surface debris included a round grain measure[42] and a grain bag[43] as well as a model vat[44] and several model figure fragments including two heads[45], another torso[46], arms and legs[47]. A model oar[48] supplements additional evidence for a model boat. The filling of Shaft 1 contained several more model figure fragments.[49] Interesting is a flat, triangular shaped element found in the side chamber of Shaft 1, that might have been the raised corner of granary.[50] The flat outer sides are painted yellow, the shorter rims show several dowel holes indicative of the original fixation.

All in all, the remnants of funerary models found in Tomb N13.1 offer an incomplete picture: The style of the oarsmen-figures is unique for Asyut, but not for the period of the transition from the First Intermediate Period to the Middle Kingdom under Mentuhotep II, to which the tomb is dated.[51] The remaining fragments show a more characteristic design. Due to the disturbed find context, it cannot be stated with certainty that they belonged to the original burial equipment of Iti-ibi(-iqer).

Tomb H11.1 ("Northern Soldiers-Tomb"/dating: 11th Dynasty)[52]

Tomb H11.1 is a complex structure: due to its heavily damaged state of preservation, the extent of its layout is not entirely clear, however, the tomb originally offered a rectangular ground plan with large above-ground hall, divided by at least two pillars and an architrave with three steps resembling the architecture in N13.1. The initial floor level is only partly preserved. More than fifteen shafts have been uncovered inside or in front of the tomb, not all of which can be linked to the original installation.[53]

---

38 Arnold 1981: 21–23, pls. 11–14.
39 Find number S06/9.
40 Compare e. g. sailor R 588, Arnold 1981: pl. 16, fig. b.
41 S07/24.
42 S06/st363.
43 Convolute S06/st346.
44 S06/st364.
45 S06/st235 and S06/st467.
46 S06/st544.
47 S06/st268, convolute S06/st346; S06/st365, S06/st396, S06/st436, S06/st448, S06/st495; convolute S06/st604.
48 S06/st268.
49 S07/st215, S07/st243, S07/st285, S07/st357.
50 S07/st1163.1.
51 Cf. Kahl 2013: 144; Kahl 2019: 33–37.
52 Kahl 2019: 34; Kilian 2019: 113; Abdelrahiem 2020: esp. 46–47.
53 Kilian 2019: 112–113; Abdelrahiem 2020: 12–16.

Wooden model material has been found scattered in the surface debris as well as in one of the shafts, including[54]

– some fragments of model figures (S14/st1764, S10/st49, S10/st7, S14/st2344, S14/st188, S14/st1741)
– a stern post (S10/st133.1), a model oar (S10/st133.2) and two oar/rudder handles (S12/st1177)
– the head of model bird, probably from an offering bearer/estate figurine (S14/st175)

Due to the disturbed find context, an allocation to the original tomb equipment cannot be stated with certainty. The heads of the model figures display a close stylistic resemblance to the figures found in the side chamber of Shaft 3 in Tomb III, which might point to a similar dating.[55]

2.2 Selected ensembles of model material discovered by earlier missions:

Tomb of Nakhti (Chassinat & Palanque's Tomb 7/dating: probably FIP, contemporary to no-marchs Kheti I or Iti-ibi or Kheti II)[56]

The tomb of the chancellor Nakhti was discovered intact by the French excavators Chassinat and Palanque during their campaign in 1903.[57] It consisted of an undecorated chapel with four burial shafts. Each contained one or two burials, equipped with different burial goods and coffins. Model equipment was found in the tomb chapel and mostly in the burial chamber of Shaft 1. Shaft 4 yielded, among others, a female offering bearer/estate figure, while Shaft 2, among other things, contained two staves. Nevertheless, the ascertainment of the exact number of model items as well as the allocation to the individual shafts and the aboveground chapel are somewhat difficult.[58] As Kilian has pointed out for the pottery, even the allocation to the tomb itself can be tentative, since finds from the adjoining Tomb 6 had been mixed with material from Tomb 7.[59] To the extent possible to reconstruct, the model material from the Tomb and its shafts consisted of:[60]

Surface/chapel:

– five offering bearers/estate figures[61] (Cairo, Egyptian Museum JE 36289, JE 36290, JE 36291; Paris, Louvre E 12029[62] and possibly Cairo, Egyptian Museum 8/4/23/7 [?][63]),
– and maybe two model boats (possibly Cairo, Egyptian Museum JE 36294 and Boston, Museum of Fine Arts Acc.no. 04.1779A–C)[64].

---

54 ABDELRAHIEM 2020: 30–33.
55 ABDELRAHIEM 2020: 31.
56 KAHL 2016c: 38–42; KAHL 2019: 43, against ZITMAN (2010a: 209–212 with further references), who suggests a date from the end of the 11th Dynasty to the early 12th Dynasty.
57 CHASSINAT & PALANQUE 1911: 29–154.
58 Cf. ZITMAN 2010b: 255. 257–260. Zitman meticulously tracked down objects from these early excavations, thus allowing the reconstruction of the approximate scope of the model equipment.
59 KILIAN 2019: 135. Furthermore, the intermixture of objects from different tombs becomes evident in the excavation report itself. For example, figure 3 on plate 2 in CHASSINAT & PALANQUE 1911 shows a compilation of bows and arrows. The caption reads: "Arcs et flèches trouvés dans les tombeaux nos 6, 14 et 20."
60 ZITMAN 2010b: 257–260.
61 The Cairo objects JE 36290 and JE 36291 are depicted in CHASSINAT & PALANQUE 1911: pls. 9–10.
62 Depicted in CHASSINAT & PALANQUE 1911: pl. 4.
63 ZITMAN 2010b: 257.
64 ZITMAN (2010b: 257 with fn. 46 and 47) allocates these boats tentatively to Tomb 7 according to the description given by CHASSINAT & PALANQUE 1911: 32, but states that they could also be the ones discovered in Tomb 20 mentioned in CHASSINAT & PALANQUE 1911: 189. ESCHENBRENNER-DIEMER (2017: 178, fn. 223) sees no basis for a convincing allocation to Tomb 7.

Shaft 1, side chamber:

The side chamber offered a variety of model items, placed on and alongside the coffin. Some were found inside the coffin, as well. These are:

— one offering bearer/estate figure (Paris, Louvre E 11992),
— one model butchery (Boston, Museum of Fine Arts Acc.no. 04.1781),[65]
— two model boats (Cairo, Egyptian Museum JE 36293 and Paris, Louvre E 12027),[66]
— one model granary (Paris, Louvre E 11938),[67]
— one model brewery/bakery[68] scene (Cairo, Egyptian Museum JE 36295),[69]
— four model ḥs.t-vases (Paris, Louvre E 12004A–B, E 12652, E 12653)[70].

The chamber contained an interesting compilation of model tool and weapon material, as well as staves:

— two[71] model shields (Paris, Louvre E 11988 and maybe Cairo, Egyptian Museum JE 36297[72]),
— two bows on the coffin (Paris, Louvre E 12020-1 and E 12020-2 [?][73]) and one inside,[74]
— two model quivers or spear cases, respectively (Paris, Louvre E 12016 and Cairo, Egyptian Museum JE 36296[75]),[76]
— eleven arrows[77] on the coffin (two probably Paris, Louvre E 12017-1 and E 12017-3)[78] and 13 arrows inside,[79]
— twelve javelins[80] (of which eleven were identified by Zitman as Paris, Louvre E 12017-2 and E 12017-4, Cairo, Egyptian Museum JE 36303 (four), Cairo, Egyptian Museum 19/11/25/6 (five tips)),[81]

---

65 Depicted in Chassinat & Palanque 1911: pl. 15.1.

66 Depicted in Chassinat & Palanque 1911: pl. 14.

67 Zitman (2010b: 257) marks the Louvre granary with a question mark, expressing doubt regarding the allocation to Tomb 7 (as for example given in Desroches Noblecourt & Vercoutter 1981: 116). He states that there were two more granaries mentioned in Chassinat & Palanque 1911, found in Tomb 20 and maybe Tomb 13. Nevertheless, the description given in Chassinat & Palanque (1911: 50) regarding the granary found in Shaft 1 of Tomb 7 matches the object Louvre E 11938 quite well apart from the measurements, which seem to be slightly inaccurate in the Chassinat & Palanque description.

68 Following Tooley's [1995: 29] interpretation that baking and brewing activities were mostly combined in a single model scene after the Old Kingdom, food production scenes combining at least certain stages of bread and beer production are labelled here as "brewery/bakery scenes" to unify contradictory labels from the literature (as an example compare the model Turin S. 8652, labeled by the excavator Schiaparelli as "scene della fabbricazione del pane" [Sbriglio 2019b: 205], termed more neutral as "food production scene" in a modern description [Sbriglio 2019a: 83], listed as "brewery" in the list of finds [Del Vesco 2019: 285] and specified as "brewery/bakery" by Zitman [2010b: 273]).

69 Zitman 2010b: 257; http://www.globalegyptianmuseum.org/record.aspx?id=15659 [25.10.2019].

70 Depicted in Chassinat & Palanque 1911: pl. 23; Desroches Noblecourt & Vercoutter 1981: 123.

71 Nibbi (2003: 175 with fns. 21–24) notes that she examined seven examples of shield models from the tomb of Nakhti in the Egyptian Museum in Cairo. Zitman (2010b: 257) was able to identify only one in Cairo (and the Louvre example, cf. footnote 72). The additional six specimens mentioned by Nibbi are neither described nor depicted in Chassinat & Palanque 1911.

72 Zitman 2010b: 257; the height of the Cairo model shield is specified as 32 cm; the Louvre item measures 50,5 cm (Desroches Noblecourt & Vercoutter 1981: 130).

73 Zitman 2010b: 258.

74 Chassinat & Palanque 1911: 111; Zitman 2010b: 258. 266.

75 Zitman 2010b: 258.

76 Depicted in Chassinat & Palanque 1911: pl. 13.1. Zitman (2010b: 258) states the height of the quivers: Paris, Louvre E 12016: 1.39 m (cf. Desroches Noblecourt & Vercoutter 1981: 130); Cairo, Egyptian Museum JE 36296: 1.45 m. On divergent measurements in Chassinat & Palanque 1911 cf. footnote 206.

77 Indicated in the sketch of the burial chamber in Chassinat & Palanque 1911: 47, fig. 3. Cf. Zitman 2010b: 258.

78 Cf. Desroches Noblecourt & Vercoutter 1981: 130, No. 126: "Provenance Assiout. Provient probablement de la tombe no 7 du chancelier Nakhti. Caveau." Cf. Zitman 2010b: 258.

79 Chassinat & Palanque 1911: 110–111; Zitman 2010b: 258.

80 These were stored inside the quivers, one of which is described as broken. 11 are indicated in Chassinat & Palanque 1911: 47, fig. 3, partly depicted on pl. 13.2. Cf. Zitman 2010b: 258.

81 Zitman 2010b: 258.

- ten model axes (four complete: Paris, Louvre E 12005B, E 12005C, E 12639 + E 12641, E 12640 + E 12646;[82] four blades: Paris, Louvre E 12635–12638; two complete: Cairo, Egyptian Museum 19/11/25/6),
- at least seven model adzes (two complete: Paris, Louvre E 12004, E 12005A; five handles: Paris, Louvre E 12647–12651; five blades: Cairo, Egyptian Museum 19/11/25/6[83]),
- one stave inside the coffin,[84]
- four model chisels/gravers[85] (one complete: Paris, Louvre E 12004; three complete: Cairo, Egyptian Museum JE 19/11/25/6),
- and four scepters (one *ḥrp/sḫm*-scepter: Paris, Louvre E 12656; two *wȝs*-scepters: Paris, Louvre E 12654–12655; one "grand scepter": Paris, Louvre E 12006).

Shaft 2, side chamber:
- two staves[86].

Shaft 4, side chamber:
- one offering bearer/estate figure (Paris, Louvre E 11991)[87].

The material from the Tomb of Nakhti shows good workmanship and careful elaboration. In contrast to the elaborate carving and painting on the contact areas of the axe handles and blades from Tomb III, however, the axes from the Tomb of Nakhti seem to have a slightly less intricate design, closer resembling the examples from Tomb V.

Tomb of Mesehti (K11.3/dating: 11th Dynasty [Mentuhotep II])[88]

The Tomb of Mesehti has recently been re-identified by the Asyut Project.[89] The unfinished and unde-corated tomb features two burial shafts, of which the first is located in the front part near the doorway, while the second is situated along the tomb axis in the rear part of the tomb. The tomb had been exca-vated and partly cleared several times between 1875 and 1906. In this time items of Mesehti's burial equipment ended up in the Egyptian Museum in Cairo.[90] Famous are the coffins[91] and the two well-known sets of wooden model soldiers. It is not possible to reconstruct the original location of the model equipment inside the tomb, leaving the inner hall or one of the tomb shafts as possibilities. In regard to model material, the tomb yielded:[92]

- one group of 'Egyptian soldiers' (Cairo, Egyptian Museum JE 30968/CG 257),
- one group of 'Nubian archers' (Cairo, Egyptian Museum JE 30969/CG 258),

---

82 DESROCHES NOBLECOURT & VERCOUTTER 1981: 127.
83 The five blades could be combined with the Louvre handles, thus summing up to at least 7 complete examples. Cf. ZITMAN 2010b: 258.
84 CHASSINAT & PALANQUE 1911: 111; ZITMAN 2010b: 258.
85 ZITMAN (2010b: 258) designates them as „pincers". DESROCHES NOBLECOURT & VERCOUTTER (1981: 129) identify a "poinçon (?)" with question mark. The depiction in DESROCHES NOBLECOURT & VERCOUTTER and the plate in CHASSINAT & PALANQUE (1911: pl. 13) indicate chisels or gravers with a rounded handle, compare the four examples from the tomb of Mesehti, now in the Petrie Collection London, UC 71241.
86 ZITMAN 2010b: 259.
87 Cf. http://cartelen.louvre.fr/cartelen/visite?srv=car_not&idNotice=3030 [25.10.2019].
88 KAHL 2019: 33. 44. Cf. ZITMAN (2010a: 164) suggests a dating between Mentuhotep II and Amenemhet I.
89 KAHL 2018: 145–147; KAHL 2019: 29–33.
90 KAHL 2018: 145–146.
91 Egyptian Museum Cairo CG 28118 and 28119.
92 ZITMAN 2010b: 210–211. The assignment of some of the objects from the Petrie Collection to the tomb of Mesehti is stated as uncertain by the collection (http://petriecat.museums.ucl.ac.uk, s. v. "UC 71244" [25.10.2019]).

- one model boat (Cairo, Egyptian Museum JE 30970/CG 4918),[93]
- one model ḥs.t-vase (Cairo, Egyptian Museum JE 30967),
- two model axes (London, University College UC 30076 and UC 30077),
- four model adzes/adze handles[94] (London, University College UC 71237),
- four chisels (London, University College UC 71241),
- maybe a small model mallet[95] (London, University College UC 71235),
- two birds of offering bearers/estate figures (London, University College UC 71234 and UC 71235),
- a possible model vessel (London, University College UC 71250),[96]
- and three (?) possible models of bows (London, University College UC 71239, 71240, 71244 [copper string]).

Noticeable is the remarkable workmanship on the soldier models as well as the boat model. The bird model UC 71234 shows elaborate painted details and careful carving, too.

Interesting in comparison to the material found by the Asyut Project is the compilation of the tool and weapon equipment. The same types were present in the side chambers of the main shafts of Tombs III and V.[97] The contact areas of the handles of the axes resembled the Tomb V specimens. A ḥs.t-vase had been found in the side chamber in Tomb V, too.

Tomb of Wepwawetemhat (Chassinat & Palanque's Tomb 14/dating: Late FIP/Early MK)[98]

The tomb of Wepwawetemhat was opened by Chassinat and Palanque as well. They state that they found it intact and present a plate in their publication, which allegedly shows the in situ position of the finds inside the hall as they found it.[99] Nevertheless, as Kilian has detected, the picture was not taken inside Tomb 14, but in front of the north wall of the large hall of Tomb III, thus showing a reproduced find complex.[100] As far as the finds can be allocated, Tomb 14 offered various wooden model material, apparently discovered in the one undecorated aboveground chamber, which also contained an undecorated and a decorated coffin:[101]

- one model bull (Boston, Museum of Fine Arts Acc.no. 04.1778),
- one model brewery/bakery scene (Boston, Museum of Fine Arts Acc.no. 04.1782),
- one offering bearer/estate figure (Paris, Louvre E 11990),
- and two model boats (Paris, Louvre E 11993 and E 11994).

---

93 For details cf. Reisner 1913: 74–80, pl. 18; Landström 1974: 71, fig. 207.

94 Zitman points out that the Petrie Collection labels them as "model wȝs-scepters" (cf. http://petriecat.museums.ucl.ac.uk [25.10.2019]), but he identifies them as „handles of model axes?" (Zitman 2010b: 211 with fn. 9). In comparison to the model tool material from Tomb III, Shaft 3 they may rather be model adzes or hoes (cf. Zöller-Engelhardt 2016: 20. 127). The wȝs-scepters show a more rounded connection and shorter head (cf. the two examples from the tomb of Nakhti, Paris, Louvre E 12654 and E 12655, Desroches Noblecourt & Vercoutter 1981: 132, no. 131a and b). Nevertheless, it is noteworthy that the side chamber of Shaft 3 in Tomb III held exactly four of this specific type, as well.

95 Zitman (2010b: 211) suspects that it could be a model mallet, but additionally points out that it could be part of a wooden model (scene) and is designated as "wooden model fruit" by the Petrie Collection (cf. http://petriecat.museums.ucl.ac.uk [25.10.2019]).

96 Cf. http://petriecat.museums.ucl.ac.uk [25.10.2019].

97 See below in conclusion.

98 Zitman (2010a: 195–198) suggests an early Middle Kingdom dating on the basis of the position of the weaponry from the tomb, the pottery, and stylistic criteria of the wooden statuary; Kilian (2019: 138–140) establishes a range from Late First Intermediate Period to Early Middle Kingdom on the basis of the pottery analysis.

99 Chassinat & Palanque 1911: pl. 34.1.

100 Kilian 2019: 138–139.

101 Chassinat & Palanque 1911: 164–166; pls. 2.3. 34–35; Zitman 2010b: 261–262. 266.

In terms of tools and weapons:[102]

- eleven arrows (Cairo, Egyptian Museum JE 36305),[103]
- and one shield handle (Paris, Louvre E 12023 [?]).

Tomb of Minhotep (dating: FIP–Early MK)[104]

The Tomb of Minhotep was excavated by Schiaparelli in 1908.[105] Since the results of the excavation were not published, the allocation of finds – today in the Museo Egizio Turin – to individual contexts is very difficult, emphasizing again the complicated excavation history of Asyut.[106] The recently published excavation diaries of Schiaparelli do not simplify the matter, since he noted only some of the finds made in the tomb,[107] while the related inventory lists comprise further material that seems to have been found in the same context.[108] Based on the coffins listed in the inventories Zitman tentatively reconstructs a maximum number of six burials in this tomb;[109] however, some of the materials cannot be assigned to the find context with certainty.

Thus, cautiously the following model material can be assigned to the Tomb of Minhotep, but not an individual burial:[110]

- one brewery/bakery scene (Turin, Museo Egizio S. 8789),
- four model boats (Turin, Museo Egizio S. 8790–S. 8793),
- and three female offering bearers/estate figures (Turin, Museo Egizio S. 8794–S. 8796).

As well as some tool and weapon material:[111]

- appr. 83 arrows (three arrows: Turin, Museo Egizio S. 8799–S. 8801; appr. 80: Turin, Museo Egizio S. 8802),
- one bow (Turin, Museo Egizio S. 8803),
- and at least three staves (two complete: Turin, Museo Egizio S. 8804 and Turin, Museo Egizio S. 8805; four further fragments: Turin, Museo Egizio S. 8806).

3. Compilation of relevant wall decorations

The extent of preserved wall decorations in Asyut to date is limited. Nevertheless, several tombs allow the description of depictions and scenes that can be compared to the model material. The descriptions are clustered in thematic groups and ordered in relative chronological sequence according to the dating of the tomb owner.

---

102 CHASSINAT & PALANQUE 1911: 164–166; pls. 2.3. 34–35; ZITMAN 2010b: 261–262. 266.
103 Partly depicted in CHASSINAT & PALANQUE 1911: pl. 2.3.
104 ZITMAN 2010a: 222. New insights have been gained from the analysis of the pottery, dating the tomb in a relative chronology before Tomb I, that means the time of Senwosret I, see KILIAN 2019: 141–142.
105 KAHL, SBRIGLIO, DEL VESCO & TRAPANI 2019: 17. 83. 155.
106 Cf. KILIAN 2019: 140–142.
107 SBRIGLIO 2019b: 205.
108 Divided into two lists [DEL VESCO 2019: 286–287].
109 ZITMAN 2010a: 219.
110 ZITMAN 2010b: 273–274; online Database of the Museo Egizio Turin (https://collezioni.museoegizio.it/ [6.11.2019]); DEL VESCO 2019: 286–290.
111 ZITMAN 2010b: 273–274.

3.1 Weaponry and soldiers/hunters

Asyut had often been a region of conflict.[112] Especially during the First Intermediate Period the ongoing war between the Heracleopolitans from northern Egypt and the southern Egyptian Theban rulers is reflected in the tomb inscriptions and wall decorations of the tombs of the local nomarchs.[113] Nevertheless, scenes with soldiers are not restricted to the area of Asyut and can be found in other tombs and on stelae of the First Intermediate Period and Middle Kingdom,[114] and might not necessarily reflect actual historical events in every case.[115]

Three tombs in particular offer scenes with troops: Tomb IV, Tomb N13.1 and the "Northern Soldiers-Tomb" H11.1, while others probably displayed similar scenes or actual fighting, but are now mostly destroyed.[116]

Tomb IV (N12.2/Khety II)[117]

The front part of the south wall of Tomb IV shows remnants of a military scene (Fig. 1). Still visible are three registers of marching soldiers, executed in sunk relief with no traces of color.[118] Red outlines at the western (right) end of the third register indicate that the decoration is unfinished, and another soldier should have been added. Red outlining above the uppermost register hints at originally planned inscriptions, which should have accompanied the scene.[119]

The first person in the uppermost register seems to portrait an overseer or troop leader, since he crosses his arms over his chest and does not carry any weapons. The following soldiers are depicted uniformly: All carry a characteristic[120] large ogival shield with pointed top and rectangular broad base in their left hand. The front of the shields is presented to the viewer and partly covers the men behind them. The right hands of the men grasp long-handled battle axes with convex blades.[121]

Tomb N13.1 (Iti-ibi(-iqer))[122]

Most instructive on scenes with soldiers and individuals with weapons are the various scenes in the partly damaged decorations of Tomb N13.1. The tomb decoration offers military scenes as well as hunting scenes.

---

112 Cf. KAHL 2007: 3–21; KAHL 2012: 1–29; KAHL 2019: 33–38.

113 Ibid.

114 EL-KHADRAGY (2006b: 150–151, fn. 21) states that in general two types of military scenes can be differentiated in this time: rows of marching soldiers equipped with different weapons and soldiers engaged in fighting. The first type is rare: He cites three examples (one from the tomb of Ankh-tifi at Mo'alla, the other two from Asyut in Tomb IV (N12.2) and Tomb H11.1 (the "Northern Soldiers-Tomb"). A fourth can be added, also from Asyut, in the Tomb of Iti-ibi(-iqer), N13.1. Related to this category are First Intermediate Period stelae depicting individual soldiers with weapons (cf. ibid). Soldiers engaged in combat are found in at least eight examples of tomb decorations from the Qubbet el-Hawa to Beni Hassan (cf. ibid).

115 WILLEMS (2014: 44, fn. 135) points out that the scenes of marching soldiers in the tombs of the nomarchs from Asyut might more general reflect a "martial frame of mind" instead of mirroring historical events, especially since the soldiers are not depicted fighting but marching. Similar ZITMAN 2010a: 20–21. 161–162. I thank Dr. Andrea Kilian for the reference to Willems.

116 A fragment of a painted wall decoration on the north wall of Tomb III (N12.1) shows traces of two Egyptian men fighting. One is shown hitting the other with two curved sticks, presumably showing the conflict between Siutian and Theban troops. It is the first depiction of the "battle for Asyut", which is attested in the historical inscription in the same Tomb. KAHL, EL-KHADRAGY & VERHOEVEN 2007: 82. 91, fig. 2.

117 A detailed description of the decoration of Tomb IV is given by EL-KHADRAGY 2008 with further references.

118 EL-KHADRAGY 2008: 226.

119 Ibid.

120 NIBBI 2003: 176–177; PARTRIDGE 2002: 52; and see below.

121 EL-KHADRAGY 2008: 227. In contrast to the soldiers depicted in Tomb H11.1, who hold axes with half-moon shaped blades, cf. ABDELRAHIEM 2020: 43–45 with figs. 24–25.

122 Cf. EL-KHADRAGY in print; a first description of the decoration of Tomb N13.1 is given by El-Khadragy 2007a.

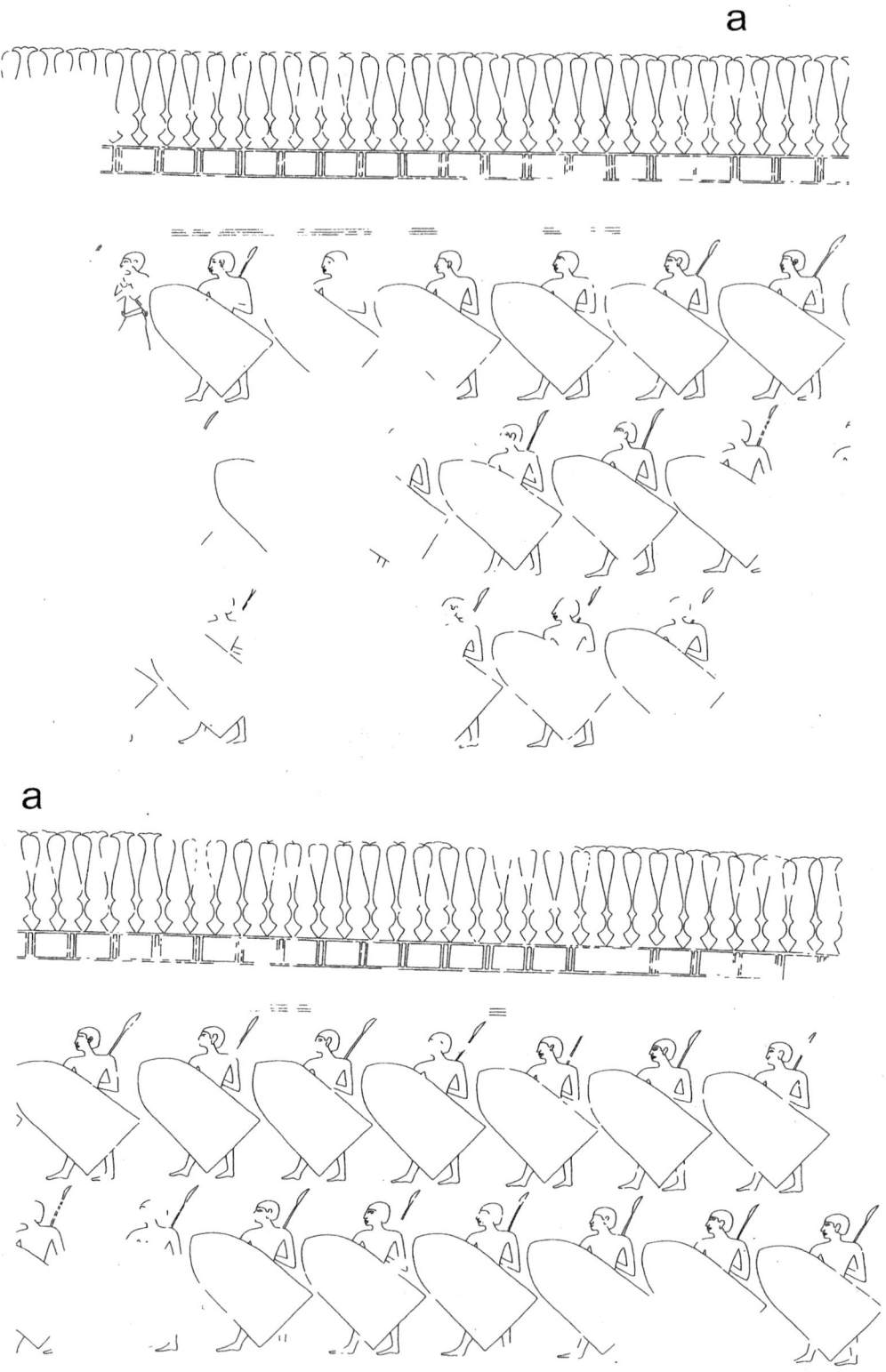

Fig. 1: Tomb IV (N12.2/Khety II), chapel, south wall (after El-Khadragy 2008: 236–237, fig. 4–5; detail);
facsimile: Sameh Shafik; © The Asyut Project.

Fig. 2: N13.1 (Iti-ibi(-iqer)), chapel, east wall, southern part (after EL-KHADRAGY 2007a: 124, fig. 4; detail); facsimile: Sameh Shafik; © The Asyut Project.

The southern part of the east wall, left of the entrance door, shows a scene with rows of soldiers (Fig. 2). In four registers troops are marching behind and under the much taller figure of the troop commander, who is facing south, probably holding a long stave in his left hand. The right hand is clenched to a fist, yet the item (a scepter?) is no longer recognizable. The soldiers are equipped differently. Register 4, the best preserved, shows from south to north (right to left):

- Two soldiers holding the characteristic ogival shields with pointed top and rectangular broad base. The shields are held with the left hand, their backside with horizontally attached handle is facing the observer. Nevertheless, the outer decorative patterns of the fronts of the shields are indicated as well, depicting various patterns of cowhides. The right hand of the second soldier grips a long straight handle of a weapon, probably a spear or javelin.[123] Some of the representations of the shields preserved little loops at the top,[124] comparable to examples in wall decorations from Beni Hassan (see below).
- The third soldier grasps a bow and bundles of arrows with his left hand and the handle of a weapon (probably an axe due to the angle in which he carries the weapon diagonally against his shoulder)[125].
- The fourth, again, carries shield and spear or javelin.
- The fifth holds a bow and arrows as well as probably an axe, too. El-Khadragy points out that this person exhibits an additional sash tied in a knot at the back.[126]
- Warriors six and seven are, in turn, carrying shields. The sixth seems to be holding an axe, while the remnants of the depiction of number seven indicate a spear or javelin.

---

123 Cf. EL-KHADRAGY 2007a: 110. For the definition of the differences between spear, javelin and lance see below.
124 I thank Eva Gervers M. A. for pointing this out to me.
125 Cf. EL-KHADRAGY 2007a: 110.
126 Cf. Ibid.

— At least three further figures complete the register, but the scene is too damaged to recognize details apart from the left hand of the ninth figure, which is holding bow and arrows.

Where recognizable, the upper three registers show a similar structure of soldiers carrying alternatingly shields and different weapons. None of the representations of the axe blades are preserved in the scene, therefore the shape of the blades cannot be determined.

Another scene on the east part of the north wall shows the tomb owner and his wife inspecting cattle and overseeing "some military activity"[127] (Fig. 3). The third and fourth register of the poorly preserved scene depict two rows of individuals carrying weapons. From east to west (right to left):

— The first three men in the lower register are holding a bow in their left hand and a handle of a weapon or a bundle of arrows in their right.[128] The leading archer wears a feather on his head and the "distinctive Nubian dress"[129] consisting of a short apron with sash and central pendant piece.
— The traces of the fourth indicate another body posture: he is not marching upright, but instead bending his knees and probably holding his arms with the weapons in hand over his head similar to the eighth person in the upper register.[130]
— The remaining figures are barely visible but seem to grasp bows in their left hands.
— The upper register is poorly preserved, as well, but displays nine people marching to the east. The third and fourth seem to hold bows. Number eight possibly holds a bundle of arrows in his right hand.

Interesting, too, is the depiction of two individuals following the tomb owner in the lower two registers at the west end of the north wall (Fig. 4). They carry two quivers/spear cases with javelins or spears protruding thereof, while leading dogs on a leash. A third individual is depicted above, carrying a tube with a strap in his right hand, which could also be a quiver.

Another scene involving weaponry is a hunting scene on the west end of the south wall (Fig. 5).[131] The six registers of the scene present desert animals and an early depiction of a mythical creature. The third and the fifth row each show one hunter at the left side of the register. The huntsman in the third register is displayed with an ostrich feather on his head in the process of drawing the string of his bow with his right hand. In front of him, at his feet, a hunting dog is added. The hunter in the fifth register carries a bow and a quiver or a bundle of arrows[132] in his left hand, while he raises his other hand about to throw a throwing stick. The archer himself is depicted with a feather on his head and wears a headband with a long ribbon at the back. His upper body is wrapped with two crossed straps that end in a high waistband. In addition, he wears a short kilt with sash and a central pendant piece. El-Khadragy characterizes him as a "Nubian hunter"[133].

Tomb H11.1 ("Northern Soldiers-Tomb"/unknown nomarch)[134]

Most remnants of the decoration in the "Northern Soldiers-Tomb" H11.1 are preserved on the south wall (Fig. 6). The decoration is painted on a thin layer of plaster, which has suffered bad damages.[135] Still identifiable are four rows of marching soldiers, strongly resembling the scene in Tomb IV. Seven men

---

127 El-Khadragy 2007a: 108.
128 The first two bows are depicted in different colors: while the first bow is shown in a yellow-ochre tone, the second one is painted in red.
129 El-Khadragy 2007a: 108.
130 Similar postures can be observed in wall decorations in Beni Hassan, cf. fig. 16.
131 El-Khadragy 2007a: 110–112. 125, fig. 5.
132 El-Khadragy 2007a: 111 identifies a quiver.
133 El-Khadragy 2007a: 111.
134 El-Khadragy 2006b. The name Djefai-Hapi was found on a block fragment which might hint at another nomarch bearing this name as tomb owner (Abdelrahiem 2020: 46–47).
135 El-Khadragy 2006b: 150; Abdelrahiem 2020: 17–26.

Fig. 3: N13.1 (Iti-ibi(-iqer)), chapel, north wall, middle section (after El-Khadragy 2007a: 123, fig. 3; detail);
facsimile: Sameh Shafik; © The Asyut Project.

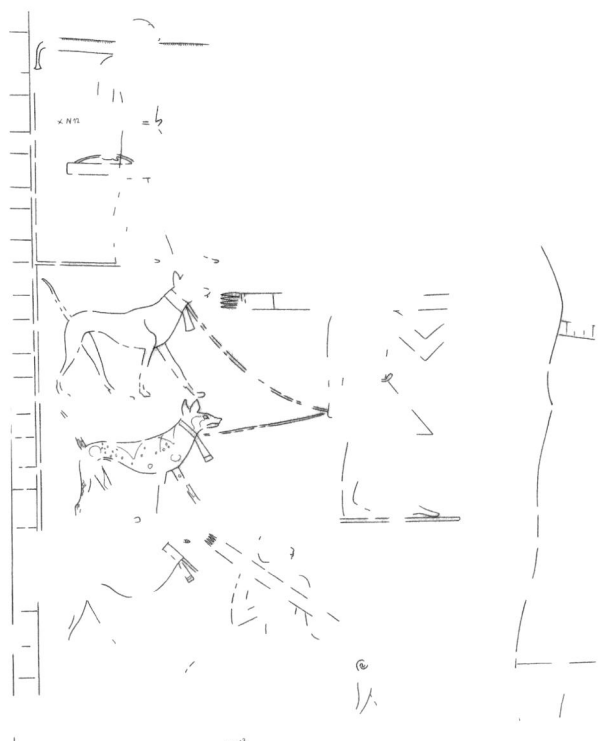

Fig. 4: N13.1 (Iti-ibi(-iqer)), chapel, north wall, western part
(after El-Khadragy 2007a: 122, fig. 2; detail); facsimile:
Sameh Shafik; © The Asyut Project.

Fig. 5: N13.1 (Iti-ibi(-iqer)), chapel, south wall, western
part (after El-Khadragy 2007a: 125, fig. 5); facsimile:
Sameh Shafik; © The Asyut Project.

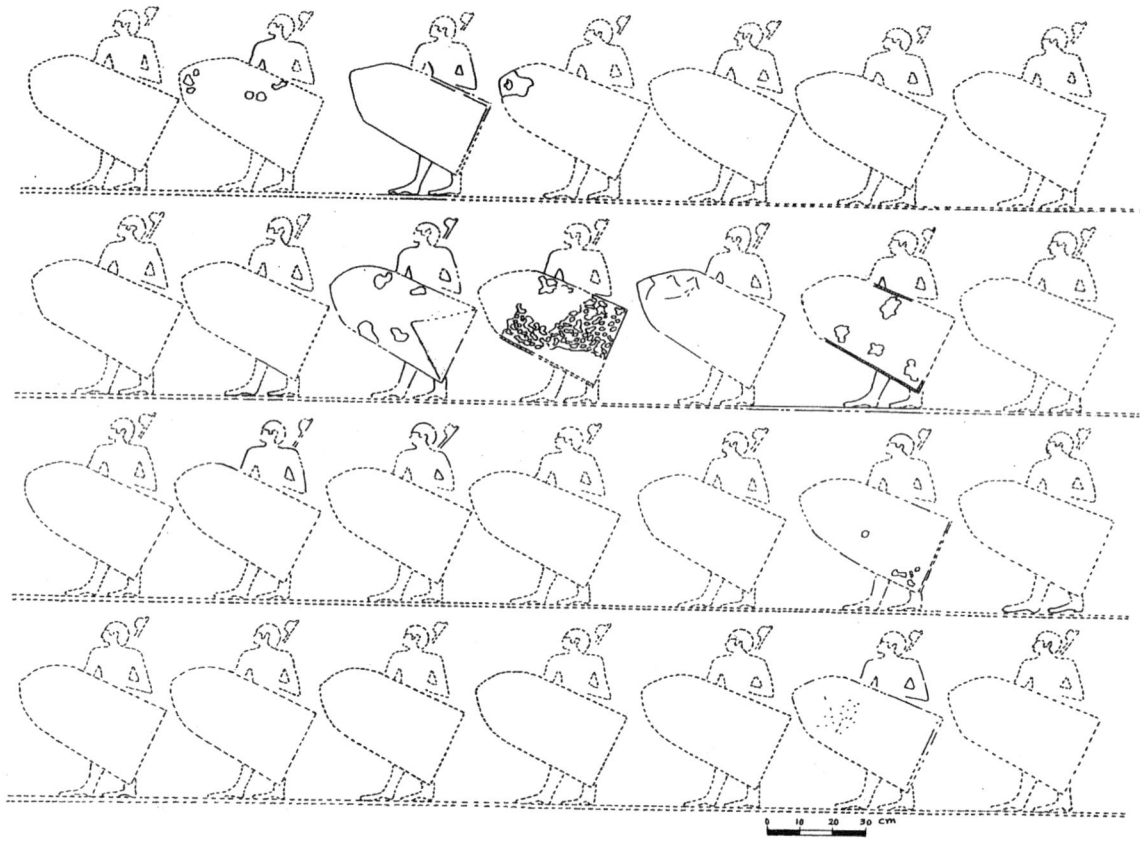

Fig. 6: H11.1 ("Northern Soldiers-Tomb"), chapel, south wall, next to the front protrusion
(after El-Khadragy 2006: 162, fig. 6); facsimile: Sameh Shafik; © The Asyut Project.

per row are reconstructable. They are carrying the characteristic large ogival shield with pointed top and
rectangular broad base in their left hand. The front of the shields is presented to the viewer and partly
covers the men behind them. In some cases, remnants of the decoration of the shields are still recognizable, showing a broad variety of designs, all outlined in brown paint:[136]

— The third shield in the uppermost register is colored in a dark yellow/ochre tone, which El-Khadragy
   interprets as antelope skin.
— The third soldier in the second row carries a shield combined of a cowhide design with red spots and
   a dark yellow/ochre triangle, pointing upwards from the base.[137]
— The fourth soldier in the second register holds a shield painted with narrowly placed small yellowish-
   brown spots, possibly imitating cheetah skin.[138]
— Several others show dark brown spots, probably cowhide, and irregular patterns.
— Noteworthy is the design of the outer edges still visible on the shield of the sixth soldier in the second
   register, imitating a seam line executed as a double brown line with a brown hatching.

The right hands of all the men grasp long-handled battle axes with semi-circular or half-moon shaped
blades, respectively, in contrast to the scene in Tomb IV, where the elongated forms of convex battle axes
were depicted.

---

136 El-Khadragy 2006b: 151; Abdelrahiem 2020: 18–19 with fig. 7 and 95, pl. 39.
137 The merging of different pieces of hides to create various patterns is not unusual in the design of shields, cf. Nibbi 2003:
      176–177; El-Khadragy 2006b: 151, fn. 25.
138 El-Khadragy 2006b: 151.

Fig. 7: N13.1, chapel, south wall, western part (cf. El-Khadragy in print: 195, Fig. 41. Pl. 93);
facsimile: Sameh Shafik; © The Asyut Project.

3.2 Tools

Some of the wall paintings in Tomb N13.1 preserved scenes including the use of tools.

On the south wall, below the tall figure of the tomb owner Iti-ibi(-iqer), three smaller registers include scenes of agriculture, food producing and crafts. The uppermost of the three registers depicts several men in the process of ploughing with a yoke of oxen, followed by a man felling a tree with an axe and another one maybe processing a piece of timber with an elongated tool, possibly a form of adze (Fig. 7). Next to them further men are engaged in ploughing. The second register preserved scenes of men tending and driving cattle, including a scene with men on a boat guiding cattle through a stream. The lower register is reserved for food producing and processing scenes, for example bread and beer production.[139] A clear instance of an adze is visible in a scene on the southern part of the west wall, where carpenters are working on iconic symbols made of wood (Fig. 8).[140]

A scene of butchering on the northern part of the west wall hints at the use of knives, however, due to the state of preservation, details are no longer visible. The lower register on the west wall depicts a man cutting off the foreleg of an ox with a broad cutting tool.

3.3 Boats

Tomb N13.1 is also the main source for the comparison of boats. The wall decorations offer several instances of boat depictions: In a large scene at the western part of the south wall, the tomb owner is standing in a shallow papyrus raft[141] with raised prow and stern ending in a flower-shaped finial, spearing fish.[142] In a smaller register below this scene, reaching further east, are more representations of boats. Still recognizable are at least four characteristic river crafts[143] and one papyrus raft[144], whose hull structure is

---

139 Cf. Kilian 2018: 49 with further references.

140 El-Khadragy 2007a: 115.

141 Comparable to Reisner's model Type III (Reisner 1913: xvii–xviii); cf. also Landström 1974: esp. 94–97. For different boat types and comparison material cf. also Göttlicher & Werner 1971; Tooley 1995; Jones 1995; Merriman 2011.

142 Two similar papyrus rafts of Type III are shown in a large scene on the north wall of the inner passage leading from the great transversal hall to the shrine in Tomb I (El-Khadragy 2007b: 127–128 with figs. 5–6).

143 Comparable to Reisner's model Type II (Reisner 1913: ix–xvi).

144 Cf. Reisner's Type III (Reisner 1913: xvii–xviii). Although Reisner has no example of this type in his catalogue, the model equipment from the tomb of Meketre at Thebes shows two of them in a fishing scene (today in Cairo, Egyptian

Fig. 8: N13.1, chapel, west wall, southern part (cf. EL-KHADRAGY in print: 194, Fig. 40. Pl. 88);
facsimile: Sameh Shafik; © The Asyut Project.

indicated in the painting. The river crafts in this register show no superstructures, but a few members of
the crew like a helmsman and some oarsmen are still recognizable. The papyrus raft carries at least two
men handling spears or lances.

A procession of at least three larger rivercraft vessels is portrayed in the lower register on the opposite
north wall. Still recognizable are several oarsmen and parts of the respective rudder structure, one preserving the depiction of the helmsman, sitting probably on top of a cabin while steering.

The most detailed illustrations, however, are painted in the lower register at the northern part of the
west wall: Four large travel boats, two under full sail, show elaborate reproductions of rivercrafts [Figs.
9–10). The most northerly boat on the west wall clearly depicts a closed cabin with a vaulted yellow-
beige roof that is slightly curved inwards. The front part of the cabin has an open-structure framework
that allows to see the sitting sailors inside. Mast and yard are stowed on two mast rests and reach above
the roof of the cabin. Visible between the two mast rests is a mast shoe. At the hoisted stern the large
rudder protrudes behind the boat and overlaps the rudder of the next boat in the procession. This boat
is smaller and under full sail, presumably travelling the opposite direction like the following two vessels.
Traces of a yellow, vaulted roof cabin are still visible. The next boat in line is better preserved. It is under
full sail, as well, and shows several sailors handling the rigging and a pilot with outstretched right arm
at the prow. Below the right part of the sail traces of an open cabin are still recognizable. One person is
kneeling in front of the structure, while another may be sitting underneath the roof. The fourth ship in
line is only partly preserved. Still visible is the stern with the large steering rudder, of the same size as the
previous boat. A standing helmsman mans the rudder, traces of another person are still visible in front
of the structure.

Museum JE 46715; cf. MERRIMAN 2011: 148, her type M1.3 with additional features. Further examples in MERRIMAN
2011: 146–149).

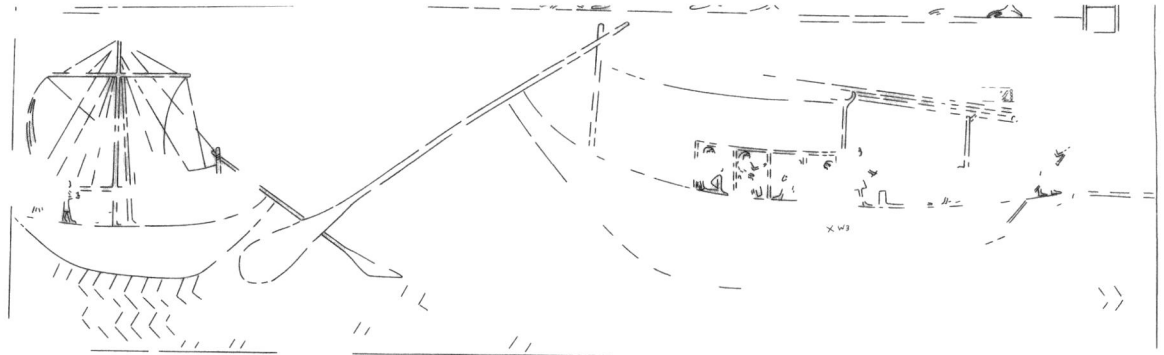

Fig. 9: N13.1, chapel, west wall, northern part (cf. El-Khadragy in print: 189, Fig. 35. Pls. 45–46);
facsimile: Sameh Shafik; © The Asyut Project.

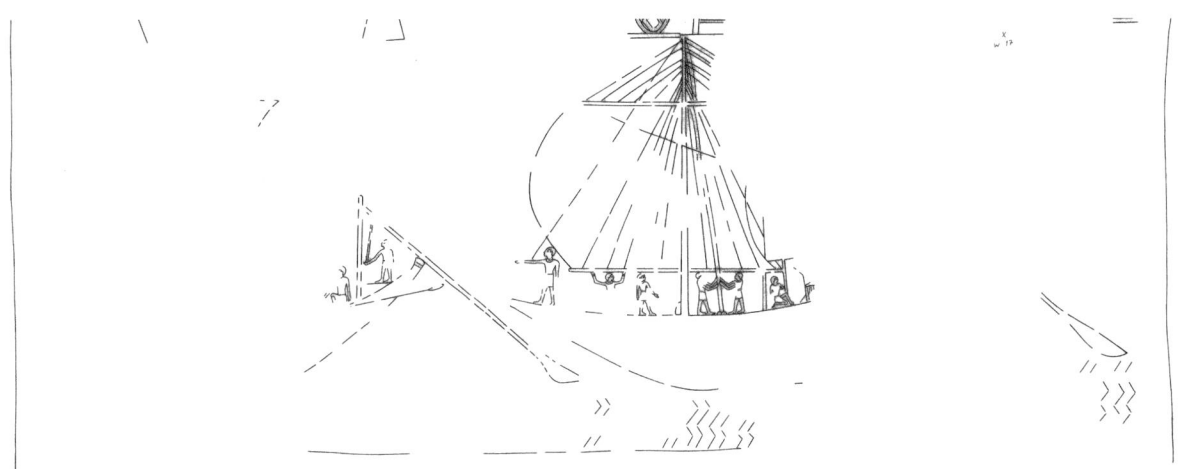

Fig. 10: N13.1, chapel, west wall, northern part II (cf. El-Khadragy in print: 190, Fig. 36. Pl. 52);
facsimile: Sameh Shafik; © The Asyut Project.

4. Comparison of the model material and the wall decorations

It is evident that several features of the weaponry as well as the images of soldiers and hunters in wall decorations are mirrored in the preserved model material. The following section compares and identifies the types of weaponry, tools and boats mirrored in the wall paintings and models.

4.1 Weaponry

4.1.1 (Battle) Axes

Different types of axes are depicted in the wall decorations and likewise present in the archaeological material:

– *'Edged-baton form'*
  Tomb IV displays axes with thin elongated blades, slightly curved, fixed high on the long shaft (Fig. 1). They could correspond to Davies' "edged-baton" form[145]. Two examples of this type are

---

145 Davies 1987: 38–39, inspired by Petrie's designation as "edged fighting batons" (Petrie 1917: 10); cf. Abdelrahiem 2020: 43.

preserved in the archaeological material from Asyut,[146] yet they are in original size and not models: Both were discovered by Chassinat and Palanque in their 1903 campaign. The first (Cairo,
Egyptian Museum JE 36300) was found in Tomb 13.[147] It shows the typical elongated thin blade, which is fixed to the shaft by plant-based strings threaded through eleven perforations at
the blades rearward edge. The handle shows notches at the lower end, which Chassinat and
Palanque interpret as marks from a wrapping for a better grip during combat.[148] They note measurements of 1.36 m overall length and 0.36 m length with 0.05 m width for the blade.[149]

The second specimen originates from Tomb 6 (Paris, Louvre E 12024), where it was found on top
of a coffin alongside one bow (Cairo, Egyptian Museum JE 36302), seven arrows (Cairo JE 36304)
and the handle of a shield (Paris, Louvre E 12022 or Cairo, Egyptian Museum JE 36298)[150].[151]
Chassinat and Palanque give measurements of 1.18 m overall length, 0.28 m length with 0.05 m
width for the blade. They describe four perforations as fixations of the blade to the shaft.[152]

The model tools/weapons from Asyut, however, display a divergent form: the round form (with lugs).

— *Round form with lugs*

The decorations in Tomb N13.1 as well as H11.1 (Figs. 2 and 6) show a different type of axe, Davies' round
form (with lugs) or maybe the lugged, perforated, round form.[153] The semi-circular blades are clearly recognizable in the preserved depictions of the axes carried by the marching soldiers, the hafting-method,
however, is not apparent. The handles are not fully visible, but seem to be at least arm's length.

The archaeological material, meanwhile, provides evidence for the round form with lugs: As presented
above, several examples of this type are documented in the tomb of chancellor Nakhti, the blades
exhibiting the semi-circular form with protruding lugs, yet without perforation. Furthermore, at least
20 and 28, respectively, examples of axe handles could be deduced from the fragments from the side
chambers of the main shafts in Tomb III and Tomb V. Here none of the original blades was preserved,
nevertheless corroded traces of metal inside the groove of the axe heads in Tomb V (and on the adze
handles and chisels from Tomb V and Tomb III)[154] prove that they were originally equipped with
such.[155] The heads including the area of contact with the blade is preserved in many of these fragments
and show remnants of the original hafting method, which consists of a narrow crisscross pattern of
cut incisions that indicates or imitates the initial fixation with interwoven stripes. These areas are darker than the surrounding wood, which could be residues from the stripes, that were usually applied
wet and contracted during the process of drying to create greater stability of the fixation.[156] Regarding
this feature, the examples from Tomb III differ from all other specimens from Asyut: they display an
accurate manufacturing or imitation of the hafting method at the contact area. The crisscross incisions are clearly cut, and the area is maybe additionally darkened by painting.

Without the blades it is hardly possible to determine if the axes were intended as weapons or tools, since
the form alone is no valid criterion for the identification.[157] The burial context allows both interpreta-

---

146 A third example of this type was found in Deir Rîfeh: Cairo, Egyptian Museum JE 38974 (Davies 1987: 39 with fn. 2.
     after Petrie 1917: 10. pl. 4).
147 Chassinat & Palanque 1911: Tf. 31.1; Davies 1987: 39, fn. 7; Zitman 2010b: 261;
148 Chassinat & Palanque 1911: 163.
149 Ibid.
150 Zitman 2010b: 256. 266.
151 Chassinat & Palanque 1911: 17. 163. pl. 2.3; Zitman 2010b: 256. 266.
152 Chassinat & Palanque 1911: 17.
153 Davies 1987: 30–35. Corresponding to Kühnert-Eggebrecht's type D and D-I (Kühnert-Eggebrecht 1969: 17–28.
     pl. 1); cf. Abdelrahiem 2020: 43.
154 Zöller-Engelhardt 2016: 21; Zöller-Engelhardt 2012b: 192.
155 Zöller-Engelhardt 2012b: 192.
156 Scheel 1989: 47.
157 Cf. Shaw (1991: 36). Axes of similar/the same outer form are displayed in different categories in *frises d'objets* of Middle
     Kingdom coffins, even labeled either as weapons or tools, respectively (Davies 1987: 32 with fn. 29; Lapp 1993: 82, figs.
     87–88). Nevertheless, the blades themselves could provide information on this distinction: Davies (1987: 24–25. 32.)

tions: Alongside the axes tools (like adzes and chisels/gravers, see above) as well as elements of weaponry (bows, arrows, [model] shields) were found.[158] However, it is noteworthy that *frises d'objets* of coffins from the Middle Kingdom mostly list the round form of the blade among the tool equipment, while the battle axes show Davies' elongated tanged form[159] among the weaponry.[160]

The model character of the axes and further tools found in Tombs V, III and the Tombs of Nakhti and Mesehti might be questioned, but seems corroborated by their reduced measurements: Compared to the battle axes in the wall depictions and the archaeological material (overall length more than 1 m) they are certainly of smaller size. In regard to their character as carpenters' tools they seem to be of reduced measurements, as well.[161]

The only completely preserved model axe handle discovered by the Asyut Project (M436)[162] measures 36.8 cm in overall length, the incision for the blade measures about 7.3 cm in length, indicating that the blade could not have been broader at this end. If the potential blade had lugs comparable to the Nakhti examples today in the Louvre Museum (Paris, Louvre E 12005B, E 12005C, E 12641 + E 12639, E 12643 + E 12636), the actual blade must have been even smaller. The sizes of the Nakhti examples vary between 27.5 cm and 29.7 cm overall length,[163] the comparable items from the Tomb of Mesehti (London, University College UC 30076 and UC 30077) are given with 32 cm and measured as 34.46 cm.[164] These comparative objects are regarded as models.[165] For Old Kingdom sources Odler additionally states that axes are always used with two hands,[166] which is also reflected in the woodcutting scene of Tomb N13.1. Axes are depicted notably longer than the model specimens, too, usually longer than a male adult's forearm.[167] Examples in Middle Kingdom tomb decoration, however, offer more diversity (Figs. 11–12): Depictions of combat in Beni Hassan Tomb 2,[168] for example, display troops using axes with blades of Davies' tanged form[169], yet they are used one-handedly and seem to have a shorter handle than the OK examples. Soldiers in depictions from Beni Hassan Tomb 15[170] use the round (maybe lugged and perforated)[171] form one-handedly, gripping the shorter handle. The same wall, two registers below, offers

states that thicker and thus heavier blades are more likely to have been used as tools than the lighter and thinner weapons' blades. These observations are corroborated by the material analysis of the British Museum material, whereof Davies (1987: 24) reports the following findings: "In particular, there is a discernible relationship between composition and function, which clearly reflects the differing hardness requirements of tool and weapon. Thus, the typical carpenter's axe of the First Intermediate Period/Middle Kingdom (the lugged round form [...]) is invariably made of unalloyed copper or low-arsenic copper, whereas the contemporary battle-axes [...] are almost all made of high-arsenic copper or of bronze, sometimes of leaded bronze. A similar distinction is noticeable in the later splayed axe." Detailed see Cowell 1987 (in Davies 1987): 96–118. For New Kingdom examples these findings have been somewhat relativized by Maeir & Ponting (2000: 275), who found that the different chemical structure of axes, especially in regard to tin content, could possibly point to high vs. low status: "Whilst it is clearly logical to make battle axes out of a hard alloy on a purely mechanical basis, it is surely no less important to have a domestic axe that also holds its edge whilst chopping timber or whatever. It can be suggested that the higher levels of tin may indeed be associated with battle-axes, but for aesthetic and status reasons rather than military practicalities." They additionally suggest that axes with medium to high tin content might have been used as tools or weapons by the "common soldiery" (Maeir & Ponting 2000: 276). Cf. also Herold 2009: 197 with fn. 63.

158 For "Early Egypt" (i.e. Predynastic and Early Dynastic Egypt) Gilbert (2004: 63–68) subsumes axes as "Weapon-Tools", his Category 2.
159 Davies 1987: 39–42. pls. 14–17.
160 Examples compiled in Lapp 1993. An exception can be found on coffin B19b (London, British Museum EA 30842), where the round/semi-circular form of axe blades is shown among the weaponry as well as the tools (Lapp 1993: 82, figs. 87–88).
161 Cf. footnote 230.
162 Zöller-Engelhardt 2016: 134.
163 Desroches Noblecourt & Vercoutter 1981: 127.
164 Petrie Collection Online Database http://petriecat.museums.ucl.ac.uk/ [13.11.2019].
165 Cf. Petrie 1917: 8. pl. 7; Petrie Collection Online Database http://petriecat.museums.ucl.ac.uk/ [13.11.2019].
166 Odler 2016: 146.
167 Compare the compilation of scenes in Odler 2016: 147–152.
168 Main chamber, East wall, south side, fourth and fifth register. Newberry 1893a: pl. 16.
169 Davies 1987: 39–42. pls. 14–17.
170 Main chamber, East wall, seventh register. Newberry 1893b: pl. 5.
171 Davies 1987: 30–35. pls. 3–7.

the tanged or maybe the edged-baton form, as well. In comparison with the depictions from Beni Hassan Tomb 2, the handle is of a comparable length, yet the blade of the axe is much shorter. The handle of the round form in the same scene is shorter.[172]

4.1.2 Shields and shield handles

The depiction of shields in the wall decorations of Asyut shows a consistent pattern: Shields are straight at the lower edge, tapering towards a pointed top, creating an ogival[173] shape or "apex design"[174]. The depictions in the tomb decorations of Tomb IV and H11.1 indicate very large shields nearly or exactly as tall as the men carrying them (Figs. 1 and 6). Only the troops on the east wall of N13.1 hold shields of a smaller size, still reaching from the head to the middle of the thigh (Fig. 2). It has been stated that the larger kind of shield could hardly have been used effectively in battle, since it would have been too heavy and unwieldy for close combat.[175] This type of shield has not been portrayed as often as the smaller "body shields",[176] thus it is interesting that it is predominantly this type which is depicted prominently in the tombs of the nomarchs from Asyut.[177] Wernick explains the size of the shields with their function as "mantelets", which were used to protect the entire body in case of "missile-fire" from fortified locations.[178]

The horizontal position of the handle in the upper third of the shield, as represented in the correlating model material, is indicated in the depictions on the east wall of Tomb N13.1, too, showing the men carrying them with the left arm, although the representations clearly show the patterned design of the front of the shields, as well (Fig. 2).[179] It is unclear, if the shield body consisted of a solid wooden plate or an open framework;[180] yet the model material consistently exhibits the latter.

The preserved model material again reflects the design of the wall decorations: The well-known model troops from the tomb of Mesehti mirror relative size and shape of the shields painted in Tomb N13.1. Their varied front design with patterns of cowhide, imitations of seams at the outer rims and the representation of patterns composed of several pieces of leather are also portrayed in the partly preserved scenes in Tomb N13.1 and H11.1.

Furthermore, the shield models from the Tomb of Nakhti and many of the fragments discovered in the side chamber of Shaft 3 in Tomb III corroborate the detailed correlation of design and form. Although fragmentary and for the most part poorly preserved, the material from the side chamber of Shaft 3 in Tomb III additionally offers a variety of designs:[181] Several examples exhibit traces of black-and-white[182], red[183] and brown[184] on white cowhide patterns. Some traces point to larger monochrome, e. g. ocher,[185] designs, which, however, cannot be stated with certainty due to the fragmentary state of

---

172 It is noteworthy that the individuals using the different types of axes are depicted differently, too. They differ in their attire, skin color and characteristics, thus seemingly signifying different groups of people with varying weapons.

173 NIBBI 2003: 177.

174 WERNICK 2016: 50–51.

175 NIBBI 2003: 175.

176 Ibid.

177 In her discussion of Egyptian shields, NIBBI (2003: 172) explicitly mentions the scene with marching soldiers in Tomb IV: "The scene is as much an artistic expression as an effort to display military strength and a readiness for war."

178 WERNICK 2016: 51 with fn. 20, explicitly pointing out the representations in Tomb IV in Asyut, and arguing against SPALINGER (2005: 16) and PARTRIDGE (2002: 52), who imply that the size of these shields was the dimension of a typical infantry shield and carried by a contingent separate from the foot soldiers.

179 NIBBI 2003: 174; WERNICK 2016: 51.

180 Cf. WERNICK 2016: 51, fn. 17.

181 Cf. ZÖLLER-ENGELHARDT 2016: 24. 142–151.

182 E. g. M509, M510, M511, M513, M525, M539, M540; ibid.

183 E. g. M517, M543; ibid.

184 E. g. M518, M537, M542; ibid.

185 E. g. M547; ibid. Compare a monochrome shield with stitched seam carried by a man in a procession of four from the tomb of Djehutynakht at Deir el-Bersha (Boston, Museum of Fine Arts Acc.no. 21.803; FREED & DOXEY 2009: 159, fig. 118).

Fig. 11: Detail of the wall decoration in Beni Hassan, Tomb 2, main chamber,
East wall, South side, fourth and fifth register (after NEWBERRY 1893a: Pl. 16).

Fig. 12: Detail of the wall decoration in Beni Hassan, Tomb 15, main chamber,
East wall, seventh register (after NEWBERRY 1893b: Pl. 5).

the items. Worth mentioning are examples with black decoration on ocher background[186] and traces of black pattern on a dark red-brown ground[187]. One shield fragment shows remnants of small closely placed ocher dots on a white background[188].

Noteworthy is the attention to detail still recognizable on the model material: Where preserved, examples from Tomb III show the imitation of a stitched seam along the outer edges, in a similar manner to the example preserved in the decoration of Tomb H11.1. The rims are executed on the front and sometimes on the back side. Maybe in correlation with the chosen pattern they are painted in different colors: many show a black rim, one with regular small red[189] lines depicting the stitching. A few preserved a white rim, one with small blue oval dots[190].

Where still recognizable, the backsides of the shields were at least covered with white plaster, sometimes with the additional decoration of the rim.[191] Even though all model shield handles were found disconnected from the shield body, the area of attachment is clearly recognizable: the area is marked by red preliminary drawing lines[192] and the remaining dowels or dowel holes. A notable difference between

186 E. g. M554 (ZÖLLER-ENGELHARDT 2016: 24. 142–151).
187 E. g. M556; ibid.
188 E. g. M568; ibid.
189 E. g. M509; ibid.
190 E. g. M556; ibid. A very similar design of the imitated stitched rim shows one of the model shields from the Tomb of Nakhti, Paris, Louvre E 11988. There are examples with a red rim and a double line white stitching, e. g. New York, Metropolitan Museum Acc.no. 17.9.3.
191 NIBBI (2003: 174) draws special attention to the practice of covering shields in gypsum before attaching the animal skin (as e. g. seen in the items from the tomb of Tutankhamun), which seems to be reflected in the models. Nevertheless, the gypsum or gesso additionally provides a background for the painting of the models, which might have been necessary to smoothen the wood and give a bright underground for lighter coloring.
192 M519, M522, M544, M573 (ZÖLLER-ENGELHARDT 2016: 24. 142–151).

the model shields from Asyut and the correlating wall decorations is the absence of a loop at the top of the shields in the model material, while some of the shield representations on the east wall of tomb N13.1 preserved these.[193]

The height of the model shields, in contrast to their form, seems to be quite variable. The height of one of the shield models from the Tomb of Nakhti (Louvre E 11988) is specified as 50.5 cm[194], while the accompanying example from the same context measures only 30 cm[195]. The maximum height of the largest fragment from Tomb III is 42 cm[196]. A completely preserved example from the Khashaba excavations, today in New York, Metropolitan Museum (Acc.no. 17.9.3) measures 71.5 cm.[197] Without the relation to a model figure or statuette holding the shield it is unclear how these differences in height reflect their accuracy in representing the different kinds of shields described above. Comparable examples coming from model scenes or boats are much smaller.[198]

Informative on the question of different sizes are also the model shield handles. Five complete or nearly complete examples, alongside 92 fragments, were discovered in the side chamber of the main shaft in Tomb III. The handles are all of the same construction, exhibiting a round central base with a raised, rounded grip, protruding in a right angle. 'Wings' project left and right from the central base and form the broad fixation and stabilization of the shield model.[199] They differ considerably in size. The complete model handles from Tomb III vary in width between 23.8 cm to 16.2 cm, pointing to varying sizes of the allocated shield models. Shield handles of original size are evident in the archaeological material from Asyut, as well. A life-size example, now either identified as Cairo, Egyptian Museum JE 36298 or as Paris, Louvre E 12022,[200] was found by Chassinat and Palanque in Tomb 6 on the lid of a coffin and measures 70 cm in width.[201]

4.1.3 Spears, lances, javelins and spear-cases/quivers

It can be difficult to distinguish spears, lances and javelins in Egyptian depictions or model representations, if they are not named explicitly in the accompanying texts.[202] The main difference between spear/lance on the one hand and javelin on the other is that the latter is a throwing weapon, while the former is a stabbing weapon.[203]

193   The depictions of shields in object friezes on Middle Kingdom coffins from Asyut partly show these, too, e. g. on coffins S18 [S10C] and S71 [S5C] (Lapp 1993: pls. 25. 30).

194   Chassinat & Palanque 1911: 52; Desroches Noblecourt & Vercoutter 1981: 130.

195   Chassinat & Palanque 1911: 52.

196   Zöller-Engelhardt 2016: 142. The shield model could have been somewhat larger, since the fragment is not preserved up to its full height.

197   https://www.metmuseum.org/art/collection/search/546270 [02.12.2019].

198   Compare, for examples, the model shields found among the model equipment of Mentuhotep II, ranging in height from 7.4 to 11.9 cm (Arnold 1981: 20. pl. 10); and model shields from Tomb 10A of Djehutynakht at Bersheh with an average height of 15 to 16 cm (Acc.no. 15-5-589a-e and 15-5-474a-e), today in Boston, Museum of Fine Arts (www.collections. mfa.org [02.12.2019]; Freed & Doxey 2009: 146, fig. 108). For a recent compilation of model boats with representation of shields on cabins see Montonati 2018.

199   Zöller-Engelhardt 2016: 25. 151–161.

200   Zitman 2010b: 256.

201   Chassinat & Palanque (1911: 18) emphasize that they found plenty of these handles during the course of their work: "Cet objet, assez commun dans les musées, a été rencontré à plusieurs exemplaires au cours des fouilles". Nibbi mentions an example (Cairo JE 36299) that bears an incised inscription reading ꜥnḫ=f, which she interprets as the name of the owner (Nibbi 2003: 174), mentioned also by Zitman (2010b: 263. 266) as maybe originating from Tomb 20. It is a noteworthy coincidence that while many shield handles have been found in excavations, actual shields are very rare (cf. ibid.).

202   Cf. e. g. the term nys.wt/ns(y).wt for javelins, Davies 1973: 224; Hoffmeier 2001: 408; TLA http://aaew.bbaw.de/tla/servlet/GetWcnDetails?u=guest&f=0&l=0&wn=88030&db=0 [17.12.2019].

203   Hoffmeier 2001: 407–408; Odler & Peterková Hlouchová 2017: 192–193. Hoffmeier (2001: 407–408) characterizes a spear as a "hand-held stabbing weapon" and writes concerning the lance: "In essence, the lance is a type of spear with a much longer shaft, although the blades could also be significantly longer than spear blades." (Hoffmeier 2001:

Without accompanying model figures, the intended size of the weapons is difficult to establish. Taking into account the potentially unproportional size ratios in model equipment and the sometimes non-existing metal heads, the identification of the weapon type can be impeded. Consequently, a clear distinction between model spear cases or model quivers (for javelins or arrows) depends on the interpretation of the content and relative size.

The only clearly recognizable quivers/spear cases in the wall decorations in Asyut are depicted on the north wall of N13.1 (Fig. 4). As described above, two men are carrying long tubes with spears or javelins protruding thereof over their shoulders, while a third holds a tube by a strap with his right hand, which might be identified as a quiver for arrows considering the smaller size. Unfortunately, the front end of the latter is lost, thus the overall length and any protruding heads of weapons are no longer preserved. The size of the remaining two containers differs: The middle one in the second register seems at least as high as the man carrying it, which might hint at lances rather than spears, while the lower one appears smaller, maybe exemplifying a difference between lance and spear or spear and javelin, respectively. Noteworthy are the coloring and the protruding heads of the weapons: The upper third of both cases in the lower registers are painted red, the remaining outer side, as far as preserved, is white. This is reflected in the model quivers, which additionally can show a cowhide pattern. Long, leaf-shaped spear- or lance-heads protrude from the larger case, which are painted black[204]. The lower, smaller case seems to contain smaller weapons, as well. Their heads are thinner and elongated. It is unclear, what kind of scene or activity the carrier figures represent: They might bring weapons for a hunting trip,[205] especially considering the dogs on the leash following them. Additionally, the desert hunting scene is pictured on the south wall, directly facing the scene on the north wall. On the other hand, the men could carry representative weapons related to the military scene further up east on the same wall.

The model material offers several examples of quivers/spear cases, e. g. from the tomb of Nakhti (Paris, Louvre E 12016 and Cairo, Egyptian Museum JE 36296), with a height of 1.39 m and 1.45 m,[206] intended for what is here considered as javelins. The height is remarkable and not mirrored in comparable specimens, as for example from the Khashaba excavations, today in the Metropolitan Museum, New York:[207] Acc.no. 17.9.4 is designated as "model spear case" with a height of 41.6 cm, with accompanying model spears (Acc.nos. 17.9.5–11) with an average height of appr. 40 cm. The spears are equipped with leaf-shaped metal heads, directly inserted into the split shaft. The ensemble was accompanied by the model shield (Acc.no. 17.9.3) described above. Two further examples of "spear cases" with a maximum height of 97 cm are kept in the Metropolitan Museum, New York, as well, yet their findspot is unknown.[208]

The design of the spear cases/quivers shows similar characteristics: They are round wooden tubes with open upper mouth and closed lower end. The upper part is painted in a monochrome red tone, mirrored in the wall scenes of N13.1. The outer body shows a cowhide design with black patches on white ground. Resembling the design of the shield models, the spear cases or quivers show details in form of imitated

---

407) He cites examples from siege scenes in tomb decorations from Beni Hassan, where soldiers are attacking a fortified town with a lance, using it like a battering ram, in contrast on the javelin: "While the spear is a thrusting weapon, the javelin is a smaller spear that is used for throwing" (Hoffmeier 2001: 408).

204 The heads of the spears/lances on the east wall of the tomb are depicted in red. I thank Eva Gervers M. A. for this information.

205 Hoffmeier (2001: 407) points out that lances could be used during the hunt to kill wounded animals. For the distinction of spear and harpoon cf. Odler & Peterková Hlouchová 2017: 192–193.

206 Chassinat & Palanque (1911: 47. pl. 13.1) state a length of 1.29 m and 1.43 m, respectively; Zitman (2010b: 258) states the measurements cited above; Desroches Noblecourt & Vercoutter (1981: 130) also give 1.39 m for the Louvre example.

207 https://www.metmuseum.org/art/collection/search/590949 [05.12.2019].

208 New York, Metropolitan Museum Acc.no. 1970.52.8a and b. The museum database shows an accompanying picture with 20 sharpened sticks arranged between the two spear cases. https://www.metmuseum.org/art/collection/search/564828 [05.12.2019]

stitching lines, the most prominent a vertical seam running along the length of the form, indicating that the cowhide was wrapped around the tube and sewn along this hem. The Metropolitan Museum example (Acc.no. 17.9.4) shows additional stitching along the transition from the red upper part to the cowhide, and the two unprovenanced items along the upper and lower rim, too. On the basis of these comparable examples, several potential quiver fragments were identified among the fragmentary model material from Tomb III, due to form, size and small traces of the original decoration.[209] Their original size and design could not be reconstructed because of their poor state of preservation, but the largest fragment shows a length of 43.8+y cm.

Regarding the weapons themselves, there is, of course, the well-known model of forty Egyptian soldiers carrying lances/spears[210] from the tomb of Mesehti (Cairo, Egyptian Museum JE 30968/CG 257). In relation to the model figures, the lances/spears are as tall as the model figures or even a bit longer. The weapons are equipped with leaf-shaped heads with midrib and clearly resemble the examples found in the tomb of Nakhti.[211] These two specimens, however, are much larger, exhibiting a length of 0.985 m and 0.978 m, respectively, corresponding to the size of the accompanying quivers.[212]

4.1.4 Bows and arrows

Similar to the limitations in specifying lances/spears and quivers/spear cases, the identification of model bows and arrows is no easy task, especially if the material is fragmentary; fragments of bows and arrows might not retain distinctive features like the arrowhead or the indicative curved tips of a bow.

The grave goods from Asyut compiled above included several identifiable life-size[213] specimens of bows and arrows, for example in the tomb of Nakhti (three bows, 24 arrows), the tomb of Mesehti (several (model?) bows), Wepwawetemhat (11 arrows) and Minhotep (at least 83 arrows and 1 bow) (Table 2). One of the bows found in the tomb of Nakhti, which is kept in the Louvre Museum today, measures 1.66 m.[214] A life-size bow still retaining remnants of the bowstring was discovered by Chassinat and Palanque in Tomb 6, measuring 1.32 m in length.[215] The accompanying arrows, consisting of hardwood elements combined with reed parts and equipped with flintstone blades ranged from 0.85 m to 0.9 m.[216] Potential fragments of model arrows might have been discovered in the side chamber of Shaft 3 in Tomb III,[217] nevertheless, they show no explicit feature of their function like e. g. a distinctive painting.[218]

---

209 ZÖLLER-ENGELHARDT 2016: 25–26. 161–164. The fragment M700 shows the characteristic red color on the upper part of the tube, an incised horizontal line at 11.6 cm below the upper rim and the hint of horizontal white dots imitating a seem. The reconstructed diameter is appr. 9 cm, the comparable example 17.9.4 from the MMA is given with 7.8 cm. https://www.metmuseum.org/art/collection/search/546271 [05.12.2019].

210 BIETAK (1985: 18) designates the weapons as "spears".

211 Cf. DESROCHES NOBLECOURT & VERCOUTTER 1981: 131, who identify the weapons found in Nakhti's tomb as "javelots".

212 Model spear cases are also known from model boats, cf. two examples from Tomb 10A of Djehutynakht with black and white cowhide decoration and black rims (Acc.no. 21.877; FREED & DOXEY 2009: 170–171, figs 129–130) and a procession of men carrying spear cases/quivers with black and white cowhide decoration and red rims as well as a red zigzag seam from the same tomb (Acc.no. 21.803; FREED & DOXEY 2009: 159, fig. 118). Further examples were discovered among the burial equipment of Mentuhotep II at Thebes, measuring about 20 cm in height ("Lanzenfutterale", ARNOLD 1981: 20. pl. 9).

213 The average length of a self-bow in dynastic times ranges between 1 and 2 m, often between 1.20 m and 1.80 m; additionally, recurve bows of comparable length might have developed during the First Intermediate Period (SHAW 1991: 37; HEROLD 2009: 206–210).

214 Louvre E 12020 (1). DESROCHES NOBLECOURT & VERCOUTTER 1981: 131, no. 128.

215 CHASSINAT & PALANQUE 1911: 17. Pl. 2.3.

216 CHASSINAT & PALANQUE 1911: 18. Pl. 2.3.

217 ZÖLLER-ENGELHARDT 2016: 26. 164–168.

218 Compare e. g. a bundle of model arrows (Boston, Museum of Fine Arts Acc.no. 21.437) from Tomb 10A of Djehutynakht at Deir el-Bersha: the tips are painted red, the opposing ends black and notched to indicate fletching. Their length is approximately 0.57 m. https://collections.mfa.org/objects/143730/bundle-of-model-arrows?ctx=9a220d7c-b68b-46a9-9587-9dd2ad3953b1&idx=123 [09.03.2020]; FREED & DOXEY 2009: 146, fig. 107.

The 'Nubian archers' from the tomb of Mesehti carry self-bows in their left hands and a bundle of three arrows each in the right. The size of the weapons and the posture of the bowmen is comparable to the archers in the rows of marching soldiers on the east wall of tomb N13.1, whose bows are all already strung. Similarly equipped are the archers in the desert hunting scene on the south wall and the soldiers on the opposite north wall.

4.1.5 Soldiers and hunters

A comparison of the figures depicted carrying weapons reveals interesting similarities between features displayed in the model material and the wall decorations of Asyut. The most famous models of soldiers are the two divisions of men from the tomb of Mesehti. They are contrasted as 'Egyptian soldiers' and 'Nubian archers' due to their different representations,[219] carrying spears/lances and shields or bow and arrows, respectively. Each division is arranged in four rows à ten men, a constellation partly mirrored – with limitations due to the state of preservation – in Tomb IV (three rows of soldiers), Tomb H11.1 (four rows) and Tomb N13.1 (four rows on the east wall).[220] The Egyptian model soldiers are represented quite uniformly, wearing white headbands, short šndj.t-kilts and carrying individually designed shields, a feature also reflected in the wall paintings of H11.1 and N13.1. The kilts, however, differ in the depictions on the east wall of N13.1, lacking the characteristic central pendant piece.

In contrast to the 'Egyptians', the 'Nubian archers' display more variety, not only regarding the height of the individual figures, but in the representation of their colorful short kilts and their jewelry, as well.[221] Of interest here are in comparison the depictions of 'Nubian archers' in the wall decorations of Tomb N13.1 described above, especially the well-preserved figure in the desert hunting scene. In contrast to the contingent of the 'Nubian archers' of Mesehti's model he is additionally equipped with a throwing stick and wearing a feather on his head. His upper body shows further attire in the form of crossed straps that are wrapped around his torso. Depicted in a similar fashion is the first archer of the second register in the scene with military activity on the north wall of the same tomb. Tomb N13.1 is the first Asyuti tomb to preserve illustrations of 'Nubian archers' in the wall decorations,[222] while Mesehti's soldier models are the earliest (known) representations in the Asyuti model material.[223]

It seems not coincidental that the decorations of Tomb N13.1 and the model equipment of Mesehti exhibit close parallels: El-Khadragy and recently in-depth Kahl point out the close connection between the owner of Tomb N13.1, Iti-ibi(-iqer), and the owner of the model soldiers, Mesehti: The latter was Iti-ibi(-iqer)'s son and successor.[224] A Mesehti(-iqer) is named in the inscriptions of N13.1; as eldest son he states that it was his responsibility to erect the tomb of his father.[225] Another close parallel is found in the representation of Mesehti's model boat, see below.

---

219 Cf. EL-KHADRAGY 2008: 228; BIETAK 1985: 87–88. Bietak designates the Egyptian group more precisely as "infantry division".

220 EL-KHADRAGY 2008: 227–228.

221 BIETAK 1985: 88–89. He interprets the differences in appearance and attire as indicator of greater individualism among the "Nubians".

222 Cf. KAHL 2019: 43 with fn. 180, following Bietak and Fischer in the assumption that Nubian mercenaries did not fight on the side of the Asyuti nomarchs until Asyut was conquered by the Thebans.

223 But not the only soldier models known: Already ZITMAN (2010a: 162) refers to further evidence from Thebes, citing the model shields from the burial equipment of Mentuhotep II (cf. footnote 198) and a group of "black soldiers with shield and spear" discovered by Naville in Shaft 5 (NAVILLE 1907: 46), comparable to the model soldiers of Mesehti. Isolated examples can be found elsewhere, e. g. an archer on a model ship from Beni Hassan (GARSTANG 1907: 157–158 with figs. 157–158), today in Oxford, Ashmolean Museum E 2301.

224 EL-KHADRAGY 2008: 228; KAHL 2019: 26–33. 44.

225 KAHL 2019: 27. Kahl emphasizes that the name of the nomarch Mesehti is given including the name component -iqer in the inscription on his boat model Cairo CG 4918, corroborating the conclusion that the well-known Mesehti is the same person as the Mesehti-iqer named in Iti-ibi-iqer's tomb.

4.2 Tools

The model material from Asyut offered a variety of model tools. The recently discovered finds included numerous wooden handles of (model) tools, among them axes, adzes and chisels/gravers.

In comparison with the wall decorations from Asyut, only the adzes and one instance of an axe can be compared. As described above, probably two woodworking scenes in Tomb N13.1 show the use of adzes (Figs. 7–8). The scene on the south wall maybe shows the processing of timber,[226] while the west wall exhibits precision woodworking. The tools are used and depicted differently: While the alleged woodcutter on the south wall grips a long tool with both hands and might be in the process of peeling off bark or branches from a piece of wood, the carpenter on the west wall holds a characteristically shaped adze in one hand and supports the Djed-pillar he is working on with the other. The suggested woodworker's tool on the south wall shows a near rectangular angle, yet the decoration is destroyed around and above the angle. The front part facing away from the workman indicates a short area with a mesh pattern of strips in a darker color, while the entire tool is depicted in a yellow-ochre tone. Although the two-handed use of larger adzes is shown for example in wall decorations of the Old Kingdom,[227] the form and coloring seem unusual in this case, as well as the vertical orientation of the piece of wood he is working on.

In contrast, the carpenter's adze is clearly visible, showing the characteristic closely bent head as well as the blade attached by rope or leather straps wrapped around the attachment point.

This type of adze is well attested in the model material from Asyut: Fragments of more than fifty adze handles were found in the side chamber of Shaft 3 in Tomb III[228] and pieces of at least forty specimens in the main Shaft in Tomb V. The tombs of Nakhti and Mesehti contained four and at least seven examples, respectively. Although there is some variation in the measurements, the shape of these adzes is quite uniform: A handle, mostly with raised tip at the lower end of the handle, leads to a rounded head with flattened broad attachment area. Many examples in the model material from Tombs III and V show a darkening of the contact area and several exhibited small traces of corroded metal, an indication that the wooden handles were originally equipped with metal blades.[229]

Again worthy of discussion is the size of the model tools: The size of the adze handles in the model material might be somewhat reduced in comparison to the examples in the wall decorations, but not of explicit miniaturization.[230] The carpenter scene on the west wall displays an adze which seems shorter than the forearm of the man holding it, the possible woodworker's adze is clearly longer. Illuminating is also the instance of the axe in the scene of tree-felling: The woodworker grips the axe with both hands and the length of the handle is about the height of the woodcutter's upper body, thus – like the battle

226 Comparable tree-felling scenes are known from Old and Middle Kingdom Tombs, for example from Mastabas at Saqqara (Moussa/Altenmüller 1971: pl. 20) or rock tombs in Beni Hassan (Newberry 1893: pl. 29). For the technique and material cf. Killen 1994; Killen 2000: 353.

227 E. g. in a woodcutting scene from the tomb of Nefer and Ka-Hay at Saqqara (Moussa/Altenmüller 1971: Tf. 20) next to men felling trees; in a carpenter scene on the south wall of the first chamber in Giza Mastaba G 6020, second registers (Weeks 1994: fig. 30) or a boat building scene in the tomb of Rahotep (Tomb 6) at Meidum (Petrie 1892: pl. 11). Odler (2016: 134–137) provides a comprehensive list of Old Kingdom examples of adzes in wall decorations.

228 There were two types of adze models: One smaller, thinner type, which probably had no separate blade attached to the head (four examples, cf. footnote 94) and the more common type reflected in wall decorations with woodworking scenes with rounded head and fastened blade. For types and forms of tool blades cf. Petrie 1917 and now especially Odler 2016.

229 Cf. footnotes 154 and 155. The comparable examples from the tomb of Nakhti (Paris, Louvre E 12006 and E 12004) were likewise found with detached blades, thus their allocation is uncertain (Desroches Noblecourt & Vercoutter 1981: 128, no. 121a–b/122a–b).

230 Well-known miniaturizations are, for example, the model tools from the "carpenter's box" from the tomb of Ankhef in Asyut (Tomb 9, Khashaba Excavations, today in the Metropolitan Museum, New York, Acc.nos. 17.9.13–17.9.25; https://www.metmuseum.org/search-results#!/search?q=Ankhef [12.02.2020]), ranging in length between 3.5 and 7.7 cm. Further examples were found by Garstang in Beni Hassan, measuring "three or four inches in length" and exhibiting copper blades (Garstang 1907: 78). The question of proportions of a collection of small chisels with iron blades found in the tomb of Tutankhamun (KV 62) is additionally discussed by Broschat et al. (2018: 5 with fn. 12). The authors mention earlier proposals which suggest a possible ritual function of the tools in connection with the Opening of the Mouth ceremony, but due to the scarce evidence cannot corroborate the hypothesis.

axes carried by the rows of soldiers described above – the axes found in the archaeological material are clearly reduced in size. Additionally, the blade of the axe in the woodworking scene seems to be of semi-circular[231] shape, a fact which corroborates the assumption that this type of axe could be depicted as tool as well as weapon in the wall decorations.[232]

4.3 Boats

In 1913 Reisner noted that „Every type of boat found among the models is also to be found in the tomb scenes."[233] This general statement is only partly supported by the scarce evidence from Asyut: Some of the boats in the wall decorations from Tomb N13.1 described above find clear counterparts in the model material, while others are not present in the archaeological evidence. Vice versa, some boat types found among the model material seem to have no obvious counterpart in the wall decorations so far, which might of course be due to the few preserved decorations or a different mode of representation of boat types in both media.

Significant features of the vessels conforming to Reisner's Type II depicted in Tomb N13.1 are the hull type with slightly raised stern, the installations of rudder, sail and rigging as well as superstructures like the vaulted, often yellow colored cabins. These characteristics, including the color scheme, are mirrored in parts of the model material.

Especially the first boat in the procession on the west wall of Tomb N13.1 (Fig. 9) finds a close parallel in the model boat from the tomb of Mesehti (CG 4918) with the solid hull structure and raised stern.[234] The vaulted cabin, although lacking its cover, mirrors the structured framework of the depicted element. The positions of the mast-shoe, the rudderpost and the crew represent the detailed wall painting in the round.

The roof of a cabin probably of a similar type was discovered in the side chamber of Shaft 3 in Tomb III.[235] Noteworthy here is the coloring that indicates a rectangular mat structure on the underside of the slightly vaulted roof by white lines with black details on a yellow ground. Three large ogival shields are painted on the upper side of the roof on the yellow background.[236]

Further model fragments discovered at the same spot indicate the presence of a funerary barque of Reisner's Type V and one or maybe two further vessels, one of which had an open structure canopy supported by thin posts.[237] The latter might resemble the superstructure on the third boat on the west wall (Fig. 10), where traces of the tomb owner sitting below a canopy might be reconstructed.[238] The tomb of Nakhti contained two funerary barques with green hull of Reisner's Type V;[239] the ends of their hulls are formed as raised papyriform finial ends painted in a light color,[240] which in profile resemble the raised prow and stern of the papyrus raft in the fishing and fowling scene of Tomb N13.1, but otherwise seem of a different hull construction.

---

231 I thank Eva Gervers M. A. for her additional information on the scene.
232 Cf. footnote 157.
233 REISNER 1913: ii. For details and critique on Reisner's model typology cf. MERRIMAN 2011: 4–8.
234 MERRIMAN (2011: 74) states a similarity of features of this type to Theban models: "Although the model is from Asyut, its stern construction has the broad counter of the Theban All Dynasty XI boats […]". For a detailed description of the model see REISNER 1913: 74–80; MERRIMAN 2011: 378–379. Another parallel in type and design, especially with the open framework of the cabin, is a travel boat from the tomb of Djehutynakht at Deir el-Bersha, today in the Boston, Museum of Fine Arts Acc.no. 21.406 a-b.
235 M261, see ZÖLLER-ENGELHARDT 2016: 99.
236 For a compilation of comparative objects cf. MONTONATI 2018.
237 ZÖLLER-ENGELHARDT 2016: 11–14.
238 I thank Eva Gervers M. A. for pointing out the details of this wall scene.
239 REISNER 1913: xxi–xxiv; MERRIMAN 2011: 222; cf. KAHL 2019: 40.
240 Cf. MERRIMAN 2011: 222.

In contrast, however, the tombs of Minhotep, Wepwawetemhat, Iti-ibi (Tomb III)[241] and others[242] contained model boats with a characteristic flat deck ending in blunt papyriform bundle ends – a feature, which Merriman characterizes as "a site-specific trait"[243] for Asyut. This popular model type has no clear parallels in the wall decorations so far.

5. Conclusion

The analysis of the selected model material and the wall decorations from Asyut has led to some interesting observations: Although the coincidence of preservation and the disruptions of the early excavations prevent a direct link between the model material from the large nomarchs' tombs of the First Intermediate Period and the Early Middle Kingdom and their decoration (Table 1), the comparison across the chronologically close tombs illustrates that the model material mirrors selected topics of the wall decorations.

Prominent examples are the soldier models of Mesehti, reflecting the scenes of marching troops in his ancestors' tombs, as well as the boat models, elaborating detailed two-dimensional depictions in the three-dimensional realm. Even changes in the socio-political environment seem to be reflected in both representations, for example in the depiction of 'Nubian archers' in wall decorations and models at the time of Iti-ibi(-iqer) and Mesehti during the transition to the Early Middle Kingdom.[244] The model material might mirror influences in artistic conventions, as well: the few squatting model figures found in the surface debris of Tomb N13.1 display a surprisingly close stylistic resemblance to model figures from the tomb of Mentuhotep II at Thebes. They are unique for Asyut so far. Mesehti's model boat, too, exhibits features of a Theban style.[245]

Noteworthy as well are the stylistic correlations of the model tool and weapon material and the two-dimensional representations: The depictions correspond in displaying the same form and construction down to imitating small details: variety, for example among the design of model shield patterns, is mirrored in wall paintings, and color schemes are accurately reproduced in both media. The Asyuti models and wall decorations generally offer a comparably high degree of attention to detail, although variations in elaboration and 'quality' occur.[246]

On the basis of the evidence from Asyut, two further correlations can be addressed: the alleged replacement of wall decorations through wooden models and the relation of model tools and weapons in regard to funerary models.

The relationship between wall decorations and Egyptian funerary models has been the subject of research for some time. One hypothesis that was prevalent in the earlier research literature is the interpre-

---

241   Documented by a prow or stern of this boat type: fragment M260 (ZÖLLER-ENGELHARDT 2016: 99).

242   E. g. the tomb of Shemes or the tomb of Hetepnebi (MERRIMAN 2011: 74. 185. 216. 244).

243   MERRIMAN 2011: 74.

244   KAHL 2019: 27. He notes several features corroborating the dating and the reflections of this change: the position of Tomb N13.1 in the Gebel Asyut al-gharbi on a different geological step in comparison to the First Intermediate Period tombs, orthographical and paleographical characteristics, the discovery of marl clay pottery and divergent artistic conventions.

245   MERRIMAN (2011: 74). Cf. footnote 234.

246   ‚Quality' in this case encompasses precise workmanship, choice of material or accuracy of painting. That "aesthetic beauty" was not a decisive factor for the functionality of models has been stated before, cf. TOOLEY 1989: 181; ESCHENBRENNER-DIEMER 2017: 174–175. 178.

tation of wooden models and their precursors, 'serving statues'[247], as substitutes for (certain types of) wall decorations.[248]

This idea has been amended in the meantime. Tooley explicitly states that models were "designed to replace or *supplement* painted scenes on tomb chapel walls"[249]. Furthermore, while Roth concedes the possibility that models can replace wall decorations in burial chambers,[250] she nevertheless points out that 'serving statues' did not have the same purpose as wall decorations. This, she states, is expressed in a limited scope of possible activities found in the serving statues.[251]

That 'serving statues' in general might allude to different concepts than funerary models has recently been emphasized by Eschenbrenner-Diemer.[252] On the replacement of wall decorations through wooden models she offers thoughts on two different concepts: Wooden models are said to serve as evolved three-dimensional substitutes of figurative decorations in the burial chamber itself and as a new form of representations of the deceased and his servants in wall decorations of the (aboveground) funerary chapel(s).[253]

The evidence from Asyut is inconclusive in the former regard: Since just one decorated burial chamber with poorly preserved remnants of its decoration has been discovered in Asyut thus far at the end of the complex burial shaft of Tomb I of the Middle Kingdom nomarch Djefai-Hapi,[254] the spectrum of motives cannot be compared to the range of model material. The representation of motives from the aboveground wall decorations is more forthright in presenting scenes and activities reflected in both media.

Especially the latter correlation has also been studied by Barker, who analyzed the wooden model material on agricultural processes and food production from the cemeteries of Meir, Deir el-Bersha and Beni Hassan and compared it to the respective wall decorations.[255] She found that although both media represented scenes and processes in similar thematic areas for the provision of the deceased in the after-life, models and wall decorations used different ways of expressing these concepts. She points out that models and wall scenes relating to bread and beer production showed a comparable number of processes, while stages in the "agricultural cycle" were significantly less represented in the model material.[256] She attributes this discrepancy to technical limitations on the side of the model production, which could not adequately reproduce scenes of sowing, harvesting and winnowing.[257] The conception of the wall

---

247 ROTH 2002.

248 Regarding "Dienerfiguren" ("servant statues"/"serving statues" [cf. ROTH 2002]), HELCK (1975: 1081–1082) for example assumed that they were intended as replacements of then missing wall decorations. According to him, the development into wooden model scenes – with the exception of offering bearers – made for a higher effectiveness of the represented work processes. LIEPSNER (1982: 169) postulates that due to the general impoverishment of the decorations of Old Kingdom tombs, models served as three-dimensional substitutes of the two-dimensional wall paintings and reliefs of the 5th and 6th Dynasty. This, he states, happened because of economical and religious reasons. LEOSPO (1988: 94–95) writes that in the tomb of Ini at Gebelein "models representing numerous activities were found which were apparently intended to take the place of painted decorations, of which there is not a trace." WILDUNG (1984: 109) supports this view: "An die Stelle der Grabreliefs des Alten Reiches und der Grabmalereien der Ersten Zwischenzeit sind in der 11. Dynastie vielfach Gruppen kleiner rundplastischer Holzfiguren getreten, die fast spielzeughaft zu ganzen Szenen zusammengestellt sind." I thank Tina Beck M. A. for the literature reference to Wildung.

249 TOOLEY 1995: 8. Italics added by the author.

250 "The burial chamber was often undecorated, but sometimes had painted scenes of offerings and daily life, similar to those in the chapel. These scenes were occasionally replaced with models of wood or stone, treating the same subjects. In both cases, the intention was to ensure by magic that the provisions and activities depicted would continue in the other world." ROTH 1988: 54.

251 ROTH 2002: 104.

252 ESCHENBRENNER-DIEMER 2017: 171.

253 ESCHENBRENNER-DIEMER 2017: 178.

254 KAHL 2017.

255 BARKER 2016.

256 BARKER 2016: 70.

257 BARKER 2016: 69. Out of the scope of Barker's analysis, counterexamples to this observation exist: The Egyptian craftsmen manufacturing the models of Meketre were not hindered by technical limitations to realize complex scenes and constructions, cf. the well-known scene of livestock census or the garden models from his tomb at Thebes, where difficult scenery with a great attention to realistic detail was produced. Cf. HUGONOT 1987: 117.

decorations in contrast to model material, however, were limited in the possibilities to represent spatial relationships and depth. In regard to the substitution of figurative decorations in burial chambers she emphasizes the fact that although animate figures were painted in burial chambers, this practice would have been quickly abandoned supposedly to prevent harm for the deceased, which raised the question, why wooden model figures posed no threat, since they should be magically come to life in the afterlife, too.[258]

Analogue to what the study of Baker has shown the correlation of model material and wall decorations in Asyut is more complex than a mere transfer of two-dimensional images into three-dimensional motives and scenes. Kilian compared the occurrences of vessels in the two-dimensional decorations of the Tomb N13.1 and Tomb I with the archaeological findings made in Asyut and found that most vessels in the decorations were integrated in scenes of food production and processing. Many of these types of vessels are present in the wooden model material from Asyut but missing from the actual ceramic corpus. She reasons that the wall decorations as well as the models aimed to represent stages in the production of necessary goods for the deceased, while the pottery equipment that was found in the tombs contained the finished products or represented – rarely – vessels intended for cultic purposes.[259]

This corroborates what has been shown for the model material presented here: some elements of the wall decorations have exact counterparts in the model equipment. Nevertheless, while the details in representation are closely connected, the configurations of model material can differ from the selection in the wall scenes.

An instructive example for this are military scenes and weaponry. As illustrated above, a salient feature of the Asyuti decoration in the First Intermediate Period and Early Middle Kingdom is military presence. Marching soldiers with axes and shields are prominent images in the tombs of the local First Intermediate Period and Early Middle Kingdom nomarchs. The newly discovered Tomb N13.1 adds scenes of further military activities including archers as well as hunting scenes. The representation of this 'military frame of mind'[260] in the model material is – as far as the scarce evidence shows – only executed by adding (model) weaponry and military equipment to the grave goods, not in the representation of military contingents or processions of figures, with the exception of Mesehti's soldier models. As is characteristic for model material not embedded in model scenes in Asyut these items are significantly larger than utensils used by model figures, but still of reduced size in comparison to life-size examples. Nevertheless, also full-size specimens were found among the burial goods from Asyut, but more individually.

The addition of model tools and weapons to the burial equipment is a well-established practice since Predynastic times.[261] Their presence among the burial equipment has been explained with defensive, protective and symbolic or cultic purposes for the weapons[262] and necessary provision for the craftsmen working on the tomb/the coffin or symbols of the property of the household of the deceased.[263] Odler combines the cultic and economic approaches and suggests a more far-reaching interpretation of model tools as an indication of a patron-craftsmen-relationship in the Old Kingdom, surpassing the idea of

---

258 BARKER 2016: 71. On the avoidance of animate figures in burial chambers of the Old Kingdom cf. also KANAWATI 2005; on the motifs of decorations in burial chambers cf. BOLSHAKOV 1997: 111–122; DAWOOD 2005; KANAWATI 2010.

259 KILIAN 2018. She especially highlights ḥs.t-vases, which occur in wooden model form in several burials in Asyut (cf. Table 2). Cf. also KAHL 2019: 25.

260 WILLEMS 2014: 44, fn. 135. Cf. footnote 115.

261 Cf. JÉQUIER 1921: 193; SWAIN 1995; ODLER 2016.

262 E. g. JÉQUIER 1921: 193; ESCHENBRENNER-DIEMER 2017: 134 with fn. 5.

263 Cf. ODLER 2016: 18 with further references. GARSTANG (1907: 78) originally suggested an association with the construction of the coffin: "[…] an adze, a drill, a saw, a bradawl, and an axe. These were all instruments necessary in constructing the wooden coffin, and they obtained thus a certain sanctity which led to the models being deposited in the tomb."

model tools as provisions or symbols of the tomb-building process.[264] Tools and weapons are also some-times found in Old Kingdom offering lists[265] and are more common motives in *frises d'objets* on Middle Kingdom coffins[266], underlining the necessity of furnishing the deceased with these items. Willems showed that the development of the Middle Kingdom object frieze has a close connection to the evo-lution of the offering list and thus with the "Speiseritual" and "object rituals" of the Old Kingdom.[267] Inspired by the royal object ritual Middle Kingdom coffins can display weapons, staves and scepters in their *frises d'objets*, partly adding additional material not included in the royal sphere. These depictions are sometimes coupled with Coffin Texts that are derivations of older Pyramid Texts dealing with ob-ject rituals.[268] He later points out a connection between the placement of three-dimensional objects or corresponding models of the conceptual realm of these object rituals in non-royal burials, which was, however, only found in a few burials (including Nakhti and Mesehti from Asyut).[269]

The recent discovery of the previously unknown high quantity of model tools and weapons in the earlier tombs of Khety I and Iti-ibi is remarkable in this regard: they reflect the types of tools and wea-pons which are subsequently depicted in object friezes of coffins from other regions dating to the Middle Kingdom, as well as from a few Asyuti examples.[270] They might thus hint at a connection to the funerary rituals outlined by Willems and add to the scarce evidence, while fulfilling the established symbolic pur-poses of a defensive and protective nature. The compilation of wooden model objects is in some contexts complemented by model *ḥs.t*-vases (Khety I, Nakhti, Mesehti) as well as wooden staves and scepters (Nakhti, Minhotep), as presented above, showing further elements of equipment evident in later object friezes. The high quantity in the cases of Iti-ibi and Khety I seems furthermore indicative of the high social status of the tomb owners. Beyond that the correlation to the wall decorations in Tomb IV, H11.1 and N13.1 is noticeable: the troops of marching soldiers in the wall decorations might additionally be reflected in the many shields and maybe the numerous axes in the funerary equipment of the nomarchs. Thus, they could perform the additional function of symbolically reinforcing the military ability and strength of the First Intermediate Period and Early Middle Kingdom nomarch beyond the more isolated occurrences of (model) weaponry hitherto documented from Asyut for the First Intermediate Period and Early Middle Kingdom.[271]

Remarkable is the situation of Mesehti's funerary equipment: the only known model with figures of soldiers from Asyut[272] came from his – unintentionally[273] – undecorated tomb, while his burial goods

---

264 ODLER 2016: 18; ODLER & PETERKOVÁ HLOUCHOVÁ 2017: 211.

265 ODLER (2016: 31–33) lists four examples from the Old Kingdom. All have a specific connection to the titles of the indi-viduals, one carpenter and three individuals connected with the "treasury", among them Kai-em-ankh, whose decorated burial chamber at Giza shows storehouses with lists of their respective contents (JUNKER 1940: 72–73 with pls. 9–10).

266 JÉQUIER 1921: 195–231. 269–280; DAVIES 1987: 32 with fn. 29.

267 WILLEMS 1988: 203.

268 Ibid.: 203–204. For critical comments see KAHL 1994.

269 WILLEMS 2014: 138–140. SEIDLMAYER (2009: 156) similarly suggests that the concept behind 'ceremonial weaponry' in relation to *frises d'objets* is based on the ritual stylization of the elite burial as a royal burial, indicating a symbolic transfer of status that had to do with the social spread of certain forms of the death ritual and royal burial attributes.

270 For coffins from Asyut, it is not clearly determinable at which point in time the depicted objects began to include weaponry, mainly because the exact dating of many Asyuti coffins is still a matter of debate (cf. WILLEMS 1988: esp. 102–104; LAPP 1993: esp. 139–146; WILLEMS 1997: 117–188; KAHL 2016c with further references), and because only a few coffins from Asyut include illustrations of weapons in the first place: The coffins of the First Intermediate Period nomarchs Khety I, Iti-Ibi and Khety II are not preserved; the coffins of Mesehti (ARQUIER 2013: 29. 41. 56–77) and Nahkti (CHASSINAT & PALANQUE 1911: 35–46) do not show weapons. LAPP (1993: 134. 137. pls. 25a. 26b. 32b) noted some examples depicting weaponry like shields, axes, quivers, bows and bundles of arrows (S17 [S12C], S18 [S10C], S70 [S9C], S71 [S5C], S84 [S1Tor/S1T], S85 [S14C]), with a dating range between the 11th and 12th/13th Dynasty (LAPP 1993: 139–146; cf. WILLEMS 1988: 102–104; WILLEMS 1997; ZITMAN 2010a and b; KAHL 2016c).

271 In contrast to symbolic weaponry, SEIDLMAYER (1999: 74–75; 2009: 156–157) sees the addition of (life-size) weapons in burial equipment furthermore as a testimony to a reassessment of displaying aggression and violence in the male self-conception of the period from the end of the Old to the early Middle Kingdom.

272 Yet, they are not the only soldier models known from Egypt in this period, cf. footnote 223.

273 The tomb is unfinished, but decoration was obviously intended, cf. EL-KHADRAGY 2008: 228–229; KAHL 2018: 147.

included a few model axes, adzes, chisels and probably bows, corresponding to the compilations of types seen in the object friezes. The special emphasis of this unique model is the display of military availability and ability, showing that the tomb owner had these troops at his disposal. Unfortunately, the find spot within the tomb is unknown, preventing information on the intended audience for this display. Positioned in the aboveground hall, the model could have taken the place of scenes of marching soldiers on the tomb walls or added to their function, if a decoration was additionally intended.

The findings from Asyut in general illustrate an overlap between the model equipment placed aboveground and the items positioned in burial chambers: The same types of model boats and offering bearers/estate figurines, for example, have been found in the superstructure of tombs as well as in burial chambers. In the case of Nakhti's models, Eschenbrenner-Diemer sees a connection between the quality of wooden models and their placement: she proposes that the most refined objects were placed in the accessible superstructure of the tomb as a way to showcase high social standing,[274] which one is tempted to assign to Mesehti's soldier models, as well. Fluctuations in quality, however, can also occur in closed contexts from one find spot[275] and in the case of Asyut, the disturbed contexts and the inadequate archaeological documentation[276] raise doubt on the accurate allocation of model material found by the early excavators, thus preventing unambiguous evidence.

Summing up, it can be stated that wooden models and wall decorations in Asyut show a strong correlation. The precise connection between tombs with extensive wall decorations on the one hand and numerous model equipment on the other hand furthermore remains inconclusive due to the coincidence of preservation: generally most of the model equipment from Asyut came from undecorated tombs, while the model material from tombs with better preserved decoration is not preserved or can no longer be allocated precisely. Vice versa, the wall paintings in tombs with allocable model material are heavily destroyed.

Nevertheless, the extended comparison showed that identical or similar modes of design are found in both media. In this regard, the conceptual realm of decorations and models overlap, both forming abstractions of real-world entities with a high degree of details. Their functional scope shows that both serve to magically provide permanent sustenance and mobility for the deceased. The model tool and weapon material might add connections to funerary rituals and the special focus on military presence in Asyut during the First Intermediate Period and the transition to the Middle Kingdom, which is additionally evident in wall depictions and two unique models of marching soldiers.

---

274 Eschenbrenner-Diemer 2017: 178.
275 For example, while the majority of models found in the tomb of Djehutynakht at El-Bersha were of a similar elaboration, the so-called "Bersha Procession" stands out, cf. Tooley 1984: 373–376.
276 Further illustrated by Kilian 2019: 138–140.

Table 1

Tomb	Model material		Wall decorations					
	chapel	burial chamber(s)	marching soldiers	figthing/hunting	woodworking/carpentry/crafts	boats	offering bearers	granary
V (M11.1)		✓						✓
III (N12.1)		✓		✓				
IV (N12.2)		(✓)ᵃ	✓					
H11.1	(✓)ᵇ		✓					
N13.1	✓ᶜ		✓	✓	✓	✓	✓	
I (P10.1)						✓	✓	✓
Nakhti	✓	✓	undecorated					
Mesehti (K11.3)	✓ᵈ		undecorated					
Wepwawetemhat	✓		undecorated					
Minhotep	✓ᵉ		undecorated					

Notes on the table:

– Model material present and allocated is marked by ✓

– If model material was found but could not be allocated to the burial chamber with certainty, the information is marked by (✓)

– If wall decorations are preserved, the information is marked by ✓

a   Found in the shaft fillings and side chambers; allocation to the original tomb equipment unclear.
b   Found in the surface debris and Shaft 11; allocation to the original tomb equipment unclear.
c   Material found scattered at the surface and in the shaft fillings.
d   Find spot within the tomb unknown.
e   Find spot within the tomb unclear, probably chapel; unclear, if tomb had burial shafts.

Table 2

Tomb	Model material													
	Weapons				Weapon/Tool	Tools			Model soldiers	ḥs.t-vases	Boats	Granaries	Food producing/processing scenes	Offering bearers/estate figurines
	Shields	Spear cases/Quivers	Javelins/Spears/Lances	Bows/Arrows	Axes	Adzes	Chisels	Other						
V (M11.1)	--	--	--	--	20+	40+	15	--	--	1	3?	--	--	--
III (N12.1) Shaft 3, sidechamber	41+	1+?	--	Arrows?	28+	56+ (2 Types)	4	--	--	--	2-3? (Type IV, Type V?)	1?	1 brewery/bakery scene? 1 slaughtering scene?	1?
III (N12.1) Shaft 2, sidechamber	--	--	--	--	--	--	--	--	--	--	1?	--	1 scene?	1?
III (N12.1) Shaft 4, sidechamber	--	--	--	--	--	--	--	--	--	--	1-2?	1?	1 scene?	1?
Nakhti	2	2	12 javelins	3 bows, 24 arrows	10	7+	4	--	--	4	2 (Type V) 2? (in chapel)	1	1 brewery/bakery scene	1 (side-chamber shaft 1) 5? (in chapel) 1 (side-chamber shaft 4)
Mesehti (K11.3)	--	--	--	bows?	2	4	4	mallet?	2 groups	1	1 (Type II)	--	--	2?
Wepwawet-emhat	1 handle (life-size)	--	--	11	--	--	--	--	--	--	2 (Type IV with blunt papyriform bundle ends)	--	1 brewery/bakery scene	1

Minhotep	–	–	–	1 bow, 83 arrows	–	–	–	–	4 (Type IV with blunt papyriform bundle ends)	–	1 brewery/ bakery scene	3

Notes on the table:

– The table lists the model material documented/preserved for the individual tombs (cf. description and remarks on the potential incompleteness of the compilations above)

– Uncertain numbers or reconstructed identifications based on fragments are marked by a question mark

– Minimum numbers are marked with a plus

– Bows, arrows or javelins might be life-size examples instead of reduced size models

– Identification of boat types is made according to the system of REISNER 1913, with additions by MERRIMAN 2011

Bibliography

ABDELRAHIEM 2020: M. Abdelrahiem, The Northern Soldiers-Tomb (H11.1) at Asyut (The Asyut Project 13; Wiesbaden 2020).

ALLEN 2006: S. Allen, Miniature and Model Vessels in Ancient Egypt, in: M. Bárta (ed.), The Old Kingdom Art and Archaeology. Proceedings of the Conference Held in Prague, May 31-Jund 4, 2004 (Prague 2006), 19-24.

ARNOLD 1981: D. Arnold, Der Tempel des Königs Mentuhotep von Deir el-Bahari III. Die königlichen Beigaben, (Archäologische Veröffentlichung 23; Mainz 1981).

ARQUIER 2013: B. Arquier, Le double sarcophagi de Mésehti S1C (CG28118) – S2C (CG28119). Recherches sur l'organisation du décor iconographique et textuel (Archéologie et Préhistoire, Université Paul Valéry-Montpellier III; Montpellier 2013). [https://tel.archives-ouvertes.fr/tel-00937051/document [08.05.2020]]

BARKER 2016: G. Barker, Funerary Models vs. Wall Scenes. A Study of Agricultural Pursuits and Food Production to the End of the Middle Kingdom (Unpublished Master Thesis, Macquarie University, Sydney 2016). [https://pdfs.semanticscholar.org/d354/7723f4f0879c317cbc68936ec34d1d73ce0f.pdf [08.05.2020]]

BIETAK 1985: M. Bietak, Zu den nubischen Bogenschützen aus Assiut. Ein Beitrag zur Geschichte der Ersten Zwischenzeit, in: P. Posener-Kriéger (ed.), Mélanges Gamal Eddin Mokhtar I (Bibliothèque d'Étude 97; Cairo 1985), 87–97.

BROSCHAT ET AL. 2018: K. Broschat, F. Ströbele, C. Koeberl, C. Eckmann & E. Mertah, Himmlisch! Die Eisenobjekte aus dem Grab des Tutanchamun (Mosaiksteine. Forschungen am Römisch-Germanischen Zentralmuseum 15; Mainz 2018).

CHASSINAT & PALANQUE 1911: É. Chassinat & Ch. Palanque, Une campagne de fouilles dans la nécropole d'Assiout, (Mémoires de l'Institut Français d'Archéologie Orientale du Caire 24; Kairo 1911).

DAWOOD 2005: K. Dawood, Animate Decoration and Burial Chambers of Private Tombs during the Old Kingdom. New Evidence from the Tomb of Kairer at Saqqara, in: L. Pantalacci (ed.), Des Néférkare aux Montouhotep. Trevaux archéologiques en cours sur la fin de la VIe dynastie et la Première Période Intermédiaire. Actes du colloque CNRS – université Lumière Lyon 2, tenu le 5–7 juillet 2001 (Travaux de la Maison de l'Orient et de la Méditerranée 40; Lyon 2005), 107–127.

DEL VESCO 2019: P. Del Vesco, Finds from the Asyut Excavations in the Museo Egizio, in: KAHL, SBRIGLIO, DEL VESCO & TRAPANI 2019: 281–308.

DESROCHES NOBLECOURT & VERCOUTTER 1981: C. Desroches Noblecourt & J. Vercoutter, Un siècle de fouilles françaises en Égypte (Cairo 1981).

EGGEBRECHT 1977: A. Eggebrecht, in: Lexikon der Ägyptologie II, 1977, 370–371, s. v. Gabenbringer.

EL-KHADRAGY 2006a: M. El-Khadragy, New Discoveries in the Tomb of Khety II at Asyut, in: The Bulletin of the Australian Centre for Egyptology 17, 2006, 79–95.

EL-KHADRAGY 2006b: M. El-Khadragy, The Northern Soldiers Tomb at Asyut, in: Studien zur Altägyptischen Kultur 35, 2006, 148–164.

EL-KHADRAGY 2007a: M. El-Khadragy, Some Significant Features in the Decoration of the Chapel of Iti-ibi-iqer at Asyut, in: Studien zur Altägyptischen Kultur 36, 2007, 105–135.

EL-KHADRAGY 2007b: M. El-Khadragy, Fishing, Fowling and Animal-Handling in the Tomb of Djefaihapi I at Asyut, in: The Bulletin of the Australian Centre for Egyptology 18, 2007, 125–144.

EL-KHADRAGY 2008: M. El-Khadragy, The Rock-cut Chapel of Khety II at Asyut, in: Studien zur Altägyptischen Kultur 37, 2008, 217–241.

EL-KHADRAGY in print: M. El-Khadragy, Tomb N13.1 of the Nomarch Iti-ibi(-iqer) at Asyut, with collaboration of U. Dubiel and E. Gervers (The Asyut Project; Wiesbaden in print).

ESCHENBRENNER-DIEMER 2017: G. Eschenbrenner-Diemer, From the Workshop to the Grave: The Case of Wooden Funerary Models, in: G. Miniaci, M. Betrò & S. Quirke (eds.), Company of Images. Modelling the Imaginary World of Middle Kingdom Egypt (2000–1500 BC). Proceedings of the International Conference of the EPOCHS Project held 18th–20th September 2014 at UCL, London (Orientalia Lovaniensia Analecta 262; Leuven et al. 2017), 133–191.

FEUGÈRE 2018: M. Feugère, Protocoles d'étude des objets archéologiques (Drémils-Lafage 2018).

FREED & DOXEY 2009: R. E. Freed & D. M. Doxey, The Djehutynakhts' Models, in: R. E. Freed, N. Picardo & D. Doxey (eds.), The Secrets of Tomb 10A. Egypt 2000 BC (Boston 2009), 151–177.

GARSTANG 1907: J. Garstang, Burial Customs of Ancient Egypt as illustrated by Tombs of the Middle Kingdom being a Report of Excavations made in the Necropolis of Beni Hassan during 1902–3–4 (London 1907).

GILBERT 2004: G. P. Gilbert, Weapons, Warriors and Warfare in Early Egypt (BAR International Series 1208, Oxford 2004).

GÖTTLICHER & WERNER 1971: A. Göttlicher & W. Werner, Schiffsmodelle im Alten Ägypten (Wiesbaden 1971).

HEROLD 2009: A. Herold, Aspekte ägyptischer Waffengeschichte, in: R. Gundlach & C. Vogel (eds.), Militärgeschichte des pharaonischen Ägypten. Altägypten und seine Nachbarkulturen im Spiegel aktueller Forschung (Krieg in der Geschichte 34; Paderborn et al. 2009), 187–216. 476–482, figs. 1–10.

HUGONOT 1987: J.-C. Hugonot, Les modeles de jardin de la tombe de Meket-Re á Thebes, in: Varia Aegyptiaca 3/2, 1987, 117–125.

JACQUET-GORDON 1962: H. Jacquet-Gordon, Les noms des domaines funéraires sous l'Ancien Empire égyptien (Bibliothèque d'Étude 34, Cairo 1962).

JONES 1995: D. Jones, Boats (London 1995).

KAHL 1994: J. Kahl, Zu den Särgen des Mittleren Reiches in Ägypten, in: Die Welt des Orients 25, 1994, 21–35.

KAHL 2007: J. Kahl, Ancient Asyut. The First Synthesis after 300 Years of Research (The Asyut Project 1; Wiesbaden 2007).

KAHL 2008: J. Kahl, Tomb N13.1: Tomb Shafts, in: J. Kahl, M. El-Khadragy & U. Verhoeven, with a contribution by Abd el-Naser Yasin, in: Studien zur Altägyptischen Kultur 37, 2008, 200–201.

KAHL 2012: J. Kahl, Tomb V: Architecture, in: J. Kahl, M. El-Khadragy, U. Verhoeven, M. Abdelrahiem, M. van Elsbergen, H. Fahid, A. Kilian, C. Kitagawa, T. Rzeuska & M. Zöller-Engelhardt, The Asyut Project: Ninth Season of Fieldwork (2011), in: Studien zur Altägyptischen Kultur 41, 2012, 190.

KAHL 2013: J. Kahl, Proportionen und Stile in den assiutischen Nomarchengräbern der Ersten Zwischenzeit und des Mittleren Reiches, in: E. Frood & A. McDonald, (eds.), Decorum and Experience. Essays in Ancient Culture for John Baines, (Oxford 2013), 141–146.

KAHL 2016a: J. Kahl, Notes from the French Mission, in: J. Kahl, N. Deppe, D. Goldsmith, A. Kilian, C. Kitagawa, J. Moje & M. Zöller-Engelhardt, Asyut, Tomb III: Objects. Part 1 (The Asyut Project 3; Wiesbaden 2016), 339–343.

KAHL 2016b: J. Kahl, Introduction, in: J. Kahl, N. Deppe, D. Goldsmith, A. Kilian, C. Kitagawa, J. Moje & M. Zöller-Engelhardt, Asyut, Tomb III: Objects. Part 1 (The Asyut Project 3; Wiesbaden 2016), i–xxii.

KAHL 2016c: J. Kahl, Zum Alter der Sargtext-Artefakte aus Assiut, in: P. Dils & L. Popko (eds.), Zwischen Philologie und Lexikographie des Ägyptisch-Koptischen. Akten der Leipziger Abschlusstagung des Akademienprojekts „Altägyptisches Wörterbuch" (Stuttgart – Leipzig 2016), 29–55.

KAHL 2017: J. Kahl, Tomb I (P10.1), in: J. Kahl, M. El-Hamrawi & U. Verhoeven, The Asyut Project: Thirteenth Season of Fieldwork (2017), in: Studien zur Altägyptischen Kultur 47, 2018, 137–142.

KAHL 2018: J. Kahl, The Tomb of Mesehti, in: J. Kahl, M. El-Hamrawi & U. Verhoeven, The Asyut Project: Thirteenth Season of Fieldwork (2017), in: Studien zur Altägyptischen Kultur 47, 2018, 137–148.

KAHL 2019: J. Kahl, Die Statue Assiut S10/16. Ein Regionalstil und seine Bewertung (The Asyut Project 11; Wiesbaden 2019).

KAHL, EL-KHADRAGY & VERHOEVEN 2005: J. Kahl, M. El-Khadragy & U. Verhoeven, The Asyut Project: Fieldwork season 2004, in: Studien zur Altägyptischen Kultur 33, 2005, 159–167.

KAHL, EL-KHADRAGY & VERHOEVEN 2006: J. Kahl, M. El-Khadragy & U. Verhoeven, The Asyut Project: Third Season of Fieldwork, in: Studien zur Altägyptischen Kultur 34, 2006, 241–249.

KAHL, EL-KHADRAGY & VERHOEVEN 2007: J. Kahl, M. El-Khadragy & U. Verhoeven, Tomb N13.1, in: J. Kahl, M. El-Khadragy & U. Verhoeven, with a contribution by Monika Zöller, The Asyut Project. Fourth Season of Fieldwork (2006), in: Studien zur Altägyptischen Kultur 36, 2007, 81–103.

KAHL & MALUR 2011: J. Kahl & J. Malur, Tomb V (M11.1), in: J. Kahl, M. El-Khadragy, U. Verhoeven, M. Abdelrahiem, H. Faheed Ahmed, C. Kitagawa, J. Malur, S. Prell & T. Rzeuska, The Asyut Project. Eighth Season of Fieldwork (2010), in: Studien zur Altägyptischen Kultur 40, 2011, 182–183.

KAHL, SBRIGLIO, DEL VESCO & TRAPANI 2019: J. Kahl, A. M. Sbriglio, P. Del Vesco & M. Trapani, Asyut. The Excavations of the Italian Archaeological Mission (1906–1913) (Studi Del Museo Egizio 1; Modena 2019).

KANAWATI 2005: N. Kanawati, Decoration of Burial Chambers, Sarcophagi and Coffins in the Old Kingdom, in: K. A. Daoud, S. Bedier & S. Abd el-Fatah, Studies in honor of Ali Radwan (Supplément aux Annales du Service des antiquités de l'Égypte 34; Cairo 2006), 55–71.

KANAWATI 2010: N. Kanawati, Decorated Burial Chambers of the Old Kingdom (Cairo 2010).

Kilian 2018: A. Kilian, Gefäße – Darstellungen in Wanddekoration und archäologischer Befund. Ein Fallbei-spiel aus Assiut, in: L. Hudáková, P. Jánosi, C. Jurman & U. Siffert (eds.), Art-facts and Artefacts. Visualising the Material World in Middle Kingdom Egypt (Middle Kingdom Studies 8; London 2018), 41–61.

Kilian 2019: A. Kilian, Untersuchungen zur Keramik der Ersten Zwischenzeit und des frühen Mittleren Reiches aus Assiut/Mittelägypten (The Asyut Project 12, Wiesbaden 2019).

Killen 1994: G. Killen, Egyptian Woodworking and Furniture (Shire Egyptology 21; Princes Risborough 1994).

Killen 2000: G. Killen, Wood [Technology], in: P. T. Nicholson & I. Shaw (eds.), Ancient Egyptian Materials and Technology (Cambridge 2000), 353–371.

Kühnert-Eggebrecht 1969: E. Kühnert-Eggebrecht, Die Axt als Waffe und Werkzeug im alten Ägypten (Münchner Ägyptologische Studien 15; Berlin 1969).

Landström 1974: B. Landström, Die Schiffe der Pharaonen. Altägyptische Schiffsbaukunst von 4000 bis 600 v. Chr. (Gütersloh et al. 1974).

Lapp 1993: G. Lapp, G., Typologie der Särge und Sargkammern von der 6. bis 13. Dynastie (Studien zur Archäologie und Geschichte Altägyptens 7; Heidelberg 1993).

Leospo 1988: E. Leospo, Gebelein and Asyut During the First Intermediate Period and the Middle Kingdom, in: A. M. Donadoni Roveri & S. Curto (eds.), Egyptian Civilization. (Egyptian Museum of Turin; Milan 1988), 82–103.

Liepsner 1982: T. F. Liepsner, in: Lexikon der Ägyptologie IV, Wiesbaden 1982, 169, s. v. Modelle.

Maeir & Ponting 2000: A. M. Maeir, M. J. Ponting, The Cutting Edge: Symbolism, Technology and Typology of a New Kingdom Egyptian Axe, in: Mitteilungen des Deutschen Archäologischen Instituts Abteilung Kairo 56, 2000, 267–276.

Merriman 2011: A. Merriman, Egyptian watercraft models from the Predynastic to Third Intermediate Periods (BAR International series 2263, Oxford 2011).

Montonati 2018: T. Montonati, Two Ancient Egyptian Models in the Historical Photographic Archive of the Museo Egizio, Turin, in: Rivista del Museo Egizio 2, 2018. [DOI: 10.29353, accessed 17.02.2020]

Naville 1907: E. Naville, The XIth Dynasty Temple at Deir el-Bahari I (Egypt Exploration Fund 28; London 1907).

Newberry 1893a: P. E. Newberry, Beni Hasan I (Archaeological Survey of Egypt 1; London 1893).

Newberry 1893b: P. E. Newberry, Beni Hasan II (Archaeological Survey of Egypt 2; London 1893).

Nibbi 2003: A. Nibbi, Some Remarks on the Ancient Egyptian Shield, in: Zeitschrift für ägyptische Sprache und Altertumskunde 130, 2003, 170–181.

Odler 2016: M. Odler, Old Kingdom Copper Tools and Model Tools (Archaeopress Egyptology 14; Oxford 2016).

Odler & Peterková Hlouchová 2017: M. Odler, M. Peterková Hlouchová, "May you receive that favourite harpoon of yours...". Old Kingdom spears/harpoons and their contexts of use, in: Studien zur Altägyptischen Kultur 46, 2017, 191–221.

Partridge 2002: R. B. Partridge, Fighting Pharaohs. Weapons and Warfare in Ancient Egypt (Manchester 2002).

Petrie 1917: W. M. F. Petrie, Tools and Weapons (British School of Archaeology in Egypt 30; London 1917).

Reisner 1913: G. A. Reisner, Models of Ships and Boats, Catalogue Générale des antiquités Égyptiennes du musée du Caire. Nos 4798–4976 et 5034–5200 (Cairo 1913).

Roehrig 2015: C. H. Roehrig, Estate Figure, in: A. Oppenheim, Do. Arnold, Di. Arnold, & K. Yamamoto (eds.), Ancient Egypt Transformed. The Middle Kingdom (New York 2015), 226–227.

Roth 1988: A. M. Roth, The Social Aspects of Death, in: S. D'Auria (ed.), Mummies & Magic. The Funerary Art of Ancient Egypt (Boston 1988), 52–59.

Roth 2002: A. M. Roth, The Meaning of Menial Labour. "Servant Statues" in Old Kingdom Serdabs, in: Journal of the American Research Center in Egypt 39, 2002, 103–121.

Ryan 1988: D. P. Ryan, The archaeological excavations of David George Hogarth at Asyut, Egypt (PhD Thesis, Cincinnati 1988).

Sbriglio 2019a: A. M. Sbriglio, Schiaparelli at Asyut, in: Kahl, Sbriglio, Del Vesco & Trapani 2019, 67–93.

Sbriglio 2019b: A. M. Sbriglio, The Excavation Journals (Transcription and Plates), in: Kahl, Sbriglio, Del Vesco & Trapani 2019, 165–228.

Scheel 1989: B. Scheel, Egyptian Metalworking and Tools (Shire Egyptology 13; Princes Risborough 1989).

SEIDLMAYER 1999: S. Seidlmayer, Kämpfende Stiere. Autorität und Rivalität unter pharaonischen Eliten, in: Gegenworte. Hefte für den Disput über Wissen 4. Von Tieren und Forschern, 1999, 73–75.

SEIDLMAYER 2009: S. Seidlmayer, Archäologische Befunde militärgeschichtlicher Aussagekraft, in: R. Gundlach & C. Vogel (eds.), Militärgeschichte des pharaonischen Ägypten. Altägypten und seine Nachbarkulturen im Spiegel aktueller Forschung (Krieg in der Geschichte 34, Paderborn 2009), 147–164.

SHAW 1991: I. Shaw, Egyptian Warfare and Weapons (Shire Egyptology 16; Princes Risborough 1991).

SPALINGER 2005: A. Spalinger, War in Ancient Egypt. The New Kingdom (Oxford 2005).

SWAIN 1995: S. Swain, The Use of Model Objects as Predynastic Egyptian Grave Goods. An Ancient Origin for a Dynastic Tradition, in: S. Campbell & A. Green (eds.), The Archaeology of Death in the Ancient Near East (Oxbow Monograph 51; Oxford 1995), 35–37.

TOOLEY 1989: A. M. J. Tooley, Middle Kingdom Burial Customs. A Study of Wooden Models and Related Material (unpubl. PhD Thesis, Liverpool 1989).

TOOLEY 1995: A. M. J. Tooley, in: D. B. Redford (ed.), Oxford Encyclopedia of Ancient Egypt II (Oxford 2001), 424–428, s. v. Models.

VAN ELSBERGEN 2019: M. van Elsbergen, Die Gefäßverschlüsse aus Grab N13.1 in Assiut (The Asyut Project 10; Wiesbaden 2019).

VANDIER 1958: J. Vandier, Manuel d'archéologie Égyptienne III. Les grandes époques: La statuaire (Paris 1958).

WERNICK 2016: N. Wernick, Ancient Egyptian Shields and their Handles. A functional Explanation of New Kingdom Developments, in: The Journal of the Society for the Study of Egyptian Antiquities (2014–2015), 2016, 47–83.

WILDUNG 1984: D. Wildung, Sesostris und Amenemhet. Ägypten im Mittleren Reich (München 1984).

WILLEMS 1988: H. Willems, Chests of Life. A Study of the Typology and Conceptual Development of Middle Kingdom Standard Class Coffins (Mededelingen en Verhandelingen van het Voorasiatisch-Egyptisch Genootschap "Ex Oriente Lux" 25; Leiden 1988).

WILLEMS 1997: H. Willems, Review of Lapp, G., Typologie der Särge und Sargkammern von der 6. bis 13. Dynastie, SAGA 7, Heidelberg 1993, in: Bibliotheca Orientalia 54/1–2, 1997, 112–122.

WILLEMS 2014: H. Willems, Historical and Archaeological Aspects of Egyptian Funerary Culture. Religious Ideas and Ritual Practice in Middle Kingdom Elite Cemeteries (Culture and History of the Ancient Near East 73; Leiden – Boston 2014).

ZITMAN 2010a: M. Zitman, The Necropolis of Assiut. A case study of local Egyptian funerary culture from the Old Kingdom to the end of the Middle Kingdom. Text (Orientalia Lovaniensia Analecta 180/1; Leuven et al. 2010).

ZITMAN 2010b: M. Zitman, M., The Necropolis of Assiut. A case study of local Egyptian funerary culture from the Old Kingdom to the end of the Middle Kingdom. Maps, plans of tombs, illustrations, tables, lists (Orientalia Lovaniensia Analecta 180/2, Leuven et al. 2010).

ZÖLLER-ENGELHARDT 2007: M. Zöller, Wooden Models from Asyut, in: J. Kahl, M.El-Khadragy & U. Verhoeven, with a contribution by M. Zöller, The Asyut Project: Fourth Season of Fieldwork (2006), in: Studien zur Altägyptischen Kultur 36, 2007, 87–88, Abb. 10, Tf. 6.

ZÖLLER-ENGELHARDT 2012a: M. Zöller-Engelhardt, Wooden Models from Asyut's First Intermediate Period Tombs, in: J. Kahl, M. El-Khadragy, U. Verhoeven & A. Kilian (eds.), Seven Seasons at Asyut. First Results of the Egyptian-German Cooperation in Archaeological Fieldwork. Proceedings of an International Conference at the University of Sohag, 10th–11th of October, 2009 (The Asyut Project 2; Wiesbaden 2012), 91–104, Tf. 6–7.

ZÖLLER-ENGELHARDT 2012b: M. Zöller-Engelhardt, Wooden Models from Tomb V, in: J. Kahl, M. El-Khadragy, U. Verhoeven, M. Abdelrahiem, M. van Elsbergen, H. Fahid, A. Kilian, C. Kitagawa, T. Rzeuska & M. Zöller-Engelhardt, The Asyut Project: Ninth Season of Fieldwork (2011), in: Studien zur Altägyptischen Kultur 41, 2012, 190–194.

ZÖLLER-ENGELHARDT 2016: M. Zöller-Engelhardt, Wooden Models, Tools and Weapons, in: J. Kahl, N. Deppe, D. Goldsmith, A. Kilian, C. Kitagawa, J. Moje & M. Zöller-Engelhardt, Asyut, Tomb III: Objects. Part 1 (The Asyut Project 3; Wiesbaden 2016), 1–172.

Online resources:

British Museum, London: https://www.britishmuseum.org/research/collection_online/search.aspx
Global Egyptian Museum: http://www.globalegyptianmuseum.org
Metropolitan Museum, New York: https://www.metmuseum.org/art/collection
Musée du Louvre, Paris: http://cartelen.louvre.fr/cartelen/visite?srv=crt_frm_rs&langue=en&initCritere=true
Museo Egizio, Turin: https://collezioni.museoegizio.it
Museum of Fine Arts, Boston: www.collections.mfa.org
Petrie Collection, University College, London: http://petriecat.museums.ucl.ac.uk/search.aspx
Thesaurus Linguae Aegyptiae: http://aaew.bbaw.de/tla/index.html

Pottery Offering Trays from Asyut*

Andrea Kilian

During the work conducted by *The Asyut Project*, 74 pieces of pottery offering trays were identified, belonging to a total of 59 individual offering trays. The individual offering trays consist mostly of sherds and only two (OT63, OT73) are completely preserved. None of the offering trays were found *in situ* and all stem from more or less heavily disturbed contexts. So far, no traces of soul houses were found in the ceramic material from Asyut, although they are very common in the neighboring site of Deir Rifeh. This article will document the offering trays that came to light during the last seasons of fieldwork and aims to provide a broader picture of tray types in use in Asyut during the First Intermediate Period/the early Middle Kingdom[1]. Most of the offering trays correspond to the material already known, but some of their features are worth highlighting, as they are new or rarely attested. As the Museo Egizio in Turin houses an extensive collection of complete offering trays from Asyut, these have been taken into consideration as well.[2] The collection comprises 14 offering trays, most of which are complete (see the catalog entries following this article).[3] Today, at least another 17 offering trays from Asyut are in the British Museum in London, eight of which are complete. Although they could only be examined using photographs that are available online, they have been included in this study as well, in order to obtain as much information as possible.

Design

In Asyut, several features were used in designing a pottery offering tray (see Tables 1–4). Generally speaking, it can be stated that almost all combinations of offerings are possible: one offering tray from Abydos even depicts a head of an ox, as well as a slain bound ox with its head still attached, but indicating the cut across the throat executed by the butcher,[4] similar to BM EA 46613 from Asyut that shows both a head and a bound animal in front of the head. However, some preferences concerning the Asyutian material are discernible:

— rectangular offering trays were preferred, although oval and horseshoe shaped offering trays occur as well (although very rarely)
— most of the rectangular trays also feature a spout, often combined with inner dividing walls forming basins that are open towards the spout

---

1 As none of the offering trays were found in an undisturbed context, the chronological reference is based on comparisons with other sites in Egypt. For a detailed analysis, see Kilian 2012a: 110seq and Leclère 2001: 118seq (including soul houses in his analysis).

2 My sincere thanks go to Roberta Accordino and Valentina Brambilla for their invaluable support and patience during my stay in the magazine of the Museo Egizio and to Dr. Paolo Del Vesco for the kind permission to publish the photographs I was allowed to take during my stay.

3 On the offering trays in the Museo Egizio di Torino, see also the latest article by Filipo Mi 2020.

4 See Manchester Museum, Acc. no. 5109: http://harbour.man.ac.uk/mmcustom/Display.php?irn=110421&QueryPage=%2Fmmcustom%2FEgyptQuery.php (accessed 08.09.2021) said to stem from Abydos. It shows the bound ox with its head turned upwards, horns touching the ground. This offering tray is unusual in many ways, as e.g. meat is depicted on the inside of the surrounding wall, thus standing vertically. The website mentions the 18th–19th Dynasties as a date for the tray.

– the head of a bovid occurs on approx. 50 % of the trays, in almost all cases placed in the center of the rear wall facing the spout. Only very few trays have the head placed in one of the rear corners[5] or even on the right or left side of the tray[6]

– on most of the trays displaying a bovid head, a leg of cattle can be found, too, combined with different kinds of meat and bread, whereas bound cattle are less frequent

– less common, but not unusual, are trays with physical vessels added to the surface (closed ones directly in the corners either on the plate or the surrounding wall; open ones inside the tray) or depictions of ḥs.t-vases, either applied or incised

– very rare are depictions of birds (not only in Asyut, but in general), mastabas along the inner wall or vessels other than the ones described above

– flat trays without rims are generally rare, as are those displaying a bḏꜣ-bread. In Asyut, this seems to be a chronological phenomenon, but references have been too scarce so far to really underline this hypothesis.

The following tables show the offerings documented for Asyut so far (Table 1), as well as the architectural elements (Table 2), vessel types that could be added (Table 3) and the shapes of the offering trays (Table 4). (Note that these tables include trays found during the fieldwork of *The Asyut Project* (OT-numbers), as well as the ones stored in the Museo Egizio (S-numbers and Provv.-numbers), the British Museum (BM EA-numbers), one in the Egyptian Museum, Cairo (JE-numbers) and one in the Museo di Antropologia ed Etnografia in Turin (*italic*). OT-numbers that are linked with a "-" denote fragments belonging to one and the same tray).

Table 1: Offerings

offering		Offering tray no.	total
parts of animals/ cattle	bound animal/cattle	OT5-9, OT6, OT7-20, OT60, S 8141, BM EA 46613, BM EA 46616, BM EA 47372 (only half preserved), *S 14974*	9
	carcass (non-identifiable animal)	OT8, OT12 (?)	2
	bovid's head	OT6, OT22-29, OT28, OT37, OT39, OT52 (?), OT63, OT65, OT68, OT74, Provv. 5537, S 8141, S 10647, S 10648, S 14848, S 14940, S 14941, S 14944, S 14946, BM EA 46607, BM EA 46608, BM EA 46609, BM EA 46613, BM EA 46614, BM EA 46615, BM EA 46616, BM EA 46618, BM EA 46619, BM EA 47372, JE 50041(1), *S 14974*	31
	leg of cattle	OT6, OT5-9, OT10-17-21, OT15, OT26, OT63, OT65, S 8141, S 9179, S 10648, S 14848, S 14940, S 14944, S 14946, BM EA 46607, BM EA 46608, BM EA 46609, BM EA 46613, BM EA 46614 (?), BM EA 46615 (?), BM EA 46616, BM EA 46618, BM EA 47372, JE 50041(1), *S 14974*	25
fowl	bird[a]	OT24 (?), OT3-16-25-33-34	2
meat	*jwꜥ*-meat	OT3-16-25-33-34, OT74, BM EA 46614 (?), BM EA 46620 (?)	4
	triangular piece of meat	OT28, OT63, OT64, OT74, S 14940, S 14941, BM EA 46607, BM EA 46608, BM EA 46609, BM EA 46613, BM EA 46618, JE 50041(1) (?)	12
	round or oval piece of meat with incisions	OT52, OT63, OT68, BM EA 46619, *S 14974*	5
	long objects/meat	OT3-16-25-33-34, OT43, OT65, OT74, S 8141, S 9179, S 10648, S 14848, S 14940, S 14946, BM EA 46607, BM EA 46614, BM EA 46615, BM EA 46616, BM EA 46620, BM EA 46622	16

---

5 OT39, OT68, OT74.
6 E. g. BM EA 46607.

bread	round, flat/spherical/conical bread loaves	OT3-16-25-33-34, OT7-20, OT10-17-21, OT19, OT26, OT22-29, OT12-30-31-32, OT52, OT53, OT60, OT63, OT72, OT74, OT75, S 8141, S 10648, S 14848, S 14941, S 14946, BM EA 46607, BM EA 46609, BM EA 46615, BM EA 46616, BM EA 46618, BM EA 46619, BM EA 46620, BM EA 47372, JE 50041(1), *S 14974*	29
	square/waisted/diamonds bread loaves	OT41, OT60, OT63, S 10648, BM EA 46618, BM EA 47372, JE 50041(1), *S 14974*	8
	triangular bread loaves	OT3-16-25-33-34, S 9179, S 14848, JE 50041(1) (?)	4
	bḏꜣ-bread	S 9179 (?), S 14944 (?), BM EA 46610, BM EA 46611	4
unknown	feather-like object	BM EA 46613, JE 50041(1)	2
	banana-shaped object, incised	BM EA 46618	1
	long objects (meat or vegetable?)	OT10-17-21, OT24, OT26, S 14940 (bread?), BM EA 46607	5
	nothing preserved	OT4-13-35, OT11, OT14, OT30, OT32, OT47, OT48, OT51, OT55, OT56, OT69	11

a) In Asyut, stone trays depicting birds have been discovered, too, see BM EA 991.

Table 2: Architectural elements

Architectural feature	Offering tray no.	total
basins	OT1, OT18, OT27, OT38, OT62, OT67, OT71, S 7979, S 14943, S 14945, BM EA 46610, BM EA 46611, BM EA 46612, BM EA 46622	14
canals	OT38, OT54, OT71, OT73, S 7979, S 10648, S 14941, BM EA 46610, BM EA 46622, JE 50041(1)	10
holes piercing walls/bases	OT73, S 7979, BM EA 46610	3
deepenings/impressed holes	OT37, OT52, OT54, S 10648	4
inner dividing walls (forming compartments or basins)	OT24, OT36, OT40, OT42, OT44, OT45, OT49, OT50, OT61, OT64, OT70, OT72, OT73, OT75, Provv. 5537, S 9179, S 10647, S 10648, S 14848, S 14940, S 14941, S 14944, S 14946, S 14949, BM EA 46607, BM EA 46608, BM EA 46614, BM EA 46615 (formed out of coils encircling a rectangular space instead of the typical L-shaped walls), BM EA 46617, BM EA 46620 (?), JE 50041(1), *S 14974*	32
spout	OT1, OT8, OT23, OT45, OT49, OT50, OT60, OT65, OT66, OT74, OT75, Provv. 5537, S 8141, S 9179, S 10648, S 14848, S 14940, S 14941, S 14944, S 14946, S 14949, BM EA 46607, BM EA 46608, BM EA 46609, BM EA 46613, BM EA 46614, BM EA 46615, BM EA 46616, BM EA 46617, BM EA 46619, BM EA 46621, BM EA 47372, JE 50041(1), *S 14974*	34
"mastaba"	OT57	1
platform/table (?)	S 9179 (may be *bḏꜣ*), S 10648, S 14944 (may be *bḏꜣ*), BM EA 46614	4

Table 3: Vessels

Kind of vessel	Offering tray no.	total
modeled open bowls or dishes/ closed bag-shaped vessel	on tray: OT3-16-25-33-34, S 10647; at corner/s of tray: OT58, OT59, OT63, Provv. 5537, BM EA 46609, BM EA 46612, BM EA 46613, BM EA 46621, BM EA 46622ᵃ, BM EA 47372	12
depictions of *ḥs.t*-flasks	OT41, OT46 (?), OT60, OT63, S 14848 (?), S 14940, S 14941 (?), BM EA 46613 (but might be meat), BM EA 46618, BM EA 46619, BM EA 46620 (might be meat), JE 50041(1), *S 14974*	13
other	OT27 (might be *ḥs.t*), S 14943 (?), S 14945 (ovoid), BM EA 46612	4

a) According to BM website, Zitman 2010: II, 217 believes BM EA 46621 and BM EA 46622 belong together; cf: https://www.britishmuseum.org/collection/object/Y_EA46622 (last accessed 06.08.2021).

None of the vessels are unique to Asyut, parallels to all of them can be found throughout Egypt:

- dishes/shallow bowls: e. g. Qubbet el-Hawa (EDEL 2008a: 1192, fig. 5, 1196, fig. 9); Edfu, MICHAŁOWSKI 1938a: pl. 42.2–3;
- ḥs.t: e. g. Kahun; PETRIE 1890: pl. 13.102; PETRIE 1891: pl. 4, no. 20, 23; Dendereh, PETRIE 1900: pl. 19.4;
- vessels in/onto corners: e. g. Sedment; PETRIE 1924: pl. 13, no. 730; Rifeh, PETRIE 1907: pl. 14, 3–4;
- ovoid vessels: e. g. Dendereh, PETRIE 1900: pl. 19.1.

Table 4: Shapes of the trays

Shape	Offering tray no.	total
rectangular	OT1, OT4-OT13-OT35, OT6, OT8, OT18, OT22-OT29, OT23, OT24, OT27, OT28, OT37, OT38, OT39, OT40, OT41, OT43, OT44, OT45, OT48, OT49, OT50, OT51, OT52, OT57, OT58, OT59, OT60, OT62, OT63, OT64, OT65, OT66, OT67, OT69, OT74, OT75, Provv. 5537, S 8141, S 7979, S 9179, S 10648, S 14848, S 14940, S 14941, S 14944, S 14945, S 14946, S 14949, BM EA 46607, BM EA 46608, BM EA 46609, BM EA 46611, BM EA 46612, BM EA 46613, BM EA 46614, BM EA 46615, BM EA 46616, BM EA 46617, BM EA 46618, BM EA 46619, BM EA 46620, BM EA 46621, BM EA 46622, BM EA 47372, JE 50041(1)	65
oval (with trapezoid/horseshoe)	OT3-OT16-OT25-OT33-OT34, OT5-OT9 (?), OT10-OT17-OT21, OT19, OT47 (OT73, S 10647, BM EA 46610)	5 (4)
unknown/not to be determined	OT7-20, OT11, OT12-OT30-OT31-OT32, OT14, OT15, OT22-OT29, OT26, OT42, OT46, OT53, OT54, OT55, OT56, OT57, OT61, OT70, OT71, OT72	18

Types of pottery offering trays attested in Asyut

While the fragments found during fieldwork suggested a great typological diversity of Asyutian pottery offering trays, the new finds, as well as the trays stored in the museums, offer a base for establishing an Asyutian offering tray typology. For the following typology, the overall shape (1: rectangular/U-shaped without spout, 2: rectancular with spout, 3: oval) was the main indicator, followed by subdivisions according to absence (2a) or presence of architectural elements (2b: compartments/basins formed by L-shaped or semicircular clay walls; 2b1: with platform) or the substitution of basins through vessels (2c). All in all, four main types can be distinguished.[7]

1. **Type 1**: rectangular offering tray, no spout, sometimes with rounded lower (?) part ("U-shaped" or slightly horseshoe-shaped), with basins deepened into the surface. The trays and basins may feature low or no rims, sometimes depictions of a vessel or bread, and canals,[8] but no other kind of offerings
2. **Type 2**: rectangular offering tray with spout
   - 2a: without compartments; the completely preserved specimens always feature a bovid head[9] placed in the center of the rear wall or – rarely – in one of the corners[10]

---

7 The following typology is based on complete specimens stored in the Museo Egizio, Turin and has been supplemented with specimens found during fieldwork and those available online on the British Museum website https://www.britishmuseum.org/collection. Note the different typology established for Asyut in MI 2020: 98, Fig. 2 which includes the bovid head as defining criterion whereas here the main focus is placed on overall form, followed by architectural elements (inner divisions/compartments), not including offerings. Mi's Type I with Variant A and B thus corresponds to Type 1; Types II, II A and II C correspond to Type 2b; Type IIB corresponds to Type 2b1, Type III to Type 2a and Type IV to Type 3. Type 2c is not present in Mi's typology.

8 Some of the trays belonging to this group strongly resemble the trays hewn into the bedrock in the chapel of Tomb N11.1, see below. (e. g. BM EA 46610 and BM EA 46611).

9 As already noted by Mi 2020: 104–105,

10 OT74.

— 2b: with inner compartments that are open towards the spout, formed by L-shaped or semicircular clay walls; they often feature a bovid head in the center of the rear wall or – rarely – in one of the corners[11]

— 2b1: like 2b, but with one or two raised platforms in the center rear part[12]

— 2c: vessels added in the corners either on the tray or on top of the surrounding wall, no frontal compartments

3. Type 3: oval offering tray with offerings, no inner compartments, no spout(?)[13]

4. Singular specimens: not matching any of the above types, but not forming a homogenous type either[14]

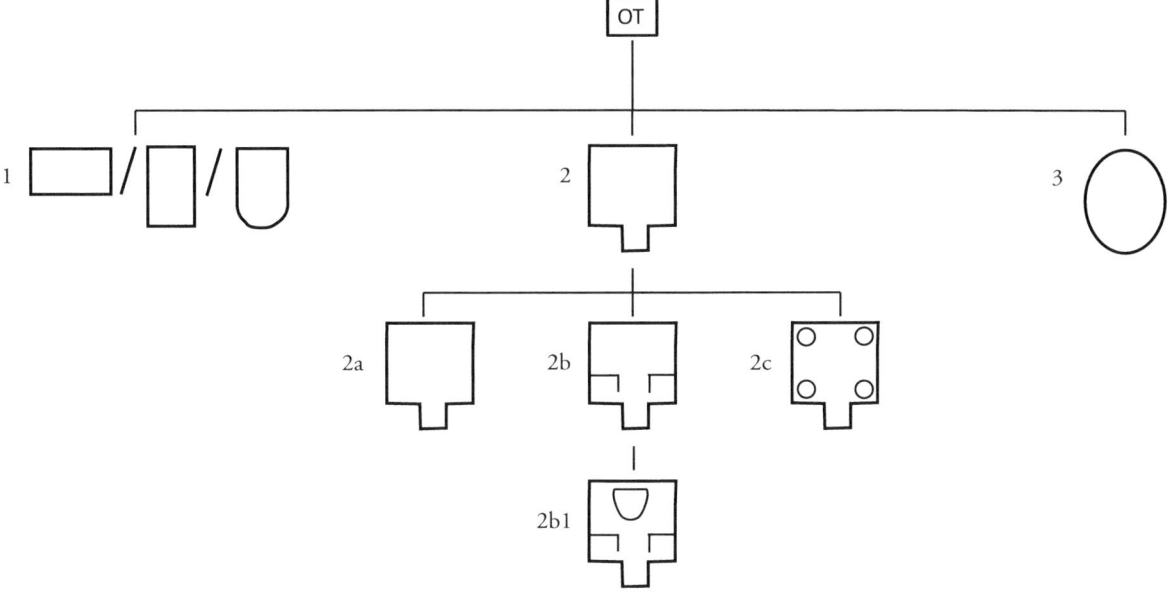

Fig. 1: Types of offering trays attested in Asyut.

Most of the offering trays are rectangular (73 %), but some taper towards the front and have an almost horseshoe-shaped appearance (S 10647, S 14943, OT73). So far, no round dish-shaped offering trays, common in Armant[15] or Gebelein[16], have been detected in Asyut.

The most common type is the rectangular tray with spout, Type 2, with subtypes 2a , 2b and 2c being almost equal in numbers; only variant 2b1 is seldom attested. Type 1 is second, but makes only 15 %. Type 3 is rare in Asyut and elsewhere in Egypt, but also attested in e. g. Kahun[17] and Denderen[18].

---

11 BM EA 46615. The L-shaped inner dividing walls are a characteristic Asyuti feature (already noted by Mᴉ 2020:

12 Either *bḏ3*-shaped or only very slightly everted rectangular.

13 OT3-16-25-33-34: OT10-17-21. The preservation of these two offering trays is not good enough to decide about the presence or absence of a spout, but a spout seems highly improbable.

14 OT1, would fit Type 1, but has a spout; OT73, featuring four basins, divided by a wall that was pierced and thus allows fluid to flow from the rear basins into the front basins that open into the spout (which would not be necessary as the rear basins are also open towards the spout), spout is formed on top of a tapering base; S 10647, being horseshoe-shaped and featuring a dish instead of offerings and a bovid head without horns and incisions on the skull; BM EA 46622, only-so-slightly deepened basins with canals, displaying a vessel in the corner and meat attached directly to the inner side of the surrounding wall similar to an offering tray from Deir Rifeh (but with the basin, canal and meat in the front half of the tray, see Pᴇᴛʀɪᴇ 1907: pl. 14. 15); BM EA 46617 forming a "tray on a tray" by adding inner dividing walls to the tray that are level with the outer surrounding wall, imitating the shape of the tray (similar to Pelizaeus-Museum Hildesheim No. 1676, where the offerings are arranged on top of a platform that has the same shape like the tray, cf. Mᴀʀᴛɪɴ-Pᴀʀᴅᴇʏ 1991: 47–48).

15 E. g. Mᴏɴᴅ/Mʏᴇʀs 1937: pl. 22, fig. 5–6.

16 Mᴉ 2020: 109ff., Type 1.

17 Pᴇᴛʀɪᴇ 1891: pl. 4.20 where the head of a bovid was placed on a round platform.

18 Pᴇᴛʀɪᴇ 1900: pl. 19.2. Cf. also RPM 5833, without provenance, presenting the offerings on a rectangular platform with a spout that looks like an "offering tray on an offering tray".

The place of the bovid head is not fixed. The most popular place is the center of the rear wall opposite the spout, but sometimes it is placed in one of the corners or at one of the side walls, independent from the type of tray. The only exception to this rule is Type 2c where the bovid head seems always to be positioned in the center of the rear wall.

Table 5: Types of pottery offering trays

Type	No. of tray	total
1[a]	OT27 (?), OT38, OT62 (?), OT71, S 7979, S 14943, S 14945, BM EA 46610, BM EA 46611, BM EA 46612	10
2	Trays listed here are known to be rectangular, but due to their state of preservation cannot be attributed to one of the subdivisions: OT4-13-35, OT6, OT5-9, OT22-29 (?), OT23, OT28, OT35, OT37, OT39, OT40, OT41, OT43, OT44, OT45, OT52, OT66	16
2a	bovid head not preserved: OT8, OT60; centered: OT65, S 8141, BM EA 46616, BM EA 46618 (?), BM EA 46619, BM EA 47372 (with a single something attached on top of the front corner (plate or vessel?); in corner: OT74 (right)	9
2b	OT75, Provv. 5537 (bovid head on rear wall, but not centered), head centered on rear wall: S 14848, S 14940, S 14941, JE 50041(1), *S 14947*; in corner: S 14946 (left), BM EA 46608, BM EA 46615 (right), centered at right wall: BM EA 46607	11
2b1	S 9179 (one platform, *bdȝ*-shape), S 14944 (two platforms, *bdȝ*-shape), S 10648 and BM EA 46614 (both with rectangular 'platform', only very slightly everted)	4
2c	OT58, OT59, OT63, BM EA 46609, BM EA 46613, BM EA 46621 and BM EA 46622 (only partly preserved, but probably belonging together, cf. ZITMAN 2010: II, 217), BM EA 47372 (front left corner (right corner missing)), Provv. 5537 (one in right rear corner). Add JE 39109, with either four vessels or four dishes placed in the corners of the tray; and JE 39110 with either vessels in all corners or two vessels in the back and two basins in front	10
3	OT3-16-25-33-34, OT10-17-21	2
4	OT1, OT18, OT73, S 10647, BM EA 46617, BM EA 466122	6

a) MI 2020: 100, Tab. 2 lists OT1, OT14 and OT44 as possibly belonging to this type. OT1 features a spout (cf. KILIAN 2012b: 200–201, Fig. 11) and therefore is arranged here with Type 4; OT14 is a fragment from the inner part of a tray (or stela) without applications (see KILIAN 2016: 182); OT44 is a corner part of a rectangular tray with surrounding and inner dividing wall, most probably belonging to Type 2, see KILIAN 2012a: Pl. 8a and below Cat. 4.

Manufacture

Offering trays were formed individually by hand; there are no traces of molding. This can be seen very clearly on the bases of e. g. OT65 or BM EA 46610 where the joints between several lumps of clay that were used to form the tray are still visible. The same holds true for the offerings: no molding techniques are discernible. All offerings were formed separately by hand before being attached to the tray. Sometimes the bottom of the tray was smoothened by hand; sometimes it was scraped carefully[19] and sometimes traces of the surface on which the trays were placed on for drying are still visible: imprints of straw or pebbles/small rocks (e.g. EA46615); sometimes even still sticking in the clay.[20] The walls of the trays often lean towards the outside, so that the upper part of the offering tray is broader than the bottom/base.

The offering trays can be covered with a red coating or left untreated; some show additional white coloring and one tray is decorated with white dots on the outside of its surrounding wall (OT44, see below), but this is so far unique and not attested otherwise.[21]

---

19 E. g. BM EA 46607 whose base is covered in a white substance while the upper side shows a red coating all over with remains of the white substance; BM EA 46622.

20 Similar observations were made for an offering tray now stored in the Gustav-Lübcke-Museum Hamm (Inv.-Nr. 8169): VON FALCK & FLUCK 2004: 118–119.

21 Decoration with white dots, however, is quite common in Asyut and can be found on vessels (not only in Asyut but also elsewhere, see KILIAN 2019: 189–191; RZEUSKA 2017: 179–187, Cat. 155–174; 303–307, Cat. 291–306). Furthermore, in

The firing conditions varied: some seem to have been baked at low temperatures, as they are crumbly in texture with worn off surfaces, while others are of a very dense and resistant, hard-burnt quality like OT41 or OT43.

Function

The function of the offering trays is not completely clear yet.[22] As canals, spouts and ḥs.t-vases suggest, fluids seem to have played a role in the use of the trays; one tray even depicts a human figure holding a vessel in front of its head, thus crossing the canals with it.[23] Ursula Verhoeven suggested that water was poured over the trays and magically absorbed the energy inherent in the food, thus magically creating a kind of consommé to nourish the deceased.[24] That the offering trays functioned somehow in provisioning for the dead seems to be supported by an offering tray that is inscribed with a part of the offering formula.[25] Interestingly enough, the Petrie Museum holds a fragment of an offering tray (or soul house) that indeed depicts a "model" offering tray that was positioned in such a manner that its spout was placed above the opening of a vessel which, in turn, was positioned in the corner of the actual tray/soul house.[26] The "model" offering tray is rectangular, bears applications of round bread and features a surrounding wall with a spout and so clearly refers to its bigger counterparts.

A singular offering tray from the Gustav-Lübcke-Museum Hamm points in a similar direction. The design of this rectangular tray with a spout reminds one of an open courtyard: four offering stands were applied, one in each corner, the center is occupied by a vessel with straight walls and outwardly rolled rim that was turned on a wheel. Each of the stands, from which one is lost and only one fully preserved, once bore a small dish on top.[27] No offerings were added, the offering stands and the vessel in the middle seem to have functioned as offering installations in miniature. Similar "installations" were found in front of some of the tombs excavated on Gebel Asyut-al gharbi[28] and some soul houses feature offering stands as well[29] (but rarely). Another hint at the use of the offering trays is the white coating on some of them, as this seems to have been used in cultic contexts.[30]

Dating

The dating of pottery offering trays is somewhat obscured by the lack of documentation, but the Asyutian trays might offer some new insights into this matter. Unfortunately, the documentation of the early excavators on this site is not very thorough, especially when it comes to these objects, but nevertheless some information can be gained.

There are some offering trays of a very simple design, displaying only two basins and an object, either a vessel or a kind of (bḏꜣ-)bread positioned in between the basins (Type 1). This arrangement very

---

Asyut it also appears on hippopotami made out of clay (see Kahl 2018: 214. Tafel 3, Abb. 1a–b; Egyptian Museum Cairo JE 44882, JE 44883).

22 For more details on this topic and different suggestions, see Kilian 2012a: 111, but especially Lundius in this volume.

23 Utah Museum of Fine Arts UMFA1952.127. I thank Eva Gervers M. A. who brought this offering tray to my attention.

24 Verhoeven 2004: 481.

25 Edel 2008b: 1626; 1627, Fig. 2; 1633, Abb. 8.

26 UC38983.

27 According to the description given in von Falck & Fluck 2004: 118–119.

28 E. g. Chassinat & Palanque 1911: 4 (mentioning stands), 160 (ovoid vessels).

29 E. g. Louvre E 26927 (depicted in Leclère 2001: 108, fig. 2); Rijksmuseum van Oudheden, Leiden: AT 99 (Boeser 1910: pl. 5.5; https://www.rmo.nl/en/collection/search-collection/collection-piece/?object=403). Maybe the cylindrical object on an offering tray from Denderah in Petrie 1900: pl. 19.7 (and maybe also pl. 19.9) are meant to be offering stands.

30 For the use of white paint in cultic contexts see e. g. Seiler 2005: 115–117.

strongly resembles installations in Tomb N11.1 at the mouth of two shafts of the very same design that were carved directly into the bedrock,[31] with another parallel, also at the mouth of a shaft, to be found in area 7 higher up on the hill in the surroundings of Tomb N13.1[32]. Tomb N11.1 can be dated to the early/middle First Intermediate Period.[33] Portable versions of these offering trays made out of stone were found in Asyut, too (now stored in the magazine at Shutb).[34]

One of the pottery offering trays of Type 1, OT62 (see catalog), was documented by *The Asyut Project* in Tomb H11.1, shaft 11, in the region around Sheikh Abu Tuq. Shaft 11 does not belong to H11.1 proper, but once was an independent structure pre-dating H11.1,[35] consisting of a rectangular entrance door with door frame, a small passage, a hall and two superimposed narrow burial chambers.[36] The only objects found inside this tomb were the remains of one coffin without an inscription, but wedjat-eyes painted on its side, one closed vessel still sealed with a stopper, but empty, resembling Hogarth's Shape 11 (and of the same type as S 7975 and S 7976 found with the pottery offering tray S 7979, see below), one bowl, bandages and bones.

Several offering trays of Type 1-design are stored in the British Museum and in the Museo Egizio. Both do not allow any conclusions concerning the exact findspot. However, one of the trays in Turin (S 7979) can still be connected with pottery (S 7975, S 7976) and one of the vessels[37] shows a strong resemblance to vessels found in the region of Sheikh Abu Tuq which seem to be of an earlier date, too. Another hint is to be found in the publication of D. P. Ryan, who describes one of the offering trays as "very rough with two pockets".[38] The material of this tray was not mentioned, but again a vessel was found together with it and again it is the same kind of vessel the Turin tray was found with, too: Hogarth's Shape 11. Shape 11 only occurs around the area of Sheikh Abu Tuq (with rare exceptions) and can be dated to a time before the late First Intermediate Period.[39]

This, albeit a bit scant, evidence suggests that in Asyut offering trays of Type 1 (simple basin-and-bread/vase-design) seem to be the earliest type of offering trays[40] that might be connected to the chronological phase predating the late First Intermediate Period. Unfortunately, it cannot be concluded if the typological sequence of Types 2 to 3 established here also mirrors the chronological development, as the information on findspots and material inventory found with the offering trays is way too sparse.

---

31 KILIAN 2019: 241–243, Abb. 16–19; see also E. LUNDIUS in this volume, esp. Table 3, Type 1 and Type 3.

32 See LUNDIUS in this volume.

33 KILIAN 2019: 52seq.

34 See LUNDIUS in this volume.

35 KILIAN 2019: 106. ABDELRAHIEM 2020: 16.

36 ABDELRAHIEM 2020: 16. ZITMAN 2010: I, 108 summarizes the architectural layout of the tombs around Sheikh Abu Tuq that were excavated by Hogarth as "basically show[ing] the same design. They are all composed of a small rock cut chapel leading out to one or more burial chambers on the same level, or sunk slightly below the floor of the chapel." The same holds true for Tomb 41 of Hogarth (IB. 118), where the offering tray BM EA 46611 (of Type 1-design) according to ZITMAN 2010: II, 227 originates. Similar observations were made by Chassinat and Palanque for their tombs 1–5: "Elles se composaient uniformément de deux petits réduits, sur plan carré irrégulier, placés tantôt en enfilade, tantôt superposés. Dans ce dernier cas, les caveaux n'atteignaient pas la hauteur d'un homme dehout. La chambre funéraire avait exactement les dimensions du cercueil qu'elle était destinée à recevoir." (CHASSINAT & PALANQUE 1911: 4). As these tombs were violated, nothing but decayed masks, bones and textile fragments are summarizingly reported to have been found there (IBD.), whereas the tombs found by Hogarth did not yield much equipment, but at least one or more vessels of his Shape 11, which dates them relatively earlier than the (richer equipped) tombs of the First Intermediate Period, which lack vessels of Shape 11 (on Hogarth's „Shapes" and the problems they pose see KILIAN 2019: 125 and PETHEN 2021). In comparison, the tombs of the late First Intermediate Period yielded much richer pottery equipment.

37 S 7976, most probably originally closed with the stopper S 7980.

38 RYAN 1988: 42.

39 Interestingly, these vessels are often reported as having been closed with a stopper. A stopper is attested with the pottery accompanying the Turin offering tray S7979, see footnote above.

40 This is in accordance with Slaters observation that the offering trays in Dendereh develop from simple to more complex designs, see SLATER 1974: 402. *Contra* Nivinski, who generally assumes the simple versions to be the last stage of development, where the original idea of a platter-like offering tray with offerings has been lost (NIWINSKI 1984: 811). Also *contra* KILIAN 2019: 106–110, correcting my assumption that the Asyutian offering trays emerge in the early Middle Kingdom.

Drawings:

Aneta Cedro (OT60, OT63, OT65, OT70, OT73–OT75)

Andrea Kilian (OT37, OT39, OT42–OT51, OT52b, OT54–OT55, OT57, OT59, OT71–OT72)

Katarzyna Molga (OT61–OT62, OT68, OT69)

Barbara Reichenbächer (OT52a, OT53)

Inkings:

Aneta Cedro

Photographs:

All photos from the pottery offering trays stored in Turin and published in the catalog were taken by the author. I thank Dr. Paolo Del Vesco for the permission to publish them.

Publications of offering trays detected by *The Asyut Project*:

Kilian 2012a   OT6: 113, Fig. 7. OT10-OT17-OT12: Pl. 9c. OT25: Pl. 8e. OT28: Pl. 8b–d. OT33: 9b. OT40: 112, Fig. 6. OT41: Pl. 9a. OT44: Pl. 8a

Kilian 2012b   OT1: 201, Fig. 11. OT26: 201, Fig. 12. OT27: 201, Fig. 13. OT38: Fig. 14

Kilian 2016   OT2–OT25, OT29–OT36, OT56, OT58

Bibliography

Abdelrahiem 2020: M. Abdelrahiem, The Northern Soldiers-Tomb (H11.1) at Asyut (The Asyut Project 13; Wiesbaden 2020).

Al-sayed Aman 2016: M. Al-sayed Aman, An Unpublished New Collection of Soul Houses Housed in the Agricultural Museum, Cairo, in: Studies on the Arab World Monuments 18, 73–93 (DOI: 10.21608/cguaa.2016.29696 [Zugriff: 2020_05_18]).

Boeser 1910: P. A. A. Boeser, Die Denkmäler der Zeit zwischen dem Alten und Mittleren Reich und des Mittleren Reiches. Zweite Abteilung. Grabgegenstände, Statuen, Gefässe und verschiedenartige kleinere Gegenstände, mit einem Supplement zu den Monumenten des Alten Reiches (Beschreibung der Ägyptischen Sammlung des Niederländischen Reichsmuseums der Altertümer in Leiden 3; Haag 1910).

Bresciani 1980: E. Bresciani, L'attivita' archeologica dell'Universita' di Pisa in Egitto: 1977–1980, in: Egitto e Vicino Oriente 3, 1980, 1–36.

Carnarvon & Carter 1912: G. E. St. M. H. Carnarvon, & H. Carter, Five Years' Explorations at Thebes. A Record of Work Done 1907–1911 (Oxford 1912).

Chassinat & Palanque 1911: É. Chassinat & Ch. Palanque, Une campagne de fouilles dans la nécropole d'Assiout (Mémoires publiés par les membres de l'Institut Français d'Archéologie Orientale du Caire 24; Kairo 1911).

Downes 1974: D. Downes, The Excavations at Esna 1905–1906 (Warminster 1974).

Dunham 1967: D. Dunham, Uronarti, Shalfak, Mirgissa. Volume II (Boston 1967).

Edel 2008a: E. Edel (eds. K.-J. Seyfried & G. Vieler), Die Felsgräbernekropole der Qubbet el-Hawa bei Assuan. I. 2 (Paderborn et al. 2008).

Edel 2008b: E. Edel (eds. K.-J. Seyfried & G. Vieler), Die Felsgräbernekropole der Qubbet el-Hawa bei Assuan. I. 3 (Paderborn et al. 2008).

von Falck & Fluck 2004: M. von Falck, C. Fluck (eds.), Die Ägyptische Sammlung des Gustav-Lübcke-Museums Hamm (Auswahlkataloge des Gustav-Lübcke-Museums Hamm 1; Bönen 2004).

Kahl 2018: J. Kahl, Ewiges Leben: Nilpferdfigurinen aus Assiut, in: A. I. Blöbaum, M. Eaton-Krauss, A. Wüthrich (eds.), Pérégrinations avec Erhart Graefe. Festschrift zu seinem 75. Geburtstag (Ägypten und Altes Testament 87; Münster 2018), 239–247.

Kilian 2012a: A. Kilian, Pottery Offering Trays: General Observations and New Material from Asyut, in: J. Kahl, M. El-Khadragy, U. Verhoeven, A. Kilian (eds.), Seven Seasons at Asyut. First Results of the Egyptian-German Cooperation in Archaeological Fieldwork, Proceedings of an International Conference at the University of Sohag, 10th – 11th of October, 2009 (The Asyut Project 2; Wiesbaden 2012), 105–118.

Kilian 2012b: A. Kilian, Pottery and offering trays from the so-called "Hogarth' Depot" in Tomb IV (N12.2), in: J. Kahl, M. El-Khadragy, U. Verhoeven et al., The Asyut Project: Ninth Season of Fieldwork (2011), in: Studien zur Altägyptischen Kultur 41, 2012, 196–201.

Kilian 2016: A. Kilian, Offering Trays, in: J. Kahl, N. Deppe, D. Goldsmith, A. Kilian, J. Moje & M. Zöller-Engelhardt, Asyut, Tomb III: Objects. Part 1 (The Asyut Project 3; Wiesbaden 2016), 173–195.

Kilian 2019: A. Kilian, Untersuchungen zur Keramik der Ersten Zwischenzeit und des Mittleren Reichs aus Assiut/Mittelägypten (The Asyut Project 12; Wiesbaden 2019).

Kitagawa 2016: C. Kitagawa, mit Beiträgen von J. Kahl und G. Vittmann, The Tomb of the Dogs at AsyuTh: Faunal Remains and Other Selected Objects (The Asyut Project 9; Wiesbaden 2016).

Kuentz 1981: Ch. Kuentz, Bassins et tables d'offrandes, in: Bulletin de l'Institut français d'archéologie orientale 81 Suppl., 1981, 243–282.

Leclère 2001: F. Leclère, Les "Maisons d'âme" Égyptiennes: une tentative de mise au point, in: B. Muller, D. Vaillancourt (eds.), «Maquettes architecturales» de l'antiquité. Regards croisés. Actes du Colloque de Strasbourg 3–5 décembre 1998 (Trauvaux du centre de recherche sur le Proche-Orient et la Grèce antiques 17; Paris 2001), 99–121.

Martin-Pardey 1991: E. Martin-Pardey, Grabbeigaben, Nachträge und Ergänzungen (Corpus Antiquitatum Aegyptiacarum, Pelizaeus Museum Hildesheim Lieferung 6, Mainz 1991).

Mi 2020: F. Mi, Ceramic Offering Trays in the Museo Egizio, Turin: Establishing Typologies and Locating Unprovenanced Specimens (Rivista del Museo Egizio 4, 2020), 94–121. DOI: https://doi.org/10.29353/rime.2020.3300

Michałowski 1938a: K. Michałowski et al., Tell Edfou 1938, Fouilles Franco-Polonaises, Rapports II (Cairo 1938).

Michałowski 1938b: K. Michałowski et al., Tell Edfou 1938, Fouilles Franco-Polonaises, Rapports III (Cairo 1938).

Müller & Forstner-Müller 2015: W. Müller & I. Forstner-Müller, A Newly Discovered "Soul House" in Assuan, in: A. Jiménez-Serrano, C. von Pilgrim (eds.), From the Delta to the Cataract. Studies Dedicated to Mohamed el-Bialy (Culture and History of the Ancient Near East 76; Leiden 2015), 189–201.

Niwinski 1984: A. Niwinski, in: Lexikon der Ägyptologie V (Wiesbaden 1984), s. v. Seelenhaus (und Opferplatte), 806–813.

Pethen 2021: H. Pethen, A New Year Pottery Corpus: Investigating Early 20th Century Excavation Methods through the Hogarth Excavation Archive at the British Museum, in: Bulletin de Liaison de la Céramique Égyptienne 30, Le Caire 2021, 231–248.

Petrie 1890: W. M. F. Petrie, Kahun, Gurob, and Hawara (London 1890).

Petrie 1891: W. M. F. Petrie, Illahun, Kahun and Gurob. 1889–90 (London 1891).

Petrie 1900: W. M. F. Petrie, Dendereh 1898 (The Egypt Exploration Fund 17; London 1900).

Petrie 1907: W. M. F. Petrie, Gizeh and Rifeh (British School of Archaeology in Egypt 13; London 1907).

Petrie 1909: W. M. F. Petrie, Qurneh (British School of Archaeology in Egypt 16; London 1909).

Petrie 1924: W. M. F. Petrie, G. Brunton, Sedment I (British School of Archaeology in Egypt 34; London 1924).

Petrie/Brunton 1924: W. M. F. Petrie, G. Brunton, Sedment I (British School of Archaeology in Egypt 34/Egyptian Research Account 27,1; London 1924).

Petrie/Quibell 1896: W. M. F. Petrie, J. E. Quibell, Naqada and Ballas. 1895 (London 1896).

Rabino Massa 2009: E. Rabino Massa, Museo di Antropologia ed Etnografia dell'Università degli Studi di Torino, in: S. Einaudi (ed.), Egitto nascosto. Collezioni e collezionisti dai musei piemontesi (exhibition catalogue San Secondo di Pinerolo, Castello di Miradolo 21 marzo–5 luglio 2009, Milano 2009).

Rzeuska 2017: T. I. Rzeuska, Chronological Overview of Pottery from Asyut. A contribution to the history of Gebel Asyut al-gharbi (The Asyut Project 7; Wiesbaden 2017).

Seiler 2005: A. Seiler, Tradition & Wandel. Die Keramik als Spiegel der Kulturentwicklung Thebens in der Zweiten Zwischenzeit (Sonderschriften des Deutschen Archäologischen Instituts Abteilung Kairo 32; Mainz 2005).

Slater 1974: R. A. Slater, The Archaeology of Dendereh in the First Intermediate Period (Pennsylvania 1974).

van Elsbergen 2019: M. van Elsbergen, Die Gefäßverschlüsse aus Grab N13.1 in Assiut (The Asyut Project 10; Wiesbaden 2019).

Verhoeven 2004: U. Verhoeven, Der Totenkult, in: R. Schulz & M. Seidel (eds.), Ägypten. Die Welt der Pharaonen (Königswinter 2004), 480–489.

Wainwright 1926: G. A. Wainwright, A Subsidiary Burial in Hap-Zefi's Tomb at Assiut, in: Annales du Service des Antiquités de l'Égypte 26, 1926, 160–166. 170.

Winlock 1955: H. Winlock, Models of daily life in ancient Egypt (New York 1955).

Catalog

Offering trays from Tomb N13.1 and surroundings on geological step 7

Cat. 1: OT37 (S07/st1161)
Tomb N13.1, shaft 3, side chamber
Nile Silt C
Rectangular
Red coating
H: 4.5, W: x+15.7+y, L: 7.1+y, Th: 2.1

Rear part with right corner. Deep impression positioned directly in the corner. A crudely manufactured bovid head leans against the surrounding wall of the tray. Horns are visible, no details (eyes, nose, mouth) given. On the inside and outside of the wall remains of red coating. Tray is covered in black sooth and very brittle.

Parallels: Petrie 1907: Pl. 14, esp. nos. 8–9, 11, 13. Ibd. no 3 has holes, not on the tray itself like OT37, but inside the corners of the surrounding wall. For the very stylized bovid head, see e. g. horseshoe-shaped offering trays in Petrie/Quibell 1896: Tf. 44.7; Downes 1974: 94, fig. 63, fig 65: left tray in upper row, Müller & Forstner-Müller 2015: 196, Fig. 15.4–5 (ibid. 198 interpreted as stairs).

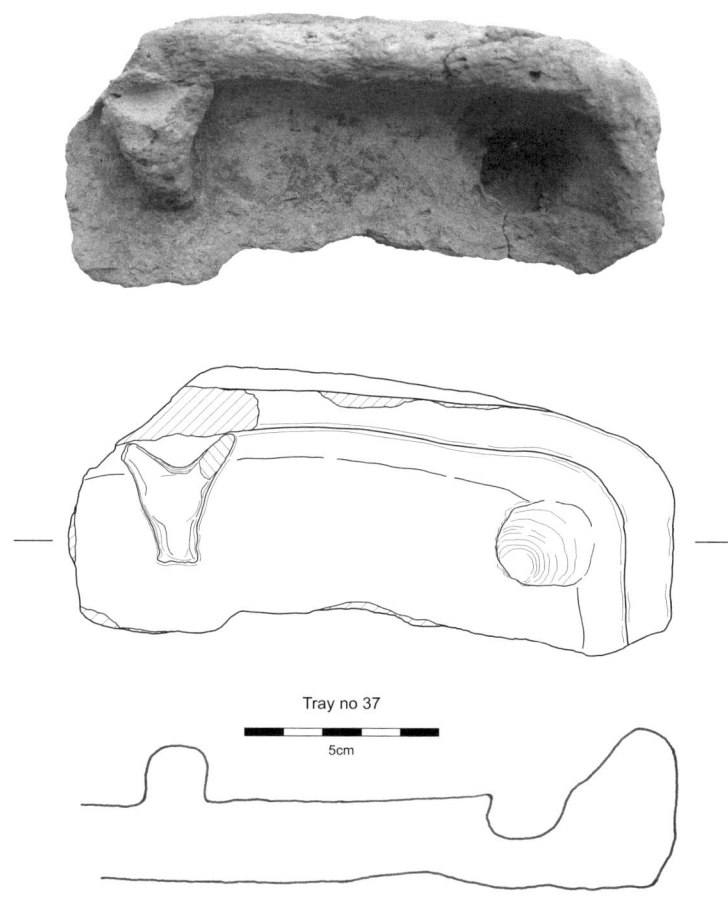

Tray no 37

5cm

Cat. 2: OT42 (S06/st83)

Tomb N12.3, shaft 1, side chamber
Nile Silt C
Red coating
W: x+6.1+y; L: x+6.4+y; Th: 1.3

Part from the middle of a tray. Kind of wall-like structure forming a right angle. Surface and breaking edges covered in black, resinous substance. Red coating on wall-like structure and inner surface.

Parallels: Petrie 1891: Pl. 4, 23.

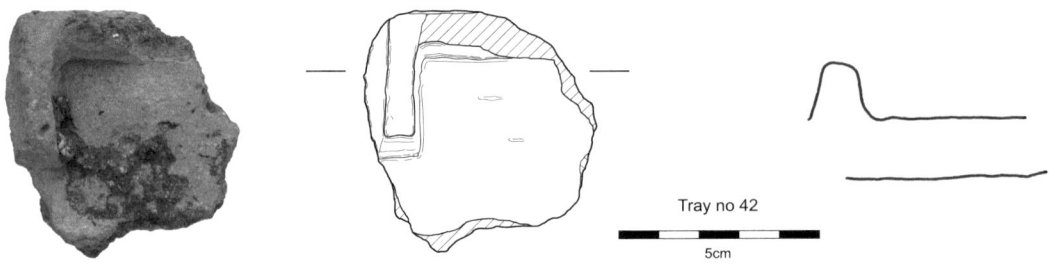

Tray no 42
5cm

Cat. 3: OT43 (S06/st361)

Tomb N13.1, southern part
Nile Silt C
Rectangular
Covered in dark red-brown coating, shimmering
H: 4.8, W: 10.0+y, L: 12.6+y, Th: 1.2

Corner piece with application of two U-shaped long objects (meat?), placed closely against each other with no space left between them.

Parallels: For similar U-shaped long objects, see OT3, Kilian 2016: 178; 191, Pl. a. S 10648, see below. Müller & Forstner-Müller 2015: 197, fig. 15.6.

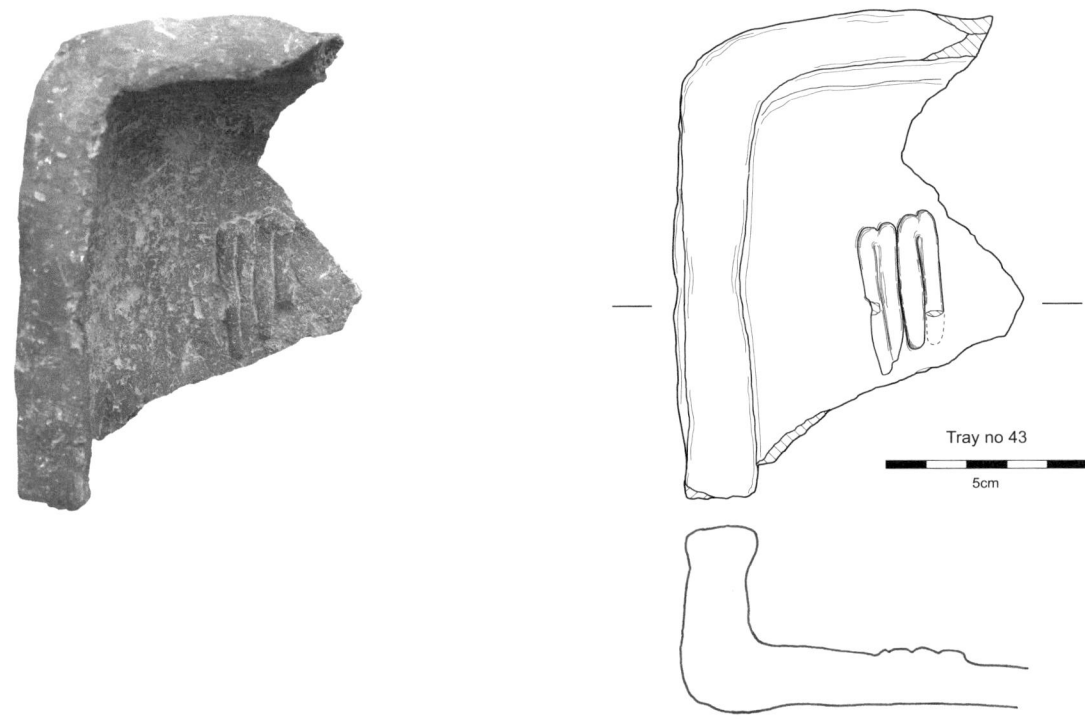

Tray no 43
5cm

Cat. 4: OT44 (S06/st426)
Tomb N13.1, depression in front of west wall
Nile Silt C
Rectangular
Red coating inside and outside with white dots on outside of the surrounding wall
H: 4.6–4.9, W: 8.1+y, L: 10.0+y, Th: 1.2

Corner piece of a rectangular tray. Inner dividing wall at a 90° angle to surrounding wall partly preserved. Upper part of the inner wall and of the connecting outer wall not preserved. On the first layer of the outer wall, a second layer was attached, with the mural crown leaning inwards. Red coating inside and outinside. Outside of the surrounding wall is decorated with irregularly dispersed white dots.

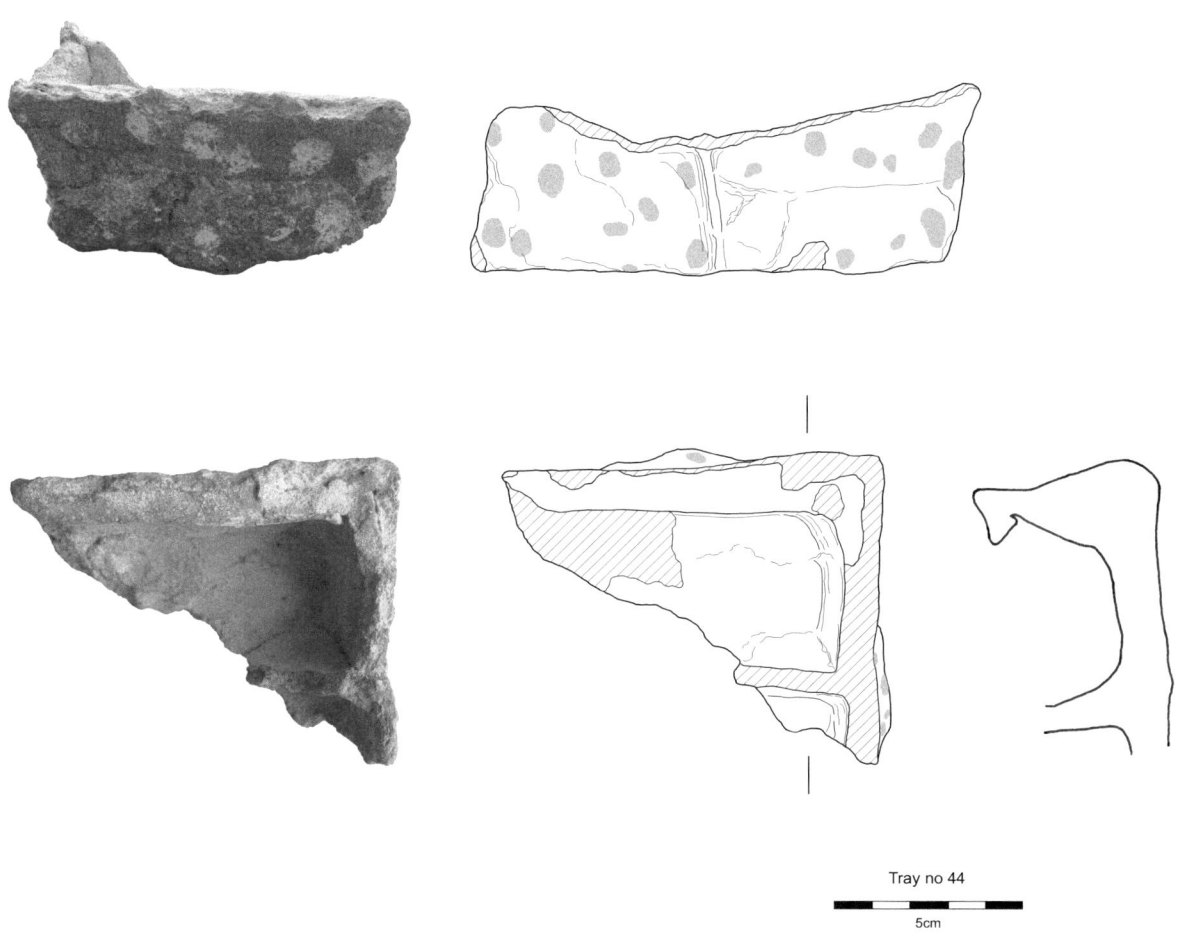

Tray no 44

5cm

Cat. 5: OT48 (S08/st1725)
Tomb N13.59
Nile Silt C
Rectangular
Red coating
H: 4.8, W: x+3.9, L: x+8.4+y, Th: 2.0

Rim piece of a rectangular tray, wall only partly preserved. Red coating inside and outside.

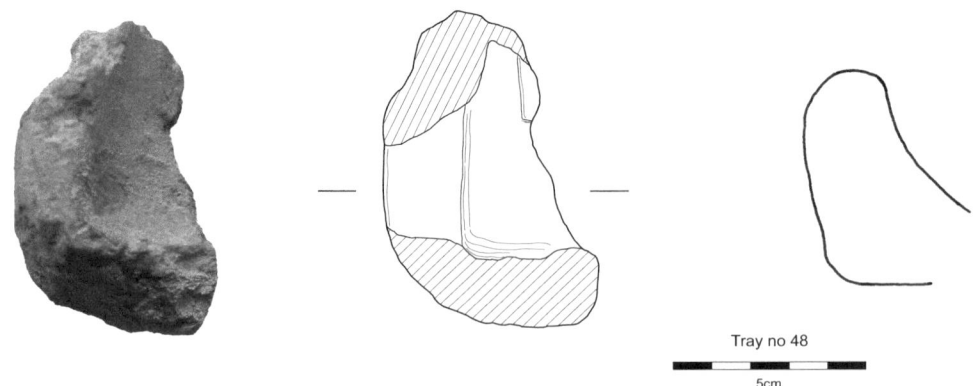

Tray no 48
5cm

Cat. 6: OT71 (S07/st1042B)
Tomb N13.24, forecourt
Nile Silt C
Rectangular
H: 3.0, W: x+15.5+y, L: 13.8+y, Th: 4.1

Front piece of a tray displaying a rectangular basin with a canal leading to the front of the tray. To the left of the basin, there is a non-identifiable elevation.

Parallels: BRESCIANI 1980: 6, T79 403; 25, pl. 6 shows a tray with meat offering at the rim of the basin.

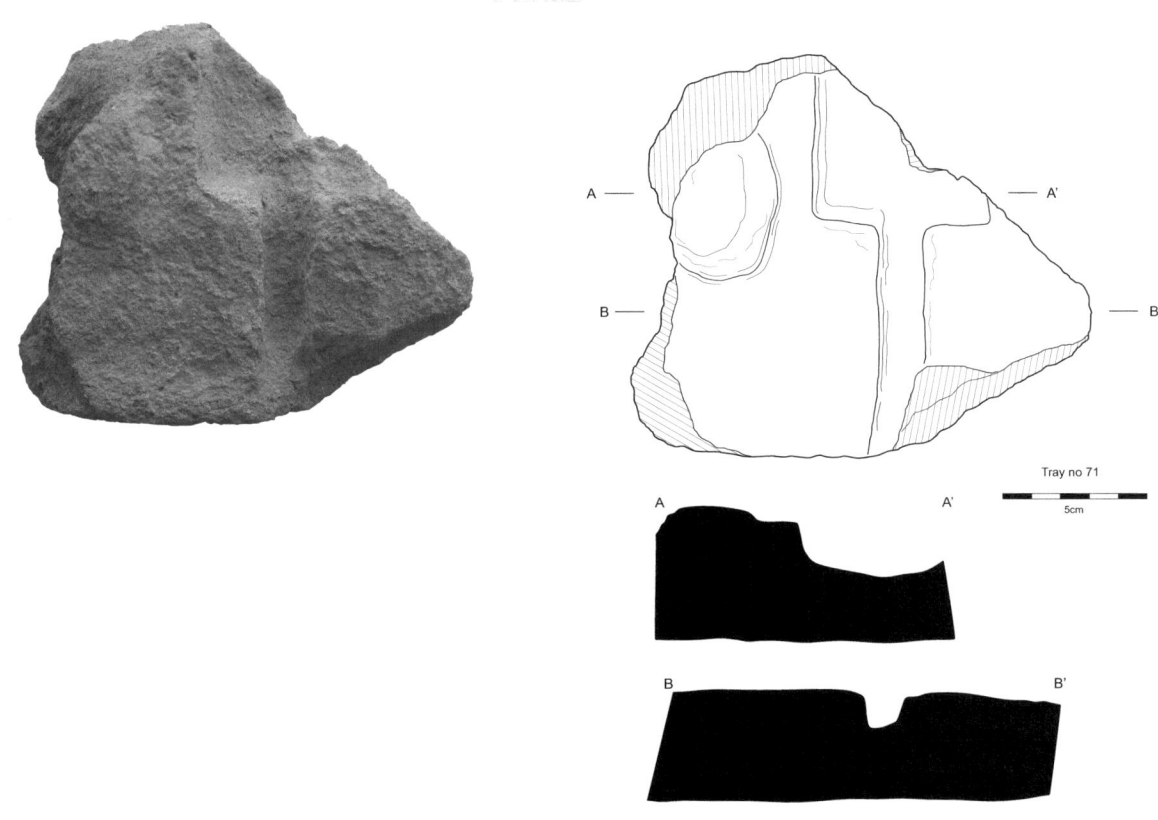

Tray no 71
5cm

Offering trays from Tomb H11.1

Cat. 7: OT52 (S12/18 (a), S11/st1071 (b))
Tomb H11.1, debris of section A3 and C2
Nile Silt B
Rectangular
Red coating on the inside
H: 3.1; W: 6.5+x (a), x+6.2+y (b); L: 12.8+x (a), 7.2+x (b); Th: 1.1

a) Lower right corner and right part of a rectangular tray. Indentation directly in the lower corner. On the left, part of a round piece of meat with incisions and a deepening.

b) Part of the rear side of the tray. Matching with the former, completes the second, upper deepening of a). Parts of another round bread (?) and probably remains of the left horn of a bovid head. Part of the surrounding wall preserved.

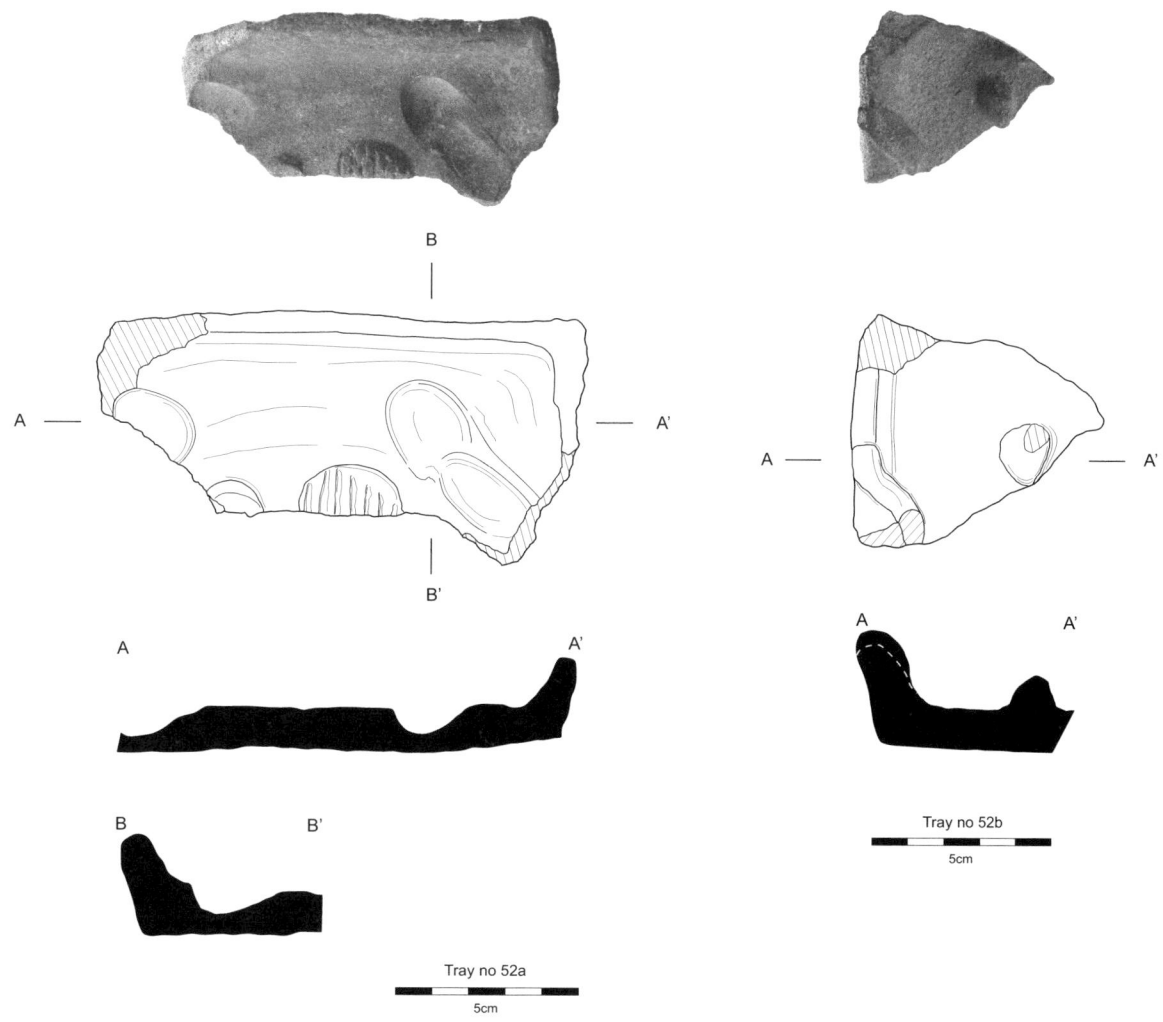

Tray no 52a
5cm

Tray no 52b
5cm

Cat. 8: OT53 (S11/st1014)
Tomb H11.1, debris of section C1
Nile Silt C
Shape unknown
W: x+11+y, L: x+6.6+y, Th: 2.8
Part of the middle of an offering tray depicting four flat and two conical loaves of bread.

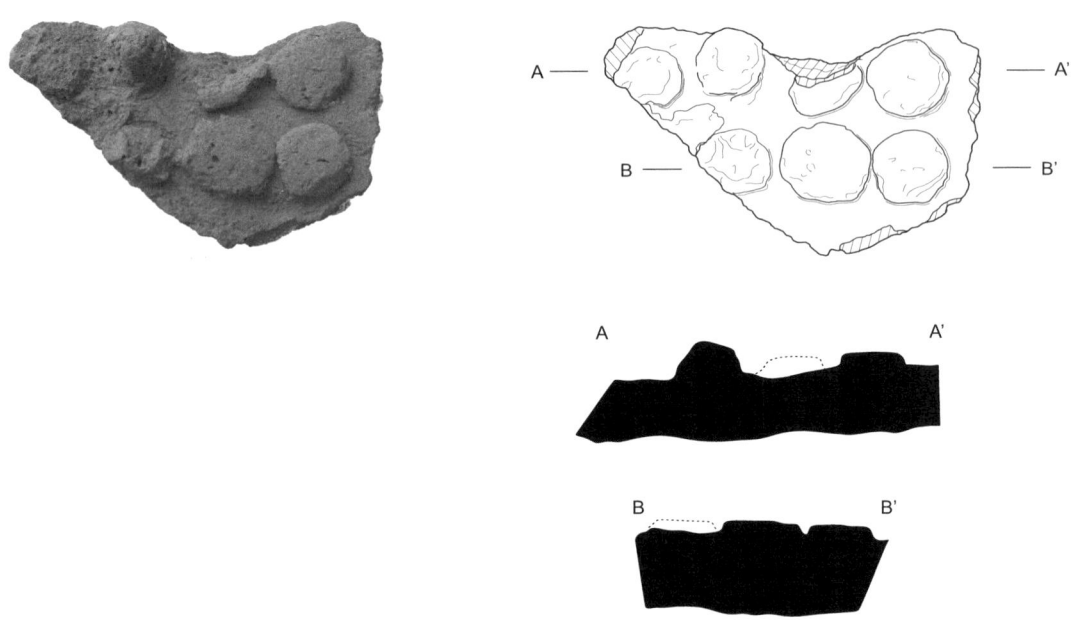

Cat. 9: OT61 (S14/st1792C)
Tomb H11.1, debris of northern part
Nile Silt C
W: x+6.0xy, L: x+8.0+y, Th: 1.3–1.7
Fragment of the inner part of a tray displaying inner dividing walls forming a right angle.

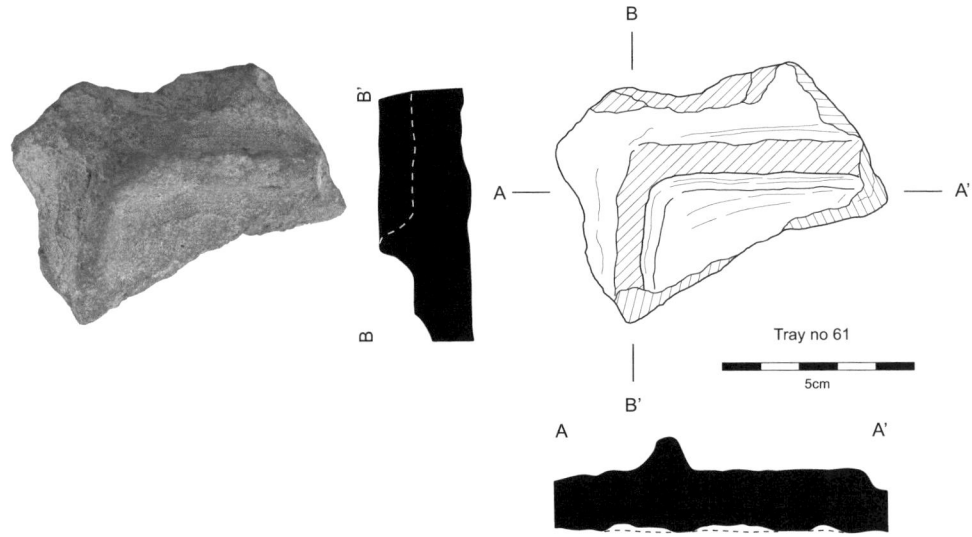

Cat. 10: OT62 (S14/st2261)
Tomb H11.1, shaft 11, second western chamber
Nile Silt C
Rectangular
Red coating
H: 5.6, W: 14.2, L: 11.0+y, Th: 2.2

Rear part of a rectangular tray with inner depressions and dividing walls forming four rectangular basins. Severely worn. Remains of red coating on the crowns of the surrounding outer and dividing inner walls.

Parallel: A tray from Uronarti shows four oval basins arranged in a single row, Dunham 1967: pl. 64.A, upper row, second from the left.

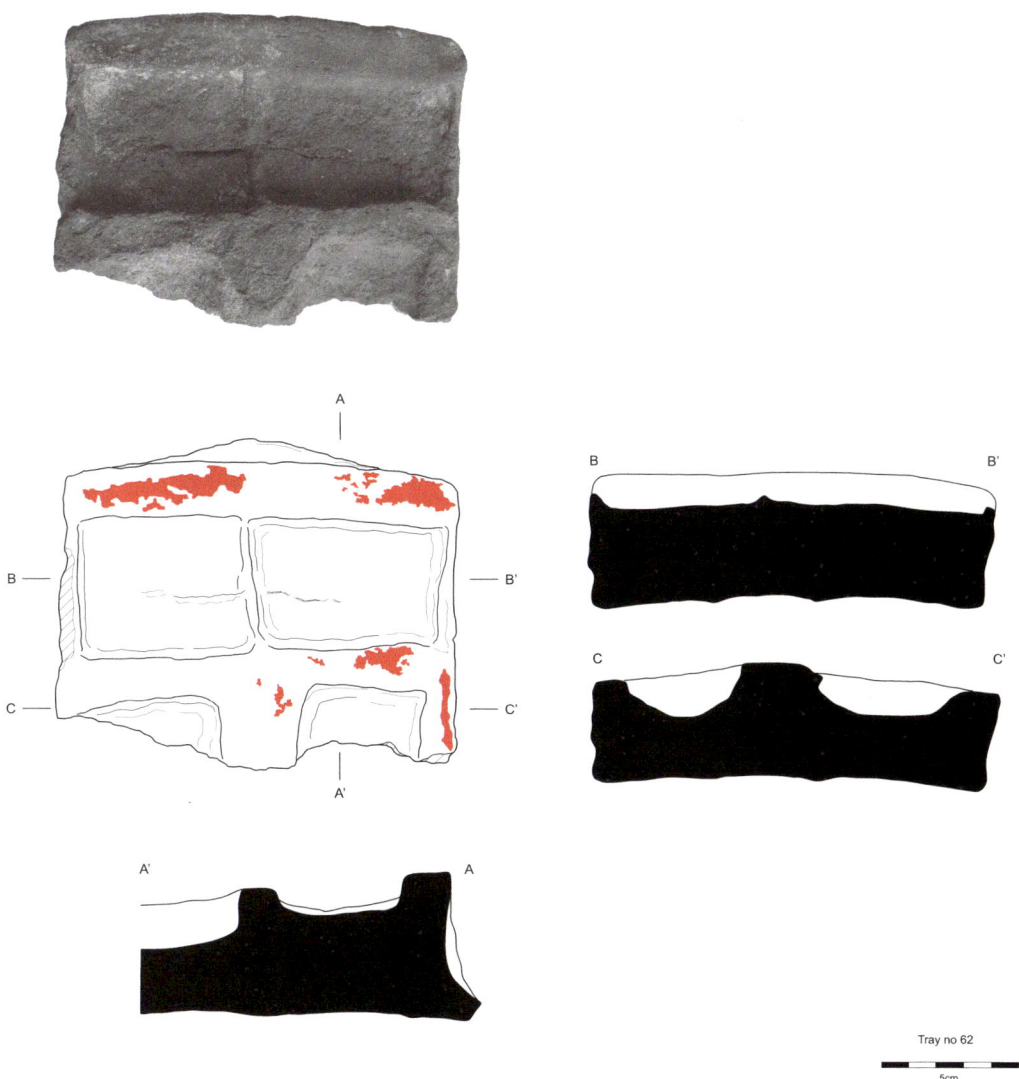

Tray no 62

5cm

Cat. 11: OT67 (S14/st2399)
Tomb H11.1, debris of eastern part, east of shaft 14
Nile Silt B
Thick red coating, shining
H: 5.0, W: x+9.0, L: x+8.1+y, Th: 2.7

Part of a rectangular tray covered in a shining thick red coating. Depression at the surrounding wall followed by an even deeper depression forming a basin. Bottom carefully scraped and also covered in red coating.

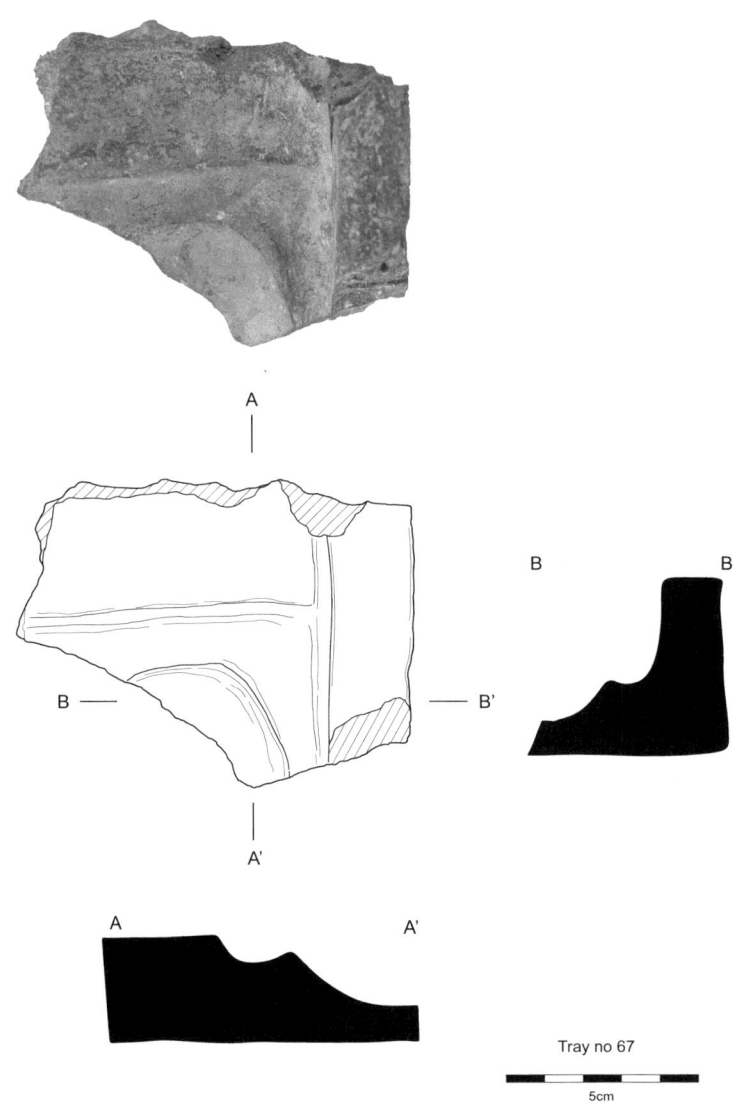

Tray no 67

5cm

Offering trays from Tomb V

Cat. 12: OT60 (S14/st1210)
Tomb V, forecourt, surface debris
Nile Silt C
Rectangular
Red coating inside
H: 3.4, W: 20.0, L: 15.4, Th: 1.7–2.6

Left half of a rectangular tray with spout, left lower corner missing. Applications of an *ḥs.t*-flask with spout and stopper and round loaves of bread at its top and bottom. Another rectangular loaf is depicted close to the missing left corner. The spout of the *ḥs.t*-flask is oriented towards a slaughtered animal with bound legs with only its rear part with tail and hind legs preserved. The surrounding wall was formed by hand and was scraped in its lower part.

Parallels: Bovid with bound legs: OT5-OT7, Kilian 2016: 179–180, Kilian 2012a: 113, Fig. 7.
ḥs.t-flask: OT27, Kilian 2012b: 201, Fig. 13. OT41, Kilian 2012a: Pl. 9. OT46, OT63, S 14848 (see below).

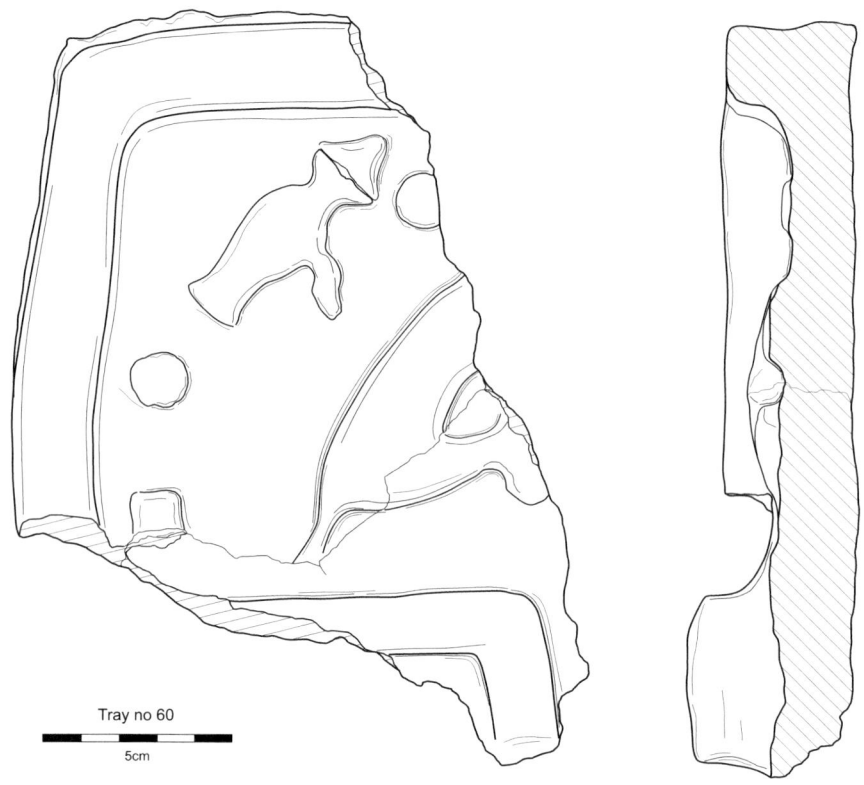

Tray no 60
5cm

Cat. 13: OT75 (S18/st434)
Tomb V, debris of southern tomb front
Nile Silt C
Rectangular
Red coating inside
H: 4.4, W: 10.0+y, L: 20.0+y, Th: 1.5

Left front corner of a rectangular tray. Left half of the spout preserved. Surrounded by an outer wall. Inner lower wall forms a basin in the corner of the tray with an opening towards the spout. Three conical loaves of bread were placed above the basin.

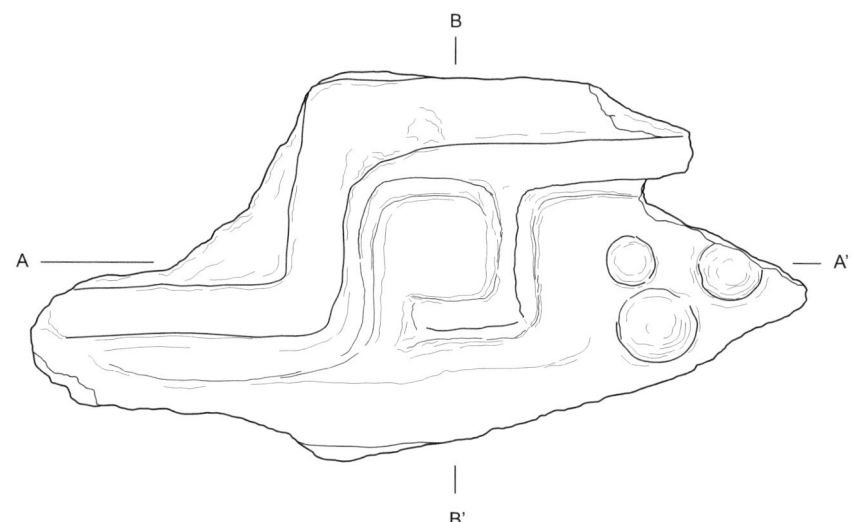

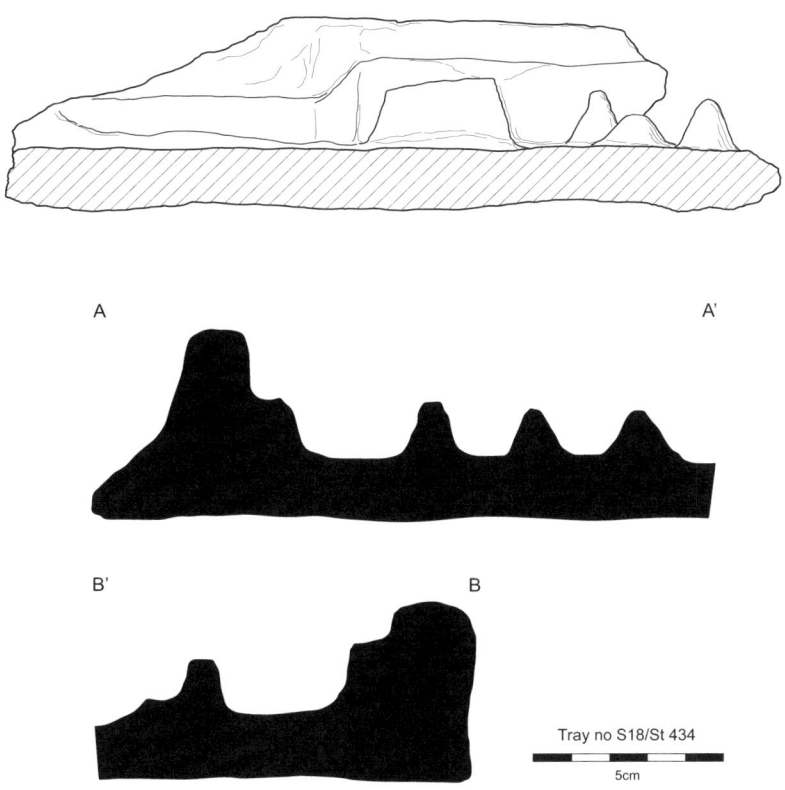

A   A'

B'   B

Tray no S18/St 434

5cm

Offering trays from Tomb IV

Cat. 14: OT57 (S05/st789)

Tomb IV, shaft 1, 0–1 m below surface

Nile Silt C

Rectangular

H: 4.3, W: 4.2+y, L: x+7.5+y, Th: 1.2

Part of the surrounding wall with a kind of mastaba attached to it.

Parallel: Such installations, often equipped with vessels, are attested on courtyards of soul houses, e. g. in Aswan: MÜLLER & FORSTNER-MÜLLER 2016: 196, fig. 15.4–5.

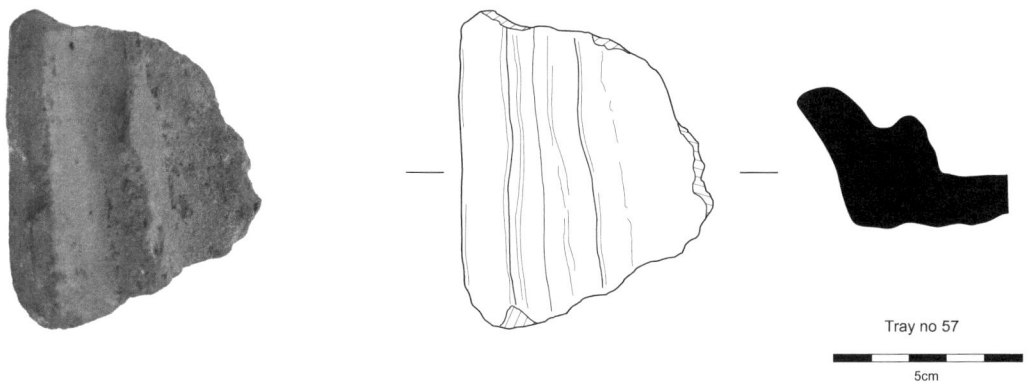

Tray no 57

5cm

Cat. 15: OT69 (S04/st221)
Tomb IV, surface of middle of southern part
Nile Silt C
Most probable rectangular
H: 6.0, W: y+7.1, L: x+7.4, Th: 3.5

Corner part of a rectangular tray.

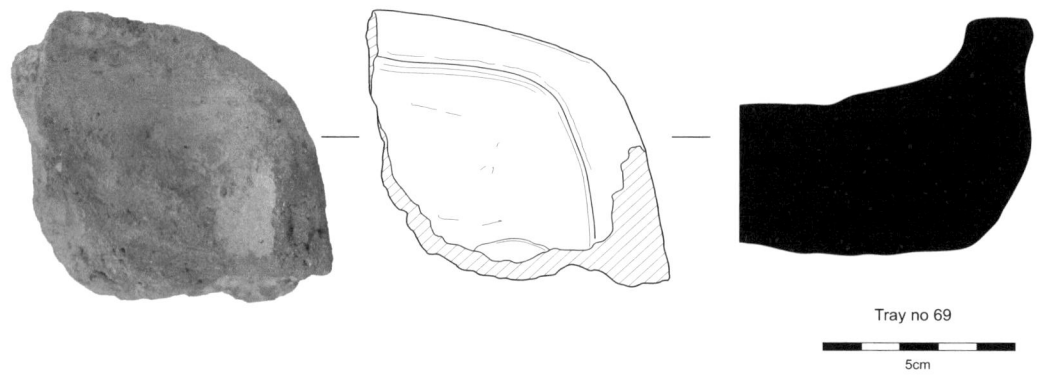

Tray no 69

5cm

Offering trays from the Tomb of the Dogs (O11.13)

Cat 16: OT45 (S08/st713)
Tomb of the Dogs, debris in front of (modern) entrance
Nile Silt C
Rectangular
Red coating
H: 3.6, W: x+14.4, L: 10.9+y, Th: 1.8

Right front corner of a rectangular tray. Right part of a broad protruding spout and small part of an inner dividing wall preserved, which connects to outer surrounding wall in a right angle. The connection to this part of the wall is unusual as in most cases L-shaped walls are attached to the sides of the trays, not to the front.

Parallels: PETRIE 1890: Pl. 13, 102.

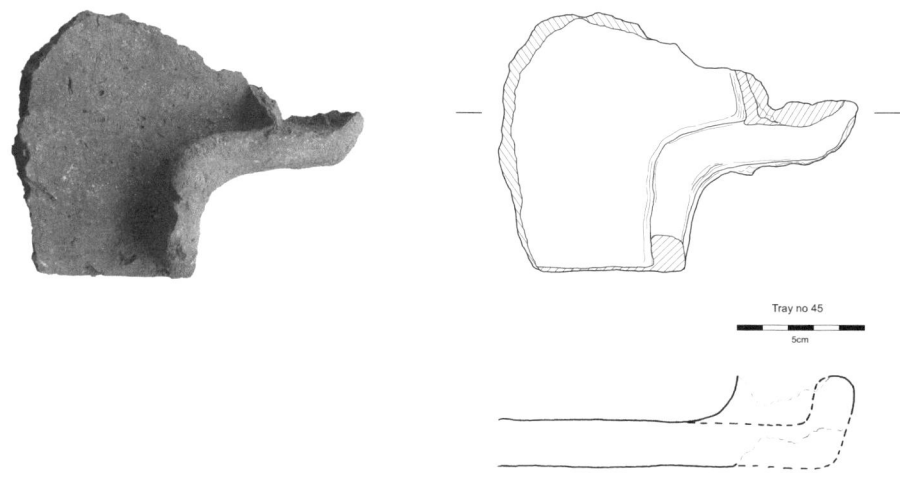

Tray no 45

5cm

Cat. 17: OT46 (S08/st730)
Tomb of the Dogs, in debris 6.5 m from (modern) entrance
Nile Silt C
Red Coating
W: x+10.7+y, L: x+6.2+y, Th: 2.7

Lowest bottom part of the surrounding wall preserved, wall itself broken off. Part of an application reminiscent of an *ḥs.-t*-flask preserved. To its left, a straight line was incised before firing.

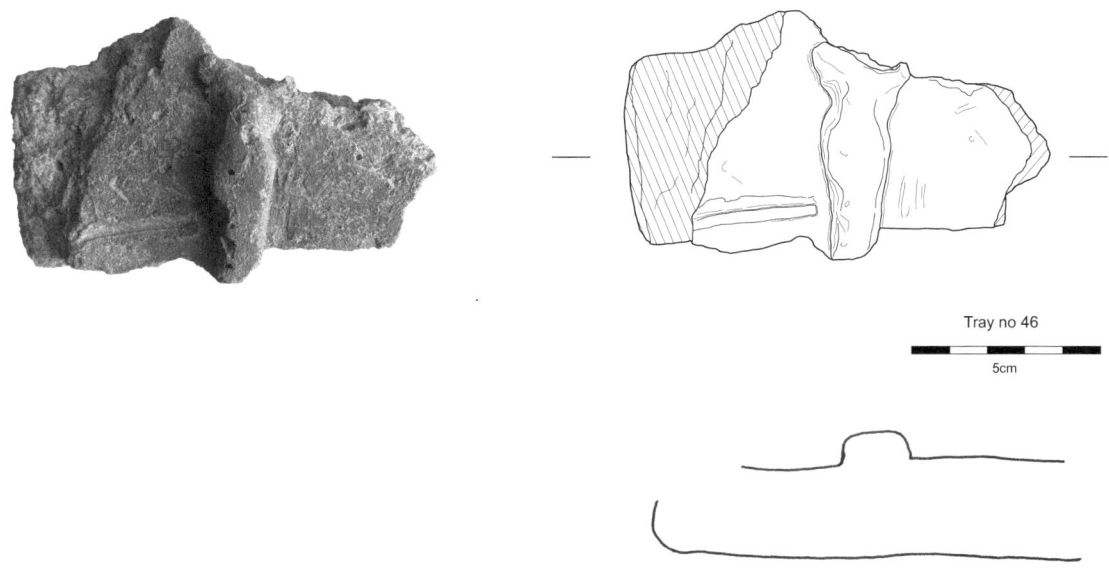

Tray no 46
5cm

Cat. 18: OT47 (S08/st758B)
Tomb of Dogs, debris in front of (modern) entrance
Nile Silt C
Rounded tray, most probably oval
H: 5.1, W: x+8.1, L: x+15.7+y, Th: 1.1–2.6

Part of an oval tray with surrounding wall. Incisions or impressions before firing, unrecognizable.

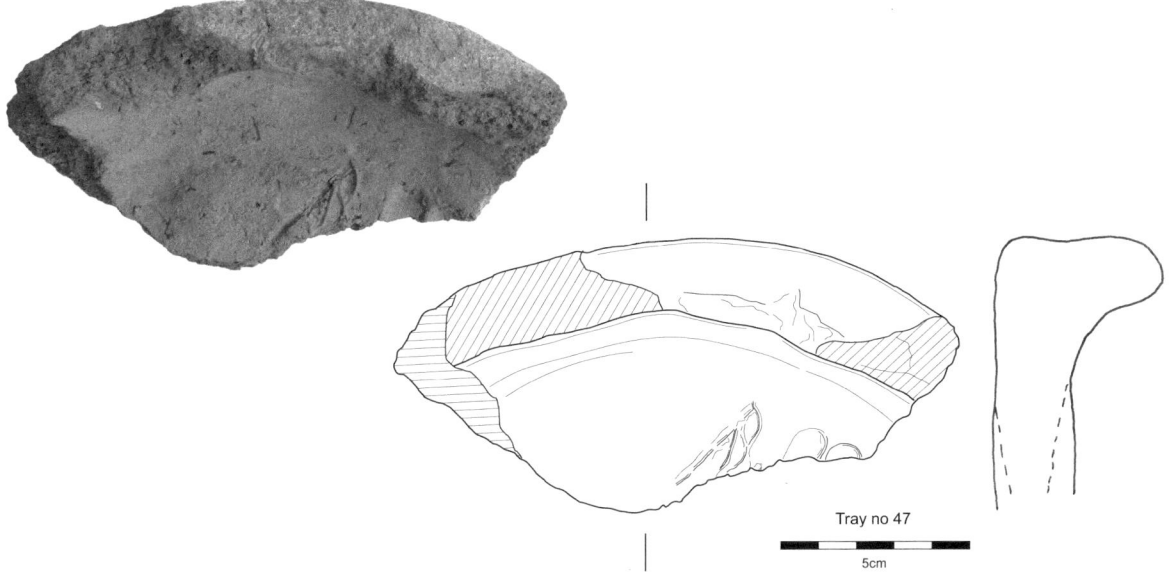

Tray no 47
5cm

Cat. 19: OT51 (S11/st422B)
Tomb of Dogs, debris north of (modern) entrance
Nile Silt C
Rectangular
H: 4.4; W: x+7.6; L: x+8.7; Th: 1.2

Corner part of an offering tray with surrounding wall.

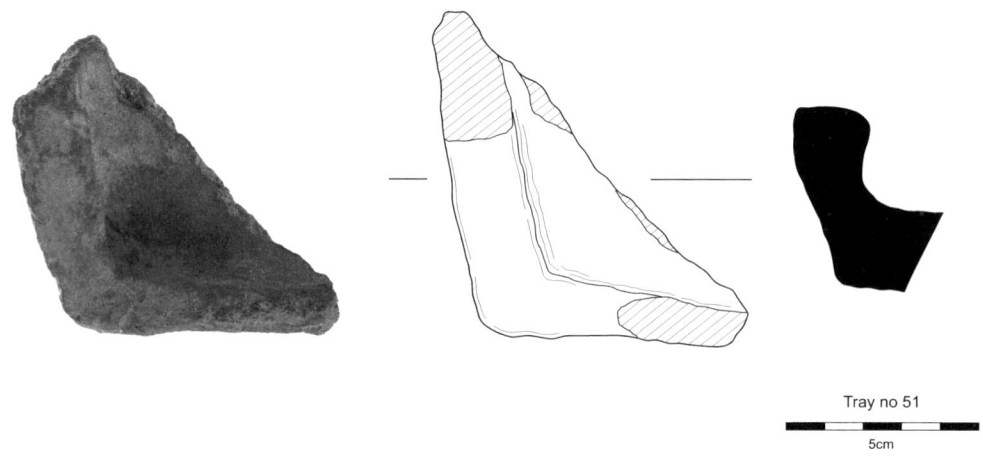

Tray no 51

5cm

Cat. 20: OT54 (S09/st1657)
Tomb of Dogs, southern debris, 114.5–113.5 m aSL
Nile Silt C
Shape unknown
Red coating inside
W: x+9.0+y; L: x+6.6+y; Th: 2.8

Part of the middle of a tray with a deepening and two canals crossing each other at right angles.

Parallels: Offering trays from Qurna, see Petrie 1909: Pl. 21, Nr. 627. 628. Deir el-Bahari: Carnarvon & Carter 1912: pl. 18.3, no. 16. See also unprovenanced offering tray in the Agricultural Museum Cairo, Reg.No. 670, Al-sayed Aman 2016: 77. My thanks go to Alexander Ilin-Tomich, who brought this article to my attention.

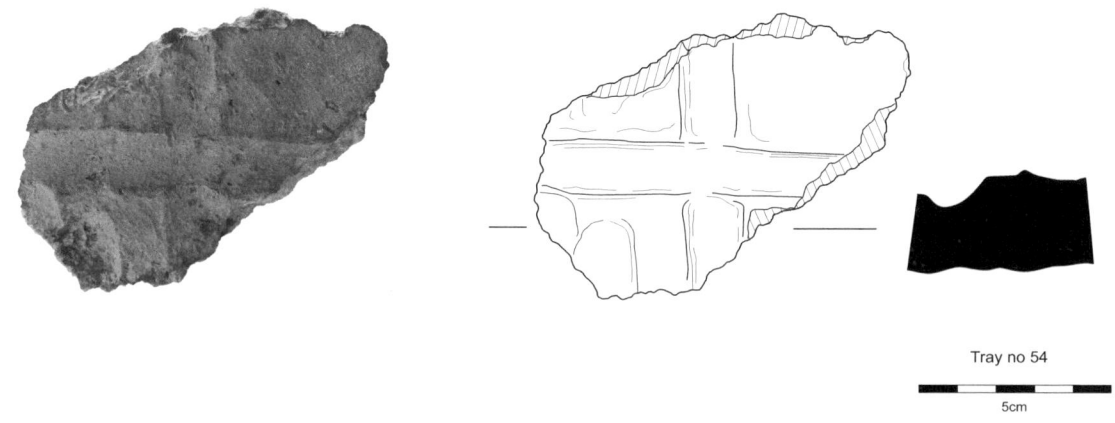

Tray no 54

5cm

Cat. 21: OT59 (S09/st1438)
Tomb of Dogs, southern debris, 114.5–113.5 m aSL
Nile Silt C
Rectangular
H: 3.8 (vessel: 4.8+y), W: 7.9+y, L: 5.9+y, Th: 1.9

Corner piece of a rectangular tray. Remains of a vessel that was applied directly in the corner, upper part lost.

Parallels: e. g. PETRIE/BRUNTON 1924: Pl. 13, no. 730. Państwowe Muzeum Archeologiczne w Warszawie, Warsaw, Inv. No. 139165. Egyptian Museum Cairo, JE 39109.

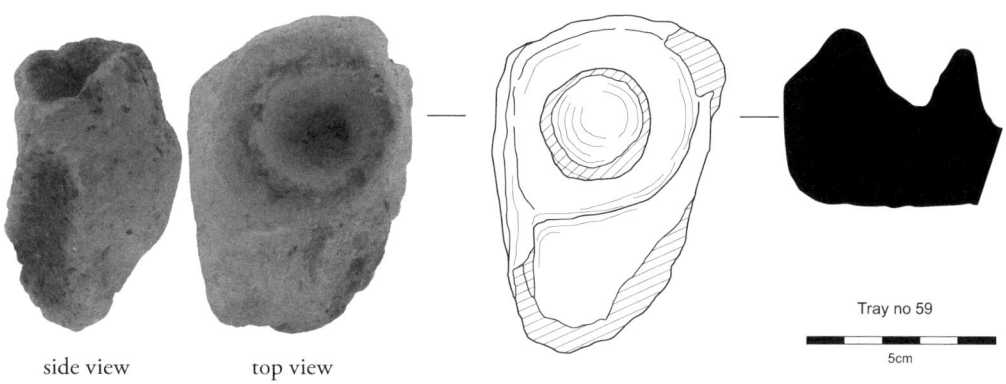

side view   top view

Tray no 59

5cm

Tomb I (P10.1) and its surroundings

Cat. 22: OT66 (S14/st1924D)
Shaft P10.4, south of Tomb I
Nile Silt C
Rectangular
H: 4.0, W: 6.0+y, L: 8.0+y, Th: 0.9

Left part of a spout and part of the surrounding wall; not matching.

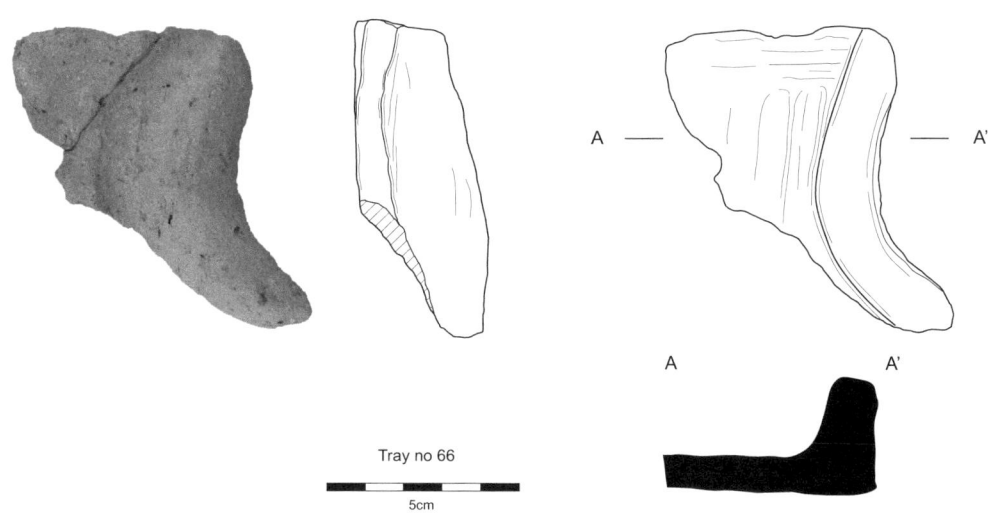

A — A'

A   A'

Tray no 66

5cm

Cat. 23: OT68 (S14/st1914C)
Tomb I, forecourt, area east of shafts
Nile Silt C
Most probably rectangular
H: 5.1+x, W: x+10.1+y, L: y+11.3, Th: 1.6

Part of outer wall preserved, against which a bovid head with horns leans. In front of it, a round piece of meat with straight incisions is depicted.

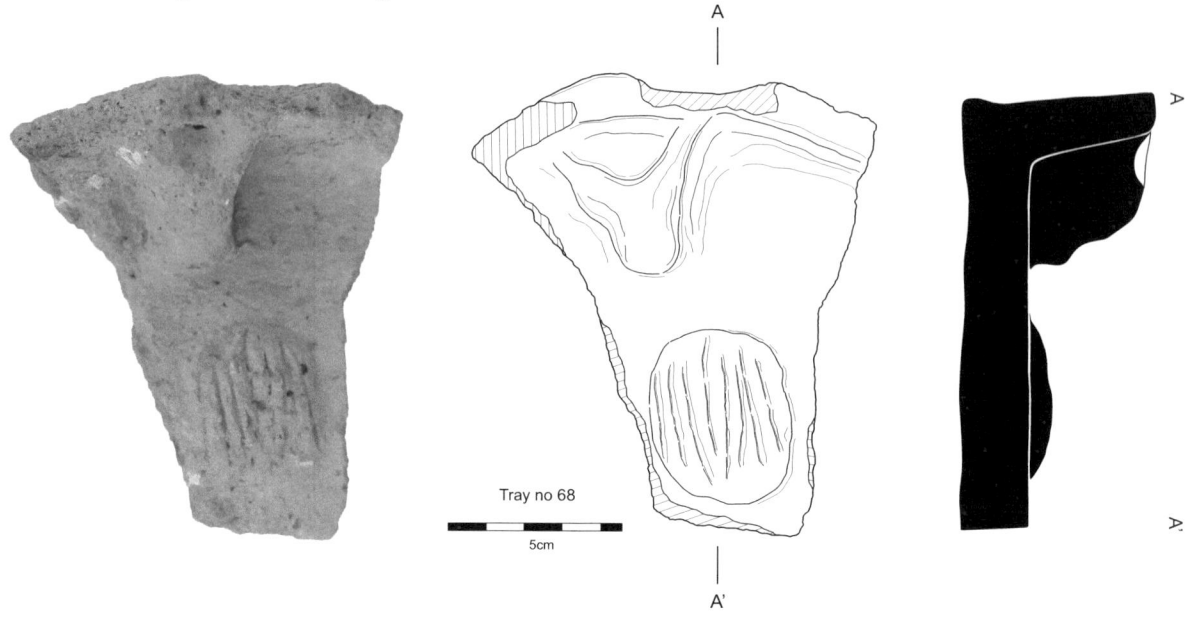

Cat. 24: OT72 (S17/st581)
Tomb I (P10.1), causeway
Nile Silt C
Red coating?
W: 7.2+y, L: x+7.2+y, Th: 2.0

Offerin tray with part of the rim preserved, unusually it does not have a surrounding wall. Inner dividing wall forming a right angle enclosing a round loaf of bread.

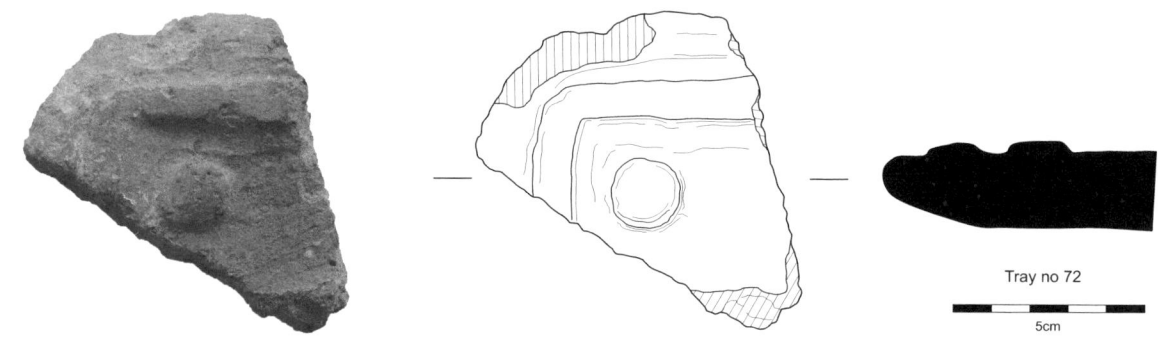

Survey Finds

Cat. 25: OT39 (S05/st1192)
Tomb II (O13.1), 12 m from entrance on the way to Deir el-Meitin
Nile Silt C
Rectangular
Red coating
H: 4.6, W: 10.8+y, L: x+8.0, Th: 2.5

Corner of a rectangular tray with an application of a very stylized bovine head directly at the corner. Wall tapers towards corner. White deposits; remains of red coating.

Parallels: OT74, S 14946 (see below). PETRIE 1909: Pl. 20, 605.

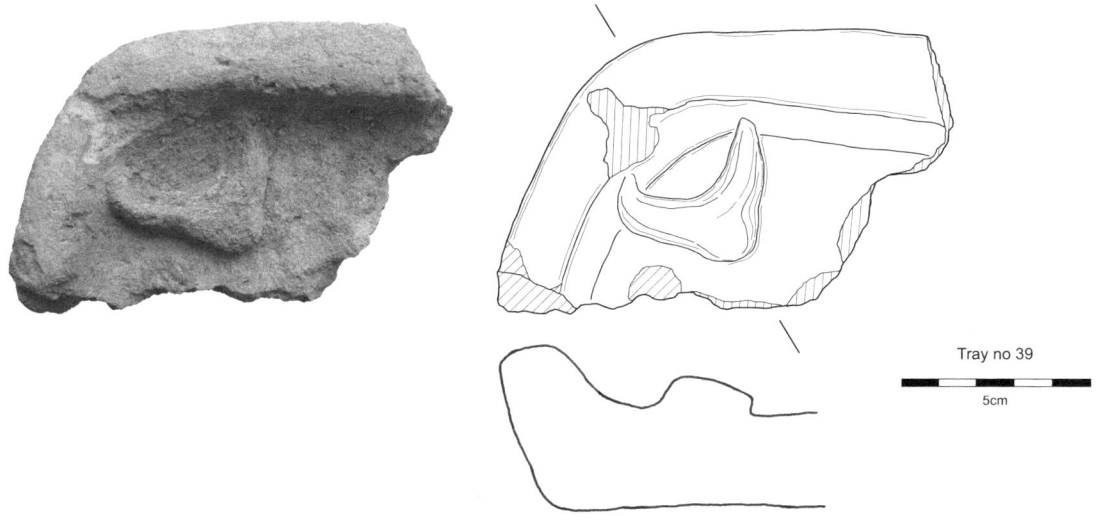

Tray no 39

5cm

Cat. 26: OT49 (S09/st843)
Deir el-Azzam
Nile Silt C
Rectangular
Red coating inside and most probably outside, but outside blackened
H: 3.5–4.5; W: 13.6+y; L: x+12.1; Th: 2.2

Lower left corner of a rectangular tray. A dividing wall in a semi-circular shape, very irregular shape separates a basin occupying the left front corner from the rest of the tray. Small part of a spout on left side preserved.

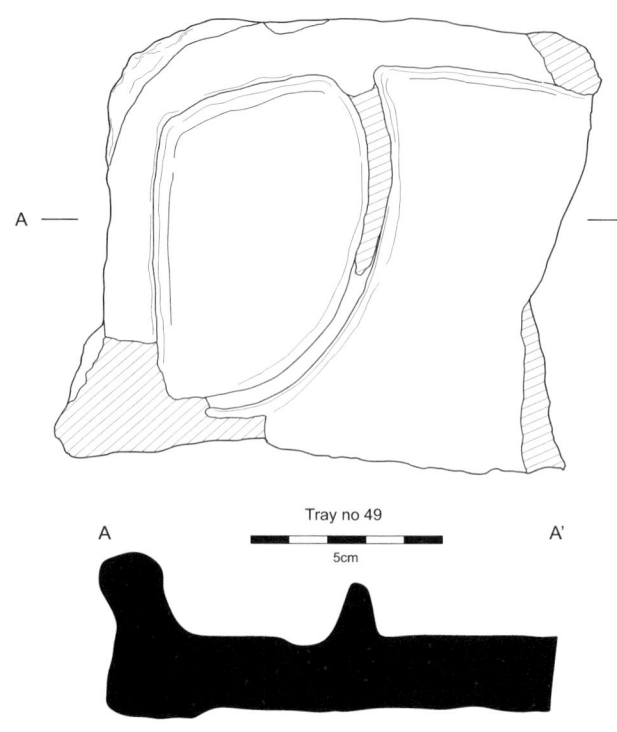

Tray no 49

5cm

Cat. 27: OT50 (S11/st611)
K12 findspot 1
Nile Silt C
Rectangular
Red coating inside and outside
H: 4.2; W: 11.0+y; L: 16.3+y; Th: 1.6

Lower left corner of a rectangular tray. Left part of a spout preserved. A low, semi-circular wall separates a basin occupying the left front corner from the rest of the tray. The lower part of the wall slopes into the spout and does not have a connection to the surrounding wall of the tray.

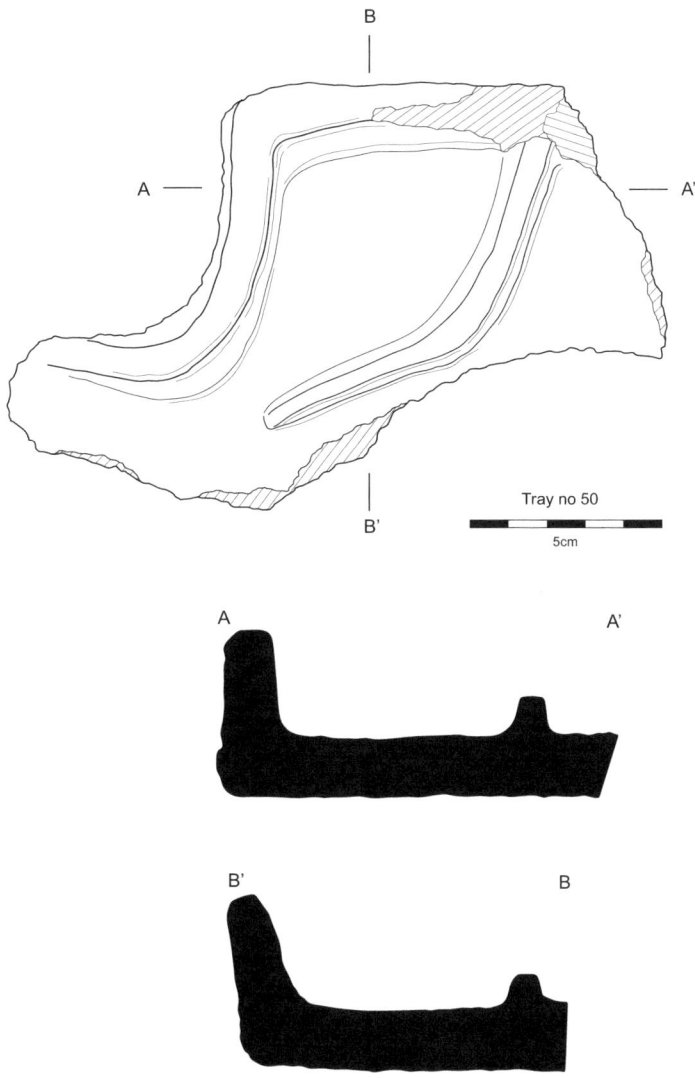

Tray no 50

5cm

Cat. 28: OT55 (S11/st1001)
Survey around Tomb K11.3
Nile Silt C
Rectangular or oval
H: 4.5, W: 3.2+y, L: x+5.5+y, Th: 1.4

Part of the rim of an oval or rectangular tray.

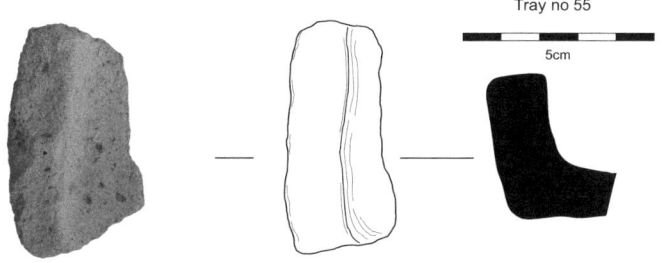

Tray no 55

5cm

Cat. 29: OT63 (S14/st809)
Survey, tombs M12.13–15
Nile Silt C
Rectangular
Red coating
H: 4.8, W: x+20.0, L: 27.5+y, Th: 2.4

Upper part of a tray with left upper corner preserved. Remains of a vessel (bottom only) that was attached directly on top of the edge of the surrounding wall. In the center, a bovid head with horns leans against the wall. In front of its mouth, a round loaf of bread is depicted, flanked by an *ḥs.t*-flask to the left and a hind leg of an ox to its right. On the right side of the leg, there is another round application with straight incisions, which might be either depicting another bread loaf or a piece of meat. Along the left side of the tray, a triangular piece of meat is shown, together with an hourglass-shaped application and the remains of another such unusual application below it.

Parallels:
This tray is unusual in several aspects as it is exceptionally big and shows hourglass-shaped applications otherwise unattested. It does not have direct parallels from Asyut although parallels for most applications are readily available in Asyut and elsewhere:
For vessels attached to an offering tray, parallels are known from e. g. Edfu: Państwowe Muzeum Archeologiczne w Warszawie, Warsaw, Inv. Nos. 138875, 139165, 139501, 139505, 141473, 141476, 141478 (published in Michałowski 1938a: 121, 179–180, 183–184, 189, 192–193. Pl. 42, Fig. 2–4. Michałowski 1938b: : 67, 82, 84, Fig. 47, 305–306, Pl. 40, 42); or Rifeh: Petrie 1907: Pl. 14.4.
For bovid heads, placed either at the corner or center of the wall, see above.
For *ḥs.t*-flasks, see OT27, Kilian 2012b: 201, Fig. 13. OT41, Kilian 2012a: Pl. 9. OT46, OT60 (see above).
For the triangular piece of meat, see OT64, OT74 (see below).
For the round piece of meat (or loaf of bread) with straight incisions, see OT52, OT68 (see above).
Round bread loaves are quite common on offering trays throughout Egypt.

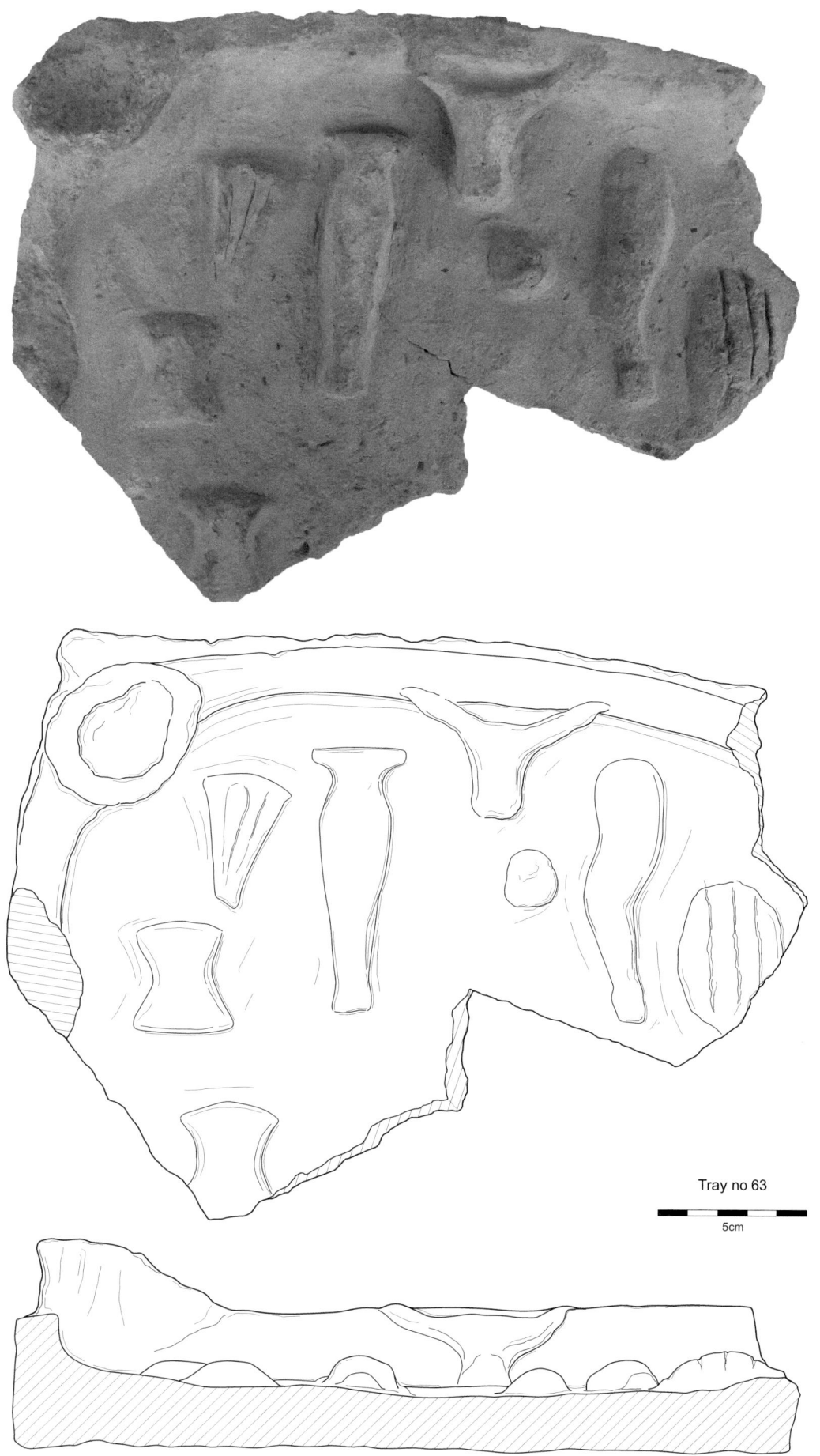

Tray no 63

5cm

Cat. 30: OT64 (S14/st809)
Survey tombs M12.13–15
Nile Silt C
Rectangular
H: 4.5, W: x+11.5+y, L: 10.5+y, Th: 1.8

Outer wall of an tray with remains of the inner plate displaying inner dividing walls forming a rectangular compartment. In this compartment, remains of a somewhat round object. Above the compartment, a trapezoid piece of meat is applied.

Parallel: Petrie 1891: Pl. 4.23

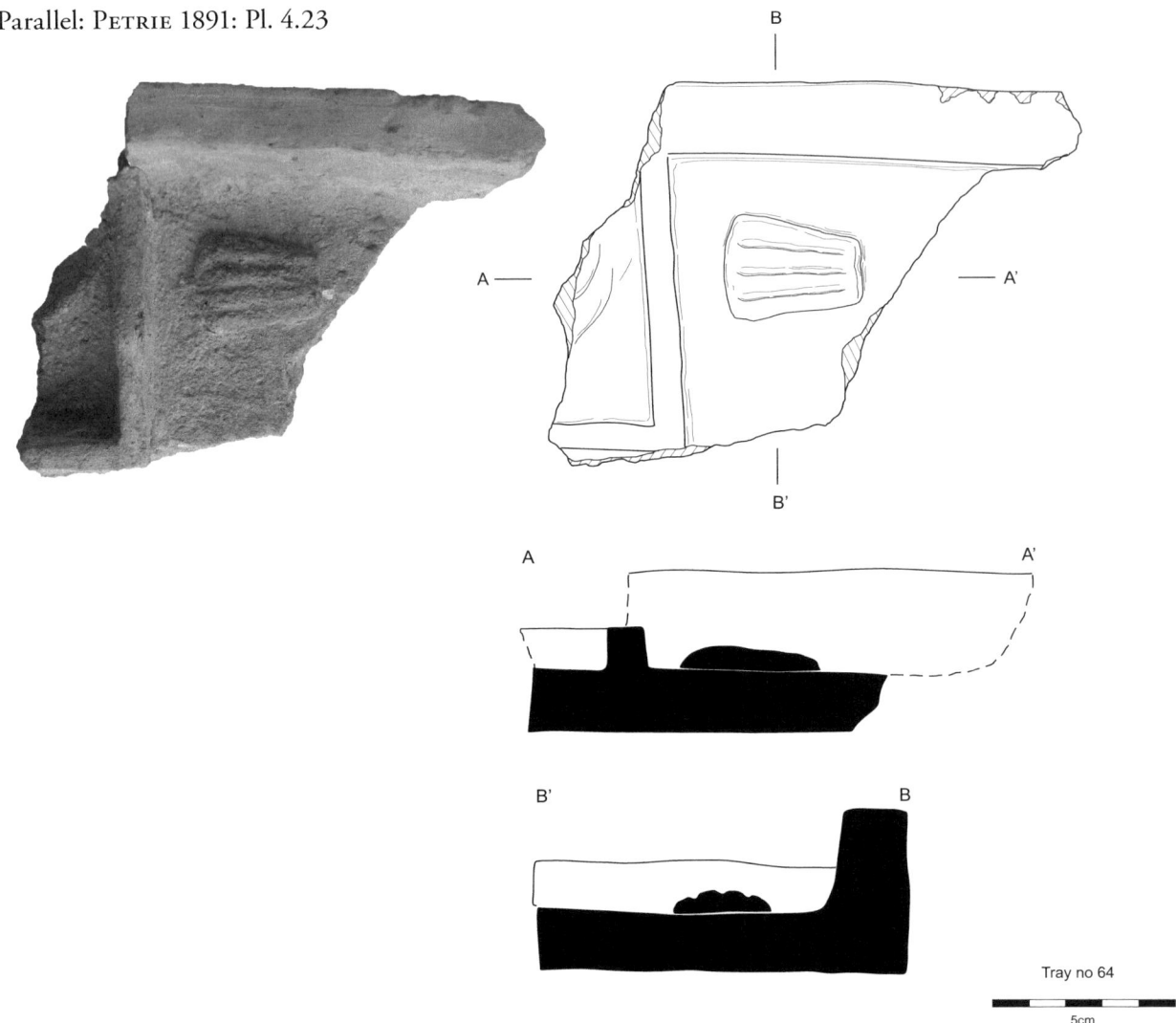

Tray no 64
5cm

Cat. 31: OT65 (S14/st809)
Survey, geological step 8
Nile Silt C
Rectangular
19.3 cm + 20.1 cm + 18.6 cm + 19.9 cm; L with spout 24.4 cm

Complete rectangular tray with spout. Surface badly eroded, surrounding wall at lower right corner missing. Application of a bovid head in the center of the back wall, in front of it, from left to right, long meat pieces and two other, no longer recognizable, offerings. In front of these offerings, one leg of an ox is shown.

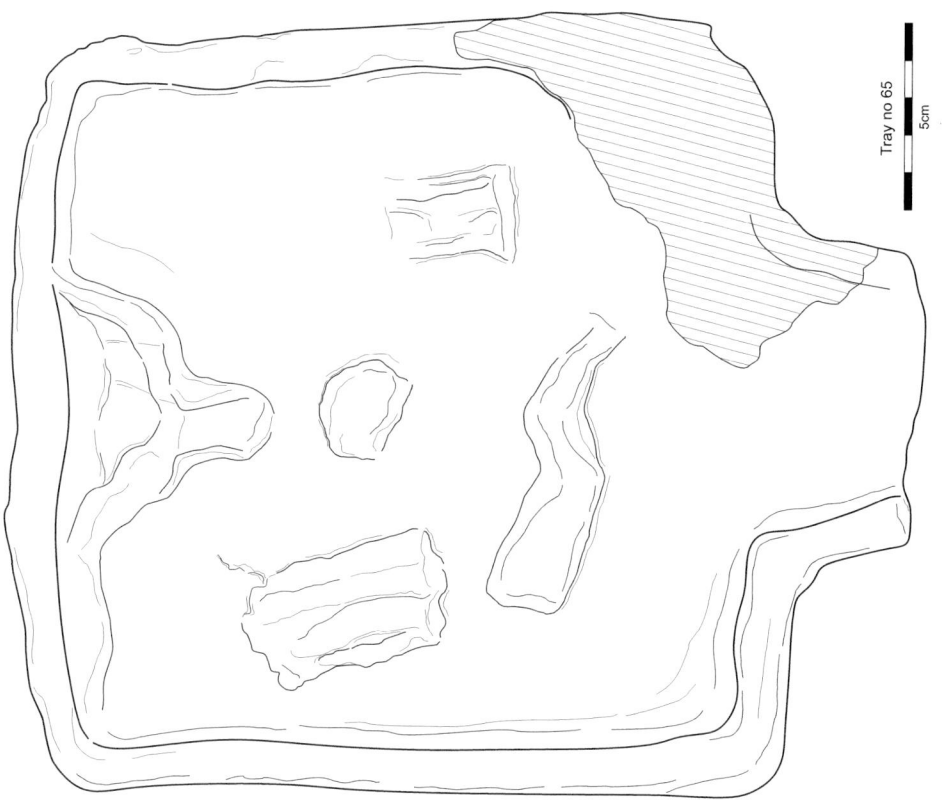

Tray no 65

5cm

Cat. 32: OT70 (S14/st840)
Survey, geological step 8, N13 findspot 2
Nile Silt C
W: x+7.0+y, L: x+7.8+y, Th: 1.5

Center piece of a tray displaying inner dividing walls forming a right angle. Bottom and parts of the surface heavily worn.

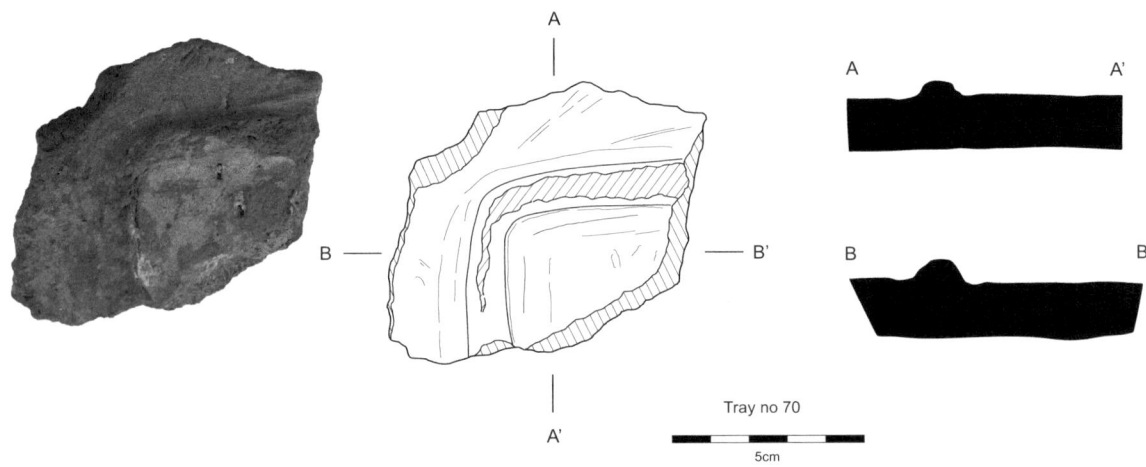

Offering trays in the Magazine in Shutb

Cat. 33: OT73 (SCA 26)
Gebel Asyut al-gharbi, exact provenance not known
Nile Silt C
Trapezoid/horseshoe-shaped
Red coating all over, including bottom
H: 4.0–7.5, W: 19.5–9.0, L: 23.5, Th: 3.3–6.2

Complete trapezoid tray that tapers towards the front. Inner dividing walls form four basins. The basins in the rear open at their middle corners respectively into a broad canal. In front of these two basins are two smaller ones, separated by walls from the bigger ones. These walls are pierced in their centers, thus connecting the bigger with the smaller basins. The smaller basins lead into canals which are parallel to the canal belonging to the big basins, the outer wall of the central canal simultaneously forming the inner wall of the smaller canals. The surface and bottom are worn, outer walls are in better condition.

Parallels: Deir el Ballas: Manchester Museum, Acc. no. 4529 (see Petrie/Quibell 1896: pl. 44, 6, but basins deepened into the surface instead of being created by adding walls). Dividing walls with holes, separating a rear from a front part, are common in Dendereh, see Petrie 1900: pl. 19, nos. 3, 6–9, 11 (there leading from the back part into a basin in the front part), 12.

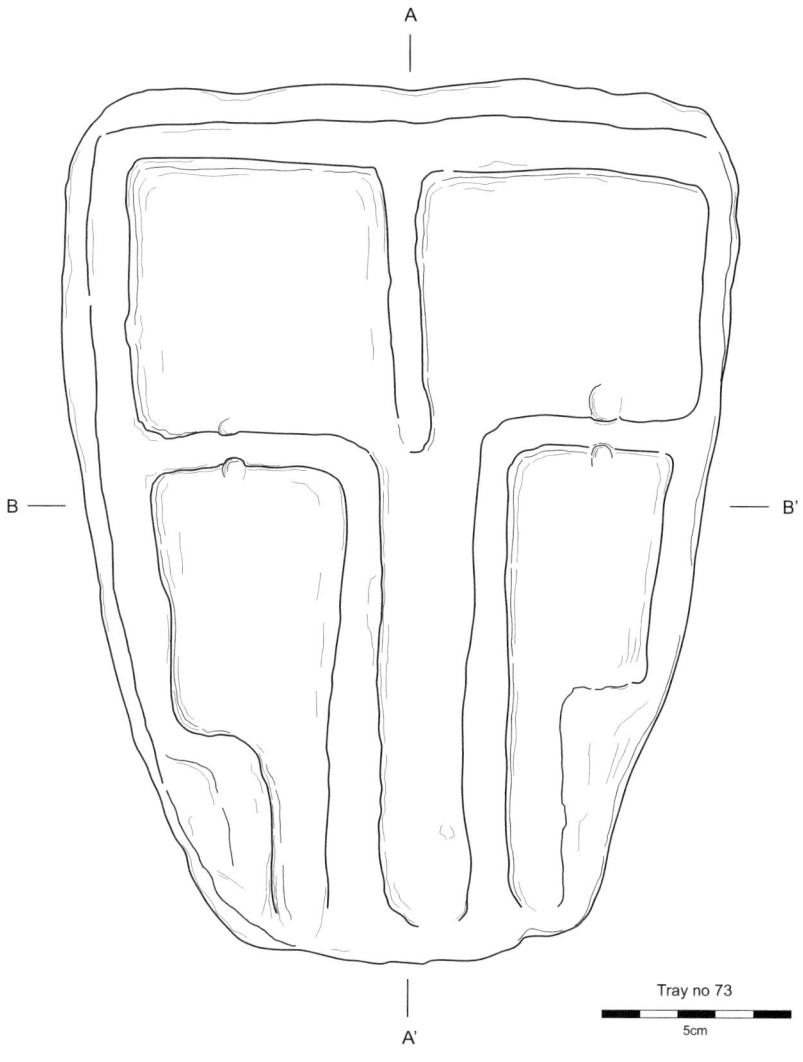

Tray no 73

5cm

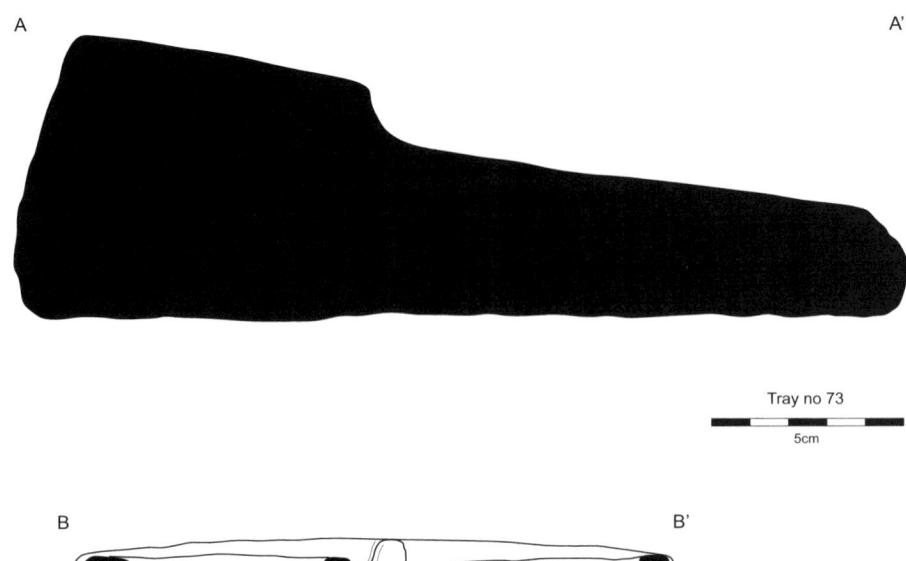

Tray no 73

5cm

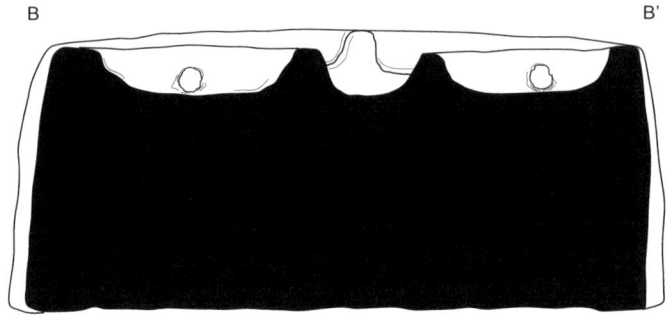

Cat. 34: OT74 (SCA 310)
Gebel Asyut al-gharbi, exact provenance not known
Nile Silt C
Rectangular
Red coating, remains of white paint
H: 5.3, W: 21.4+y, L: 33.8, Th: 2.1–2.6

Rectangular tray with spout, right part missing. Displays a bovid head with eyes indicated, placed in the right upper corner, with its horns stretched across the outer wall. In front of it, different offerings were applied: two long pieces of meat with straight incisions, between them a *jwᶜ*-meat and round bread loaves. In the center, a triangular piece of meat with straight incisions is shown, its right corner missing. A oval-round object in front of the bovid head is broken off. Surface and bottom worn, outer walls in good condition. Red coating on sides and surface, in right lower part traces of white coating on meat pieces and the rear part of the surrounding wall.

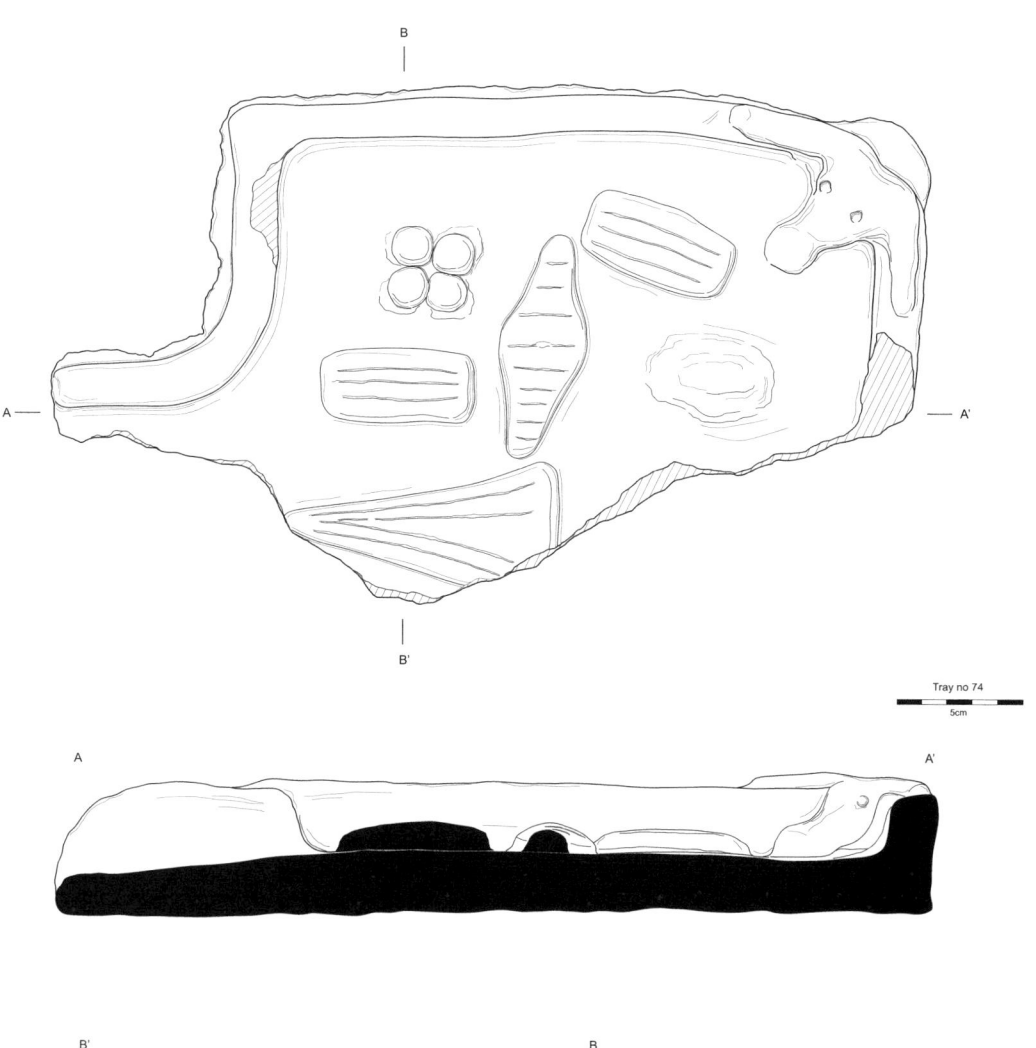

Tray no 74
5cm

Offering trays stored in the Museo Egizio, Turin[41]
Cat. 35: Provv. 5537
Gebel Asyut al-gharbi, exact provenance not known
Nile Silt C
Rectangular
Remains of red coating
W: 21.0, L: x + 22.8/25.4

Rectangular tray, front wall almost completely broken, with only the left part of the spout preserved. Manufacturing technique discernible: first, manufacturing of a rectangular platter, then surrounding wall that forms a spout in the front part. Then, inner walls forming compartments/basins were added, as well as a vessel in the right rear corner that was attached to the platter using clay; preserved are only the clay particles that once fastened the vessel to the platter. Somewhat dislocated, not centered, but shifted to the left, are the remains of a bovid head. Surface is heavily eroded in this area.

41 For better quality photos in color, see Mi 2020.

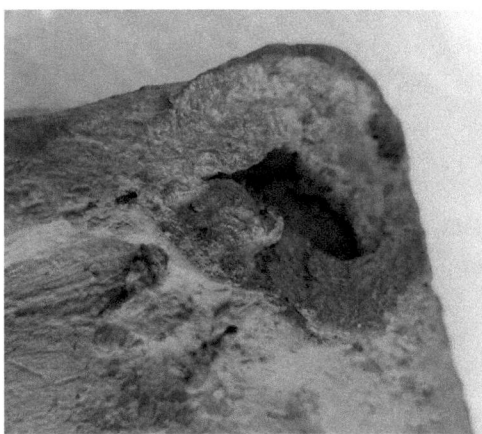

Cat. 36: S 7979

Gebel Asyut al-gharbi, "Tomba N. 2"[42]
Nile Silt C
Rectangular
Red coating on the upper side, clay colored on the underside
17.7 cm x 24.5 cm x 16.2 cm x 24.8 cm; Th.: 4.0–5.0 cm

Rectangular tray with two basins that were deepened into the surface, one oval shaped and the other rectangular with rounded corners. Both were connected via a small canal scraped into the surface. In between the basins, a lozenge-shaped object was added to the tray, its small end crossing the canal that continues underneath it. The tray is flat and does not have a surrounding wall nor a spout, but the wall of the rectangular basin was pierced on the small side opposite the canal connecting it to the other basin so that water can flow from the tray in a controlled direction. The surface of this hole that was made before firing is blackened.

The tray was found by Schiaparelli in 1906[43] in "Tomba N. 2". The exact location of this tomb is unknown, but it can still be linked with some pottery: S 7975, S 7976, S 7977 and a stopper[44] S 7980.

S 7975 is the upper part of a bag-shaped vessel similar to those found in the region of Sheikh Abu Tuq,[45] which can be linked to the earlier phase of the First Intermediate Period (predating the late First Intermediate Period). It was made of Nile Silt B and covered with red paint on the outside and on the upper part of the inside of the neck. S 7976 is the same kind of vessel like S 7975, but smaller and with the complete profile preserved. The bottom shows the typical scrape marks.

S 7977 is a miniature bag, made of Nile Silt B1, with a clay colored surface and scrape marks on the bottom. The mouth diameter is 5.4 cm; the height 9.8 cm.

S 7980 actually is not a vessel, but a stopper made of unbaked Nile mud. Interestingly, vessels of the type like S 7975 and 7976 reportedly were found still closed with a stopper.[46]

---

42 According to Sbriglio, in: KAHL ET AL. 2019, 75–81, 141–142, 169–170, it should be located in the area of Tombs II–V. I thank Jochem Kahl for this and the following references to the findspots of Schiaparellis excavations.

43 ZITMAN 2010: II, 269seq. but mentioning the year 1905 instead of 1906.

44 Listed in ZITMAN 2010: II, 270 as "lid of a vase (?) (sic)". Apparently, he was translating Schiaparellis notes and did not have access to the object itself. ZITMAN ibd. further mentions a "skull, apparently found in front of a large tomb", a head rest (S 7975) and an unidentified artefact (S 7979). According to Del Vesco, in: KAHL ET AL. 2019: 283, the following items were found in "Tomba N. 2": S 7975(sic)–S 7977 (pottery vases), S. 7978 (unknown object, limestone), S 7979 (pottery offering tray) and S 7980 (lid). According to Sbriglio, in: KAHL ET AL. 2019: 142, the skull S 7974 should be added.

45 For these vessels, see KILIAN 2019: 126. 387–390, Dok. 7–12.

46 KILIAN 2019: 108. 252, Abb. 38. 359, Kat. 490. Pl. 11b. For the stopper, see also VAN ELSBERGEN 2019: 37–38. 165, Tf. 5. This kind of stopper is well attested in Asyut, parallels can be found in VAN ELSBERGEN 2019: 37, Fig. 13 and ibd. in the catalog under the entry "Kleine Gefäßverschlüsse (GV1-290)" on pp. 53–85 (e.g. p. 53, GV7, GV8, p. 54, GV 10, etc.).

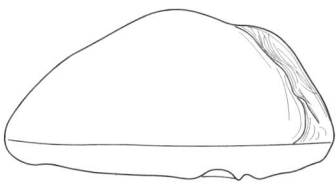

S 7980	Gebel Asyut, Tomba No 2	
Nile mud	Ø 8.4–8.5	H: 4.3 + x cm
Unbaked. No impressions, surface worn. Sketch, appr. 1:2.		

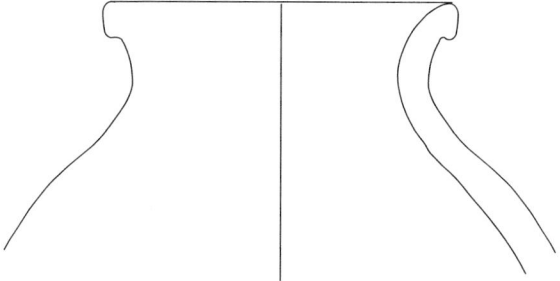

S 7975	Gebel Asyut, Tomba No 2		
Nile B	Ø ~ 9 cm	H: 8.3 cm x y	~ 160°
Surface: red coloured.			
Sketch, appr. 1:2			

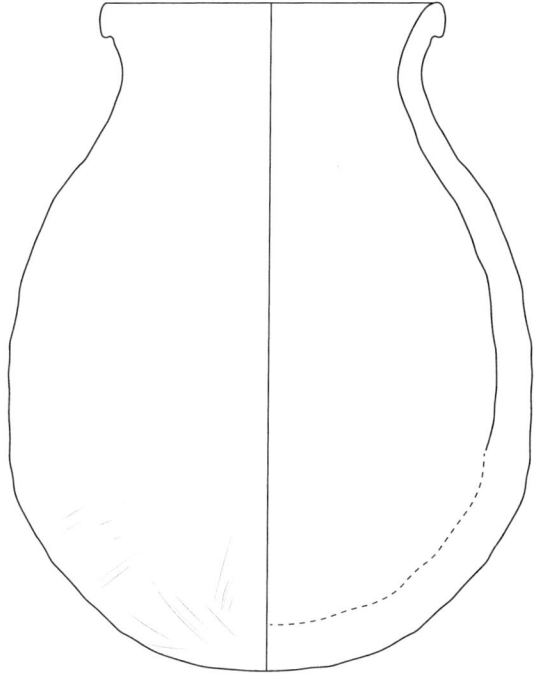

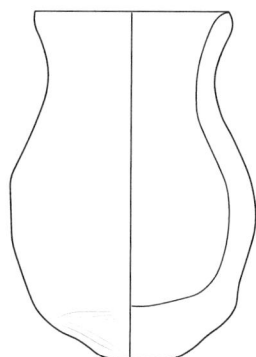

S 7976	Gebel Asyut, Tomba No 2		
Nile	Ø ~ 9 cm	H: 17.8 cm	~ 160°
Surface: red coloured.			
Bottom shows irregular scraping marks. Sketch, appr. 1:2.			

S 7977	Gebel Asyut, Tomba No 2		
Nile B	Ø 5.4 cm	H: 9.7 cm	360°
Surface: clay coloured.			
Bottom has been cut into shape. Sketch, appr. 1:2.			

Cat. 37: S 14943
Gebel Asyut al-gharbi, exact provenance not known[47]
Nile Silt
Rectangular with rounded front
Red coating all over (including base)
L: 27.3 cm; W: 21.1 cm; Th.: front 4.5 (right) – 3.7 (left); middle part with application: 5.0 cm

Rectangular tray with a rounded front, flat without surrounding or dividing walls. Surface heavily worn. Two small basins were deepened into the surface approx. in the middle of the tray. Their upper parts are rounded, their fronts show a canal opening to the rounded and tapering front part of the tray. This tapering part of the tray has an irregular surface with the right side being higher than the left. In between the basins, a very worn application remains visible, but is no longer discernible (might have been a vessel, similar to S 14945).

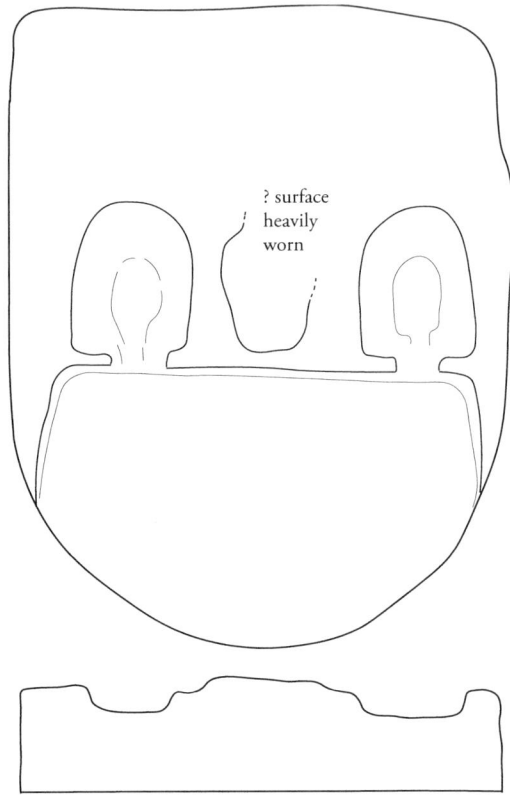

Sketch of S 14943,

Cat. 38: S 14945
Gebel Asyut al-gharbi, exact provenance not known[48]
Nile Silt C
Rectangular
Red coating on the upper side
21.3 cm x 12.2 cm x21.0 cm x 12.0 cm; Th: left: 4.0 cm, right: 2.3 cm + x

---

47 According to KAHL ET AL. 2019: 76–77, 294ff., the possible findspots include the area around Sheikh Abu-Tug, H11.1, the Salakhana Tomb, Tombs II–V and the area between the latter and Tomb I.

48 The possible findspots are the same as those mentioned in the above footnote.

Rectangular tray with red coating on the surface (excluding base). Right side heavily eroded; parts of the upper surface chipped. No wall, no spout, even surface that is a little bit higher towards the rim. Two basins were deepened into the surface of the front (?) quarter, the left one with a rounded lower side, the right one rectangular, with slightly elevated rims. In between the basins an ovoid object was attached. This might be an ovoid vessel with its mouth directed at the outside of the tray, but as its surface shows a depression in what would be the belly of the vase, I am not sure if some kind of offering (bread?) was meant instead.

Maybe the flat rear part was used as a "table" for real offerings. This would fit with the trays featuring clay offerings with basins that are always positioned in the front part where they open into the spout of these offering trays.

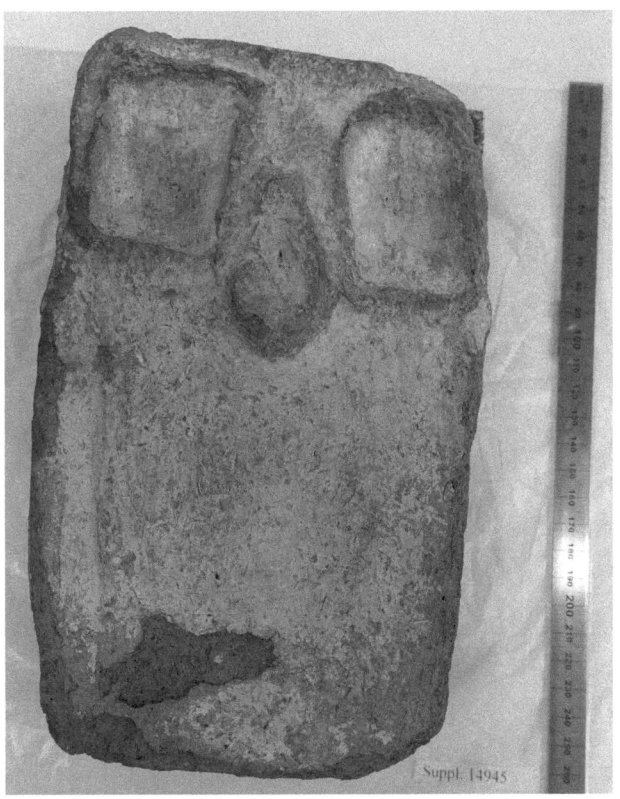

Cat. 39: S 9179
Gebel Asyut al-gharbi, exact provenance not known[49]
Nile Silt C
Rectangular
Thick red coated surface and sides, clay colored base
24.8 cm x 21.8 cm x 23.0 cm x 23.1 cm, length with spout 19.3 cm

Rectangular tray with a spout and surrounding wall. The rear two thirds feature a flat *bḏꜣ*-bread (?),[50] on top of which a leg and a triangular bread loaf were added. To the right of the *bḏꜣ*, four long objects

---

49 According to Sbriglio, in: KAHL ET AL. 2019: 76–77, 285ff, the findspot must be located on Step 3 or south of Tomb I.

50 The bread-making tables in Meketre's brewery show a very similar form, so maybe, in this case, the offering tray shows an installation of a kind of table or platform with offerings on top (instead of a *bḏꜣ*, as placing offerings onto a giant *bḏꜣ* seems somewhat strange); cf. WINLOCK 1955: pl. 23 and the drawing thereof on pl. 64. On the other hand, *bḏꜣ*-breads could be depicted in exactly the same way as here, e. g. the (stone) offering table 1976/114/a/2065 from Ihnasiya el-Madina/ Herakleopolis in the Museo Arqueológico Nacional, Madrid. However, it is hard to decide in favor of one or the other, because the bread can be depicted without its characteristic "stem", which makes it look very similar to Meketre's tables.

(most probably meat), each formed separately, are to be found. The front third of the tray was separated via inner dividing walls forming basins that are open towards the spout. The basin walls are even with the surrounding wall.

Parallels: A very close parallel to this offering tray is Liverpool Museum 1973.1.362. Unfortunately, the provenance is not known. Similar is also Pelizaeus-Museum Hildesheim No. 1676 with unknown provenance: MARTIN-PARDEY 1991: 47–48. Interestingly, instead of having inner dividing walls separating a rear from a front part, this tray has an elevated rear part with its own spout, thus resembling a tray having been put on a tray.[51] Bovid heads placed on either a bread or a kind of platform are also attested at Kahun: PETRIE 1891: pl. 4.15; Dendereh: PETRIE 1900: pl. 19.2.

    For Asyut, platforms seem to be the more likely option, as the breads normally feature a stem and a "true" platform is attested e. g. on S 10648.

51 For a very unusual depiction of an offering tray on an offering tray, see UC 38983.

Cat. 40: S 14944
Gebel Asyut al-gharbi, exact provenance not known[52]
Nile Silt C
Rectangular
Surface red coated, but heavily worn, so not many traces left, but in the upper right part of the surrounding wall and the outer side of this wall; black paint dripped down on some spots
19.8 cm x 18.8 cm x 18.7 cm x 17.8 cm, with remains of spout 20.8 + x cm; H: 4.0; Th: 1.3–1.6 cm

Rectangular offering tray. The rear two thirds of it display two *bḏꜣ*-breads or platforms (see above) with the pointed side directed towards the now lost spout, upon which offerings are depicted: the left bears a head of a bovid of which even the ears and holes for the nostrils are depicted (which is a rare feature), the right one shows a leg and maybe something small (bread?) in front of the leg, but due to the badly eroded surface this is not recognizable any longer.

The front third is occupied by two basins formed by adding inner dividing walls that are open in the front part where they meet the spout, which is not preserved.

Parallels: Liverpool Museum 1973.1.362, see S 9179.

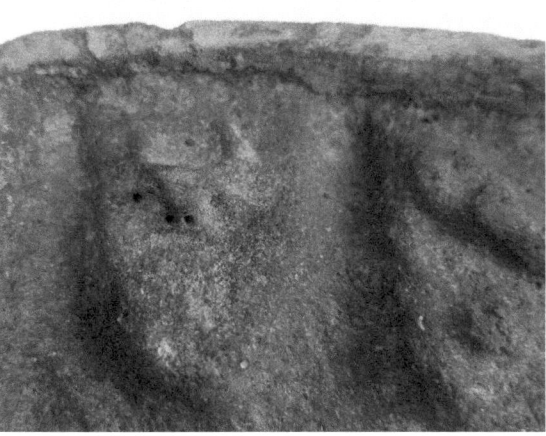

---

52 According to KAHL ET AL. 2019: 76–77, 294ff., the possible findspots include the area around Sheikh Abu-Tug, H11.1, the Salakhana Tomb, Tombs II–V and the area between the latter and Tomb I.

Cat. 41: S 8141
Gebel Asyut al-gharbi, exact provenance not known[53]
Nile Silt C, very rough
Rectangular
Clay colored
W: 16.5 cm; L: 17.0 cm, L + spout: 24.0 cm; H: right: 5.0 cm, left: 3.0 cm, spout: ~ 1.0 cm

Rectangular tray, tapering in height from the right to the left side. Application of a bovid head with ears in the middle of the rear wall facing the spout; its horns bending across the crown of the wall onto the outside. In front of it, feet facing the head, a decapitated bound bovid lies, with a tail indicated, followed by an oval object with three incisions (piece of meat). Along the left side, a leg is to be found, along the right, four round loaves of bread.

Cat. 42: S 10648
Gebel Asyut al-gharbi, exact provenance not known[54]
Nile Silt C?
Rectangular
Clay colored (but surface very worn off)
23.0 cm x 20.5 cm x 21.0 cm x 20.5 cm; Length with spout: 30.0 cm; spout: 6.8 cm

Rectangular tray with spout. On the rear wall, facing the spout, a very stylized bovid head with horns was attached. In front of it, a slight elevation forms a kind of "platform"[55] on which offerings were positioned: from left to right a leg, an oval lump with three incisions (meat), a conical bread loaf (bd_3), two long, "U-shaped"[56] pieces; in front of this row are two rows with two square loaves of bread each. Between the conical bread loaf and the "U-shaped" pieces is a small hole (not piercing the base).

The front quarter is occupied by two basins that are open towards the spout. They were formed out of low dividing walls that taper towards the spout. In these basins, additional, slightly sunken round basins were added. An ever-so-slight sunken "canal" leads in a straight line from the platform into the spout.

The outer wall shows either a triangular incision that was made before firing or the remains of a large part of a plant stalk. The latter seems more probable as it is highly unusual for pottery offering trays to show any kind of "markings" or inscriptions.

---

54 According to Kahl et al. 2019: 76–77, 291, the possible findspot could have been either close to the modern cemetery around Tomb K6.1 or between Tomb N11.1 and Step 3 above Tomb I.

55 For a similar arrangement with offerings displayed in an enclosure formed by a low wall, see soul house E 26927 in the Louvre,

56 Cf. also OT43, either meat or bread. For the interpretation as bread, see (although of 5th Dynasty date) MfA 03.1739–03.1744: https://collections.mfa.org/search/objects/*/votive%20loaf (accessed 02/2020).

Cat. 43: S 14848
Gebel Asyut al-gharbi, exact provenance not known[57]
Nile Silt C
Rectangular
Red coated
26.8 cm x 23.0 cm x 23.8 cm x 11.0 cm; L with spout 29.8 cm; H: 3.4 cm; Th: at spout ~ 0.8 cm

Rectangular tray with spout, broken into five pieces. Approx. two thirds of the left surrounding wall and the wall forming the right basin are missing.

Bovid head in the center of the rear wall, leg in front of it; in both rear corners conical loaves of bread. The next row displays four separately formed, long objects touching one another, most probably meat; a triangular loaf of bread, an *ḥs.t*-flask[58] and another triangular loaf of bread. The front quarter is occupied by two basins formed out of crescent shaped clay coils that taper towards the spout. The basins are open on their sides where they meet the spout part.

---

57 According to Kahl et al. 2019: 76–77, 294ff., the possible findspots include the area around Sheikh Abu-Tug, H11.1, the Salakhana Tomb, Tombs II–V and the area between the latter and Tomb I.

58 It is not completely to be excluded that in this case, it might not be an *ḥs.t*, but a piece of meat as their respective forms sometimes intermingle when it comes to depictions on pottery offering trays, cf. the choices of meat on S 9179 that might easily be misinterpreted if only half of them were preserved.

Cat. 44: S 14941
Gebel Asyut al-gharbi, exact provenance not known[59]
Nile Silt C
Rectangular
Surface unknown, heavily eroded all over and for the most part, original surface has vanished
23.7 cm x 21.6 cm x 22.8 cm x 22.0 cm; L with spout: 26.3 cm; H: 3.1 cm, Th: at spout 0.9 cm

Rectangular tray, heavily worn; some applications broken off. The overall design is, as far as recognizable, similar to S 14941: bovid head in center of the rear wall, facing the spout; conical loaves of bread in both rear corners, the left one broken off; in front of head: either triangular bread with $hs.t$-flask below, or only $hs.t$-flask with the triangular application being the stopper of the flask (similar to OT60) or triangular bread with leg instead of $hs.t$-flask. As the lower part of the flask/leg is missing, that is hard to decide. To the left of this feature: triangular piece of meat with incisions, parts of which are broken off; to the right: long object, broken off (bread or leg?).

The front quarter of the tray shows two basins formed out of clay coils, open towards the spout; the right basin's wall is completely missing. The spout is relatively broad and somewhat lopsided (maybe due to erosion); a canal was impressed in its middle.

59 According to KAHL ET AL. 2019: 76–77, 294ff., the possible findspots include the area around Sheikh Abu-Tug, H11.1, the Salakhana Tomb, Tombs II–V and the area between the latter and Tomb I.

Cat. 45: S 10647
Gebel Asyut al-gharbi, exact provenance not known[60]
Nile Silt
Rectangular/horseshoe-shaped
Surface red coated (traces discernible on outer wall)
W: 14.8 cm at spout, 19.5 cm at rear wall; L: 22.8 cm; H: 4.6 cm; Th: 1.8–2.0 cm

Offering tray with unusual form and applications: rectangular-horseshoe shaped tray with a head or
skull of a bovid in the middle of the rear wall. Horns are missing, the snout is very elongated and the top
part (the skullcap, if a skull is meant) shows five vertical incisions, so I guess instead of a head, a skull
might be indicated here. In the left corner, between the skull and the front left basin, a dish or flat bread
was installed from which a low wall emanates that leads to the right front basin. The two basins in the
front occupy two thirds of the tray and were formed by inner dividing walls. They are not, as usual, open
towards the spout, instead, their respective walls lead to the end of the tray meeting the front part, thus
creating a small "canal" in between them. Thus, in this case, the tray does not really have a spout, but
instead tapers towards an open front creating the mere appearance of a spout.

60 According to Kahl et al. 2019: 76–77, 291, the possible findspot could have been either close to the modern cemetery
   around Tomb K6.1 or between Tomb N11.1 and Step 3 above Tomb I.

Cat. 46: S 14946
Gebel Asyut al-gharbi, exact provenance not known[61]
Nile Silt C
Rectangular
Red coating all over
25.5 cm x 21.0 cm x 23.5 cm x 18.0 cm, L with spout 27.2 cm; H: 3.6 cm; Th: 2.7 (middle)–2.1 cm

Rectangular offering tray with a heavily eroded surface, once covered in thick red coating that is still visible all over the surrounding wall, on the conical bread loaf in the middle of the rear wall, on the long objects next to it, on the inner wall of the basin and on the underside of the tray, the latter having been carefully smoothened. The surrounding wall leans outwards, so that the surface of the tray is broader than the base.

Several objects were applied: a bovid head in the left corner instead of in the middle of the rear wall, where a conical loaf of bread is to be found instead, followed by four long objects in the right corner, most probably meat. Beneath, a very stylized leg was added, next to which a ladder-like object was applied. Below this row of offerings two baguette-shaped objects were centered, reaching between two basins that were formed by inner dividing walls that are open towards the spout, occupying the front quarter of the tray. Whereas most basins are regular and mirror-images to one another, the ones on this tray were formed irregularly and were installed at slightly different distances to the spout.

To the right of the leg, an unusual and so far not attested element was added that is shaped like a ladder. Its meaning is unclear to me. So far, only meat, bread, sometimes fowl and vegetables are depicted, supplemented by containers, such as $ḥs.t$-flasks, bag-shaped closed or dish-shaped open vessels, as well as basins. So the ladder-like object might also fit into one of these categories. My colleague, Dr. Nadine Gräßler, suggested it might be patches for growing vegetables which seems the most likely idea so far.[62]

Parallels: OT39 featuring the same kind of head, similarly shaped, also in a corner instead of the center of the rear wall. In Dendereh, the ladder-like object might find a parallel in Petrie 1900: pl. 19.3 where a ladder seems to have been incised into the surface. Unfortunately, the upper part is missing so that this cannot be stated with certainty.

S 14946, detail of ladder-shaped application

---

61 According to Kahl et al. 2019: 76–77, 294ff., the possible findspots include the area around Sheikh Abu-Tug, H11.1, the Salakhana Tomb, Tombs II–V and the area between the latter and Tomb I.

62 See, e. g., the offering trays from Edfu featuring small fields and a hut (?) in the center of the rear wall (Michałowski 1938a: Pl. 42.4) or Deir el-Bahari that is completely comprised of fields of different sizes (Carnarvon & Carter 1912: Pl. 47.2). The latter show holes pierced onto the surrounding wall and/or the walls in the center of the offering tray, reminiscent of vine bowers. For an interpretation as gardens or fields ("bassins agricoles"), see Kuentz 1981: 246seq.

Cat. 47: S 14940
Gebel Asyut al-gharbi, exact provenance not known[63]
Nile Silt
Rectangular
Thick brown-red coating on surface, base clay-colored
28.2 cm x 19.6 cm x 27.8 cm x 19.0 cm, L with spout 30.0 cm; H: rear wall 4.5 cm, left: 4.0 cm, right: 4.2 cm, front: 3.2 cm; Th: at spout 1.2 cm

Rectangular red-coated tray that was divided in half by low inner dividing walls that are open towards the spout, the left front edge of which is missing.

In the rear half, a small bovid head with horns was applied in the center of the rear wall, facing the spout, its horns reaching only to the middle of the wall; the left side is occupied by a large leg, the right by a long object with three incisions (meat) and an oval lump of clay, most probably symbolizing a loaf of bread.

The front half was delimited from the rear part by two low walls that bend forward, normally thus forming two basins that are open towards the spout. In this case, the intention as basin seems no longer to prevail as two further applications were added in this area: to the left, an *ḥs.t*-flask with an aperture directed towards the spout; to the right, a triangular piece of meat with three incisions. The incisions are hardly visible due to the thick red coating the tray was covered with.

---

63 According to Kahl et al. 2019: 76–77, 294ff., the possible findspots include the area around Sheikh Abu-Tug, H11.1, the Salakhana Tomb, Tombs II–V and the area between the latter and Tomb I.

Cat. 48: S 14949
Gebel Asyut al-gharbi, exact provenance not known[64]
Nile Silt C
Rectangular
Clay colored (?)
H: 4.0 (wall), W: y + 8.6, L: x + 13.2, Th: 2.4 (plate)

Left front corner of a rectangular tray. Inner dividing wall forming a basin is intact, as usual this wall is open towards the spout, which is not preserved. Dividing walls are flush with outer surrounding wall.

Suppl. 14949

---

64 According to Kahl et al. 2019: 76–77, 294ff., the possible findspots include the area around Sheikh Abu-Tug, H11.1, the Salakhana Tomb, Tombs II–V and the area between the latter and Tomb I.

The Asyuti Offering Tables:
an attempt at reconstructing funerary ritual in the ancient necropolis of Asyut

Esmeralda Lundius

1. Introduction

1.1 The Ancient Egyptian Offering Table

In ancient Egyptian rituals, offering tables constituted a link between the living and the sphere of the dead/divine. They were mainly used in temples and/or tombs in funerary complexes, believed to provide nourishment to the deceased.[1] Their size, shape, material and placement indicate the social status of their users as well as their function. Offering tables were made from a wide variety of materials and their design depends on context, use, origin and time period. The surface of several stone offering tables may be covered with depictions of victuals, vessels and vegetation in raised relief, though motifs and their combinations vary significantly. However, a common feature in most of their iconography is its connection with water.[2] Offering tables do not only indicate regional characteristics and are not only useful for dating tombs, but more importantly suggest the nature and development of funerary rituals and the importance of the necropolis in ancient Egypt.

1.2 Previous Research

Unfortunately, the far-reaching significance of this artefact has often been overlooked, especially in the field of ancient Egyptian funerary ritual. Much research remains to be done in connection with offering tables, not only within the realm of Egyptology, but also within the general archaeological record.[3] How to cope with death is central to human existence; funerary and ancestor cults are part of human reality and an essential ingredient in cultural expressions.

Offering tables are generally found in museum collections, though so far they have seldom been studied in an all-encompassing manner and only occasionally been connected with their ritual and topographic context.[4] This study is an intent in that direction and is concentrated to Asyuti offering tables, found both *in situ* and in different museum collections.

---

1 Bolshakov 2001.

2 Information based on an ongoing compilation of a catalogue of offering tables and similar objects in collections in Egypt, Europe and the USA.

3 This paper is based on a PhD thesis begun in 2016 at the Department of Archaeology at Durham University UK.

4 Important publications concerning the classification and interpretation of offering tables include Regina Hölzl's doctoral thesis (Hölzl 2002) where she describes, catalogues and analyses an extensive sample of stone offering tables (as well as some pottery offering trays) ranging from the Old to the New Kingdom. Using samples from numerous museums she identifies and categorises different types of offering tables, arranging them in accordance with clear and useful typologies. Extensive museum catalogues also describe offering tables, such as Ahmed Kamal's 1909 Cairo Museum catalogue (Kamal 1909), as well as Labib Habachi's 1977 Turin Museum catalogue (Habachi 1977).

1.3 Previous research on the Asyuti Offering Tables

Over the course of the centuries, over one hundred tombs of the ancient necropolis of Asyut in Middle Egypt have been excavated and analysed. All these tombs have been cut out in a stratified limestone cliffside,[5] both in the shape of rock-cut tombs and shaft tombs. Even if most of the tombs, and their content, have been thoroughly researched and scientific excavations continue to be carried out, the offering tables found at the site have so far to a high degree been neglected. Offering tables brought from Asyut can be found in Egyptian collections around the world, while some are still left *in situ* or have been stored in the excavation magazine located in the village of Shutb. Several offering tables, both intact and fragmented, have been discovered during recent campaigns. Only in 2016 were fragments of five different offering tables discovered.

The Asyuti offering tables have been recently studied by scholars, for example by Ilin-Tomich, who mostly addresses the 'elaborate' type offering tables and their complex provenance.[6] Since the tables present in museum collections are of a high quality and often filled with inscriptions, they have received the most attention, especially since they have been studied and analysed for museum catalogues. The work of Ilin-Tomich is vital for the understanding of how workshops functioned and the importance of ancient Asyut whose role as a cultural hub for local production is often overlooked. The production of funerary equipment such as offering tables and steles was more complex and abundant in this area than previously thought.[7] Another important publication mentioning Asyuti offering tables and their possible archaeological context is that of Marcel Zitman, who addresses offering tables present in museum collections.[8] These complex funerary utensils still present in and around Asyut's necropolis, as well as those found in museums around the world, highlight the importance of this site, not only as an ancient Egyptian town, but also as a garrison town, pilgrimage site and a necropolis for *nomarchs*.[9] Andrea Kilian has also contributed to the study of Siutian offering tables, specifically pottery offering trays, which have a few similarities to the stone tables and were found in similar archaeological contexts.[10]

The following description and analysis of offering tables found in the necropolis of Asyut is the result of an opportunity provided by Prof. Dr. Jochem Kahl as part of *The Asyut Project*.[11] The specific environment of Asyut and the remains of offering tables still found in their original setting strengthened a resolve to try to analyse offering tables in a "socio-anthropological" manner, namely trying to trace their ritual function/use within their original context and relate it to ideas and traditions of people living in the world in which they were used. This paper constitutes an attempt at not only describing and classifying some of the numerous offering tables found in Asyut, it also intends to present some theories regarding their potential use and the importance they had for people living in a liminal world; a border city placed between desert and fertility, between warring factions, and between life and death.

---

5 The porous limestone is both layered and compact, giving the cliff-face a "honeycomb" like appearance. KAHL 2007: 3.

6 ILIN-TOMICH 2018a, b.

7 ILIN-TOMICH 2018a, b.

8 ZITMAN 2010.

9 KAHL 2017: 15.

10 KILIAN 2012, KILIAN 2016.

11 Part of the excavation season in 2018. „*The Asyut Project*": "Die altägyptische Nekropole von Assiut: Dokumentation und Interpretation" (DFG) (2005–2019) is a collaboration between the Johannes Gutenberg-Universität Mainz, Freie Universität Berlin and Sohag University. https://www.aegyptologie.uni-mainz.de/the-asyut-project-feldarbeiten-in-mittelaegyptenfieldwork-in-middle-egypt/ [accessed: 07.08.2019].

2. The Geographical, Historical and Socio-Religious Context

A point of departure for the study of a ritual object is to place it in connection to the specific geographic/ spatial context where it has been found and furthermore relate to the time period during which it was in use. Such an approach could then be further developed through an anthropological approach, intending to connect the use and appearance of the artefact to its assumed spatial and ritual context, thus tracing the meaning and importance it once had for the people of a specific time and place.

2.1 The Origin and Rise of Asyut

Asyut first emerged in importance during the *Old Kingdom*, as evidenced by its mentioning in *Pyramid Texts* dating back to the 6th Dynasty.[12] From approximately 2500 BCE, Asyut was the capital of the 13th Upper Egyptian *nome* (province), known all over ancient Egypt for its fertile farmland.[13] The name Asyut is derived from the early Egyptian *Sauti (s3w.tĭ)*, meaning *The Guardian*, apparently referring to the strategic importance of the town.[14] During Graeco-Roman times Asyut was called *Lycopolis*, Wolf City. *Wepwawet*, the main deity of Asyut,[15] was depicted in the shape of a canid, though the Greeks apparently considered Wepwawet's appearance to be similar to that of a wolf.[16] As a hunter and a warrior, Wepwawet was believed to be a guardian against menacing powers. He also served as a guide for the dead and a guardian of cemeteries.[17] Dogs were often painted inside coffins found in Asyut's necropolis, affirming the status of Wepwawet as the town's protective deity and a companion to the Duat.[18] Wepwawet was labelled as "the Opener of Ways", guarding access to mountains and oases and he was thus considered to be a "liminal deity".[19] As "opener" and a chthonic god Wepwawet has furthermore been associated with the *Opening of the Mouth* ceremony possibly due to his liminality (see section 7).[20]

To the east of Asyut, a mountain range faces the Nile, which at this point contains dangerous currents and intersects a route which leads from Darfur to the Kharga Oasis. To the West, Asyut is also protected by a vast mountain range.[21] This means that Asyut is not only sheltered by natural barriers, it also has a unique position at the crossroads of waterways and caravan routes. Furthermore, Asyut's importance was connected with the veneration of its gods. Its temples were centres of economic activity, controlling extensive landholdings. Equipped with small industries like kitchens, bakeries and workshops the temples provided jobs for local residents, who also benefited from the fertile lands and Asyut's strategic position.[22] Unfortunately, the ancient city of Asyut and its temples have not been explored in detail due to the rising of the alluvial plain and also due to the fact that the modern city has been built over the entire area of ancient Asyut.[23]

2.2 Topographic, Stylistic and Political Liminality

Asyut was once the most prominent religious centre of ancient Egypt, after Thebes in the south, and Herakleopolis and Memphis to the north. Its position between these two power centres proved to be both prodigious and precarious. Asyuti art, craftmanship, cults and power-structures were influenced by both Thebes and Herakleopolis, influences that created a unique syncretistic culture.

---

12 Kahl 2007: 35.
13 Regulski & Golia 2018.
14 Kahl 2007: 14.
15 An inscription from the temple of Aset/Isis in Philae describes Wepwawet as the Great God in Asyut (Junker 1958: 115).
16 Kahl 2007: 108.
17 Pinch 2004.
18 Ibid. 56.
19 Kahl 2007: 39.
20 Wilkinson 2003: 191.
21 Kahl 2007.
22 Regulski & Golia 2018: 17.
23 Kahl 2007: 3.

As a city it maintained its influence and importance, both artistically and economically, between the 11th and 12th Dynasties.[24] However, it was constantly influenced by its precarious position between two even more influential power spheres. After the 8th Dynasty, there was no centralised government in Egypt, consequently the country was divided into several regions governed by local rulers. It has often been stated that Asyut did not recover from the Herakleopolitan defeat and that it ended up as a provincial town of little importance. However, recent archaeological findings have proved that this was not the case.[25]

Throughout its long history Asyut has been a liminal place, a border town of strategic importance, receiving influences from various parts of the antique world, facilitated by its position as a trading and pilgrimage site. For much of its existence Asyut was also a garrison town containing a vast number of soldiers from other areas.[26] Asyut absorbed influences not only from its allies, in particular the Herakleopolitan kingdom, but also from Thebes and other areas, mingling them with local styles and belief systems. The town sometimes ended up as a battle ground and was occasionally for longer periods forced to succumb to hostile forces.

2.3 Religion, Wealth and Power

Religious beliefs and funerary rituals of Asyut seem to reflect its unique position as a liminal realm. Asyut's grandest building was the temple of Wepwawet, a world of its own; a political and administrative centre, important employer, and influential trendsetter. However, Wepwawet's temple was not alone in this role. Asyut was not only an important grain producer, a powerful garrison town and economic centre, it also attracted pilgrims and it appears that both locals and pious people from other parts of the Egyptian realm wanted to be buried close to their venerated deities: mighty protectors and guardians against evil like Wepwawet, Anubis and Osiris. For centuries, Asyut remained an important religious centre for both Middle and Upper Egypt.[27] A preeminent religious festival was celebrated for five days by the end of a year. As part of the festivities Wepwawet's statue was carried from the city centre to the home of Anubis, a site probably situated by the edge of the necropolis. Other important temples apart from the ones of Wepwawet and Anubis, were dedicated to Hathor and Thoth.[28] Asyut was historically linked to Osiris, whose temple has been recorded in the First Intermediate Period and functioned for more than two millennia. An important pilgrimage site and sanctuary was established in the Greco-Roman Period dedicated to the cult of Osiris known as *The House of the Eight Trees*.[29]

The temples and the funerary cult were controlled and supervised by the local elite. In the tomb of Djefai-Hapi I, ten contracts related to mortuary rituals have been found, listing details concerning the burial ceremonies and addressing the administrators of proceedings connected with Djefai-Hapi's funeral.[30] Contracts mention the erection of a statue within a complex which included a garden at the lower edge of a causeway leading from the cultivated areas to the forecourt of his tomb. They explicitly proclaim him to be worshiped as a god as evidenced by the recounting of priests, whose duties were to be similar to those concerning the cult executed at the temples of Wepwawet and Anubis.[31] The organization of everything around elaborate burials, the treatment of corpses, the furnishing and construction of tombs, etc., apparently constituted an important and profitable business in Asyut, actively supported by functionaries and administrators. Furthermore, during the 11th and 12th Dynasties the chief priests of

---

24 Kahl 1999: 336–337. Zitman 2010a: 182.
25 Kahl 2007: 8. Elaborate tombs, complete with grave goods including wooden models and exquisite coffins have been discovered and analysed in great detail. A re-examination of the tomb of Djefai-Hapi I, which is the largest known Middle Kingdom tomb in Egypt, has in fact proven this point. Ibid. 9.
26 Ibid. 12.
27 Kahl 1999: 339–348.
28 Kahl 2007: 35–58.
29 Kahl 2007: 35.
30 Ibid. 45.
31 Kahl et al. 2015: 121–126.

the Wepwawet and Anubis temples served as *nomarchs*, rulers, of the Asyut province. The cults, festivities and the officials mentioned may explain the presence of numerous steles as well as elaborate offering tables dedicated to these deities from a variety of time periods, but also dedicated to the nomarchs buried within the necropolis.[32]

3. The Necropolis

The people of Asyut buried their dead in the mountain range to the west of their city, where the necropolis extended several kilometres along the edge of the cultivated plain. Tombs belonging to Asyut's ancient elite overlooked the city from the side of the mountain *Gebel Asyut al-gharbi*.[33] The tombs of the wealthy came with a view since they were impressive rock-cut tombs carved into the limestone cliff. The cliff itself is steeply inclined and divided into eleven limestone layers, with numerous elaborate tombs and shaft tombs which stretch from at least 1 km east to west.[34] The tombs of high officials are almost always accompanied by smaller shaft tombs in the vicinity or even the courtyard of the tombs which may have belonged to members of the household, officials and dependants.

3.1 The Dynamic World of the Dead

In general terms, wealthy tombs were equipped with coffins, statues, wall paintings, models and figurines, while lower status tombs contained funerary equipment often inscribed with names and titles of officials to provide access to the cult above (although this is not a frequent feature at Asyut).[35] Offering tables found in the tombs of the wealthy were cut out directly from the bedrock, or placed inside them, often in front of the burial chambers. By the shaft tombs offering tables could also have been cut out directly from the rock, though it was probably more common that portable offering tables were placed beside them, mostly depending on their date and context within the necropolis.

Even if the necropolis was a liminal area, set apart from the living and referred to as *The Mountain of the Desert Edge*,[36] it was nevertheless frequently visited by mourners, pilgrims and others who carried with them votive offerings. The inner, burial chambers of elite tombs were sealed off, though some were equipped with specific cult chapels, some decorated with reliefs and paintings depicting Egyptian landscapes and human activities, thus constituting versions of the Egyptian cosmos, complete with actions repeated for eternity, transforming the cult chapel into a reflection of real life.[37] Specifically in the case of Asyut, First Intermediate Period tombs have a large hall containing vertical shafts leading to the burial chambers below (e.g. Tomb N12.1).[38] From the Middle Kingdom onwards more rooms were added for specific cults (e.g. Tomb P10.1) as well as a more complex system of shafts which lead to numerous chambers below. The tomb functioned as liminal space centred around the offering table as the essential tool for a ceremony that not only united the world of the living with the one of the deceased, but also served as a vehicle bringing vital forces to deceased ancestors, reviving the entire mortuary space.

Provincial cemeteries throughout Middle Egypt like the one in Asyut, boasted large rock-cut tombs dedicated to their most powerful officials, especially the nomarchs, but also high priests of local cults.

---

32 KAHL 2007: 57. Royal cults were common throughout Egypt. These rulers were venerated in ka-houses along processional routes such as the ones present in Asyut, including the impressive causeway outside the tomb of Djefai-Hapi I. The venerated "saints" at Asyut include Pepy I, Ramesses Meryamun as well as Djefai-Hapi, worshipped from the Second Intermediate Period all the way through the New Kingdom. See KAHL 2012: 163–188.
33 REGULSKI & GOLIA 2018: 50.
34 ZITMAN 2010a: 13.
35 ARNOLD ET AL. 2015: 319.
36 KAHL 2007: 59.
37 HARRINGTON 2015.
38 KAHL 2007: 73–77.

The cultic paraphernalia in such tombs dating back to the First Intermediate Period exhibit a regional style. However, later tombs may often be made in conformity with the royal style of the early 12th Dynasty, mixed in with own stylistic choices and regional influence as is evidenced in the tomb chapel of Djefai- Hapi I.[39]

Deities alluded to on offering tables, as well as other objects, inscriptions and paintings, are numerous and several extend beyond Asyut. Khnum is frequently mentioned, which is not so unusual since his cult may have originated in the neighbouring town of Shutb.[40] The most common deities in Asyut include not only Wepwawet but also Isis, Anubis and Osiris, Amun etc. Local cults also included the veneration of important nomarchs as well as pharaohs, which is also evidenced by the presence of inscribed offering tables as well as steles.[41] Several ka houses and chapels have also been mentioned in texts, being dedicated to local deities such as Pepy I, Ramesses Meryamun and Djefai-Hapi, who were venerated throughout the *New Kingdom*.[42]

Between the *First Intermediate Period* and the 12th Dynasty, the necropolis was separated into a sacred area and until then no quarrying had been carried out within the burial area. However, by the beginning of the 18th Dynasty, the more ancient tombs began to be quarried for stone and new quarries were eventually opened all over the mountain.[43] During the *New Kingdom* it was not uncommon for older tombs to be reused, especially throughout the *Late Period* and into the *Ptolemaic era*. Centuries later, when the ancient religion had largely been forgotten, as well as the language inscribed in tombs and temples, the Coptic communities of Asyut adapted the burial grounds to their specific needs. In addition to burying their dead there, the Copts built monasteries and some of the ancient tombs were transformed into chapels.[44]

3.2 Geological characteristics

The Asyut Necropolis is composed of at least four superimposed series of rock-cut tombs. The first would be the *Old Kingdom* tombs at the top of the cliff. However, activity in the *First Intermediate Period* seems to have been low but not absent, especially since the area has not been explored in sufficient detail to reveal reliable data, as evidenced by the numerous offering tables potentially dating back to this period. In the early *Middle Kingdom* numerous tombs emerged of important officials in the north-western lower cliffs.[45]

The geological properties of the mountain have had a significant effect on the preservation of the rock-cut tombs in the necropolis. The *gebel* is composed of 11 layers, each with several distinct properties within the limestone (Table 1).

Geological Step	Time Period/Featured Tomb	Description of Step
Step 1	Middle Kingdom? – Tombs have been subject to looting and are very damaged due to their easy access from the modern road.	Limestone of roughly 5 m thickness. Area very damaged due to modern destruction and natural erosion. Limestone is light-grey in color, significant karstification.

---

39 Kahl 2007: 9–12.
40 Ibid. 57.
41 DuQuesne 2009: 79.
42 Kahl 2007: 57–58.
43 Kahl 2007: 61–62.
44 Kahl 2007: 102–106; Kahl 2014.
45 Zitman 2010a: 182–183.

Step 2–4	Middle Kingdom Step 2 = Tomb of Djefai-Hapi I "Djefai-Hapi-unity"	Step 2 is described as roughly 15 m thick containing karstified hard limestone and an 8 m thick layer composed of marly limestone with clay liners. These features seem to continue up to Step 4. Limestone light-grey in color with karst holes and fossil features.
Step 5–7	First Intermediate Period, Middle Kingdom Step 6 = Tomb of the Soldiers "Khety-unity"	Hard limestone plains – karst cavern formation decreases in frequency. Fewer or non-existent fossil remains and is lighter in color compared to lower layers.
Step 8	First Intermediate Period, Middle Kingdom Tomb L12.1	Subdivided by 15 cm thick layers of merlons (marl/clay liners). Limestone starts to become coarser since it shows signs of calcification.
Step 9	Presence of numerous small tombs, dates not yet confirmed.	White limestone step with 10 cm thick black (magnesium rich?) karst filling with some traces of alabaster-like structures. Limestone is significantly coarser due to calcification and is therefore more porous in nature.
Step 10 (Step 11 inaccessible)	Presumably early in date, however the site is inaccessible.	Each layer is roughly 8 m thick and include a combination of marl and limestone beds and hard limestone re-emerges after the 7th step.

Table 1: Geological steps of limestone and corresponding time-periods and tombs.
Based on KLEMM & KLEMM 2005 and KAHL 2007: 59–106.

Dietrich and Rosemarie Klemm have studied the numerous chisel marks that are still visible on the tomb walls and used them to date the tombs.[46] The tomb chambers were cut with copper chisels, which before the 18th Dynasty left tracks that were five to eight centimetres long. Up until then the tracks formed chaotic patterns, though from the 18th Dynasty onwards the entrance angles become regular and the chiselled walls present a "fish bone pattern". During the New Kingdom the tracks become longer, generally up to 20 cms, and during Coptic times the tracks have broad entrance angles and are 2.5 cm x 4 cm long.[47]

The characteristics of the limestone and chisel marks existing in the Asyut necropolis may not only be used to identify the age of the tombs, they may also inform about the origin and previous positions of the numerous offering tables found within the perimeters of the necropolis. Several of the preserved offering tables, as well as numerous fragments, have been removed from their original sites, making it hard to date them, as well as it aggravates an interpretation of their use and importance in the mortuary cult.

3.3 The Present State of the Necropolis

While studying an artefact like an offering table originating from Asyut you have to take into account not only how the necropolis where it was found functioned and looked like at the time it was created and used. The site has over time suffered a lot of damage, also evidenced by the poor condition of most tables in the sample. Torrential rains and earthquakes, combined with ruthless plundering and quarrying that occurred already in antiquity and then continued throughout the centuries, have left clefts that continuously damage the tombs, sometimes burying them in rubble. Early ill-advised excavations have contributed to the devastation of the site, even dynamite was used to open-up the tombs.[48] Records kept during earlier excavations are often inadequate or missing all together. Artefacts like offering tables

---

46 KLEMM & KLEMM 2005.
47 Ibid.
48 KAHL 2007: 3.

were carelessly removed, or even thrown away and destroyed while excavators were searching for "more valuable" finds. Findings were haphazardly documented and spread to collections all over the world.[49] Excavations have been numerous.[50] Most important so far have been Charles Palanque's excavations in 1903, unearthing twenty-six tombs, all but five of which were intact.[51] Extraordinary objects from this expedition are housed in the Egyptian Museum of Cairo and the Louvre Museum of Paris. Outside of Egypt, the largest group of artefacts from Asyut is in the Turin Museum.[52] In the course of seven seasons of fieldwork, 1906–1913, the team of Ernesto Schiaparelli uncovered over three thousand artefacts. However, Schiaparelli who worked on the south-eastern portion of the necropolis soon had to leave the western part to be explored by the Englishman David George Hogarth. The British mission lasted only between December 1906 and March 1907 and Hogarth did not publish his findings. He did however compile a detailed fieldwork archive and brought seven hundred or so artefacts to England.[53] In 1913, Ahmed Pasha Kamal excavated in Asyut on behalf of a private collector. Kamal published lists of the recovered items, but his assembled collection was soon dispersed worldwide.[54] An attempt at contextualising finds from these excavations by consulting field notes as well as archival material and artefacts present in museums such as the British Museum and the Museo Egizio in Turin has been made by Zitman in his 2010 publication and by Kahl, Sbriglio, Del Vesco and Trapani in their 2019 publication.[55]

4. The Sample

By observing offering tables, especially *in situ*, and trying to establish their original context within a funerary setting, conclusions may be reached regarding the use and significance they had for the individuals living within the socio-religious realm of Asyut, as well as the role they played in the sacred landscape surrounding them. Most offering tables were placed in tombs, in the vicinity of false doors or statues representing members of the elite. However, few offering tables can now be found *in situ*, most of them are found in museum collections, though the majority are rarely exhibited, mainly due to their size, poor state of conservation, as well as a limited public interest in them. Furthermore, many offering tables are stored without any information whatsoever about their provenance and original context. This is one reason to why a study of Asyuti offering tables is valuable. At least four offering tables directly carved into the bedrock are still in place and may thus reveal something about their original function. A study of these tables as well as 86 others, not found exactly in their original location but with a clear and specific provenance, provides a unique possibility to connect them with a specific, topographical context.

Any analysis of the 90 offering tables presented in this study has so far not been published. The sample consists of four tables still in situ, 48 tables found in the so-called Hogarth Depot in Asyut,[56] 38 tables which context and exact location are described in archaeological reports, and four tables from an unidentified context. Most of the tables are of a similar size, varying between 20–40 cm in width and 15–30 cm in length and almost all of the tables are made out of limestone, which is the most common material used for manufacturing offering tables. Most of the studied offering tables appear to have been cut directly inside the tomb, using the natural limestone bedrock. The varying qualities of the limestone may indicate a table's original location, considering the quite easy definition of the various limestone layers (see Table 1) present in the gebel (mountain) of Asyut. Some offering tables are made of limestone

---

49 ZITMAN 2010a.
50 KAHL 2007: 21–33.
51 CHASSINAT & PALANQUE 1911.
52 Ibid.; KAHL, SBRIGLIO, DEL VESCO & TRAPANI 2019.
53 See RYAN 1988.
54 KAHL 2007: 29.
55 ZITMAN 2010a; KAHL, SBRIGLIO, DEL VESCO & TRAPANI 2019.
56 KILIAN 2012: 196–201; CzyŻEWKA-ZALEWSKA 2015: 104–116.

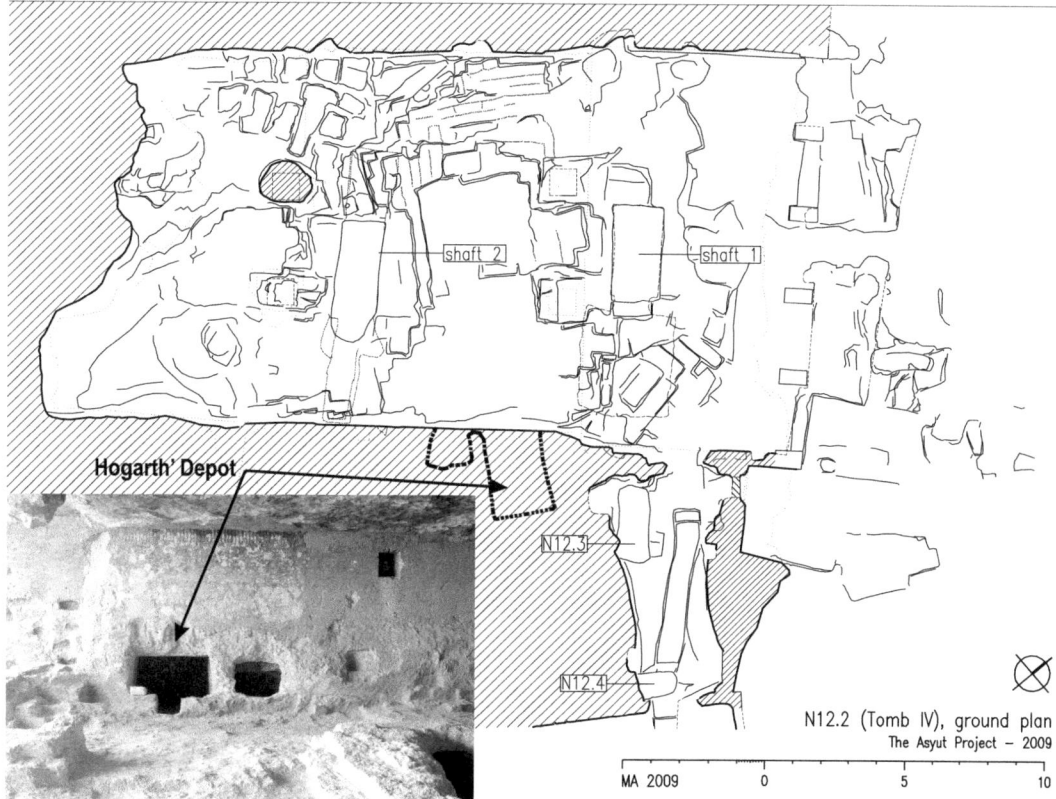

Fig. 1: Plan of tomb N12.2 (Tomb IV) and the location of the so-called "Hogarth's Depot"
(from: Kahl et al. 2015: 104, Fig. 1).

not found in this place. They have a much whiter hue and a more compact density than the limestone found on the gebel. Furthermore, does the absence of chisel marks on their bases indicate that they were free-standing and commissioned elsewhere than in the necropolis.

4.1 Context Typology

Most of the analysed offering tables originate from Steps 5–7 (see Table 1), which also include the four offering tables still *in situ*. Most offering tables have been found inside two niches cut into the southern wall in Tomb IV, which did not belong to its original design. These niches contained mixed artefacts from various time periods, deposited there by earlier excavators of the site.[57] 38 of the 90 analysed offering tables derive from this deposit, the so-called *Hogarth Depot*. In spite of the originally "jumbled" state of this site, it is nevertheless possible to make some conclusions about the origin of the offering tables found there (Fig. 1). According to their fixture, offering tables may be described as:

Fixed: Meaning that the table was carved directly from the limestone bedrock of the tomb (see examples in N11.1; Fig. 5) indicated by their irregular bases and sides as well as the presence of large, irregular chisel marks (e.g. S04/47; Figs. 2–3). Most offering tables have been removed either at an early stage, or by archaeologists later on. The approximate time for their removal may be indicated by chisel marks. These offering tables are often placed close to or directly above tomb shafts and/or inside the tombs. Usually strategically placed by the entrance to the burial chamber, with their spout facing the shaft, or canal, entering the chamber. They were assumedly used during official ceremonies performed by priests.

57 Kilian 2012: 196–201.

Fitted: These offering tables may be large or small, though with sloping edges and a smoothened base, indicating that they have been fitted into another kind of structure (e.g. S05/408, S04/168, S12/35, etc., also see Tor S.09178). Chisel marks on the sides and bottom are regular and smoothened. These offering tables are often "monumental" and placed in front of ka statues or stelae in the tombs of wealthy or influential people.

Handheld: Most such offering tables may be classified as votive offerings due to their size and the fact that they are often made of materials other than limestone, such as alabaster (e.g. S09/6, etc., also see Leiden AP 82. For an example of an amulet see MM10006). Such tables may also be made of pottery and are accordingly easy to transport. The stone tables and/or basins are often quite elaborate, and some have apparently been made in a workshop, commissioned on demand to be placed in a public area as offerings presented to the deceased by her/his relatives. Usually it is impossible to place these offering tables within a specific context.

Six of the 90 tables can be considered as having been fitted. Twenty-eight of the tables may be classified as handheld. Examples of such tables are those with remnants of four legs, or with a flat base. Such offering tables are not as heavy or large as those which are fitted or fixed. Offering tables classified as "votive offerings" are significantly smaller than regular tables, include miniature tables in the shape of amulets and/or small models. The sample contains one offering basin made of calzite-alabaster, which may be classified either as handheld or fitted.

Twenty-one of the tables show indications of having been painted, though only three of them have with all certainty been painted, preserving red, and blue/black pigmentation. Without microscopic analysis it cannot be established whether the others have been painted, their reddish hue may have been caused by the use of red limestone which occurs naturally within the necropolis.

4.2 Provenance

As indicated above, provenance is a complicated matter in archaeological contexts. However, since most offering tables found in the Asyut necropolis date back from the First Intermediate Period and onwards, as well as their original location may be considered as fairly assured their origin may at least be assumed to have been Middle Egypt. Alexander Ilin-Tomich assumes that the manufacture of Asyut may have three basic origins:[58]

Centralised production meaning that offering tables have been produced at prestigious workshops in other places than Asyut, where they have been purchased and brought to the Asyut necropolis by private buyers, or their contractors. In the case of Asyut, comparisons of certain characteristics may indicate that such a manufacturing centre could have been Abydos.

Localised production. Asyut offering tables produced in local workshops, supported by local patrons and applying local/regional design.

Mobile production. Itinerant artists originating from different areas were hired to construct tombs and the various artefacts used in mortuary rituals, not the least offering tables.

By comparing objects from a large sample of stone offering tables found in Asyut, Ilin-Tomich has been able to identify artisans from various local workshops. Originally these artisans seem to have been exclusively inspired by local traditions. However, during the Middle Kingdom new features emerged among the products of these workshops. According to Ilin-Tomich a Theban style was from then on incorporated into the design of most trays, as well as offering tables, indicating that the artisans were copying iconography and styles preferred by Theban artists.[59] Furthermore, Ilin-Tomich assumed that several of the portable offering tables found in Asyut were manufactured in other places, most probably

---

58 Ilin-Tomich 2018a: 82.
59 Ibid. 92.

Fig. 2: Surface of offering table S04/47 (photo: Fritz Barthel 2018; © The Asyut Project).

Fig. 3: Side-view of the offering table S04/47 showing irregular and prominent chisel marks
across the surface. Photograph by author 2018.

and commonly in Herakleopolis.[60] Ilin-Tomich also states that there are few preserved offering tables
from the 11th Dynasty,[61] though I am inclined to disagree. There is significantly more varieties in the
shape and form of offering trays and tables emanating from the Middle Kingdom, such as soul houses,
pottery offering trays, as well as other votive offerings, which even if they earlier have not been labelled
as *offering plates/tables*, nevertheless may have served the same purpose as utensils that exclusively have
been denominated as *offering plates/tables*. Differences in shapes and aspects may have been due to the
rise of new "personal" styles and tastes, as well as an adaption to styles from other areas. Asyut was a
melting pot of diverse influences.

---

60 Herakleopolitan workshops were during the 9th–10th Dynasties (First Intermediate Period), important producers of offering tables, as indicated by such tables found in Qubbet el-Hawa, Mo'alla, Dendera, Akhmin, Bersheh, Beni Hasan,
Saqqara, Abusir, Herakleopolis, and Sedment. Ilin-Tomich 2018b: 58–87; own observations in research.
61 Ilin-Tomich 2018b: 59.

There appear to have been several workshops in Asyut producing grave goods and cutting tombs. Marcel Zitman has pointed out that inscriptions in the coffins, i.e. offering formulae and names, are similar to those formulae inscribed on some offering tables, something that may indicate that several coffins and offering tables were manufactured by the same workshop.[62] Offering tables were made from local limestone, after all – the entire *gebel* that overshadows the town was created by limestone, the preferred material for laymen tombs. Comparing Asyuti offering tables with those produced in other places Ilin-Tomich found that the execution and iconography of some offering tables found in Asyut were excellently done, but that the inscriptions were often clumsily executed, something he interpreted as if the tables had been purchased from workshops in other towns, while the inscriptions had been added and custom-made in Asyut.[63] Furthermore, the iconography on some offering tables had been adapted to Asyut preferences. For example, *ḥs.t* vases recurrent on offering plates/tables from other places in Asyut have been replaced by tilted *ḥs.t* vases. Depictions of such vases on offering trays and tables may indicate local, religious/funerary rituals.[64] It is a well-known fact that ancient Egyptian religious practices and beliefs differed quite a lot from one place to another. Both Ilin-Tomich and Zitman indicate that Asyut constituted an eclectic, but nevertheless highly active, unique and innovative artistic environment, receiving influences from both local and regional sources.

4.3 Materials

As mentioned above, offering tables were generally made of limestone, which is easily carved as well as readily available. However, more valuable, prestigious, or monumental offering tables, generally found in mortuary temple contexts, may be made of more exquisite limestone, alabaster, granite, basalt, etc. According to previous research, less valuable materials may include sandstone and even coarse ware. Such materials are often porous and not impermeable, a fact which may indicate specific ritual functions.[65]

As expected, the most common limestone used for the analysed offering tables was of a *marly* kind, i.e. slightly dense, but also quite fine, flaky and easily subject to wear. 38 % of the analysed offering tables are made of material coinciding with layers 5–7 (see Table 1). This is also where the four offering tables still *in situ* can be found. More than half of the offering tables made of this particular material are of the *fixed* type, while a third of the offering tables made of this type of limestone can be classified as *handheld*. This is not uncommon in other sites as well, since most offering tables are actually made from marly limestone.[66]

As indicated by Table 2 below, all offering tables made from dense limestone can be classified as *handheld*, indicating that they were **manufactured** from limestone not quarried in, or in vicinity of the necropolis, but commissioned from workshops situated elsewhere (see Chart 1). However, the difference between dense limestone and the marly kind is quite insignificant and to be quite sure about the different nature of limestone used to manufacture offering tables petrographic analysis has to be applied.[67]

---

62 Zitman 2010a: 245–343.

63 Ilin-Tomich 2018a: 92.

64 Ibid. 83–84. *ḥs.t* vases are depicted as spilling a stream of liquid through an external spout structure, a ritual carried out by priests within a funerary setting. *Ḥs.t* vases are occasionally depicted together with Wepwawet and this unique iconography may thus allude to local rituals. Possibly a local variant of the *Opening of the Mouth* ceremony, since *ḥs.t* vases played an important role in this ritual.

65 Porous, absorbing materials, especially sandstone, might be assumed to preserve the force of water, since the moisture remains in the stone. A material like steatite, soapstone, furthermore, erodes easily and water flowing across it could be considered to release and carry with it "magic" force previously absorbed through the offering table's contagious quality. See Aston et al. 2000.

66 Based on own research.

67 Aston et al. 2000: 40–44.

Type of Limestone/Material	Fixed	Fitted	Handheld	Undetermined	TOTAL	Percentages
Dense/Marly	0	0	7	0	7	7.8%
Flaky/Marly	35	5	19	3	62	68.9%
Porous	16	0	2	0	18	20%
Striped/Magnesium Fillings	1	0	0	0	1	1.1%
Other	1	1	0	0	2	2.2%
TOTAL	53	6	28	3	90	

Table 2: Classification of offering tables in the sample according to dimensions and material.

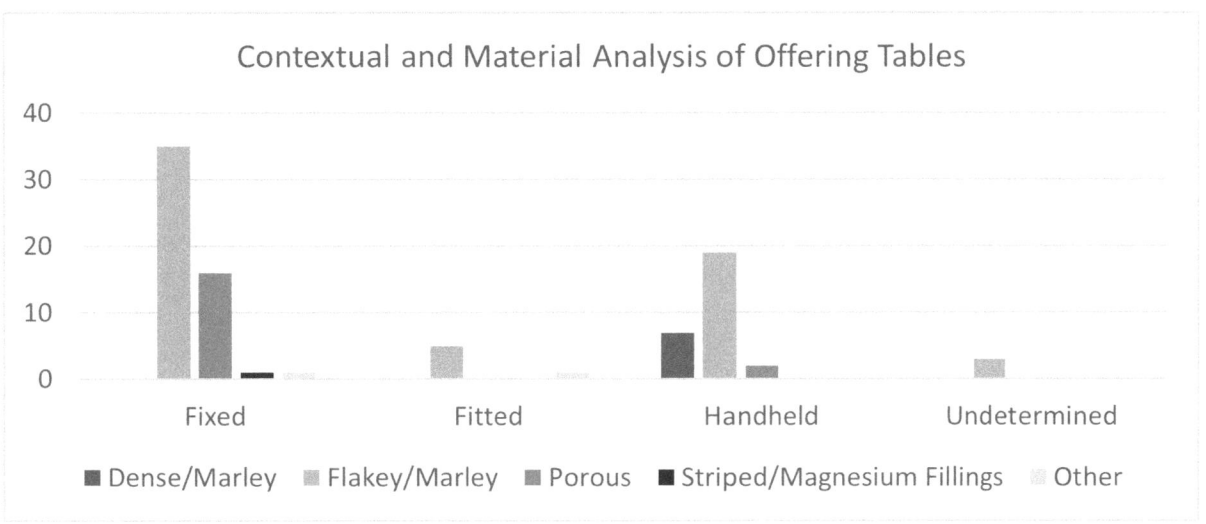

Chart 1: Classification of offering tables in the sample according to dimensions and material.

4.4 Iconography

55 tables out of the 90 in the sample have a central *ḥtp* sign in raised relief (see Chart 2). It is the most common feature on offering tables. The sign is first evidenced in predynastic tombs and may be considered in connection to offerings, such as the *šꜥ*-shaped bread, placed on reed mats next to the deceased, it could then be considered as an abstract rendering of the ritual.[68] Some stone offering tables are inscribed with, or even have the shape of the *ḥtp* sign, explained to mean "to be satiated" or "offering".[69] This sign may thus be considered as making the table a tool for offering life-giving liquids to the deceased, during the Old Kingdom the Pharaoh in his semblance of Osiris, a connection later on transferred to deceased laymen as well. The sanctified water might thus have been considered as a reference of the efflux of Osiris, which within the Nile water brings rejuvenation to the land.

The other two most common features of the Asyuti tables are *ḥs.t* vases (eight tables) and irrigation fields (six tables). Followed by bovine head/leg (three tables) and round bread, which is actually generally common on offering tables, though not so in Asyut (three tables).[70] The most prominent connotation

---

[68] Bolshakov 2001; Taylor 2001.

[69] Betrò 2010: 56. ⬚ *ḥtp* sign – this triliteral sign originates from the predynastic offering ritual of placing loaves of bread and other victuals on a reed mat in front of the deceased within grave-pits. Bolshakov 2001; Taylor 2001.

[70] Ilin-Tomich who analysed another sample from Asyut than the one I have investigated, mainly offering tables at important museum collections, states that triangular bread is more common than round bread in Asyuti iconography and this appears to be a unique feature for depictions of offerings among Asyuti artisans. Ilin-Tomich 2018a: 89.

apparent on the offering tables is water management – basins and/or canals leading to an external spout structure. The offering tables *in situ* illustrate how the ceremony of filling them with water may have functioned – water was poured over the *ḥtp* sign and then flowed towards the basins which were filled up to the brim, after which the water was conducted by the small, drainage canals until it reached the spout and flowed down into the burial chamber, or tomb shaft.

This paper deals exclusively with stone offering tables, though the iconography is similar to the one found on pottery offering trays, which have been studied in more detail by Andrea Kilian. Pottery offering trays contain canals, basins, oxen, bread, vegetables, etc. – similar to the design of stone offering tables. Differences are in the depiction of *ḥs.t* vases as well as the *ḥtp* and pottery trays do not usually have inscriptions.[71] They all have a rim, and some kind of spout such as a drainage hole. The pottery trays are not mass produced and most of them do apparently not come from a workshop, since no tray is similar to another, all have minor differences as well as in the fabric itself.[72]

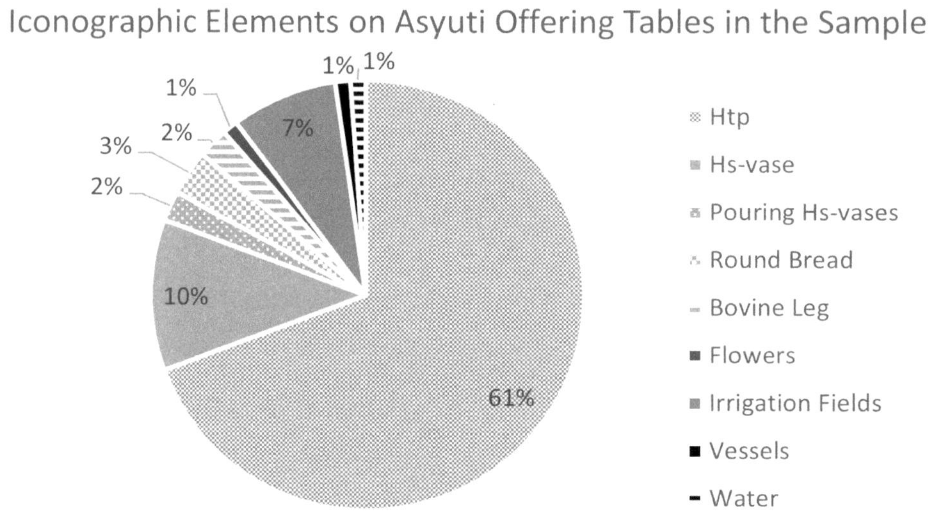

Chart 2: Percentages of the main iconographic elements present on Asyuti offering tables in the Sample.

5. Categorisation

The 90 offering tables in the sample may be classified in 6 general types and 14 sub-types as illustrated by these sketches (Table 3). Type 7 is classified as non-identifiable mostly because of the poor condition of the table or if it is too fragmented.

---

71 For an example of an offering tray with an inscription of an offering formula from Qubbet el-Hawa see KILIAN 2016: 174.
72 KILIAN 2012: 109.

Type Description	Hölzl Categorisation, Dating	Similar Tables in Museums
Type 1: A-F Rectangular/square shaped with two rectangular basins on either side of a central *ḥtp* sign in raised relief. Each basin has a small, often diagonal, canal oriented towards the centre and outer edge of the table. If not *in situ* it often has irregular edges and base indicating that it was originally fixed.	Typ B+C: Opfertafeln mit Becken und Napfkuchen bzw. *ḥtp*-Zeichen – Typen des Alten Reiches (p. 23) Typ B+C: Opfertafeln mit Becken und Napfkuchen bzw. *ḥtp*-Zeichen – Typen des Mittleren Reiches (p. 34) FIP/early MK	BM EA 973 Tor. S14939 (Tor-Provv. 0314) RMO LX15 RMO F1901/F1.63 MM NME047 Hölzl Examples: OK = Cairo CG 1355, Cairo CG 1335, Cairo CG 1363, Louvre D70 MK = Tor N.22012, Tor N.22014, Tor N.22011, Tor N. 22024
Type 2: G Rectangular shaped with a sunken area at one end containing a *ḥtp* flanked by two large *ḥs.t* vases with spouts facing inwards, with streams of liquid flowing to the external spout structure, both creating a canal extending from the *ḥtp* at one end to the spout structure. Edges are often smoothened outwards to a certain extent, then become irregular as well as the base, something which indicates that the table was originally fixed.	Typ B+C: Opfertafeln mit Becken und Napfkuchen bzw. *ḥtp*-Zeichen – Typen des Mittleren Reiches (p. 34) Early MK	BM EA 46611 (pottery offering tray) MM10006 Tor S.14939 – offering tables of Hetepneb Hölzl Examples are similar to the previously described Type 1 (see above)
Type 3: H, I Rectangular shaped offering basin/table with two rectangular sloping-edged basins which may have contained organic residue (to be analyzed further). The edges and base are irregular, indicating it was originally fixed.	Typ B2: Opfertafeln mit Becken – Typen des Alten Reiches (p. 17–18) Late OK	Hölzl Examples: OK = Cairo CG 1334, AR-8, Cairo CG 1326, Cairo CG 1367
Type 4: J, K Rectangular/square shaped with a central raised area which may contain a *ḥtp* in raised relief. The table also has an external spout structure containing a canal which flows from around the raised area to the end of the spout. The sides of the table may be sloping to a certain extent, but the rest is highly irregular indicating that the tables may have been fixed.	Typ C2: Opfertafeln mit Darstellungen des Napfkuchens oder *ḥtp*-Zeichens – Typen des Mittleren Reiches (pp. 32) MK	Hölzl Examples: MK = Cairo CG 23063, Cairo CG 23109

Table 3: Categorisation of the offering tables present in the sample according to certain typologies identified using Hölzl's typology charts, according to time-periods (based on HÖLZL 2002: 9–51).

Type Description	Hölzl Categorisation, Dating	Similar Tables in Museums
Type 5: L Rectangular/square shaped with a geometric design alluding to irrigation fields. The table contains a t-shaped sunken area at the top usually incorporating a *ḥtp* sign in raised relief. A canal connects the sunken area to a central horizontal basin and then all the way down to the external spout structure. On either side of the sunken area and central basin are two vertical rectangular basins, followed by a large horizontal area divided into two basins via an intersecting canal. The interlinking canals and varied-sized basins with sloping edges allude to the canal systems and basins present even in modern-day Egyptian irrigation fields. The edges and base of such tables are smoothened, and chisel marks are faintly visible. The edges are often slanted creating a "floating effect" for the table. They may have been handheld or fitted.	Typ B+C: Opfertafeln mit Becken und Napfkuchen bzw. *ḥtp*-Zeichen – Typen des Mittleren Reiches (p. 37). MK	BM EA 990 Tor S.09178 Tor S.09176 Tor S.09177 Hölzl Examples: MK = Leiden AP 82, Tor N. 22022, Tor CG 23068, Tor CG 23028
Type 6: M, N Rectangular/square shaped table/basin which may have a long external spout structure containing a canal extending from a central sloping-edged basin inside a sunken area to the end of the spout. There may be depictions of offerings in raised relief in the sunken area. The edges and base have all been smoothened and the chisel marks are hardly visible indicating that the offering table was handheld.	Typ B1 und B2: Einzelne Kultbecken (Typ B1) oder Opfertafeln mit Becken (Typ B2), Opfertafeln mit Becken und Napfkuchen bzw. *ḥtp*-Zeichen (Typ B+C) – Typen des Neuen Reiches Late MK/early NK	Hölzl Examples: NK = Tor CG 23086, NR-10, Tor CG 23084
Type 7: Undetermined These tables are too worn or fragmented. Most fragmented tables in this category have smoothened bases and edges and are small in size, which may indicate that they were handheld and put in precarious areas which may explain why they are so fragmented – votive offerings or commissioned tables – they present inscriptions, paint and elaborate depictions of offerings.		

Table 3 continued: Categorisation of the offering tables present in the sample according to certain typologies identified using Hölzl's typology charts, according to time-periods (based on HÖLZL 2002: 9–51).

What is interesting to note here is that the most frequent type is Type 1, specifically Type A which is mostly composed of fixed offering tables (see Chart 3). The types which are mostly handheld are those which are more elaborate in nature such as Type 5 which is composed of tables with an irrigation fields design. They are also the most numerous in the unidentified field. This must be due to their archaeological context since they could be easily moved and therefore damaged.

Types 1 and 3, which are most common, can be dated back to the First Intermediate Period or even earlier, especially Type 3, if based on design. What is interesting is that the design is very similar to that of offering tables found in Saqqara, which also date back to the First Intermediate Period[73], perhaps alluding to external and earlier influences from the north.

---

73 LEGROS 2008: 241, fig. 6 and 7 illustrate tables with similar typological features present on most tables dating back to the FIP in the sample from Asyut. The offering tables present in Legros' study allude specifically to the mid–late half of the

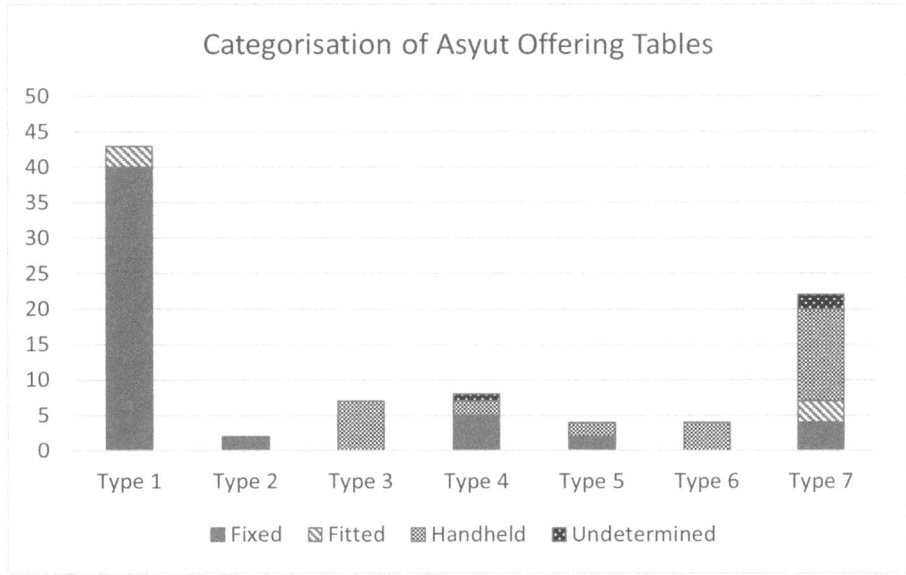

Chart 3: Numbers of offering tables/basins present in each typology and fixture.

Types 2, 4 and 5 can be dated back to the Middle Kingdom, specifically 12th Dynasty, while Type 6 may even be dated to the early New Kingdom, based on the sloping edged basins as well as the elaborate offerings present on some tables. I assume most of these tables date back to the First Intermediate Period and the Middle Kingdom, in accordance with the classification charts published in Hölzl's 2002 publication. The more elaborate ones may have been manufactured somewhat later. Generally speaking, few offering tables can be dated back to the Old Kingdom.

Apart from the offering tables studied at Asyut and the Antiquities Magazine at Shutb, up until now in my research I have examined two Asyut tables in the British Museum (EA973, EA990), five in Turin (S14939, S09178, S09176, S09177, S09175) and one in Medelhavsmuseet, Stockholm (MM10006). About 24 stone offering tables are documented by Zitman,[74] 18 were recorded in connection with Hogarth's excavations[75] (including ES973-437, ES976-440, ES978-442 at the British Museum), three are described in Schiaparelli's listings[76], two are recorded by Chassinat & Palanque (Boston BMFA 04.1891 and CPA 50-51), and another has been identified from the Khashaba collection now in Berlin.[77] As seen in Table 3, they are just a few examples which can be categorised and compared to the unpublished offering tables in the sample. Unfortunately, only six offering tables out of the 90 are inscribed and are all fragments of larger offering tables with only parts of the general offering formula and obscure names.

FIP. It is important to note that the tables included in Type 1 include the two tables in tomb N11.1, which can be dated to early–mid FIP.

74 Zitman 2010a: 264–279.

75 The offering tables recorded by Hogarth and listed in the Zitman 2010 publication can even be associated to specific tombs accompanied by a plan. Unfortunately, most of the Hogarth tombs have not been identified, however, it may be interesting to note that 19 offering trays were also recorded by Hogarth and that out of the tombs containing offering tables, only seven contained only stone offering tables, and five contexts contained both. Ibid. 264–279.

76 The three tables are at the Museo Egizio in Turin, two of which Zitman has directly associated to coffins: Tor. Suppl. 14939 joins with coffin 14462 of a male Ḥtp-nb(=i) and Tor. Suppl. 8931-9187 joins with S15Tor coffin of Pꜣ Ibid. 264–279.

77 The offering table of Šmsw dating back to the Middle Kingdom. Kamal 1916: 95–96 (no. 111).

6. Placement of Offering Tables

In general terms, most offering tables found *in situ* in ancient Egyptian funerary contexts are generally placed in tomb courtyards, inside the main offering chapel beneath the *ka* statue of the deceased, or by a false door, depending on their time-period and function. They also tend to be placed in the proximity of offering lists, as well as painted offering scenes including the deceased.

Offering tables served as a means of communication with deceased ancestors and the divine realm. As cultic objects, they were at the very centre of attention during rituals and their specific aspects may have influenced their placement within a royal funerary temple, or in the badly lit intimacy of a private tomb chapel.[78] Since pouring of water over them was an essential part of the ceremony most offering tables are equipped with a spout from which the water came forth to be collected after flowing across the "energizing" surface of the tables and poured into the tombs, bringing nourishment and force to the inhabitants of another realm.[79]

The size, shape, material and placement of offering tables indicated the intentions and social status of their users. Offering rituals performed in the vicinity of burial chambers and tombs were generally separated from the actual burial chamber by a wall and/or a shaft and were in some cases later even replaced by symbolic practices and rituals carried out in separate offering chapels.[80] Nutrition for the dead was offered by family members, or in the case of the royal funerary/elite cult by priests (*ḥmw-kꜣ*).[81] They entered accessible areas of the tomb, or nearby chapels and used the offering tables in combination with rituals activating depictions of offering lists and following instructions that were depicted and/or written on the walls.[82]

At Asyut, it appears as if 66 of the analysed offering tables (73 %) were found inside, or close to, shafts (see Chart 4). However, 48 of these offering tables had been disposed of in *Hogarth's Depot* (see Fig. 1). Only one out of the 90 analysed tables was found inside a burial chamber, rather than in the forecourt of a tomb, or near a shaft. Nevertheless, it is nearly impossible to provide these offering tables with a reliable context, unless they had been directly cut out of the bedrock and left there, as is the case with only four of the tables (see Figs. 4–7).

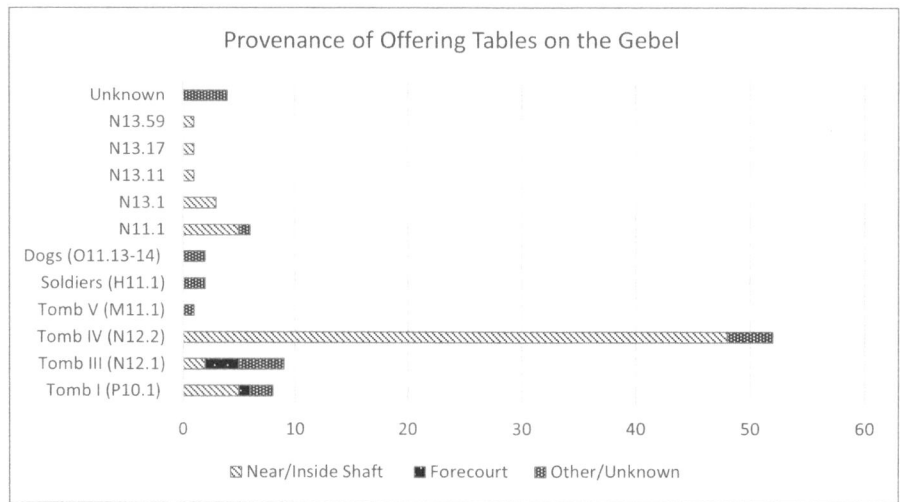

Chart 4: Provenance/ archaeological context of offering tables present in the sample.

---

78 HARRINGTON 2015.

79 Similar ritual processes involving the different phases of water which occur in the *Opening of the Mouth Ceremony* as described in ROTH 1993 as well as the act of planting grain seeds in wooden Osiris Mummy effigies. As you would water the seeds, the grain would grow, just as the inundation would cause the banks of the Nile to overflow with produce. CENTRONE 2005.

80 HARRINGTON 2015, 138.

81 See EATON 2013; CAUVILLE 2012.

82 TAYLOR 2001: 175; STRUDWICK 2005: 270.

Fig. 4: Offering table at one of the shafts on step 7 (photo: Fritz Barthel 2018; © The Asyut Project).

Fig. 5: Two offering tables (Cat. 81, 82) positioned by shafts 5 and 6, one of which is facing one of the entrances to tomb N11.1, Gebel Asyut (photo: Fritz Barthel 2018; © The Asyut Project).

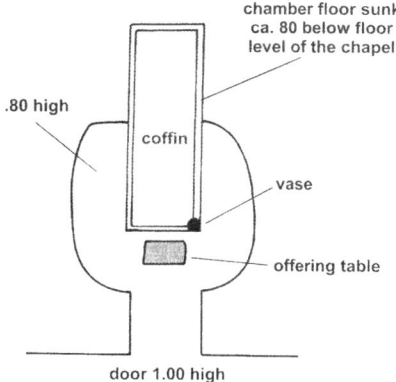

Fig. 6: Plan of Hogarth Tomb 21, now lost. This is described as a small tomb dating back to the late MK with a single chamber containing a coffin and an offering table inside the burial chamber (after Zitman 2010b: Pl. 31).

It is difficult to exactly locate the offering tables found in Hogarth's depot to the tombs where they were originally located. Hogarth's notes are often too vague, though thanks to Zitman's investigations of notes and sketches and research within the site most of them can be connected to specific tombs and it has even been possible to find where in the chambers they have been placed. Nevertheless, the location of the tombs is now unknown.

Schiaparelli's generally too vague notes nevertheless mention that four offering tables, now in the Turin Museum (Tor. Suppl. 8142–8145), were found in front of the First Intermediate Period tombs of Khety I and Khety II, though without a context and it has so far been impossible to establish their exact placement.[83] These offering tables were probably all cut directly from the bedrock and they were thus an essential part of the architecture of the entire tomb structure. In tomb N11.1, two tables can still be found *in situ* (see Fig. 5). Each of them are positioned over a shaft leading into a burial chamber below. Both tables are orientated towards the shaft itself. One of the tables (Cat. 81) is positioned over shaft 6 which may have directly faced the original main entrance/forecourt to the tomb. Tomb N11.1, however, has a very particular design and is still under investigation.[84] Table Cat. 80, positioned near shaft 5 is orientated towards another chamber and potential secondary entrance to the north-east. Nonetheless, both tables are facing liminal areas within the tomb structure. A large number of the Asyut tombs date back to the FIP onwards and usually contain a large shaft at the entrance and several other shafts inside (although this is not always the case – cf. Tomb III). These shafts all lead to burial chambers below.[85]

It is also important to note that from the First Intermediate Period onwards smaller offering tables have been found inside the burial chamber near the deceased (see Fig. 6). This may be the case for most of the pottery offering tables as well as smaller votive-sized stone offering tables. Kilian does in her analyses of pottery tables found in Asyut mention that several of them have been found in the vicinity of the corpse's head.[86] It is possible that there is a relation between the iconography and placement of such handheld offering trays/tables and the iconography and placement of the fixed offering tables in Asyut. They may be an indication of a specific mortuary ritual, like the one of the *Opening of the Mouth* ceremony, as will be discussed later.

Most handheld offering tables are either from a disturbed context or found along a causeway/forecourt, with the exception of a large fixed offering table in front of Tomb III[87] (see Fig. 7). Out of 23, only two were found in the vicinity of a shaft. This may indicate their use as a moveable cultic object, perhaps placed in front of statues and/or steles along the causeway or in public areas such as the forecourt, while fitted or more likely fixed tables were used for official funerary rituals performed directly over or by the burial chamber.

---

83 Zitman 2010b: 120. Kahl, Sbriglio, Del Vesco & Trapani 2019: 75–77, 284.

84 Cf. Kilian 2019: 12–14, 239–243.

85 It is important to note that there is always a level of uncertainty whilst dating the tombs at Asyut, not only due to their poor preservation but also since a significant amount of data is missing whilst observing smaller tombs such as those observed by early excavators.

86 Kilian 2012: 110. As stated in the Ryan 1988 publication as well as in Zitman 2010 discussed previously, both stone and pottery offering tables have been found in the same tomb, although in different archaeological contexts. As stated by Kilian, offering trays were placed in the burial chamber while offering tables were placed in the offering chapel or in the forecourts, possibly for the same ritual but in different scenarios and for different audiences.

87 Kahl 2012: 186–187, Pl. 19; Kahl 2016: xxii.

Fig. 7: Large fixed offering table (Cat. 79) in the forecourt of Tomb III, which may date back to the New Kingdom and then altered in the Greco-Roman period as evidenced by the presence of red mortar. Photograph by author 2018.

7. A Link Between the Realm of the Dead and that of the Living

As suggested by Regina Hölzl,[88] even though it is not explicitly outlined in ancient Egyptian sacred texts, offering tables may have played a major role in almost all ancient Egyptian rituals, expressed initially as part of an offering ritual and then as a more abstract libation ritual. They appear to have been at the very centre of the liminal space between the living and the dead constituted by an ancient Egyptian tomb.

7.1 The ritual landscape and water ritual

Throughout my research on offering tables, one major theme which reoccurred was the relationship they have with their surrounding ritual landscape. The design of offering tables may reflect architectural as well as the natural elements in their surroundings. This is evidenced by their semblance to irrigation fields as well as their direct association to objects/fixtures found within tombs such as steles, false doors and the ritual texts inscribed on the walls or even within the tomb itself. Rituals centred around an offering table were enacted within a liminal space, a *twilight zone* between the profane world of the living and a sacral world of dead. An Asyut tomb, with its burial chamber and forecourt/chapel was constructed with the inclusion of the offering table in the ground plan, and its placement and entire design were

88 Hölzl 2002: 159–161.

Fig. 8 (left): Offering table (Cat. 81) above shaft 6 in Tomb N11.1. One of the basins has been filled with water, illustrating how the water flows from the table down a canal to the shaft below. Photograph by author 2018.
Fig. 9 (right): Offering Table S09/6 with an "irrigation fields" design corresponding to Type 5
(photo: Fritz Barthel 2018; © The Asyut Project).

Fig. 10: Filled irrigation fields outside the village of Sa el-Hagar in the Delta Region. Photograph by author 2018.

thoroughly characterized by its function as a link between the living and the dead and as a tool which with the help of flowing water transferred vital force into the realm of the dead.

The action of pouring liquids over the table covered in depictions of offerings in raised relief, as well as canals and basins was all done as an activation process. To get an impression of the ritual proceedings and their mimicking of real life it may be illuminating to compare them to techniques still used in Egyptian agriculture, where fields are flooded and separated by canals, similar to the imagery upon and the processes indicated by offering tables (see Figs. 9–10). Like the surface of an offering table a field is filled with water and then drained after the water has soaked the ground. Water acted as a courier between the spheres of the living and the dead. The offering table was thus designed in such a manner that its surface, with depictions of canals and basins, water symbols, vegetation, offerings, as well as symbols of life and fertility, like the *ḥtp* sign, was believed to be able to empower the water that was poured over it. Endowing it with a life-giving force, just like the Nile water and Osiris's efflux. The offering table was placed so the vitalized water through a shaft could reach the abode of the dead person, at the same time as the participants in the ritual were enabled to witness how the water reached the underworld (see Fig. 8). The area of the dead was blocked from the one of the living by a wall, or closed, false door, while the offering table was placed in an intermediate, liminal space between these two worlds.[89]

7.2 A link to the Opening of the Mouth ritual[90]

The offering table thus served as a utensil supporting a *death cult* in the sense that it was intended to transform an individual from being alive into being deceased person. From being a living member of well-defined social existence and become a dead being endowed with the status and actions necessary to exist in the otherworld, the *Duat*. This transformation was achieved through the *Opening of the Mouth* ceremony in which the offering table may have had a decisive role. Furthermore, the offering table was also essential for an *ancestor cult,* in which all actions concerned the relationship between the deceased and the survivors.[91]

The *Opening of the Mouth* ceremony was a ritual performed on a mummy and/or statue in order to animate it and make it functional by restoring all its essential parts. The utensils probably used in the ceremony and depicted in sacred texts, as well as in the imagery present on some offering tables and tomb walls include an *adze*, an ax with the cutting-edge perpendicular to the handle, a censer, a blade, as well as a calf's leg. Other utensils present at the ceremony are *ḥs.t* vases, a copper sieve, copper offering tables, and several miniature containers. The "miniature containers" could probably be the pottery offering trays and miniature offering tables that often have been found inside burial chambers, rather than in the offering chapels or courtyards. As mentioned above, Andrea Kilian described how pottery trays have been found by the heads of mummies in Asyut, just as they have been found in similar rock-cut tombs in near-by Deir el-Bersha (Fig. 11, 12). Harco Willems states that mouth opening rituals were carried out beside the corpse in the course of a funeral, though they could also be staged in other places in different contexts, like commemoration ceremonies in tomb forecourts.[92] This might partly explain the permanence of fixed offering tables by tomb shafts and the fact that they often are unchiselled with symbolic signs probably connected with the *Opening of the Mouth* ceremony. This may be a later development, as evidenced by a change in the dimensions and designs of offering tables from the First Intermediate Period to the early Middle Kingdom onwards.

---

89 Willems 2016: 80.
90 To be further discussed in the upcoming thesis.
91 Fitzenreiter 1994: 74.
92 Willems 2016: 168.

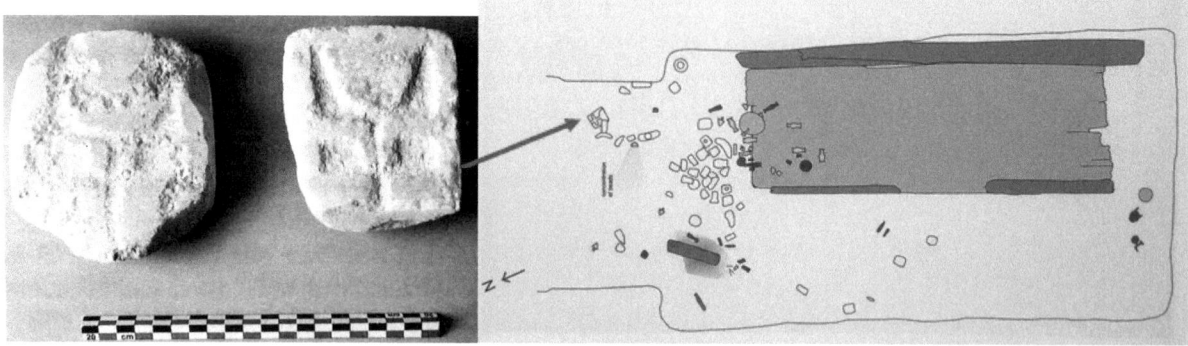

Fig. 11 (left): Two miniature alabaster offering tables (after Willems 2016: 163, Abb 13).
Fig. 12 (right): Spatial distribution of funerary finds within the burial chamber of Djehutinacht I(?) at Deir el Bersha. The objects in white are made of calcite-alabaster and include utensils commonly used in the *Opening of the Mouth* ceremony including two miniature offering tables (Fig. 12, left; Fig. 11; after Willems 2016: 148, Abb. 5).

Most of the analysed offering tables found in Asyut do not exhibit the wealth of symbols and depictions of victuals and other paraphernalia as offering tables that have been found in other sites, at least the ones studied in this sample. However, they often depict canals and basins indicating the life-providing flow of the Nile water across agricultural plains, and most of them also depict *ḥtp* signs, indicating the nourishment of the deceased. By the Middle Kingdom, the *Opening of the Mouth* ceremony appears to have been a funerary, "nourishment" ritual, occurring repeatedly and performed in front of, or as in Asyut, above the burial chamber, probably using the offering table.[93] It is also interesting to note that similar offering tables dating back to the First Intermediate Period are similar in placement and design have been found in Saqqara as stated earlier. The Asyuti tables then resemble the Middle Kingdom offering tables found by Willems inside the burial chamber but are smaller and possibly votive offerings, something that may be assumed by their material (see Fig. 11, 12). Their design, however, is almost identical to the Asyuti First Intermediate Period and later Middle Kingdom offering tables (Fig. 13). We are perhaps looking at the evolvement of funerary ritual, expressed in numerous ways. In the Middle Kingdom, the Asyuti tables begin to be similar to southern styles, such as the irrigation fields design. Although more work is needed in trying to interpret the exact funerary function of offering tables and their significance within the funerary cult, it is nevertheless interesting to note that these utensils may have been in more frequent use than previously believed. Although these objects vary significantly in design, material, size, etc., they may be expressions of the same ritual process, only expressed in different ways and used in different contexts. This may be the basis for future research on this specific series of ritual utensil.

7.3 The Liminal Landscape of Asyut

The offering tables at Asyut provide insight into the dynamics of ancient Egyptian funerary ritual, especially whilst considering their social context and surrounding landscape. The landscape of Asyut is dramatic and liminal, a contrast between extremes. Barren mountains rising above the fertile plains and the life-giving, intensely venerate river Nile. It has been said that deceased ancestors from their abode on the naked slopes of Gebel Asyut al-gharbi could look down upon their industrious descendants toiling on their fertile fields and worshipping them from their renowned temples. The deceased were assumed to exist in the necropolis, some of them even surrounded by painted images and wooden replicas of the world below them. Several areas were venerated through the ages, dedicated to numerous gods, even deified officials such as Djefai-Hapi I. The causeways, forecourts, *ka* chapels, etc. have all been filled

---

93 Ibid. 60–64.

Fig. 13: Limestone offering table S16/st102 (Cat. 37) at Asyut, potentially dating back to between the 11th and 12th Dynasty. The table originates from the disturbed shaft 7 in the First Hall of Tomb I (P10.1), which dates to the 12th Dynasty. However, since the shaft was disturbed, the date is not exact since the table has been chiseled out from its original location. Even though there is uncertainty regarding its date, it may be interesting to note the similarities in design compared to the votive offering tables found at Deir el-Bersha. They may therefore be used in similar ceremonies; however, their shape and material may indicate that they were meant to be used at different occasions. Photograph by author 2018.

with offering tables from the Middle Kingdom onwards, as evidenced by the numerous steles[94] and the development of new tombs inside ancient ones. This may indicate that offering tables were not only "cenotaphs" for the deceased inhabitants of Asyut, but also areas for the performance of libations and an indication of a pious veneration to the ancestral leaders of the land. Asyut therefore is an extremely important site for the interpretation of funerary ritual in general, since its history is so dynamic and its position within a sacred landscape so evident.

---

94 The Salakhana tomb at Asyut contained numerous steles from the 18th Dynasty onwards, giving an insight into the funerary cult during the New Kingdom on the gebel. These objects could have been positioned in numerous places around the gebel and moved in later times, but the sheer volume of votive material indicate a need to for ancestor cult and commemoration, something to be compared with objects such as offering tables at Asyut. DUQUESNE 2009: 80–87.

8. Conclusion

The offering tables at Asyut demonstrate the same, or at least a similar funerary ritual, though expressed in different ways, evidenced by the diversity of not only their shape and size, but also according to their fixture and assumed original archaeological context. In a sense, the inhabitants of Asyut expressed their pertinence to the city via the sacred landscape of the *gebel* as well as their unique material culture. This is why the offering tables at Asyut are vital for an understanding of the dynamics of funerary ritual during the First Intermediate Period and early Middle Kingdom within Middle Egyptian necropoleis. These utensils present an almost perfect chronological sequence, though with contextual differences that cannot be neglected. Further research is needed, especially efforts to place them within a funerary setting. As expressed by Zitman, offering tables may have a direct connection to coffins found at Asyut and therefore also the Coffin Texts. It is therefore essential to further study funerary inscriptions present on tomb walls in the vicinity of offering tables, as well as any other associated funerary texts present inside the burial chambers and coffins. Another important step would be to link offering tables to other utensils with an assumed similar function, such as pottery offering trays as well as any equipment used in funerary ceremonies found in the burial chamber. Offering tables from surrounding necropoleis have only briefly been mentioned, however there are interesting examples found at similar Middle Egyptian sites such as Beni Hasan, Meir, Qau el-Kebir, Deir El-Bahari, etc. (just to mention a few) and these will be examined more closely in future research, together with findings from both the north (Herakleopolis, Saqqara and Memphis) and the south (Abydos, Thebes, El-Kab, etc.) in order to discern similarities and differences in the progression of certain styles as well as the placement of various types of offering tables.

All in all, the connection between offering tables and the deceased is evident throughout the Asyuti funerary landscape. The processions that from the numerous temples meandered to the edge of the mountain and its necropolis reflect the connection between the living and the dead, via the protection and assurance of the libation made on numerous offering tables. Funeral corteges also entered the necropolis and its honeycomb of tombs and tomb shafts, which could be viewed from the city below, reflecting a living cult which was continuously transformed and yet endured through the ages. The study of offering tables, especially their link to ritual texts, and how they were envisioned and used, may deepen our understanding of how funerary rituals were enacted and how they reflected the dynamic and impressive liminal landscape of ancient Asyut.

Ackowledgements
I would like to thank the generosity and interest of Prof. Dr. Jochem Kahl, who graciously granted access to the offering tables at Asyut and Shutb. I am very grateful for all his support during my research and also for involving me in *The Asyut Project*. I would like to thank all the members of the 2018 season, especially Dr. Andrea Kilian, who helped me to locate numerous tables present at the site as well as in the storage facilities, and Fritz Barthel who graciously photographed all the important offering tables both *in situ* on the gebel and at the Shutb magazine. I am also grateful for the assistance offered from the SCA as well as Zoza Room, who was also of significant help. I would like to thank all the curators and staff responsible for the ancient Egyptian collections at the following cited museums and institutions who kindly assisted me in my research and granted me unlimited access to their collections: British Museum in London, Rijksmuseum van Oudheden in Leiden, Medelhavsmuseet in Stockholm and the Museo Egizio di Torino. Much credit must be given to my supervisor Dr. Penelope Wilson at Durham University who has always believed in me and my research. A special thank you to the Helge Ax:son Johnsons Stiftelse in Stockholm, the Egypt Exploration Society in London, the European Commission as well as the The German Academic Exchange Service (DAAD).

Cited offering tables present in the sample:
S04/47 (Cat. 64 – Shutb Magazine, SCA Room, Box 04)
S09/6 (Cat. 42 – Shutb Magazine, SCA Room)
S16/st102 (Cat. 37 – Gebel Asyut al-gharbi, stored in Tomb III)
Cat. 79 (Gebel Asyut al-gharbi, forecourt of Tomb III; Kahl 2012: 186–187, Pl. 19; Kahl 2016: xxii)
Cat. 80 (Gebel Asyut al-gharbi, Tomb N11.1, Shaft 5)
Cat. 81 (Gebel Asyut al-gharbi, Tomb N11.1, Shaft 6)
Cat. 82 (Gebel Asyut al-gharbi, Shaft N12.11, in front of N13.1)
*Catalogue numbers correspond to author's database entry numbers

Cited offering tables from Asyut present in museum collections:
BM EA 973 (unpublished, examined in museum)
BM EA 976 (Zitman 2010b: 177, 241; Ilin-Tomich 2018a:89, 92)
BM EA 978 (BM online catalogue; Zitman 2010b: 241; Ilin-Tomich 2018a: 92–93)
BM EA 990 (examined in museum; Hölzl 2002: 36)
BM EA 46611 (examined in museum; Zitman 2010b: 227)
Tor Provv. 0314* (unpublished, examined in museum)
Tor S.09178 (unpublished, examined in museum)
Tor S.09176 (unpublished, examined in museum)
Tor S.09177 (unpublished, examined in museum)
Tor S.14939 (examined in museum, Zitman 2010a: 64)
Tor S.09175 (unpublished, examined in museum)
Tor S.8931–9187 (Zitman 2010a: 64)
Tor S.8142 (Zitman 2010a: 120)
Tor S.8143 (Zitman 2010a: 120)
Tor S.8144 (Zitman 2010a: 120)
RMO LX15* (examined in museum; Boeser 1907: Pl. 39)
RMO F1901/F1.63* (examined in museum; Boeser 1907: Pl. 5)
MM NME047* (unpublished, examined in museum)
MM ME1006 (examined in museum; available online: http://collections.smvk.se/carlotta-mhm/web/object/3012944)
*from an unknown context, but similar in design and also corresponding to similar time period

Cited offering tables present in museum collections published in Hölzl 2002:
Tor N.22022 (Hölzl 2002: 34–37; Habachi 1977: 21)
Tor N.22012 (Hölzl 2002: 34–37; Habachi 1977: 21–22)
Tor N.22014 (Hölzl 2002: 34–37; Habachi 1977: 22)
Tor N.22011 (Hölzl 2002: 34–37; Habachi 1977: 21)
Tor N.22024 (Hölzl 2002: 34–37; Habachi 1977: 29)
Cairo CG 1355 (Hölzl 2002: 23; Borchardt 1937: 674)
Cairo CG 1335 (Hölzl 2002: 23; Borchardt 1937: 17)
Cairo CG 1363 (Hölzl 2002: 23; Borchardt 1937: 768)
Cairo CG 1326 (Hölzl 2002: 18; Borchardt 1937: 458)
Cairo CG 1367 (Hölzl 2002: 18; Borchardt 1937: 579)
Cairo CG 1334 (Hölzl 2002: 18; Borchardt 1937: 16–17)
Cairo CG 23063 (Hölzl 2002: 32; Kamal 1909: 54)
Cairo CG 23109 Hölzl 2002: 32; Kamal 1909: 90–91)
Cairo CG 23068 (Hölzl 2002: 37; Kamal 1909: 58)
Cairo CG 23028 (Hölzl 2002: 37; Kamal 1909: 23–24, Taf. 11)

Cairo CG 23086 (Hölzl 2002: 42; Kamal 1909: 70–71)
Cairo CG 23084 (Hölzl 2002: 46; Kamal 1909: 69, Taf. 18)
RMO AP82 (Hölzl 2002: 37; Boeser 1910: Nr. 1, Taf. 1)
Louvre D 70 (Hölzl 2002: 23)
AR-8 (Hölzl 2002: 18; Junker 1943: 231, Abb. 94)
NR-10 (Hölzl 2002: 42; Balcz & Bittel 1932: 40, Taf. 5; Wildung 1985: 28, Abb. 18)

Abbreviations:

BM   British Museum, London
CG   Catalog General at the Cairo Museum
FIP   First Intermediate Period
Louvre Louvre Museum, Paris
MK   Middle Kingdom
MM   Medelhavsmuseet, Stockholm
NK   New Kingdom
OK   Old Kingdom
RMO   Rijksmuseum van Oudheden in Leiden
Tor   Museo Egizio Torino

Bibliography

Arnold et al. 2015: D. Arnold, F. Arnold, M. Blelak, L. Gabolde, L. Giddy, J. Karmin & J. Wegner, Selected sites: Elephantine, Thebes: East Bank (Karnak and Luxor), Thebes: West Bank, Abydos, Middle Egypt, The Fayum, Lisht, Dashur, Memphis, The Delta, in: A. Oppenheim, D. Arnold, K. Yamamoto (eds.), Ancient Egypt transformed: The Middle Kingdom (New Haven – London 2008), 315–325.

Aston et al. 2000: B. G. Aston, J. A. Harrel, I. Shaw, Stone, in: T. Nicholson, P. T. Shaw (eds.), Ancient Egyptian Materials and Technology (Cambridge 2000), 5–77.

Balcz & Bittel 1932: H. Balcz, K. Bittel, Grabungsbericht Hermopolis 1932, in: Mitteilungen des Deutschen Archäologischen Instituts Kairo 3, 1932, 9–45.

Betrò 2010: M. Betrò, Geroglifici: 580 Segni per Capire l'Antico Egitto (Milano 2010).

Boeser 1907: P. A. A. Boeser, Catalogus van het Rijksmuseum van Oudheden te Leiden, Egyptische afdeeling. (The Hague: Ministerie van Binnenlandsche Zaken 1907).

Boeser 1910: P. A. A. Boeser, Beschreibungen der Ägyptischen Sammlung des niederländischen Reichsmuseums der Altertümer in Leiden. Die Denkmäler der Zeit zwischen dem Alten und Mittleren Reich und des Mittleren Reiches (Leiden 1910).

Bolshakov 2001: A. O. Bolshakov, Offerings: offering tables, in: D. B. Redford (ed.), The Oxford Encyclopaedia of Ancient Egypt: Volume 2 (Oxford 2001), 572–576.

Borchardt 1937: L. Borchardt, Catalogue Général: Denkmäler des Alten Reiches, Band 1 (Cairo 1937).

Cauville 2012: S. Cauville, Offerings to the Gods in Egyptian temples (Leuven – Paris 2012).

Centrone 2005: M. C. Centrone, Behind the corn-mummies, in: K. Piquette, S. Love (eds.), Current Research in Egyptology 2003: proceedings of the fourth annual symposium which took place at the Institute of Archaeology, University College London, 18–19 January 2003 (Oxford – Oakville 2005), 11–28.

Chassinat & Palanque 1911: É. Chassinat & Ch. Palanque, Une campagne de fouilles dans la nécropole d'Assiout (Mémoires publiés par les membres de l'Institut Français d'Archéologie Orientale du Caire 24; Kairo 1911).

Czyżewska-Zalewska 2015: E. Czyżewska-Zalewska, Painted pottery from the so-called "Hogarth Depot" in Tomb IV of the Asyut necropolis, in: J. Kahl, M. El-Khadragy, H. Faheed Ahmed, U. Verhoeven, M. Abdelrahiem, I. Regulski, M. Becker, E. Czyzewska-Zalewska, A. Kilian, M. Stecher & T. Rzeuska, The Asyut Project: Eleventh Season of Fieldwork (2014), in: SAK 44, 2015, 103-161 (104–116).

DuQuesne 2009: T. DuQuesne, The Salakhana Trove: votive stelae and other objects from Asyut (Oxfordshire communications in Egyptology 7; London 2009).

Eaton 2013: K. Eaton, Ancient Egyptian temple ritual: performance, pattern, and practice (New York 2013).

Fitzenreiter 1994: M. Fitzenreiter, Zum Ahnenkult in Ägypten, in: Göttinger Miszellen 143, 1994, 51–72.

Habachi 1977: L. Habachi, Tavole d'offerta, are e bacilli da libagione, n. 22001–22067 (Torino 1977).

Harrington 2015: N. Harrington, Creating visual boundaries between the 'sacred' and 'secular' in New Kingdom Egypt, in: M. Dalton, G. Peters, A. Tavares (eds.), Seen and Unseen Spaces (Archaeological Review From Cambridge, 30.1, 2015), 143–149.

Hölzl 2002: R. Hölzl, Ägyptische Opfertafeln und Kultbecken: eine Form- und Funktionsanalyse für das Alte, Mittlere und Neue Reich (Hildesheimer ägyptologische Beiträge 45; Gerstenberg 2002).

Ilin-Tomich 2018a: A. Ilin-Tomich, Centralized and Local Production, Adaptation, and Imitation Twelfth Dynasty offering tables, in: G. Miniaci, C. Moreno Garcia, S. Quirke & A. Stauder (eds.), The Arts of Making in Ancient Egypt: Voices, images, and materials of material producers 2000–1550 BC (Leiden 2018), 81–100.

Ilin-Tomich 2018b: A. Ilin-Tomich, Ikonografische Datierungskriterien für Privatopfertafeln der 12. Dynastie, in: Studien zur Altägyptischen Kultur 47, 2018, 57–87.

Junker 1943: H. Junker, Excavations at Giza, Die Mastaba des *Kȝjmꜥnh* (Kai-em-anch), Vol. 4 (Cairo 1943).

Junker 1958: H. Junker, Der Grosse Pylon des Tempels der Isis in Philä (Österreichische Akademie der Wissenschaften, Philosophisch-Historische Klasse; Wien 1958).

Kahl 1999: J. Kahl, Siut – Theben. Zur Wertschätzung von Traditionen im alten Ägypten (Probleme der Ägyptologie 13; Leiden – Boston – Köln 1999).

Kahl 2007: J. Kahl, Ancient Asyut: The First Synthesis After 300 Years of Research (The Asyut Project 1; Wiesbaden 2007).

Kahl 2012: J. Kahl, Regionale Milieus und die Macht des Staates im Alten Ägypten: Die Vergöttlichung der Gaufürsten von Assiut, in: Studien zur Altägyptischen Kultur 41, 2012, 163–188.

Kahl 2014: J. Kahl, Gebel Asyut al-gharbi in the First Millennium AD, in: E. R. O'Connell (Ed.), Egypt in the First Millennium AD. Perspectives from New Fieldwork (British Museum Publications on Egypt and Sudan 2, Leuven – Paris – Walpole, Ma 2014) 127–138.

Kahl 2016: J. Kahl, Introduction, in: J. Kahl, N. Deppe, D. Goldsmith, A. Kilian, C. Kitagawa, J. Moje, M. Zöller-Engelhardt, Asyut, Tomb III: Objects. Part 1 (The Asyut Project 3; Wiesbaden 2016) xi–xxii.

Kahl et al. 2015 : J. Kahl, M. El-Khadragy, H. Faheed Ahmed, U. Verhoeven, M. Abdelrahiem, I. Regulski, M. Becker, E. Czyżewska-Zalewska, A. Kilian, M. Stecher & T. Rzeuska, The Asyut Project: Eleventh Season of Fieldwork (2014), in: Studien zur Altägyptischen Kultur 44, 2015, 103–161.

Kahl, Sbriglio, Del Vesco & Trapani 2019: J. Kahl, A. M. Sbriglio, P. Del Vesco & M. Trapani, Asyut. The Excavations of the Italian Archaeological Mission (1906–1913) (Studi del Museo Egizio 1; Modena 2019).

Kamal 1909: A. Kamal, Catalogue Général des Antiquités Égyptiennes du Musée du Caire, Nos 23001–23256: Tables d'offrandes (Cairo 1909).

Kamal 1916: A. Kamal, Fouilles a Deir Dronka et a Assiout (1913–1914), in: Annales du Service des Antiquités de l'Égypte 16, 1916, 65–114.

Kilian 2012: A. Kilian, Pottery offering trays: general observations and new material from Asyut, in: J. Kahl, M. El-Khadragy, U. Verhoeven, A. Kilian (eds.), Seven Seasons at Asyut. First Results of the Egyptian-German Cooperation in Archaeological Fieldwork. Proceedings of an International Conference at the University of Sohag, 10th–11th of October, 2009 (The Asyut Project 2; Wiesbaden 2012), 105–118.

Kilian 2016: A. Kilian, Offering trays, in: J. Kahl, N. Deppe, D. Goldsmith, A. Kilian, C. Kitagawa, J. Moje & M. Zöller-Engelhardt, Asyut, Tomb III: Objects. Part 1 (The Asyut Project 3; Wiesbaden 2016) 173–195.

Kilian 2019: A. Kilian, Untersuchungen zur Keramik der Ersten Zwischenzeit und des frühen Mittleren Reichs aus Assiut/Mittelägypten (The Asyut Project 12, Wiesbaden 2019).

Klemm & Klemm 2005: R. Klemm & D. Klemm, Vorläufiger Bericht zum Asyut-Projekt 2005 (unpublished).

Legros 2008: R. Legros, Approche méthodologique pour une datation des tables d'offrandes de la Première Période intermédiaire, in: Bulletin de l'Institut français d'archéologie orientale 108, 2008, 231–252.

Pinch 2004: G. Pinch. Egyptian Mythology: A Guide to the Gods, Goddesses and Traditions of Ancient Egypt (New York 2004).

Roth 1992: A. M. Roth, The *psš-kf* and the 'Opening of the Mouth' Ceremony: A Ritual of Birth and Rebirth, in: The Journal of Egyptian Archaeology 78, 1992, 113–147.

Ryan 1988: D.P. Ryan, The Archaeological Excavations of David George Hogarth at Asyut, Egypt 1906/1907 (PhD thesis, Cincinnati 1988).

Strudwick 2005: N. Strudwick, Texts from the Pyramid Age (Atlanta 2005).

TAYLOR 2000: J. H. Taylor, The Third Intermediate Period, in: I. Shaw (ed.), The Oxford History of Ancient Egypt (Oxford 2000), 330–368.

TAYLOR 2001: J. H. Taylor, Death and the Afterlife in Ancient Egypt (London 2001).

THE ASYUT PROJECT: "The Asyut Project": The Ancient Egyptian Necropolis of Assiut: Documentation and Interpretation (DFG), Institut für Altertumswissenschaften, Fachbereich Ägyptologie, Letzte Aktualisierung: Juli 8, 2019: https://www.aegyptologie.uni-mainz.de/the-asyut-project-feldarbeiten-in-mittelaegyptenfieldwork-in-middle-egypt/ [accessed 07.08.2019].

WILDUNG 1985: D. Wildung, Die Kniefigur am Opferbecken. Überlegungen zur Funktion altägyprischer Plastik, in: Münchner Jahrbuch der bildenden Kunst 36, 1985, 17–38.

WILKINSON 2003: R. H. Wilkinson, The Complete Gods and Goddesses of Ancient Egypt (London 2003).

WILLEMS 2016: H. Willems, Die Grabkammer des Djehutinakht (I.?) in Dayr al-Barshā – methodologische Aspekte der Rekonstruktion des Ablaufs des Bestattungsrituals anhand eines neuentdeckten Beispiels, in: A. H. Pries (ed.), Die Variation der Tradition: Modalitäten der Ritualadaption im Alten Ägypten. Akten des Internationalen Symposions in Heidelberg vom 25.–28. November 2012 (Orientalia Lovaniensia Analecta 240; Leuven – Paris – Bristol, CT 2016), 133–170.

ZITMAN 2010a: M. Zitman, The Necropolis of Assiut: A Case Study of Local Egyptian Funerary Culture from the Old Kingdom to the End of the Middle Kingdom. I: Text (Orientalia Lovaniensia Analecta 180,1; Leuven 2010).

ZITMAN 2010b: M. Zitman, The Necropolis of Assiut: A Case Study of Local Egyptian Funerary Culture from the Old Kingdom to the End of the Middle Kingdom. II: Maps, Plans of Tombs, Illustrations, Tables, Lists (Orientalia Lovaniensia Analecta 180,2; Leuven 2010).

Additional Remarks on Ushebtis from Early Excavations in the Necropolis of Asyut

Jan Moje

This article presents new information on the ushebtis found in the rock necropolis at Asyut in Middle Egypt from the collections of Sayed Bey Khashaba and the Museo Gregoriano in Città del Vaticano. These objects were first edited by the author and published in *The Ushebtis from Early Excavations in the Necropolis of Asyut, Mainly by David George Hogarth and Ahmed Bey Kamal. With Remarks on Ushebti Iconography and Related Burial Practices in Asyut from the New Kingdom to the Ptolemaic Period* (The Asyut Project 4; Wiesbaden 2013).

1. New sources for ushebtis from Asyut

Since the publication of my book on the Asyut ushebtis,[1] I have been able to collect more information on funerary figurines from Asyut. Furthermore, Donald P. Ryan kindly provided me with details on the history of the collection in the Museo Gregoriano Egizio in Città del Vaticano[2].

The first new source is the typewritten manuscript of William Christopher Hayes, entitled "*Selective Catalogue of Egyptian Antiquities from the Collection of Sayed Pasha Khashaba, Assiut, Upper Egypt,*" the origin or date of which is unknown.[3] It consists of 81 bound cardboard folios with 48 photos mounted on them. The original, which was last housed in the *Metropolitan Museum of Art, Watson Library,* is missing today.[4] Fig. 1 shows a photo of nine ushebtis from the Khashaba collection (**UL-13–UL-16**).

The photos are stamped with the name "Badr" in Arabic and Roman letters; this is presumably the work of Egyptian photographer Muhammad Badr, who possessed a photo studio in Cairo from 1907 throughout the first and second decades of the 20th century.[5] Little is known about the photo studios owned by Egyptians in the beginning of this century and located in Cairo, Alexandria, and Luxor.

It is not entirely clear why Hayes compiled this selective catalogue, but from information like "needs cleaning" it can be assumed that it was a sales catalogue intended to market of parts of the Khashaba collection. With this also the hiring of Badr and his Cairo studio fits well. Unfortunately, the greatest amount of the artifacts in this regional museum was sold worldwide during the first half of the 20th century, and no information about the Egyptian dealers or the European and American buyers survives. By 1952, the remaining artifacts in the Khashaba collection were transferred into state control.

---

1   MOJE 2013. The study was conducted within the framework of the DFG project "The ancient Egyptian necropolis of Asyut: documentation and interpretation". I am indebted to James Moore for checking my English.

2   Email 11th of June, 2013. I would like to express my thanks to him for sharing this new information with me, and to allow me to include them in this article.

3   I am indebted to Sandy Wallace and Deirdre Lawrence for providing scans of the photo pages from the Brooklyn Museum Library's Xerox copy of this volume.

4   Email from the library administration, August 2015.

5   For him see BARON 2007: 90; GOLIA 2010: 56, 85, 178 note. 1.

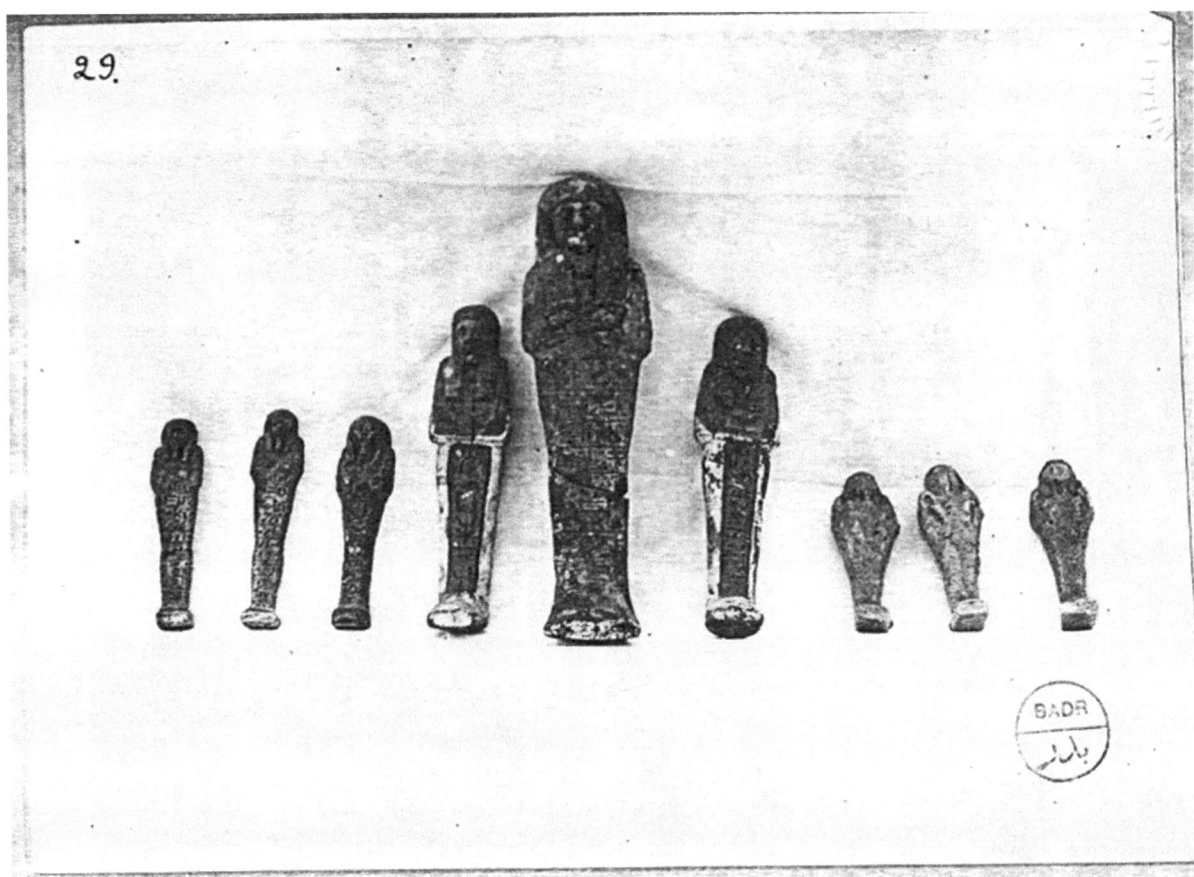

Fig. 1: From Hayes, n. d.: pl. 29.

In 2013, M. Al-Sayed Aman delivered a paper concerning 14 ushebtis from the Al-Salam School in Asyut,[6] but most of them seem to originate not from Asyut, but from Thebes or Deir Rifeh.[7] There are no parallels to the ushebtis in the corpora from the Hogarth excavation or from *The Asyut Project* excavation.

In 2015, a short article was published in the online newspaper *The Cairo Post*[8] about the seizure of artifacts from private diggings in Asyut. The accompanying photograph shows 18 ushebtis (**UL-17–UL-20**) beneath lamps and coins.[9]

---

6 Aman 2013.
7 Already briefly mentioned by Aman 2013: 76.
8 English website version of the Arabic daily newspaper اليوم السابع (Youm7).
9 Mostafa 2015, currently unavailable, but cf. http://egitalloyd.blogspot.de/2015/12/recovered-artifacts-asyut-police-seize.html?m=1. I am indebted to U. Verhoeven for information on this article (email 29.12.2015). It states: "CAIRO: Tourism and Antiquities policemen have seized a set of 47 ancient artifacts at a house of a farmer in Upper Egypt's governorate of Asyut, Youm7 reported Friday. The seizure came hours before the artifacts were prepared for sale. Spanning several periods of the ancient Egyptian historical periods, the artifacts in question include 29 coins, five pottery lanterns, 14 statues made of blue faience along with four incomplete statues made of clay."

2. Additional ushebtis from Asyut

UL-13 (= UM-12?) One mummiform ushebti of Si-Ese III

Mat: Limestone, painted.
Dim: H: 30 cm. W: ? cm. T: ? cm.
Dat: New Kingdom, 19th Dynasty.
Mus: Unknown.
Prov: Asyut, *ex* collection Sayed Bey Khashaba (possible excavation, A. Kamal 1913/14).
Publ: HAYES, n. d.: chap. G, photo 29, no. 5.

This ushebti has a mummiform body. Its long and tripartite wig with flat and broad laps was once pain-ted blue, while all details of the flat and round face were highlighted in red. The arms are crossed over the chest, right over left, both hands were painted in red. On the body, eight lines of hieroglyphs are incised and painted blue. The object is nearly complete: the surface is partially chipped, and the lower part has been broken and reattached with some material loss along the broken edges. The paint is mainly worn and faded. According to Hayes, the piece "needs cleaning."

Hayes noted that the owner of this ushebti is identical with that of the huge granite sarcophagus from a tomb in Asyut.[10] Thus the assignment of this ushebti to Si-Ese III is certain.

It is currently unclear whether or not the ushebti UM-12, published in my volume,[11] is identical with this piece. The given size of 30 cm is identical, but the ushebti UM-12, as mentioned by Kamal,[12] was made from wood and broken into three pieces. Unfortunately, he does not supply photos. The photo of UL-13 shows clearly a stone ushebti, but it is broken into three pieces, at the neck and at the knees. In my opinion, Kamal's identification of UM-12 as wood is erroneous. Thus UL-13 may be identical with UM-12. Due to the unknown whereabouts of the latter this remains a point of speculation.

UL-14,1–15 Fifteen mummiform ushebtis of Wepwawet-nakht

Mat: Wood, painted.
Dim: H: 23 cm. W: ? cm. T: ? cm.
Dat: New Kingdom: 19th –20th Dynasty.
Mus: Unknown.
Prov: Asyut, *ex* collection Sayed Bey Khashaba (possibly excavation A. Kamal 1913/14).
Publ: HAYES, n. d.: chap. G, photo 29, no. 4 and 6.

The ushebtis from this family are mummiform and "summarily modeled". They wear a long, tripartite and black painted wig. The faces are carved round. The eyes are shadowed in black, and all skin parts are painted in red. Both arms are crossed over the chest with only the hands visible. They hold red painted *mr*-hoes. Below the laps and on the entire chest, a yellowish painted collier is visible. From the hands downwards, their bodies show white groundings. All statuettes bear a column of black painted hiero-glyphs with yellow shade and red frames. They read:

s:ḥḏ Wsjr Wpj-wꜣj.wt-nḫt
"He may be illuminated, the Osiris Wepwawet-nakht."
These ushebtis were, according to Hayes, in "perfect condition", but the accompanying photo shows two of them to be chipped and to have tension cracks.

---

10 MOJE 2013: 51 with note 18.
11 MOJE 2013: 50 –52.
12 KAMAL 1916: 77 sub no. 55

UL-15,1–25 Twenty five mummiform ushebtis of "Ra-erpa"

Mat: Quartz ceramic, glazed.

Dim: H: 14 cm. W: ? cm. T: ? cm.

Dat: Late Period (30th Dynasty)–Early Ptolemaic Period.

Mus: Unknown.

Prov: Asyut, *ex* collection Sayed Bey Khashaba (possibly excavation A. Kamal 1913/14).

Publ: HAYES, n. d.: chap. G, photo 29, nos. 1–3.

These ushebtis are mummiform and tall. They wear a short, tripartite wig with divine beard, and are "modeled in great details". The arms are crossed over the chest, with only the hands visible. They hold faintly visible implements, presumably *mr*-hoes. On the bodies are 11 lines of an incised hieroglyphic inscription, which is surely the late version of the ushebti spell BD 6. The flat feet are mounted on a rectangular base. The condition is, according to Hayes, "excellent." Only name and title of the owner are mentioned. They read:

sẖ n(j) ḥw.t-nṯr n(j) Wpj-wȝj.wt "Ra-erpa".

"Scribe of the temple of Wepwawet 'Ra-erpa'".

I am not sure which name Hayes meant, unfortunately he had not provided a transcription.

UL-16,1–250 Twohundred and fifty mummiform ushebtis

Mat: Quartz ceramic, bright blue glazed.

Dim: H: 10 –12 cm. W: ? cm. T: ? cm.

Dat: Late Period (30th Dynasty)

Mus: Unknown.

Prov: Asyut, *ex* collection Sayed Bey Khashaba (possibly excavation A. Kamal 1913/14).

Publ: HAYES, n. d.: chap. G, photo 29, nos. 7–9.

These ushebtis are mummiform and wear short, tripartite wigs in black color. Also the beard is black. The body is made with "fine", bright blue glaze. They are "summarily modeled" and in complete condition. Parallels for these bichrome ushebtis include the Late Period statuettes London, British Museum EA 47451 and Città del Vaticano, Museo Gregoriano Egizio 38352 from Asyut[13] with a similar shape of the body. Their exact number is not definitely clear; Hayes mentions only "about Two hundred and fifty" examples.

UL-17,1–3 Three mummiform ushebtis

Mat: Light brown pottery, black core.

Dim: H: ? cm. W: ? cm. T: ? cm.

Dat: New Kingdom, Ramesside Period, 19th –20th Dynasty.

Mus: Unknown.

Prov: Asyut, private diggings.

Publ: MOSTAFA 2015. Cf. for similar items MOJE 2016: 197–318, Cat. U53, U68 ff.

Presumably all three ushebtis show a thick mummiform body. They wear a large, long and tripartite wig and have no beards. The arms are crossed over their chests, and hold implements. The feet are missing. Color is not visible on the photo.

---

13 MOJE 2013: 85 –86, Cat. UM-50 and UM-51.

UL-18 One mummiform ushebti

Mat: Brown pottery.

Dim: H: ? cm. W: ? cm. T: ? cm.

Dat: New Kingdom, Ramesside Period, 19th–20th Dynasty.

Mus: Unknown.

Prov: Asyut, private diggings.

Publ: MOSTAFA 2015. Cf. for parallels MOJE 2016: Cat. U53, U68ff.

This ushebti shows a slender tripartite wig. Both arms are outward and against each other, as though they once carried implements. The feet are missing. Color is not visible on the photo. The statuette is taller than UL-17,1–3.

UL-19 One overseer ushebti

Mat: Light brown pottery.

Dim: H: ? cm. W: ? cm. T: ? cm.

Dat: New Kingdom, Ramesside Period, 19th–20th Dynasty.

Mus: Unknown.

Prov: Asyut, private diggings.

Publ: MOSTAFA 2015.

This ushebti wears a duplex wig without beard. Both arms are crossed over the chest, and holding implements. The lower part of the body is covered with a long and protruding apron with a trapezoid shape. The feet are missing. Color is not visible on the photo.

UL-20, 1–13 Thirteen mummiform ushebtis

Mat: Quartz ceramic, light blue glazed.

Dim: H: ? cm. W: ? cm. T: ? cm.

Dat: Late Period, 26th–30th Dynasty.

Mus: Unknown.

Prov: Asyut, private diggings.

Publ: MOSTAFA 2015.

All ushebtis of this family have a tall mummiform body. They wear a thin long and tripartite wig with divine beard. Only the hands are visible wearing hoe and adze; both are carved already in the mould. The feet are rested on a small square base.

3. Additional information on the published Asyut ushebtis in the Museo Gregoriano Egizio

Due to information Donald P. Ryan kindly provided to me[14], he was able to link the Asyut ushebtis, which are housed in the Museo Gregoriano in Città del Vaticano, definitely to the excavation of David George Hogarth. In his study on that early "excavator", Ryan was not able to identify the initials "R.N.", which appear often in the Hogarth notebooks[15]. Now it is known that these are the initials of an American

---

14 Email 11th of June, 2013. Most of the information in this chapter is from this communication, and I am indebted to him for the possibility to include his information in my paper.

15 RYAN 1988: 57–58 ("History of the excavation").

scholar named Richard Norton (*1872 – †1918)[16]. He was appointed director of the American School of Classical Studies in Rome in 1899 and held this position until 1907.

During Hogarth' diggings, Norton was one of his assistants, as Hogarth mentions him in his autobiography – rather hidden – as "Mr. Richard Norton, a comrade ... at Siut".[17] After his return to Rome in 1907, Norton presented the 170 objects[18] donated to him by Hogarth to the museum of the American School of Classic Studies. This was noted by him in the Annual report 1906–07:

> "The School museum has grown considerably during the year, the chief addition being a large number of vases and some other antiquities from XII Dynasty tombs excavated at Assiut by D.G. Hogarth, Esq., and myself during my absence from the School. An accurate and complete catalog was made during the year by Mr. Harmon." [19]

In 1948, a third of the Egyptian objects, including all Asyut ushebtis, were transferred from the American Academy (merged with the American School in 1913) to the Vatican museum, as the relevant report mentions:

> "Egyptian Museum of the Vatican. This Museum has received a notable and unexpected accretion, by gift from the American Academy in Rome, of a number of vases, wooden effigies and other objects, the equipment of Twelfth Dynasty tombs excavated at Assiut by David G. Hogarth and Richard Norton in 1907, which at the time had been presented to the old American School of Classical Studies by Mr. Norton. The incorporation of this homogenous group in the larger collection not only will ensure its proper maintenance but will render it of service to a wider group of scholars as well as make it better known and more readily accessible to the general public. Part of the opening meeting of the Pontifical Roman Academy of Archaeology on March 19, 1948, was devoted to the announcement and illustration of the gift."[20]

Bibliography

AMAN 2013: M. Al-Sayed Aman, An Unpublished New Collection of Shabtis 'Ushebtis' Housed in Al-Salam School Museum in Assiut, Egypt, in: Abgadiyat 8, 2013, 75 –91.

BARON 2007: B. Baron, Egypt as a Woman. Nationalism, Gender, and Politics (Berkeley 2007).

BRADFORD WELLES 1948: C. Bradford Welles, Archaeological News, in: American Journal of Archaeology 52, 1948, 501 –502.

GEFFCKEN 2015: K. A. Geffcken, The history of the Collection, in: L. Bonfante & H. Nagy, The Collection of Antiquities of the American Academy in Rome (Ann Arbor MI), 21 –33.

GOLIA 2010: M. Golia, Photography and Egypt (London 2010).

HAYES, n. d.: W. Ch. Hayes, Selective Catalogue of Egyptian Antiquities from the Collection of Sayed Pasha Khashaba, Assiut, Upper Egypt (no place, no date).

HOGARTH 1910: D. G. Hogarth, Accident's of an Antiquaries Life (London 1910).

KAMAL 1916: A. Kamal, Fouilles à Deir Dronka et à Assiout (1913–1914), in: Annales du Service des Antiquités de l'Égypte 16, 1916, 65–114.

MOJE 2013: J. Moje, The Ushebtis from Early Excavations in the Necropolis of Asyut, Mainly by David George Hogarth and Ahmed Bey Kamal. With Remarks on Ushebti Iconography and Related Burial Practices in Asyut from the New Kingdom to the Ptolemaic Period (The Asyut Project 4; Wiesbaden 2013).

MOJE 2016: J. Moje, The Ushebtis from Tomb III and its Surroundings (Seasons 2004–2007), in: J. Kahl, N. Deppe, D. Goldsmith, A. Kilian, C. Kitagawa, J. Moje & M. Zöller-Engelhardt, Asyut, Tomb III: Objects. Part 1 (The Asyut Project 3; Wiesbaden 2016).

---

16 GEFFCKEN 2015: 21–33.
17 HOGARTH 1910: passim.
18 GEFFCKEN 2015: 32.
19 WEST & NORTON 1907: 29.
20 BRADFORD WELLES 1948: 501–502.

Mostafa 2015: R. Mostafa, Police seize 47 artifacts in farmers house in Asyut, in: The Cairo Post December 27 (2015); http://thecairopost.youm7.com/news/184487/news/police-seize-47-artifacts-in-farmers-house-in-asyut

Ryan 1988: D. P. Ryan, The Archaeological Excavations of David George Hogarth at Asyut, Egypt (PhD thesis, Cincinnati 1988).

West & Norton 1907: A. F. West & R. Norton, Twelfth Annual Report of the Managing Committee of the American School of Classical Studies in Rome, in: American Journal for Archaeology 11, 1907, Supplement: Annual Reports 1906 –1907, 22 –35.

Fragmente reliefierter lotusförmiger Fayencekelche aus Assiut[*]

Ana Sofia de Carvalho Gomes

Während der Feldkampagne 2008 wurde ein Oberflächensurvey im zentralen Bereich des Gebel Assiut al-gharbi durchgeführt, in dem das Hundegrab (Tomb of the Dogs, O11.13) vermutet wurde. Diese Vermutung bestätigte sich im Verlauf der Kampagne.[1] Neben zahlreicher sogenannter *Animal Necropolis Ware*, die im Abraum um das Hundegrab gefunden wurde und seit jeher mit dem großen Ibisfriedhof in Tuna el-Gebel assoziiert wird,[2] wurde ein weiterer, weitaus seltener Fund gemacht,[3] der durch seine erste umfassende Bearbeitung durch George A. D. Tait[4] ebenfalls mit Tuna el-Gebel in Verbindung gebracht werden kann: ein Fragment eines hellblauen reliefierten lotusförmigen Fayencekelches (S08/st751, Abb. 1). In den Jahren 2010 (S10/st1354, Abb. 2) und 2011 (S11/st448, Abb. 1) folgten zwei weitere Fragmente von Fayencekelchen. Während S11/st448 das gleiche Relief wie das Fragment S08/st1354 zeigt und eventuell ein weiterer Teil desselben Kelches sein könnte, handelt es sich bei dem Fund aus dem Jahr 2010 gesichert um den zweiten lotusförmigen Fayencekelch, der in Assiut entdeckt worden ist.

Die ersten lotusförmigen Reliefkelche gelangten im beginnenden 19. Jahrhundert als Geschenke oder Souvenirs vorwiegend in privaten Besitz[5] und in europäische Museen, wie beispielsweise der Kelch im Berliner Museum (ÄM 4563) und der Kelch in Athen (National Museum, Inv. Nr. 566). Durch Verkauf oder Nachlass von Privatsammlungen steigt die Zahl dieser Fundgruppe in Museen bis zum heutigen Tag stetig an.[6] Eine wissenschaftliche Bearbeitung der Objekte findet erst seit dem späten 19. und frühen 20. Jahrhundert statt.[7] Die umfassendste Bearbeitung erfuhren die Kelche durch Tait im Jahr 1963, der neben den wenigen vollständigen Exemplaren auch zahlreiche Kleinfragmente der Reliefkelche bearbeitete und identifizierte. So gelang es ihm, Fragmente unterschiedlicher Museen miteinander in Beziehung zu setzen. Durch seine detaillierten Beschreibungen und Abbildungen gab er in seiner Arbeit einen guten Überblick über die ihm bis dahin bekannten Exemplare.[8] Danach beschränkte sich das Interesse an den Kelchen auf Einträge in diversen Ausstellungskatalogen zum Thema Fayence.[9] Seit 2009 ist das Interesse an den lotusförmigen Kelchen erneut erwacht und von Bissings Idee des Motivtransfers in phönizische Metallschalen wurde weiterentwickelt.[10]

---

[*] Dieser Artikel entstand im Rahmen des Forschungsprojektes „Asyut – centre of ancient trade", gefördert durch die Deutsche Forschungsgemeinschaft (DFG) - Projektnummer 426702318 und Narodowe Centrum Nauki.

[1] Drei Vorratsbehälter, die in die 25.–26. Dynastie datieren, sind bislang die frühesten Belege einer Nutzung des Hundegrabes. Kitagawa 2016: 15; Rzeuska 2017: 496–497, 520–525.

[2] Siehe dazu Nicholson 2005.

[3] Kahl et al. 2009: 121.

[4] Tait 1963.

[5] Hufft 2016.

[6] Tait 1963: 94.

[7] Wallis 1898, 1900; Ricketts 1918; Hufft 2016.

[8] Tait 1963.

[9] Bspw. Schneider et al. 2003.

[10] Hufft 2016.

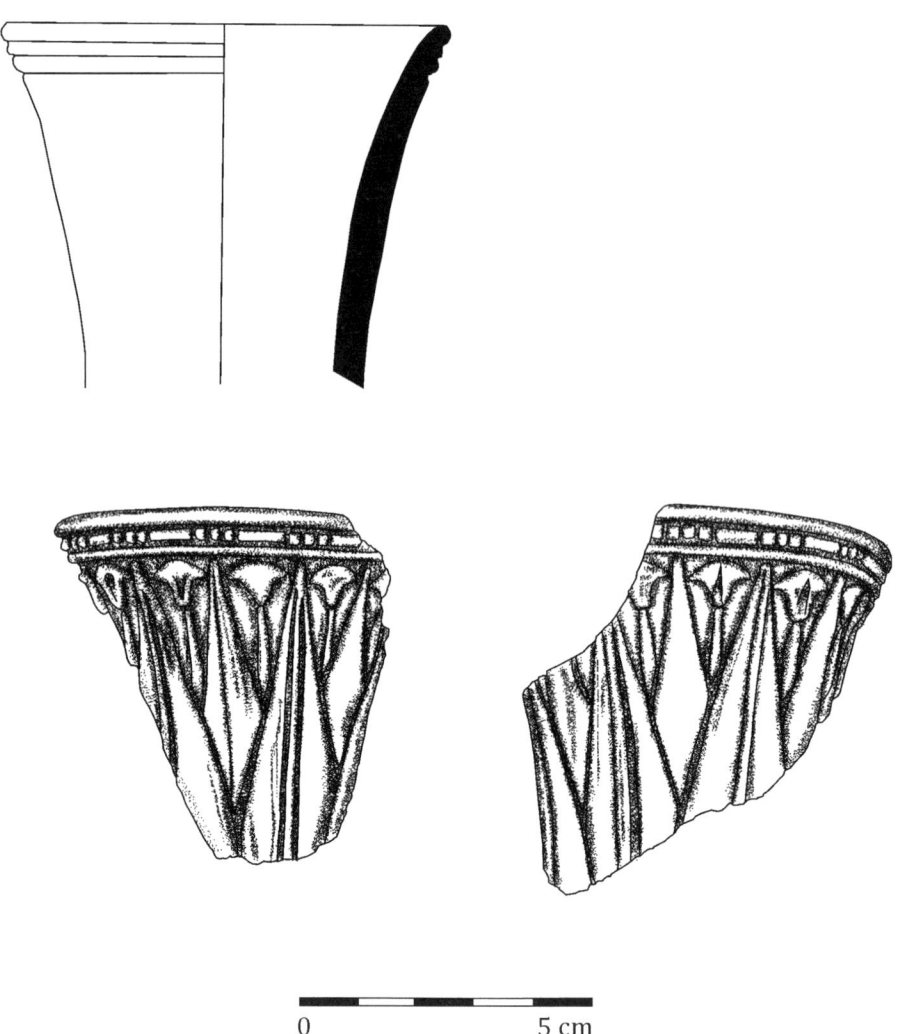

0   5 cm

Abb. 1: S08/st751, S11/st448, Umzeichnung: K. Molga.

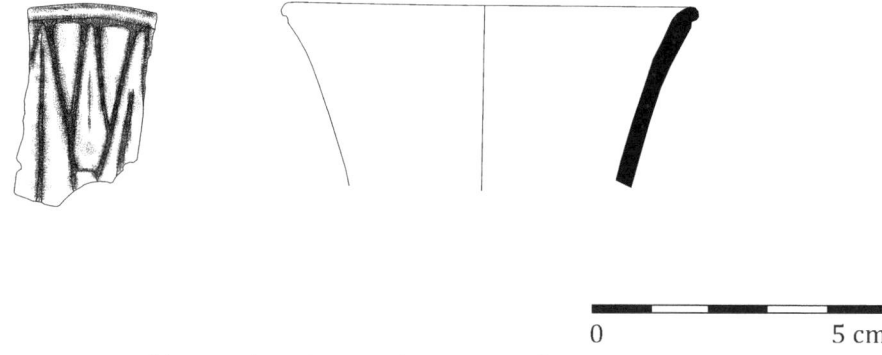

0   5 cm

Abb. 2: S10/st1354, Umzeichnung: K. Molga.

1. Herkunft und Datierung der lotusförmigen Fayencebecher

„Der Fundort Tuna an sich, der für mehrere Gefässe der Art überliefert ist, bedeutet nichts."[11] Sowohl Wallis als auch MacGregor und Myers sollen Stücke aus der Nekropole des antiken Hermopolis Magna eingekauft haben, welche in den 1890er Jahren von der dort ansässigen Bevölkerung geplündert worden ist. Die dort gefundenen Objekte wurden stückweise durch die Bewohner verkauft. Zahlreiche reliefierte Fayencekelche stammen aus den Ankäufen von Wallis, MacGregor und Myers.[12] Tait etablierte in seiner Bearbeitung Tuna el-Gebel als ursprünglichen Herkunftsort dieser Kelchart[13], gibt jedoch für einige der von ihm aufgelisteten Kelche und Kelchfragmente einen Ankauf in Kairo, Qurna oder Luxor an.[14] Die Tatsache, dass unterschiedliche Museen einzelne Fragmente ein und desselben Kelchs in ihrer Sammlung haben, zeigt, dass die Kelche und Fragmente nicht als Sammlung an einen einzelnen Aufkäufer verkauft worden sind und die Antikensammler ihre Einkäufe in derselben Region getätigt haben.[15] Die von Tait zusammengetragenen Argumente sind schlüssig, beweisen jedoch nicht, dass die existierenden Kelche aus Tuna el-Gebel stammen oder exklusiv dort hergestellt worden sind. Die Plünderungen der 1890er Jahre in der Nekropole machen eine Rückverfolgung der einzelnen Funde unmöglich und keiner der Käufer hat die Fayencekelche bei seinen Einkäufen explizit vermerkt.[16] Die Wahrscheinlichkeit, dass einige Museumsstücke aus dieser Zeit der Plünderung des Friedhofs stammen, ist zwar hoch, die Exklusivität Tuna el-Gebels als einziger Herkunftsort jedoch nicht gesichert. Bereits Wallis sprach in seiner Bearbeitung von „Tuneh Find"[17] und ging fest davon aus, dass die Fayencekelche aus den Plünderungen der Nekropole stammen. Für ihn schien dieser Umstand einzig für die Datierung der Kelche schwierig zu sein, die Herkunft zweifelte er nicht an.[18] Dies mag als Indiz gewertet werden, dass Wallis die Herkunft der aufgekauften Stücke genau kannte, allerdings erweckt sein Kommentar dazu nicht den Eindruck, als hätte Wallis die Stücke direkt bei den Plünderern der Nekropole erstanden.

In den Museen sind aktuell unterschiedlichste Herkunftsangaben zu finden. Dabei fällt auf, dass Tuna el-Gebel relativ selten als eindeutige Provenienz angegeben wird. Angaben wie „Tuna ware" assoziieren zwar eine gewisse Nähe zu Tuna el-Gebel als Fundort, die vage Angabe „Egypt" erscheint jedoch den meisten Museen angebrachter (siehe Abb. 3).

Tuna el-Gebel wird seit Jahren intensiv bearbeitet. Die zahlreichen Grabungen des frühen 20. Jahrhunderts[19] förderten eine große Anzahl an Funden zu Tage. Diese sind, wenn überhaupt, nur unzureichend dokumentiert.[20] Günther Roeder[21] erwähnt in seinem Expeditionsbericht Fayencegefäße und weitere Gegenstände aus Fayence, spricht aber nicht von reliefierten Kelchen. Der 2010 erschienene Zwischenbericht zu den aktuellen Ausgrabungen in Tuna el-Gebel[22] gibt einen Überblick über die mengenmäßige Verteilung der einzelnen Fundgruppen. Reliefierte Fayencekelche oder Fragmente davon sind in den letzten Jahren nicht vermerkt worden. Die in Museen verwendete Fundortangabe

---

11 Bissing 1902: XVII.

12 Tait 1963: 94 f.

13 „I have no doubt that all these fragments were sold piecemeal by the Tuna villagers", Tait 1963: 95.

14 Vgl. Tait 1963; Hufft 2016.

15 Sowohl MacGregor als auch Wallis und Myers waren zur gleichen Zeit in der gleichen Region Ägyptens unterwegs. Vgl. Tait 1963: 95.

16 Bzw. die betreffenden Tagebücher sind nicht mehr erhalten. Siehe dazu Tait 1963: 95.

17 Wallis 1898.

18 „The excavation was made by natives, so no pains were taken to preserve the record of any circumstances bearing on the date of the tombs", Wallis 1898, Einleitung.

19 Beispielsweise die 1902/1903 durch A. Gombert im Auftrag des Institut français d'archéologie orientale (IFAO) oder die zwischen 1931 und 1952 durch S. Gabra im Auftrag der Ägyptischen Universität Kairo durchgeführten Grabungen.

20 Flossmann-Schütze et al. 2015.

21 Roeder 1959.

22 Helmbold-Doyé 2010.

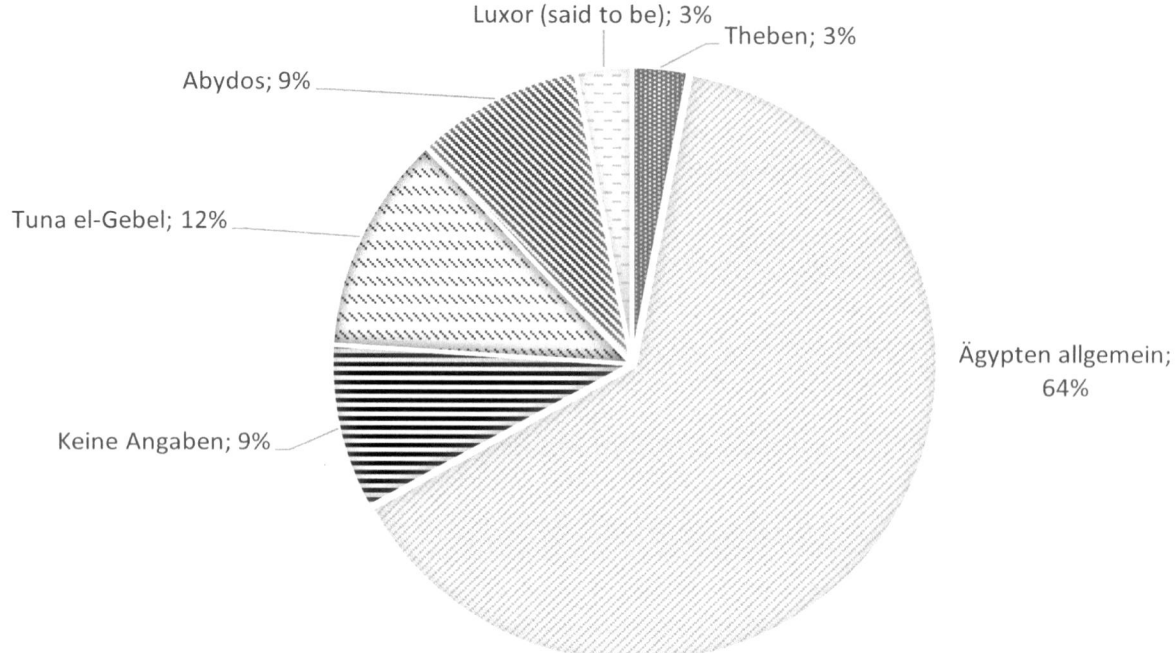

Abb. 3: Herkunftsvermutungen nach Museumsangaben, vollständige und fast vollständige Gefäße.

„said to be from Tuna el-Gebel" oder „Tuna ware" basiert somit einzig auf der durch Tait etablierten Annahme, dass die Exemplare aus Tuna el-Gebel stammen. Die wenigen gesicherten Fundorte der Kelche oder Kelchfragmente wie beispielsweise des Bostoner Kelches 01.7396 aus Abydos, eines Kelches aus Saqqara[23] und der neu entdeckten Fragmente aus Assiut sprechen für eine Nutzung und Verortung im mittelägyptischen Raum, zu dem auch, aber nicht einzig, Tuna el-Gebel gehört.[24]

2. Das Bildprogramm der reliefierten lotusförmigen Fayencekelche

Im Allgemeinen werden die lotusförmigen Kelche in zwei Kategorien aufgeteilt, wobei das Bildprogramm maßgeblich für die Datierung herangezogen wird. Komplexe Szenendarstellungen werden hierbei deutlich jünger als die einfachen Blütendarstellungen datiert.[25] Der Aufbau der Kelche gleicht sich bei allen bekannten Exemplaren. Dem Standfuß des Kelches folgt, wie bei seinem natürlichen Pendant, der

---

23 Zaki Y. Saad leitete zwischen 1939 und 1940 eine Grabung im Gebiet zwischen der Stufenpyramide des Djoser und dem Aufweg zur Unas-Pyramide. Das Grabungsgebiet zeigt deutliche Spuren vorheriger Grabungstätigkeiten. Einige Funde stammen aus dem Abraum zwischen den beiden Pyramiden und können keiner Bestattung sicher zugewiesen werden. Dies gilt auch für den reliefierten Fayencekelch, von dem es zwar eine Abbildung gibt, der im Bericht jedoch keine Erwähnung findet. SAAD 1940: 675.

24 Der Bostoner Kelch 01.7396 aus Abydos liefert darüber hinaus eine gesicherte Datierung in die 18. Dynastie. Der Lotuskelch MFA 01.7396, der sich seit 1901 im Besitz des Bostoner Museums befindet, stammt aus den Ausgrabungen des Egypt Exploration Fund in Abydos, die von 1899 bis 1949 durchgeführt wurden. Unter den Funden befinden sich zwei Skarabäen und ein Siegel mit der Kartusche Thutmosis III., die eine Datierung in oder kurz nach der Regierungszeit Thutmosis III. erlauben. Siehe dazu PEET & LOAT 1913; FRIEDMAN 1998.

25 HUFFT 2016: 138.

Pflanzenstiel. Dieser ist oftmals mit Wasserlinien oder umgekehrten Kelchblättern geschmückt. Die Kelchblätter folgen und bilden alternierend mit den plastisch ausgearbeiteten Blütenblättern den eigentlichen Kelch. Bei den „einfachsten" Varianten des Kelches macht dies die gesamte Gestaltung aus.[26] Die meisten Kelche zeigen jedoch eine Aufteilung in drei Register, vereinzelt sind auch vier vorhanden.[27] Der Innenteil der Kelche ist, außer bei einem Kelch (Berlin ÄM 4563), undekoriert. Der äußere Aufbau ähnelt sich zwar im Motiv, variiert jedoch in der Gestaltung. Die Dekorelemente wie Blockrand (Farbleiter), Udjat-Augen, Tier- und Menschenmotive unterscheiden sich ebenso wie die Anzahl an Registern und deren Breite. Die einfachste Variante des reliefierten Lotuskelches mit Bildmotiven zeigt drei Szenenregister. Das unterste Register nimmt meist die Dekoration des Standfußes auf und zeigt ausgearbeitete Sepalen und Blütenblätter des Lotus. Das breiteste mittlere Register - das Hauptregister - zeigt Tier- oder Menschenmotive. Diese sind hauptsächlich linksläufig angebracht.[28] Das oberste und meist schmalste Register zeigt entweder einen Fries aus Vögeln, Nestern mit Eiern, zeitweise Udjat-Augen oder einen Blockrand im Stil einer Farbleiter.[29] Das Grundmotiv der dargestellten Bildmotive erscheint in beiden Gruppen gleich: Darstellungen des Papyrusdickichts mit Lotus und Papyrus, Wasservögeln, Eiern und Kälbern oder der Lotusblume als Urpflanze in ihrer einfachsten Form, aus der die Welt entstand und die eng mit dem Gott auf der Blume[30] assoziiert ist. Sie weisen, wie die Darstellungen des Königs beim Trinken an der göttlichen Brust[31] oder auch die Darstellung ithyphallischer Gottheiten[32] und tanzender Besfiguren, auf den mythologischen Kreislauf der Wiedergeburt und Erneuerung hin. Somit muss deutlich gemacht werden, dass die grobe Aufteilung zwischen den Bildmotiven in Szenen aus dem Papyrusdickicht, mythologische Szenen und Darstellungen einfacher Lotusblüten zwar möglich ist, aber nur eine strukturelle Aufteilung der dargestellten Motive sein kann, da alle Kelche denselben symbolischen Charakter haben. Eine zeitliche Einteilung anhand des gewählten Bildmotives ist somit nicht ausschließlich zielführend. Betrachtet man die wenigen Museumsangaben zur Datierung, scheint dies jedoch die gängige Herangehensweise zu sein.

3. Das Bildprogramm der Assiuter Fragmente – eine Rekonstruktion

Alle drei in Assiut gefundenen Stücke gehören zu den Kelchen mit Lotusdarstellungen. Das Fragment S10/st1354 ist, wie die anderen zwei gefundenen Fragmente, ein Randstück, was die Rekonstruktion der Dekoration und der Kelchform weitestgehend ermöglicht. Der Rand ist undekoriert. Spitz zulaufende Kelch- und Blütenblätter wechseln sich ab. Andere Dekorationselemente sind nicht vorhanden. Der Kelch ist wenig ausgestellt und ähnelt in Dekoration und Aufbau vermutlich dem Kelch ÄM 12578 aus dem Berliner Museum. Boden und Standfuß sind nicht zu rekonstruieren, die restliche Ausgestaltung des Kelches lässt aber die Vermutung zu, dass beides undekoriert gewesen sein könnte.

Die zwei weiteren Fragmente aus Assiut, S08/st751 und S11/st448, teilen das gleiche Bildprogramm. Auch diese Stücke gehören zu den Kelchen mit Lotusdarstellung. Ihre Ähnlichkeit lässt darauf schließen, dass beide Stücke zum selben Kelch gehören.[33] Die diagnostische Scherbe erlaubt eine Rekonstruktion

---

26 Siehe z. B. British Museum 26226, Florenz 3254.

27 HUFFT 2016: 146.

28 Sodass der Blick des Betrachters nach rechts gelenkt wird.

29 HUFFT 2016: 146.

30 MORENZ & SCHUBERT 1954. Besonders ab der 21. Dynastie tritt die Ikonographie des Sonnenkindes auf der Blüte in seiner typischen Erscheinungsform als nackter Knabe, die Hand an den Mund geführt, mit Flagellum oder Krummstab, auf der Blüte sitzend stärker hervor. Siehe dazu SCHLÖGL 1977: 25.

31 FEUCHT 1984.

32 Vergleiche dazu die Rolle von Min und Osiris als ithyphallische Gottheiten.

33 Allerdings schließen beide Fragmente nicht unmittelbar aneinander an.

Abb. 4: Kelchfragmente aus Assiut, S10/st1354 (oben),
S08/st751 (unten links), S11/st448 (unten rechts) (© The Asyut Project).

der Dekoration (siehe Skizze der Dekoration Abb. 6) und der äußeren Form. Der Kelchkörper selbst
ist wenig ausgestellt. Eine so ausgeprägte Glockenform oder Auswölbung wie bei dem Kelch Louvre
E 11349, der eine ähnliche Dekoration aufweist, ist nicht zu erkennen. Die Gefäßlippe zeigt eine
Farbleiterdekoration, bei der sich jeweils drei Quadrate mit einem rechteckigen Balken abwechseln.
Eingefasst ist diese Farbleiter durch ein Band. Darunter sind spitz zulaufende Kelchblätter mit einer
plastisch ausgearbeiteten Blattader dargestellt. Zwischen den Kelchblättern befinden sich Blütenblätter,
die bis zum Boden des Kelches zwischen den Sepalen zu sehen sind. Die Blütenblätter werden durch jeweils eine Papyrusdolde auf beiden Seiten eingerahmt. Im Gegensatz zum Kelch Louvre E 11349 behält
der Kelch aus Assiut jedoch seine runde Grundform bei und zeigt keine Auswölbung der Gefäßlippe
oder weitere Ausgestaltungen der Blütenblätter oder der Papyrusdolden. Sein Standfuß ist nicht erhalten
und kann auf Grund der großen Vielfalt der Formen nicht mit Sicherheit nachvollzogen werden.

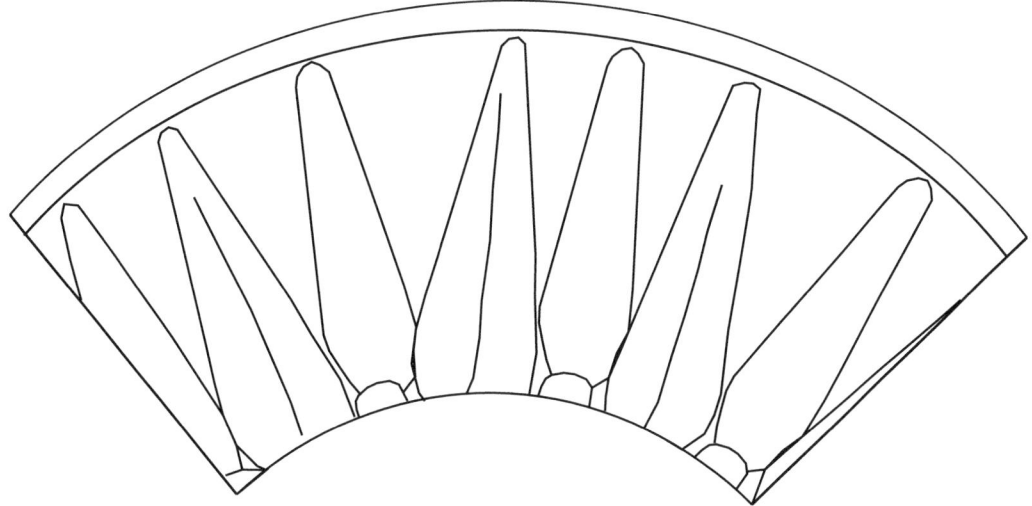

Abb. 5: Skizze der Dekoration von Kelch S10/st1354, Zeichnung: A. S. de Carvalho Gomes.

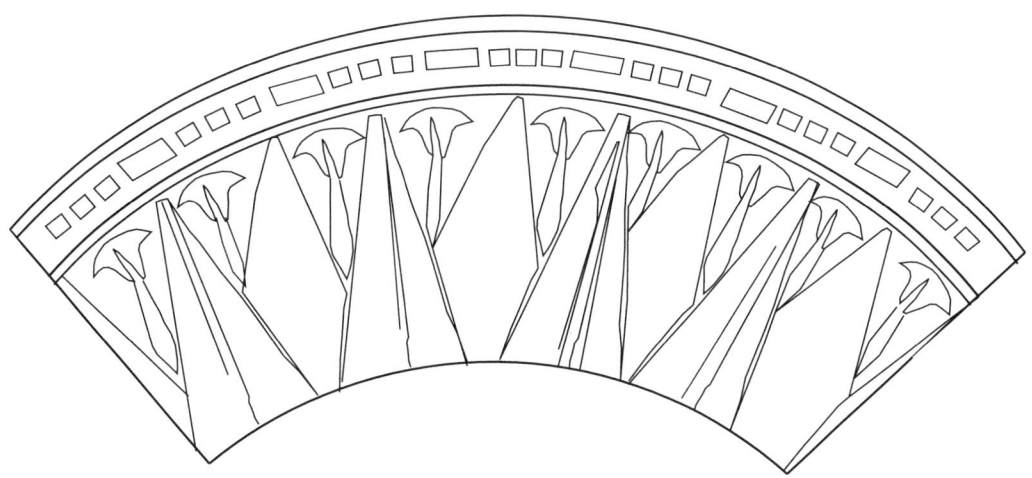

Abb. 6: Skizze der Dekoration, Kelch S08/st751 und S11/st448, Zeichnung: A. S. de Carvalho Gomes.

4. Mögliche typologische und stilistische Entwicklung

Gefäße in Kelchform sind bereits aus dem Mittleren Reich belegt.[34] Die Abbildung an der Westwand der Hauptkammer von Grab 2 in Beni Hassan zeigt beispielsweise Kelche mit schmalem Körper, jedoch mit breitem, kompaktem Standfuß.[35] Die Gefäße erscheinen nicht rot, sondern grünlich, was gegen gewöhnliche Tonware spricht. Auch Metallgefäße sind auszuschließen, da die Produktion dieser Waren im darüber befindlichen Register dargestellt wird und die Arbeitsschritte auf die Verarbeitung von Ton oder tonähnlichem Material hinweisen, was Gefäße aus Kupfer gleichfalls unwahrscheinlich erscheinen lässt. Ob es sich tatsächlich um die Darstellung der Fayenceverarbeitung handelt, müsste weiter verifiziert

---

34 Bissing 1902.
35 Newberry 1893: pl. 11.

werden. Ein reliefierter Lotuskelch ist bei einer Auswahl an Vasen aus der Regierungszeit Thutmosis III. bezeugt.[36] Das dort dargestellte Exemplar zeigt Kelch- und Blütenblätter und einen breiten, gedrungenen Blütenstiel. Zu sehen sind die Weihgeschenke an Amun nach der erfolgreichen Heimkehr Thutmosis III. an einer Wand neben dem Sanktuar des großen Tempels von Karnak,[37] die somit in die 18. Dynastie zu datieren sind. Eine Typologisierung anhand dieser wenigen Darstellungen ist jedoch schwierig, da es sich nicht um den gleichen Werkstoff handeln muss und die Verarbeitung von Fayence durch die Beschaffenheit des Materials eine andere ist als die von Ton oder Metall. Technische Kriterien könnten zur Entwicklung der äußeren Form beigetragen haben.

Die Typologische Methode wurde von Oskar Montelius bereits im 19. Jahrhundert entwickelt und beruht auf der Annahme einer mehr oder weniger kontinuierlichen Entwicklung einer Form aus einer vorherigen, einfacheren Grundform.[38] Diese Grundform wird durchgängig weiterentwickelt und ausgestaltet, die Herstellungstechnik wird verfeinert und die Verzierungen werden ausgeprägter und feiner. Da es sich bei den Fayencekelchen um eine Adaption von Kelchen aus einem anderen Werkstoff handelt, könnte man von einer kontinuierlichen Weiterentwicklung ausgehen. Lotusförmige Becher aus unterschiedlichen Werkstoffen sind weit verbreitet, beispielsweise die aus Gold gearbeiteten Kelche aus Tell-Basta (Bubastis, heute im Kairo Museum) mit einer Kartusche der Tausret oder ähnlich aussehende Kelche aus Alabaster[39]. Fayence weist als Werkstoff jedoch einige Besonderheiten auf, die eine technische Weiterentwicklung verlangen und eine eher kompakte erste Variante wahrscheinlich machen. Eine rein ikonographisch orientierte Typologisierung des vorliegenden Materials, wie sie Tait teilweise vorgenommen hat, erscheint durch den symbolischen Zusammenhang der Abbildungsarten, wie bereits erwähnt, nicht zielführend. Um eine Typologisierung vornehmen zu können, bedarf es einer Einbeziehung stilistischer Merkmale. Form und Aufbau, aber auch besonders die technischen Merkmale der Bearbeitung, können einen Hinweis auf die Entwicklung dieser Fundgattung geben.

5. Der Versuch einer Typologisierung

Wie bereits erörtert, sind die Fundlage und die Datierung der Fundgruppe schwierig. Die Inschrift am Kelch ÄM4563 ist die einzig feste Datierungsmöglichkeit, die bislang gegeben ist. Die hier genannte 22. Dynastie muss als *terminus a quo* verstanden werden. Ein weiterer zeitlicher Hinweis, wenn auch ein nicht so gesicherter wie der des Kelches aus Berlin, sind die Kelche aus dem Grab D115 in Abydos, die in die 18. Dynastie datiert werden. In Anbetracht der übrigen Grabbeigaben ist die zeitliche Einordnung wahrscheinlich, wenn auch nicht völlig gesichert.[40] Bei der Museumsrecherche tauchen jedoch immer wieder zeitliche Einordnungen der einzelnen Kelche auf. Meist besteht ein direkter Zusammenhang zwischen dem Bildprogramm und der gewählten Datierung oder sie orientiert sich an der zeitlichen Einordnung von Wallis oder Tait, die maßgeblich Bezug auf von Bissings Theorie des Motivtransfers nehmen.[41] Dabei werden äußerliche, technisch bedingte Kriterien wie Form des Standfußes oder Ausprägung der Glockenform des Kelches außer Acht gelassen. Bezieht man diese äußeren Komponenten mit ein und verwendet nur die bereits genannten Daten als Orientierung, ändert sich die typologische Reihe.

---

36 Prisse d'Avennes 1991.
37 Prisse d'Avennes 1991.
38 Eggers 2006: 88–105.
39 Bspw. New York, MMA 26.7.1434 aus der Zeit Thutmosis III.
40 Die Publikation zu dieser Grabung gibt zum Zustand des Grabes bei seiner Auffindung wenig Aufschluss, siehe Peet & Loat 1913: 16. Als Orientierungshilfe soll sie dennoch einbezogen werden.
41 Von Bissing sieht einen direkten Zusammenhang mit phönizischen Metallschalen, siehe Tait 1963: 93.

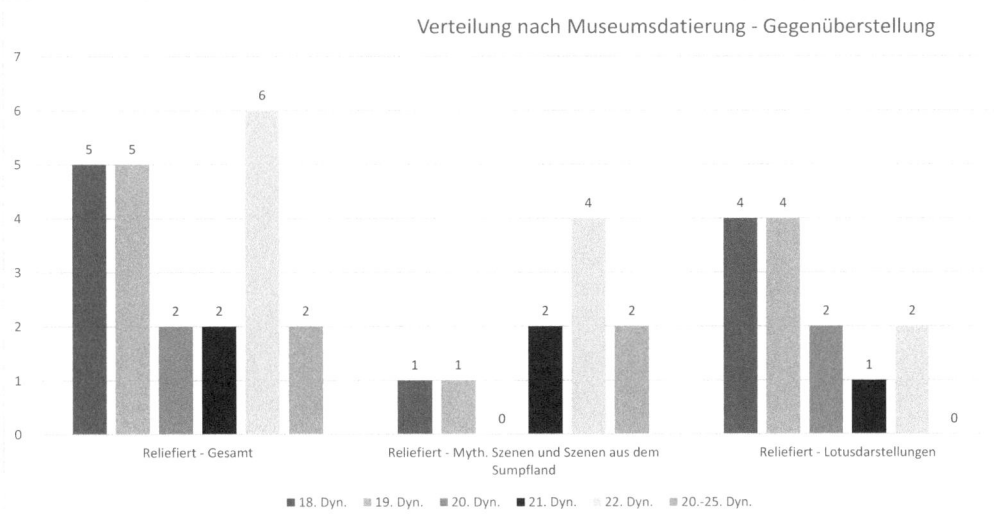

Abb. 7: Zeitliche Einordnung nach Museumsangaben.

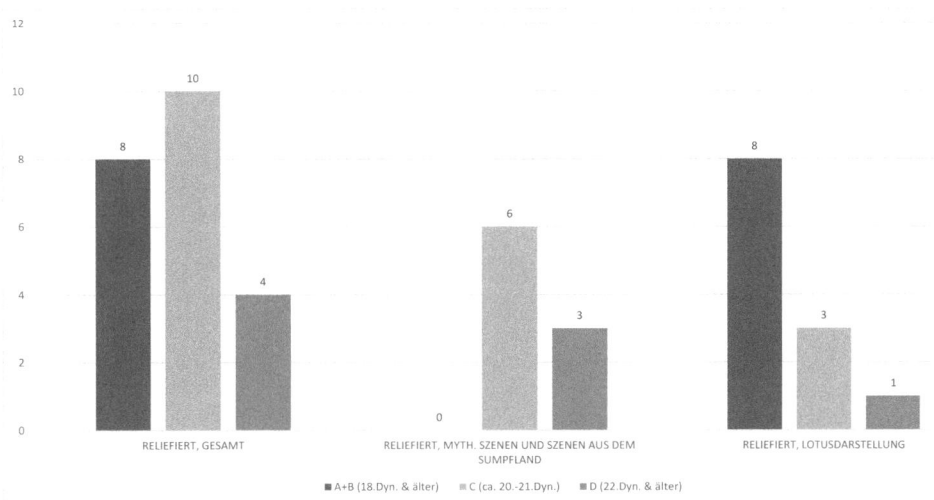

Abb. 8: Veränderung der zeitlichen Einordnung durch die Typologisierung.

Die im Folgenden vorgelegte typologische Einordnung basiert auf der Annahme, dass sich durch die Beschaffenheit des Werkstoffs eine Entwicklung von eher gedrungener Form mit breitem Rand, wenig ausgeprägter Glockenform und Ausstülpung des Randes hin zu einer schmaleren Grundform mit ausgeprägter Glockenform zeigt und die Entwicklung der verzierten und unverzierten Werkstücke parallel verläuft. Die Gefäße werden also höher und schlanker, Merkmale wie Gefäßlippe und Glockenform werden ausgeprägter. Die grobe Einteilung in Gruppe A+B, C und D bedeutet also:

Gruppe A + B: Gedrungene Grundform, breiter und kurzer Standfuß, Glockenform des Bechers kaum ausgeprägt, Gefäßlippe kaum oder gar nicht abgesetzt, allgemein robuste Erscheinung.	Royal Athena Galleries	-
	Bolton Museum	1900 5449
	Museum of Fine Arts Boston	01.7396
	Museum of Fine Arts Boston	01.7397
	Louvre	E 22452
	The Petrie Collection	45500
	Metropolitan Museum of Art	26.7.973
	The Fitzwilliam Museum Cambridge	E 255.1939
Gruppe C: Höhere Ausführung, breiter, aber höherer Standfuß, leicht ausgeprägte Glockenform des Kelches mit deutlich abgesetzter Gefäßlippe, allgemein eleganter als Typ A.	Metropolitan Museum of Art	66.7.971
	Metropolitan Museum of Art	26.7.972
	Metropolitan Museum of Art	26.7.975
	Metropolitan Museum of Art	26.7.976
	The Brooklyn Museum	49.133
	The Petrie Collection	UC 14556
	British Museum	EA 26.226
	Louvre	E 11349
	The Walters Art Museum	45.414
Gruppe D: Hohe und schmale Ausführung, Standfuß ebenfalls hoch und schmal, Glockenform des Kelches ist stark ausgeprägt, die Gefäßlippe ist deutlich abgesetzt. Möglicherweise Sonderformen. Kelche erscheinen filigran.	Toledo Museum of Art	1983.12
	Museo Egizio di Firenze	-
	Neues Museum Berlin	ÄM 4563

6. Fazit

Die Idee, eine typologischen Reihe anhand dieser geringen Fundmenge zu erstellen, ist schwierig, dennoch demonstriert der gewählte Ansatz wie einfach die bisher geltende zeitliche Einordnung verändert werden kann. Erhalten bleibt eine Entwicklungsübereinstimmung, die die Kelche mit einem Bildmotiv im Durchschnitt deutlich älter als die Kelche mit zwei oder drei Bildreihen einstuft. Zu sehen ist jedoch, dass diese Darstellungen deutlich jünger vorstellbar sind, sobald äußerliche Elemente wie ausgeprägte Glockenform oder ähnliches zugefügt werden. Die Kriterien für die von mir vorgenommene Typologisierung nach äußerer Form, Standfuß und Ausprägung der Glockenform wären sicherlich noch zu verfeinern. Auch die Auseinandersetzung mit der Idee des Motivtransfers der Kelche und ihr Zusammenhang mit der Levante und dem phönizischen Raum sollten weiter untersucht werden. Die Einordnung der Assiuter Kelchfragmente in die typologische Reihe anhand äußerer Faktoren kann nur als Versuch gewertet werden. Da der Standfuß der zwei bzw. drei Kelche nicht vorhanden und schwer zu rekonstruieren ist, basiert die Einordnung einzig auf der Rekonstruktion des Kelchkörpers. Auch wenn ich dargelegt habe, dass das Bildprogramm an sich durch seine Gemeinsamkeit des symbolischen Inhalts in der Entwicklung der vorliegenden Sammlung zeitunabhängig zu werten ist, sollte man zukünftig die Art der Ausgestaltung miteinbeziehen. Taits Theorie zum zentralen Anfertigungsort und damit verbunden einer sehr begrenzten Anzahl von Herstellern kann ich nicht folgen.

Die einzige Aussage, die getroffen werden kann, ist, dass die meisten reliefierten Fayencekelche aus der Region in und um Mittelägypten stammen, obwohl sich die großen Stätten der Fayenceherstellung – nach heutigem archäologischen Kenntnisstand – während des Neuen Reichs und der Spätzeit in

Amarna, Lisht, Memphis und Naukratis befunden haben.[42] Tuna el-Gebel als einzigen Herstellungsort dieser Fundgattung zu vermuten, ist möglich, aber beweisen lässt sich diese Annahme nicht. Gerade das Auffinden der Assiuter Kelche sollte daran erinnern, dass zahlreiche Produktionsstätten durch moderne Überbauung nicht entdeckt und untersucht werden können. So bedeutet der fehlende Nachweis für eine Fayencewerkstatt nicht, dass beispielsweise in Assiut keine Fayencekelche hergestellt wurden.

Der typologischen Reihe nach bewegen sich die Kelchfragmente aus Assiut zwischen den Gruppen B und C. Wie durch die typologische Reihe nachgewiesen werden konnte, kommt das Bildprogramm der Assiuter Fragmente in der gesamten Zeitreihe vor. Weitere Kriterien wie die Ausarbeitung der Kelchform rücken diese Stücke jedoch in den älteren Bereich der Typologie.

Bibliographie

BISSING 1902: F. W. von Bissing, Fayencegefäße (Catalogue Général des Antiquites Égyptiennes du Musee du Caire 6; Cairo 1902).

EGGERS 2006: H. J. Eggers, Einführung in die Vorgeschichte (München – Zürich 2006).

FEUCHT 1984: E. Feucht, Verjüngung und Wiedergeburt, in: Studien zur Altägyptischen Kultur 11, 1984, 401– 417.

FLOSSMANN-SCHÜTZE ET AL. 2015: M. C. Flossmann-Schütze, F. Hoffmann & D. Kessler, Die Petosiris-Nekropole von Tuna El-Gebel. Band I. Unter Mitarbeit von J. Helmbold-Doyé, Ch. Klein, L. Lembke & T. Meyer, (Tuna el-Gebel 6; Vaterstetten 2015).

FRIEDMAN 1998: F. D. Friedman, Gifts of the Nile. Ancient Egyptian Faience (London 1998).

HELMBOLD-DOYÉ 2008: J. Helmbold-Doyé, Tuna el-Gebel – Fundgruppen, Werkplätze und Öfen. Ein Zwischenbericht, in: Culture and History of the Ancient Near East 41, 2008, 133–148.

HUFFT 2006: B. Hufft, Motivtransfer und Rezeption? Ein Beitrag zu den ägyptischen reliefierten Lotuskelchen der 3. Zwischenzeit, in: Studien zur Altägyptischen Kultur 45, 2006, 137–168.

KAHL ET AL. 2009: J. Kahl, M. El-Khadragy, U. Verhoeven, A. El-Khatib & C. Kitagawa, The Asyut Project: Sixth Season of Fieldwork (2008), in: Studien zur Altägyptischen Kultur 38, 2009, 113–130.

KITAGAWA 2016: C. Kitagawa, mit Beiträgen von J. Kahl und G. Vittmann, The Tomb of the Dogs at Asyut: Faunal Remains and Other Selected Objects (The Asyut Project 9; Wiesbaden 2016).

MORENZ & SCHUBERT 1954: S. Morenz & J. Schubert, Der Gott auf der Blume. Eine ägyptische Kosmogonie und ihre weltweite Bildwirkung (Artibus Asiae, Supplementum XII; Zürich 1954).

NEWBERRY 1893: P. E. Newberry, Beni Hasan I (Archaeological Survey of Egypt 1; London 1893).

NICHOLSON 2005: P. T. Nicholson, The sacred animal necropolis at North Saqqara: the cults and their catacombs, in: S. Ikram (Hg.): Divine Creatures: Animal Mummies in Ancient Egypt (Cairo 2005), 44–71.

PEET & LOAT 1913: T. E. Peet; W. L. S. Loat, The Cemeteries of Abydos. 3: 1912–1913 (Egypt Exploration Fund 35; London 1913).

PRISSE D'AVENNES 1991: E. Prisse D'Avennes, Atlas of Egyptian Art (reprint, Cairo 1991).

RICKETTS 1918: Ch. Ricketts, Two Faience Chalices at Eton College from the Collection of the Late Major W. J. Myers, in: The Journal of Egyptian Archaeology 5,3, 1918, 145–147.

ROEDER 1959: G. Roeder, Hermopolis 1929–1939. Ausgrabungen der Deutschen Hermopolis-Expedition in Hermopolis, Ober-Ägypten, in Verbindung mit zahlreichen Mitarbeitern (Hildesheim 1959).

RZEUSKA 2017: T. I. Rzeuska, Chronological Overview of Pottery from Asyut. A contribution to the history of Gebel Asyut al-gharbi (The Asyut Project 7; Wiesbaden 2017).

SAAD 1940: Z. Y. Saad. A Preliminary Report on The Excavations at Saqqara 1939–1940, in: Annales du Service des Antiquités 40, 1940, 675–713.

SCHNEIDER ET AL. 2003: H. D. Schneider et al., The Small Masterpieces Of Egyptian Art: selections from the Myers Museum at Eton College (Leiden 2003).

---

42 FRIEDMAN 1989.

SCHLÖGL 1977: H. A. Schlögl, Der Sonnengott auf der Blüte. Eine ägyptische Kosmogonie des Neuen Reiches (Aegyptiaca Helvetica 5, Genève 1977).

TAIT 1963: G. A. D. Tait, The Egyptian Relief Chalice, in: The Journal of Egyptian Archaeology 49, 1963, 93–139.

WALLIS 1898: H. Wallis, Egyptian Ceramic Art. The MacGregor collection; a contribution towards the history of Egyptian pottery (London 1898).

WALLIS 1900: H. Wallis, Egyptian Ceramic Art: Typical Examples of the Art of the Egyptian Potter (London 1900).

Totenbuch Spruch 72 des *P(ꜣ)-ṯi̯-ỉmn(.w)* auf der Mumienkartonage S05/71 aus Assiut

Mahmoud El-Hamrawi

„Meinem verehrten Lehrer Prof. Mohamed Saleh
zum 80. Geburtstag gewidmet".

The following article deals with an unpublished copy of the spell 72 of the Book of the Dead which was written on the mummy cartonage S05/71 of the deceased *P(ꜣ)-ṯi̯-ỉmn(.w)* from Asyut. It was found in Gebel Assiut al-gharbi, the necropolis of the nomarchs of the 13ᵗʰ Upper Egyptian nome during the fieldwork in the season 2005 by the Egyptian-German Mission. It is now housed in the antiquities-magazine at the village of Shutb. Not only the vignette of the spell 72 from Asyut but also the text is studied with help of 25 parallels which are dated from the 18ᵗʰ Dynasty to the Ptolemaic Period. The parallel versions of the spell 72 are written on papyri, coffins, sarcophagi and tomb walls. A new translation, commentary and dating are given.

0. Vorbemerkung

Die alte Stadt ⊗𓄿𓏏 *sꜣw.t* (> cop. ϭⲓⲟⲟⲩⲧ, ϭⲓⲟⲟⲩⲑ, ⲥⲓϣⲟⲩⲧ > äg.arab. *syūṭ* سيوط > arab. *ʾasyūṭ, ʾasyūṭ* أسيوط)[1] war die Hauptstadt des 13. oberägyptischen Gaues, dessen altägyptischer Name *Nčf.t ḫnt.t* war. Die Ausdehnung des Gaues konnte in der Kapelle des Königs Sesostris I. mit etwa 6 *ỉtrw* und 6 *ḫꜣ* identifiziert werden, d.h. 66,138 km² oder 65,90 km.[3] Der Gau erstreckte sich von km 335 beim Dorf Um al-Qusour nördlich von Assiut, bis km 378, ca. drei bis vier Kilometer südlich von Assiut. Die weite Entfernung zwischen der Nord- und der Südgrenze nähert sich etwa 42 km gemäß der Ausdehnung der

---

* Dieser Aufsatz ist die Überarbeitung eines Vortrags, der im Rahmen des Kolloquiums „Terra Incognita: Archaeological Fieldwork in Asyut and Middle Egypt" an der Freien Universität Berlin vom 20.–22. Juni 2019 gehalten wurde. Für die Einladung und die Finanzierung danke ich Herrn Prof. Jochem Kahl. Ihm bin ich auch dankbar dafür, dass er mir die Veröffentlichung der Mumienkartonage gestattet hat; ebenso danke ich ihm für wertvolle Diskussionen bei der Kollation. Prof. Ursula Verhoeven, Prof. Jochem Kahl und Dr. Andrea Kilian gebührt mein Dank, dass sie die Arbeit im Manuskript gelesen und mit wertvollen Literaturhinweisen gefördert haben. Ich danke auch den Personen, die diese Arbeit ermöglichten: Dr. Sameh Shafik für das Faksimile, Herrn Fritz Barthel für die Fotos, Herrn Medhat Tadros, Direktor von Shutb-Magazin, für seine Hilfsbreitschaft. Mein Dank geht an Frau Tina Beck und Frau Angela Böhme, die mein Deutsch korrigiert haben. Für verbleibende Mängel übernehme ich natürlich die Verantwortung. Als Transkriptionssystem wird das von Prof. Wolfgang Schenkel gebrauchte System benutzt: *ỉ* für *j*, *y* für *jj*, *s* für *z*, *ś* für *s*, *ḳ* für *q*, *č* für *ṯ*; *ṱ* für *d*, *ç* für *ḏ*, siehe Schenkel 2012: 19–25; ders. 2005: 31–36; ders. 1990: 1–6; siehe auch Rössler 1971: 163–326. Mit dem Zeichen – bezieht sich die Endung *k(ỉ)–/kw–* auf kein Determinativ (Gardiner sign-list A1); mit dem Zeichen + bezieht sich die Endung *k(ỉ)₊ / kw₊* auf ein Determinativ, siehe auch El-Hamrawi 2016: passim.

1 Timm 1984: I, 235–251.
2 Helck 1974: 104.
3 Leitz 2006: 418. Leitz ist der Ansicht, dass es sich bei den Maßangaben der Sesostriskapelle um Flächenmaße handelt, d.h. die Fläche des 13. oberägyptischen Gaues ist 6 *ỉtrw* und 6 *ḫꜣ* etwa 689,3 km, siehe Leitz (2006: 411).

Eisenbahn, während die tatsächliche Entfernung zwischen der Nord- und der Südgrenze entlang des Nils auf 63 km geschätzt wird.[4]

Die Nekropole der Gauhauptstadt befindet sich auf dem Gebel Assiut al-gharbi. Sie enthält die Felsengräber der Gaufürsten, die den Gau in der Ersten Zwischenzeit und im Mittleren Reich regierten. Eines davon ist das Felsengrab des Gaufürsten *Itỉ-ỉbỉ* (Grab Siut III = Grab N12.1), der den Gau in der Zeit des Königs Nebkare (des Vaters von König Merikare) am Ende der 10. Dynastie regierte.[5]

Es besteht aus zwei Seitenkammern (Abb. 1) vor einer großen Halle (Abb. 2) mit vier Schächten, wobei jeder Schacht zu einer Grabkammer führt. Der zuvor in der Forschung unbekannte Schacht Nr. 4 (Abb. 3) wurde im Jahr 2005 durch das *Asyut Project* freigelegt.[6] Der Schachtinhalt war massiv durchwühlt, dennoch konnten bei den Freilegungsarbeiten u. a. Reste von Mumien, Körperteilen, Bandagen und Kartonage geborgen werden. Dabei wurde auch die Mumienkartonage (S05/71) entdeckt, welche heute im Shutb-Magazin aufbewahrt wird.[7]

Schacht 4 wurde wohl – wie die anderen Schächte auch – in der Spätzeit und in der Ptolemäerzeit wiederverwendet, was unter anderem dort gefundene massiv gestörte Mumienbestattungen bezeugen. Eine der Mumien war wohl ursprünglich mit der Kartonage bedeckt, die aus Leinen mit Gips gemacht worden ist. Nach den Inschriften auf der Kartonage zu urteilen, gehörte sie einem Mann namens *P(ȝ)-ṯỉ-ỉmn(.w)*. Sie wurde zuerst mit dunkelgelber Farbe bemalt. Darauf sind die Szenen und Bilder bunt gemalt.

Die Mumienkartonage kann in drei Teile geteilt werden (Abb. 4a–b):[8]

A. Der obere Teil der Mumienkartonage

1. Das erste Register
    1.1 Die letzte Szene der 12. Stunde des Pfortenbuchs hinter dem Kopf
    1.2 Die Geburt von Horus

2. Das zweite Register
    2.1 Die Szene des Usech-Halskragens
    2.2 Die Geburt von Khepri
    2.3 Die Szene der rechten Seite
    2.4 Die Szene der linken Seite

3. Das dritte Register
    3.1 Die Szene der Göttin Nut
    3.2 Die Geburt von Re
    3.3 Die Szenen der rechten Seite
    3.4 Die Szenen der linken Seite

---

4   Gardiner 1947: II 74; Montet 1961: II, 135–137; Lacau & Chevrier 1969: Tf. 3; Helck 1974: 104–106, Tf. 2; Gomaá 1986: I, 100–101; Leitz 2006: 418.

5   Franke 1987: 52; Kahl 2007: 74–77; El-Khadragy 2008: 221; Kahl et al. 2016: passim. Vor ihm regierte Cheti I. (Grab Siut V = M11.1) den Gau, während nach ihm sein Sohn Cheti II. (Grab Siut IV = N12.2) folgte, der den Gau in der Zeit des Königs Merikare regierte, siehe El-Khadragy 2008: 221 Anm. 3. Zu verschiedenen Ansichten zum Vater von Merikare siehe El-Khadragy 2008: 221 Anm. 6. Die Felsengräber der Gaufürsten des 13. oberägyptischen Gaues werden systematisch und neu durch das *Asyut Project* nummeriert. Deshalb wird das Grab des Nomarchen *Itỉ-ỉbỉ* mit der neuen Nummer „Grab N12.1" anstelle von „Grab/Siut III", wie in der älteren Literatur angegeben, bezeichnet, siehe Kahl, El-Khadragy & Verhoeven 2006: 241–242; Kahl 2007: 17; 74–83; El-Khadragy 2008: 221 Anm. 2.

6   Vgl. Kahl, in Kahl et al. 2016: 21.

7   Kahl 2007: 74, 75, fig. 51.

8   Der Verfasser arbeitet noch an diesen Gliederungen und wird die Kartonage zu einem späteren Zeitpunkt in Gänze veröffentlichen.

1. Die Vignette des Tb-Spruchs 72 von *P(ꜣ)-ṯi-ỉmn(.w)* (Abb. 5a–b)

Der Verstorbene *P(ꜣ)-ṯi-ỉmn(.w)* ist stehend mit Blick nach links abgebildet. Er trägt einen langen weißen gefalteten Schurz, während der Kopf, der Oberkörper und die Füße nackt und dunkelrot gefärbt sind. Er erhebt seine Hände in Anbetung zum Gott Osiris, der dem Verstorbenen gegenüber auf seinem Thron in steifer aufrechter Haltung sitzt und den Blick auf *P(ꜣ)-ṯi-ỉmn(.w)* gerichtet hat. Er trägt seine charakteristische Krone, die als Atef-Krone bekannt ist. Sie ist dunkelblau gefärbt und besteht aus einem hohen konischen Mittelstück (das in seiner Form der Weißen Krone entspricht) mit einer Feder zu beiden Seiten. Sein Körper ist in dunkelrote Binden gewickelt, aus denen seine Arme herausragen, um das Flagellum zu halten, während der Krummstab nicht dargestellt ist. Sein Thron ist dunkelrot und dunkelblau gefärbt.[9] Dazwischen gibt es einen Opfertisch, auf dem eine einzelne große Lotosblüte und ein rundes Brot liegen.[10]

Über der Szene finden sich kurze Kolumnen mit Beischriften zur Szene:

– vor dem Verstorbenen:

|¹ṯwꜣ.w nčr(.w) sp 2 {4}   „Anbetung des Gottes, zweimal".

– über dem Verstorbenen:

|¹čṯ mṯw ỉn wśr(.w)   „Worte zu sprechen von Osiris
|²{čṯ mṯw} P(ꜣ)-ṯi-ỉmn(.w) <mꜣꜥ-ḫrw>   Padiamun, <dem Gerechtfertigten>",

---

9   Die Vignette ist vergleichbar mit V Tb 72 bei pTurin Tf. 27 über dem Spruch, re; pMilbank1 Pho.-Tf. 69 über dem Spruch, re; pHor Pho.-Tf. 6 über dem Spruch, li; pRyerson Pho.-Tf. 24 über Kol. 48, mi; pKöln über Kol. 37; pNachtamun (Ba) Naville 1886: I, Tf. 84; pNeferuebenef (Pb) Naville 1886: I, Tf. 84; pBaksu (Ax) Naville 1886: I, Tf. 84; pNebseni (Aa) Naville 1886: I, Tf. 84; siehe auch Mosher 2016: 379–380.

10   Zur Beschreibung der Vignette von pIahtesnacht siehe Verhoeven 1993: 1, 55 und der Vignette von pHor siehe Munro 2006: 60. Zur geschichtlichen Zusammenfassung der Vignette siehe Milde 1991: 140–143.

– über dem Gott Osiris :

| ³n wśr(.w) nb |²ỉmn.tt   „für Osiris, den Herren des Westens,

|⁴ nčr ꜥ nb ꜣbč(.w)   den großen Gott, den Herren von Abydos".

Kommentar und Analyse

Die Vignette des Tb-Spruchs 72 ist wohl eine besondere Darstellung auf der Mumienkartonage von *P(ꜣ)-ṯi̯-ỉmn(.w)* aus Assiut, weil sie den Verstorbenen vor einem einzigen Gott zeigt, nämlich vor Osiris. In der Spätzeit und Ptolemäerzeit wird der Verstorbene üblicherweise in Anbetung vor zwei oder drei Göttern dargestellt, die vor einem Opfertisch sitzen.[11] Die Götter werden als Osiris, der die Atef Krone trägt, und Tekem, dem die Vorräte dargebracht werden, identifiziert.[12]

Im Neuen Reich wird der Verstorbene in Anbetung vor drei hockenden Götterfiguren dargestellt, gelegentlich vor einem Schrein oder einer Tür.[13] Die Vignette der Assiuter Mumienkartonage enthält zudem ein besonderes Motiv, und zwar eine einzige große Lotusblume, die auf dem Opfertisch liegt, wohingegen bei pTurin, pMilbank, pRyerson und pKöln zwei Lotosblüten dargestellt sind.

2. Text des Tb-Spruchs 72 von *P(ꜣ)-ṯi̯-ỉmn(.w)* (Abb. 6a–b)

Unter der Vignette ist die Mumienkartonage S05/71 von *P(ꜣ)-ṯi̯-ỉmn(.w)* mit einer Kopie des Tb-Spruchs 72 ohne Titel und Nachschrift beschriftet.[14] Der Text besteht aus fünf Kolumnen, in denen die Richtung der Hieroglyphenschrift nach rechts zeigt. Die Inschriften sind schwarz gefärbt, während der Hintergrund der Kolumnen in verschiedenen Farben bemalt ist. Die erste und die fünfte sind dunkelgelb, die zweite und die vierte hellblau und die dritte Kolumne hellgelb gemalt.

2.1 Lesung des Tb-Spruchs 72 anhand der Parallelen[15]

pNespa.   [Titelzeile] *r̓ n(.ỉ) pri̯<.t> m hrw w*|²⁸,¹³*b̓ꜣ ỉmḥ.<t> m ỉmn.tt*

ₛKairo₃₄₆₄₈   [Titelzeile] <..> <..> <...> <.> <...> <...> <...>

ₛₐKammar   [Titelzeile] <..> <..> <...> <.> <...> <...> <...>

pKöln   [Titelzeile] *r̓ n(.ỉ) pri̯<.t>* |³⁴,²*m hrw wb̓ꜣ ỉmḥ.{w} m ỉmn.tt*

ₛTurin₂₂₀₁   [Titelzeile] <..> <..> <...> <.> <...> <...> <...>

ₛOxford₁₉₄₇.₂₉₅   [Titelzeile] <..> <..> <...> <.> <...> <...> <...>

ₛₐKairo₄₁₀₅₈   [Titelzeile] <..> <..> <...> <.> <...> <...> <...>

ₛLondon₉₇₁   [Titelzeile] <..> <..> <...> <.> <...>

---

11 pRyerson Tf. 24, XLVIII; pMilbank Tf. 69, 440–449 obere Hälfte; pTurin Tf. 27 siehe auch Milde 1993: 142 Anm. 10; Mosher 2016: 379–380.

12 Allen 1960: 43.

13 Hornung 1990: 457.

14 Der Text des Spruchs 72 wird auf der Mumienkartonage gekürzt wiedergegeben, siehe ₖAssiut Z. 1–5. Für den kompletten Text sind die folgenden Parallelen zu beachten: Mitt.Ptol. (2.–1. Jh. v. Chr.): pTurin Tf. 27, 1–11; pEmory 1, 11–22; sBerlin Inv.-Nr. 46 Abb. 1, 1–10; pMilbank Pho.- Tf. 69, 440–449 (M₁); 76, 654–659 (M₂). Früh.Ptol. (3.–2. Jh. v. Chr.): sKairo JE 6291 Z.1–9; sKairo TR (13/1/21/8) Z. 1–12; pHor Tf. 6, 133–141; pKairo Pho.- Tf. 23, 1–2; 24, 3–12. Pers.-Ptol.: pRyerson Pho.-Tf. 24 Kol. 49, 1–42; sPhiladelphia E 16135 Z. 1–4; sLondon EA 971 Z. 1–4. 30.–26. Dyn.: sOxford 1947. 291 Z. 1–9. 26. Dyn.: pNespasefy Tf. 28, Kol. B9, 12–18; 29, Kol. B10, 1–11; sKairo JE 34648 Z. 1–14 nach Maspero 1900: 259–260; saKamar Z. 229–238 nach Maspero 1902: 179; pKöln 34, 1–13; sTurin 2201 Z. 10–25 nach Piehl 1886: Tf. 86E–89F; Roccati 1989: 30, Abb. 14, Z. 16–25); Heise 2007: 270–273; sKairo 41058 Z. 7–47 nach Gauthier 1913: 348–349. 26.–25. Dyn.: Grab TT 34 nach Rosati 2006: 299, Tf. 2b, 3, 21, 1–12. 18. Dyn.: pNebseni (Aa) Tf. 3, 1–15 nach Budge 1898: I, 159–162; pMesemneter (Ca) Naville 1886: I, Tf. 84, 1–14; pBaksu Tf. 2, 43–55; pNu Lapp 1997: Tf. 20, 1–14+1; Quirke 2013: 173–174. Vgl. auch die unlängst publizierte Fassung im Grab des Monthemhet (TT 34): Gestermann et al. 2021: 295–308. Vgl. weiter die Belege von Tb 72 auf www.totenbuch.awk.nrw.de

15 Für die Übersetzung des Spruchs 72 vgl. Allen 1960: 146–147; Keller 1984: 62; Hornung 1990:152–153; Verhoeven 1993: 1, 168–170; Heise 2007: 270–273; Quirke 2013: 173–174; Mosher 2016: 354–357; 359; 361–362; 366–368. Zur Zusammenfassung des Spruchs vgl. Hornung 1990: 459.

ₖAssiut	[Titelzeile]	<..> <..> <...> <.> <...> <...> <...>[16]
pHor	[Titelzeile]	*rʾ n(.i) ꜥḥꜥ(.t) m-bȝḥ psč̣.t iri=s mȝꜥ-ḫrw=f*
pEmory	[Titelzeile]	*rʾ n(.i) pri<.t> m hrw*[1, 12]*wbȝ imḥ.t m imn.tt*
ₛBerlin₄₆	[Titelzeile]	<..> <..> <...> <.> <...> <...> <...>
pTurin	[Titelzeile	*rʾ n(.i) pri<.t> m hrw wbȝ imḥ.t*
pMilbank₁	[Titelzeile]	[69, 440]*rʾ n(.i) wbȝ imn.tt m hrw{m ḥ wbȝ}{rʾ n(.i)św}*
pMilbank₂	[Titelzeile]	<..> <..> <...> <....> <.> <...>

pNespa.	*č̣t mṯw in wśr(.w) ḥm-nčr Nś-pȝ-śf* <...-...>
ₛKairo₃₄₆₄₈	|[1]*č̣t mṯw in wśr(.w) imi-rʾ ś.t Pȝ-ṯi-n(.i)-ȝś.t mȝꜥ-ḫrw*
ₛₐKammar	|[229]*č̣t mṯw in wśr(.w) wr snw Pśmč̣k* <...-...>
pKöln	*č̣t mṯw in wśr(.w) iꜥḥ-t(ȝy)=ś-nḫt* <...-...>
ₛTurin₂₂₀₁	|[3]*č̣t mṯw in wśr(.w) ḥrp ḥ.wt ..*|[9]*.. č̣ȝ.ti Gmi.n=f "rʾ(.w)-bȝk* <...-...>
ₛOxford₁₉₄₇.₂₉₅	|[1]*č̣t mṯw in wśr(.w) imi-rʾ pr(.w) Ptḥ-ḥtp(.w) mȝꜥ-ḫrw mśi.n NN*
ₛₐKairo₄₁₀₅₈	|[1]*č̣t mṯw in* |[2]*wśr(.w) nb.t pr* |[3]*šps.t tȝbč̣.t*|[4] *mȝꜥ-ḫrw*
ₛLondon₉₇₁	|[1]*č̣t mṯw in wśr(.w) iyi-m Ḥtp mȝꜥ-ḫrw sȝ NN iri.n NN*
ₖAssiut	|[1]*č̣t mṯw*[17] *in* <....> <..-..-....> <...-...> [18]
pHor	|[6, 133]*č̣t mṯw in wśr(.w) ḥm-nčr Ḥr(.w) mȝꜥ-ḫrw*
pEmory	*č̣t mṯw in wśr(.w) imi-rʾ pr(.w) Pȝhb mȝꜥ-ḫrw sȝ NN iri.n*|[1, 13]*NN*
ₛBerlin₄₆	|[1]*č̣t mṯw in wśr(.w) ... Wn-nfr mȝꜥ-ḫrw ...*
pTurin	|[27, 1]*č̣t mṯw in wśr(.w) iw=f-ꜥnḫ(.w) mȝꜥ-ḫrw*
pMilbank₁	<...> <...> <..> <...> <..-..-....> <...-...>
pMilbank₂	<...> <...> <..> <...> <..-..-....> <...-...>

pNespa.	*i:nč̣ ḥr=tn nb.w mȝꜥ.t* |[28, 14]*šwi̯.ø m iśf.t*
ₛKairo₃₄₆₄₈	<i>nč̣{t} ḥr=tn nb.w mȝꜥ.t {ś}wi̯.ø* |[2]*m iśf.t*
ₛₐKammar	*i:nč̣ ḥr=čn nb.w mȝꜥ.t šwi̯.ø m iśf.t*
pKöln	*i:nč̣ ḥr=tn nb.w mȝꜥ{ḫrw}.t šwi̯.ø [.] iśf.{i}*
ₛTurin₂₂₀₁	|[10]*i:nč̣ ḥr=tn nb.w mȝꜥ-ḫrw šwi̯.ø m iś{w}f.(t)*
ₛOxford₁₉₄₇.₂₉₅	*i:nč̣ ḥr=tn nb.w mȝꜥ.ti šwi̯.ø m iśf.t*
ₛₐKairo₄₁₀₅₈	|[7]*i:nč̣ ḥr=tn nb.w mȝꜥ.t šwi̯.ø* |[8]*m iśf.{i}*
ₛLondon₉₇₁	*i:nč̣ ḥr=č[.] [...] [...] [...] [.] [...]*
ₖAssiut	*i:nč̣ ḥr=čn*[19]*nb.w mȝꜥ.t šwi̯.ø m iśf.*<.> [20]
pHor	*i:nč̣ ḥr=čn nb.w mȝꜥ.t šwi̯.ø m iśf.t*
pEmory	*i:nč̣ ḥr=tn nb.w mȝꜥ.t šwi̯.ø m iśf.{i}*

---

16 Bei ₖAssiut ist der Text ohne Titelzeile; bei pKairo ist die Titelzeile zum Teil gut erhalten; bei pHor findet sich ein ungewöhnlicher Spruchtitel, siehe MUNRO 2006: 23 a; bei pMilbank₁ ist der Titel verderbt, vgl. auch *rʾ n(.i) pri(.t) m hrw wbȝ imḥ.t m imn.tt* pRyerson Tf. 24, Kol. 49; *rʾ n(.i) pri(.t) m hrw wbȝ imḥ.<t> in sḫȝ.w Nb-sny mȝꜥ-ḫrw* pNebseni (Aa) Tf. 3, 1; *rʾ n(.i) pri(.t) m hrw wbȝ imḥ.<t> in im.i ś.t ꜥȝ n(.i) Imn(.w) sḫȝ.w Mśi-m-nčr iri.n NN mśi.n NN* <...-...> pMesemneter (Ca) Tf. 34, 1–2; *rʾ n(.i) wbȝ Imḥ.t* pNu Tf. 20, 1; QUIRKE 2013: 173; siehe auch MOSHER 2016: 354 Anm. 2.

17 Hier weist *č̣t mṯw* eine abgekürzte Schreibung auf, vgl. Wb V 625, 3; zu unterschiedlichen Schreibungen der Formel *č̣t mṯw in ...* vgl. Wb V 625, 13–15; 626, 1–3.

18 Bei ₖAssiut ist die Textzeile (*č̣t mṯw* Formel) zum großen Teil ausgelassen. Der Rest der Formel wird in schwarz geschrieben, vgl. auch *č̣t mṯw in wśr(.w) NN mȝꜥ-ḫrw* pRyerson Tf. 24 Kol. 49, 1–2; *č̣t=f* pNebseni (Aa) Tf. 3, 1; *č̣t=f* pMesemneter (Ca) Tf. 34, 2.

19 Hier ist *inč̣ ḥr=tn* eine Begrüßungsformel, die vor einem Suffixpronomen und seinem resumptiven Substantiv am Anfang einer Anrede steht, Wb II 372, 10–22; weitere Begrüßungsformeln lauten: *hnw n=k* „Jubel sei dir" Wb II 493, 18; *śn tȝ n=k* „Erde küssen für dich" Wb IV 154, 9 und *śwȝš n=k* „Preisen dir" Wb IV 64, 24.

20 Bei ₖAssiut ist die Textstelle gut erhalten, vgl. *i:nč̣-ḥr=tn nb.w mȝꜥ.t šwi̯.Ø m iśf.t* pRyerson Tf. 24 Kol. 49, 3; <i:nč̣-ḥr>=čn nb.w mȝꜥ.t šwi̯.Ø m iśf.t Grab TT 34, 1 nach ROSATI 2006: Tf. 21, 1; *i:nč̣-ḥr=<.> nb.w <kȝ.w> <šwi̯.Ø> m iśf.t* pNebseni (Aa) Tf. 3, 1–2; *i:nč̣-ḥr=čn nb.w kȝ.w šwi̯.Ø m iśf.t* pMesemneter (Ca) Tf. 34, 2; *i:nč̣-ḥr=čn nb.w mȝꜥ.t šwi̯.y/w m iśf.t* pNu Tf. 20, 2; QUIRKE 2013: 173.

sBerlin46	*ỉ:nč ḥr=čn nb.w mȝꜥ.t šwỉ.ø m ỉśf.t*
pTurin	*ỉ:nč ḥr=tn nb.w mȝꜥ.t šwỉ.ø m ỉśf.t*
pMilbank1	|[69, 441]*ỉ:nč ḥr=tn nb.w mȝꜥ(.t) šwỉ.ø* |[69, 442]*ỉśf.t*
pMilbank2	|[76, 654]*ỉ:nč ḥr=tn nb.w mȝꜥ.t šwỉ.ø ỉś<f.t>*

pNespa.	*wnn.w ꜥnḫ r nḥḥ {sp 2} ḥn.tỉ č.t*
sKairo34648	*wnn.w ꜥnḫ r nḥḥ ḥn.t{t} r č.t*
SaKammar	*wn.w ꜥnḫ* |[230]*r (n)ḥḥ ḥn.tỉ č.t*
pKöln	*wnn.w ꜥnḫ r nḥḥ*|[34, 3]*ḥn.tỉ č.t*
sTurin2201	*wnn.w ꜥnḫ r nḥḥ* |[11]*{sp 2} ḥn.{w}tỉ č.t*
sOxford1947.295	*wn.y/w ꜥnḫ r (n)ḥḥ ḥn.tỉ r č.t*
SaKairo41058	*wnn.w ꜥnḫ r* |[9]*nḥḥ {sp 2} ḥn.{wy} č.t*
sLondon971	*[....] [...] r (n)ḥḥ ḥn.tỉ č.t*
KAssiut	*wnn.w ꜥnḫ r (n)ḥḥ*[21]*{sp 2}ḥn.tỉ*[22] *n(.ỉ) č.t*[23]
pHor	|[6, 134]*wnn.w ꜥnḫ r nḥḥ ḥn.tỉ č.t*
pEmory	*wnn.w ꜥnḫ r* |[1, 14]*(n)ḥḥ ḥn<.t> n.t č.t*
sBerlin46	*wnn.w ꜥnḫ r nḥḥ ḥn{n}.tỉ č.t*
pTurin	*wnn.w ꜥnḫ* |[2]*r (n)ḥḥ ḥn.tỉ č.t*
pMilbank1	*wnn.w ꜥnḫ r (n)ḥḥ ḥn.tỉ {r}č.t*
pMilbank2	*wnn.w ꜥnḫ r (n)ḥḥ ḥn.tỉ {r}č.t*

pNespa.	*wbȝ=tn <..> r* |[28, 15]*tȝ*
sKairo34648	*wbȝ=<ỉ>r=čn*
SaKammar	*ȝb=tn wỉ r tȝ*
pKöln	*wbȝ=tn <.>=ỉ r tȝ*
sTurin2201	*wb<ȝ>=tn <.>=ỉ r tȝ*
sOxford1947.295	*wb<ȝ>=ỉ r=tn*
SaKairo41058	|[10]*wbȝ=tn <..> r tȝ*
sLondon971	*wbȝ=tn r tȝ pn n(.ỉ) mȝꜥ.tỉ*
KAssiut	*wbȝ*|[2]*=tn <..> r {tȝ.wỉ}*[24]
pHor	*[.]bȝ=čn <..> r tȝ*
pEmory	*wb<ȝ>=ỉ r <t>n*
sBerlin46	*wbȝ=tn wỉ r tȝ*
pTurin	*wbȝ=tn*|[27, 2]*wỉ r tȝ*
pMilbank1	*wb<ȝ>=tn wỉ r tȝ*
pMilbank2	*wbȝ=tn wỉ r tȝ*

pNespa.	*tw=ỉ ȝḫ.kw+ m ỉrw=tn*
sKairo34648	*ȝḫ.k(ỉ)_*|[3]*m ỉrw=<ỉ>*
SaKammar	*ȝḫ.kw+ m ỉr(w)=tn*
pKöln	*tw=ỉ ȝḫ.kw+ m ỉrw=tn*

---

21 *r nḥḥ* „bis in Ewigkeit" Wb II 301, 1 gegenüber *n nḥḥ* „für die Ewigkeit" Wb II 301, 7.

22 Bei KAssiut wird das Wort *ḥn.tỉ* wie in den meisten Parallelen als Dual geschrieben; diese Dualschreibung ist seit der 18. Dynastie belegt. Das Wort *ḥn.t* bedeutet „Bereich" Wb III 105, 9; zur Übersetzung vgl. VERHOEVEN 1993: 1, 168; QUIRKE 2013: 173; MOSHER 2016: 354 Anm. 4.

23 Bei KAssiut ist der Text an dieser Stelle gut erhalten, vgl. *wnn.w ꜥnḫ r-(n)ḥḥ ḥn.tỉ č.t* pRyerson Tf. 24 Kol. 49, 4–5; *wnn.(w) [...] [.-...] [....] [...]* Grab TT 34, 1–2 nach ROSATI 2006: Tf. 21, 1–2; *wnn.y/w <ꜥnḫ> r-nḥḥ ḥn.tỉ č.t* pNebseni (Aa) Tf. 3, 2; *wnn.y/w ꜥnḫ r-nḥḥ {sp 2} ḥn.tỉ č.t* pMesemneter (Ca) Tf. 34, 2; *wnn.y/w ꜥnḫ r nḥḥ ḥn.tỉ č.t* pNu Tf. 20, 2; QUIRKE 2013: 173.

24 Bei KAssiut ist der Text an dieser Stelle zum Teil weggebrochen und weist Schreibfehler auf, vgl. *wbȝ=tn p.t tȝ* pRyerson Tf. 24 Kol. 49, 5; *[...=..] [..] [.] tȝ* Grab TT 34, 2 nach ROSATI 2006: Tf. 21, 1; *wbȝ.n=ỉ r=tn* pNebseni (Aa) Tf. 3, 2; *wbȝ.n=ỉ r=tn* pMesemneter (=Ca) Tf. 34, 2–3; *wbȝ=ỉ r=tn* pNu Tf. 20, 2–3; QUIRKE 2013: 173.

ₛTurin₂₂₀₁	*tw=ỉ 3ḫ{t}.kw₊ m ỉrw=tn*
ₛOxford₁₉₄₇.₂₉₅	*3ḫ.kw₊ m ỉrw=ỉ*
ₛₐKairo₄₁₀₅₈	*tw=ỉ 3ḫ.kw|¹¹₊ m ỉr{tt}w=tn*
ₛLondon₉₇₁	*3ḫ{t}.k(ỉ)₋ m ỉr(w)=tn*
ₖAssiut	*{p}w=ỉ 3ḫ{t}.kw₊ m ỉrw{t}/y=tn²⁵*
pHor	*tw=ỉ 3ḫ.kw₊ m ỉr|⁶, ¹³⁵w=tn*
pEmory	*3ḫ{t}.k(ỉ)₋ m ỉrw.w=ỉ*
ₛBerlin₄₆	*tw=ỉ 3ḫ.kw₊ |²m ỉrw.w=tn*
pTurin	*tw={y} 3ḫ.kw₊ m ỉrw.w=tn*
pMilbank₁	*<t>w=ỉ |⁶⁹, ⁴⁴⁴3ḫ.kw₊ m ỉrw.w=tn*
pMilbank₂	*<t>w=ỉ 3ḫ.<k>w₊ m|⁷⁶, ⁶⁵⁵ỉrw.w=tn*
pNespa.	*šḫm.kw₊ m ḥk3{w}=tn*
ₛKairo₃₄₆₄₈	*ᶜpr.k(ỉ)₋ m ḥk3=<ỉ>*
ₛₐKammar	*šḫm.kw₊ m ḥk3=tn*
pKöln	*šḫm.kw₊ m ḥk3{w}=tn*
ₛTurin₂₂₀₁	*|¹²šḫm.kw₊ m ḥk3{w}=tn*
ₛOxford₁₉₄₇.₂₉₅	*ᶜpr.kw₊ m ḥk3.{t}=ỉ*
ₛₐKairo₄₁₀₅₈	*šḫm.kw|¹²₊ m ḥk3{w}=tn*
ₛLondon₉₇₁	*ᶜpr.k(ỉ)₋ <m> ḥk[3=tn]*
ₖAssiut	*šḫm.kw₊ <.> ḥk3{t}={r'=ỉ}=<tn>²⁶*
pHor	*šḫm.k{t}w₊ m ḥk3{t}=tn*
pEmory	*ᶜpr.kw₊ m ḥk3{w}=ỉ*
ₛBerlin₄₆	*šḫm.kw₊ m ḥk3{w}=čn*
pTurin	*šḫm.kw₊ m ḥk3{t}=tn*
pMilbank₁	*šḫm.|⁶⁹, ⁴⁴⁵kw₊ m ḥk3{t}=tn*
pMilbank₂	*šḫm.kw₊ m ḥk3=tn*
pNespa.	*ỉp=kw₊ m ỉp.{w}=<..>*
ₛKairo₃₄₆₄₈	*3tp.k(ỉ)₋ m 3ḫ.w=<ỉ>*
ₛₐKammar	*ỉp=k |²³¹w₊ m ỉp.<.>=tn*
pKöln	*ỉp=kw₊ m ỉp.<.>=tn*
ₛTurin₂₂₀₁	*ỉp=kw₊ m ỉp=tn*
ₛOxford₁₉₄₇.₂₉₅	*3tp.|²kw₊ m 3ḫ{.t}<=ỉ>*
ₛₐKairo₄₁₀₅₈	*ỉp=k|¹³w₊ m ỉp.{w}=<tn>*
ₛLondon₉₇₁	*[3tp.k(ỉ)₋] [m] [3ḫ.w=tn]*
ₖAssiut	*[..]=[.]w₊|³m ỉp.{w}t=t<.>²⁷*
pHor	*ỉp=k{t}w₊ m ỉp.{w/y}=<..>*
pEmory	*3tp.|¹, ¹⁵kw₋ m 3ḫ{.t}=ỉ*
ₛBerlin₄₆	*ỉp=kw₊ m ỉp=čn*
pTurin	*ỉp=kw₊ m ỉp.t=tn*

---

25 Bei ₖAssiut ist die Textstelle zum Teil weggebrochen und weist Schreibfehler auf, vgl. *tw=ỉ 3ḫ.kw₊ m ỉrw=tn* pRyerson Tf. 24 Kol. 49, 6; *tw=ỉ 3ḫ.kw₊ m ỉrw=[..]* Grab TT 34, 2–3 nach Rosati 2006: Tf. 21, 2–3; *3ḫ.kw₊ m ỉrw=ỉ* pNebseni (Aa) Tf. 3, 3; *3ḫ.kw₊ m ỉrw=ỉ* pMesemneter (=Ca) Tf. 34, 2–3; *3ḫ.kw₊ m ỉrw.w=ỉ* pNu Tf. 20, 3; Quirke 2013: 173.

26 Bei ₖAssiut ist die Textstelle zum Teil ausgelassen und weist Schreibfehler auf, vgl. *šḫm.kw₊ m ḥk3{w}=tn* pRyerson Tf. 24 Kol. 49, 6–7; es fehlt beim Grab TT 34 vgl. Rosati 2006: Tf. 21, 3; *šḫm.kw₊ m ḥk3{w}=ỉ* pNebseni (Aa) Tf. 3, 3; *šḫm.kw₊ m ḥk3{w}=ỉ* pMesemneter (=Ca) Tf. 34, 3; *šḫm.kw₊ m ḥk3{w}=ỉ* pNu Tf. 20, 3; Quirke 2013: 173.

27 Bei ₖAssiut ist der Text an dieser Stelle zum Teil weggebrochen, vgl. *ỉp=kw₊ m ỉp.t=tn* pRyerson Tf. 24 Kol. 49, 7–8; *[.]p=kw₊ m ỉp.{w}=tn* Grab TT 34, 3 nach Rosati 2006: Tf. 21, 3; *ỉp=kw₊ m 3ḫw=<.>* pNebseni (Aa) Tf. 3, 3; *ỉp=kw₊ [.] 3ḫw=ỉ* pMesemneter (Ca) Tf. 34, 3–4; *3tp=kw₊ m 3ḫ.w=ỉ* pNu Tf. 20, 3–4; Quirke 2013: 173. Zur Schreibung: *ỉp.t=tn* „Anzahl" bei ₖAssiut sowie pRyerson, pMilbank₁ und pTurin gegenüber *3ḫw=ỉ* bei den Parallelen der 18. Dyn.

pMilbank₁ |⁶⁹, ⁴⁴⁶ỉp=kw₊ m ỉp.t=tn

pMilbank₂   ỉp{.t}=kw₊ m ỉp.t=tn

pNespa.   nḥm=|²⁸, ¹⁶tn <..> m-ꜥ ꜣṭ tꜣ pn n(.ỉ) mꜣꜥ.t

ₛKairo₃₄₆₄₈   nḥm=čn w|⁴<ỉ> m-ꜥ ꜣṭ ỉmỉ tꜣ pn n(.ỉ) mꜣꜥ.tỉ

ₛKammar   nḥm=tn wỉ m-ꜥ ꜣṭ ỉmỉ tꜣ pn n(.ỉ) {tꜣ.wỉ}

pKöln   nḥm=tn <.>ỉ m-ꜥ ꜣṭ |³⁴, ⁴tꜣ pn mꜣꜥ.t

ₛOxford₁₉₄₇.₂₉₅   nḥm=tn wỉ m-ꜥ ꜣṭ wnm rꜣ pn n(.ỉ) mꜣꜥ.tỉ

ₛTurin₂₂₀₁   nḥm=tn|¹³<w>ỉ m-ꜥ ꜣṭ n(.ỉ) tꜣ pn n(.ỉ) mꜣꜥ.tỉw

ₛₐKairo₄₁₀₅₈   nḥm=|¹⁴tn wỉ m<-ꜥ> ꜣ{ꜥ}ṭ tꜣ pn|¹⁵n(.ỉ) mꜣꜥ.t

ₛLondon₉₇₁   [...]= |³tn <wỉ> m-ꜥ {ỉčỉ} ꜣṭ tꜣ pn mꜣꜥ.tỉ

ₖAssiut   nḥm=čn <.>ỉ m-ꜥ ꜣṭ tꜣ pn <n(.ỉ)> mꜣꜥ.tỉw ²⁸

pHor   nḥm=|⁶, ¹³⁶čn <.>ỉ m-ꜥ ꜣṭ tꜣ pn n(.ỉ) mꜣꜥ.tỉw

pEmory   nḥm=tn wỉ m-ꜥ ꜣṭ wnm rꜣ pn mꜣꜥ.tỉ

ₛBerlin₄₆   nḥm=tn wỉ m-ꜥ ꜣṭ m tꜣ pn n(.ỉ) mꜣꜥ.tỉ

pTurin   nḥm=tn wỉ m-ꜥ ꜣṭ tꜣ pn|²⁷, ³n(.ỉ) mꜣꜥ.t

pMilbank₁ |⁶⁹, ⁴⁴⁷nḥm=tn wỉ m-ꜥ {w}ṭ ỉm.ỉ|⁶⁹, ⁴⁴⁸tꜣ pn n(.ỉ) mꜣꜥ.tỉ

pMilbank₂   nḥm=tn wỉ m-ꜥ ꜣṭ ỉm.ỉ tꜣ pn n(.ỉ) mꜣꜥ.tỉ

pNespa.   čč=tn n=ỉ rꜣ=ỉ mṭ.t=ỉ ỉm=f

ₛKairo₃₄₆₄₈   ỉw n=<ỉ> rꜣ=ỉ mṭu=ỉ ỉm=f

ₛKammar   čỉ=tn n=ỉ rꜣ=ỉ mṭ.t=ỉ ỉm=f

pKöln   čč=tn n=ỉ rꜣ=ỉ mṭ.t={f}ỉm=f

ₛTurin₂₂₀₁   čč=tn n=ỉ rꜣ=ỉ mṭ.t=ỉ |¹⁴ỉm=f

ₛOxford₁₉₄₇.₂₉₅   ỉw <n>=ỉ rꜣ=ỉ mṭu=ỉ ỉm=f

ₛKairo₄₁₀₅₈   čỉ.t=tn n=ỉ rꜣ=ỉ |¹⁶mṭ.t=ỉ ỉm=f

ₛLondon₉₇₁   čỉ=tn n=ỉ rꜣ=ỉ mṭ.t=ỉ ỉm=f

ₖAssiut   čỉ=tn n=ỉ rꜣ=ỉ [.]ṭ.[.=.] ỉm=<.>²⁹

pHor   čỉ=tn n=ỉ rꜣ=ỉ mṭ.t=ỉ ỉm=f

pEmory   ỉw n=ỉ rꜣ=ỉ mṭ.t=ỉ ỉm=f

ₛBerlin₄₆ |³čỉ=tn n=ỉ rꜣ=ỉ mṭu=ỉ ỉm=f

pTurin   čỉ=tn n=ỉ rꜣ=ỉ mṭ.t=ỉ ỉm=f

pMilbank₁   čỉ=tn n=ỉ rꜣ=ỉ mṭ.t=<.> |⁶⁹, ⁴⁴⁹ỉm=f

pMilbank₂   čỉ|⁷⁶, ⁶⁵⁶=tn n=ỉ rꜣ=ỉ {rꜣ=ỉ}mṭ.t=<.> ỉm=f

pNespa.   ỉw čỉ.tw n=ỉ ꜣw(.t)-ꜥ |²⁸, ¹⁷m-bꜣḥ=tn

ₛKairo₃₄₆₄₈   čỉ.t<.> n=<ỉ>|⁵ ꜣw.<t>-ꜥ m-bꜣḥ=čn

ₛKammar   ỉw|²³²čỉ.tw n=ỉ ꜣw.t m-bꜣḥ=tn

pKöln   ỉw čč.tw n=ỉ ꜣw.<t>-ꜥ m-bꜣḥ=tn

ₛTurin₂₂₀₁   ỉw čč.tw n=ỉ ꜣw.<t>-ꜥ m-bꜣḥ=tn

ₛOxford₁₉₄₇.₂₉₅   čỉ n=<ỉ> ꜣw.<t>-ꜥ m-bꜣḥ=tn

ₛₐKairo₄₁₀₅₈   ỉw čỉ.tw |¹⁷n=ỉ ꜣw.<t>-ꜥ m-bꜣḥ=tn

ₛLondon₉₇₁   <..> <..> <.=.> <...> <.-...=..>

---

28 Bei ₖAssiut ist die Textzeile gut erhalten, vgl. nḥm=tn <wỉ> m-ꜥ ꜣṭ tꜣ pn n(.ỉ) mꜣꜥ.t pRyerson Tf. 24 Kol. 49, 8–9; es fehlt beim Grab TT 34 Rosati 2006: Tf. 21, 4; nḥm=tn wỉ m-ꜥ ꜣṭ.w n(.ỉ) tꜣ pn n(.ỉ) mꜣꜥ.t pNebseni (Aa) Tf. 3, 4; nḥm=tn wỉ m-ꜥ ꜣṭ n(.ỉ) tꜣ pn {r} mꜣꜥ.tỉw pMesemneter (Ca) Tf. 34, 4; nḥm=čn wỉ m-ꜥ ꜣṭ.w n(.ỉ) ỉw pn n(.ỉ) mꜣꜥ.tỉw pNu Tf. 20, 4; Quirke 2013: 173.

29 Bei ₖAssiut ist der Text an dieser Stelle zum Teil weggebrochen, vgl. čỉ=tn n=ỉ rꜣ=ỉ mṭ.t=ỉ ỉm=f pRyerson Tf. 24 Kol. 49, 9–10; [..=..] [.=.] [..=.] [...=.] ỉm=f Grab TT 34, 3 nach Rosati 2006: Tf. 21, 3; čỉ=tn <n>=ỉ rꜣ=ỉ mṭu=ỉ ỉm=f pNebseni (Aa) Tf. 3, 5; <..=.> <.=.> rꜣ=ỉ mṭu=ỉ ỉm=f pMesemneter (Ca) Tf. 34, 4; rꜣ=ỉ n=ỉ mṭu=ỉ ỉm=f pNu Tf. 20, 4–5; Quirke 2013: 173.

ₖAssiut	*či<.t>n|⁴{wi} 3w.<t>-{ib}{wi}-ᶜ m-b3ḫ=tn³⁰*
pHor	*|⁶, ¹³⁷iw či.tw n=i 3w.<t>-ᶜ m-b3ḫ=tn*
pEmory	*či=tn |¹, ¹⁶ 3w.<t> m-b3ḫ=tn*
ₛBerlin₄₆	*iw či.tw n=i 3w.<t>-ᶜ m-b3ḫ=tn*
pTurin	*iw či.tw n=i 3w.<t>-ᶜ m-b3ḫ=tn*
pMilbank₁	*|⁷⁶, ⁶⁵⁶rči.w n=i 3w.<t> m-b3ḫ=tn*
pMilbank₂	*rči.w n=i 3w.<t> m-b3ḫ=tn*
pNespa.	*ḥr n.tt tw=i rḫ.kw₊ rn=tn*
ₛKairo₃₄₆₄₈	*ḥr n.t{t} tw=<i> rḫ.<k(i)_> čn rḫ. k(i)_ rn=čn*
ₛₐKammar	*ḥr n.t{t}tw=i rḫ.kw₊ tn rḫ.kw₊ rn=tn*
pKöln	*ḥr n.ti tw=<.> rḫ.kw₊ rn=tn*
ₛTurin₂₂₀₁	*ḥr n.t{t} tw=i rḫ.kw₊ rn=tn*
ₛOxford₁₉₄₇.₂₉₅	*ḥr n.t{t} tw=i rḫ.<k(i)_> tn rḫ.kw₊ rn=tn*
ₛₐKairo₄₁₀₅₈	*ḥr n.ti |¹⁸tw=i rḫ.kw₊ rn=tn {rḫ.k|¹⁹w₊ rn=tn}*
ₛLondon₉₇₁	*<..> <..> <.=.> <...> <.-...=..>*
ₖAssiut	*ḥr n.ti tw=i rḫ.k(i)_ rn.w=čn³¹*
pHor	*ḥr n.ti tw=i rḫ.k(i)_ <.>n.w=čn*
pEmory	*ḥr n.ti <tw=i> rḫ.k(i)_ rn=tn*
ₛBerlin₄₆	*ḥr n.ti tw=i rḫ.kw₊ rn=tn*
pTurin	*ḥr n.ti tw=i rḫ.kw₊ rn=tn*
pMilbank₁	*ḥr n.t<i> <t>w=i rḫ.{t}<kw₊> <rn=tn>*
pMilbank₂	*ḥr n.t<i> <t>w=i rḫ.<kw₊> <rn>=t<n>*
pNespa.	*rḫ.kw₊ rn n(.i) nčr pfy ᶜ3*
ₛKairo₃₄₆₄₈	*iw=<i> |⁶rḫ.k(i)_ nčr pf ᶜ3*
ₛKammar	*rḫ.kw₊ rn n(.i) nčr pf ᶜ3*
pKöln	*rḫ.kw₊ rn n(.i) nčr pfy ᶜ3*
ₛTurin₂₂₀₁	*rḫ.kw₊ rn n(.i) nčr pwy ᶜ3*
ₛOxford₁₉₄₇.₂₉₅	*iw=i rḫ.kw₊ nčr pf ᶜ3*
ₛₐKairo₄₁₀₅₈	*rḫ.kw₊ rn n(.i) nčr {ᶜ3} pf ᶜ3*
ₛLondon₉₇₁	*<....> <..> <.=.> <...> <.-...=..>*
ₖAssiut	*rḫ.kw₊ nčr pwy {r}3"³²*
pHor	*rḫ.kw₊|⁶, ¹³⁸rn n(.i) nčr pwy ᶜ3"*
pEmory	*rḫ.k(i)_ rn nčr pf ᶜ3*
ₛBerlin₄₆	*rḫ.kw₊ rn n(.i) nčr|⁴pwy ᶜ3*
pTurin	*rḫ.kw₊ rn n(.i) nčr|²⁷, ⁴pwy ᶜ3*
pMilbank₁	*<...> <..> <.> <...> <...> <..>*
pMilbank₂	*<...> <..> <.> <...> <...> <..>*
pNespa.	*čč=tn čf3.w r fn|²⁸, ¹⁸.t=f*
ₛKairo₃₄₆₄₈	*či.t=čn čf3.w r fnč=f*

---

30 Bei ₖAssiut weist der Text teilweise Schreibfehler auf, vgl. *iw či.tw n=i 3w.t-ᶜ m-b3ḫ=tn* pRyerson Tf. 24 Kol. 49, 9–10; *iw či.tw n=i 3w.[.-.]* Grab TT 34, 4–5 nach Rosati 2006: Tf. 21, 4–5; *iw či.tw n=i 3w.t-ᶜ{ᶜ.wi=i}m-b3ḫ=tn* pNebseni (Aa) Tf. 3, 5; *iw či.tw n=i 3w.t-ᶜ=i m-b3ḫ=tn iw či.tw <n>=i ᶜ3=i m-b3ḫ=tn* pMesemneter (=Ca) Tf. 34, 4–5; *iw či.tw n=i 3w.<t>-ᶜ m-b3ḫ=čn* pNu Tf. 20, 5; Quirke 2013: 173.

31 Bei ₖAssiut ist die Textzeile gut erhalten, vgl. *ḥr n.tt tw=i rḫ.kw₊ rn=tn* pRyerson Tf. 24 Kol. 49, 10–11; es fehlt beim Grab TT 34, 5 vgl. Rosati 2006: Tf. 21, 5; *ḥr n.tt tw=i rḫ.kw₊ [tn] rḫ.kw₊ rn.w=čn* pNebseni (Aa) Tf. 3, 5–6; *ḥr n.tt tw=i rḫ.kw₊ tn rḫ.kw₊ rn.w=tn* pMesemneter (Ca) Tf. 34, 4–5; *ḥr n.tt [tw=i] [rḫ.kw]₊ čn rḫ.kw₊ rn.w=čn* pNu Tf. 20, 5; Quirke 2013: 173.

32 Bei ₖAssiut ist hier die Textstelle teilweise ausgelassen, vgl. *rḫ.kw₊ rn n(.i) nčr pwy ᶜ3* pRyerson Tf. 24 Kol. 49, 11–12; *<.>ḫ. kw₊ rn n(.i) nčr pwy ᶜ3* Grab TT 34, 5 nach Rosati 2006: Tf. 21, 5; *rḫ.kw₊ rn n(.i) nčr pwy ᶜ3* pNebseni (Aa) Tf. 3, 6–7; *rḫ.kw₊ rn n(.i) nčr ᶜ3* pMesemneter (Ca) Tf. 34, 5; *iw=i rḫ.kw₊ nčr pwy ᶜ3* pNu Tf. 20, 6; Quirke 2013: 173.

ₛₐKammar	|²³³*či̯=tn čf<ꜣ.w> r fnč=f*
pKöln	*či̯.t=tn*|³⁴, ⁵*čfꜣ.w r fnč=f*
ₛTurin₂₂₀₁	*čč=tn čfꜣ.w r fnṯ=f*
ₛOxford₁₉₄₇.₂₉₅	*či̯=tn čfꜣ.w r fnč=f*
ₛₐKairo₄₁₀₅₈	*či̯=tn čfꜣ.w r fnč=f*
ₛLondon₉₇₁	*či̯=tn čf<ꜣ>.w r fnṯ/t=<f>*
ₖAssiut	*či̯=tn čf<ꜣ>.w r fn.tỉ=f*³³
pHor	*či̯=tn čf<ꜣ>.w r fnṯ/t=f*
pEmory	*či̯=tn čf<ꜣ>.w*|¹, ¹⁷*[.] [...=.]*
ₛBerlin₄₆	*či̯=tn čf<ꜣ>.w r fnṯ=f*
pTurin	*či̯=tn čf<ꜣ>.w r fn.t=f*
pMilbank₁	*<..=..> <....> <.> <...=f>*
pMilbank₂	*<..=..> <....> <.> <...=.>*

pNespa.	*tkm(.w) rn=f*
ₛKairo₃₄₆₄₈	*Rkm.(w) rn=f*
ₛₐKammar	*tkm.w rn=f*
pKöln	*tkm.w rn=f*
ₛTurin₂₂₀₁	|¹⁶*čṯ tkm rn=f*
ₛOxford₁₉₄₇.₂₉₅	*Rkm.(w) rn=f*
ₛₐKairo₄₁₀₅₈	|²¹*ky čṯ tkm.w rn=f*
ₛLondon₉₇₁	*tk[m](.w) [rn=f]*
ₖAssiut	*tkm(.w) rn=f*³⁴
pHor	*tkm(.w) rn=f*
pEmory	*[Rkm] [..=.]*
ₛBerlin₄₆	*tkm.w rn=f*
pTurin	*tkm(.w) rn=f*
pMilbank₁	*<....> <..=.>*
pMilbank₂	*<....> <..=.>*

pNespa.	*ỉw wbꜣ=f r ꜣḫ.t {ỉmn.tt} n.t p.t*
ₛKairo₃₄₆₄₈	*ỉw=f wbꜣ=<.> <.> <...> <...> <..> <..>*
ₛₐKammar	*ỉw ꜣb=f r ꜣḫ.t ỉꜣb.t n.t p.t*
pKöln	*ỉw wbꜣ=f r ꜣḫ.t ỉꜣb.tt n.t p.t*
ₛTurin₂₂₀₁	*ỉw=f wb<ꜣ>=f r ꜣḫ.t ỉꜣb.tt n.t p.t*
ₛOxford₁₉₄₇.₂₉₅	*ỉw*|³*=f wb<ꜣ>=f m ꜣḫ.t ỉꜣb.tt n.t p.t*
ₛₐKairo₄₁₀₅₈	*<ỉw=f>w*|²²*bꜣ=f r ꜣḫ.t ỉꜣb.*|²³*tt n.t p.t*
ₛLondon₉₇₁	vorzeitiger Abbruch des Spruchtexts
ₖAssiut	*ỉw=f wbꜣ{t}{ḥ}=f r ꜣḫ.t ỉꜣb.tt <n>.t p.t*³⁵
pHor	*ỉw=f*|⁶, ¹³⁹*wbꜣ=f r ꜣḫ.t ỉꜣb.tt n.t p.t*
pEmory	*[..=.] [.]bꜣ=f m ꜣḫ.t ỉꜣb.tt n.t p.t*
ₛBerlin₄₆	*ỉw=f wbꜣ=f r ꜣḫ.t ỉꜣb.tt n.t p.t*

---

33 Bei ₖAssiut ist die Textstelle gut erhalten, vgl. *či̯=tn čfꜣ.w r fnṯ=f* pRyerson Tf. 24 Kol. 49, 12–13; *či̯=tn [....] [.] [...=f]* Grab TT 34, 5–6 nach Rosati 2006: Tf. 21, 5–6; *čč=tn čfꜣ.w r fnṯ* pNebseni (Aa) Tf. 3, 6–7; *čč.w=tn čfꜣ.w r fnṯ=<.>* pMesemneter (Ca) Tf. 34, 5–6; *čč=čn čfꜣ.w [r] fnṯ=f* pNu Tf. 20, 6; Quirke 2013: 173.

34 Bei ₖAssiut ist die Textstelle gut erhalten, vgl. *rkm(.w) rn=f* pRyerson Tf. 24 Kol. 49, 13; es fehlt beim Grab TT 34, 6 vgl. Rosati 2006: Tf. 21, 6; *tkm(.w) r[.]=f* pNebseni (Aa) Tf. 3, 7; *rkm(.w) <..>=f* pMesemneter (Ca) Tf. 34, 6; *čkm rn=f* pNu Tf. 20, 6; Quirke 2013: 173.

35 Bei ₖAssiut ist die Textstelle gut erhalten, vgl. *ỉw=f wbꜣ=f ꜣḫ.t ỉꜣb.tt n.t p.t* pRyerson Tf. 24 Kol. 49, 13–14; *<..>=f <...=.> m ꜣḫ.t ỉꜣb.tt n.t p.t* Grab TT 34, 6 nach Rosati 2006: Tf. 21, 6; *ỉw=f wb<ꜣ>=f m ꜣḫ.t ỉꜣb.tt n.t p.t* pNebseni (Aa) Tf. 3, 7; es fehlt beim pMesemneter (Ca) Tf. 34, 6; *ỉw=f wbꜣ=f m ꜣḫ.t ỉꜣb.tt n.t p.t* pNu Tf. 20, 6–7; Quirke 2013: 173.

pTurin	*ỉw=f wbꜣ*|[76, 657]*=f r ꜣḫ.t ỉꜣb.tt n.t p.t*
pMilbank₁	*ỉw=f wbꜣ=f r ꜣḫ.t {ỉmn.tt} n.t p.t*
pMilbank₂	*ỉw=f wbꜣ=f r ꜣḫ.t {ỉmn.tt} n.t p.t*
pNespa.	*ỉw wbꜣ=f r ꜣḫ.t {ỉꜣb.tt} n.t p.t*
ₛKairo₃₄₆₄₈	*<..=.> ḥp=f m ꜣḫ.t ỉmn.t <...> p.t*
ₛₐKammar	*ỉw ꜣb=f r ꜣḫ.t ỉmn.t n.t p.t*
pKöln	*ỉw=f wbꜣ=f r ꜣḫ.t ỉmn.tt n.t p.t*
ₛTurin₂₂₀₁	*ỉw=f wb<ꜣ>=f r ꜣḫ.t ỉꜣb.tt n.t p.t*
ₛOxford₁₉₄₇.₂₉₅	*ỉw=f ḥp=f m ꜣḫ.t ỉmn.tt n.t p.t*
ₛₐKairo₄₁₀₅₈	*ỉw=f wb*|[24]ꜣ*=f r ꜣḫ.t {ỉꜣb.tt}*|[25]*n.t p.t*
ₖAssiut	*ỉw=f wb[ꜣ]=f* [36] vorzeitiger Abbruch des Spruchtexts
pHor	*ỉw=f wbꜣ=f r <...> ỉmn.tt n.t p.t*
pEmory	*[ỉ]w=f ḥp=f m ꜣḫ.*|[1, 18]*t ỉmn.tt n.t{ỉ} p.t*
ₛBerlin₄₆	*ỉw=f ḥtp=f m ꜣḫ.t ỉmn.tt n.t p.t*
pTurin	*ỉw=f wbꜣ=f r ꜣḫ.t ỉmn.tt n.t p.t*
pMilbank₁	*ỉw=f wbꜣ=f r ꜣḫ.t {ỉꜣb.tt} n.t p.t*
pMilbank₂	*ỉw=f wb<ꜣ>*|[76, 657]*=f r ꜣḫ.t {ỉꜣb.tt}n.t p.t*

2.2 Übersetzung des Tb-Spruchs 72 von Padiamun

<Der Spruch des Herausgehens am Tage
   und des Öffnens des Totenbereichs>[37]
Worte zu sprechen
von <Osiris> <*P(ꜣ)-ṯi̯-ỉmn(.w)*>,
   <dem Gerechtfertigten>:[38]
Seid gegrüßt,
   (Oh) Herren der Wahrheit,
   die ihr frei von Sünde seid,
   und die ihr lebendig bis in Ewigkeit
   (im) Bereich der Unendlichkeit existiert.
Möget ihr den Ausgang der Erde öffnen;[39]
ich bin verklärt in eurer Gestalt,[40]
   indem ich <in> [eurem] Zauber mächtig bin,[41]

---

36 Bei ₖAssiut endet der Text des Tb-Spruchs 72 mit *ỉw=f wb<ꜣ>=f*, vgl. *ỉw=f wbꜣ=f ꜣḫ.t ỉmn.tt n.t p.t* pRyerson Tf. 24 Kol. 49, 14–15; *ỉw=f wb<.=f> <.> <...> <.....> <..> <.>* Grab TT 34, 6 nach Rosati 2006: Tf. 21, 6; *ỉw=f ḥn=f m ꜣḫ.t ỉꜣb.tt n.t p.t* pNebseni (Aa) Tf. 3, 7–8; *ỉw=f wbꜣ=f ꜣḫ.t ỉmn.tt n.t p.t* pMesemneter (Ca) Tf. 34, 6; *ỉw=f ḥn=f m ꜣḫ.t ỉmn.tt n.t p.t* pNu Tf. 20, 7; Quirke 2013: 173. Zur Schreibung: *ỉw=f wbꜣ=f* ... gegenüber *ỉw=f wbꜣ=f* ... *ỉw=f ḥn=f* ... bei pNebseni und pNu oder *ỉw=f wbꜣ=f* ... *ỉw=f wbꜣ=f* ... bei den anderen Parallelen. *ꜣḫ.t ỉꜣb.tt* ... *ꜣḫ.t ỉmn.tt*... bei den meisten Parallelen gegenüber *ꜣḫ.t ỉmn.tt* ... *ꜣḫ.t ỉꜣb.tt* bei pMilbank₂ und pNespasefy.

37 Im Titel des Tb-Spruchs 73 sind *ỉmḥ.t* und *ṯꜣ.t* austauschbar, deshalb ist *ỉmḥ.t* ein Synonym für *ṯꜣ.t* mit der Bedeutung „Unterwelt". Im Tb-Spruch 149 gibt es einen Bereich in der Unterwelt mit dem Namen *ỉmḥ.t*. Es ist auch möglich, dies als Grab zu deuten, siehe Milde 1991: 140.

38 Es fehlen der Name und die Affiliation.

39 Der Ausdruck *rʾ tꜣ* bezieht sich wohl auf die Bedeutung „Gang/Ausgang der Erde" als Bezeichnung für einen Bereich in der Unterwelt, vgl. Wb II 398, 7–10. Gemäß des Tb-Spruchs 72 ist der Hauptwunsch des Verstorbenen, dass ihm die anbetenden Götter einen Ausgang in der Erde öffnen, damit er aus der Unterwelt herausgehen kann, vgl. auch Hornung 1990: 459.

40 Das Wort kommt oft in der Singularform im Ausdruck *m ỉrw n(.ỉ))* „in der Gestalt von (Person/Sache)" vor, Wb I 113, 13.

41 *šḥm* „mächtig sein" Wb II 245, 10, vgl. „Ich verfüge über eure Zauberkräfte" Verhoeven 1993: I, 169; pNu der 18. Dynastie schreibt *šḥm.kw₊ m ḥkꜣ{w}=ỉ* „Ich bin mit meinem Zauber mächtig" nach Quirke 2013: 173; siehe auch Mosher 2016: 354 Anm. 7.

und indem [ic]h eur<er> Anzahl [zugezählt] bin.[42]

Möget ihr <mi>ch vor dem Wütenden
  dieses Landes der Gerechten retten.[43]

Möget ihr mir meinen Mund geben,
  damit [ich] mit [ihm] [reden] kann.

Möget [ih]r [mir] Geschenke[44] vor euch geben,
  denn ich kenne eure Namen,
    und ich kenne (den) jene<s> großen Gottes,
    an dessen Nase ihr Nahrung gebt:

Tekem ist sein Name.

Er öffnet den östlichen Horizont des Himmels.

Er öffnet[45] <den westlichen Horizont des Himmels>.

3. Exkurs

Der Tb-Spruch 72 wird auf der Mumienkartonage S05/71 von *P(3)-ṯi-ỉmn(.w)* aus Assiut nicht in Gänze wiedergegeben. Es fehlt fast die gesamte zweite Hälfte des Spruchs, die von dem Wunsch der Erfüllung aller materiellen Bedürfnisse für den Verstorbenen handelt[46] sowie die Nachschrift. Stattdessen sind die rechte und linke Seite des unteren Teils der Mumienkartonage mit zwei Opferformeln beschriftet, wobei jede Formel in eine senkrechte Kolumne aufgeteilt ist.

3.1 Die Opferformel auf der rechten Seite (Abb. 7b)

ḥtp ṯi nśw	„Ein Opfer, das der König gibt,
n wśr(.w) ḫn.tỉ ỉmn.tt	dem Osiris, dem Ersten des Westens,
nčr(.w) ˁ3 nb 3bč(.w)	dem großen Gott, dem Herrn von Abydos,
n ỉnp(.w) ḫn.tỉ śḥ-nčr(.w)	und dem Anubis, der der Gotteshalle vorsteht,
ỉm.ỉ-wt	der in der Balsamierung befindlich ist,
nb {čśr} t3{.wỉ}<čśr>	dem Herrn des heiligen Landes,
či=f {prỉ(.w)} prỉ(.t) ḫrw	damit er ein Totenopfer geben möge
<t3> ḥ(n)ḳ.t	(aus) <Brot> und Bier,
k3.w 3pt.w	Rindern und Geflügel,
ỉrp{t} ỉrt.t	Traubensaft und Milch,
n k3 n(.ỉ) wśr(.w)	für den Ka des Osiris,
P(3)-ṯi-ỉmn(.w) m3ˁ-ḫrw	Padiamun, den Gerechtfertigten,
mśỉ.n [...]	den [NN] geboren hat".

---

42 *ỉp* „zuzählen" Wb I 66, 4; *ỉp.t* „Anzahl" Wb I 66, 24, vgl. „Ich bin in euren Prüfungen geprüft" Verhoeven 1993: I, 169; pNu der 18. Dynastie schreibt *3tp.kw, m 3ḫ.w=ỉ* „Ich bin mit meinem Ach beladen" nach Quirke 2013: 173.

43 Bei ₖAssiut sowie ₛTurin₂₂₀₁ Z. 13 der 26. Dynstie wird der Ausdruck *t3 pn <n(.ỉ)> m3ˁ.tỉw* „dieses Land der Gerechten" als Bezeichnung des Totenreichs verwendet, Wb II 21, 10; beim pHor emendierte Munro die Textstelle in *m3ˁ.tỉw* Munro 2006: 23f, Anm. Tb 72 gegenüber *m3ˁ.t* „die Göttin der Wahrheit" als Personifikation der Wahrheit und des Rechts, als Genossin des Thot und des Re, Wb II 20, 10–11, oder *m3ˁ.tỉ* „die beiden Wahrheiten" als Name zweier Göttinnen beim Totengericht, Wb II 21, 1; siehe auch Mosher 2016: 354 Anm. 1 u. 10.

44 Bei pMilbank *3w.t* „Speisen" Wb I 5, 2 gegenüber *3w.t-ˁ* „Geschenk" bei den anderen Parallelen. Bei ₖAssiut weist die Schreibung eine Kombination von *3w.<t>-ỉb* „Fröhlichkeit" Wb I 5, 16–17 und *3w.t-ˁ* „Geschenk" Wb I 5, 7 auf; bei ₖAssiut und pHor wird das Zeichen ˁ richtig hinter dem Determinativ (Y1) geschrieben. In allen anderen Parallelen wird es dem Determinativ Y1 vorangestellt.

45 Hier endet der Text des Spruchs 72 von Padiamun aus Assiut.

46 Hornung 1990: 459.

3.2 Die Opferformel auf der linken Seite (Abb. 7a)

ḥtp ṯi nśw	„Ein Opfer, das der König gibt,
n Ḥr(.w)-3ḫ.t(i) nčr ꜥ3	dem Harachte, dem großen Gott,
nb p.t šw.tỉ	dem Herrn des Himmels, dem Schatten,
prỉ.ø m 3ḫ.tt	der aus dem Horizont herausgeht[47],
<n> (ỉ)tm(.w) nb t3.wỉ	und dem Atum, dem Herrn der beiden Länder,
Iwn{t}.<wy>	dem Heliopolitaner,[48]
či=f n(=k) śḫ.t-ỉ3r.w	damit er dir das Binsengefilde gibt und damit
či=f n=k 3ḫ.t<ỉ> n.t p.t	er dir die beiden Horizonte des Himmels gibt,[49]
ḫr Rꜥ(.w) wśr{t} m t3.wỉ	bei Re, der in den beiden Ländern mächtig ist[50]
ḫr G{k}b....	und bei Geb .... .

Zu Füßen der Verstorbenen wird Anubis liegend auf seinem Schrein dargestellt. Vor ihm ist die folgende Hieroglypheninschrift in einer Kolumne zu lesen:

[ỉrỉ] rsy ḥr wśr(.w)	Hält Wache über den Osiris,
<P(3)>-ṯi-<ỉmn(.w)> m3ꜥ-ḫr<w>	Padiamun, den Gerechtfertigten.

4. Anmerkungen zur Graphie der Textfassung von Tb-Spruch 72

Der Terminus „Graphie" bedeutet, dass man einen Text oder ein Textstück (z. B. ein Wort) auf eine besondere Art schreibt bzw. geschrieben hat.[51] Die lokale Kopie des Tb-Spruchs 72 von Padiamun aus Assiut weist auf der Mumienkartonage einige Besonderheiten und Schreibfehler auf.

4.1 Richtungsumkehrung

╬ (M40) in: ⟦hieroglyphs⟧ Z. 1;

    vgl. ⟦hieroglyphs⟧, ⟦hieroglyphs⟧ *ỉsf.t* „Sünde" Wb I 129, 11–12.

Das Zeichen ╬ (M40) wird seitenverkehrt bei ₖAssiut sowie pHor, pEmory und pTurin geschrieben. Alle anderen Parallelen weisen die richtige Richtung ╬ auf.

4.2 Determinative

4.2.1 Determinativlosigkeit

Meistens werden die Lexeme beim Tb-Spruch 72 auf der Mumienkartonage des *P(3)-ṯi-ỉmn(.w)* aus Assiut mit Determinativen versehen. Es gibt aber manche, bei denen sie fehlen, was entweder als Schreibfehler oder als Schreibvarianten betrachtet werden kann:

– ⟦A1⟧ (A1), ⟦A40⟧ (A40) oder ⟦G7⟧ (G7) fehlt in: ⟦hieroglyphs⟧ *nb.w* „Herren" Z. 1;

    vgl. ⟦hieroglyphs⟧ „Herr" Wb II 227, 5.

– ⟦A2⟧ (A2), fehlt in ⟦hieroglyph⟧ *rn* Z. 5;

---

47 Als Bezeichnung für Harachte; vgl. *šw.t nčr* „Schatten eines Gottes" Wb IV 433, 2; *šw.t Rꜥ(.w)* „Schatten des Re" Wb IV 433, 3.

48 *ỉwn.wy* „der von der Stadt Heliopolis ist" als Beiname Atums Wb I 54, 7–8.

49 *3ḫ.t* „Horizont, Lichtland", wo die Sonne auf- und untergeht; *3ḫ.tỉ* „die beiden Horizonte"; *3ḫ.t ỉmn.tt* „westlicher Horizont"; *3ḫ.t ỉ3b.tt* „östlicher Horizont" Wb I 17, 12–14.

50 *Rꜥ(.w) wśr{t} m t3.wỉ* als Eigenschaft des Re vgl. auch *wśr m m3ꜥ.t* „....., der in der Wahrheit mächtig ist" Wb I 361, 20.

51 Bussman 1990: 294; Bartschat & Conard 1981: 100–101. Zur Graphie der abydenischen Denk-und Grabsteintexte aus dem Mittleren Reichs siehe El-Hamrawi 2002: 211–218.

vgl. 𓂋𓏤 „Name" Wb II 425, 1;

vgl. auch *ḥk3* mit 𓀀 (A2) in:

𓀀𓄿𓏭𓏜	*ḥk3*	„bezaubern"	Wb III 177, 7;
𓀀𓏭𓄿𓏭𓏜	*ḥk3.w*	„der Zauberer"	Wb III 177, 10;
𓀀𓂋𓏭𓄿𓏭𓏜	*ḥk3w.t*	„Zauberei"	Wb III 177, 6.

– 𓏤 (Y1) fehlt in: 𓄿𓏠𓏭 *ip.t{w}* Z. 3,

vgl. 𓏠𓏭 „Anzahl" Wb I 66, 24.

fehlt auch in: 𓄿𓏠𓏜 *ḥk3{t}* Z. 2,

vgl. 𓏠𓏜 „Zauber" Wb III 175;

fehlt auch in: 𓂋𓐍 *rḫ* Z. 4,

vgl. 𓂋𓏤𓐍 „kennen" Wb II 442.

fehlt auch in: 𓂝𓊃 *{r}ᶜ(3)* Z. 5,

vgl. 𓏭𓄿𓂝𓈖 , 𓂋𓏤 „groß" Wb I 161.

– 𓀀 (G A40) fehlt in: 𓏠𓂝𓊃 *m3ᶜ.tiw* Z. 3,

vgl. 𓀀𓄿𓂝𓏥𓊃 „die Gerechten" Wb II 21, 13.

4.2.2 Der Füllstrich

Der Füllstrich wird gebraucht:

a) in der ideographischen Schreibung wie 𓊪𓏏 *p.t* „Himmel" Z. 5.

b) ungewöhnlicher Füllstrich kommt vor:

– bei der Präposition 𓅓 *m* in: 𓅓 „in" Z. 1; 2; 3.

– auch bei inlautendem 𓅓 *m* in: 𓈖𓅓𓎛 *nḥm* „retten" Z. 3.

c) ungewöhnliche Füllstriche kommen oft als Füllzeichen vor:

– 𓏠𓂝𓊃 *m3ᶜ.t* Z. 1;

vgl. 𓏠𓂝𓊃 „die Wahrheit" Wb II 18, 12.

– 𓏠𓂝𓊃𓊪𓊪 *isf.t* Z. 1;

vgl. 𓊃𓂝𓊪𓊪 „Sünde" Wb I 129, 11–12.

4.3 Fehler

4.3.1 Falsche Zeichen

Die Kopie des Tb-Spruchs 72 des *P(3)-ṯi-imn(.w)* wurde auf der Mumienkartonage mit manchen falschen Zeichen versehen. Sie werden nicht als Schreibvariante, sondern als Schreibfehler betrachtet und mittels der Zeichenliste von Gardiner emendiert.

– 𓌉 (?) statt 𓌉 (S43) in: 𓌉 Z. 1,

vgl. 𓌉 *ḏt mtw* „Worte zu sprechen" Wb V 625, 3.

– 𓈇 (N17) statt 𓏠 (Y1) in: 𓏠𓂝𓊃 Z. 1,

vgl. 𓏠𓂝𓊃 *m3ᶜ.t* „die Wahrheit" Wb II 18, 12,

auch in 𓏠𓂝 Z. 4,

vgl. 𓅓𓂝𓄿 *m-b3ḥ* „vor" pHor Taf. 6, 137; 𓅓𓂝 pEmory Fig. 1, 16.

– 𓏥 (M16) statt 𓇋 (M2) in: 𓎛𓎛𓏥𓏭 Z. 1,

vgl. 𓎛𓎛𓏥𓏭 *ḥn.ti* „Bereiche" vgl. Wb III 105, 10–11; 106, 8–13.

— ⬒ (Y1) statt ▬ (O34) in: 𓏥𓈖𓏌𓏲 Z. 1,

         vgl. ⟨⟩ *isf.t* „Sünde" Wb I 129, 11–12.

— ⌐ (?) statt ▬ (N17) in: ⌐ Z. 1,

         vgl. ⌐ *č.t* „Unendlichkeit" Wb V 504, 4.

— 𓅆 (G25) statt 𓅀 (G29) in: ▬𓅆𓏛𓏏 Z. 1; ▬𓊃𓅆𓏛𓏏 Z. 5,

         vgl. ▬𓅆𓏛𓏏 *wbȝ* „öffnen", „bohren" Wb I 290, 8 u. 1–2.

— 𓊪 (Q3) statt 𓏏 (X1) in: 𓃀𓊪 Z. 2,

         vgl. 𓀀𓃀𓊪 *tw=i* „ich" bei den Parallelen.

— (O34) statt ▬ (N35) in: 𓃀𓊃𓎵 Z. 3,

         vgl 𓂝𓃀𓎵 *nḥm* „retten" Wb II 295, 12.

— 𓂧 (D42) statt 𓂞 (D40) in: 𓃀𓂧𓎵 Z. 3,

         vgl. 𓂝𓃀𓎵 *nḥm* „retten" Wb II 295, 12.

— 𓂉 (G20?) statt 𓅓 (G17) in: 𓉐𓂉 Z. 4,

         vgl. 𓅓𓂉 *m-bȝḥ* „in der Gegenwart von" pHor Taf. 6, 137,   𓂉▬ pEmory fig.1, 16.

— 𓀀 (A1) statt 𓀁 (A2) in: 𓀀𓃀𓃭▬ Z. 1,

         vgl. 𓀁𓂋▬ *rn.w* „Namen" Wb II 427, 15.

— 𓂋 (D21) statt 𓂝 (O29) in: 𓂋𓏏 Z. 5,

         vgl. 𓂝𓏏 *ʿȝ* „groß" Wb I 161.

— 𓎯 (V30) statt 𓎰 (V31) in: 𓀀𓅆𓎯 Z. 5,

         vgl. 𓅆𓀀𓎯 *tkm(.w)* „Gott Tekem" Wb V 333, 8.

— 𓀀 (A1) statt 𓀙 (A40) in: 𓀀𓅆𓎯 Z. 5,

         vgl. 𓀙𓅆𓎯 *tkm(.w)* „Gott Tekem" Wb V 333, 8.

— 𓈌 (N26) statt 𓈍 (N27) in: 𓈌𓏏 Z. 5,

         vgl. 𓈌𓏏 *ȝḥ.t* „Horizont" Wb I 17, 12.

— 𓏤𓏤𓏤 (Z2) statt 𓏤 (Z1) in: 𓏤𓏤𓏤𓈌𓏏 Z. 5,

         vgl. 𓈌𓏏 *ȝḥ.t* „Horizont" Wb I 17, 12.

4.3.2 Falsche Wörter

— ▬𓊃𓅆𓏛𓏏 Z., 5 statt ▬𓅆𓏛𓏏 *wbȝ* „öffnen"; „bohren" Wb I 290, 1–2, 8.

Wahrscheinlich handelt es sich um eine Kombination von 𓏛𓏏 *wb<ȝ>* und ▬𓊃𓅆 *ȝḥ.t* „Horizont" Wb I 17, 12, also um Wortgruppen.

— 𓈌𓏏 Z. 2 statt 𓏤𓏏 *tȝ* „Land" bei den Parallelen.

— 𓉐𓀀𓃀𓏌 Z. 4 statt 𓏤𓃀𓏌 *ȝw.t-ʿ* „Geschenk" Wb I 5, 7.

Der Schreiber dachte wahrscheinlich gleichzeitig an die folgenden Wörter:

𓏤𓏤𓏤𓏤𓉐𓃀𓏌, 𓏌𓏌 *ȝw.t-ỉb* „Art Myrrhe" Wb I 5, 1.

     𓏤𓃀𓏌   *ȝw.t-ʿ* „Geschenk" Wb I 5, 7.

     𓉐𓃀𓏌   *ȝw.t* „Speisen" Wb I 5, 2.

     𓏤𓃀𓏌   *ȝwi̯-ʿ* „den Arm ausstrecken" Wb I 5, 4.

     𓂧𓃀   *ȝw.t-ʿ* „mit ausgestrecktem Arm" Wb I 5, 6.

     𓏌𓃀   *ȝw.t-ỉb* „Fröhlichkeit, Freude" Wb I 4, 17.

4.3.3 Zusätzliche Wörter

– ⸗ *sp* 2 Z. 1; auch beim Sarkophag Kairo 41058 Z. 9 aus der 26. Dynastie und pNespasefy Z. 14 aus der Zeit des Pharaohs Psammetich I.

4.4 Wortgruppen

4.4.1 Füllzeichen

Bei manchen Wörtern werden manche Zeichen zusätzlich geschrieben und dürfen nicht gelesen werden, deshalb werden sie als Füllzeichen betrachtet. Sie sind:

a) ⸗ *t* (X1) als Füllzeichen:

– ⸗ Z. 2;
    vgl. ⸗ *3ḫ* „verklären" pTurin Taf. 27, 2; Sargkammar Z. 230.
– ⸗ Z. 2;
    vgl. *irw* „Gestalt" Wb I 113, 8–12.
– ⸗ Z. 4;
    vgl. *čn* „ihr".
– ⸗ Z. 2;
    vgl. *ḥk3* „Zauber" Wb III 175.

b) ‖ (Z4) als Füllzeichen:

– ⸗ Z. 2;
    vgl. *irw* „Gestalt" Wb I 113, 8–12.

4.5 Auslassungen und Lakunestellen

4.5.1 Auslassung

a) Laute

– Anlautendes
    w in <w>*i* „mich", in: *nḥm=čn* <w>*i m 3ṯ(.w)* Abb. 4a, b, Z. 3.
    n in: <n>*.t* „Genitivpartikel" in: *3b.tt* <n>*.t p.t.* Abb. 4a, b, Z. 5.
– Postlautendes
    t in: *isf.*<t> „Sünde" Z. 1.
    n in: *ip.t{w}=t*<n> „eurer Anzahl" Z. 3.
    3 in: *čf*<3>*.w* „Speisen" Z. 5.

b) Andere

– *m* in: *sḥm.kw* <m> *ḥk3{t}* „indem ich <in> <eurem> Zauber mächtig bin" Z. 2 nach den Parallelen.
– Die Pluralstriche ⁞⁞⁞ in: *či=tn čf*<3>*.w* „Möget ihr Speisen geben" Z. 5.

4.5.2 Lakunestellen

– Ende Zeile 2: Die Parallelen schreiben für diese Textstelle, bzw. pHor:

śḥm.kw̟₊ <m> ḥk3{t}{r=i}[=tn] „indem ich <in> [eurem] Zauber mächtig bin,
[ỉp].[k]w|³₊ m ỉp.t{w}=t<n>   und indem [ic]h in eur<er> Anzahl [zugezählt] bin“.

– Ende Zeile 3: Die Parallelen schreiben für diese Textstelle, bzw. pHor:

č̣ị=tn n=ỉ r'=ỉ   „Möget ihr mir meinen Mund geben,
[m]ṯ.[t=ỉ] ỉm=<.>   damit [ich] mit [ihm] [reden] kann.
č̣ị=<t>n|⁴wỉ Möget ihr mir ......“.

4.6 Schreibweise

– für ⁓ (N35) in:

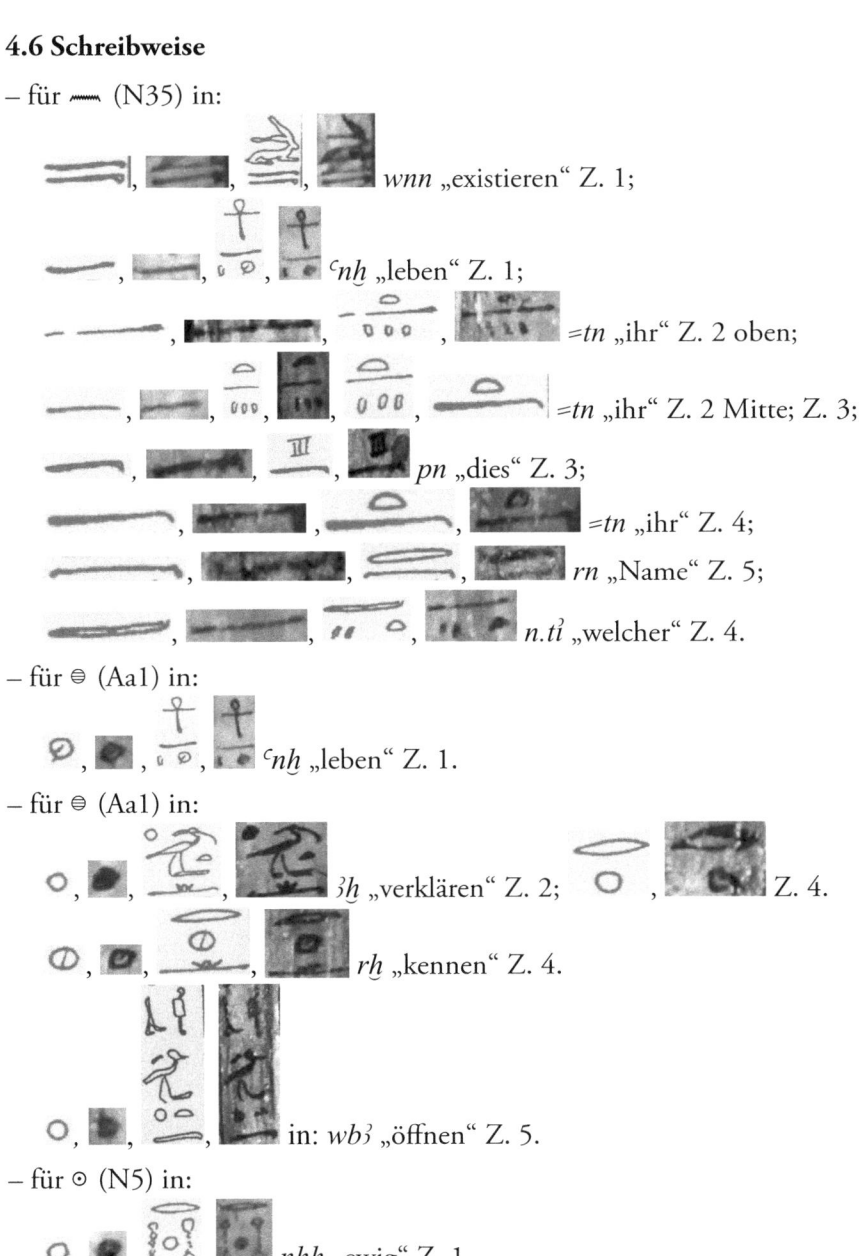

wnn „existieren“ Z. 1;

ᶜnḫ „leben“ Z. 1;

=tn „ihr“ Z. 2 oben;

=tn „ihr“ Z. 2 Mitte; Z. 3;

pn „dies“ Z. 3;

=tn „ihr“ Z. 4;

rn „Name“ Z. 5;

n.tỉ „welcher“ Z. 4.

– für ⊖ (Aa1) in:

ᶜnḫ „leben“ Z. 1.

– für ⊖ (Aa1) in:

3ḫ „verklären“ Z. 2;   Z. 4.

rḫ „kennen“ Z. 4.

in: *wb3* „öffnen“ Z. 5.

– für ⊙ (N5) in:

nḥḥ „ewig“ Z. 1.

– für ⊚ (O50) in:

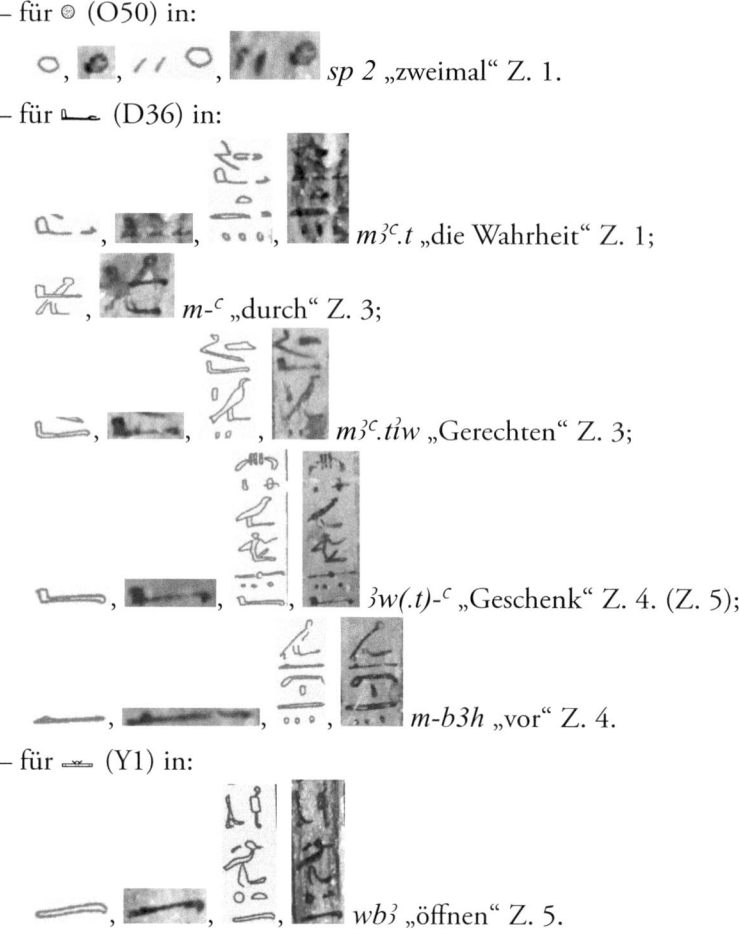

○ , , / / ○ , , *sp 2* „zweimal" Z. 1.

– für ⌐ (D36) in:

⌐ , , , *m3ꜥ.t* „die Wahrheit" Z. 1;

, , *m-ꜥ* „durch" Z. 3;

, , , *m3ꜥ.tíw* „Gerechten" Z. 3;

, , , *3w(.t)-ꜥ* „Geschenk" Z. 4. (Z. 5);

, , , *m-b3h* „vor" Z. 4.

– für ⚊ (Y1) in:

, , , *wb3* „öffnen" Z. 5.

5. Datierung der Mumienkartonage

Die Abschrift des Tb-Spruchs 72 auf der Mumienkartonage des *P(3)-ṭi-ỉmn(.w)* aus Assiut soll zuerst mit den Parallelen verglichen werden, wobei der Textvergleich sich gut als Kriterium eignet, um die Mumienkartonage datieren zu können. Weitere Hinweise können zur Verstärkung herangezogen werden:

a) pEmory wird von Keller in das 2.–1. Jahrhundert v. Chr. datiert, nachdem er bewiesen hatte, dass er pTurin sehr nahe steht.[52]

pNespa.	*tw=ỉ 3h.kw₊ m ỉrw=tn*
ₛKairo₃₄₆₄₈	*3h.k(ỉ)_∣³m ỉrw=<ỉ>*
ₛₐKammar	*3h.kw₊ m ỉr(w)=tn*
pKöln	*tw=ỉ 3h.kw₊ m ỉrw=tn*
ₛTurin₂₂₀₁	*tw=ỉ 3h{t}.kw₊ m ỉrw=tn*
ₛOxford₁₉₄₇.₂₉₅	*3h.kw₊ m ỉrw=ỉ*
ₛₐKairo₄₁₀₅₈	*tw=ỉ 3h.kw∣¹¹₊ m ỉr{tt}w=tn*
ₛLondon₉₇₁	*3h{t}.k(ỉ)_ m ỉr(w)=tn*
ₖAssiut	*{p}w=ỉ 3h{t}.kw₊ m ỉrw{t}/y=tn*
pHor	*tw=ỉ 3h.kw₊ m ỉr∣⁶,¹³⁵w=tn*

52 KELLER 1985: 60–61, 66. Zur Datierung des pTurin 1791 siehe SPIEGELBERG 1923: 152–153.

pEmory	*ʒḫ{t}.k(ỉ)_ m ỉrw.w=ỉ*
ₛBerlin₄₆	*tw=ỉ ʒḫ.kw₊ |²m ỉrw.w=tn*
pTurin	*tw={y} ʒḫ.kw₊ m ỉrw.w=tn*
pMilbank₁	*<t>w=ỉ |⁶⁹, ⁴⁴⁴ʒḫ.kw₊ m ỉrw.w=tn*
pMilbank₂	*<t>w=ỉ ʒḫ.<k>w₊ m|⁷⁶, ⁶⁵⁵ỉrw.w=tn*

Der Textvergleich des Tb-Spruchs 72 zeigt, dass die Datierung von Keller zum großen Teil übernommen werden kann, denn pEmory schreibt das Wort *ỉrw.w* „Gestalten" in der Pluralform ebenso wie pTurin und pMilbank₁ gegenüber *ỉrw* „Gestalt" in der Singularform bei den anderen Parallelen.

b) In Saqqara wird die Sargkammer von Psammetich in die Zeit des Königs Amasis datiert.[53] Der Sarkophag Kairo 34648 wird hingegen in die Zeit von Psammetich I. bis Amasis datiert.[54] Der Sarkophag Oxford 1947.295 von Ptaḥḥotep aus Giza wird in die Zeit von der 26. bis zur 30. Dynastie datiert.[55]

pNespa.	*ḥr n.tt tw=ỉ rḫ.kw₊ rn=tn*
ₛKairo₃₄₆₄₈	*ḥr n.t{t} tw=<ỉ> rḫ.<k(ỉ)_> čn rḫ. k(ỉ)_ rn=čn*
ₛₐKammar	*ḥr n.t{t}tw=ỉ rḫ.kw₊ tn rḫ.kw₊ rn=tn*
pKöln	*ḥr n.tỉ tw=<.> rḫ.kw₊ rn=tn*
ₛTurin₂₂₀₁	*ḥr n.t{t} tw=ỉ rḫ.kw₊ rn=tn*
ₛOxford₁₉₄₇.₂₉₅	*ḥr n.t{t} tw=ỉ rḫ.<k(ỉ)_> tn rḫ.kw₊ rn=tn*
ₛₐKairo₄₁₀₅₈	*ḥr n.tỉ |¹⁸tw=ỉ rḫ.kw₊ rn=tn {rḫ.k|¹⁹w₊ rn=tn}*
ₛLondon₉₇₁	*<..> <..> <.=.> <...> <.-...=..>*
ₖAssiut	*ḥr n.tỉ tw=ỉ rḫ.k(ỉ)_ rn.w=čn*
pHor	*ḥr n.tỉ tw=ỉ rḫ.k(ỉ)_ <.>n.w=čn*
pEmory	*ḥr n.tỉ <tw=ỉ> rḫ.k(ỉ)_ rn=tn*
pTurin	*ḥr n.tỉ tw=ỉ rḫ.kw₊ rn=tn*
pMilbank₁	*ḥr n.t<ỉ> <t>w=ỉ rḫ.{t}<kw₊> <rn=tn>*
pMilbank₂	*ḥr n.t<ỉ> <t>w=ỉ rḫ.<kw₊> <rn>=t<n>*

Der Textvergleich zeigt, dass die drei Parallelen die Konstruktion *tw=ỉ rḫ.kw₊ tn rḫ.kw₊ rn=tn* „ich kenne euch und kenne euren Namen" schreiben gegenüber *tw=ỉ rḫ.kw₊ rn=tn* „ich kenne euren Namen" bei den anderen Parallelen. Es ist zu bemerken, dass die Konstruktion *rḫ.kw₊/k(ỉ)_ tn/ čn rḫ.kw₊/kỉ_ rn=tn/čn* ab der 26. Dynastie durch die Konstruktion *rḫ.kw₊/k(ỉ)_ rn=tn/čn* allmählich ersetzt wird.

Deshalb lehne ich mich an den Textvergleich als Kriterium zur Datierung der Mumienkartonage S05/71 des *P(ʒ)-ṯi-ỉmn(.w)* aus Assiut an. Die folgenden Kriterien sind zu betrachten:

a) Der Ausdruck *{sp 2}* in ₖAssiut anhand der Parallelen:

pNespa.	*wnn.w ꜥnḫ r nḥḥ {sp 2} ḥn.tỉ č.t*
ₛKairo₃₄₆₄₈	*wnn.w ꜥnḫ r nḥḥ ḥn.t{t} r č.t*
ₛₐKammar	*wn.w ꜥnḫ |²³⁰r (n)ḥḥ ḥn.tỉ č.t*
pKöln	*wnn.w ꜥnḫ r nḥḥ|³⁴, ³ḥn.tỉ č.t*
ₛTurin₂₂₀₁	*wnn.w ꜥnḫ r nḥḥ |¹¹{sp 2} ḥn.{w}tỉ č.t*
ₛOxford₁₉₄₇.₂₉₅	*wn.y/w ꜥnḫ r (n)ḥḥ ḥn.tỉ r č.t*
ₛₐKairo₄₁₀₅₈	*wnn.w ꜥnḫ r |⁹nḥḥ {sp 2} ḥn.{wy} č.t*
ₛLondon₉₇₁	*[....] [...] r (n)ḥḥ ḥn.tỉ č.t*
ₖAssiut	*wnn.w ꜥnḫ r (n)ḥḥ{sp 2}ḥn.tỉ n(.ỉ) č.t*
pHor	*|⁶, ¹³⁴wnn.w ꜥnḫ r nḥḥ ḥn.tỉ č.t*
pEmory	*wnn.w ꜥnḫ r |¹, ¹⁴(n)ḥḥ ḥn<.t> n.t č.t*
ₛBerlin₄₆	*wnn.w ꜥnḫ r nḥḥ ḥn{n}.tỉ č.t*

---

53 MASPERO 1900: 166–188.
54 BUHL 1959: 213; Totenbuchprojekt Bonn, TM 90671.
55 BUHL 1959: 140–141, 213, fig. 82, K1; Totenbuchprojekt Bonn, TM 9135509.

pTurin   *wnn.w ꜥnḫ |²r (n)ḥḥ ḥn.tỉ č.t*

pMilbank₁   *wnn.w ꜥnḫ r (n)ḥḥ ḥn.tỉ {r}č.t*

pMilbank₂   *wnn.w ꜥnḫ r (n)ḥḥ ḥn.tỉ {r}č.t*

Der Textvergleich zeigt, dass ₖAssiut den zusätzlichen Ausdruck *{sp 2}* aufweist, ebenso pNespasefy aus der Zeit des Königs Psammetich I.[56], ₛₐKairo 41058 von Tabatjat aus der 26. Dynastie aus Theben[57] und ₛTurin 2201 von Gemnefhorbak aus der 26. Dynastie aus Sais.[58]

b) Das Wort *mꜣꜥ.tỉw* „die Gerechten" in ₖAssiut anhand der Parallelen:

pNespa.   *nḥm=|²⁸, ¹⁶tn <..> m-ꜥ ꜣṯ tꜣ pn n(.ỉ) mꜣꜥ.t*

ₛKairo₃₄₆₄₈   *nḥm=čn w|⁴<ỉ> m-ꜥ ꜣṯ ỉmỉ tꜣ pn n(.ỉ) mꜣꜥ.tỉ*

ₛₐKammar   *nḥm=tn wỉ m-ꜥ ꜣṯ ỉmỉ tꜣ pn n(.ỉ) {tꜣ.wỉ}*

pKöln   *nḥm=tn <.>ỉ m-ꜥ ꜣṯ |³⁴, ⁴tꜣ pn mꜣꜥ.t*

ₛTurin₂₂₀₁   *nḥm=tn|¹³<w>ỉ m-ꜥ ꜣṯ n(.ỉ) tꜣ pn n(.ỉ) m̲ꜣ̲ꜥ̲.̲t̲ỉ̲w̲*

ₛOxford   *nḥm=tn wỉ m-ꜥ ꜣṯ wnm rꜣ pn n(.ỉ) mꜣꜥ.tỉ*

ₛₐKairo₄₁₀₅₈   *nḥm=|¹⁴tn wỉ m<-ꜥ> ꜣ{ꜥ}ṯ tꜣ pn|¹⁵n(.ỉ) mꜣꜥ.t*

ₛLondon₉₇₁   *[...]= |³tn <wỉ> m-ꜥ {ỉčỉ} ꜣṯ tꜣ pn mꜣꜥ.tỉ*

ₖAssiut   *nḥm=čn <.>ỉ m-ꜥ ꜣṯ tꜣ pn n(.ỉ) m̲ꜣ̲ꜥ̲.̲t̲ỉ̲w̲*

pHor   *nḥm=|⁶, ¹³⁶čn <.>ỉ m-ꜥ ꜣṯ tꜣ pn n(.ỉ) m̲ꜣ̲ꜥ̲.̲t̲ỉ̲w̲*

pEmory   *nḥm=tn wỉ m-ꜥ ꜣṯ wnm rꜣ pn mꜣꜥ.tỉ*

ₛBerlin₄₆   *nḥm=tn wỉ m-ꜥ ꜣṯ m tꜣ pn n(.ỉ) mꜣꜥ.tỉ*

pTurin   *nḥm=tn wỉ m-ꜥ ꜣṯ tꜣ pn|²⁷, ³n(.ỉ) mꜣꜥ.t*

pMilbank₁   *|⁶⁹, ⁴⁴⁷nḥm=tn wỉ m-ꜥ {w}ṯ ỉm.ỉ|⁶⁹, ⁴⁴⁸tꜣ pn n(.ỉ) mꜣꜥ.tỉ*

pMilbank₂   *nḥm=tn wỉ m-ꜥ ꜣṯ ỉm.ỉ tꜣ pn n(.ỉ) mꜣꜥ.tỉ*

Der Textvergleich zeigt auch, dass ₖAssiut das Wort *mꜣꜥ.tỉw* „die Gerechten" aufweist, ebenso ₛTurin 2201 von Gemnefhorbak aus der 26. Dynastie aus Sais und pHor aus der frühen Ptolemäerzeit gegenüber *mꜣꜥ.t* „die Wahrheit" oder *mꜣꜥ.tỉ* „die beiden Wahrheiten" bei den anderen Parallelen. Es ist auch zu bemerken, dass ₖAssiut und pHor das Wort *mꜣꜥ.tỉw* mit dem Zeichen G4 schreiben.[59]

c) Das Wort *rn.w* „Namen" in ₖAssiut anhand der Parallelen:

pNespa.   *ḥr n.tt tw=ỉ rḫ.kw₊ rn=tn*

ₛKairo₃₄₆₄₈   *ḥr n.t{t} tw=<ỉ> r̲ḫ̲.̲<̲k̲(̲ỉ̲)̲ ̲>̲ čn rḫ. k(ỉ)₋ rn=čn*

ₛₐKammar   *ḥr n.t{t}tw=ỉ r̲ḫ̲.̲k̲w̲₊̲ ̲t̲n̲ r̲ḫ̲.̲k̲w̲₊̲ rn=tn*

pKöln   *ḥr n.tỉ tw=<.> rḫ.kw₊ rn=tn*

ₛTurin₂₂₀₁   *ḥr n.t{t} tw=ỉ rḫ.kw₊ rn=tn*

ₛOxford₁₉₄₇.₂₉₅ *ḥr n.t{t} tw=ỉ r̲ḫ̲.̲<̲k̲(̲ỉ̲)̲ ̲>̲ tn rḫ.kw₊ rn=tn*

ₛₐKairo₄₁₀₅₈   *ḥr n.tỉ |¹⁸tw=ỉ rḫ.kw₊ rn=tn {rḫ.k|¹⁹w₊ rn=tn}*

ₛLondon₉₇₁   *<..> <..> <.=.> <...> <.-...=..>*

ₖAssiut   *ḥr n.tỉ tw=ỉ rḫ.k(ỉ)₋ rn.w=čn*

pHor   *ḥr n.tỉ tw=ỉ rḫ.k(ỉ)₋ <.>n.w=čn*

pEmory   *ḥr n.tỉ <tw=ỉ> rḫ.k(ỉ)₋ rn=tn*

ₛBerlin₄₆   *ḥr n.tỉ tw=ỉ rḫ.kw₊ rn=tn*

pTurin   *ḥr n.tỉ tw=ỉ rḫ.kw₊ rn=tn*

pMilbank₁   *ḥr n.t<ỉ> <t>w=ỉ rḫ.{t}<kw₊> <rn=tn>*

pMilbank₂   *ḥr n.t<ỉ> <t>w=ỉ rḫ.<kw₊> <rn>=t<n>*

Weiterhin zeigt der Textvergleich, dass auf ₖAssiut die Schreibung *rn.w=čn* „eure Namen" verwendet wird, ebenso auf pHor aus der frühen Ptolemäerzeit, ganz im Gegensatz zur Schreibung *rn=tn* „euer

---

56 Verhoeven 1999: passim.

57 Gauthier 1913: I, 348; Totenbuchprojekt Bonn, TM 1352622.

58 Piehl 1886: Tf. 86E–89F; siehe auch Mosher 2016: 354 Anm. 4.

59 Munro 2006: 23 Anm. Tb 72, f; Wb II 21, b); siehe auch Mosher 2016: 354 Anm. 1 u. 9.

Name" bei allen anderen Parallelen. Es ist zu bemerken, dass auf pNebseni, pMesemneter und pNu der 18. Dynastie der Ausdruck *rn.w=čn* geschrieben steht, der durch *rn=čn* in der Spätzeit ersetzt wird. In der Ptolemäerzeit steht wieder *rn.w=čn* in den Quellen.

d) Der Ausdruck *nčr pwy ꜥȝ* „jener große Gott" in _KAssiut anhand der Parallelen:

pNespa.	*rḫ.kw₊ rn n(.ỉ) nčr pfy ꜥȝ*
_SKairo₃₄₆₄₈	*ỉw=\<ỉ\>* |⁶*rḫ.k(ỉ)₋ nčr pf ꜥȝ*
_{Sa}Kammar	*rḫ.kw₊ rn n(.ỉ) nčr pf ꜥȝ*
pKöln	*rḫ.kw₊ rn n(.ỉ) nčr pfy ꜥȝ*
_STurin₂₂₀₁	*rḫ.kw₊ rn n(.ỉ) nčr pwy ꜥȝ*
_SOxford₁₉₄₇.₂₉₅	*ỉw=ỉ rḫ.kw₊ nčr pf ꜥȝ*
_{Sa}Kairo₄₁₀₅₈	*rḫ.kw₊ rn n(.ỉ)* |²⁰*nčr {ꜥȝ} pf ꜥȝ*
_SLondon₉₇₁	\<....\> \<..\> \<.=.\> \<...\> \<.-...=..\>
_KAssiut	*rḫ.kw₊ nčr pwy {r}ȝ"*
pHor	*rḫ.kw₊*|⁶, ¹³⁸*rn n(.ỉ) nčr pwy ȝ"*
pEmory	*rḫ.k(ỉ)₋ rn nčr pf ꜥȝ*
_SBerlin₄₆	*rḫ.kw₊ rn n(.ỉ) nčr*|⁴*pwy ꜥȝ*
pTurin	*rḫ.kw₊ rn n(.ỉ) nčr*|²⁷, ⁴*pwy ꜥȝ*
pMilbank₁	\<...\> \<..\> \<..\> \<...\> \<...\> \<..\>
pMilbank₂	\<...\> \<..\> \<..\> \<...\> \<...\> \<..\>

Darüber hinaus kann durch den Textvergleich gezeigt werden, dass lediglich auf _KAssiut der Ausdruck *nčr pwy ꜥȝ* „jener große Gott" Verwendung findet, ebenso auf _STurin 2201 von Gemnefhorbak aus der 26. Dynastie aus Sais und auf pHor aus der frühen Ptolemäerzeit, diese Schreibung steht im Gegensatz zur Schreibung *nčr pf/y ꜥȝ*, die bei den anderen Parallelen benutzt wird.[60]

e) Andere Beweise

– Das Zeichen (M40) wird seitenverkehrt bei _KAssiut sowie pHor, pEmory und pTurin geschrieben. Alle anderen Parallelen weisen die richtige Richtung auf.

– Der Tb-Spruch 158 ist, sowie auch Tb-Spruch 159 und 157, nur aus späten Handschriften bekannt, nämlich pMarseille 291 der 26. Dynastie und pTurin der Ptolemäerzeit. Jeder Papyrus enthält die Vignette und den Text, dessen Titel lautet:

pIuefankh Tf. 76, 1[61]

rʾ n(.ỉ) wsḫ.t n(.ỉ) nbw	„Spruch des Usech-Halskragens aus Gold
ṯi̯ r ḥḥ	der am Hals plaziert ist".

Die drei Sprüche befinden sich besonders auf den Amuletten am Hals des Verstorbenen.[62]

– Es ist zu bemerken, dass die *sḫm.ti̯*-Krone (das Doppelte) in der Ptolemäerzeit oft als Zusatz zu anderen Kronen getragen wurde.[63]

Daher kann die Mumienkartonage stark mit den Quellen der Spätzeit und der frühen Ptolemäerzeit verglichen werden, insbesondere pHor, wobei beide manche Besonderheiten, die vielleicht zu einer anderen Hauptquelle gehören, enthalten. Daher gehe ich davon aus, dass die Mumienkartonage in die frühe Ptolemäerzeit zu datieren ist.

---

60 Siehe auch MOSHER 2016: 354 Anm. 11.
61 Für den Tb-Spruchtext 158 siehe LEPSIUS 1842: Tf. 76, 1–2.
62 HORNUNG 1990: 336.
63 COLLIER 1996: 132, Fig. 64, table 24.

6. Zusammenfassung

Die Untersuchung führt zu den folgenden Ergebnissen:

– In Assiut ist die Mumienkartonage S05/71 des Padiamun mit den ersten fünf Zeilen des Tb-Spruchs 72 beschriftet worden.
– Der Textvergleich zeigt, dass die Mumienkartonage große Ähnlichkeit mit den Quellen der Spätzeit und der frühen Ptolemäerzeit aufweist.
– Die Kopie des Tb-Spruchs 72 des Padiamun aus Assiut ist besonders gut vergleichbar mit dem pHor (pBerlin P. 10477) aus der frühen Ptolemäerzeit. Beide enthalten gemeinsame Besonderheiten, so dass die Mumienkartonage in die frühe Ptolemäerzeit datiert werden kann.
– Der Tb-Spruch 72 des Padiamun ist neben dem Totenbuchpapyrus des Pa-di-Nemti[64] und Uschebtis mit Tb-Spruch 6 die erste Kopie für das Totenbuch vom Gebel Assiut al-gharbi, der Nekropole der Gauhauptstadt Assiut.

7. Anhang

Textkritische Zeichen
[...]   Eckige Klammern umschließen Zerstörtes, vom Bearbeiter evtl. Ergänztes.
⌜...⌝   Eckige Halbklammern umschließen Teilzerstörtes, vom Bearbeiter evtl. Ergänztes.
<...>   Spitze Klammern umschließen im Original versehentlich Ausgelassenes, vom Bearbeiter evtl. Eingefügtes.
{...}   Geschweifte Klammern umschließen im Original versehentlich zuviel Geschriebenes.
(...)   Runde Klammern umschließen im Original korrekt nicht Vorhandenes, vom Bearbeiter der Klarheit wegen Zugefügtes.

Abkürzungen
Abb.   = Abbildung
Anm.   = Anmerkung
bzw.   = beziehungsweise
Dyn.   = Dynastie
evtl.   = eventuell
frühptol.   = frühptolemäisch
Früh.Ptol.   = Frühe Ptolemäerzeit
G   = Grab
Inv. Nr.   = Inventar-Nummer
Jh.   = Jahrhundert
K   = Kartonage
Kol.   = Kolumne
li   = links
mi   = Mitte
Mitt.Ptol.   = Mitte Ptolemäerzeit
p   = Papyrus
pers.-ptol. = persisch-ptolemäisch
Pho.-Tf.   = Photo-Tafel

64 Kahl 2007: 136 mit weiterer Literatur; Moje 2013.

Ptol.	= Ptolemäerzeit
ptol.	= ptolemäisch
re	= rechts
ₛ	= Sarkophag
ₛₐ	= Sarg
Tf.	= Tafel
u.	= und
u. a.	= unter anderem
v. Chr.	= vor Christus
Z.	= Zeile

Besitzer der benutzten Parallelen für die Kopie des Tb-Spruchs 72 aus Assiut

Iꜥḥ-t(ꜣy)=ś-nḫt	= pColon. Aeg. 10207
Iyi-m-ḥtp	= ₛLondon 971 (1303), British Museum
Iw=f-ꜥnḫ(.w)	= pTurin 1791, Museo Egizio
Ir.tỉw-r.w	= pMilbank = pOIM 10486
Wnn-nfr	= ₛBerlin Inv.-Nr. 46
Bꜣk-św (ꜣḫ)	= Hannover, Kestner-Museum (pKM 1970.37)
Pꜣ-hb	= pEmory
P(ꜣ)-ṯi-bꜣśt.t	= ₛPhiladelphia E 16135, Pennsylvania Museum
P(ꜣ)-ṯi-n(.ỉ)-ꜣśt	= ₛKairo JE 34648, Ägyptisches Museum
Psmčk	= ₛₐKammar, Nordwand
Ptḥ-htb(.w)	= ₛOxford 1947.295, Ashmolean Museum
Mnč(.w)-m-ḥꜣt	= Grab TT 34
Mśi-m-nčr (Ca)	= pMesemneter (Ca) = Paris, pLouvre E.21324
Nꜣḫ.t(ỉ)-ỉmn(.w) (Ba)	= pBerlin P. 3002
Nw	= London, pBM EA 10477
Nb-sny (Aa)	= London, pBM EA 9900
Nfr-wbn=f (Pb)	= pLouvre 3092
Nś-pꜣ-śfy	= pKairo JE 95714 + pAlbany 1900.3.1 + pKairo JE 95649
Nś-šw-tfn.t ?	= pRyerson = Chicago, pOIM 9787
Nś-tfn.t	= ₛKairo JE 6291 (TR 15/1/21/4), Ägyptisches Museum
Ḥr(.w)	= pBerlin P. 10477
Ḥr(.w)-ỉr-ṯi-ś	= ₛKairo TR 13/1/21/8, Ägyptisches Museum
Gmi.n=f-Ḥr(.w)-bꜣk	= ₛTurin Inv. Nr. 2201, Museo Egizio
Tꜣ-bꜣ-čꜣ.t	= ₛKairo CG 41058, Ägyptisches Museum

Verzeichnis der in vorliegender Untersuchung benutzten Parallelen für die Kopie des Tb-Spruchs 72 aus Assiut

pBaksu	18. Dyn.	Munro 1995: Tf. 2, 43–55
ₛBerlin Inv.-Nr. 46	Mitte/Späte Ptol.	Kakosy 1974: 113–118, Abb. 1
CT	MR	de Buck 1935–1961
Grab TT 34	26-25. Dyn.	Rosati 2006: 299, Tf. 21, 1–12
pEmory	Mitte/Späte Ptol.	Keller 1985: Fig. 1, 55–67
pHor	Frühe Ptol.	Munro 2006: Tf. 69, 133–141
ₛKairo JE 34648	Psammetich I-Amasis	Buhl 1959: 20–21, Fig. 82, A1; Maspero 1900: 259–260; PM III 175

sKairo JE 6291	Frühe Ptol.	BUHL 1959: 111–112, fig. 65, F, b1; Tb-Projekt Bonn, TM 112682
sKairoTR 13/1/21/8	Frühe Ptol.	BUHL 1959: 98–99 F, a); KAMAL 1902: 7_14); PM IV, 8; Tb-Projekt Bonn, TM 90743
saKairo CG 41058	26. Dyn.	GAUTHIER 1913: 348–349, Tf. 23; ELIAS 1993: 483, 526, (III–1) n. 528, 776, 822 no. 147); PM I.1 2nd, 644; Tb-Projekt Bonn, TM 134964
sAKammar	Amasis	MASPERO 1902: 179; GESTERMANN 2001: Nr. 52, 127–149; Tb-Projekt Bonn, TM 134964
pKöln	26. Dyn.	VERHOEVEN 1993: II S. 48–49, Z. 34, 1–13
sLondon 971 (1303)	30. Dyn.–1. Hälfte 2. Jh. v. Chr	BUHL 1959: 81–82, fig. 43, E, b 18); Tb-Projekt Bonn, TM 90726
pMesemneter (Ca)	18. Dyn.	NAVILLE 1886: 1, Tf. 84, 1–14
pMilbank	Mitte Ptol.	ALLEN 1960: Tf. 69, 440–449 (pMilbank$_1$); Tf. 76, 654–659 (pMilbank$_2$)
pNachtamun (Ba)	19. Dyn.	NAVILLE 1886: 1, Tf. 84
pNebseni (Aa)	18. Dyn.	pNebseni Tf. 3, 1–15, in: BUDGE 1898: I, 159–162
pNeferuebenef (Pb)	18. Dyn.	NAVILLE 1886: 1, Tf. 84
pNespasefy	Anf. 26. Dyn.	VERHOEVEN 1999: Tf. 28, Kol. B9, 12–18; Tf. 29, Kol. B10, 1–11)
pNu	18. Dyn.	LAPP 1997: Tf. 20, 1–14+1; QUIRKE 2013: 173–174
sOxford 1947.295	26. Dyn.	BUHL 1959: 140–141 K1, fig. 82; LD III Tf. 277c; Texts I, p. 101; PM III 57; Tb-Projekt Bonn, TM 135509
sPhiladelphia E16135	Pers.-Ptol.	BUHL 1959: 86–89, Fig. 50, E, b 23; Tb-Projekt Bonn, TM 90731
pRyerson	Pers.-Ptol.	ALLEN 1960: Pho.-Tf. 24 Kol. 49, 1–42
pTurin 1791	Mitte/Späte Ptol.	LEPSIUS 1842: Tf. 27, 1–11.
sTurin Inv. Nr. 2201	26. Dyn.	PIEHL 1886: pls. 86E–89F; BUHL 1959: 120–122, 176–177, fig. 73, Tf. 7–9, Gb 2; ROCCATI 1989: 30, Abb. 14, Z. 16–25; HEISE 2007: 270–273

Bibliographie

ALLEN 1960: T. G. Allen, The Book of the Dead or Going Forth by Day (Studies in Ancient Oriental Civilization 37; Chicago 1960).

BARTSCHAT & CONRAD 1981: B. Bartschat & R. Conrad, Kleines Wörterbuch sprachwissenschaftlicher Termini, 3. Auflage, Leipzig 1981.

DE BUCK 1935–1961: A. de Buck, The Egyptian Coffin Texts, 7 Bde (Oriental Institute Publications 34; Chicago 1935–1961).

BUDGE 1898: E. A. W. Budge, The Book of the Dead, The Chapters of Coming forth by Day, 2 Bde (London 1898).

BUHL 1959: M. L. Buhl, The Late Egyptian Anthropoid Stone Sarcophagi (Kopenhagen 1959).

COLLIER 1996: S. A. Collier, The Crowns of Pharaoh: Their Development and Significance in Ancient Egyptian Kingship (PhD, University of California; Los Angeles 1996).

EL-HAMRAWI 2002: M. El-Hamrawi, Anmerkungen zur Graphie der abydenischen Denk-und Grabsteintexte aus dem Mittleren Reich, in: Lingua Aegyptia 10, 2002, 211–218.

EL-HAMRAWI 2016: M. El-Hamrawi, Das transitiv-aktivische und passivische Pseudopartizip-Perfekt 1. Sg. ohne vordere Erweiterung in der Sprache des Alten und Mittleren Reichs, in: Lingua Aegyptia 24, 2016, 67–88.

ELIAS 1993: J. P. Elias, Coffin Inscription in Egypt after the New Kingdom. A Study of Text Production and Use in Elite Mortuary Preparation (Chicago 1993).

EL-KHADRAGY 2008: M. El-Khadragy, The Decoration of the Rock-cut Chapel of Khety II at Assiut, in: Studien zur Altägyptischen Kultur 37, 2008, 219–241.

EL-KHADRAGY 2012: The Nomarchs of Asyut during the First Intermediate Period and the Middle Kingdom, in: J. Kahl, M. El-Khadragy, U. Verhoeven & A. Kilian (eds.), Seven Seasons at Asyut. First Results of the Egyptian-German Cooperation in Archaeological Fieldwork (The Asyut Project 2; Wiesbaden 2012), 31–46.

FRANKE 1987: D. Franke, Zwischen Herakleopolis und Theben. Neues zu den Gräbern von Assiut, in: Studien zur Altägyptischen Kultur 14, 1987, 49–60.

GARDINER 1947: A. H. Gardiner, Ancient Egyptian Onomastica II (Oxford 1947).

GAUTHIER 1913: H. Gauthier, Cercueils anthropoides des prètres de Montou (CG 41042–41072) (Catalogue général des antiquités égyptiennes du Musée du Caire; Kairo 1913).

GESTERMANN 2001: L. Gestermann, Grab und Stele von Psametich, Oberarzt und Vorsteher der Tjemehu, in: Revue d'Égyptologie 52, 2001, 127–149.

GESTERMANN ET AL. 2021: L. Gestermann, C. Teotino, M. Wagner, Die Grabanlage des Monthemhet (TT 34) I. Der Weg zur Sargkammer (R 44.1 bis R 53) (Studien zur spätägyptischen Religion 31; Wiesbaden 2021).

GOMAÁ 1986: F. Gomaá, Die Besiedlung Ägyptens während des Mittleren Reichs. 1. Oberägypten und das Fayyūm (Beihefte zum Tübinger Atlas des Vorderen Orients. Reihe B (Geisteswissenschaften) 66, 1; Wiesbaden 1986).

HEISE 2007: J. Heise, Erinnern und Gedenken. Aspekte der biographischen Inschriften der Ägyptischen Spätzeit (Orbis Biblicus et Orientalis 226; Freiburg 2007).

HELCK 1974: W. Helck, Die altägyptischen Gaue (Wiesbaden 1974).

HORNUNG 1990: E. Hornung, Das Totenbuch der Ägypter (2. Auflage, München 1990).

KAHL 2007: J. Kahl, Ancient Asyut. The First Synthesis after 300 Years of Research (The Asyut Project 1; Wiesbaden 2007).

KAHL 2016: J. Kahl, Ornamente in Bewegung. Die Deckendekoration der großen Querhalle im Grab von Djefai-Hapi I. in Assiut (The Asyut Project 6; Wiesbaden 2016).

KAHL ET AL. 2016: J. Kahl, N. Deppe, D. Goldsmith, A. Kilian, Ch. Kitagawa, J. Moje & M. Zöller-Engelhardt, Asyut. Tomb III: Objects. Part 1 (The Asyut Project 3; Wiesbaden 2016).

KAKOSY 1974: L. Kakosy, Ein Sarkophag aus der Ptolemäerzeit im Berliner Ägyptischen Museum, in: G. Poethke, U. Luft & S. Wenig (Hgg.), Festschrift zum 150jährigen Bestehen des Berliner Ägyptischen Museums (Mitteilungen aus der Ägyptischen Sammlung – Staatliche Museen zu Berlin 8; Berlin 1974), 113–118.

KAKOSY 1998: L. Kakosy, A Late interpretation of the Name Osiris, in: Archív orientální 66, 1998, 243–248.

KAMAL 1903: A. Kamal, Tell FarAon (Bouto), in: Annales du Service des Antiquités de l'Égypte 3, 7–14.

KELLER 1985: C. A. Keller, A Late Book of the Dead in Emory University Museum, in: Bulletin of the Egyptological Seminar 6, 1985. 55–67.

LACAU & CHEVRIER 1969: P. Lacau & H. Chevrier, Une Chapelle de Sesostris Ier a Karnak (Kairo ³1969).

LAPP 1997: G. Lapp, The Papyrus of Nu (BM EA 10477) (Catalogue of Books of the Dead in the British Museum 1; London 1997).

LAPP 2002: G. Lapp, The Papyrus of Nebseni (BM EA 9900). The Texts of Chapter 180 with the New Kingdom Parallels (British Museum Occasional Paper 139; London 2002).

LAPP 2004: G. Lapp, The Papyrus of Nebseni (BM EA 9900) (Catalogue of the Books of the Dead in the British Museum 3; London 2004).

LAPP 2006: G. Lapp, Totenbuch Spruch 17. Synoptische Textausgabe nach Quellen des Neuen Reichs (Totenbuchtexte 1; Basel 2006).

LAPP 2011: G. Lapp, Die *prt-m-hrw*-Sprüche (Tb 2, 64–72). Synoptische Textausgabe nach Quellen des Neuen Reiches (Totenbuchtexte 7; Basel 2011).

LD: C. R. Lepsius, Denkmäler aus Ägypten und Äthiopien, 6 Abteilungen in 12 Bänden, Berlin 1849–1859 (Nachdruck Genève 1971–1972).

LEITZ 2006: Ch. Leitz, Die Größe Ägyptens nach dem Sesostris-Kiosk in Karnak, in: G. Moers et al. (Hgg.), *jn.t dr.w* – Festschrift für Friedrich Junge, Band II, Göttingen 2006, 409–427.

LEPSIUS 1842: C. R. Lepsius, Das Totenbuch der Ägypter nach dem hieroglyphischen Papyrus in Turin (Leipzig 1842; Nachdruck Osnabrück 1969).

MASPERO 1900: G. Maspero, Les inscriptions du tombeau du Péténisis, in: Annales du Service des Antiquités de l'Égypte 1, 1900, 234–261.

MASPERO 1902: G. Maspero, Les inscriptions de la chambre de Psammétique, in: Annales du Service des Antiquités de l'Égypte 3, 1902, 166–184.

MASPERO 1914–1939: G. Maspero, Sarcophages des époques persane et ptolémaïque (CG 29301–29323) (Catalogue général des antiquités égyptiennes du Musée du Caire; Cairo 1914–1939).

MILDE 1991: H. Milde, The Vignettes in the Book of the Dead of Neferrenpet (Egyptologische Uitgaven 7; Leiden 1991).

MOJE 2013: J. Moje, The Ushebtis From Early Excavations in the Necropolis of Asyut, Mainly by David George Hogarth and Ahmed Bey Kamal (The Asyut Project 4; Wiesbaden 2013).

MONTET 1961: P. Montet, Géographie de l'Égypte ancienne II (Paris 1961).

MOSHER 2017: M. Mosher, The Book of the Dead, Saite through Ptolemaic Periods. A Study of Traditions Evident in Versions of Texts and Vignettes, volume 4 (BD Spells 50-63, 65-77) (London 2017).

MUNRO 1988: I. Munro, Untersuchungen zu den Totenbuch-Papyri der 18. Dynastie (Studies in Egyptology; London 1988).

MUNRO 1995: I. Munro, Das Totenbuch des Bak-su (pKM 1970.37/ pBrocklehurst) aus der Zeit Amenophis' II. (Handschriften des Altägyptischen Totenbuchs 2; Wiesbaden 1995).

MUNRO 2006: I. Munro, Der Totenbuch-Papyrus des Hor aus der frühen Ptolemäerzeit (pCologny Bodmer CV+pCincinnati 1947.369+pDenver 1954.61) (Handschriften des Altägyptischen Totenbuches 9; Wiesbaden 2006).

NAVILLE 1886: E. Naville, Das Ägyptische Totenbuch der XVIII. bis XX. Dynastie aus verschiedenen Urkunden (3 Bde, Berlin 1886).

PIEHL 1886: K. Piehl, Inscriptions hiéroglyphiques recueillies en Europe et en Égypte I (Leipzig 1886).

PM: B. Porter & R. Moss, Topographical Bibliography of Ancient Egyptian Hieroglyphic Texts, Reliefs, and Paintings (Oxford 1960–1964).

QUIRKE 2013: S. Quirke, Going out in Daylight – *prt m hrw*. The Ancient Egyptian Book of the Dead, translation, sources and meanings (Golden House Publications Egyptology 20; London 2013).

ROCCATI 1989: A. Roccati, Kunst und Technik der Schrift, in: Donadoni Roveri, A. M. (Hrsg.), Ägyptisches Museum Turin. Das Alte Ägypten. Das Alltagsleben (Mailand 1989).

ROSATI 2006: G. Rosati, Glimpses of the Book of the Dead in the Second Court of the Tomb of Montuemhat TT 34, in: B. Backes, I. Munro & S. Stöhr (Hgg.), Totenbuch-Forschungen: Gesammelte Beiträge des 2. Internationalen Totenbuch-Symposiums Bonn, 25. bis 29. September 2005 (Wiesbaden 2006), 279–324, Tf. 1–24.

RÖSSLER 1971: O. Rössler, Ägyptisch als semitische Sprache, in: F. Altheim & R. Stiehl (Hgg.), Christentum am Roten Meer I, (Berlin – New York 1971), 262–326.

SCHENKEL 1990: W. Schenkel, Einführung in die altägyptische Sprachwissenschaft (Darmstadt 1990).

SCHENKEL 2005: W. Schenkel, Tübinger Einführung in die klassisch-ägyptische Sprache und Schrift (Tübingen 2005).

SCHENKEL 2012: W. Schenkel, Tübinger Einführung in die klassisch-ägyptische Sprache und Schrift (Tübingen 2012).

SPIEGELBERG 1923: W. Spiegelberg, Die Datierung des Turiner Totenbuchs, in: Zeitschrift für Ägyptische Sprache und Altertumskunde 58, 1923, 152–153.

TIMM 1984: S. Timm, Das christlich-koptische Ägypten in arabischer Zeit (Wiesbaden 1984–1992).

VERHOEVEN 1993: U. Verhoeven, Das saitische Totenbuch der Iahtesnacht: P. Colon. Aeg. 10207 (Papyrologische Texte und Abhandlungen 41; 3 Bände, Bonn 1993).

VERHOEVEN 1999: U. Verhoeven, Das Totenbuch des Monthpriesters Nespasefy aus der Zeit Psammetichs I., pKairo JE 95714+pAlbany 1900.3.1+pKairo JE 95649, pMarseille 91/2/1 (ehem. Slg. Brunner)+pMarseille 291 (Handschriften des Altägyptischen Totenbuches 5; Wiesbaden 1999).

VERHOEVEN 2001: U. Verhoeven, Untersuchungen zur späthieratischen Buchschrift (Orientalia Lovaniensia Analecta 99; Leuven 2001).

VERHOEVEN 2017: U. Verhoeven, unter Mitarbeit von Sandra Sandri, Das frühsaitische Totenbuch des Monthpriesters Chamhor C (Beiträge zum Alten Ägypten 7; Basel 2017).

Wb: A. Erman & H. Grapow, Wörterbuch der ägyptischen Sprache (5 Bde; Bd. 6, 1950; Bd. 7, 1971, Berlin).

Inernetquellen

Tb-Projekt Bonn: http://totenbuch.awk.nrw.de//

Abb. 1: Vorhof des Grabes N12.1 (Grab III) von *Itỉ-ỉbỉ (*Foto: Jochem Kahl 2005; © The Asyut Project).

Abb. 2: Innere Halle des Grabes N12.1/Grab III von *Itỉ-ỉbỉ* (Foto: Fritz Barthel 2007, © The Asyut Project).

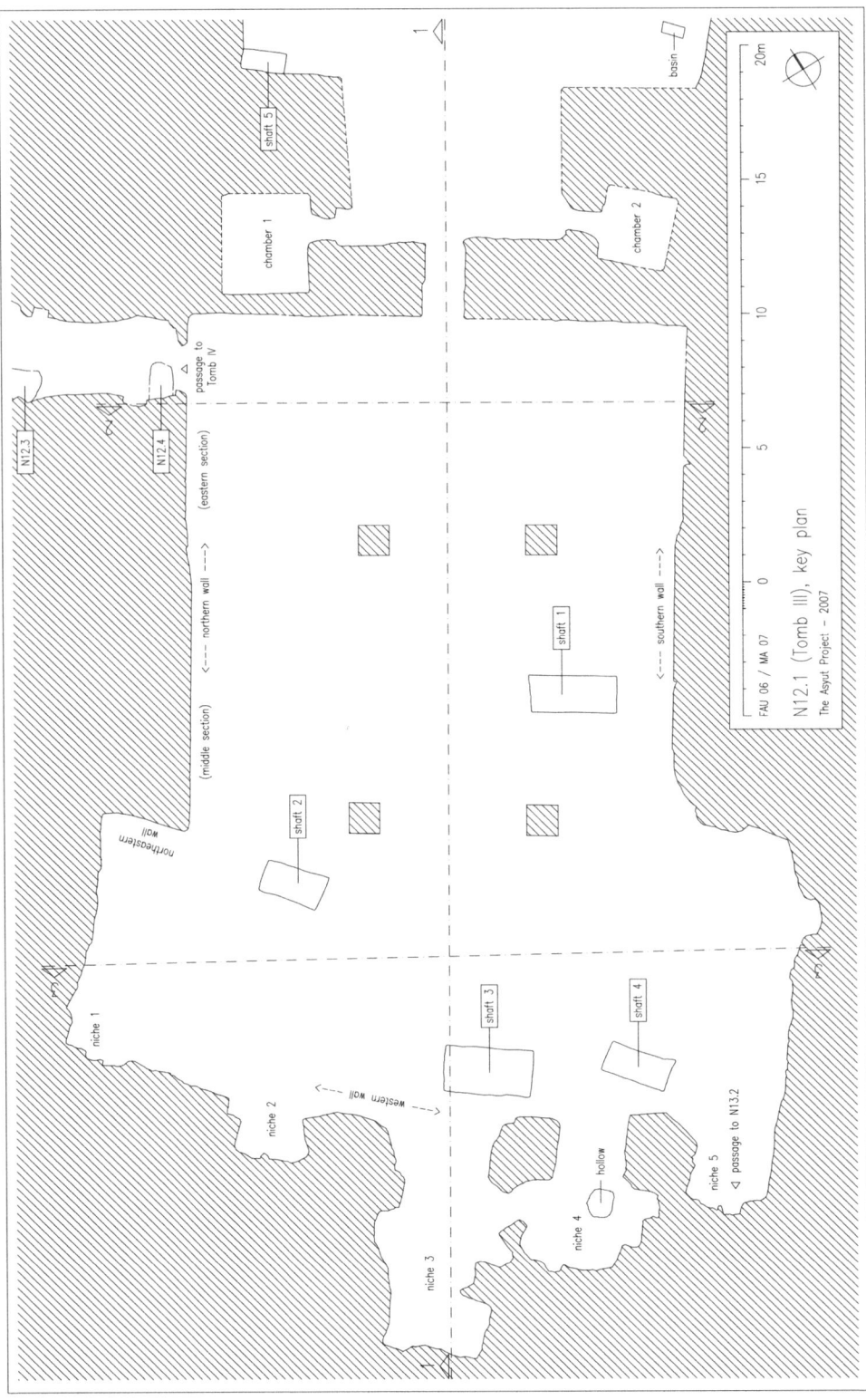

Abb. 3: Grundriss von Grab N12.1/Grab III von *Itỉ-ỉbỉ* (©The Asyut Project).

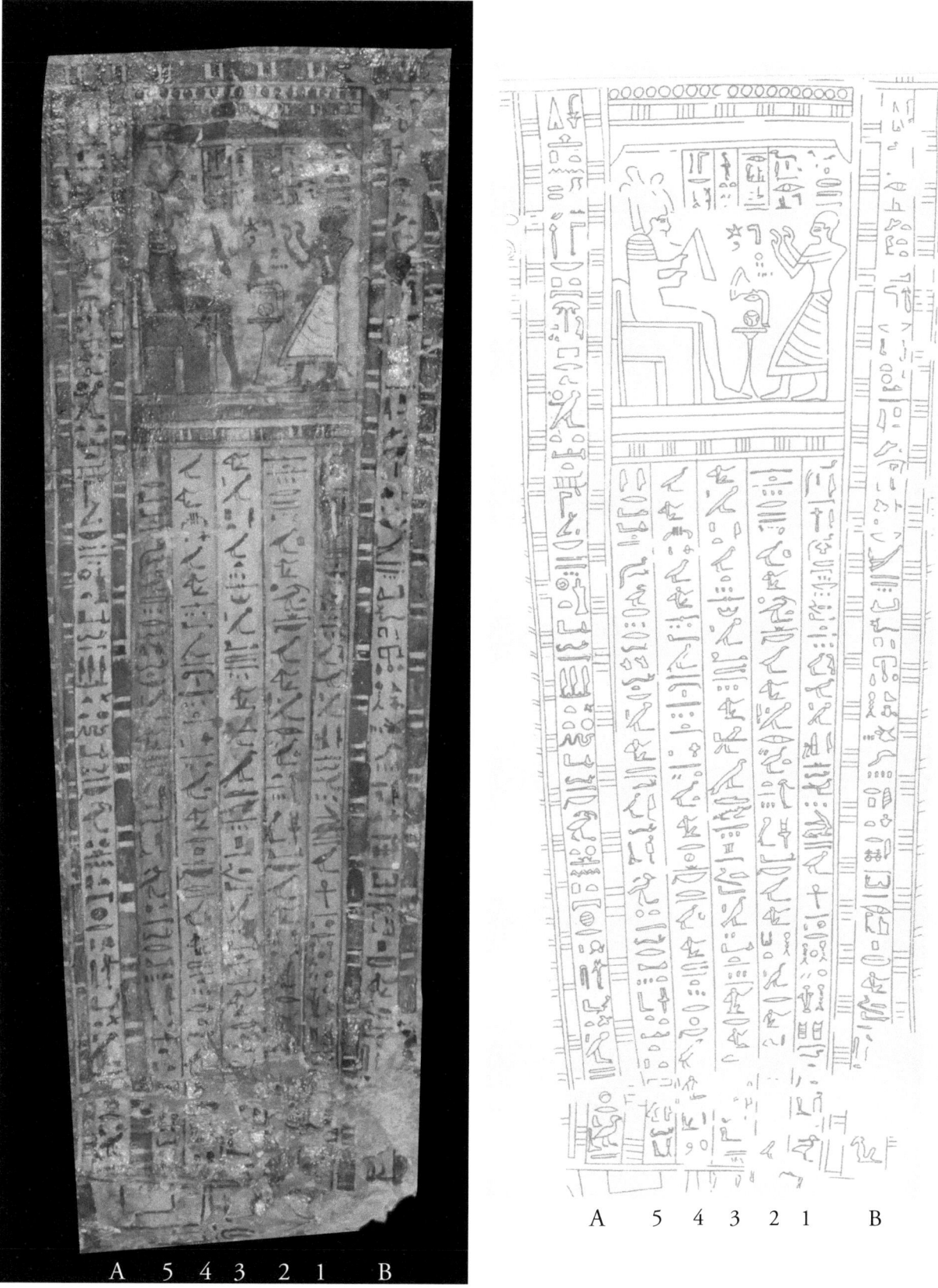

Abb. 4a (links): Tb-Spruch 72 aus Assiut (Foto: Fritz Barthel 2017; © The Asyut Project).
Abb. 4b (rechts): Faksimile des Tb-Spruchs 72 (Sameh Shafik; © The Asyut Project).

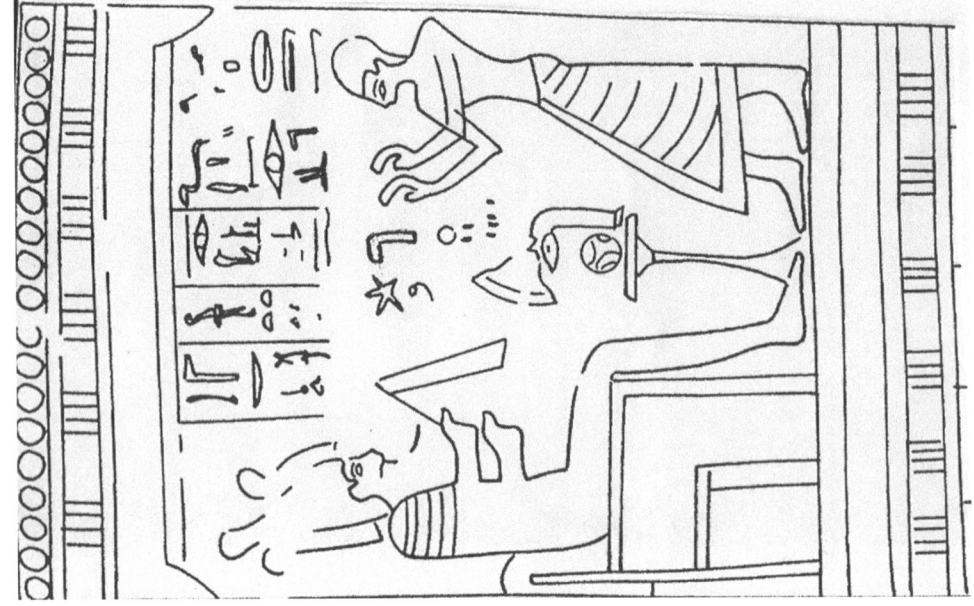

Abb. 5a (links): Vignette des Tb-Spruchs 72 aus Assiut (Foto: Fritz Barthel 2017; © The Asyut Project).
Abb. 5b (rechts): Faksimile der Vignette des Tb-Spruchs 72. (Sameh Shafik; © The Asyut Project).

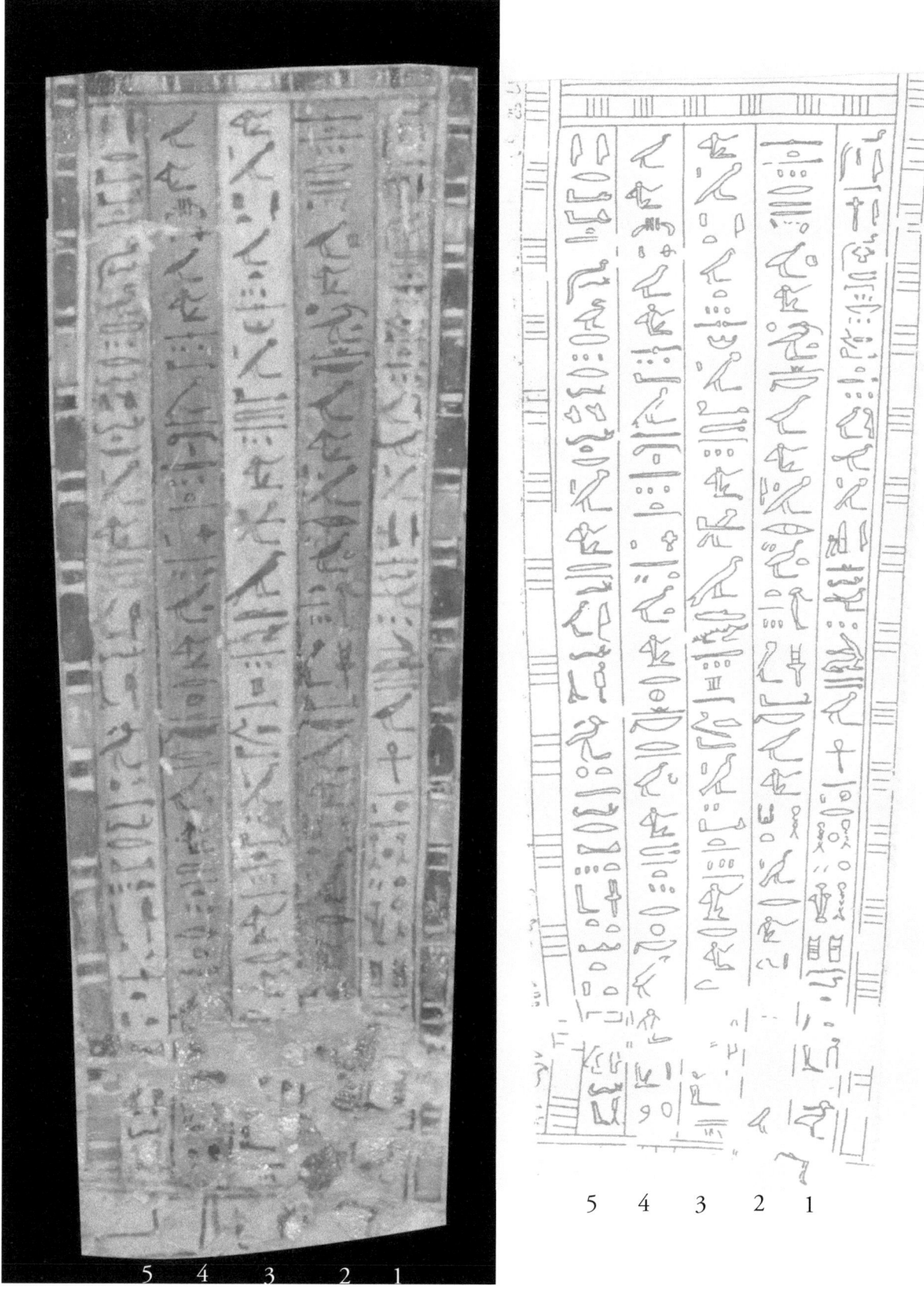

Abb. 6a (links): Kopie des Tb-Spruchs 72 aus Assiut (Foto: Fritz Barthel 2017; © The Asyut Project).
Abb. 6b (rechts): Faksimile des Tb-Spruchs 72 (Sameh Shafik; © The Asyut Project).

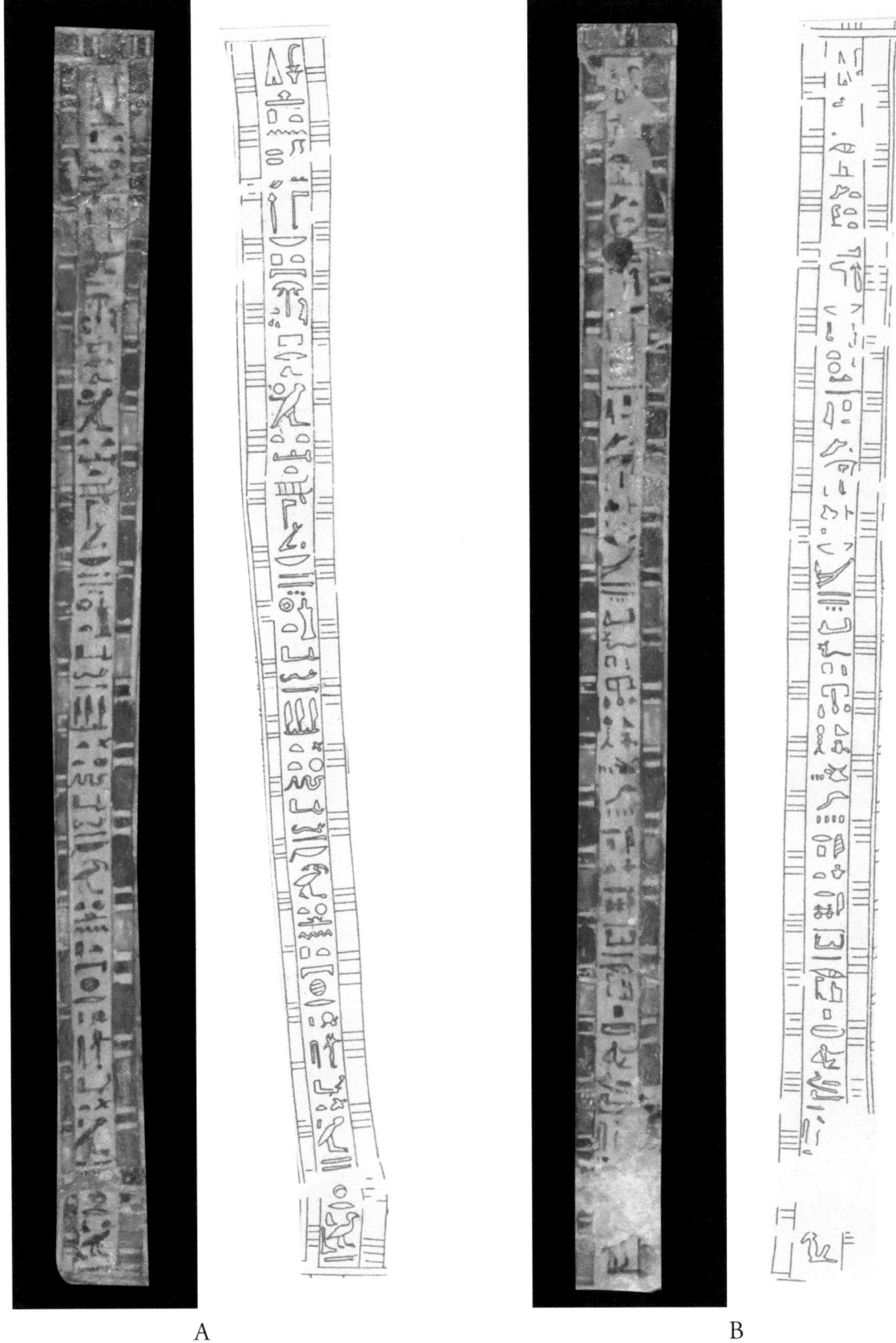

A   B

Abb. 7a (links): Opferformel der linken Seite. Abb. 7b (rechts): Opferformel der rechten Seite
(Fotos: Fritz Barthel 2017; Faksimiles: Sameh Shafik; © The Asyut Project).

Christliche Grabstelen aus Assiut

Philipp Scharfenberger

Im Antikenmagazin von Shutb befinden sich einige christliche[1] Grabstelen mit koptischen oder griechischen Inschriften, von denen drei Gegenstand der vorliegenden Arbeit sind. Die Provenienz der Stücke ist zumindest teilweise rekonstruierbar: Sie wurden im Jahr 1961 aus Assiut an das Ägyptische Museum Kairo verschickt, um von dort dann 2008 ins Antikenmagazin von Shutb zu gelangen, in dem sie sich bis heute befinden und zusammen mit weiteren Objekten in einem von Jochem Kahl und Mohamed Abdelrahiem geleiteten Projekt bearbeitet werden. Ursprünglich stammen die Stücke mit größter Wahrscheinlichkeit vom Gebel Assiut al-gharbi, dem westlich von Assiut gelegenen Berg.[2] Dort gab es mindestens zwei christliche Klöster, Deir el-Azzam und Deir el-Meitin, die spätestens im 15. Jh. n. Chr. aufgegeben wurden, aber noch archäologisch nachweisbar sind.[3] Neben diesen Klosteranlagen und ihren Friedhöfen lassen sich auf dem Berg zahlreiche Spuren von Christen finden, wie beispielsweise Kapellen, Keramikfunde oder von Eremiten neugenutzte pharaonenzeitliche Felsgräber. Aus verschiedenen Gründen sind viele dieser Anfang des 20. Jahrhunderts noch sichtbaren christlichen Relikte Zerstörungen anheimgefallen und für immer verloren.[4] Somit ist die rekonstruierbare Herkunft der hier vorgestellten Grabstelen von zweifacher Bedeutung: Die Anzahl der bekannten christlichen Relikte vom Gebel Assiut al-gharbi mehrt sich und die Epigraphik erhält für ihre Forschung topographisch zuordenbare Objekte. Der letzte Punkt ist von besonderer Relevanz, da die mit Inschriften versehenen christlichen Grabstelen Ägyptens häufig keine geklärte Provenienz aufweisen[5] – ein Faktum, das die epigraphischen Studien erschwert.

1. Die Objekte

Um an Präzision bei der Objektverortung zu gewinnen, wurden den Grabstelen Inventarbezeichnungen zugeordnet. Diese setzen sich aus dem Objektbesitzer Supreme Council of Antiquities (SCA), dem Aufbewahrungsort (Shutb) und einer Nummer (nach dem Ordnungssystem des von Kahl und Abdelrahiem geleiteten Aufarbeitungsprojektes) zusammen. So ergeben sich für die drei Grabstelen die Bezeichnungen SCAShutb4, SCAShutb7 und SCAShutb9.

---

1   In den terminologischen Bezeichnungen der Grabstelen folge ich Bianca Tudor, sodass generell von christlichen Grabstelen die Rede ist und je nach Sprache der Inschriften die einzelnen Grabstelen die Attribute koptisch, griechisch oder griechisch-koptisch erhalten (vgl. Tudor 2011: 13). Weiterhin sind hier generell nur die christlichen Grabstelen gemeint, die in ebenjenen Sprachen verfasst wurden. Die Tradition christlicher Inschriften in diesen Sprachen in Ägypten beginnt sich im 4. Jh. n. Chr. zu entwickeln und nimmt ab dem 9. Jh. n. Chr. ab (vgl. van der Vliet 2017: 482a–83b).

2   Allerdings ist eine Herkunft aus der Stadt nicht völlig auszuschließen. An dieser Stelle sei Jochem Kahl für die Bereitstellung von Fotos ebenjener Objekte und für seine Unterstützung herzlich gedankt. Von ihm stammen auch die der Arbeit zugrunde liegenden Berichte zur Provenienz.

3   Vgl. Kahl 2007: 99–106; Kahl 2014: 130a–b; van der Vliet 2015.

4   Vgl. Kahl 2007: 59, 71–72, 99–106; Kahl 2014: 130a–131b; für einen Lageplan siehe Kahl 2014: 129. Die Bedeutung der Klöster zeigt bereits der Friedhof von Deir el-Azzam, der um die 1400 Bestattungen umfasste (vgl. Kahl 2007: 100–102, Abb. 85; Kahl 2014: 130a). Obwohl Assiut und gerade der Gebel Assiut al-gharbi als wichtige Orte christlicher Einrichtungen eine Vielzahl an christlichen Grabstelen erwarten ließen, sind doch nur wenige erhalten (siehe bspw. die spärlichen Nennungen von Stelen aus Assiut bei Tudor 2011: 71–72).

5   Vgl. Tudor 2011: 1–2.

1.1 SCAShutb4

Hinter der Bezeichnung SCAShutb4 stehen sechs unterschiedlich große Kalksteinfragmente[6] (Abb. 1), die zusammengesetzt eine fast vollständige Grabstele ergeben (Abb. 2). Wie die digitale Zusammensetzung der mit einem Maßstab versehenen Fragmente belegt (Abb. 1 und Abb. 2), hat das zusammengesetzte Stück eine Größe von 51 cm x 37 cm x 7 cm.[7] Die Inschrift befindet sich in einem rechtwinklig in den Stein gehauenen Rahmen. Während dessen Seitenlinien einfach gehalten sind, sind die horizontalen Linien, die die Zeilen und den Rahmenrand begrenzen, stets als Pärchen angeordnet. Es ist keine weitere Dekoration zu erkennen. Die Buchstaben halten die Zeilen fast immer ein und überschreiten die Trennlinien nur in wenigen Fällen; ihre Ausführung ist von elaborierter Qualität. Nimmt man die in ihrer Gänze rekonstruierten Zeilen als Maßstab, so standen pro Zeile ca. 8–10 Buchstaben. Der Text ist fast komplett erhalten und erstreckt sich über zehn Zeilen. Lediglich in den ersten vier Zeilen fehlen die Zeilenenden. Die Inschrift ist auf den Fragmenten 3 und 4 (von oben nach unten und links nach rechts gezählt) schlechter erhalten als der übrige Text, aber noch lesbar. Die Textbearbeitung zeigt, dass es sich bei der Einleitungsformel um eine Bilingue in griechischer und koptischer Sprache handelt: Sie beginnt in der ersten Zeile griechisch und wird nach der Nennung des Verstorbenen mit dem koptischen Pendant in Zeile 3 fortgesetzt.[8]

Zeile	Koptisch	Deutsch
1	ἐκεμήθ[η ὁ μα(κάριος),]	Er legte sich zur Ruhe[, der selige]
2	ⲁⲡⲁ ⲑⲱⲙⲁ[ⲥ]	Apa Thomas,
3	ⲛⲧⲁⲃⲙⲧⲟⲛ [ⲙ]	der sich zur Ruhe begab
4	ⲙⲟⲃ ⲛⲥⲟⲩ ⲥ[ⲁ]	am 7. Tag
5	ⲱϥ ⲙⲡⲁϣⲟⲟⲛ	des Paschons
6	ⲥ ⲡⲣⲱⲧⲏⲥ ⲛⲓⲛ(ⲇⲓⲕ)	des ersten Indiktionsjahres.
7	ⲕ(ⲧⲓⲱⲛⲟⲥ), ⲉⲣⲉⲡⲛⲟⲩⲧⲉ	Möge Gott
8	ⲣ ⲟⲩⲛⲁ ⲛⲉⲙⲁ	Mitleid mit
9	ⲃ ϩⲛ ⲛ̅ⲧⲟⲡⲟⲥ	ihm haben an den Orten,
10	ⲛⲧⲁⲃⲱⲕ ⲉⲣⲟⲟ<ⲩ>	zu denen er gegangen ist.

1 ἐκεμήθ[η l. ἐκοιμήθη; [ο μα,] stel. **3** ⲛⲧⲁⲃ l. ⲛⲧⲁϥ **3–4** [ⲙ]|ⲙⲟⲃ l. ⲙⲙⲟϥ **6** πρῶτος **6–7** ⲓⲛ|ⲕ, stel. (ἰνδικτιῶνος) **8–9** ⲛⲉⲙⲁ|ⲃ l. ⲛⲙⲙⲁϥ **9** τόπος **10** ⲛⲧⲁⲃⲱⲕ l. ⲛⲧⲁϥⲃⲱⲕ; ⲉⲣⲟⲟ st.

1 ὁ μα,, der vorhandene Platz lässt diese oder eine ähnliche Abkürzung von μακάριος erwarten.[9]
6–7 ⲛⲓⲛ|ⲕ,, das ⲛ des Genitivs ist bemerkenswert, weil griechische Ordinalzahlen keinen nachfolgenden koptischen Genitivanschluss benötigen. Außerdem ist die nicht bei Förster belegte Abkürzung ⲓⲛⲕ, auffällig. Möglicherweise wurde sie gemäß der in koptischen Texten belegten Tendenz gebildet, die ersten beiden Buchstaben von ἰνδικτιῶνος nur durch ein Ny auszudrücken (ⲛⲇⲓⲕⲧⲓⲟⲛⲟⲥ). Vgl. Förster 2002: 347–352.
    Eine weitere sprachliche Auffälligkeit des Textes ist die durchgehende Verwendung von Beta anstatt eines im Sahidischen üblichen Fai als Suffixpronomen der 3. Person Singular Maskulinum. Da auf der

---

6   Da der Gebel Assiut al-gharbi geographisch Teil einer Kalksteinformation ist, konnten Kalksteinobjekte wie SCAShutb4 vor Ort hergestellt werden (vgl. Kahl 2007: 59; Kahl 2014: 127a–b; Klemm & Klemm 2008: 112b–115a).

7   Alle Maße basieren auf den Fundzetteln des von Jochem Kahl und Mohamed Abdelrahiem geleiteten Projekts.

8   Die Schwierigkeit, eine Grabstelen-Inschrift als Bilingue zu bezeichnen, wird von Tudor diskutiert (vgl. Tudor 2011: 13). In Bezug auf bilinguale Inschriften gibt Jacques van der Vliet an: „The epigraphy of Christian Egypt was essentially bilingual, as was Egyptian society itself. [...] Greek and Coptic may be used next to each other in a single text ("code switching"), but real bilingual inscriptions that render more or less identical texts in two languages are rare." (van der Vliet 2017: 482b). Daher wird lediglich der angesprochene Textteil als eine Bilingue deklariert.
    Der Anschluss durch ⲛⲧⲁϥ kann als zweites Tempus oder relativisch (wie in der Übersetzung) interpretiert werden.

9   Die unten aufgeführten Inschriften von SCAShutb9 und der Grabstele der Ama Lo belegen das regelmäßige Auftreten von ὁ μακάριος/οἱ μακαρία NN nach ἐκοιμήθη in christlichen Epitaphen aus Assiut.

Stele vier Belege für diese sprachliche Eigenheit in unterschiedlichen grammatikalischen Konstruktionen vorliegen, handelt es sich bei der Sprache des koptischen Textteils um ein destandardisiertes Sahidisch mit ausgeprägten regionalen Merkmalen.[10] Die verwendeten Formeln sind gut belegt.[11]

Der Name des Verstorbenen ist rekonstruierbar: Für „Thomas" spricht sowohl die Beleglage des Namens[12] als auch der verbleibende Raum in der Zeile. Da er den Ehrentitel „Apa" trug, bekleidete Thomas wahrscheinlich ein Amt in der Kirchenhierarchie,[13] möglicherweise in einem der Klöster des Berges. Aus anderen Quellen ist er, meines Wissens, nicht bekannt. Anhand des Textes lässt sich das Todesdatum von Apa Thomas auf Tag, Monat und Indiktionsjahr festlegen. Eine absolute Datierung ist nicht möglich.

1.2 SCAShutb7

Die Grabstele SCAShutb7 besteht im Gegensatz zur vorher beschriebenen aus nur einem einzelnen Fragment mit den Maßen 33 cm x 23 cm x 6 cm (Abb. 3). Die oberen zwei Drittel der Stele werden von zwei großen, im versenkten Relief gestalteten Kreuzen eingenommen. Im unteren Teil findet sich die eingravierte koptische Inschrift. Mit Ausnahme der Trennung durch den Relieftypwechsel sind keinerlei Rahmen oder Trennlinien um den Text erhalten. Die Buchstaben wurden zwar den einzelnen Zeilen zuordenbar und so dick geschrieben, dass die Lesbarkeit gewährleistet wird, doch wirkt die Ausführung nicht hochwertig. Durch die Kreuze über der ersten Zeile wird ersichtlich, dass diese die erste Textzeile ist. Es sind drei Zeilen erkennbar und es bleibt offen, wie viel Text nach der letzten Zeile fehlt.

Zeile	Koptisch	Deutsch
1	ⲡⲛⲟⲩⲧⲉ	Gott,
2	[ⲉ]ⲣ ⲟⲩⲛⲁ ⲙ[ⲛ	habe Mitleid mit
3	ⲁ]ⲡⲁ ϣⲟⲓ […]	Apa Schoi […].

2 [ⲉ]ⲣ, weil der Anfang der Zeilen 2 und 3 nicht erhalten und es nicht sicher ist, ob die letzten Buchstaben der Zeilen das jeweilige Zeilenende markieren, wurde bei Emendationen der Zeilenumbruch ggf. nach Wortzugehörigkeit vorgenommen.

Die verwendete Eingangsformel ist reichlich in koptischen Epitaphen belegt[14] und daher gut zu ergänzen. Dass „Schoi" wahrscheinlich der vollständige Name des Verstorbenen ist, beweisen die vielen Belege des Namens in dokumentarischen Texten.[15] Mit ihm ist ein weiterer Träger des Ehrentitels „Apa" vom Gebel Assiut al-gharbi bekannt, der, meines Wissens, noch nicht in anderen Quellen belegt ist. Das Kreuz als christliches Symbol schlechthin ist ein gängiges Dekorationselement christlicher Grabstelen Ägyptens.[16] Eine Datierung ist nicht möglich.

---

10 Bzgl. dieses Phänomens vgl. KAHLE 1954: 136–138.
11 Für ein weiteres Beispiel der Kombination der griechischen Eingangsformel mit dem koptischen Gebet um Mitleid siehe BIONDI 1907: 163, Nr. 38 (vgl. HASITZKA 1993: 158, Nr. 439). Die Kombination aus der griechischen Formel und beiden koptischen Formeln existiert auch in erweiterter Form (siehe bspw. ŁAJTAR 1998: 29–30 (vgl. HASITZKA 2004: 198, Nr. 1231; HASITZKA & ŁAJTAR & MARKIEWICZ 1999: 26, Nr. 50). Siehe bzgl. der Formeln auch TUDOR 2011: 161–162, 178–181, 196, 263–267, 298–304 (für eine Erweiterung des Gebets um eine Ortsangabe siehe TUDOR 2011: 304).
12 Vgl. HASITZKA 2007: 39a. 25 Kilometer südlich von Assiut liegt das Kloster des Apa Thomas (Wadi Sarga; vgl. O'CONNELL 2014: 122–123; CHOAT 2015: 407).
13 Vgl. ATIYA 1991: 152b.
14 Vgl. Fußnote 11.
15 Vgl. HASITZKA 2007: 113b.
16 Vgl. bspw. CRUM 1975: 124, Nr. 8582, Tf. XXXII, Nr. 8582.

1.3 SCAShutb9

SCAShutb9 ist ein einzelnes, mit einer Inschrift versehenes Fragment einer Grabstele aus Kalzit-Alabaster; es hat die Maße 50 cm x 24 cm x 5 cm (Abb. 4). Der obere Teil der Stele war abgerundet. Es sind keinerlei Rahmen, Zeilentrennstriche oder Dekorationen zu erkennen. Möglicherweise bilden die Gravur-Überreste in der unteren rechten Ecke eine Ausnahme: Es könnte sich um den oberen Teil eines Kreuzes handeln. Der in den Stein gehauene griechische Text scheint mit der ersten erkennbaren Zeile zu beginnen. Links vom ersten Buchstaben befindet sich die mit blauer Farbe geschriebene arabische Ziffer 28, die ohne Weiteres keine hier brauchbaren Informationen liefert und möglicherweise einer modernen Inventarisierung dient. Es sind fünf Textzeilen identifizierbar. Von allen Zeilen ist nur der Anfang erhalten. Die Buchstaben sind mit dünnen Linien lesbar, aber ohne besondere Qualität in den Stein gehauen. Über die mögliche Buchstabenanzahl pro Zeile lässt sich nur spekulieren.

Zeile	Griechisch	Deutsch
1	ἐκη[μήθη]	Er legte sich zur Ruhe,
2	ὁ μακ[άριος]	der selige
3	Κολλο[υθος]	Kollo[uthos]
4	αφου [Φαμεν]	(Sohn des) Aphou [Parem-]
5	ώθ †(?) . [...]	hat †(?) [...].

1 ἐκη[μήθη l. ἐκοιμήθη.

3 Κολλο[υθος], denkbar wäre auch eine Variante des Namens (vgl. Hasitzka 2007: 50b–51a).
5 ωθ, ist das Ende einer Monatsangabe. Die Buchstabenanzahl pro Zeile weist auf Φαμενώθ anstatt des ebenfalls denkbaren Θώθ hin.

Die ersten drei Textzeilen sind trotz der Zerstörung gut zu rekonstruieren. Die Eingangsformel entspricht der von SCAShutb4. Der Name Kollouthos ist gut belegt[17] und mit der Region verbunden: So existierte gemäß Abu Salih auch ein Kloster des Kollouthos in Assiut.[18] Aphou ist ebenfalls ein gut belegter Name.[19] Dafür, dass die Inschrift nicht in Zeile 5 endet, sprechen drei Gründe: 1. Am Ende von Zeile 5 findet sich eine Linie, die Teil eines Buchstabens gewesen sein könnte (hier sind Untersuchungen am Objekt notwendig). 2. Sollte es sich bei der Dekoration um ein Kreuz handeln, böte die Stele noch viel Platz für Text. 3. Nach dem Monat könnte die Monatsangabe durch eine Tages- und möglicherweise eine Jahresangabe erweitert gewesen sein.[20] Eine Datierung ist nicht möglich.

2 Erkenntnisse

Sowohl SCAShutb4 als auch SCAShutb9 beginnen mit derselben griechischen Todesformel („ἐκοιμήθη ὁ μακάριος"). Diese findet häufig Anwendung in griechischsprachigen christlichen Epitaphen Ägyptens.[21] So auch in dem Text der Grabstele der Ama Lo, die vor rund 100 Jahren in einem Haus in Assiut von der Polizei beschlagnahmt worden ist. Hier heißt es: „[...] ἐκοιμήθη οι μακαρία αμα Λω [...]"(„[...] Sie legte sich zur Ruhe, die selige Ama Lo [...]".[22] Während die Eingangsformel von SCAShutb9 damit Teil einer gut belegten Formeltradition ist, scheinen hingegen vergleichsweise wenige Parallelen zu der grie-

---

17 Vgl. Hasitzka 2007: 50b–51a.
18 Vgl. Evetts & Butler 1895: 251; Timm 1984: 244.
19 Vgl. Hasitzka 2007: 18b.
20 Vgl. Tudor 2011: 143.
21 Vgl. Tudor 2011: 161–162, 263–267.
22 Vgl. Lefebvre 1915: 138, Nr. 848. Eigene Übersetzung.

chisch-koptischen bilingualen Eingangsformel von SCAShutb4 bekannt zu sein.[23] Da die Herkunft von SCAShutb4 als weitestgehend gesichert gelten kann, ist die Überlegung anzustellen, ob vergleichbare bilinguale Grabstelen mit unbekannter Provenienz möglicherweise in einem örtlichen Zusammenhang zu der Region um Assiut stehen könnten.[24] Es benötigt selbstverständlich eine viel größere Anzahl an untersuchten christlichen Grabstelen vom Gebel Assiut al-gharbi und der Umgebung, um fundierte Aussagen tätigen zu können. Gleichwohl ist das dreifache Auftreten der griechischen Formel („ἐκοιμήθη ὁ μακάριος/ οἱ μακαρίᾳ") in einem kleinen untersuchten Korpus bemerkenswert.[25] Da die lokalen Werkstätten üblicherweise ein limitiertes Repertoire an Formeln verwendeten, sind diese regionaler Variation unterworfen.[26] So kann begründeter Weise die vorläufige Vermutung angestellt werden, dass die besagte Formel gebräuchlicher Bestandteil des lokalen Formelbestands aus der Umgebung Assiuts gewesen ist.

Neben den Formeln verdienen auch die in den Inschriften auftretenden Namen besondere Aufmerksamkeit: Apa Thomas, Apa Schoi, Kollouthos und Aphou können jetzt in die Sammlung bekannter Namen aus der Region aufgenommen und mit anderen lokalen Quellen abgeglichen werden. Die beiden Erstgenannten standen aufgrund ihres „Apa"-Titels wahrscheinlich in Verbindung zu den Klosteranlagen des Berges und können diesen unter Vorbehalt zugeordnet werden. Aus anderen Untersuchungen sind bereits einige Apas bekannt, die mit Assiut, dem Gebel Assiut al-gharbi und der Region auf unterschiedliche Weise verbunden sind.[27] Eine lohnenswerte Aufgabe wäre es, diese Namen zu sammeln und in Hinblick auf verschiedene Aspekte zu sortieren (Diachronie, griechische gegenüber ägyptischen Namen, Kontext der Erwähnung, Fundumstände des Textträgers etc.). Erst dann können fundierte Aussagen zum Potenzial eines solchen Registers getätigt werden. Abzugleichen wäre ebenfalls die unwahrscheinlich erscheinende Möglichkeit, dass der in SCAShutb9 genannte Kollouthos mit dem bei Abu Salih erwähnten Kloster des Kollouthos in Assiut in Verbindung stehen könnte.[28]

Weiterführende Untersuchungen christlicher Grabstelen vom Gebel Assiut al-gharbi und seiner Umgebung (insofern diese noch aufgefunden werden) böten also Aufschluss über lokale Formulartraditionen und könnten dazu dienen, ein Register regionaler Personennamen zu erstellen (wie Kahl es für das 5. und 6. Jahrhundert andeutet)[29]. Auch um sprachliche Eigenheiten wie die von SCAShutb4 besser greifen zu können, wären solche Untersuchungen möglicherweise nützlich. Die vorgestellten Objekte konnten zeigen, dass nicht absolut datierbare, christliche Grabstelen Ägyptens mit bekannter Provenienz ein beachtliches Potenzial für die Erforschung der christlichen Historie Ägyptens (lokal und überregional) aufweisen.[30] Diese Erkenntnis widerspricht der Aussage Timms, wenn er schreibt: „Auch für einige koptische Grabsteine wird Asyūṭ als Herkunftsort genannt. Sie geben aber für die Lokalgeschichte des Christentums nichts her."[31] Stattdessen kann gerade aufgrund der bekannten Provenienz eine Untersuchung weiterer Epitaphe aus Assiut Aufschlüsse über die christliche Lokalgeschichte der Stadt liefern.

---

23 Vgl. die Fußnoten 8 und 11.

24 Ein solches Objekt ist bspw. das bereits genannte aus Łajtar 1998: 29–30 (vgl. Hasitzka 2004: 198, Nr. 1231; Hasitzka & Łajtar & Markiewicz 1999: 26, Nr. 50).

25 Im Vorfeld wurden vom Autor insgesamt sieben der unpublizierten christliche Grabstelen aus dem Antikenmagazin von Shutb untersucht, die alle vom Gebel Assiut al-gharbi stammen. Zwei der sieben Grabstelen wiesen diese Formel auf. Mit der Stele der Ama Lo tragen sie also drei von acht Grabstelen.

26 Vgl. van der Vliet 2017: 483b.

27 Siehe beispielsweise Clédat 1908: 220–221 (für eine Bearbeitung und Übersetzung siehe Lefebvre 1910: 56–58); Palanque 1903: 127; Timm 1984: 237–238, 240–242, 244–246; Wagner & Coquin 1971: 170–172.

28 Vgl. Evetts & Butler 1895: 251; Timm 1984: 244.

29 Vgl. Kahl 2007: 122.

30 Bzgl. des Potenzials von Statistiken zur geographischen Verteilung von Formeln und Formularen siehe Tudor 2011: 6–8.

31 Timm 1984: 246. Van der Vliet unterstreicht die Bedeutung von Epigraphen, indem er sie beschreibt als: „[…] a firsthand witness to the social and religious practices of local Christian communities" (2017: 482a).

Bibliographie

Atiya 1991: A. Atiya, Apa, in: The Coptic Encyclopedia Band 1: Abab–Azar (New York 1991) 152b–153a.

Biondi 1907: G. Biondi, Inscriptions copes (suite et fin), in: Annales du Service des antiquités de l'Égypte 8, 1907, 161–183.

Clédat 1908: Jean Clédat, Notes d'archéologie copte, in: Annales du Service des antiquités de l'Égypte 9, 1908, 213–220.

Choat 2015: M. Choat, Narratives of Monastic Genealogy in Coptic Inscriptions, in: Religion in the Roman Empire 1,3, 2015, 403–430.

Crum 1975: W. E. Crum, Coptic Monuments, in: Catalogue général des antiquités du Musée du Caire, Nos 8001–8741 (Osnabrück 1975; Reprint der Erstedition von 1902).

Evetts & Butler 1895: B. T. A. Evetts; A. J. Butler (Hgg.), The Churches and Monasteries of Egypt and Some Neighbouring Countries. Attribut to Abû Ṣâliḥ, the Armenian (Anecdota Oxoniensia, Semitic Series 7; Oxford 1895).

Förster 2002: H. Förster (Hg.), Wörterbuch der griechischen Wörter in den koptischen dokumentarischen Texten (Texte und Untersuchungen zur Geschichte der altchristlichen Literatur. Archiv für die Ausgabe der Griechischen Christlichen Schriftsteller der ersten Jahrhunderte (TU), Band 148; Berlin – New York 2002).

Hasitzka 1993: M. R. M. Hasitzka (Hg.), Koptisches Sammelbuch I <KSB I> (Mitteilungen aus der Papyrussammlung der Österreichischen Nationalbibliothek (Papyrus Erzherzog Rainer); Neue Serie, Folge 23, Band 1; Wien 1993).

Hasitzka 2004: M. R. M. Hasitzka (Hg.), Koptisches Sammelbuch II <KSB II> (Mitteilungen aus der Papyrussammlung der Österreichischen Nationalbibliothek (Papyrus Erzherzog Rainer); Neue Serie, Folge 23, Band 2; Wien 2004).

Hasitzka 2007: M. R. M. Hasitzka, Namen in koptischen dokumentarischen Texten. Als Open-Source-Datei verfügbar unter: http://onb.ac.at/fileadmin/user_upload/PDF_Download/1_PAP_kopt_namen.pdf, 2007 (zuletzt eingesehen am 31.07.2019).

Hasitzka & Łajtar & Markiewicz 1999: M. R. M. Hasitzka; A. Łajtar; T. Markiewicz, Coptic Inscriptions in Egyptian Collections. Some Notes on Recent Publications, in: Journal of Juristic Papyrology 29, 1999, 13–32.

Kahl 2007: J. Kahl, Ancient Asyut. The First Synthesis after 300 Years of Research (The Asyut Project 1, Wiesbaden 2007).

Kahl 2014: J. Kahl, Gebel Asyut al-gharbi in the First Millennium AD, in: E. R. O'Connell (Hg.), Egypt in the First Millennium AD. Perspectives from New Fieldwork (British Museum Publications on Egypt and Sudan 2, Leuven – Paris – Walpole, Ma 2014) 127–138.

Kahle 1954: P. Kahle (Hg.), Bala'izah. Coptic Texts from Deir el-Bala'izah in Upper Egypt, Band 1 (London 1954).

Klemm & Klemm 2008: D. D. Klemm; R. Klemm, Stones and Quarries in Ancient Egypt (Übersetzung der deutschen Originalausgabe von 1993; London 2008).

Łajtar 1998: A. Łajtar, Griechische und koptische Inschriften im Koptischen Museum Kairo. Eine Fortsetzung, in: Journal of Juristic Papyrology 28, 1998, 25–30.

Lefebvre 1910: G. Lefebvre, Égypte chrétienne, in: Annales du Service des antiquités de l'Égypte 10, 1910, 50–65.

Lefebvre 1915: G. Lefebvre, Égypte chrétienne, in: Annales du Service des antiquités de l'Égypte 15, 1915, 113–139.

O'Connell 2014: E. R. O'Connell, R. Campbell Thompson's 1913/14 excavation of Wadi Sarga and other sites, in: British Museum Studies in Ancient Egypt and Sudan 21, 2013, 121–192.

Palanque 1903: Ch. Palanque, Notes de fouilles dans la nécropole d'Assiout, in: Bulletin de l'Institut français d'archéologie orientale 3, 1903, 119–128.

Timm 1984: St. Timm, Das christlich-koptische Ägypten in arabischer Zeit. Teil 1 (A–C) (Beihefte zum Tübinger Atlas des Vorderen Orients, Reihe B (Geisteswissenschaften), Nr. 41/1; Wiesbaden 1984).

Tudor 2011: B. Tudor, Christian Funerary Stelae of the Byzantine and Arab Periods from Egypt (Marburg 2011).

van der Vliet 2015: J. van der Vliet, Snippets from the Past. Two Ancient Sites in the Asyut Region: Dayr al-Gabrawi and Dayr al-ʿIzam, in: G. Gabra & Hany N. Takla (Hgg.), Christianity and Monasticism in Middle Egypt. Al-Minya and Asyut (Cairo – New York 2015) 161–168.

van der Vliet 2017: J. van der Vliet, Epigraphy: Coptic, in: P. C. Finney (Hg.), The Eerdmans Encyclopedia of Early Christian Art and Archaeology, Band 1: A–J (Grand Rapids 2017) 481b–484b.

Wagner & Coquin 1971: G. Wagner; R.-G. Coquin, Stèles grecques et coptes d'Égypte, in: Bulletin de l'Institut français d'archéologie orientale 70, 1971, 161–172.

Abbildung 1: SCAShutb4 (Foto: Jochem Kahl; © The Asyut Project).

Abbildung 2: SCAShutb4 – zusammengesetzt (© Philipp Scharfenberger & Jochem Kahl).

Abbildung 3: SCAShutb7 (Foto: Jochem Kahl; © The Asyut Project).

Abbildung 4: SCAShutb9 (Foto: Jochem Kahl; © The Asyut Project).

Plates

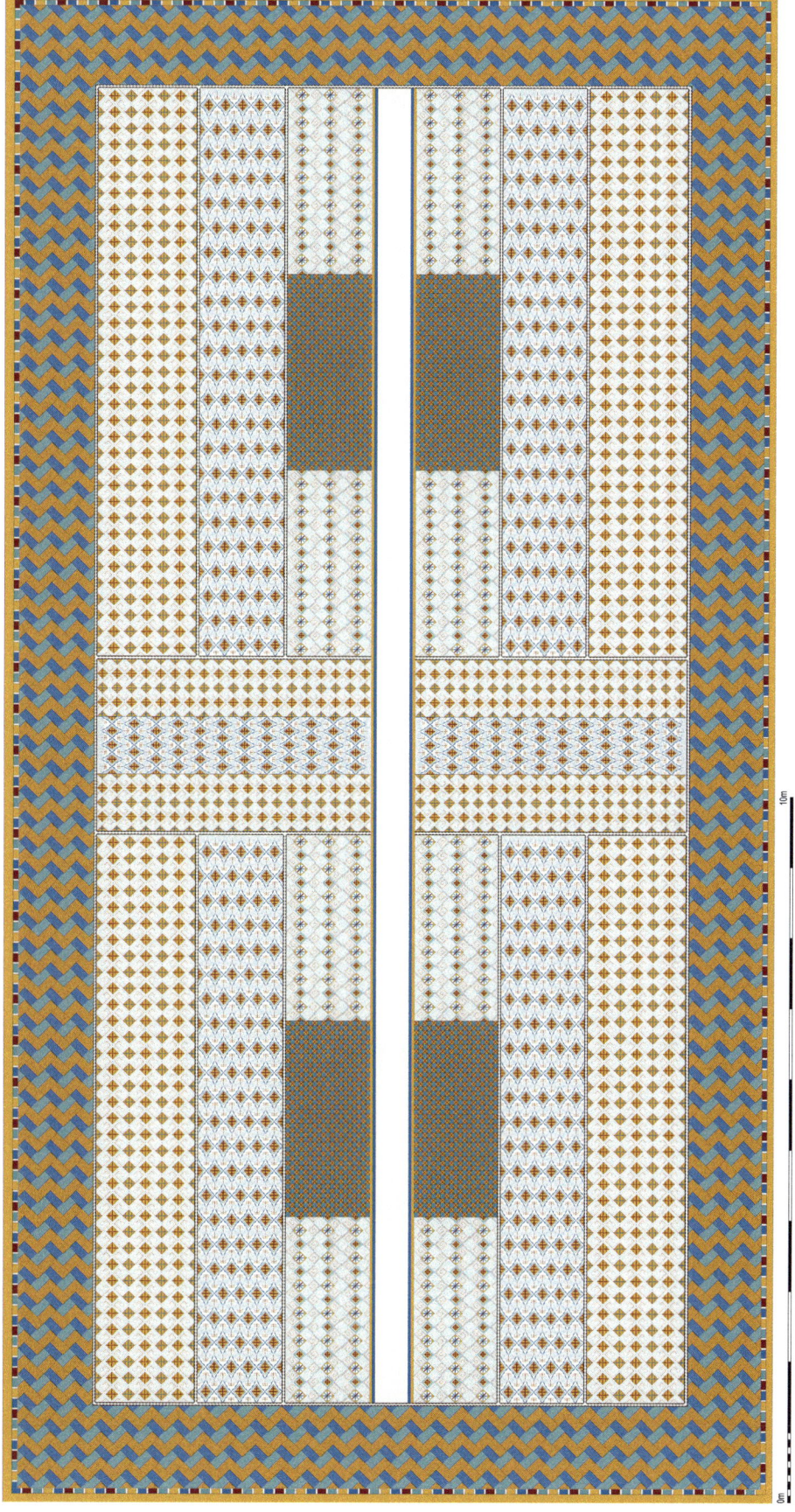

Pl. 1: Tomb I, Great Transverse Hall, ceiling, computer-based reconstruction, (Philipp Jansen 2016; © The Asyut Project).

Plate 2   Jochem Kahl

Pl. 2a: Tomb I, Great Transverse Hall, ceiling, detail (photo: Fritz Barthel 2014; © The Asyut Project).

Pl. 2b: Tomb I, Second Corridor, southern wall, detail (photo: Fritz Barthel 2007; © The Asyut Project).

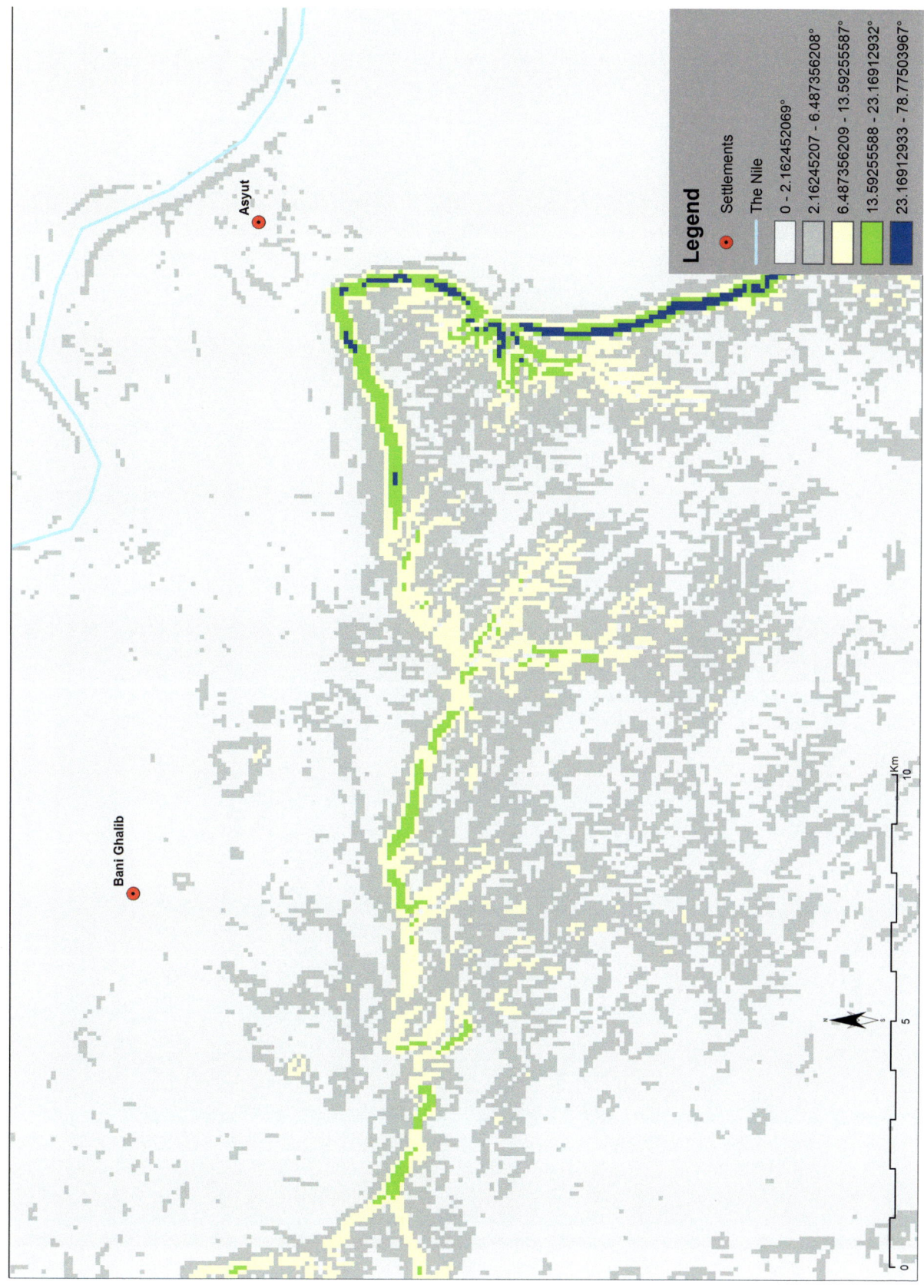

Legend

⊙ Settlements

— The Nile

☐ 0 - 2.162452069°

☐ 2.16245207 - 6.48735620°

☐ 6.487356209 - 13.59255587°

☐ 13.59255588 - 23.16912932°

☐ 23.16912933 - 78.77503967°

Asyut

Bani Ghalib

Pl. 3: Gebel Asyut al-gharbi, slope angle (© Mohamed Osman /The Asyut Project). Spatial analysis using ArcGIS & Grass GIS; after: NASA SRTM V3.0, 3 arcsec, http://gdex.cr.usgs.gov/gdex/

Plate 4   Mohamed Osman & Jochem Kahl

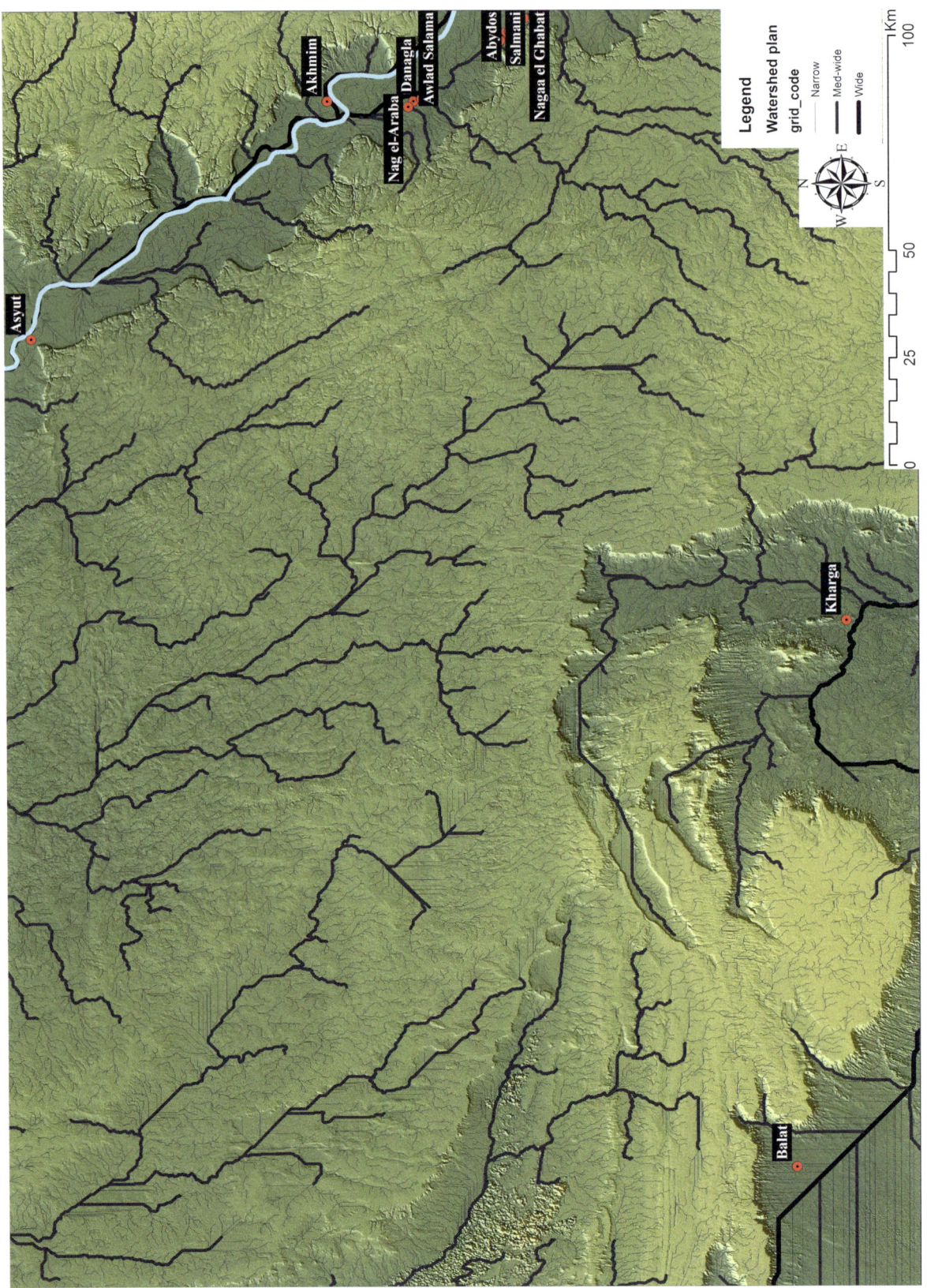

Pl. 4: Western Desert, watershed plan (© Mohamed Osman /The Asyut Project). Spatial analysis
using ArcGIS & Grass GIS; after: NASA SRTM V3.0, 3 arcsec, http://gdex.cr.usgs.gov/gdex/

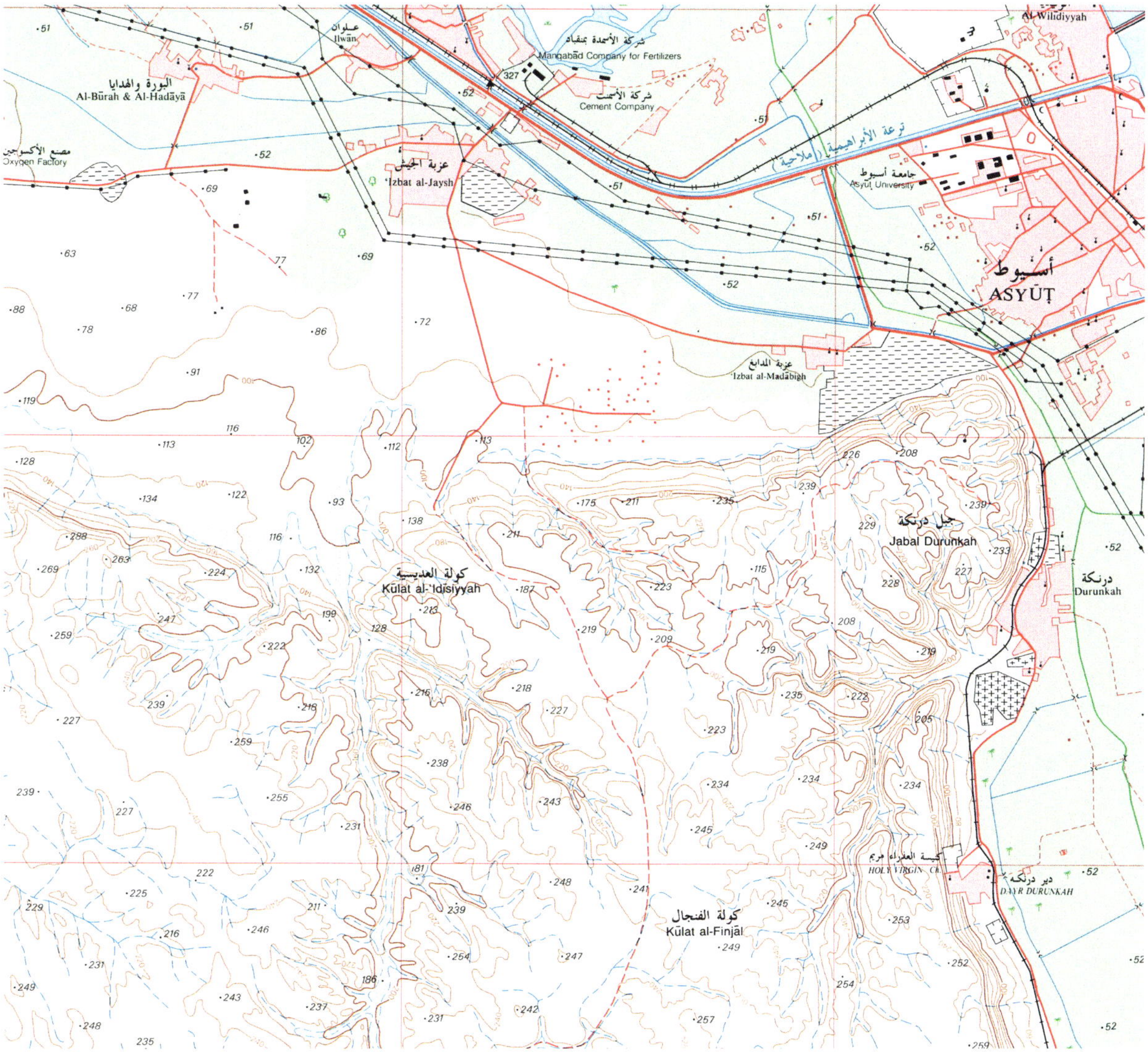

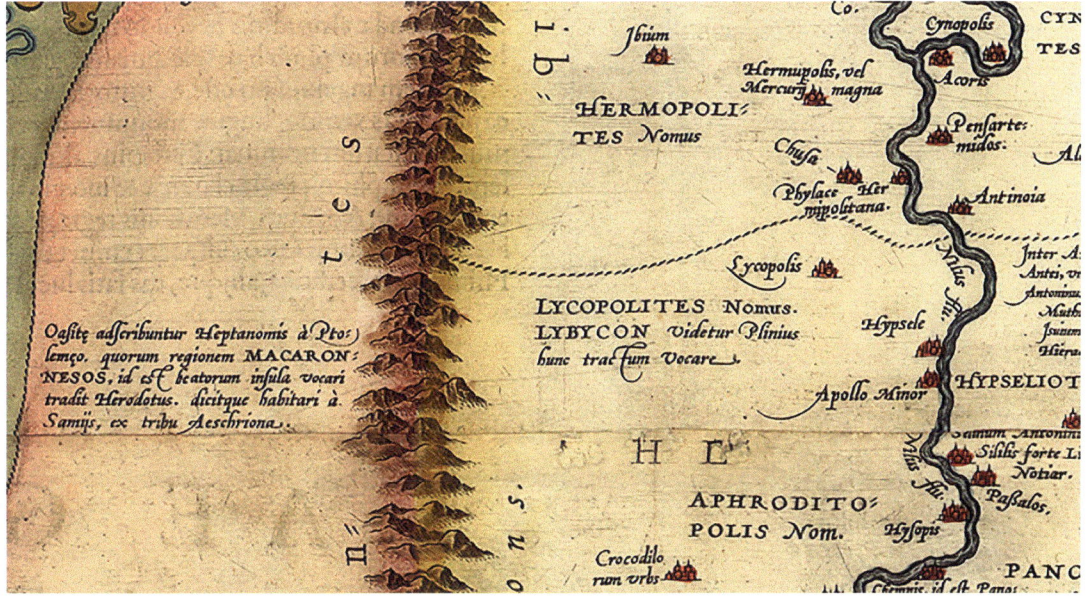

Pl. 5a: Asyut and Gebel Asyut al-gharbi (Topographical Map, Survey of Egypt).

Pl. 5b: Abraham Ortelius "Aegyptus Antiqua" (Antwerp 1584), detail.

Plate 6   Mohamed Osman & Jochem Kahl

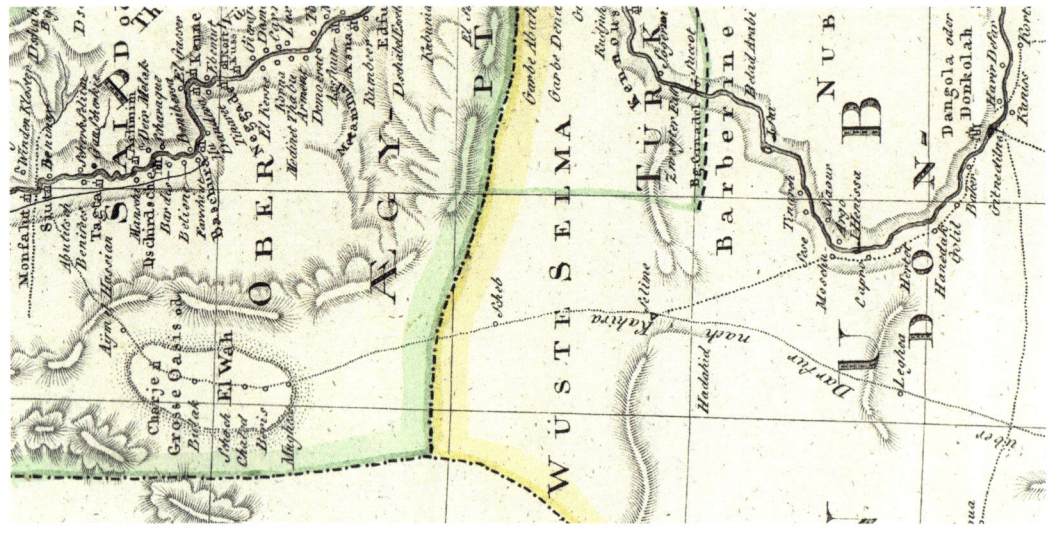

Pl. 6c: "Charte vom Nil Strome, Aegypten, Nubien und Habesch" (Map of the Nile River, Egypt, Nubia, and Abyssinia), detail. (Adam Christian Gaspari, Allgemeiner Hand-Atlas der Ganzen Erde: nach den besten astronomischen Bestimmungen, neuesten Entdeckungen und kritischen Untersuchungen entworfen und zu A.C. Gaspari vollstaendigem Handbuche der neuesten Erdbeschreibung bestimmt. Weimar, Verlag des Geographischen Instituts, 1817).

Pl. 6b: Nicolas de Fer, L'Empire des Turcs en Europe, en Asie, et en Afrique (Paris 1715), detail.

Pl. 6a: Carte de l'Égypte, de la Nubie, de l'Abissinie &c. Par Guillaume de L'Isle de l'Académie Royale des Sciences; Desrosiers sculp. Atlas Géographique contenant la Mappemonde et les quatre partie, 1707, detail.

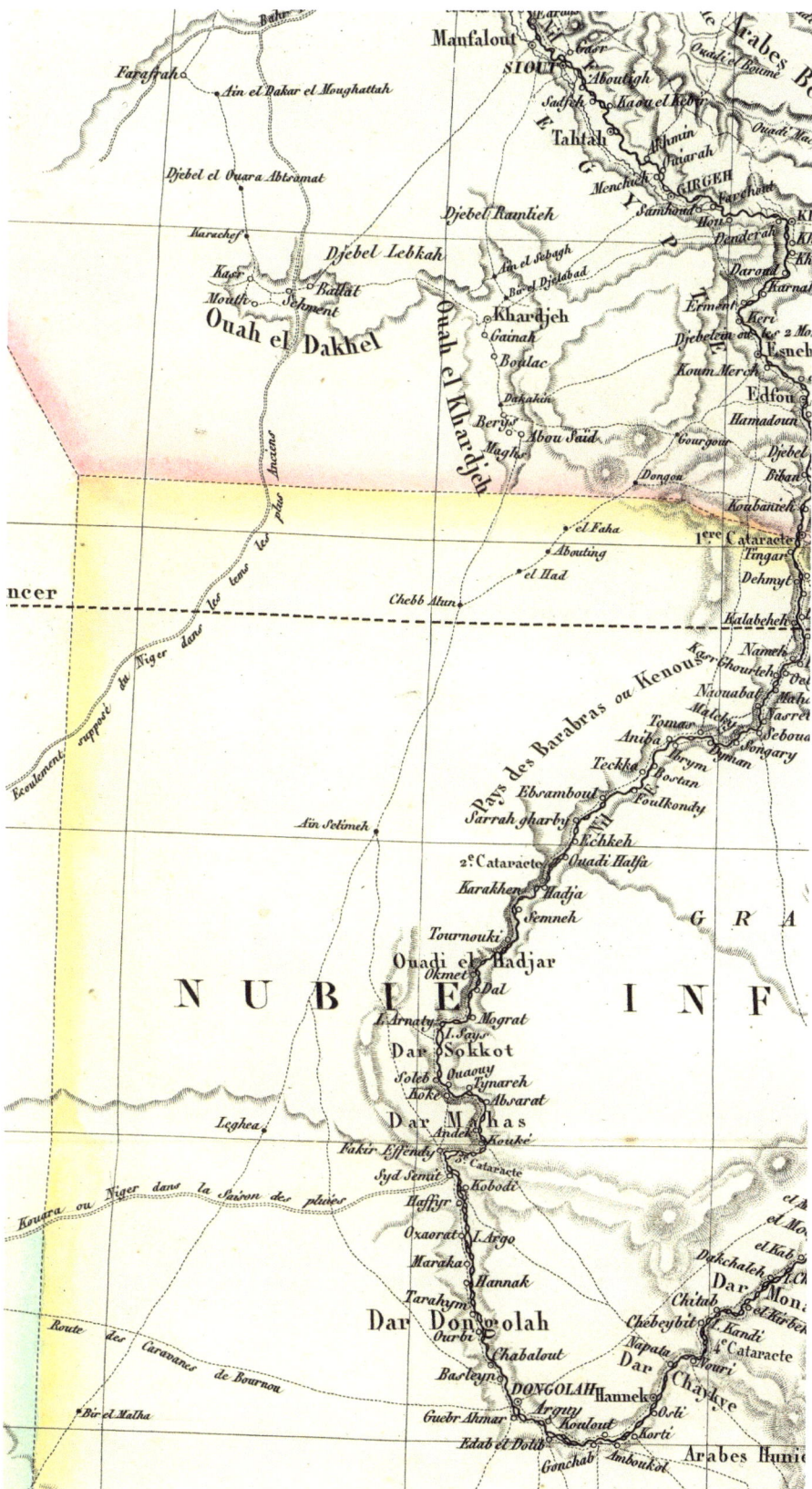

Pl. 7: Carte de l'Égypte, de la Nubie, de l'Abissinie, du Kourdofan et d'une partie de l'Arabie. Dressée par M. Lapie, 1er. Géographe du Roi et M. Lapie Fils, Géographe de S.A.R.M. le Dauphin. Paris, 1829. Chez Eymery Fruger et Cie., Rue Mazarine No. 30. La gravure dirigée et executée par Lallemand, detail.

Plate 8   Mohamed Osman & Jochem Kahl

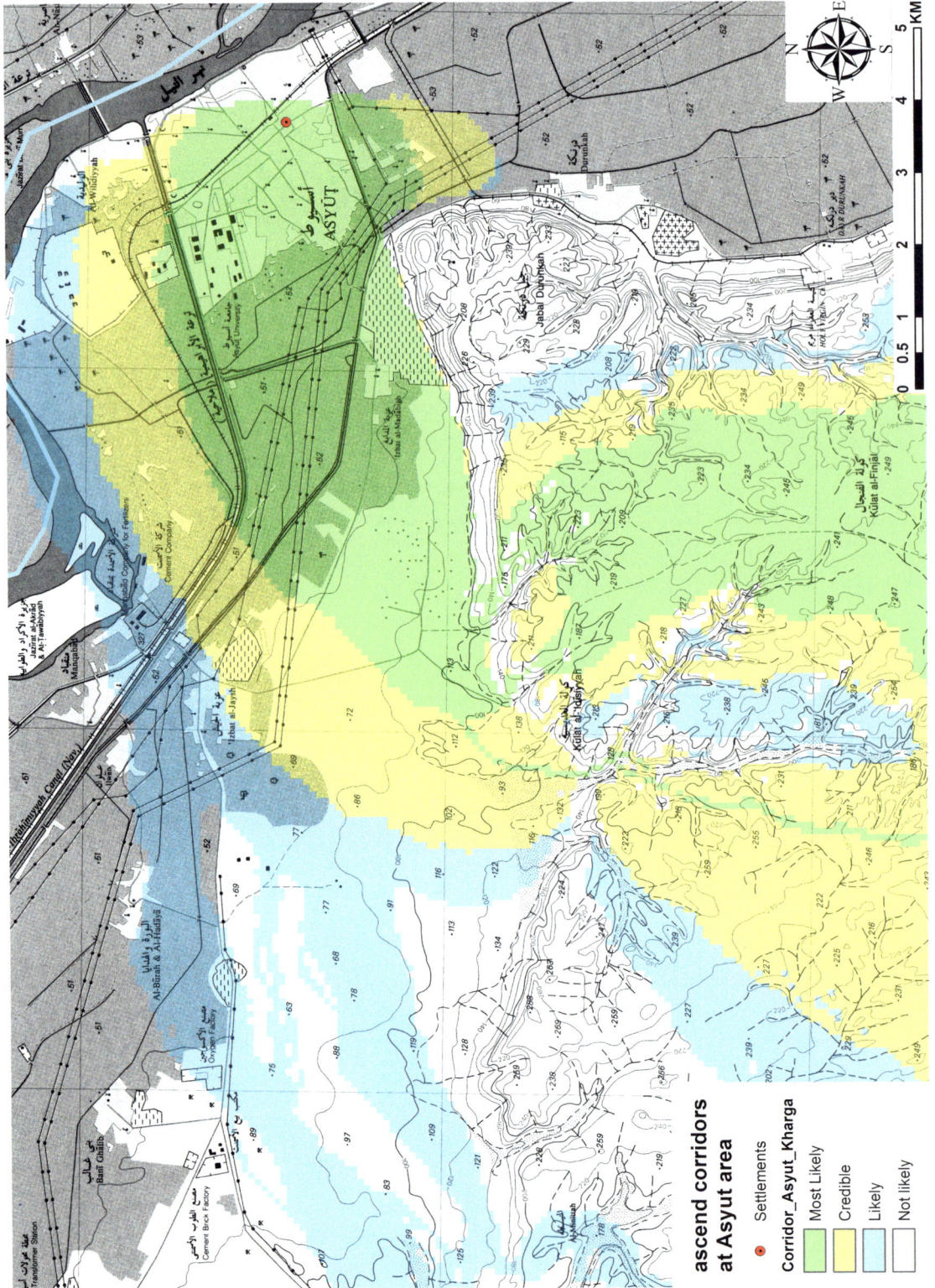

Pl. 8: Ascend corridors at Asyut area (© Mohamed Osman/The Asyut Project). Spatial analysis using ArcGIS & Grass GIS; after: NASA SRTM V3.0, 3 arcsec, http://gdex.cr.usgs.gov/gdex/

Pl. 9a: Google Earth Satellite image, showing locations where caravan traces could be seen
(© Mohamed Osman/The Asyut Project).

Pl. 9b: Google Earth Satellite image, zoom in into the ascending area at Wadi Kulit el Edissiyah.
Marking locations of caravan traces (© Mohamed Osman/The Asyut Project).

Plate 10   Mohamed Osman & Jochem Kahl

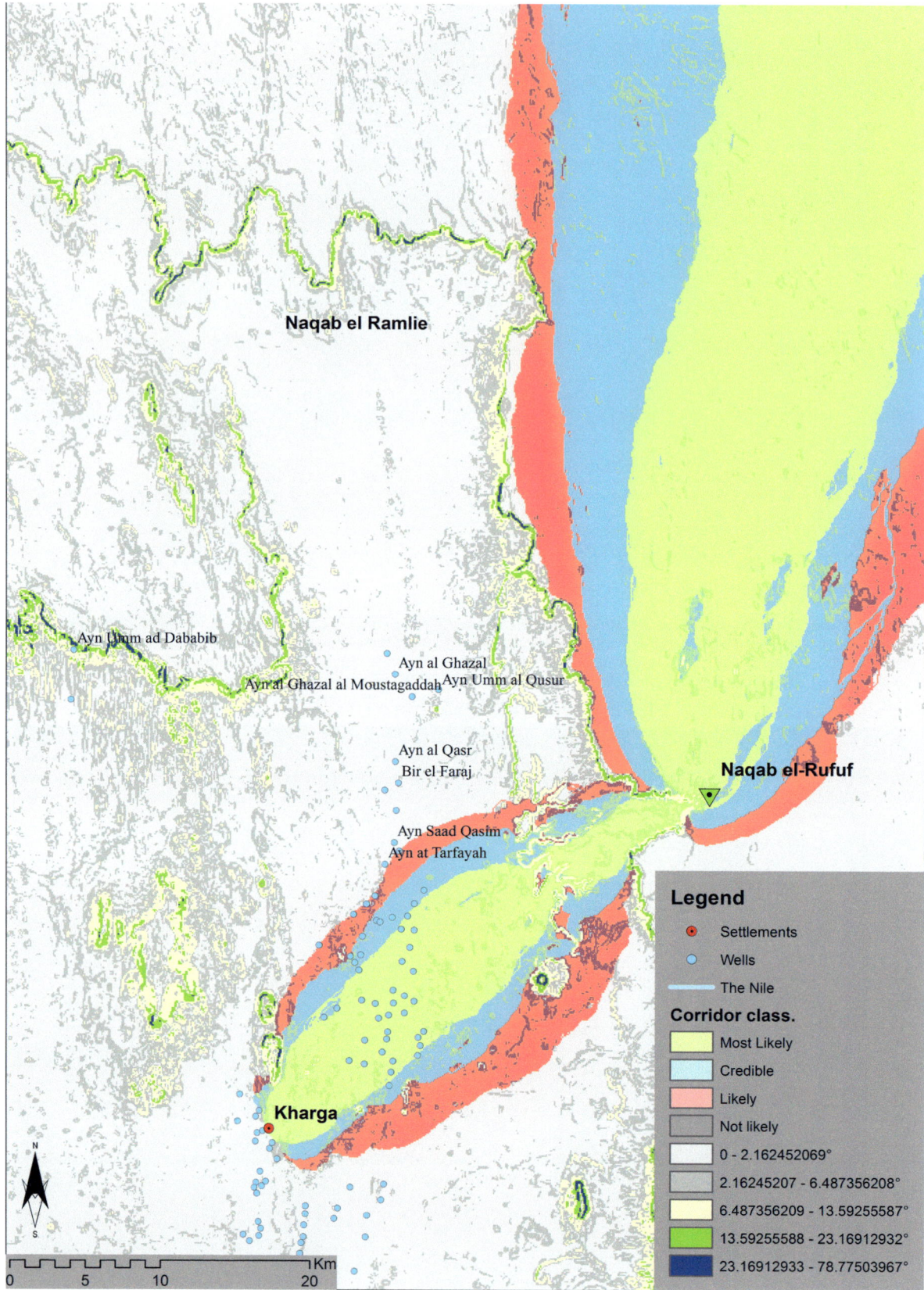

Pl. 10: Corridor analysis model for the route between Asyut and Kharga (zoom in on the descent are into the Kharga depression). The map is based on slope model of the area. (© Mohamed Osman/The Asyut Project). Spatial analysis using ArcGIS & Grass GIS; after: NASA SRTM V3.0, 3 arcsec, http://gdex.cr.usgs.gov/gdex/

Plate 12   Jochem Kahl & Mohamed Abdelrahiem

Pl. 12a: Tempelblock, Antikenmagazin Shutb SCA Z36/4 (TA 4)
(Foto: Fritz Barthel 2016; © Ägyptologisches Seminar, Freie Universität Berlin).

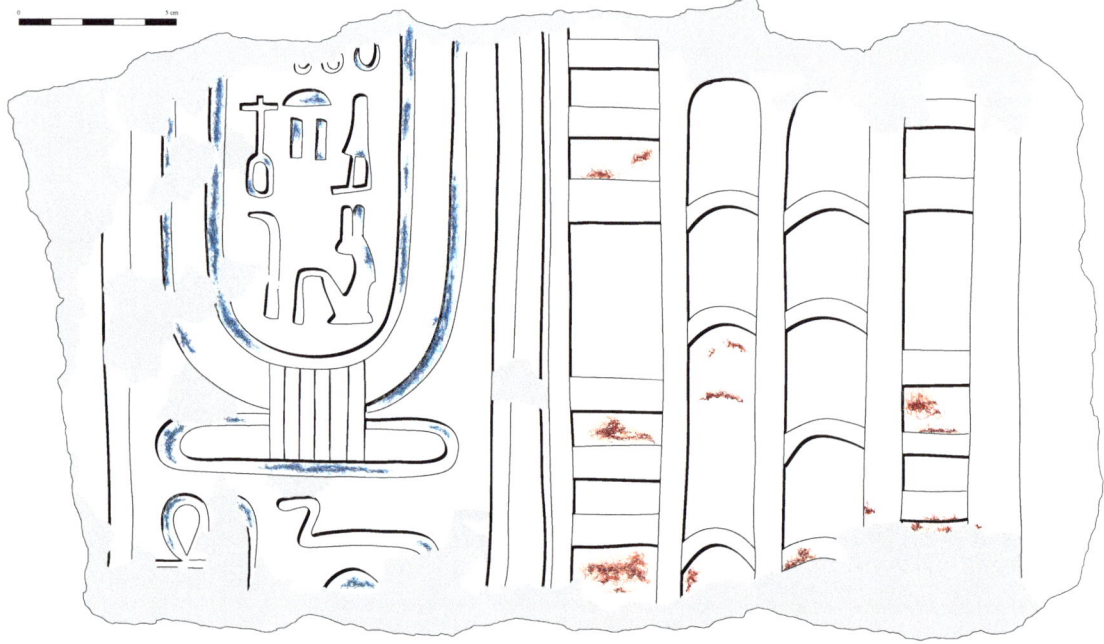

Pl. 12b: Tempelblock, Antikenmagazin Shutb SCA Z36/4 (TA 4)
(Faksimile: Anja Hilbig 2016; © Ägyptologisches Seminar, Freie Universität Berlin).

Pl. 13a: Tempelblock, Antikenmagazin Shutb SCA Z41/1 (TA 16)
(Foto: Fritz Barthel 2016; © Ägyptologisches Seminar, Freie Universität Berlin).

Pl. 13b: Tempelblock, Antikenmagazin Shutb SCA Z41/1 (TA 16)
(Faksimile: Anja Hilbig 2016; © Ägyptologisches Seminar, Freie Universität Berlin).

Pl. 14a: Tempelblock aus der Zeit Sethos' I., 2015 (heute im Museum in Sohag); Foto: http://english.ahram.org.eg/NewsContent/9/40/152042/Heritage/Ancient-Egypt/Egypt-recovers-Stolen-relief-of-King-Seti-I-from-L.aspx

Pl. 14b: Tomb I10.1, areas 1–3 in the south-west corner (photo: Svenja A. Gülden 2010; © The Asyut Project).

Pl. 15b: Area 1 on the south wall, detail of decoration (j[n] ḥꜣ[tj]-ꜥ [...]mr[...])
(photo: Ursula Verhoeven 2006; © The Asyut Project).

Pl. 15a: Area 1 on the south wall, detail of decoration ([mꜣ]ꜣ kꜣt)
(photo: Ursula Verhoeven 2006; © The Asyut Project).

Plate 16   Ursula Verhoeven

Pl. 16: Area 1 on the south wall, detail of decoration (ḥ[s]y) (photo: Ursula Verhoeven 2006; © The Asyut Project).

Pl. 17: Area 2 on the west wall, at the south end (photo: Svenja A. Gülden 2010; © The Asyut Project).

Plate 18　　　　　　　　　　Ursula Verhoeven

Pl. 18: Area 3 on the west wall, at the south end (photo: Ursula Verhoeven 2005; © The Asyut Project).

Pl. 19: Area 3 on the west wall, at the south end, detail (photo: Ursula Verhoeven 2006; © The Asyut Project).

Plate 20   Ursula Verhoeven

Pl. 20a: Area 4 on the west wall, north of the doorway (photo: Svenja A. Gülden 2010; © The Asyut Project).

Pl. 20b: Area 5 on the west wall, at the north end (photo: Ursula Verhoeven 2007; © The Asyut Project).

Pl. 21: Area 6 on the north wall. View facing local north (photo: Fritz Barthel 2016; © The Asyut Project).

Plate 22   Ursula Verhoeven

Pl. 22a: Area 6 on the north wall, at the west end, uppermost part with palanquin (?)
(photo: Ursula Verhoeven 2016; © The Asyut Project).

Pl. 22b: Area 6 on the north wall, at the west end, upper part (photo: Ursula Verhoeven 2005; © The Asyut Project).

Pl. 23a: Area 6 on the north wall, at the west end, middle part (photo: Ursula Verhoeven 2005; © The Asyut Project).

Pl. 23b: Area 6 on the north wall, at the west end, lower part (photo: Ursula Verhoeven 2005; © The Asyut Project).

Plate 24   Ursula Verhoeven

Pl. 24a: Area 6 on the north wall, at the west end, detail from register x+2, col. x+2
(photo: Ursula Verhoeven 2007; © The Asyut Project).

Pl. 24b: Area 6 on the north wall, at the west end, detail from register x+3, col. x+3
(photo: Ursula Verhoeven 2007; © The Asyut Project).

Pl. 25: Area 6 on the north wall, at the west end, detail from register x+4, col. x+1–2
(photo: Ursula Verhoeven 2007; © The Asyut Project).

Plate 26   Ursula Verhoeven

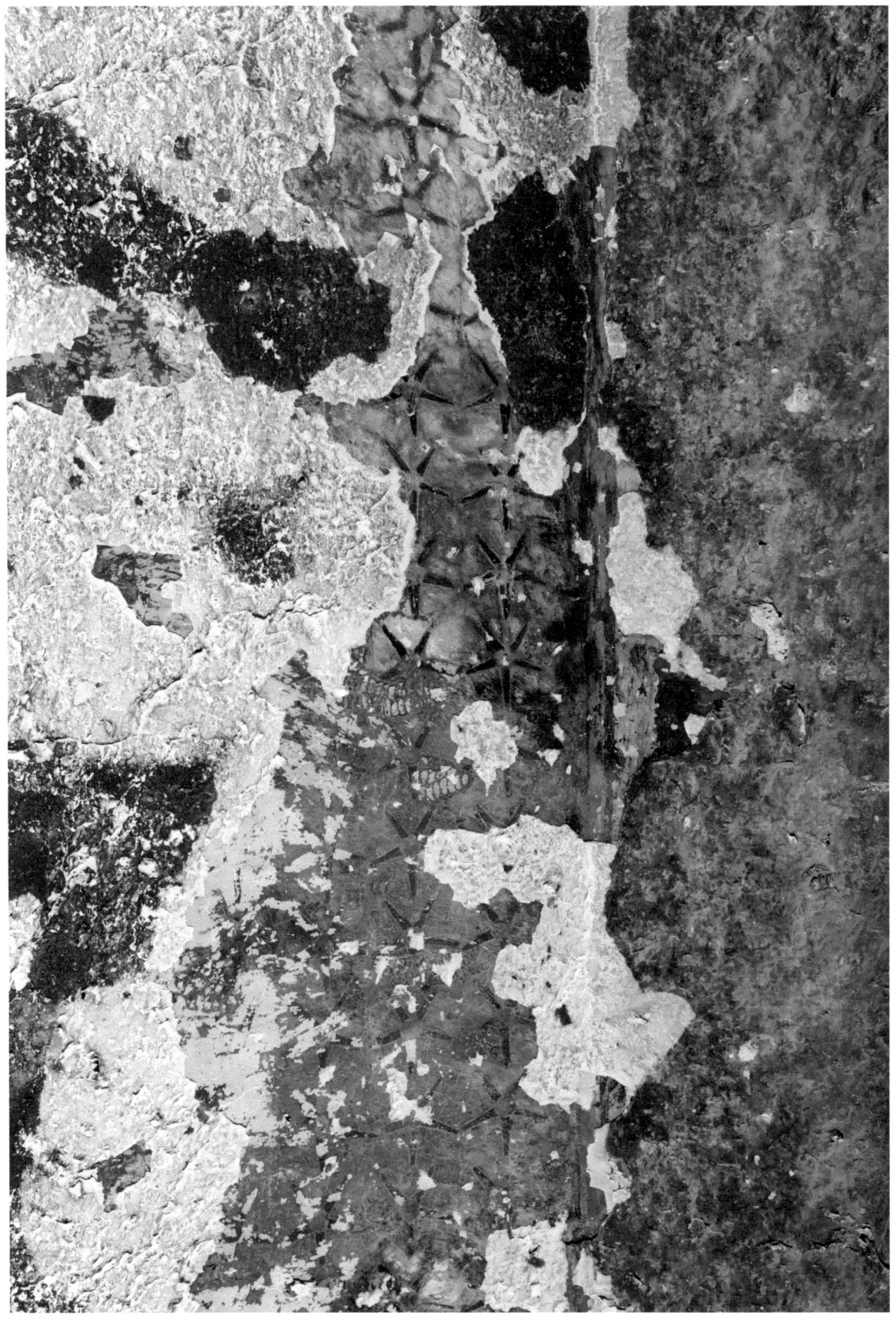

Pl. 26: Area 7 in corridor B, south wall, ceiling (photo: Fritz Barthel 2016; © The Asyut Project).

Pl. 27a: Area 7 in corridor B, south wall, upper part of the wall, line 1 left (photo: Fritz Barthel 2016; © The Asyut Project).

Pl. 27b: Area 7 in corridor B, south wall, upper part of the wall, line 1 right (photo: Fritz Barthel 2016; © The Asyut Project).

Plate 28   Ursula Verhoeven; Mohamed Abdelrahiem

Pl. 28a: Area 8 in corridor B, north wall (photo: Fritz Barthel 2016; © The Asyut Project).

Pl. 28b–e: Head of a Female Statuette from Asyut (photos: Fritz Barthel; © The Asyut Project).

Pl. 29a: Udjataugenpaar auf dem Sarg des J, Museo Egizio, Turin, S. 8875, S4Tor (© Museo Egizio, Turin, photo by G. Lovera).

Pl. 29b: Udjataugenpaar auf dem Sarg des Basa, Museo Egizio, Turin, S. 8876, S5Tor
(© Museo Egizio, Turin, photo by G. Lovera).

Plate 30   Nadine Gräßler

Pl. 30a: Udjataugenpaar auf dem Sarg der Upuautemhat, Museo Egizio, Turin, S. 8912+8922, S7Tor
(© Museo Egizio, Turin, photo by G. Lovera).

Pl. 30b: Udjataugenpaar auf dem Sarg des Minhotep, Museo Egizio, Turin, S. 8919, S10Tor
(© Museo Egizio, Turin, photo by P. Del Vesco).

Pl. 31a: Udjataugenpaar auf dem Sarg Museo Egizio, Turin, S. 8807, S11Tor (© Museo Egizio, Turin, photo by G. Lovera).

Pl. 31b: Udjataugenpaar auf dem Sarg des Mesehti, Museo Egizio, Turin, S. 8923+8926+8929, S12Tor
(© Museo Egizio, Turin, photo by P. Del Vesco).

Plate 32   Nadine Gräßler; Mohamed Abdelrahiem

Pl. 32a: Udjataugenpaar auf dem Sarg der Upuautemhat, Museo Egizio, Turin, S. 8924+8927, S13Tor
(© Museo Egizio, Turin, photo by N. Dell'Aquila).

Pl. 32b: Exterior of the coffin of Nakhti (S1Shu)
(photo: Mohamed Abdelrahiem 2016; © Shutb Magazine Project).

Pl. 33a: Inner side of the lid supported by wooden props, coffin of Nakhti (S1Shu)
(photo: Fritz Barthel 2018; © Shutb Magazine Project).

Pl. 33b: The interior of the coffin of Nakhti (S1Shu)
(photo: Fritz Barthel 2018; © Shutb Magazine Project).

Pl. 33c: Lid of the coffin of Nakhti (S1Shu)
(photo: Fritz Barthel 2017; © Shutb Magazine Project).

Plate 34

Mohamed Abdelrahiem

Pl. 34a (left/above): Front side of the coffin of Nakhti (S1Shu) (Photo: Fritz Barthel 2017; © Shutb Magazine Project).
Pl. 34b (right/below): Back side of the coffin of Nakhti (S1Shu) (Photo: Fritz Barthel 2017; © Shutb Magazine Project).

Pl. 35b: Foot end of the coffin of Nakhti (S1Shu)
(photo: Fritz Barthel 2017; © Shutb Magazine Project).

Pl. 35a: Head end of the coffin of Nakhti (S1Shu)
(photo: Fritz Barthel 2017; © Shutb Magazine Project).

Plate 36

Jochem Kahl & John Moussa Iskander

Pl. 36a (oben): Sarg S1Mal (Mallawi Antiquities Museum, no. 566, photo: Dr. Nassef Abdelwahed).
Pl. 36b (unten): Sarg S1Mal, Unterseite des Deckels (Mallawi Antiquities Museum, no. 566, photo: Dr. Nassef Abdelwahed).

Pl. 37: Sarg S1Mal, Unterseite des Deckels, rechter Teil (Mallawi Antiquities Museum, no. 566, photo: Dr. Nassef Abdelwahed).

Plate 38   Jochem Kahl & John Moussa Iskander

Pl. 39a–b: Model figures from Tomb N13.1 (Convolute S06/8; left figure: height: x+8.7 cm, width: 3.9 cm, depth: 3.25 cm; right figure: height: 10.6 cm; width: 3.2 cm, depth: 2.2 cm [head]) (photo: Jochem Kahl; © The Asyut Project).

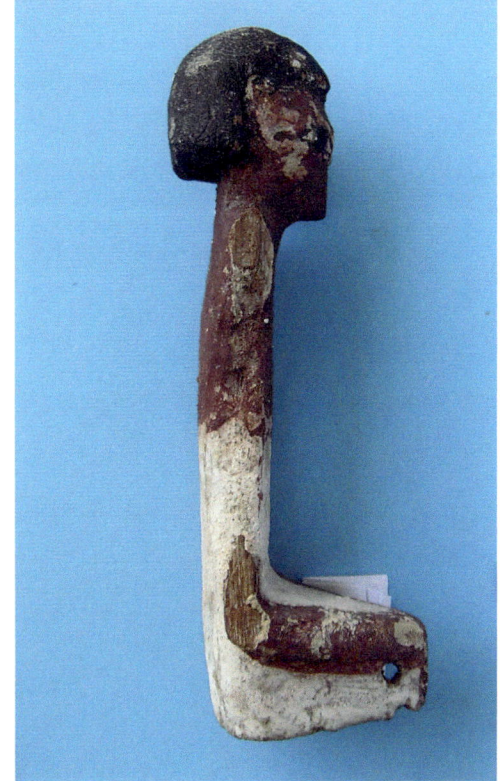

Pl. 39c–d: Model figure from Tomb N13.1 (S07/7; height: 12.6 cm, width: 3.5 cm, depth: 4.6 cm)
(photo: Monika Zöller-Engelhardt; © The Asyut Project).

Plate 40   Monika Zöller-Engelhardt

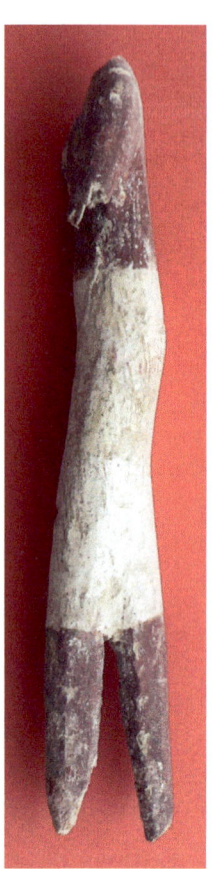

Pl. 40a–b: Model figure from Tomb N13.1 (S06/9; height: x+18.0+y cm, width: x+3.3 cm, depth: 2.2 cm)
(photo: Jochem Kahl; © The Asyut Project).

Pl. 40c–d: Model figure from Tomb N13.1 (S07/24; height: 10.9 cm, width: x+3.5+y cm, depth: 3.5 cm)
(photo: Jochem Kahl; © The Asyut Project).

The Asyut Project

Edited by **Jochem Kahl, Ursula Verhoeven, Mahmoud El-Khadragy and Andrea Kilian**

14: Ina Eichner

Der Survey der spätantiken und mittelalterlichen christlichen Denkmäler in der Nekropole von Assiut/Lykopolis (Mittelägypten)

Mit einem Beitrag von Thomas Beckh
(Die Keramik aus dem Survey am Gebel Assiut al-gharbi)

2020. X, 152 Seiten, 112 Abb., 14 Tabellen, gb
170x240 mm
ISBN 978-3-447-11457-8
⊙ *E-Book: ISBN 978-3-447-39028-6*
je € 54,– (D)

15: Ursula Verhoeven (Hg.)

Dipinti von Besuchern des Grabes N13.1 in Assiut

Band 1: Teil 1: Besuchertexte, Lehren und Lieder des Neuen Reiches von Ursula Verhoeven unter Mitarbeit von Svenja A. Gülden, Teil 2: Zeichnungen von Besuchern des Neuen Reiches von Eva Gervers, Teil 3: Texte und Zeichnungen aus islamischer Zeit von Youssef Ahmed-Mohamed
Band 2: Tafeln

2020. 1. Band: XII, 494 Seiten, 17 Abb., 83 Tabellen;
2. Band: 370 Seiten, 368 Tafeln , gb
210x297 mm/240x345 mm
ISBN 978-3-447-11523-0
€ 198,– (D)

Der wohl wichtigste Faktor für die überregionale Bedeutung des Gebel Assiut al-gharbi in der Spätantike und im Mittelalter war die Eremitage des berühmten Asketen Johannes von Lykopolis, des Sehers der Thebais, der sich im 4. Jahrhundert n. Chr. in den drei größten pharaonischen Grabanlagen niedergelassen hatte. Schon zu Lebzeiten, aber auch über seinen Tod hinaus war sein Wirkungsort Anziehungspunkt für Pilger aus allen Regionen der antiken Welt. Parallel dazu besiedelten auch andere Anachoreten den Berg und bewohnten ältere pharaonische Grabanlagen. Inschriften, Graffiti und Alltagsgegenstände im Oberflächenschutt, aber auch gebaute Strukturen und die Überreste zweier Klosteranlagen geben Zeugnis von dieser intensiven monastischen Besiedlung des Berges.

Ina Eichners Studie widmet sich den spätantiken und mittelalterlichen koptischen Monumenten, die während einer fünfwöchigen Surveykampagne im Sommer 2009 auf dem Gebel Assiut al-gharbi untersucht wurden. Die koptischen Überreste am Berg, soweit sie obertägig erhalten bzw. zugänglich waren, werden wissenschaftlich analysiert und dokumentiert und geben Auskunft über das Ausmaß der koptischen Besiedlung. Damit werden die koptischen Monumente am Berg, abgesehen vom Kloster Deir el-Azzam und zweier christlich genutzter und dekorierter Grabkapellen, erstmals Gegenstand einer archäologischen Untersuchung.

Das Felsgrab N13.1 im oberen Bereich des Bergmassivs westlich von Assiut/Mittelägypten stammt aus der Zeit um 2000 v. Chr. und bietet einen weiten Blick über Stadt und Umland. 214 Tuschegraffiti, sogenannte Dipinti, die an seinen Wänden entdeckt wurden, zeigen, dass das Grab zwischen 1550 und 1100 v. Chr. ein Ziel für Schreibkundige war, die die lokalen Tempel und Fürstengräber bewundern wollten. Sie hinterließen ihre Namen, formulierten Wünsche an die Nachwelt oder Opferformeln für die Vorfahren, lobten die Schönheit der vergöttlichten Felswand und schrieben teils umfangreiche Exzerpte aus berühmten Lebenslehren, Reden und Hymnen an die Wände. Bilddipinti von Gottheiten, Menschen und Tieren zeugen ebenso wie manche der Texte davon, dass man die alte Grabdekoration studierte und respektierte. Besuchergraffiti kennt man für die Epoche des Neuen Reiches auch aus anderen Denkmälern Ägyptens, Umfang und Vielfalt sind in diesem Grab aber bislang einzigartig. Mehr als zweitausend Jahre nach dem Ende des Neuen Reiches diente das alte Grab für die Bestattung eines islamischen Scheichs, wovon eine Grabnische, eine Gebetsnische sowie großformatige Koranverse zeugen, die mit roter Farbe auf die Wände gemalt sind. Daneben finden sich religiöse, literarische und andere Texte von arabisch schreibenden Besuchern.

VERLAG PUBLISHERS
HARRASSOWITZ

The Asyut Project

Edited by Jochem Kahl, Ursula Verhoeven, Mahmoud El-Khadragy and Andrea Kilian

---

16: Jochem Kahl, Sameh Shafik

Gottesworte in Assiut

Eine Paläographie der reliefierten Monumentalhieroglyphen der Ersten Zwischenzeit und der 12. Dynastie

2021. VIII, 298 Seiten, 5 Abb., 1 Tabelle, 12 Tafeln, gb
210x297 mm
ISBN 978-3-447-11733-3
⊙ E-Book: ISBN 978-3-447-39214-3
je € 78,– (D)

Seit 2003 arbeitet das deutsch-ägyptische *The Asyut Project* auf dem Gebel Assiut al-gharbi, dem im Westen der mittelägyptischen Stadt Assiut gelegenen Wüstenberg. Ein Bestandteil des Forschungsvorhabens ist die epigraphische Aufnahme der Inschriften in den Gaufürstengräbern I, III, IV und V aus der Ersten Zwischenzeit und der 12. Dynastie. Jochem Kahl und Sameh Shafik stellen die reliefierten Hieroglyphen aus diesen gut datierten Gräbern in einer Paläographie zusammen und beschreiben die angewandten Werktechniken der Grabbeschriftung. Mit dieser Publikation liegt nun ein zeitlich wie regional genau erfasster Satz an Hieroglyphenformen für das 21. und 20. Jahrhundert v. Chr. vor.

17: Mahmoud El-Khadragy

Tomb N13.1 of the Nomarch Iti-ibi(-iqer) at Asyut

with collaboration of Ulrike Dubiel and Eva Gervers

2022. VI, 360 pages, 48 figures, 156 plates, 3 tables, hc
210x297 mm
ISBN 978-3-447-11778-4
⊙ E-Book: ISBN 978-3-447-39255-6
each € 98,– (D)

One of the important outcomes of the long-term Egyptian-German cooperation in archaeological fieldwork at the necropolis of Asyut is the discovery of Tomb N13.1 in 2005. The tomb was discovered by the members of *The Asyut Project* while surveying the necropolis of Asyut for the purpose of mapping. Tomb N13.1 belongs to the late First Intermediate Period/early Eleventh Dynasty Siutian Nomarch Iti-ibi(-iqer).

This discovery is the only available source of information introducing the then unknown Siutian nomarch Iti-ibi(-iqer). It provides us with a possible evidence connecting the well-known Siutian family of nomarchs, who ruled Asyut during the later part of the First Intermediate Period, i. e., Khety I, Iti-ibi and Khety II, and the celebrated nomarch Mesehti, owner of the two sets of model-soldiers representing Egyptian spearmen provided with shields (Cairo CG 258) and Nubian archers (Cairo CG 257), in addition to the two coffins (Cairo CG 28118, 28119). The tomb's decoration is one of the best preserved late First Intermediate Period/early Eleventh Dynasty tombs known to us up to date. Its iconographic details present one of the earliest known examples of a fabulous creature in a hunting scene in a private tomb and the earliest known example of goddess Sekhet dominating a fowling scene in a non-royal context.

VERLAG PUBLISHERS
HARRASSOWITZ

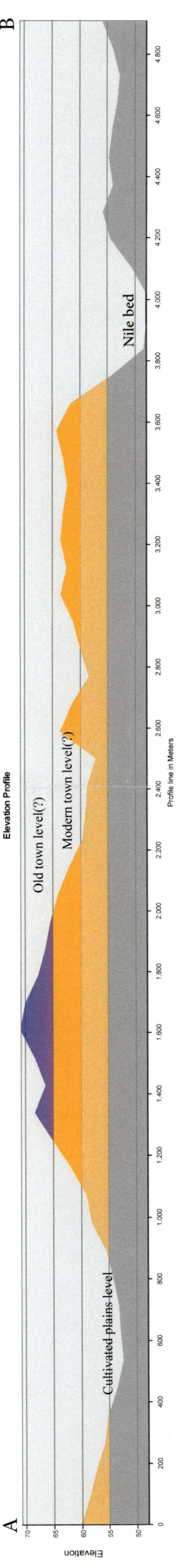

Beilage 3a: Höhenprofil von Assiut: Schnitt vom Gebel Assiut al-gharbi zum Nil (Mohamed Osman 2019; © Ägyptologisches Seminar, Freie Universität Berlin).

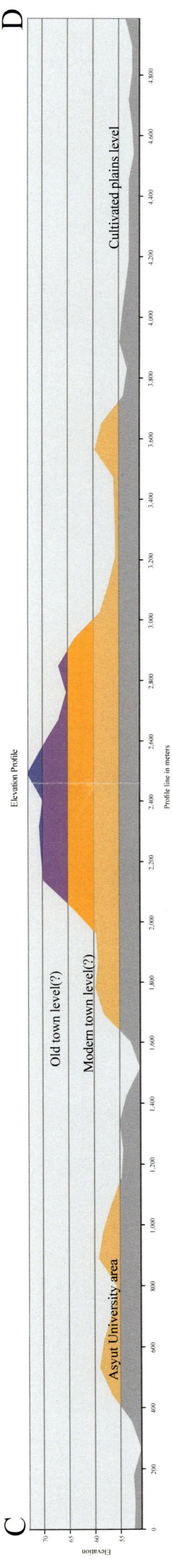

Beilage 3b: Höhenprofil von Assiut: Schnitt vom Gebiet der Assiut-Universität zu den Feldern im Südosten (Mohamed Osman 2019; © Ägyptologisches Seminar, Freie Universität Berlin).

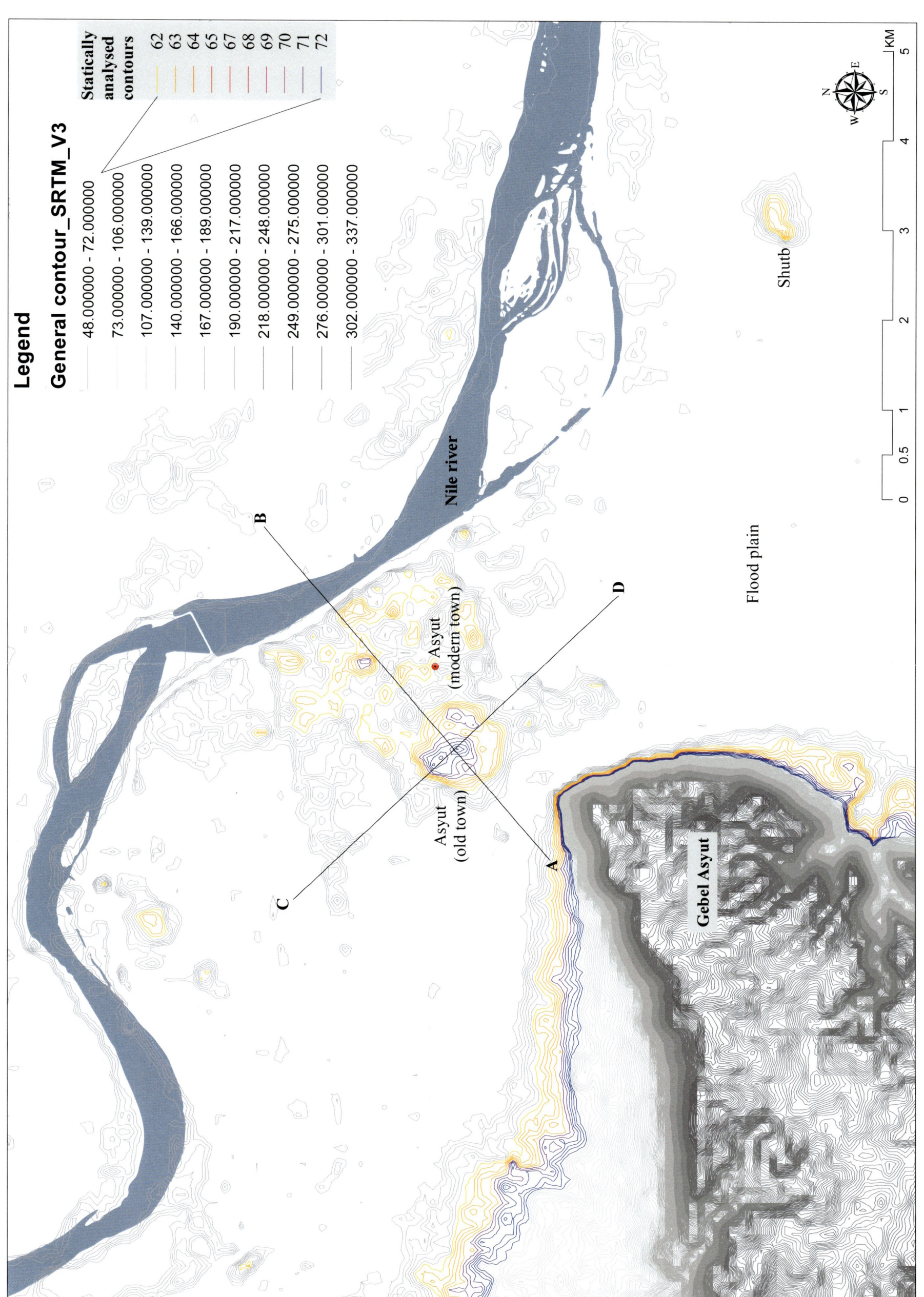

Beilage 2: Konturanalyse mit Satellitenbild von Assiut (Mohamed Osman 2019; © Ägyptologisches Seminar, Freie Universität Berlin).

Legend

General contour_SRTM_V3

	48.000000 - 72.000000	
	73.000000 - 106.000000	
	107.000000 - 139.000000	
	140.000000 - 166.000000	
	167.000000 - 189.000000	
	190.000000 - 217.000000	
	218.000000 - 248.000000	
	249.000000 - 275.000000	
	276.000000 - 301.000000	
	302.000000 - 337.000000	

Statically analysed contours

62
63
64
65
67
68
69
70
71
72

Nile river

Asyut (modern town)

Asyut (old town)

Flood plain

Gebel Asyut

Shutb

A B C D

0 0.5 1 2 3 4 5 KM

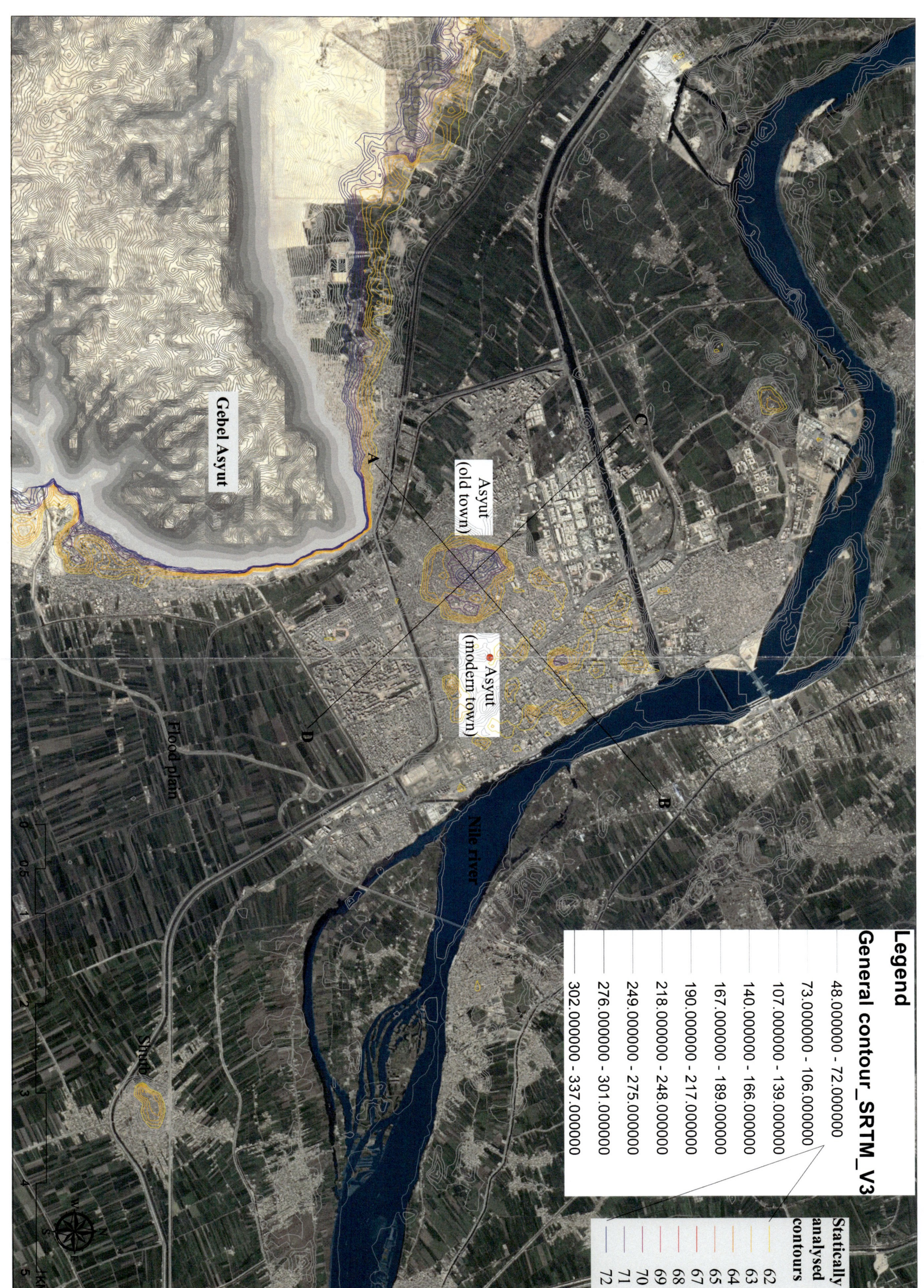

Beilage 1: Konturanalyse mit Satellitenbild von Assiut (Mohamed Osman 2019; © Ägyptologisches Seminar, Freie Universität Berlin).

Legend

General contour_SRTM_V3

	48.000000 - 72.000000
	73.000000 - 106.000000
	107.000000 - 139.000000
	140.000000 - 166.000000
	167.000000 - 189.000000
	190.000000 - 217.000000
	218.000000 - 248.000000
	249.000000 - 275.000000
	276.000000 - 301.000000
	302.000000 - 337.000000

Statically analysed contours

62
63
64
65
67
68
69
70
71
72

Gebel Asyut

Asyut (old town)

Asyut (modern town)

Flood plain

Nile river

Shutb

A
B
C
D